# The Journey of Adulthood

# The Journey of Adulthood



**Helen L. Bee**

**Macmillan Publishing Company**
New York
**Collier Macmillan Publishers**
London

Printed in the United States of America



Macmillan Publishing Company
866 Third Avenue, New York, New York 10022

Collier Macmillan Canada, Inc.

**Library of Congress Cataloging-in-Publication Data**

Bee, Helen L.
The journey of adulthood.

Includes index.
1. Adulthood—Psychological aspects. 2. Developmental psychology. I. Title.
BF724.5.B44 1987 155.6 86-5169
ISBN 0-02-308090-6

Printing: 1 2 3 4 5 6 7 Year: 7 8 9 0 1 2 3

ISBN 0-02-308090-6

**To Carl,
who journeys with me**

# Preface

This is a book about adult development. Such a simple statement, but it implies a lot. This is not just a catalogue of facts about adults, or a personality text that deals with the origins of personality in childhood, or a discussion of old age. Instead, this book is about adults over the full range of adult years, and, most importantly, it is about the ways in which they change or develop in systematic and individual ways over those years. My interest is first in the process of development, in the biological or psychological or social rules or laws that may govern the changes or the continuities we see. But at the same time I am fascinated by the ways in which individual adults differ from one another, and by the effects those differences have on the processes or patterns of adult development. These abiding interests lead me to ask certain questions again and again, about each aspect of development: What changes (if any) do we observe with age? How do those patterns of change or continuity differ for different groups or individuals? And how can we explain the age changes and the individual differences? What rules or theories best describe the process?

Answers to such questions are divided in this book into three basic parts. In the first three chapters I have laid the groundwork, describing some of the key dimensions on which adults differ as they start their journeys through adulthood, and introducing some of the major concepts and theories of adult development. The second part, Chapters 4 through 10, is the empirical, descriptive core of the book. In each of a series of domains of adult functioning—physical functioning, mental skill, social roles, patterns of relationships, work experience, personality, and systems of meaning or spirituality—I have laid out our current knowledge of age changes or continuities, based on the most recent research. These chapters are not devoid of theory or synthesis, but the major emphasis is descriptive. In the final three chapters of the book, some of the threads are pulled together again. Included here is a chapter on stress (and its effect on the changes already described in Chapters 4 through 10), a chapter on death and dying, and a final chapter in which I have integrated information from all of the previous chapters in several ways. Thus, although the major structure of the book is topical rather than chronological, there is enough synthesis throughout so that you will not lose sight of the whole human being, progressing through the adult years.

## Some Other Key Features

Research on adulthood, and on adult development, is highly interdisciplinary, as is this book. I approach the subject as a developmental psychologist (hence my fascination with and emphasis on the processes of development), but the adult years have also been studied extensively by sociologists (particularly family sociologists), demographers, epidemiologists, industrial psychologists, vocational specialists, gerontologists, and physicians. You will find all of these different disciplines represented in the research I have described in this book, which gives the book both breadth and depth. I have found it personally fascinating to delve into the literature of fields other than my own, and have been frequently intrigued not only by the new questions raised in my mind by the findings from other disciplines, but also delighted with the congruities I have found.

In describing this varied literature, I have aimed at an especially challenging combination of empirical detail, theoretical clarity, and practical relevance. I personally have never liked texts that were mere catalogues of facts; nor do I like texts that offer opinion and theory without describing the findings on which those opinions are based. My preference is for a text that offers both facts and theory and that simultaneously tells the reader how all those facts and theories apply to real life. Emphasizing the practical relevance of findings or theories seems particularly important here, since this book is really about *us*—about you, and me, our parents, our grown children, our friends, and about how we may (or may not) mature as we face the inevitable tasks of adult life.

In part to foster that sense of relevance to the real tasks of adult life, I have written this book as if I were talking directly to you, the reader, and I have included a number of personal anecdotes to illustrate points. You will end the book knowing a good deal about me, as well as about adult development! I hope, in the process, that I will also convey clearly that I find being an adult a fascinating, challenging, enjoyable process. To me, the material in this book is not just a set of facts or abstract theories, but a set of provocative ideas, food for thought about my own life. I hope you will find it food for thought about yours as well.

There are also, of course, pedagogical features to the book that I hope will make learning easier. Each chapter includes boldfaced key words, which are defined in a glossary at the end of the book. A chapter-ending summary and an annotated list of suggested readings are also included in each chapter. Within each chapter I have paused regularly to summarize the material up to that point, emphasizing key points, or pointing out inconsistencies. In addition, each of Chapters 4 through 10 includes a summary table that shows the main changes with age in that particular domain. Each of these features will help you to integrate the many findings and theories as you go along.

Finally, I should say a word about the inclusion in the book of a highly unusual topic—the development of systems of meaning or spiritual development. Clearly this is an area of deep personal interest for me. I was reared in a family that took discussions of such questions for granted and was exposed early in life to the literature and teachings of most of the world's major religions and philosophies. The inclusion of such material in this book is, in a sense, an attempt to integrate this life-long personal interest with my professional knowledge of human development. But I would not have included the material purely for the personal interest. I am also convinced that this is a relevant—even a central—aspect of adult development, and that to understand adulthood fully, we must understand the systems of meaning that adults bring to, or that emerge from, the process of development.

## Some Bouquets

It may seem to authors, as they sit over their keyboards, gazing endlessly at their computer screens, or while reading stacks of journals and books, or mulling and pacing, that writing a book is an entirely individual, solitary process. But in our saner moments we all know that such an enterprise cannot be completed without a great deal of help and support.

My own thanks go first to the many students in classes on adult development I have taught who criticized my early attempts at synthesis, let me know in no uncertain terms when I was being fuzzy, and willingly shared the details of their own journeys. This book is really written to them and to all others like them.

Thanks, too, to those members of my own "convoy"—that collection of friends and family members who have accompanied me on my own journey—who offered very concrete help with this project. Linda Jo Pym and Sandra Mitchell both read early drafts of the chapter on spiritual development, as did my father, and all offered useful and constructive criticism. Many others listened carefully and sympathetically when I needed a willing ear. I have learned from them all.

Thanks to UPS and the U.S. Postal Service for not losing the 27 boxes of books, papers, computer, and printer that were moved (along with the author, of course) three times during the writing of this book. (Nothing like adding a little stress to the system!)

Finally, thanks to the eight reviewers who offered detailed evaluations of the first draft of the book. They were both helpfully positive and appropriately picky, and I am grateful for all their suggestions: Diana L. Veith, Hutchings Psychiatric Center, Syracuse, NY; Alan M. Dahms, Metropolitan State College, Denver, CO; Carol K. Sigelman, Eastern Kentucky University, Richmond, KY; Paul E. Panek, Eastern Illinois University, Charleston, IL; Ruth G. Lyell, San Jose State University, San Jose, CA; Clara C. Pratt, Oregon State University, Corvallis, OR; Lesley A. Diehl, SUNY, Oneonta; and Bert Hayslip, Jr., North Texas State University.

Helen L. Bee
Madison, WI

# Contents

## 8 Work and Work Roles in Adulthood 212



## 9 Changes in Personality, Motivation, and Values over the Adult Years 246



## 10 Spiritual Development and the Search for Meaning 280

# 1

# Defining the Journey: Some Assumptions, Definitions, and Methods

It seems in retrospect that I have uprooted myself every five to seven years and gone off in a different direction. Sometimes these changes have been physical, moving from place to place; sometimes they have been inner changes, when there has been a turning inward or a turning away from.

After college, I completed a Ph.D. in four years and started off on a traditional academic career with a first job at Clark University, and then quickly a shift to the University of Washington (in my hometown, Seattle, which was a big draw). I spent a total of eight years in this traditional frame, doing all the usual things: teaching huge classes as well as seminars, ''doing'' research, sitting on endless committees, and having anxiety attacks about whether I'd get tenure or not (I did). I loved the teaching, eventually enjoyed the research, hated the anxiety, and in the end disliked the life of a professor as a whole. After a year's sabbatical during which I went around the world looking at child care arrangements in other countries (Russia, Israel, Scandinavia, France, and spots in between), I quit my tenured job completely. For me, the ''average day'' as a professor contained too many things I did not like and too few that brought pleasure or satisfaction. And it was too much the life of the mind. I felt constrained. So at the age of 32 I quit (to the astonishment of a great many people).

Shortly afterward I married and we moved with my husband's two children (ages 3 and 11 at the time) to a small island north of Seattle, where we lived for six years. I now think of this as my ''back to the land'' phase, though it was much more than that. I began to write books as a way to earn a living, which turned out to be both enjoyable and successful. I spent three years at the thankless but fascinating community job of school board director, grew a huge garden, learned how to can and make bread and butter and jam and all those other lovely, domestic things. I also grew up in some quite different ways, and discovered some parts of myself that logic didn't touch.

Unfortunately, the marriage did not hold together. Eventually I moved back to Seattle, where I began work on some research with colleagues, began teaching again, and generally stuck my toe back into the traditional academic waters. (For a while there I was in at least up to my waist, but I have resisted any further immersion.) At the same time I became much more interested in what I now think of as the ''inner journey,'' the search for understanding of what each of us is all about. Over the past five years I have begun to read the literature of mysticism, meditation has become part of my daily routine, and I have struggled with the problem of applying fundamental ethical principles to my everyday living. My friendships have deepened; my capacity to care for others has grown; my willingness to make commitments to others has expanded. I am sure there is more—vastly more—growing to do, but I am finally feeling like a grown-up person. Looking forward a bit, I plan to be a very eccentric old lady, and to enjoy to the hilt the many good years between now and then.

As you may well have guessed, this is my own life I am describing. I have taken this excerpt from the description I wrote recently for my college's 25th reunion yearbook. Since the women in my family live to be *very* old (typically into their late 90s), I am, at 46, right in the middle of my expected span of years.

I have quoted this somewhat self-revealing passage not only so that you can have at least a brief acquaintance with the person who will be talking to you in these pages, but also to help me raise some issues about development among adults. (You may want to think about your own life thus far, or your parents' lives, or your grandparents' lives, as further illustrations.)

First of all, when I think about myself and read what I wrote, I experience both a sense of continuity and a sense of change. I'm still very much an intellectual, so that is constant. Yet I feel that my relationships with others have changed greatly. Is this typical? How much do people really change in adulthood? Most of us like to think that we are maturing, growing, getting ''better.'' But are we really? How much do we just take ourselves with us through the years, bringing the same patterns, the same styles to each new situation? This issue of continuity versus change will form one of the major themes of this book.

A second issue that may have struck you as you read my brief life history is the occurrence of episodes, phases, or even stages. I established stable life patterns, then reassessed them and changed, only to establish a new life pattern for a number of years. And each of these periods or stages seemed to be focused on a different set of tasks, goals, or issues: Getting a career started and achieving success; rearing a family and exploring the tenderer side of myself; searching for the reasons, the meaning. Is this kind of life pattern typical? Is adult life made up of phases or stages? If it is, are these stages shared by all adults? Are the tasks and issues the same for all 20-year-olds, or all 40-year-olds, or all 70-year-olds? Is there, in other words, a predictable rhythm to adult life? This theme, too, will recur as we work our way through this book.

Still a third theme has to do with inner versus outer changes. My life has gone through a variety of ''outer'' changes—shifts in the jobs I held, in the people I lived with, the roles I tried to fill with those people. I went from student to professor to wife and parent to researcher, for example. At the same

**Figure 1–1** *Is this man in the midst of a "midlife crisis?" Has he thrown out the old pattern of his life, searching for something new and better? Does everyone go through such a change at midlife? When we make changes like this, are the changes only external, or are there inner transformations as well—changes in values, goals, or temperament? These are all questions that are part of the study of adult development. (Source: Ed Lettau, Photo Researchers Inc.)*

time I changed physically—my hair turned nearly white, I gained and then lost weight, I lost fitness and then regained it. All of these changes can be seen by someone observing from the outside, and represent, in a sense, an "outer journey" through the adult years.

But we can talk about an inner journey as well, a set of changes that are experienced by the individual but that may not be so obvious to someone on the outside. My own sense of "growing up" is one such inner change, as is the shift I described from a preoccupation with success and family to a recent preoccupation with inner growth and spiritual development.

I do not at all mean to imply that these inner and outer changes are independent of one another. They are not, as we will see again and again through the book. The shifts we all experience in the roles we fill (e.g., student, spouse, parent, young worker, older worker, mentor, friend) affect the way we feel about ourselves and the issues that concern us. The physical changes, too, influence our inner processing. The day (at age 38) that I realized that walking up a flight of stairs made me puff was not just a recognition of a physical change; it was a shock to my image of myself. I felt middle–aged for the first time, and that realization changed my inner perspective. The influences go the other way, too. The inner shifts influence our outward behavior in significant ways as well. Thinking of myself as middle-aged resulted in a new exercise program, weight loss, and a significant change in my appearance. Another adult may change jobs at age 30 or at 40 because of a significant shift in the issues that preoccupy him. One of my tasks in this book is to try to sort out the causal links between the inner and the outer threads of change.

# The Basic Questions

These fundamental themes can be described a bit differently. My questions about adult development are of two basic kinds: descriptive and explanatory.

## Descriptive Questions

The first task with any scientific endeavor is description. What happens? What kinds of changes occur over the adult years? What kinds of continuities exist? Are these changes or continuities widely shared or universal or, alternatively, are there subgroups that seem to share distinctive patterns of change and continuity? To understand development, we must be able to answer such questions about each facet or aspect of human functioning: the way the body works, the way the mind works, the kinds of roles and relationships adults have, the inner patterns such as personality or temperament, and the issues of concern to the individual.

Merely describing such change and continuity is no small task. And as you will discover very quickly, we lack the data to provide good, basic description in a great many areas. Still, we can begin.

## Explanatory Questions

Equally important are questions that ask ''how'' or ''why.'' We will be searching for causes, both for shared patterns of change and for individual variations. For example, we will see in chapters 4 and 5 that beginning in perhaps their

30s or 40s, adults experience some decline in the speed with which they can do mental tasks. By age 60 or 70, this difference in speed is quite noticeable. How could we account for this? Such a loss of speed could certainly be the result of one or more physical changes, such as the speed with which the nervous system conducts signals. But slower performance of mental tasks could also result from a change in the amount of time older adults, compared to younger adults, spend doing complex mental tasks. Maybe they are just out of practice! Still a third possibility is that older adults may be much less motivated to compete or to strive to succeed at such tasks. Working quickly may simply not be a high value.

Virtually every pattern of change or continuity over adulthood that we can identify or describe has such multiple possible explanations. In most instances, we are a very long way from understanding the causes of the patterns we observe. But over the past decade or so, psychologists and sociologists who study adult development (e.g., Baltes, Reese, & Lipsitt, 1980; Riley, 1976) have at least reached preliminary agreement that we can divide the basic sources of influence into three groups: (1) shared, "age-graded" change; (2) cohort effects; and (3) unique experiences. Since I will use this classification of potential causes of change (or continuity) throughout the book, let me pause here to describe it in some detail.

## Change in Adults: The Basic Explanations

### Shared, Age-Graded Changes

This type of change is probably what you assume when you hear the phrase "adult development." These are changes linked to age in some way and shared by most or all adults, in every generation. I find it useful to divide this further into three subtypes:

**Biologically Influenced Changes.** Some of the changes we see in adults are shared by all of us because we are all biological organisms, undergoing natural aging processes. Our hair turns gray, we lose taste buds, our skin becomes drier. The speed with which we process information seems to decline as the synapses in the brain become less efficient. The *rate* at which these (and equivalent) changes occur varies quite a lot from one adult to another, but the *sequence* seems to be highly similar. Biological explanations of adult change have not been terribly popular (perhaps because most of us, including the researchers and the theorists, don't like to think about our own physical aging), but this is a possibility we need to keep steadily in mind. For example, could some of the "crises" of midlife be due to the hormone changs of the menopause (and the equivalent changes in men)? Can changes in work attitudes be linked in any way to a decline in physical or mental efficiency? We need to keep an open mind about such possibilities.

**Figure 1–2** *Our bodies change as we get older. The older person has more gray hair, more wrinkles, probably also fewer taste buds and drier skin. Are these inevitable changes in the body as we get older? (Source: Suzanne Szasz, Photo Researchers Inc.)*

**Changes Produced by Shared Experiences** Another highly significant source of shared changes is simply shared experience. There are obvious individual variations, but most of us move through adulthood encountering similar tasks, similar options, similar experiences. These are *cultural* and not biological patterns. Adults living in quite different cultures (or those within our own society who participate in highly different subcultures) may experience somewhat different sequences of changes in adulthood, as shaped by their own common experiences.

Most importantly for our purposes, these shared experiences are organized at least roughly by age. Sociologist Matilda White Riley and her colleagues (Riley, 1976; Riley, Johnson, & Foner, 1972) point out that virtually all societies are organized into **age strata**—periods in the life span which have shared demands, expectations, privileges. In our culture, for example, we have quite different expectations of, and attitudes toward, 18-year-olds, 35-year-olds, and 60-year-olds. We expect them to do different things, to form different kinds of relationships, and we afford them different amounts of recognition, responsibility, or power. Such collections of expectations and responsibilities for each age constitute the **age norms** for that culture or subculture. Over the course of adulthood, each individual passes through the sequence of age strata with their accompanying norms, and this shared age-graded experience exerts a powerful influence on the pattern of change we see in individuals over their lifetimes.

One of the most significant elements in age stratification and age norms in virtually all cultures is the pattern of experiences associated with marriage and family life—what the sociologists call the **family life cycle.** In the United States, for example, about 90% of adults marry (and that number has been stable through this century). Further, the vast majority (80%–90%) of married couples have children (Glick, 1979). Once the first child is born, the parents are locked into a powerful sequence of experiences linked to the child's developmental stage: infancy, toddlerhood, school age, adolescence, and finally departure from home. Each of these periods in the child's life makes a different set of demands on the parents, and this sequence of demands shapes 20 or 30 years of most adults' lives.

The impact of such a shared pattern may extend well beyond the family relationships themselves. For example, one of the findings I'll talk about in chapter 7 is an intriguing decline in friendship formation between approximately ages 30 and 45. This seems to be a widely shared pattern, but how can we explain it? I can think of no obvious biological explanation, but it might well be one of the offshoots of the family life cycle. When your children are small, your energy is focused on the relationships in the immediate family. There is less time, and perhaps less opportunity, for forming and maintaining new friendships.

There are a great many widely shared, age-related, cultural patterns other than the family life cycle. To take just one more example: For the past several generations at least, most adults have become more physically (and mentally) sedentary with age. Our jobs are becoming more automated, we read less, move less. This fact suggests the intriguing possibility—one I'll explore in some detail in Chapter 4—that some of the changes in our bodies that might seem to be biologically inevitable are really the result of disuse and not unavoidable deterioration.

**Internal Change Processes.** A third kind of shared, age-graded change is more difficult to describe because it involves inner processes. It is precisely this kind of shared, inner change that most theorists of adult development have attempted to describe. The basic idea is that each of us must face and cope with a set of tasks or dilemmas in our adult life. In the process of coping, we undergo a series of inner adjustments. We may become more "integrated," we may learn to express a wider range of emotions, we may become more "mature." Movement through the family life cycle or other shared experiences may be part of what triggers this set of inner changes, but the internal transformations may go beyond this. For some adults at least, values change, ways of thinking change.

For example, one of the current notions is that in early adulthood, particularly after the birth of children, there is a kind of exaggeration of masculine or feminine qualities for many adults. Then at midlife, men and women both seek to "balance" their feminine and masculine qualities more completely (e.g.,

Giele, 1982b). For most of us, this means expanding the expression of the less "practiced" aspect. If this is true, then we might find that men at midlife become more emotionally expressive and warm, while women become more assertive and independent. In fact there is some evidence that such a "cross-over" does occur in many cultures, as I'll describe more fully later. For now my point is simply that this is an example of the kind of internal change, linked to age but neither caused by biological change nor entirely defined by age norms, that theorists suggest may occur over the adult years.

If we are to understand adult development, we must eventually be able to sort out the effects of and the interactions among these several types of age-graded change. If we observe the same pattern of change between age 20 and age 60 in many cultures, and in many generations in the same culture, we still will not know whether that particular change is biologically based, culturally defined, or results from some natural or inevitable internal psychological change, or some combination of the three.

## Cohort Differences

A second major explanation of observed differences betwen young and old is based on variations in experiences in succeeding generations. Suppose I study a group of men and women now in their 40s or 50s, and another group of men and women now in their 20s. I have each person fill out a questionnaire that tells me something about his or her ideas about appropriate male and female sex roles (e.g., Just how egalitarian should family tasks be? How appropriate is it for women to work when they have small children?). When I add up the results, I find that the adults in their 40s and 50s hold much more "traditional" ideas about sex roles than do the 20-year-olds. I have observed an age difference, haven't I? Older adults are more traditional than younger adults. How can this difference be explained?

Biological differences seem an implausible source of explanation. I might appeal to the family life cycle changes, and argue that with increasing age adults become more traditional in their sex role ideas because they have lived through the years of rearing children and have discovered how difficult truly egalitarian arrangements really are. The younger adults may be idealistic, but not realistic.

But I can hear you rebutting me: "Come on! It's much simpler than that. The current 20-year-olds have been influenced by the women's movement and the change in values about adult sex roles. The older group grew up at a different time, when values were different." Precisely. The difference between the 20-year-olds and the 40-year-olds in this case is probably not really a change in the individuals over time. It reflects a change in society. The current 40-year-olds probably held much the same values when they were 20, and the current 20-year-olds probably will not get more traditional as they get older (though that is an empirical question). Thus what looks like an age change is most likely to be a **cohort difference.**

The term **cohort** may be new to you. It is frequently used as a rough synonym for "generation," but psychologists and sociologists also use it with narrower time references. In general, a cohort is a group of individuals who were born in the same time interval and share the same major experiences throughout their lives. A cohort thus shares some set of historical experiences distinct from those of adjacent cohorts. In the example I just gave, 20-year-olds are clearly in a different cohort from 40-year-olds, but there are also several cohorts in between, each of which had somewhat different historical experiences. The cohort of adults now in their middle to late 30s for example, arrived at college at just about the height of the Vietnam war protests; those of you who were born a bit later hit college just as the severe gas shortages of 1973–74 occurred. Each of these experiences, and thousands of others like them, may shape the attitudes or values you and your cohort will have about particular issues for the rest of your lives.

Obviously, many adjacent cohorts experience the same historical events. I was certainly around during the Vietnam war protests and during the gas shortages. But these experiences happened at different points in my own life span than is true for younger cohorts. The key is that each cohort passes through a specific set of experiences at particular ages. The timing of the events interacts with the tasks, issues, or age norms for that age, producing unique patterns of influence for each cohort.

The phrase "cohort effect" is used to describe those differences between groups of different ages that are due not to age or aging or to any other developmental process, but simply to the fact that the different age groups have grown up in different cultural circumstances. Cohort effects abound in research on adult development. A few examples will help make this clearer:

Early researchers studying IQ changes in adulthood compared average IQ scores of adults of different ages (e.g., Matarazzo, 1972 Wechsler, 1955;). They found that the older the group, the lower the average score. Alas, it looked as if we all declined in mental power as we aged. But there is a cohort effect lurking in the data: Older cohorts in this culture have had significantly less education than have younger cohorts. So it could be education, and not age, that is related to IQ. As you'll see in chapter 5, that is roughly what researchers have found when they approached the problem in other ways.

Glen Elder, in his detailed studies of the effects of the depression on children and adults, has also shown clear cohort effects. Those who were teenagers in the depths of the depression showed fewer long-term effects than did those who had been in early elementary school when the depression struck full force. The younger cohort spent a greater portion of their childhood under conditions of economic hardship. The hardship altered family interaction patterns, educational opportunities, and even the personalities of the children, so that the effects could still be detected as adults (Elder, 1974, 1979; Elder, Liker, & Cross, 1984).

As we look at descriptions of changes in adulthood in the rest of this book, we need to be steadily alert for possible cohort differences. Cohort differences make it harder to develop broad, general statements or universal principles about adult development. But such differences are not just "noise" in the system. They are interesting in and of themselves. They tell us something about how major social forces shift the developmental patterns for adults.

## Unique, Nonshared Events

For any one individual, changes over the adult years are also shaped by a wide range of experiences that are not shared with all adults, or even with all members of a cohort. Having your parents die when you are a child, or in your 20s or 30s; a significant illness early in life; the early death of a spouse; the death of a child; loss of a job; whether you marry early or late (or not at all); whether

**Figure 1–3** *All of us experience unique or unusual events in our adult lives. This young adult has to cope with the unusually early death of her father, an "off-time" event that may have a large impact on her development. (Source: Rhoda Sidney, Leo de Wys Inc.)*

you have a special teacher in highschool who inspires you to go on for a specific kind of training—all of these and hundreds more experiences like them can alter the pathway a particular individual will follow through adulthood. Even experiences like marital separation or divorce, which are widely shared, belong in this category of unique or nonshared events, since divorce is neither universal nor age-graded. As you'll see as we go along, the timing of particular unique events seems to be a highly significant factor influencing the degree or direction of impact. Bernice Neugarten (1979), in particular, has emphasized that events that are "on time," that follow a "normal expectable life cycle" are less disruptive or difficult than those that are "off time." So having your parents die when you are in your 20s (which is "off time") is more difficult to deal with, more likely to lead to significant life-disruption, than is the death of your parents when you are in your 40s or 50s. Similarly, losing your job in your 30s is harder to handle than is retirement at 65. In some sense, this is another way of saying that those adults who deviate from the age norms in significant ways are likely to show more distinctive or unusual patterns of development than do those whose lives more closly follow the culturally defined age norms.

Obviously, in a book like this I cannot begin to explore the effects of every possible combination of unique and shared experiences in the lives of adults. But I can and will try to search for any underlying patterns that may exist that will help us understand types of unique events, their timing, and their combined effects.

## Some Definitions

Before I go further, I think it is important to pause and define some terms. Perhaps you have already been confused by having so many different words used apparently interchangeably—words like "development," "change," "aging," and "maturing." So far I have used these words rather loosely, but if I am going to create any order at all out of the evidence and the theories, I need to be more precise and more strict in the way I label various concepts. At the very least we need terms for the following processes or concepts: (1) basic physiological change that is an inevitable accompaniment of the passage of years; (2) "improvements" that occur with age, such as greater personality flexiblity, or successful completion of a series of tasks or dilemmas; (3) "declines" that may occur with age (that may or may not be physiologically based); and (4) all other patterns of variation in behavior or attitudes that are associated or linked with age but that don't fit the other categories.

My choices for terms to describe these different patterns may not altogether fit your preconceived notions, but I will use these terms consistently throughout the book.

***Adulthood.*** I will define adulthood as that period from age 18 to death. Eighteen is an arbitrary age, but it represents (in our culture at least) the time when young people graduate from high school, and many then immediately take on the duties and responsibilities of adulthood. To be sure, many other young people continue in a semidependent status for some years after 18, but it is still a convenient demarkation.

***Age.*** This one is straightforward: I'll use the word simply to refer to chronological years since birth.

***Aging.*** To be consistent, I will use this term to describe simply the passage of years, although the everyday meaning also includes the notion of decline or "getting worse," as in "She's certainly aged since we saw her last, hasn't she?" I will make every effort to avoid that sort of implication.

***Maturation.*** This is a term used commonly in the study of children's development to refer to those processes of change with age that are governed by underlying physiological processes, largely determined by the genetic code. We can speak, for example, of the maturational changes that underlie the infant's progression from sitting to crawling to walking, or the maturational changes of puberty. I will use it in the same way in this book to describe any sequence of physical changes that appears to be governed by systematic, shared genetic or other biological processes. For example, the complex sequence of changes associated with the loss of reproductive capacity between the ages of 40 and 60 (referred to most generally as the climacteric in both men and women, also called menopause in women) is a maturational change parallel to the changes of puberty. Note that maturation, in this sense, is quite different from the common parlance word "maturing," which often connotes "becoming wiser" or "becoming psychologically better balanced." Any increase in wisdom or balance might be the result of fundamental maturational (physiological) processes, but could also reflect any one of a host of other growth or development processes as well. Note also that a maturational change might involve either the addition or the loss of skills or physical functions. With increasing age, adults lose taste buds but gain ear size; we lose speed in nerve synapses, but gain plaque in our blood vessels.

***Development.*** I will use this term to mean "maturing." In this usage I am following, at least roughly, the definitions given by Heinz Werner and Bernard Kaplan (Kaplan, 1983; Werner & Kaplan, 1956), who define development in terms of increasingly higher, more integrated levels of functioning. Whether development in this sense of the word actually exists or not in adulthood is one of the key questions I will be asking in this book. Do some adults, or all adults, become "more mature," "wiser," more altruistic and compassionate? Obviously, the decision of what constitutes "better" or "more mature" is a question as much of values and philosophy as fact. But I am not content merely to describe strings of changes with age without at least addressing the question of value or "growth."

***Gain*** and ***Decline.*** These two terms I will use, as nonperjoratively as possible, to describe changes that involve increases or decreases in some function or skill over age. It is important to be clear about the fact that development, as I have defined it here, may result from either gains or declines. It is possible, for example, to gain in wisdom as a result of loss of health: Illness causes some people to examine themselves and their lives in constructive and beneficial ways.

***Change.*** Where it is not clear whether some pattern of change with age is a gain, or a loss, or reflects some development, I will simply talk about change. Descriptions of change or stability will nearly always be the beginning point in our explorations of adulthood. What is the pattern of frequency and depth of friendship over the adult years? What is the pattern of hearing retention or loss in older adults? What happens to scores on IQ tests over time in adulthood? All of these are questions that call for data on change or stability over age. But once we have such data, we then need to understand the basis of the change or stability we have found. Are these maturational changes (i. e., governed by automatic or shared physiological change)? Are these cohort effects, or has the same pattern of change been observed over several generations? Finally, can we legitimately describe this set of changes as development, as gain, or as loss, whatever the cause?

## Collecting the Information to Answer the Questions

To answer questions like these is no simple task. More importantly, the specific research methods an investigator chooses have a powerful effect on the range of questions that can be answered with that particular study. Examining research methodology is always an important part of understanding the findings in any field, but never more so than in studying adult change or development.

Let me take as an example the issue I pointed to just a few paragraphs back: What is the pattern of change or stability in frequency, duration, or quality of friendships over the adult years? What decisions would I have to make in trying to answer such a question? Here are some of the key ones:

Should I study groups of people of different ages, or should I study the same group of people over time, or some combination of the two? This is a question dealing with basic research design.

How shall I find out about friendships in the subjects I decide to study? Shall I simply ask people to tell me how many friends they have? How shall I define "friend" for this purpose? Shall I ask about specific relationships, and how close they are? Should I do this with a questionnaire or an interview? What else would I want to know about each subject aside from numbers of friendships and age?

How shall I analyze and interpret the responses that people give me? Is it enough merely to determine the average number of friends described by subjects of each age group? What else would I want to do in order to tease out some of the possible explanations?

You need to have at least a basic working knowledge of the options involved in such research decisions if you are going to be able to interpret the findings from the research I'll be describing in the book.

# Research Design

Choosing a research design is perhaps the most crucial decision the researcher makes. This is true in any area of psychology or sociology, but there are special considerations when the subject of study is change or development with age. There are essentially three choices: (1) You can pick different groups of subjects at each of a series of ages and compare their responses. This is called a **cross-sectional design**. (2) You can study the *same* subjects over a period of time, observing whether their responses remain the same or change in systematic ways. This is called a **longitudinal design**. (3) You can combine the two in any of several ways, collectively called **sequential designs** (Achenbach, 1978; Schaie, 1983a).

## Cross-sectional Designs

The essential characteristic of cross-sectional studies is that they include *different* groups of subjects at *different* ages. Each subject is tested only once. Such comparisons tell us about age differences, but they do not tell us directly about age change.

As an example, suppose once again that I am interested in friendship changes over the adult years. I could select a group of adults in their 20s, another group of adults in their 30s, and so forth. I could then compare the average number of friends reported by subjects in each age group. The results from one study like this are in Figure 1–4 (Lowenthal, Thurnher, & Chiriboga, 1975).

These results tell us that numbers of friendships are different in different age groups, with a low point in the 30s. It is also possible to read these findings as if they said that friendships decline in one's middle years, and then rise again later. But there are several problems with drawing conclusions about age changes from results like these. First and foremost, there is a "cohort problem" here. The 60-year-olds are from a distinctly different generation than are the 25-year-olds. There is no way for us to tell whether the different levels of friendships represent genuine, life-cycle changes that would occur with successive generations, or whether these are simply cohort differences. That is, we cannot assume that today's 25-year-olds, when they are 60, will show the same pattern of friendships that current 60-year-olds show. The technical term for such built-in coexistence of effects is **confounding**. Thus *in any cross-sectional study, age and cohort are totally confounded*. They vary simultaneously, so that we cannot ascribe an observed pattern of age differences unequivocally to either age or cohort.

A second difficulty in this particular study is that the subjects at each age were actually selected not for their age per se, but because they occupied particular statuses or roles. The youngest group is made up of high school students; the next oldest group included only newlyweds (in their first marriages),

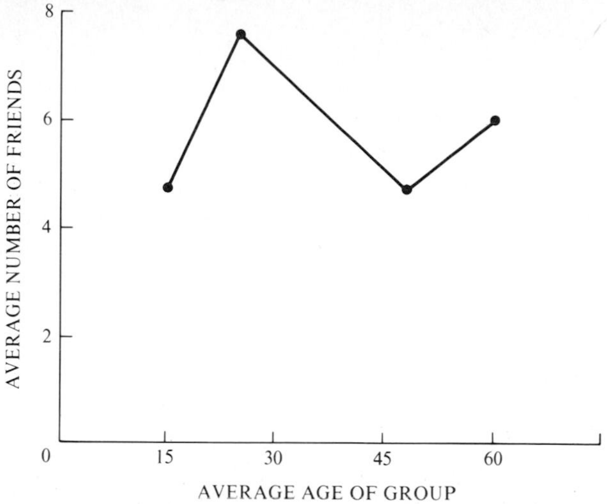


***Figure 1–4*** *Lowenthal and her colleagues studied four separate groups of adults, of differing ages, asking each one how many friends he or she had. These cross-sectional results tell us about an age difference in number of friends, but they do not tell us that friendship patterns change with age. (Source: Lowenthal, Thurnher, & Chiriboga, 1975, data from Table 4, p. 50.)*

who ranged in age from 20 to 38; the middle-aged group, (average age 50) were all married and had children nearly grown and ready to leave home; the oldest group consisted of married adults whose children had left home and who were about ready to retire. Thus these results, if they tell us anything, tell us more about the relationship between family life status and friendships than they do about age and friendships. We would need to look at other adults in their 20s who were not newlyweds, or who had been married for some years, to see if the pattern was actually linked to age.

The selection of subjects based on their stage in the family life cycle is very common in research by family sociologists. For example, a great deal of what we know about marriages over the adult years is based on research following such a design. Sociologists also commonly use another variant of a cross-sectional design. Instead of selecting subjects initially in specific age groups, they simply sample randomly across a wide age range. The group of subjects may be chosen so as to represent the characteristics of the total population, or it may include only women who work, or only families that have telephones, or the like. If all ages are included in the group, then the researcher can later either combine the subjects into groups on the basis of age, or can look at age as a continuous dimension. But research of this kind, although it may give us more information, does not solve the cohort problem. Age and cohort are still confounded.

## Longitudinal Designs

One obvious solution to the cohort problem is to follow the same subjects over time. This tells us about change or continuity over age in a particular group of people. It also tells us, as cross-sectional studies never can, how consistent or inconsistent each individual is over time. Do some people consistently have more friends than others? Do most adults show the same patterns of change and stability, or do people vary in their pathways through the adult years? These questions can only be answered by longitudinal studies.

When cross-sectional and longitudinal results differ markedly from one another, it tells us that some kind of cohort effect is at work. For example, as I pointed out earlier (and as I'll detail more fully in chapter 5), cross-sectional studies of IQ consistently showed that IQ declined over the adult years, beginning in middle-age or even earlier. But when longitudinal studies were done, declines were not found until quite late in old age (e.g., Schaie, 1983b). The obvious explanation was that the older subjects in the cross-sectional studies had had less education and less exposure to standardized tests. So as a group, they performed less well. But as individuals they had probably not shown declines in IQ over their own lifetimes.

It may seem from this that a longitudinal study solves all our problems. Longitudinal studies have their own built-in difficulties, of which three are particularly troublesome.

**The Dropout or Selective Attrition Problem.** Whenever you study the same people over a period of time, it turns out to be impossible to keep in touch with all of them. Some move and you can't find them again. Some decline to participate at later testing points. Some die or become too ill to participate. In general, the healthiest and best educated subjects are more likely to continue to participate in longitudinal research, so that over time your sample becomes narrower and narrower, and biased more and more toward those with the best functioning. This is a problem with all longitudinal research, but a particularly troublesome one in studies of the final decades of life. Since the least healthy older adults die, we may underestimate the degree of actual decline in some function (such as memory speed, or IQ, or whatever) because each succeeding test includes only those healthy enough to have survived.

An excellent example of this effect comes from an analysis by Ilene Siegler and her colleagues (Siegler, McCarty, & Logue, 1982) of some findings from the first Duke Longitudinal Study of Aging, which you can see in Figure 1–5. The subjects, who initially ranged in age from 63 to 87, were tested repeatedly over 16 years on a wide range of measures. This particular figure shows scores on a test of verbal memory for the oldest subjects, those who were 71 or older at the beginning of the study. As you can see, in this group those who remained in the study the longest had initially had the highest verbal memory scores. Findings like these mean we must be cautious about overly optimistic conclusions from longitudinal studies about retention or improvement in skill or performance with increasing age.

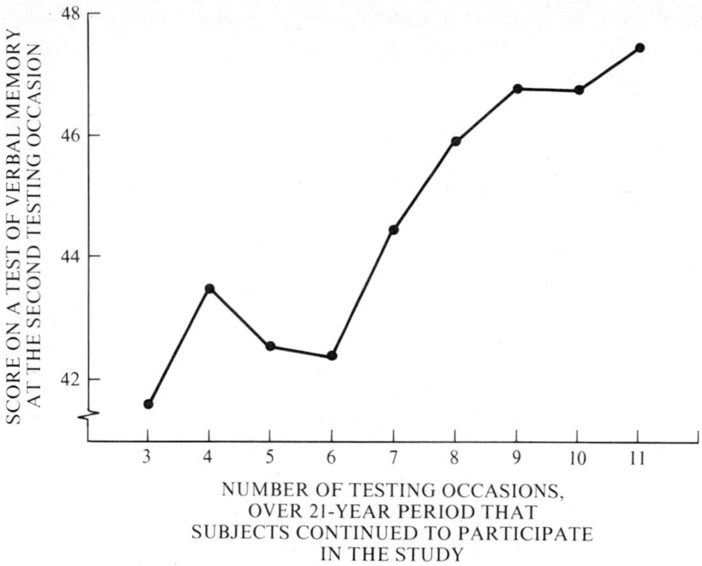


**Figure 1–5** *Selective attrition—the steady loss of the least healthy, the least educated, or other subjects over repeated testings—is a serious problem in longitudinal research. These results from the first Duke Longitudinal Study show that for adults who were 71 years or older when the study began, those who lasted the longest in the study had started out with higher scores on the verbal memory test. Since these initially brighter subjects are the only ones left at later ages, we may end up underestimating the effects of aging on memory loss or maintenance. (Source: Siegler, McCarty, & Logue, 1982, Figure 1, page 179. Reprinted by permission of the* Journal of Gerontology, *1982, 37, 176–181.)*

**Time of Measurement or Historical Effects.** A second problem is that a longitudinal sample is drawn from a single cohort—so we haven't really gotten rid of the cohort problem entirely. We cannot be sure that any pattern of age change we observe in our longitudinal study would also describe another cohort studied longitudinally. The example I gave earlier, of changes in attitudes about sex roles, may help make this clear. If I had studied sex role attitudes longitudinally in a group of adults born in 1925 (those now about 60), I might well find that the subjects' attitudes had become more egalitarian in their late 40s and in their 50s. But would such a change really reflect some age-linked or developmental process that normally occurs at midlife, or does it reflect merely the fact that for this cohort, the women's movement coincided with their 40s and 50s?

This is an especially important issue given the fact that many of the most thorough longitudinal studies—those that have examined the widest range of adult functioning and followed the subjects for the greatest number of years—involve essentially the same cohort: those born between about 1920 and 1930 (e.g., Eichorn, Clausen, Haan, Honzik, & Mussen, 1981; Vaillant, 1977a).

And this is in some respects a highly atypical group. They grew up during the depression, lived through World War II, formed their families during that unusual time immediately following the war when women returned to full-time homemaking and birth rates soared. Both preceding and succeeding cohorts had very different life experiences. The basic point is that even when we look at results from longitudinal studies, we must be sensitive to the potential impact of experiences unique to that cohort.

**Changing Theories and Measures.** A third frustration for longitudinal researchers is that they usually find, five or 10 or 20 years into the study, that they are now interested in somewhat different aspects of development than they were at the beginning, and find that they did not measure initially the qualities or aspects they now find intriguing. Theories change, new data emerge that alter the way issues are framed, new tests and measurement strategies are devised. With a longitudinal study, one is locked into a set of measurement decisions that had to be made in a different era. (Having been involved myself in one 10-year study, I know how frustrating this can be!)

## Sequential Designs

A third type of research design was developed to combine the best of both worlds—to achieve the relative speed and flexibility of cross-sectional designs while at the same time retaining the study of sequence and consistency that is the hallmark of longitudinal research. Collectively, these are called sequential designs, and each involves studying more than one cohort.

The simplest strategy is to do a set of parallel cross-sectional studies, each several years apart (what Warner Schaie calls a **time-sequential design**). For example, Majorie Lowenthal and her colleagues could study the friendship patterns of new groups of young, middle-aged, and older subjects in 1985, ten years after the original comparisons were made (a design described in Table 1–1). Such a study would still be essentially describing age differences,

**TABLE 1–1 An Example of a Possible Time Sequential Research Design: Lowenthal's Cross-sectional Study of Friendship Patterns, with a Hypothetical Second, Parallel Series of Cross-sectional Comparisons 15 Years Later**

| | Year of Birth of Subjects in Each Group | | |
|---|---|---|---|
| | *Young (age 25)* | *Middle-aged (age 50)* | *Older (age 60)* |
| Year in which subjects are interviewed: | | | |
| 1970 | 1945 | 1920 | 1910 |
| 1985 | 1960 | 1935 | 1925 |

| COHORT | AGE AT START OF STUDY | BORN IN YEAR: | AGES AT WHICH SUCCESSIVE TESTS WERE GIVEN<br>45 47 49 51 53 55 57 59 61 63 65 67 69 71 73 |
|---|---|---|---|
| A | 45–49 | 1919–1923 | 1968 1970 1972 1974 |
| B | 50–54 | 1914–1918 | 1968 1970 1972 1974 |
| C | 55–59 | 1909–1913 | 1968 1970 1972 1974 |
| D | 60–64 | 1904–1908 | 1968 1970 1972 1974 |
| E | 65–69 | 1899–1903 | 1968 1970 1972 1974 |

***Figure 1–6*** *The design of the Duke Longitudinal Study illustrates a "cross-sequential" design. Each cohort was studied on four occasions—1968, 1970, 1972, and 1974. If we compare the scores for the five cohorts in 1968, or in 1972, or 1974, we would have a cross-sectional study. If we look at each cohort over time, we have a longitudinal study. And if we look at the scores for different cohorts at the same age, we can see whether different cohorts exhibited the same age-linked behaviors. (Source: Palmore, 1981.)*

rather than age change, but if the same trends appeared in each cross-sectional comparison, then an age-change hypothesis becomes much more tenable.

Other types of sequential designs are much more powerful and complex. In each case, the researcher selects subjects from several cohorts and follows each cohort longitudinally. In a **cross-sequential design**, the groups are different ages at the beginning of the study and each group is followed over time. One of the Duke Longitudinal Studies, shown schematically in Figure 1–6, is an excellent example of this type of research program (Palmore, 1981; Siegler, 1983).

The researchers began with five groups, ages 45, 50, 55, 60, and 65 at the start of the study. Each group was retested three more times, at two-year intervals. Thus they have four separate longitudinal studies, each lasting six years. They also have potentially a series of cross-sectional studies: At each testing year, they can compare the responses of subjects of differing ages. But because the ages of the cohorts began to overlap as the longitudinal study progressed, the researchers also have a third option: They can compare the responses of different cohorts at the same ages. For example, they could see whether Cohort A at age 50 responded similarly on their tests as had Cohort B when they were 50—six years earlier.

A somewhat similar kind of cross-sequential analysis is common in survey research in sociology. In such studies, a large group of subjects of varying ages is selected so as to represent some population as well as possible. The entire sample, or representative subsamples, are then studied again at subsequent intervals. For example, the Retirement History Study, conducted by the Social Security Administration, included originally over 11,000 men and women who were between 58 and 63 years of age when the study began in 1969. These subjects were then contacted again every two years until 1979 (Keith, 1985; Murray, 1979; Palmore, Burchett, Fillenbaum, George, & Wallman, 1985).

A related analysis, which Schaie calls a **cohort-sequential design**, is like the cross-sequential design in that it involves studying a series of cohorts longitudinally. But in this case each cohort is studied at the same ages. A researcher might study one cohort for a 10 year period, say from age 35 to 45, and then start over with a second group at age 35 and follow them for 10 years. This strategy avoids the time of measurement problem in longitudinal research by providing a check on the consistency of age trends in several cohorts.

When all three of these types of sequential designs are combined, as Schaie has done in the Seattle Longitudinal Study (Schaie, 1983b; Schaie & Hertzog, 1983), remarkably rich and powerful data may emerge. Schaie first selected and gave IQ tests to a series of cohorts seven years apart in age, ranging from 25 to 67 at the start of the study. This first study was thus cross-sectional. Then a subset of the subjects at each age were followed longitudinally (a cross-sequential analysis), with retesting at seven-year intervals for 21 years. Every seven years Schaie also selected another set of cross-sectional samples aged 25 to 67, and followed some of them longitudinally as well. In the end he had one set of parallel longitudinal subjects he had followed for 21 years, another set he had followed for 14 years, and others he had followed for seven years. He also had four full cross-sectional studies, seven years apart. It is a remarkable study. Few researchers have had either the patience or the resources to complete designs of this complexity. But all the sequential designs allow us to shift from talking merely about age differences, to talking about age changes and their variations. They also allow us to separate out the impact of unique cohort experiences (time of measurement effects) from that of more enduring developmental patterns.

## Choosing the Subjects: Sample Selection

In addition to questions of when and how often one will observe or assess subjects, and at what ages, a critical element in research design is the selection of the actual individuals to be included as subjects. Ideally, the sample should accurately represent the population the researcher is hoping to describe. If we are really searching for age changes or developmental patterns valid for all adults, we should select random samples of adults from all cultures of the world. Since that—or anything even close to it—is clearly impractical, researchers make a variety of compromises in selecting subjects, each of which may affect the generalizability of the findings. As you can see from the descriptions of some key studies in Table 1–2, the most representative samples are typically found in the large sociological survey studies, in which subjects are selected randomly within one or more cities, or from across the country. In contrast, most of the longest-term, in-depth longitudinal studies include relatively small samples (100–300), more middle class than working class, and usually predominantly white subjects. Many frequently quoted studies include only men. As a consequence, we know more about the adult development of white middle-class American men born between 1920 and 1930 than we do about any other group.

Given the enormous investment of time and effort required to do research of this kind, it is remarkable that there are as many decent studies as there are. But we do need to keep limitations in both design and sampling in mind as we move through the various chapters of the book.

## Collecting Information About Subjects

Once the research design is determined, the next major set of decisions has to do with the ways in which information will be collected from subjects. Each of the basic strategies has distinct advantages. Since you have probably encountered descriptions of these techniques in other reading, I will assume that each of you has at least some knowledge of the pros and cons of the alternatives, and describe them only very briefly.

**Observation.** The most open-ended way to explore adult behavior is to observe adults in natural surroundings. This is a common technique in studies of children, but is rarely done with adults. Even structured observations, or observations of adults in specially created or artificial situations, are relatively rare. Most of what we know about adulthood comes from asking people about themselves in one way or another.

**Interviews.** Interviews are extremely common in research on adulthood. The longitudinal studies described in Table 1–2 all included extensive interviews in their test procedures; many sociological studies of aspects of adult life also involve structured interviews. Sometimes the transcripts of subjects' responses to interview questions are later rated on broad dimensions by other psychologists or researchers; sometimes the data from the interviews are coded in a more direct fashion.

**Questionnaires.** Still more structured is a questionnaire in which the alternative answers are provided. The questions may request factual information about the subject (age, occupation, number of friends of various types, marital status, income, etc.); they may be standardized instruments designed to assess attitudes or aspects of personality, such as sex role attitudes or rigidity/flexibility.

**Other Standardized Tests.** IQ tests and tests of other specific ablities are also used widely, sometimes administered individually, sometimes given in groups.

Most of the longitudinal studies have included all or most of these techniques in their testing procedures, yielding a very rich body of data. Most of the shorter-term longitudinal studies, or the cross-sectional studies, involve a more focused set of questions and a narrower range of assessment techniques.

**TABLE 1–2 Design and Sampling Characteristics of Some Major Longitudinal and Sequential Studies**

| Name of Study | Recent Source | Years of Study | Average of Range of Ages of Ss at Start (and End) of Study | Birth Year of Oldest Cohort | Number of Ss at Start (and End) of Study | Sample Characteristics | Design and Measures |
|---|---|---|---|---|---|---|---|
| *Long-term Longitudinal Studies* | | | | | | | |
| Grant Study | Vaillant, 1977 | 1937–1970 | 19 (49) | 1918 | 268 (95) | Harvard undergraduates, all male | longitudinal; psychological adjustment, health |
| Berkeley Intergenerational Studies | Eichorn, Clausen, Haan, Honzik, & Mussen, 1981 | (a) 1928–1970 | birth (40) | 1928 | 248 (144) | sample from Berkeley, CA, male & female, mostly middle class, mostly white | longitudinal; personality, IQ, health |
| | | (b) 1932–1970 | 10–12 (48) | 1920 | 212 (107) | sample from Oakland, CA, all white, middle class & working class | longitudinal; personality, IQ health |
| AT&T Longitudinal Studies | Bray & Howard, 1982 | 1956–1976 | 24–30 (44–50) | 1926 | 422 (226) | all male, beginning managers at AT&T, college and noncollege; white | longitudinal; work success, personality |
| Terman Study of Gifted | Sears, 1977 | 1922–1972 | 11 (62) | 1911 | 1,528 (916) | children with IQs of 135 or above, from California | longitudinal; work success, personality |

| | | | | | | | |
|---|---|---|---|---|---|---|---|
| *Sequential Studies* | | | | | | | |
| Duke Studies of Aging | Palmore, 1981 | (a) 1955–1976 | 59–94 (76–102) | 1870 | 270 (44) | Southeastern city, reasonably representative, white & black | cross-sequential; health, personality, IQ, work history |
| | | (b) 1968–1976 | 46–70 (51–77) | 1899 | 502 (375) | Southeastern city, all white, more middle class, male & female | cross-sequential; health, personality, work, IQ |
| Seattle Longitudinal Study | Schaie, 1982 | 1956–1977 | 25–67 (46–88) | 1889 | 21 year study: 120; 14 year study: 300 | Seattle, Washington, participants in a Health Maintenance Organization, male & female, mixed social class | cross-sequential and time-sequential; Heavy focus on intellectual measures |
| Baltimore Longitudinal Studies of Aging | Costa, McCrae, & Arenberg, 1982 | 1958–1978 | 17–77 (37–97) | 1881 | 769–171 | all male volunteers; quite well educated | cross-sequential; though less systematic; personality, health |
| Michigan Survey Research Center Study of Mental Illness & Health | Veroff, Douvan, Kulka, 1981 | 1957 & 1976 | 21 and older in each sample | approx. 1877 | 2,460 in 1956 2,267 in 1977 | National probability sample, all social classes & races | time-sequential: two cross-sectional studies 20 years apart. Values, family, work, health |
| National Longitudinal Surveys | Parnes, 1981 | 1966–1976 | 45–59 (55–69) | 1907 | 5,020–3,185 | All male, with blacks intentionally overrepresented; national sample | cross-sequential; work history, family economics |

## Understanding the Answers

Once the data have been collected, researchers must make another set of decisions about how to analyze the findings. Some of the statistical methods now being used are extremely sophisticated and complex. I'll be describing a few of these in later chapters, as I discuss specific studies that include them. At this early point, all I want to do is talk about the two most common ways of looking at the results of studies of adult change and continuity.

The most common way to describe age differences is simply to calculate average (mean) scores on some measure for each of several different age groups, then compare the means. When longitudinal data are available, a comparison of mean scores at different ages is also involved. In each case, we are usually looking for a trend, a pattern of scores linked to age.

If the sample studied is large enough, it is often possible to subdivide it and look for age differences or equivalences separately in the subgroups, such as women versus men, working class versus middle class, those with young children versus those without young children, and the like. If every group shows essentially the same pattern over age, and if the same pattern occurred in longitudinal studies as well, we'd be much more likely to conclude that this is a significant age-linked or developmental pattern. If the changes and continuities are very different for different sub-groups, (as is often the case, by the way), then we are led to ask other kinds of follow-up questions: Why might the groups differ? What do the differences tell us about the possible pathways through adulthood?

Let me give you a quick example. One of the consistent findings in sociological research on families is that marital satisfaction is related to the presence and age of children. Figure 1–7 shows the results from one of the early studies (Rollins & Feldman, 1970). You can see that the percentage of couples who say they are happy ''all the time''goes down with the birth of the first child, and stays relatively low until retirement age. I'll be talking much more about this intriguing pattern in chapter 6. For now I merely want to have you think about the way in which these findings are analyzed and interpreted. These are cross-sectional comparisons, so we don't know if individual families actually go through this sequence. All we know from this study is that when we compute separate means for each age/family stage group, we find a robust pattern of age or stage differences. Since other researchers reported the same results (Rollins & Galligan, 1978), confidence in the consistency of this pattern is increased.

But recent research shows that this curvilinear pattern is much more typical of some families than of others. Stephen Anderson and his colleagues (Anderson, Russell, & Schumm, 1983) looked at this same pattern for three different kinds of spouses: those who were high, medium, or low in ''marital conventionalization.'' Subjects high in conventionalization were those who agreed with statements like ''My marriage is a perfect success'' or ''Every new thing I have learned about my husband has pleased me,'' and disagreed with statements like ''I have some needs that are not being met by my marriage.'' (Sub-

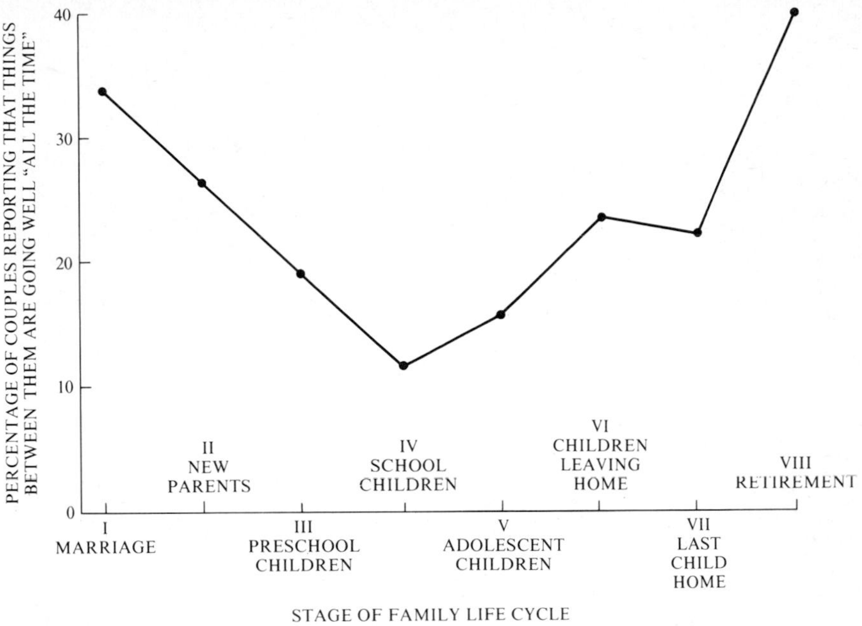


**Figure 1–7** *These cross-sectional findings, replicated by other researchers in other cohorts, show a consistent pattern of age differences related to stage of family life cycle: Couples with young children are less satisfied with their marriages than are couples with no children, or with children gone from home. (Source: Rollins & Feldman, 1970, data from Tables 2 and 3, page 24. Copyrighted 1970 by the National Council on Family Relations, 1910 West County Road B, Suite 147, St. Paul, MN 55113. Reprinted by permission.)*

jects low in marital conventionalization showed the reverse pattern and thus reported a few warts and wrinkles in their marriages.) When they looked at the relationship between marital satisfaction and age/family stage in each of these three groups, the results in Figure 1–8 emerged.

As you can see, the clearest curvilinear pattern emerged for those couples low in conventionalization. Intriguing, isn't it? This could mean that children have a negative effect on marital satisfaction only for those couples who are already lower in satisfaction, or it could mean that those couples who are more honest in their description of their marriage are also more willing to acknowledge negative reactions to the birth of a child. The point for now, though, is that all of this information emerges from quite simple techniques: the comparison of mean (average) scores for different age or life stage subgroups.

Comparisons of means for different age groups, either cross-sectionally or longitudinally, can give us some insights about possible age changes or developmental patterns, but they cannot tell us whether there has been continuity or change within individuals. For this, a different type of analysis is required, namely, correlational techniques. A **correlation** is simply a statistic that tells us the extent to which two sets of scores on the same people tend to vary

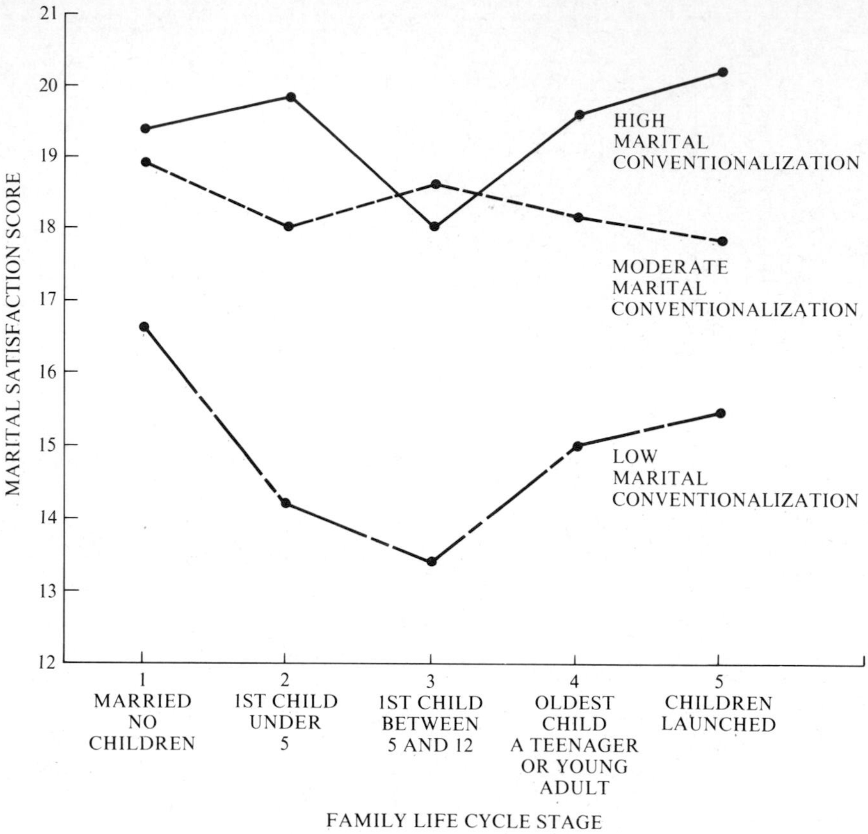


**Figure 1–8** *Compare the curves in this figure with those in Figure 1–7. Here we see that the drop in marital satisfaction after the birth of a child, and when children are young, occurred clearly only in one subgroup, those with low "marital conventionalization." By using analyses like these, even simple comparisons of mean scores in cross-sectional studies can be very informative. (Source: Anderson et al., 1983, Figure 2, page 135. Copyrighted 1983 by the National Council on Family Relations, 1910 West County Road B, Suite 147, St. Paul, MN 55113. Reprinted by permission.)*

together. Correlations (symbolized **r**) can range from +1.00 to −1.00, with a positive correlation showing that high scores on the two dimensions occur together. A negative correlation tells us that high scores on one dimension go with low scores on the other. The closer the number to 1.00, the stronger the relationship. A correlation of .00 indicates no relationship.

For example, height and weight are positively correlated: Taller people generally weigh more, shorter people less. But the correlation is not perfect (*not* 1.00) because there are some short, heavy people and some tall, light people. If you are on a diet, the number of pounds you lose is negatively correlated with the number of calories you eat—high calories go with low weight loss.

But this correlation, too, is not perfect (as any of you who have dieted know full well!).

When we go searching for continuities or discontinuities in individual patterns over adulthood, the correlation is the main tool we use. A researcher will measure some skill or quality in each member of a sample at several time points and then use the correlation statistic to describe the degree to which the scores at any two time points are similar to one another. For example, do adults who have high IQs at 20 still have high IQs at 40? Yes. In one study, Dorothy Eichorn and her colleagues (Eichorn, Hunt, & Honzik, 1981) found a correlation between IQ at 18 and at 40 of about .80, which is very high indeed.

Correlations are also used to search for explanations for patterns of change or continuity that we may have already observed. If we were interested in why some adults remain satisfied with their lives into old age, while others do not, (as Palmore, 1981, has been) we could look at the correlations between life-satisfaction and a wide range of other measures, such as education, or income, or presence of family members, or availability of friends, or health.

There are many variations on these analytical themes, but nearly all the research on adult development involves one or the other (or both) of these basic techniques.

## Experimental Designs

The type of research design I have not mentioned thus far—an omission you may have noted, particularly if you are familiar with research in other areas of psychology—is the **experiment**. In an experiment, the researcher systematically controls or manipulates one or more variables, assigning subjects randomly to various treatment or nontreatment groups. Because the questions we are interested in when we study development have to do with changes or continuities with age, and since we cannot assign subjects randomly to age groups, nor manipulate or speed up the process of aging, there is not a great deal of experimental research in the study of adult development. But there are important ways in which experiments can help to explore alternative explanations of age-related patterns that may be observed in cross-sectional or longitudinal studies.

Take, for example, the observed reduction in speed with which older adults, compared to younger adults, perform many intellectual tasks. There are several possible explanations of this pattern, several of which I sketched earlier: It could reflect fundamental maturational changes in the brain or nervous system; it could reflect differences in practice at such tasks; it could reflect differences in motivation to compete or achieve; or it could conceivably reflect a cohort difference caused by education differences between the old and the young in today's society.

Controlled experiments might help us choose among these alternatives. We could, for example, select groups of young, middle-aged, and older subjects, and assign half of each group (at random) to a training group in which extra practice was given on some particular intellectual task. The other half of the subjects at each age might be given no training, or might be given training at some other kind of task altogether. If we then tested all the subjects before and after training, we could determine whether the performance of the older group benefited more, equally, or less from training than did the younger groups. If they benefited more, it would provide support for the "lack of practice" explanation for speed differences.

Perhaps there are so few experiments of this kind in the study of adult development because we are still, in this field, primarily concerned with problems of description rather than explanation. In those areas in which the basic descriptive research is more complete—such as the study of changes in intellectual performance over adulthood—experiments like this are done, and we will encounter a few as we go along. But at the moment, systematic, controlled experimentation is not one of the major modes of research in this field.

# A Final Word

Since I began this chapter on a personal note, let me end it the same way. I approach the topic of this book both as a psychologist and as an adult. My interest is both scientific and personal. I want to understand how it all works and why, both because that is inherently interesting to me, and because it may help me to understand and deepen my own development. Your own journey through adulthood will be like my own in many ways, and very unlike it in others. What I am searching for in this book are the basic rules or processes that account for both those similarities and differences. I hope you can share with me the sense of adventure in the scientific search, as well as in the personal journey.

## Summary

1. Several central themes run through the study of adult development: Is there continuity, or is there change within the individual? Are there stages or phases? Is there both inner and outer change? In each instance we will look at both description and attempts at explanation.

2. Three major kinds of influences help to produce change in adulthood. Shared, age-graded experiences are the first. This includes both shared, inevitable biolological change as part of aging; shared cultural experiences, such as those associated with the family life cycle; and internal changes that may be shared.

3. A second source of influence is the impact of experiences unique to individual cohorts.

4. Unique experiences encountered by each adult, shared neither within cohort nor across cohorts, form a third source of influence.

5. The term *maturation* will be used to describe those age-graded changes due to fundamental, universally shared biological changes. The term *development* will be used to describe changes with age that involve improvement or growth.

6. Researchers exploring questions of adult continuity and change must decide on basic research designs. Cross-sectional designs involve studying separate groups at each of several ages or stages; longitudinal designs involve repeated study of the same group of individuals over time; sequential designs involve several more complex combinations of longitudinal and cross sectional strategies.

7. Cross-sectional designs inevitably confound age and cohort, while longitudinal studies involving assessment of a single cohort over time confound age change and time of testing. Longitudinal designs also suffer from problems of selective attrition. Sequential designs can help sort out the differing effects.

8. A second series of decisions for the researcher concerns the way in which information will be collected from subjects. The most common strategies in adult research are variations on questionnaires and standardized tests, with interviews also common.

9. Analysis of findings typically involve one of two techniques: comparison of means for groups of different ages (or for the same people across age); or calculation of correlations between scores for the same people at different ages, or the same people at the same time on different measures.

10. True experiments, in which the experimenter systematically manipulates one or more variables and assigns subjects at random to experimental and control groups, are not common in the study of adult development, although they can help to choose among competing explanations for patterns of change or continuity over age.

# Suggested Readings

ACHENBACH, T. M. (1978). *Research in developmental psychology.* New York: Free Press.

If you are interested in some of the intricacies of research design and analysis, this is a good source. I especially recommend pages 89–104.

SCHAIE, K. W. (1983a). What can we learn from the longitudinal study of adult psychological development? In K. W. Schaie (Ed.), *Longitudinal studies of adult psychological development.* New York: Guilford Press.

Schaie is the originator of many of the more complex and elegant sequential designs for studying adult development. In this chapter he lays out some of the possibilities clearly and in more detail than I have given here.

VAILLANT, G. E. (1977). *Adaptation to life.* Boston, MA: Little, Brown.

If you are dying to get started reading about some real people actually moving through adulthood, try this book. I have found it to be one of the most intriguing of the descriptions of longitudinal evidence, full of fascinating case studies as well as provocative theory.

# 2

# The Journey Takes Shape: Starting Points and Continuities Through Adulthood

Let me introduce some people to you—each at the starting point of the journey of adulthood, but already with many of their qualities established and significant choices made.

Tom Kleck, 22, is a big, rawboned, friendly young man with a thick blond moustache and neatly cut hair. He has a ready smile, is outgoing and easy to talk to. His steady girlfriend, Marianne, says he was one of the most popular kids in their high school class. He is usually pretty optimistic about himself and his future, and is hard to rile.

Tom grew up in a working class neighborhood with his parents, two brothers, and a sister. His father is a truck driver; his mother mostly stayed home to care for the children, taking odd jobs only when the family needed the money. Neither of his parents went to college, but his father had higher hopes for Tom. So after Tom did well in high school his folks encouraged him to go to the local community college, where he finished a two-year business degree. He's now working as a low-level manager in the same trucking firm for which his father drives, which pleases them both. Although he has his own apartment, he sees his folks often, usually having supper with them on Sundays.

Tom likes the routine his life has fallen into—time for Marianne and for his folks, time for some sports with his high school buddies, a few beers at the tavern. But he is also constantly looking for new experiences, new chances. He's planning to take some more college courses, likes to try new sports and new foods. Just for a lark, last year he even taught himself to bake bread. When he looks down the road a few years, he sees himself married and with a family, but maybe with a different job, one with more challenge and variety.

Cathy Stevens, also 22, might fit your image of the "All American Girl." When you first meet her, it is her smile that strikes you, and her face is open, guileless. She laughs often and her face is already developing a few smile wrinkles.

She went through many of the usual stages and phases in childhood—a tomboy stretch when you could hardly get her out of the nearest tree (with a broken arm from a fall as a reminder of those days)—braces on her teeth, Girl Scouts. Since her family was always well off (her father's a banker, and both her parents went to college), she also had some special advantages like horseback riding lessons and ballet classes. These days she stays in shape with aerobic dancing classes and rides whenever she can find the time.

From earliest days (according to her parents, at least), Cathy had a remarkably sunny disposition. Unlike her brother and sister, she was usually obedient and rarely made trouble. In high school, while her parents worried about her brother and sister, they always trusted Cathy. Her grades were only average, but they were good enough to get her into the local state university. She has never thought of herself as a great brain, but she enjoyed school and graduated last year with a degree in psychology. She was lucky to find a job right away as a secretary and girl Friday for a mental health clinic in her home town. Within a few months she plans to marry Pete, whom she met in college. He's just finishing his master's degree in business administration and hopes to get a good job with a local brokerage firm. After they marry, Cathy is planning to work until their first child is born, and then to stay home with the kids while they are little. She thinks that later she may want to go back to school and get a degree in something like social work, but that is all a long way off right now.

Laura Rogers' life has been sharply different from either Cathy's or Tom's, something you might guess when you meet her; she already has a permanent frown line between her eyebrows. Otherwise she is an attractive woman with intense brown eyes.

Her folks were working class people. Her dad worked in a steel mill, and her mom worked a lot of the time as a clerk in a nearby drugstore. It seemed to her that they didn't have much time for her. On the other hand, Laura wasn't such an easy child to raise. She was a bit cranky, didn't sleep regularly as a baby, got upset easily, and became a somewhat willful teenager. But she was also outgoing and usually friendly, so although she was not the most popular girl in school, she had a group of friends she enjoyed.

Life changed abruptly at 15 when she got pregnant. Her family, and her boyfriend's family, pressured them to marry, so by 16 Laura was married and the mother of an infant. She dropped out of high school and quickly got pregnant for the second time. She is now 22, divorced with two children to rear on her own. Her ex-husband is not very good about making child support payments, and things are very tight financially. Right now she has a pretty good job as a waitress, but mostly she's been on welfare since the divorce. Both sets of grandparents help out when they can, but she often feels quite hopeless about her future. She takes pains with her appearance, but you can see the fatigue in her face, in her posture. One of her hopes is that she will eventually marry again—someone steady and more mature than her first husband.

Like Laura, Walter Washington has had a rockier start to his life than either Tom or Cathy. His father left when he was about three and Walter has seen his dad only occasionally since then. His mother was left with four kids to bring up (Walter was the youngest) and had to make ends meet on her pay as an aide in a nursing home. They lived in a crowded apartment in a black neighborhood in Chicago, and all the kids spent a lot of their time on the streets. Walter was part of a street gang for a while when he was in his early teens, and several times he was picked up by the police. But in high school things turned around a bit for him.

Walter was tall enough, and just good enough, to make the varsity basketball team at his high school, and the coach happened to be a man who pushed the kids hard to study and get good grades as well as to play ball. Walter just scraped by in English, and always hated history, but somewhat to his surprise he found that he liked math and science. There was something about the orderliness of both subjects that appealed to him, and he was good at them both. When he got out of high school, his coach and his science teacher helped to get Walter into a TV repair training program, which at least used a little of his technical interests. For three years now Walter has had a pretty good job as a repairman.

But Walter is not satisfied. He wants more—a better job, more money, more education. He is fascinated with computers and is taking night school classes in computer programming and engineering. It is this ambition, this drive, that most distinguishes Walter at 22. His long, lean face has a firmness around the mouth, an unsmiling quality, that is quite striking. It is not an angry expression—although he can get quite angry about the discrimination against blacks in the computer field—rather, it is a quality of determination.

Socially, Walter is a loner. He has had a few girlfriends, but he would rather spend his time tinkering with computers or machines than with people. He plays a little pick-up basketball, sees his family once in a while, but mostly he lives a pretty solitary life—and that suits him fine.

The fifth member of this quintet of young people is Christopher Linton, who at 22 is just starting his last year of law school. He's a couple of years ahead of most of his peers in school since he skipped a grade in elementary school. He learned to read when he was four, and his parents had a hard time keeping his nose out of a book from then on. Needless to say, Chris did extremely well in school, but he didn't have many friends. An only child of highly educated and financially successful parents, he seemed quite content with the company of his books, his parents, and their friends.

**Figure 2–1** *Class reunions can be both shocking and fascinating, both warm and surprising. Some people have changed a great deal in appearance, others seem much the same. What kinds of consistency can we see here? If we had a measuring rod, we would find that everyone has gotten a bit shorter, but the tallest man is still the tallest. But is the shyest person still the shyest? (Source: Nancy Kaye, Leo de Wys, Inc.)*

Chris doesn't look much like the stereotypical egghead. He's quite broad shouldered and well muscled and dresses the part, wearing mostly tweeds and crewneck sweaters. Women find him attractive, but they sometimes have a hard time getting past his shyness. At the moment he does not have a steady girlfriend, though he is dating more now than he did in high school. Aside from being shy, Chris's major problem is that he tends to take things very hard—things like setbacks in his school work or rejection by a girlfriend. He tends to brood about such things, to be pessimistic and grumpy. If you ask him if he's happy, he guesses he is "OK." but not much better than that.

When he looks forward, he sees himself as a partner in a top law firm, probably involved in corporate or tax law. Marriage seems far off, although he says he'd like to have children "eventually." He also assumes that whoever he marries will probably have a career, just as his mom did. But his mom also did all the cooking and most of the housework, and Chris figures his wife will probably do most of that, too.

These five young people illustrate an absolutely critical point about development in adulthood: Each of us begins adulthood already strongly shaped by such built-in characteristics as gender or race, by internal qualities such as intelligence or personality, by such external conditions as our family background, and by the amount of education we complete. At 22, these five young adults differ along all these dimensions. As a result, they have already embarked on different pathways through adulthood. These pathways, or trajectories, are not permanently fixed; no one's adulthood is completely determined by these starting points. People can and do shift from one pathway to another. But for most of us, there is a line of least resistance, a pathway that opens in front of us in early adulthood, shaped by our family background, our school experiences, our abilities, and our personalities.

What I want to do in this chapter is to ask two questions about each of these basic starting conditions: (1) How persistent or consistent is this condition throughout adulthood? (e.g., Does intelligence or personality remain the same as we age? Do adults follow the same occupational or social paths as do their parents?) (2) How is the adult pathway shaped by differences in each of these basic qualities or conditions? Do adults with more education have very different life experiences from those with less education? Do extroverted adults (like both Tom Kleck and Cathy Stevens) experience adulthood differently from those who are more introverted (like Chris Linton or Walter Washington)?

In the remainder of the book I will be spending most of my time searching for, and talking about, patterns of *shared change* in adulthood—ways in which all (or most) adults change as they age. In such a search, it is easy to overlook several crucial things about adulthood and about adult development: There are wide individual variations among adults in skills, qualities, and background; those variations are already present at the very beginning of adulthood, and affect the rate, sequence, or pattern of adult change we may see for different individuals. On some of these dimensions of individual difference, it is not change that distinguishes the adult years, but consistency.

## A Word About Consistency and Change

Before I explore the impact of some of these dimensions of individual difference and consistency, let me say just a bit more about what is meant by consistency, and how it is usually measured.

Any one of four different meanings can be implied by a statement that some quality or behavior is "consistent" over time (Kagan, 1980):

1. A characteristic is consistent if individuals show minimal change in the *absolute* level of that quality over time. Physical qualities like height show this kind of consistency in the early years of adulthood. Some psychological qualities may also be consistent in this sense.
2. A characteristic is consistent if individuals retain the same *relative* position, compared to other individuals, on measures of that characteristic over time. For example, we would say that IQ is consistent in this sense if those adults who achieve the highest scores when they are 20 still have among the high-

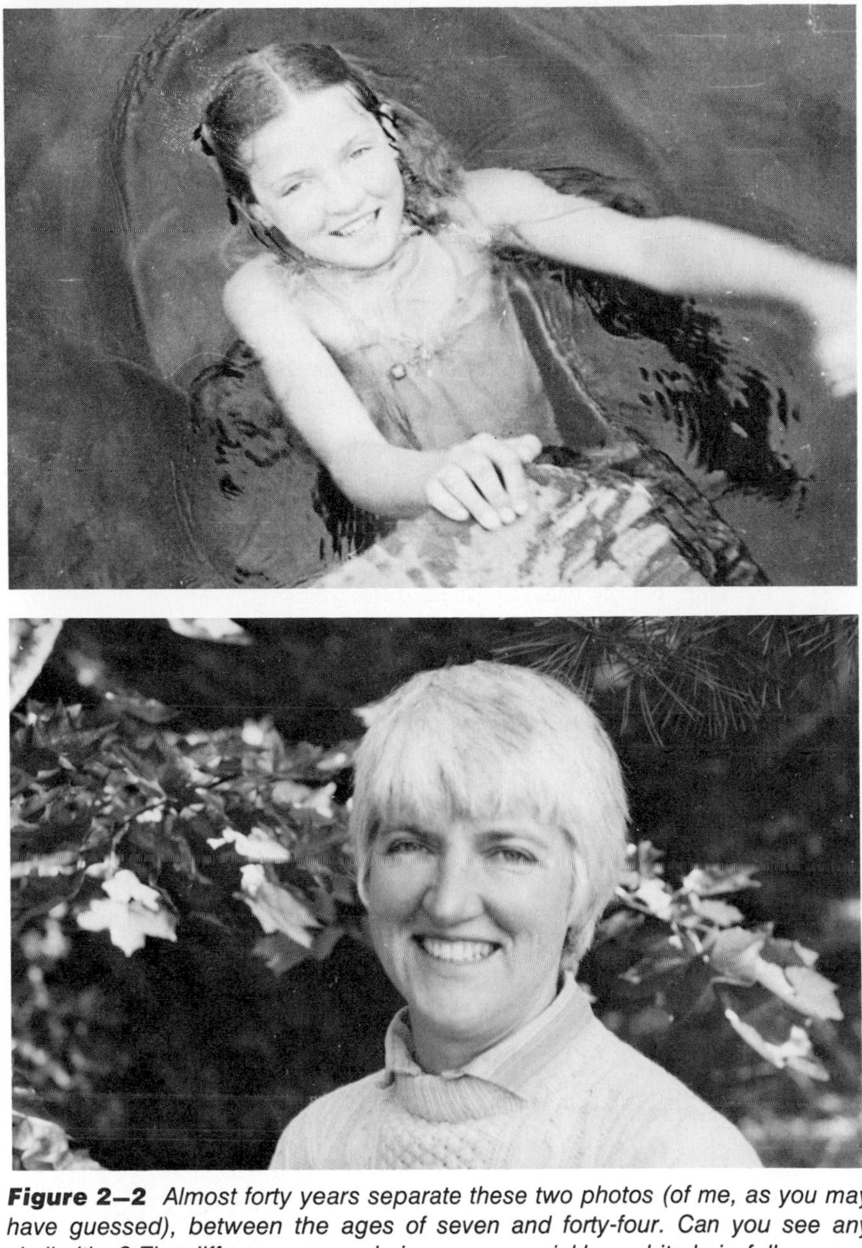

**Figure 2–2** *Almost forty years separate these two photos (of me, as you may have guessed), between the ages of seven and forty-four. Can you see any similarities? The differences are obvious—more wrinkles, white hair, fully grown. But I still feel like the same person in many respects, despite the maturing. (Source: Helen L. Bee, author.)*

est scores when they are 40 or 50, while those who originally had low scores still show low scores, even if the average score of the whole group has gone up or down. Or, to give another example, if we measure height in the same individuals at 20 and again at 70, we would find that everyone's height had gone down. But since we all shrink at about the same rate, most adults would still be in the same relative position in the group.

3. A third type of individual consistency occurs when a set of qualities or characteristics remain at the same relative strength *within an individual* over time. For example, if you take a test of vocational preference, one outcome is a profile of your scores in each of a series of interest areas. If you took the same test five years later, we could measure the consistency of your interest by comparing the profiles to see whether your interests had remained in the same rank order.
4. Finally, we may search for patterns of underlying or "trait" consistency even when overt behavior has changed. Suppose, for example, that we wanted to study dependency and its consistency or change in adulthood. We might argue that some underlying quality of dependency on others would remain constant, but that the outward manifestation of this quality would change with age. Young people might show dependency by calling home a lot, or spending every vacation at home; 45-year-olds might show dependency by spending all leisure time with the same person (such as a spouse), without branching out into independent activities. Thus, the dependency may be the same, but the behavior might differ.

Virtually all the research on consistency I am going to talk about in this chapter is focused on one of the first two kinds of consistency: We are looking for either absolute or relative stability over time. As I have already emphasized, however, it is important to bear in mind that both relative individual consistency and group change with age are possible on the same dimension or quality. Stability does not preclude change. But since most of the book will deal with change, let me put a few stones in the other side of the balance scale and talk about some key consistencies and about the impact of individual differences on adult pathways.

Specifically, let me look at the consistency of, and the impact of, six qualities or conditions: gender, race, intelligence, personality, family status, and educational achievement.

## Gender Differences in Adult Lives

Since we do not change gender during our adult years (barring a sex change operation), I don't need to talk about how consistent gender is over adulthood. Children discover at about age five that they are stuck with whatever gender they are, and by adulthood each of us is well socialized into the roles for our gender. Since gender roles vary somewhat from one culture to the next, what I can say about the impact of gender on adult lives is necessarily culture specific. But the basic point is not culture specific: Gender affects adult lives profoundly, determining choices (or whether you will have certain choices at all), relationships, and sequences of experiences.

Since I will be talking about sex differences in adult lives in virtually every chapter of this book, I will not give you a detailed analysis here, but let me list a few of the most significant differences:

- Women's work patterns are much more likely to be interrupted by periods of nonwork than are men's (see Giele, 1982b, for a review). (This is true

**Figure 2–3** *This young couple may seem to be starting out on the journey of adulthood with similar advantages and opportunities. But merely because one is male and one is female, there are likely to be differences in the life pathways they will follow. The young woman is likely to change a great many more diapers, to wash many more dishes, to work fewer years, and to have more friends. The young man is likely to make more money, but to have a shorter life span. (Source: John Vincent Veltri, Photo Researchers Inc.)*

even today, when many more women show patterns of continuous work involvement than was true a few decades ago.) This occurs both because of childbearing and childrearing, and because women are often not the primary wage earner in a family. The interrupted work pattern, in turn, affects job advancement, success, and income.

- Women's family roles include much more child care, housework, and nurturing of both children and spouse than do men's family roles (e.g., Geerken & Gove, 1983; Maret & Finlay, 1984; Rossi, 1980a), even when both spouses are employed full time. This fact has implications not only for the relationship between the spouses, but also for the sequence in which women and men take up the various emotional and developmental "tasks" of adulthood. For men, for example, nurturance and emotional expressiveness appear to flower in middle age, while for women they are expressed strongly in the 20s and 30s.
- Men and women have different patterns of relationships with friends. Women's friendships are more intimate, with more personal disclosure, while men's friendships are more based on shared activities or interests (Bell, 1981; Reisman, 1981). Women also typically have more friends than do men (Lowenthal, Thurnher, & Chiriboga, 1975). These differences have an impact throughout life, but perhaps most strongly when an individual adult is facing high levels of stress or personal crisis. Many men, lacking a close personal confidant, find dealing with such crises as the death of a spouse, or unexpected unemployment, far more traumatic than do women.
- Women live longer than men do. Among other things, this means that most women will be widowed, and will have to deal with living alone in old age (e.g., Verbrugge, 1984).

If we look at the lives of the five young people I described at the beginning of the chapter, we can make some educated guesses about their life paths, knowing only their gender. To be sure, there is a great deal of variation in life patterns within each gender. There are many women (of whom I have been one) who follow a more typical "male" occupational and family pathway, working continuously throughout adulthood, sharing family duties, or having no children. There are certainly many men with deep and intimate friendships, and many who share fully in the rearing of children. But it is no accident that the first thing we ask about any newborn baby is "is it a boy or a girl?" We expect boys and girls to be different, and to lead different lives. Those expectations are grounded in the facts of gender roles in our culture.

## Racial and Ethnic Differences in Adult Life

Like gender, race is an unchangeable characteristic of the individual, and like gender, a person's race has a profound effect on the patterns of adulthood.

Most of what I can say about racial differences in the experiences of adults in the United States relates to black/white comparisons. There has been relatively little research on Spanish-surname adults, still less on Asians, and least of all on Native Americans. So if, in the following summary statements, I seem to be saying mostly "blacks" and "whites," take that as a reflection of the state of our knowledge, rather than a statement about the importance of other racial groups.

- Life expectancy is five to six years longer among whites than among nonwhites for both men and women (U.S. Bureau of the Census, 1984a). A white girl born in the United States in 1981 could expect to live to be 78.5 years old; a black girl could expect to live till age 73. (The equivalent figures for males are 71.1 and 64.4 years, respectively.) Life expectancies are still shorter for Mexican Americans, and shortest of all for Native Americans. The racial difference is very clear in Figure 2–4, which shows the number

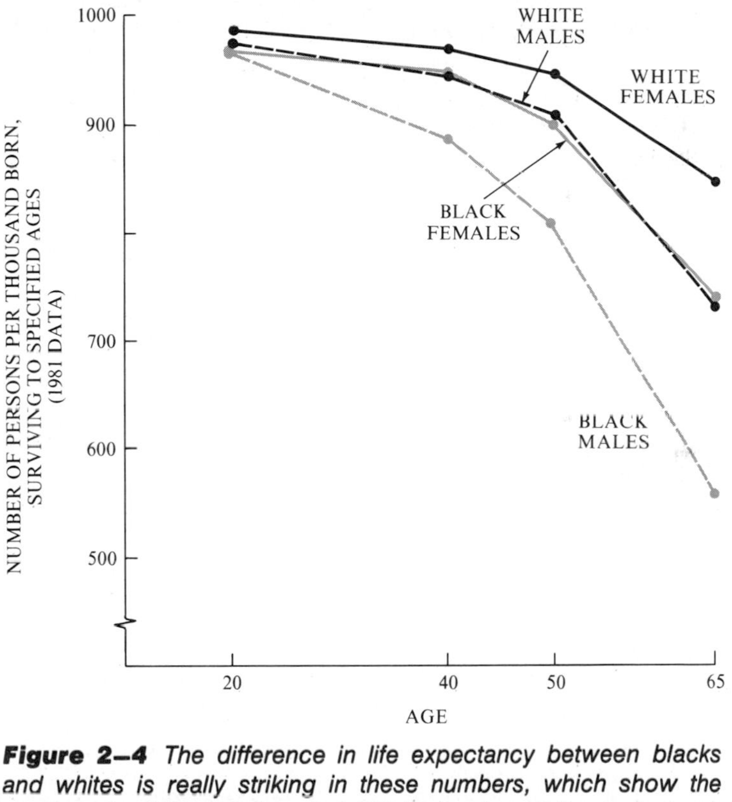


***Figure 2–4*** *The difference in life expectancy between blacks and whites is really striking in these numbers, which show the number of adults out of each 1,000 born who will live to be each of several ages. As you can see, women have higher survival rates than do men, but blacks are consistently lower than whites. In particular, black males show a marked drop in survival between age 50 and 65. (Source: U.S. Bureau of the Census, 1984a, Table 103, p. 69.)*

of black and white adults, out of each 1,000 born, who could expect to live to various ages. As you can see, the largest difference is in the likelihood that a black male will reach the age of 65. Interestingly, however, this racial difference in life expectancy largely disappears for those adults who reach the age of 65. For example, a white woman who had reached the age of 65 in 1981 could expect to live an additional 18.8 years, while a black woman of the same age could expect to live an additional 17 years (U.S. Bureau of the Census, 1984a). By age 75, the pattern has reversed, with nonwhite adults having longer life expectancies than whites (Verbrugge, 1985).

- Blacks have lower social status, less well paying jobs, and lower incomes than do whites. In 1983, for example, the average household income of blacks was $16,531, while that of whites was $26,455. (For Spanish-surname households, the average was $19,369.) In that same year (a year of economic recession) over 30% of black households were below the poverty line, compared to about 11% of white households (U.S. Bureau of the Census, 1984a). These differences exist at all ages (Palmore, Burchett, Fillenbaum, George, & Wallman, 1985). Among the elderly, over half of blacks are living below the poverty line, compared to approximately 15% to 20% for whites (Staples & Mirande, 1980).
- Family experiences are, on average, quite different in black and white families. Table 2–1 shows some typical differences in divorce rates for the cohort of women born between 1930 and 1939 (now 46 to 56). In this age group, a third of the black women had been divorced, compared to a quarter of the whites (Norton, 1983). In addition, Bianchi & Farley (1979) estimate that as many as 50% of the black children born in 1976 were born to an unmarried mother, compared to 8% among whites. Collectively, these differences mean that there are a great many more black households headed by women, and that a large minority of black children—like Walter Washington—grow up without a father present. Spanish surname adults, in contrast, have divorce rates that are similar to whites' (Norton, 1983).
- Blacks have traditionally received fewer years of education than have whites. In 1960, for example, the median years of school completed was 10.9 for

**TABLE 2–1 Patterns of Divorce and Remarriage in the U.S. Population of Women Born Between 1930 and 1939**

| | White Women | Black Women | Spanish-surname Women |
|---|---|---|---|
| Percent of women who have been divorced at least once | 25.7% | 33.1% | 25.5% |
| Percent married twice | 11.1% | 12.0% | 9.7% |
| Average number of children born to those women married at least once | 3.27 | 4.40 | 3.76 |

**Source:** Norton, 1983.

whites and 8.0 for blacks (U.S. Bureau of the Census, 1984a). But by 1983 this difference had shrunk to almost nothing (12.6 versus 12.4 years). Spanish surname adults, however, still receive about a year less education on average.

- On average, blacks report lower overall life satisfaction than do whites (Campbell, 1981; Harris, 1981), no doubt in part because of lower income, fewer job opportunities, and outright prejudice encountered throughout life. Interestingly, however, suicide rates are higher for whites than for blacks (McIntosh, 1985), particularly among those 30 and older, and particularly for men.

The overall picture is one of an extra set of hurdles for blacks and for those of other minority races. Since all the summary statements represent averages, not individuals, we can be quite sure that a great many minority race adults surmount those extra hurdles and achieve not only satisfaction in their lives, but genuine development or growth. Still, in this culture, at this moment, the pathways of adulthood are strewn with more obstacles for blacks and other minority group adults than they are for the average white. Given his determination and the good fortune of having had encouragement from teachers, Walter Washington may well pull himself up by his economic bootstraps and achieve considerable occupational and financial success. But because of persisting prejudice in the workplace (and elsewhere) that task will be harder for him than it would be for a young white man in similar circumstances.

## Intelligence Differences in Adult Life

Unlike gender and race, intelligence is not a quality that is directly visible, but differences in intelligence nonetheless have a notable effect on the pathways individuals follow through adulthood. I am not going to delve into the question of whether intelligence, as measured by an IQ test, is inherited or determined by environment. It is both, in about equal measure (Scarr, 1981). But whatever their origins, differences between children in intellectual "power," in ability to remember things, analyze ideas, or recognize relationships, are well established and quite stable from about age five or six (Bloom, 1964). Scores on intelligence tests (IQ scores) are positively correlated (about .60) with school performance in elementary and high school (Sattler, 1974). Higher IQ children also are more popular with their peers and are likely to have a somewhat easier time weathering the storms of adolescence (Asher, Renshaw, & Hymel, 1982; Rowe & Marcia, 1980). It seems reasonable to assume that differences in intelligence—whatever their source—would have equal impact on adults. To determine how much this is so, we need to know two things: How consistent are IQ scores over adulthood, and what influence do IQ scores have on the shape or experience of adult life?

## Consistency of Intelligence over Adulthood

It is important to understand that what I am looking for here is the second type of consistency I discussed a moment ago—whether adults stay in roughly the same rank order of measured intelligence through adulthood. I am not asking whether, for adults as a group, intelligence goes up or down with age. The latter is a question of intellectual change or development, which I will discuss in detail in chapter 5. Here I am concerned with the issue of individual differences and their persistence.

Results from the several longitudinal studies addressing this question have converged on quite a clear answer: IQ shows strong individual consistency over the adult years. A typical finding is from the Berkeley Intergenerational Studies (recall Table 1–2) (Eichorn, Hunt, & Honzik, 1981). In this sample, there was a correlation of .83 for men and .77 for women between IQ scores at 17 and those achieved by the same adults between the ages of 36 and 48. These are strong relationships, but they still leave a good deal of room for individual shifts within the range. In this particular sample, 11% of the subjects gained 13 or more IQ points over this age span, while another 11% showed losses of six points or more.

Gainers were likely to have gone to school longer, to have traveled abroad, or to have married someone with a higher IQ. Personally, gainers were likely to be tolerant of ambiguity, to be "intellectually efficient," and to show general psychological health. IQ losers, in contrast, were likely to have developed physical diseases or disabilities which impaired performance, or to be heavy or problem drinkers.

Overall, IQ scores at the start of adulthood are highly predictive of IQ scores at later ages, but psychologically significant individual change can and does occur.

## The Influence of IQ Variations on Adult Life

The more significant question is whether people with different levels of intellectual skill (as measured by an IQ test, or by school grades, or the equivalent) have different kinds of life experiences. It will not surprise you to know that they do. Let me give you a brief list of some of the larger differences.

- Higher IQ teenagers complete more years of school than do those with lower IQ (Brody & Brody, 1976; McCall, 1977).
- Higher IQ young adults are more likely to end up in higher prestige occupations (Brody & Brody, 1976), and earn higher incomes (Hauser & Dickinson, 1974).
- Higher IQ adults show less decline in intellectual ability in old age than do lower IQ adults (e.g., Jarvik & Bank, 1983).

The relationship between IQ and occupational success, however, is more complex than this list may imply. Many occupations have "entrance requirements,'' including IQ-like measures. To get into law school or medical school, for example, a student must do well on special examinations. There are minimum IQ requirements for other jobs, too, such as police officer or army officer. In these occupations, among those who pass the entrance requirement, IQ does *not* predict ultimate job success (see Brody & Brody, 1976, for a review of this research). Lawyers with IQs of 150 do not earn more money or make better advocates than those with IQs of 120. Higher IQ police officers do not make more arrests or solve domestic squabbles more effectively than lower IQ officers.

However, among jobs that have fewer or weaker intellectual entrance requirements but that nonetheless demand skill—jobs like secretary or bookkeeper or even midlevel managers in businesses—IQ scores are correlated with both income and promotions (Bray & Howard, 1983; Brody & Brody, 1976). So IQ serves as a credential for higher status jobs, and as a predictor of significant job-related skills in lower status jobs.

If you look at the list I have just given, you may well suspect that in many instances the impact of IQ is indirect, rather than direct. It is not that high IQ causes higher income, or retention of greater intellectual skill in old age. Instead, IQ influences such things as the years of education or interest in intellectual pursuits (reading, doing crossword puzzles, playing intellectual games), and these in turn affect the life patterns. Still, differences in intelligence among young adults may suggest a good deal about the direction of their future lives.

## Temperament and Personality Differences in Adult Life

Another inner or built-in quality of young people that appears to have a major effect on the pattern of adult development is what psychologists call **personality** or **temperament**. Personality is the broader term, referring to ''the individual's distinctive, consistent, patterned methods of relating to the environment'' (Houston, Bee, & Rimm, 1983). The term *temperament* is normally used more narrowly, to describe individual variation on a small number of constitutionally based, relatively stable aspects of personal style or emotional response to stimulation (Buss & Plomin, 1984; Rothbart & Derryberry, 1981; Thomas & Chess, 1977). Such aspects as basic sociability or emotionality are now typically described as temperament, while such characteristics as levels of aggressiveness or dependency or altruism would be described as personality. Temperamental differences—which can be identified in early infancy—may thus be some of the building blocks of later, more complex personality patterns.

The personal styles of the four young people I described at the beginning of the chapter differ in a number of significant ways. Both Tom Kleck and Cathy Stevens are outgoing, sociable people, while Chris Linton is shy and somewhat reclusive and Walter Washington is a loner. Laura Rogers and Chris are both somewhat negative in their response to problems, while both Tom and Cathy are characteristically more cheerful and optimistic. They also differ in their degree of rigidity or openness to experience. Tom Kleck seeks out new experiences, as does Walter Washington; Chris and Cathy like to avoid them, preferring predictable routine.

## The Consistency of Temperament and Personality in Adulthood

The question of whether personality is consistent across situations or from one year to the next has been a matter of hot debate within psychology for several decades (e.g., Costa & McCrae, 1980; Mischel, 1968, 1984). Two questions have to be separated in order to make sense out of this dispute. First, do people describe themselves (or are they described by others) similarly on basic personality dimensions from one time to the next? The answer to this seems to be "yes," at least for some dimensions. Each of us experiences ourself as being in some ways "the same" over time. We approach problems in similar ways, have characteristic moods, and enduring motives.

Second, do these relatively consistent personality or temperamental characteristics translate consistently or predictably into behavior? The answer to this is "not always." A person who describes himself as shy at 25 is likely to still describe himself as shy at 45, and in many situations he will behave "shyly." But there will also be variations in his shy behavior as a function of circumstances. If he badly wants to impress his boss, or is with close friends, he may show no more shy behavior than would someone who describes himself as more outgoing. Thus the trait may be stable, but its expression is partially affected by the context.

The strongest evidence for consistency of personality or temperament in adulthood comes from the work of Paul Costa and Robert McCrae (1980a 1984; Costa, McCrae, & Arenberg, 1983). They propose three basic personality dimensions, which I've summarized in Table 2–2. In their Baltimore Longitudinal Study of Aging, they have studied men who range in age from 20 to 90, testing and retesting each man every six years. (Recently, they have also begun to study women, but do not yet have any longitudinal results for women.) Table 2–3 shows the correlations between self-reported personality characteristics over 12-year intervals for men in three different age groups. These cor-

**TABLE 2–2 Three Stable Aspects of Personality**

| | |
|---|---|
| Neuroticism | Included in this dimension of personality are such tendencies as: hostility, impulsiveness, vulnerability, self-consciousness, a tendency toward depression, and high levels of anxiety. A person low on this dimension would be low on all of these qualities. |
| Extraversion | An individual high in extraversion (vs. intraversion) shows high levels of activity, positive emotions, excitement seeking, gregariousness, assertiveness, and attachment to others. |
| Openness | An individual high in openness shows willingness to explore new values, new actions, new aesthetics or fantasy, a wide range of feelings and ideas. |

**Source:** from Costa & McCrae, 1980.

**TABLE 2–3 Correlations Between Scores on Several Personality Dimensions Obtained 12 Years Apart on a Large Group of Men of Different Ages**

| | Age Groups | | | |
|---|---|---|---|---|
| | *22–44* | *45–59* | *60–76* | *Entire Group* |
| **Personality Dimensions Relating to Extraversion:** | | | | |
| General Activity | .77 | .82 | .78 | .77 |
| Ascendance | .61 | .74 | .76 | .83 |
| Sociability | .64 | .81 | .66 | .74 |
| **Dimensions Relating to Lack of Neuroticism** | | | | |
| Emotional Stability | .63 | .76 | .71 | .70 |
| Objectivity | .66 | .76 | .59 | .69 |
| Friendliness | .74 | .68 | .87 | .74 |
| Personal Relations | .78 | .64 | .73 | .68 |

**Source:** Costa, P. T., jr, McCrae, & Arenberg, 1983, adapted from Table 7.5, p. 247. Reprint by permission of the Guilford Press, New York.

relations are quite remarkably high, suggesting strong consistency at least over periods of a decade. In separate analyses, they found somewhat lower consistency for their domain of Openness, with 10-year correlations ranging from .44 to .63 (Costa & McCrae, 1980a). Other researchers have also found high levels of consistency on similar measures, particularly measures that tap a general dimension of "negative affectivity" or maladjustment (Pogue-Geile & Rose, 1985; Watson & Clark, 1984).

Costa and McCrae conclude that "personality dispositions are extraordinarily stable in adulthood" (1984a, p. 149). Other researchers, particularly those who have studied adults over longer stretches of time than 10 years, have reported less striking stability (e.g., Block, 1971; Mussen, Honzik, & Eichorn, 1982). Norma Haan, who has studied personality consistency and change in the Oakland and Berkeley longitudinal samples over periods from adolescence to middle age, comes to a more cautious conclusion: "The implication seems to be that people change slowly, while maintaining some continuity" (Haan, 1981, p. 128).

Three points stand out for me from my reading of this literature. First, individual adults do show consistency—sometimes remarkable consistency—in some aspects of personality or temperament over long periods of time. Costa and McCrae appear to have identified several general qualities, extraversion and neuroticism, which are among the most consistent aspects. But a great many dimensions of personality or temperament do not show similar consistency over the adult years. In the Berkeley Intergenerational Studies (Eichorn et al., 1981), for example, measures of nurturance and hostility show only very weak consistency (low correlations) over the years from 20 to 30, or 30 to 40, a pattern also found between adolescence and young adulthood in the Fels longitudinal study (Kagan & Moss, 1962).

A second key point for me is that even on those dimensions on which considerable stability occurs, change does occur—perhaps fairly slowly, over decades rather than over years, but it does occur.

The third point, which is not apparent in the findings I have reported but which I find most intriguing of all, is that some people seem to be more stable than others. Some of us (perhaps those who are characteristically more open to new experiences?) change markedly from adolescence to middle or late adulthood; others are remarkably consistent and predictable over the same years. The traditional methods of analysis, such as the correlations shown in Table 2–2, mask this variability in consistency. Jack Block draws what I think is the right conclusion about this variability:

> We should not be asking the question: Are people consistent over time? Some are and some are not. We should be asking instead such questions as: What kinds of people are consistent and what kinds are not? Is consistency a sign of positive change or a sign of failure to grow? Is inconsistency an indicator of positive change or of negative change or is it simply a sign of transformation? Can we identify the conditions and circumstances related to various kinds of personality change and personality continuity? (1981, p. 36)

I will be returning to precisely these questions in the last chapters of the book, when I come back again to the issue of individual pathways through adulthood.

## The Impact of Personality or Temperament on Adult Pathways

Since by definition personality or temperament describe characteristic ways of responding to the world around us, differences in personality are bound to have an impact on our day to day lives. Those aspects of personality that are stable over decades should have a still more pervasive effect, influencing our choices of jobs or friends, our response to crises, even our overall satisfaction with our lives. The cumulative effect of these choices and responses over the adult years should be substantial.

The evidence is fragmented, but let me give you a few examples to illustrate the kind of effect personality or temperament can have on adult lives.

As you might expect, job choice is related to personality, particularly to extraversion. Extraverts are more likely to prefer occupations like social work, business administration, advertising, or law. Introverts prefer such occupations as architecture, physics, or carpentry (Costa, Fozard, & McCrae, 1977).

Once in a job, personality may have some effect on success. Within the business world, at least in the United States, certain aspects of "openness," lack of rigidity, or lack of authoritarianism seem to be related to success, as are high levels of achievement motivation. In the AT&T studies of success in management over a 20-year period (Bray & Howard, 1983; Rychlak, 1982),

**Figure 2–5** *Which of these young business executives will be president of the company in 30 years? You can't tell by looking at them, since they are all "dressing for success." Most likely, the one with the most education, the highest ability, the highest achievement motivation, the strongest commitment to work, and the most open personality will succeed. (Source: Michael Kagan, Monkmeyer Press.)*

men who advanced further in the corporate hierarchy started out not only brighter (higher IQ), but also with wider interests, greater dominance, and greater achievement motivation. Rychlak describes these men as "enlargers." Their goals included change, innovation, and growth, much of which sounds a great deal like the dimension of openness listed by Costa & McCrae. This is not to say that success in all jobs requires these same qualities. There are doubtless many jobs that require stability, thoroughness, even repetition (bookkeeping or accountancy comes to mind). For an adult life course, what may be particularly significant is whether a given adult finds herself in a job with demands and payoffs that match her own temperament or style. When this occurs, the individual is likely to be more successful at that job.

The most general impact of personality on adult life is on overall life satisfaction. Costa and McCrae have found, for example, that adults high on aspects of neuroticism are consistently less satisfied with their lives, while those high in extraversion are consistently more satisfied. Openness appears to have little link to satisfaction (Costa & McCrae, 1984b). The correlations are only of moderate magnitude (on the order of .35 to .50), but they have been found repeatedly. More impressive is the fact that Costa and McCrae can show that measures of neuroticism or extraversion at one point in adult life can predict happiness or satisfaction 10 or even 20 years later.

> To the extent that wellbeing depends on personality, it follows that an individual's wellbeing can be predicted years in advance by assessment of personality. Psychologists are not prophets, and we cannot predict whether life will hold wealth or poverty, health or illness, love or loss. But if our model is correct, we can predict how individuals will evaluate whatever life circumstances they encounter, whether they will be happy or unhappy with their lot. (Costa & McCrae, 1984b, p. 150–151)

It appears not to be maturity, or wisdom, or even wealth or success that are the primary determinants of happiness or life satisfaction. Rather, it is the adult's tendency to respond to life with optimism and cheerfulness, or with depression and complaint, that is the most significant factor. Personality thus affects not only specific occupations, or life success; it helps to shape the emotional fabric of adult life.

## Social Class and Family Background Differences in Adult Life

Each of the four elements I have talked about so far is a built-in or internal quality of adults: their gender, their race, their intelligence, and their personality. These are all significant influences on adult patterns. But broader social forces are also at work. Most particularly, the general economic or social conditions in which a young person grows up has a powerful influence on the course he or she will follow through adulthood.

Every society is divided into strata of some kind. In addition to the age strata I described in chapter 1, there are also strata defined by some kind of **social status**. There are bosses and workers, or rich and poor, or even explicit castes. In Western societies, an individual's social status or **social class** is typically defined or measured in terms of three dimensions: education, income, and occupation. Thus, a person with higher status is one with more education, higher income, and a more prestigious occupation. (In other societies, the dimensions of status would be different, but some status differences exist in every society.) Distinctions between "blue collar" and "white collar," or "middle class" and "working class," are fundamentally status distinctions.

Each of us was reared to young adulthood in a family occupying some position in the status hierarchy. Walter Washington grew up in a poverty-level or lower-class familiy; Both Tom Kleck and Laura Rogers grew up in working-class families; Cathy Stevens and Chris Linton grew up in middle-class families. We can see the effects of these differences in family background in a host of ways in early adulthood—in education levels, in life expectations, in attitudes. But to what extent is a young person's own eventual social status determined by that of his or her parents? And what is the long-term effect of a person's own social status on his or her experience of adult life?

## The Persistence of Social Status Through Adulthood

Societies differ markedly in the permeability of the boundaries between social classes. What sociologists call **social mobility**—the movement of an individual from one social status level to another—is much more visible in some cultures than in others, and at different times in the same cultures. So what I will have to say here is necessarily culture-and time-specific. In the United States over the past several generations at least, 60 percent to 70 percent of men end up in occupations at the same broad level of social status as their fathers. You can see this effect in Figure 2–6, from data collected in 1972 (Featherman, 1980;

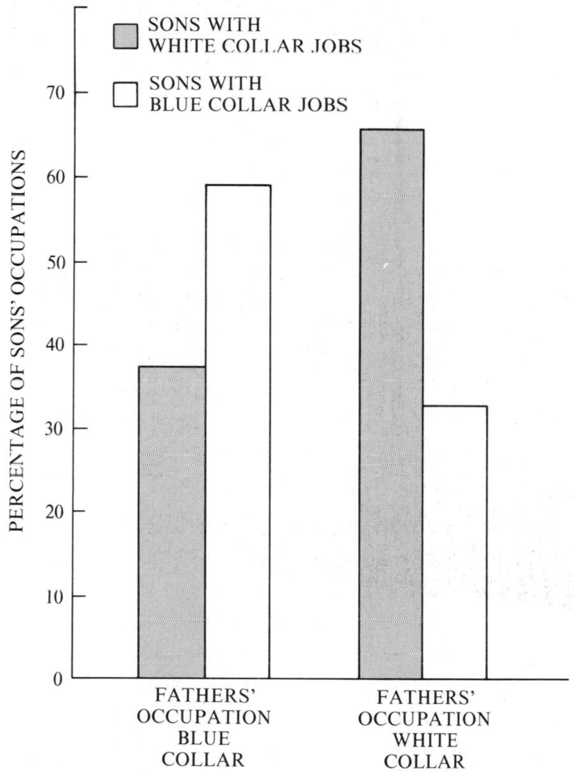


***Figure 2–6*** *The majority of young men from both blue-collar and white-collar families will end up spending their adult lives in the same social class as their fathers. But significant minorities will show shifts, either upward or downward in social class. (Source: Featherman, 1980, p. 704, and Featherman & Hauser, 1975.)*

Featherman & Hauser, 1975). About 60 percent of men from blue-collar families were themselves in blue-collar jobs, while two thirds of those from white-collar families had similar jobs themselves. There is a good deal more movement within levels than Figure 2–6 suggests, of course, such as between higher and lower status white collar jobs, or higher and lower status blue collar jobs. But if we look just at the two broad social strata in our culture, there is quite a strong degree of persistence from one generation to the next.

Still, it is clear that mobility from one status to the other is also quite common. Thus, while there is a bias in the system in favor of consistency in status, any one adult is not fixed into a particular social class because of the family in which he or she grew up.

For women, by the way, the persistence of social status positions from one generation to the next operates not primarily through jobs but through choice of husband. The principle of **marital homogamy** says that people tend to marry those like themselves—in religious background, in race, in social status (Lewis & Spanier, 1979). So women from working class backgrounds tend to marry men from the same background, and the couple is then likely to remain in that broad social status group throughout adulthood, as a function of the husband's occupation.

For me, the most interesting question about these facts is not why people tend to remain in the same social class group as their parents, but why some people do *not* do so. Is upward (or downward) mobility just a question of luck or chance? Or can we identify some qualities of young adults that might lead us to predict which ones will be upwardly mobile, which will not? Some results from several of the longitudinal studies I described in Table 1–2, the Berkeley Intergenerational Studies (Clausen, 1981) and the AT&T study of managers (Bray & Howard, 1983; Rychlak, 1982) give us a few clues.

Upwardly mobile men in the Berkeley studies had, as teenagers, placed a stronger value on intellectual matters and appeared brighter to the adults who interviewed them than did those who turned out to be less mobile. They were also rated as more socially perceptive, more dependable, and more highly motivated to achieve (Clausen, 1981). Similarly, men in the AT&T study who had moved up to management from working-class beginnings, and then went on to be successful at the management level, had somewhat higher IQ scores, a wide range of interests, and strong internal motivations to achieve (Bray & Howard, 1983). Both Tom Kleck and Walter Washington, whom you met at the beginning of this chapter, have a number of these qualities, and both are already at higher occupational levels than their parents. We might predict, from these studies, that Tom and Walter will continue to move upward in the occupational and social ladder.

Overall, there is a strong but not dominant tendency for young people to spend their adult lives in the same broad social status group as their parents. In recent decades, as the number of blue-collar jobs has declined and the number of white-collar jobs has increased, there has been an overall increase in status throughout our society. But there remains a strong correlation between parents' and children's economic and social life circumstances.

## The Impact of Social Status on Adult Pathways

One of the dominant facts about adult life is that adult pathways are heavily influenced by social status. In our society, working-class and middle-class people experience adulthood very differently. Let me give you only a partial list of the differences. Those adults with higher social status, compared to those of lower status:

- are less likely to experience periods of unemployment in their adult lives (Pearlin & Lieberman, 1979). As an example, in March, 1984, the unemployment rate for adults with only a high school education was 7.2%, while the rate for those with four or more years of college was 2.7%.
- are healthier and live longer (Palmore & Stone, 1973). They are also more likely to be sexually active in late adulthood (especially true for women).
- have more stable and satisfying marriages (Campbell, 1981; Locksley, 1982).
- retain a higher level of intellectual functioning longer into old age (Palmore, 1981).
- are, in general, more satisfied with their lives, (Campbell, 1981) and more likely to show "development" over adulthood in the sense in which I am using that word. For example, Farrell and Rosenberg (1981), in a study of young and middle-aged working-class and middle-class men, found that the working-class men showed not growth but a kind of alienation and disintegration of personality at midlife.

Because proportionately many more blacks than whites are in the working class, there are obvious parallels between this list and the earlier one describing racial differences. And the same overall point needs to be made: Working-class status does not doom a man or woman to an unfulfilling or unsatisfying life, just as a middle-class status does not guarantee happiness and success. But it is clear that the status with which one starts adulthood profoundly shapes the choices, opportunities, and obstacles an adult is likely to face, as well as the way in which those choices and obstacles are met.

# Education Differences in Adult Life

A final significant element in the predictive equation—one that is almost the resultant of the other five—is level of education. In our society, the number of years of education a young adult completes has an even stronger impact on his adult life pattern than does any quality of his parents' social status (Featherman, 1980), or even his intelligence.

## Consistency of Educational Patterns over Adulthood

In the United States, as elsewhere in the Western world, the number of years of education the average person completes has been going up steadily for many decades. The rate of increase is now slowing down, but the difference is still striking between many cohorts. For example, men born during the Depression, who completed their schooling after World War II, on the average had three or four more years of education than had their fathers (Hauser & Featherman, 1976). Yet despite this overall shift, it is still true that within each adjacent pair of generations there is a moderate and steady correlation of around .45 between the number of years of fathers' and sons' education. That is, those fathers with higher levels of education in their generation had sons with higher levels of education in theirs. Still, a correlation of .45, however steady, leaves a good deal of room for shifting, too. Some of the other variables that seem to have the effect of pushing some adults (both men and women) toward greater

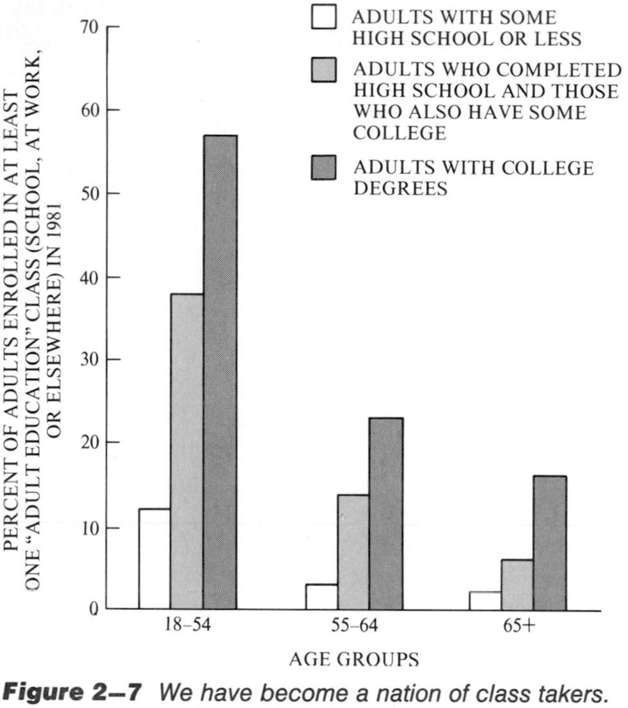


**Figure 2–7** *We have become a nation of class takers. Based on a national survey taken in 1981, Harris estimates that 29% of all adults over 18 are taking at least one "adult education" class at any one time. As you can see in the figure, though, better educated adults are more likely to continue their education in this way, thus increasing the differences in education over the years of adulthood. (Source: Harris, 1981, data from Table I–16, p. 34.)*

education, and others away from it, include intelligence or school grades, the education plans of peers, specific encouragement from parents and teachers, the timing of marriage, and the young person's own aspirations (Featherman, 1980; Lowe & Witt, 1984).

Most of these analyses of educational attainment have focused on high school and college. The assumption is that young people go to school continuously for some number of years, stop schooling to take a job or to marry, and then don't get much education after that point. But there are educational opportunities throughout life, either through a return to a regular school or college, or through some form of adult education. Estimates of the number of adults enrolled in such classes vary, depending on whether students in regular high school or college classes are included. The National Center for Educational Statistics (1981) estimates 13% of adults 17 or over were participating in some kind of "adult education," including those who might also have been in regular high schools and colleges. When actual enrollment in such regular school classes are included, the estimates rise. Harris, in a national survey taken at about the same time (Harris, 1981), found 29% of all adults 18 and over were enrolled in some kind of class, as you can see in Figure 2–7.

You can also see in Figure 2–7 that adult education is more common in the early years of adulthood. The National Center for Educational Statistics (1981) puts the peak between the ages of 25 and 34. But older adults are also in school in quite striking numbers. Most adults take these classes in order to acquire new or better job skills, or to expand their general knowledge about some subject or hobby (Harris, 1981).

What is also apparent in the figure is that such further education is much more common among those adults who had the most traditional schooling in their teens and 20s. Thus, early differences in educational attainment tend to get larger over the years of adulthood as the well educated take more courses, and the least educated take few or none.

## The Influence of Variations in Education on Adult Lives

The effects of these different amounts of education on adults' life patterns are quite striking.

It is through job patterns that education appears to play its largest role.

Laura Rogers' life course is strongly shaped by the fact that because she dropped out of high school when she got pregnant, she is not eligible for any but the lowest levels of jobs. More specifically, education influences a person's first job, and that first job in turn affects later jobs as well (a pattern I will describe in detail in chapter 8). Put another way, how far you can travel on the "job ladder" over your lifetime is strongly influenced by the rung at which you enter it. And the rung-of-entry is itself strongly influenced by the years of education you have completed.

For example, in an extremely complete recent study of workers for a large corporation over a 13-year period, James Rosenbaum (1984) found that the level of entry was one of the biggest factors in determining a worker's job level or income 13 years later. Level of entry, in turn, was strongly influenced by whether the worker had a BA degree or not. And in the longitudinal studies of AT&T workers, Bray and Howard (1983) found that even when basic ability (IQ or acquired job skill) was roughly equated, promotions more often went to workers with college degrees.

For women, education is also strongly related to work success. Featherman (1980) points out that because many women move in and out of the work force, rather than having continuous job patterns, their level of education continues to influence the sorts of jobs they are able to get. For someone who has been continuously employed, a strong work history may override low education in a hiring or promotion decision. But in evaluating a job candidate who has been out of the job market for a time, an employer may place greater emphasis on the credential of a BA degree or other educational achievement.

Of course it is also true that more intellectually able young people are more likely to go to school longer. So perhaps these findings simply tell us that capable people both go to school longer and are have more successful work histories. To some extent that is true. But the amount of education a young person receives is only partially predicted by school grades or achievement test scores. At the level of job entry, it appears to be the credential (or lack of it) conferred by a BA degree or some other educational achievement that has the major effect. And when ability is held constant, as in the AT&T studies, amount of education is still a strong predictor of later job success.

There are Horatio Alger stories out there—men and women with little education who, by dint of hard work and ability, are able to achieve job success and the economic stability that goes with it. Ability does matter. But it is surprisingly hard to override the impact that education has on the size of that first step into the world of work.

In talking here about the impact of education on work lives I do not want to imply that education has no effect on other aspects of adult life. That is far from the truth. Better educated adults share the advantages of higher status adults that I listed earlier: They have better health, remain mentally alert longer into old age, are more satisfied with their marriages and with their lives. Doubtless the financial security that typically accompanies higher education is part of the reason for those differences. But education may also create, or reinforce, habits that will affect later life experiences as well: a habit of reading and discussing ideas; a tendency to be active socially and politically; analytic skills that assist in real-life problem solving.

## Beginnings and Continuities: A Final Look

The six elements I have talked about—gender, race, intelligence, personality, social class, and education—do not exhaust the list of characteristics of young people that will affect their later life courses. We could make a much longer list, including such physical qualities as stature, body type, physical attractiveness, coordination, or athletic skill. (For OJ Simpson, at 22, the most significant characteristic was not the family he came from, how bright he was, or what his personality was, but the fact that he was a phenomenally good football player.) We could also include many other qualities of family life, such as whether the young person's parents are divorced, whether she has brothers or sisters, or whether she is first born or later born in the family. Each of these elements, too, has an impact on adult lives. But the six I have mentioned help to set the agenda for adulthood for each of us. We do not begin the adult years with equal characteristics, equal choices, or equal opportunities. And to the extent that the initial qualities and choices remain stable or consistent over the adult years, adults will tend to remain on the same trajectory on which they first began the journey.

In the rest of the book I will be searching for ways in which adult lives move in the same ways, for developmental shifts, for shared changes. But there are also powerful forces creating differences in develomental patterns. If we are to understand adulthood, we have to understand the ways in which these two sets of forces interact.

## Summary

1. Adults do not begin the journey of adulthood with clean slates. They already differ in ways that will have a major impact on the pathways they will follow. Particularly significant are differences in gender, race, intelligence, personality, social class, and level of education.

2. Gender differences are pervasive, affecting family roles, work patterns, and the sequencing of the tasks of adult life.

3. Race differences, too, are predictive of different family patterns, work opportunities, health and longevity, and life satisfaction.

4. Intelligence differences, present in young adulthood, are highly persistent through the adult years. Nonetheless, some people show notable increases or decreases in IQ.

5. Intelligence levels influence educational attainment, occupational success, and intellectual vigor in old age.

6. Personality is less consistent through adulthood than is intelligence, but several dimensions of personality seem to be particularly stable: extraversion and neuroticism. Openness to new experiences shows more modest stability.

7. Personality differences affect job choices, and the match between an adult's personality and the demands of the job may affect job success. Most pervasively, personality or temperament appears to affect overall emotional tone or life satisfaction.

8. The majority of adults spend their adult life in the same broad social class strata as did their parents. However, 40% or more show shifts in social class. Upward mobility is predicted by higher levels of education, and by higher IQ, as well as by some personal qualities.

9. The social class in which an adult spends his or her adult years has a major effect on a wide range of adult experiences, including job security, marital satisfaction, life satisfaction, and health.

10. Like social class, a young person's amount of education is somewhat predicted by his or her father's years of education, but there is less consistency here than in the

case of social class. Within the adult years, many adults continue to seek out education, but this is more true of the better educated than the less well educated.

11. Differences in years of education achieved, at least in this culture, have a powerful impact on work history and thus on social class. Education is thus a key link in the chain of elements that shape adult lives.

12. Other differences, present in young adulthood, also have significant effects on adult lives. But these six, in combination and in interaction, are especially important. Shared developmental patterns over adult life are played against the background of these fundamental differences.

## Suggested Readings

COSTA, P. T. JR., & MCCRAE, R. R. (1984) Personality as a lifelong determinant of wellbeing. In C. Z. Malatesta & C. E. Izard (Eds.), *Emotion in adult development.* Beverly Hills, CA: Sage Publications.

I find this collection of work extremely interesting, and these authors describe complex findings with both clarity and verve.

FEATHERMAN, D. L. (1980). Schooling and occupational careers: constancy and change in worldly success. In O. G. Brim, Jr., & J. Kagan (Eds.), *Constancy and change in human development.* Cambridge, MA: Harvard University Press.

This dense but excellent chapter will introduce you to some of the complexities of studying the effects of education, intelligence, and social class on adult lives.

# 3

# Theories of Adult Change or Development

Having just spent an entire chapter persuading you that adult life is powerfully shaped by persistent, durable characteristics of individuals, it may seem contradictory to turn now to an examination of the ways in which adult lives move in the same directions or share similar patterns. But the fact that both of these ways of looking at adulthood are simultaneously true is one of the basic points I want to make in this book. Each of us may enter and move through adulthood on a somewhat different trajectory, but all adult trajectories may still have important elements in common. We are both all alike and all different.

The empirical search for the common elements is the subject of the seven chapters in the next section. Before looking at the data, though, I want to lay the groundwork by talking about theories of adult continuity and change. I find these theories fascinating in themselves. But they also serve to point us at some of the critical questions that research might answer, and to illustrate the variety of ways of thinking about adulthood.

## Varieties of Theories

Twenty-five years ago, any discussion of theories of adult development would have been almost totally dominanted by one theory: Erik Erikson's model of psychosocial development. Erikson's view is still highly influential, but today there has been a real flowering of ideas, some of them distinctly different from Erikson's views.

This wide variety of existing theories will form a better framework for later discussions if I organize the approaches along several dimensions, as I have done in Figure 3–1. Any categorization scheme, including this one, is inevitably an oversimplification. Each theory contains its own unique combination of ideas. But we can still use the two dimensions shown in Figure 3–1 as a helpful basis for organizing the options.

The first dimension on which theories may be organized is their relative

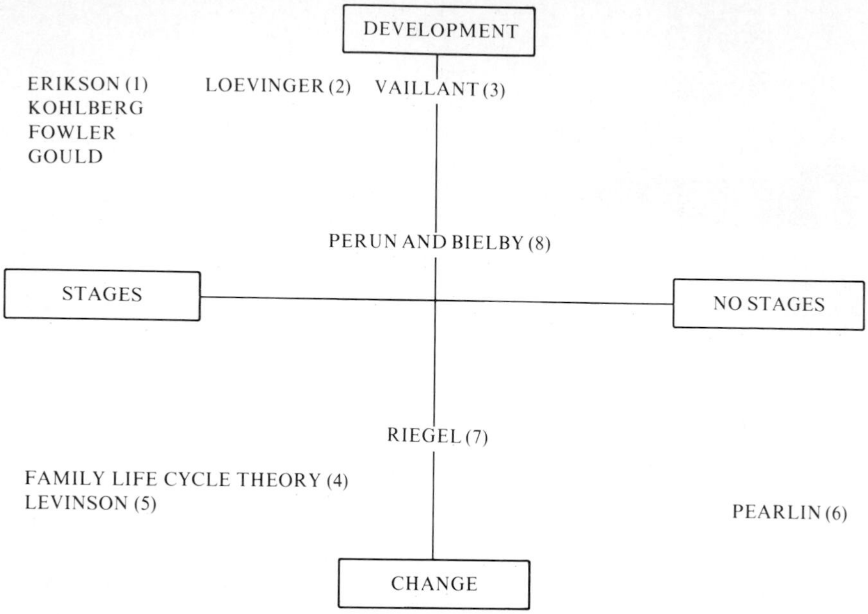


***Figure 3–1*** *This two-dimensional grid, with development versus change as one dimension, and stage versus nonstage theories as the other, allows us to contrast several of the major theories of adult development. (The numbers in parentheses indicate the sequence with which these theories are discussed in the chapter.)*

emphasis on development versus change. The fundamental difference—as I am using the terms development and change in this book—is that a development theory assumes there is some goal or end point toward which the adult moves, and that this end point is potentially "better" or more mature than what is seen at earlier ages. A theory of adult change, in contrast, assumes no such end point or goal nor any "improvement" or growth. Among developmental theorists, for example, Erikson talks about "ego integrity" as being the final state, accompanied by wisdom. Vaillant describes a developmental continuum from immature to more mature forms of defense mechanisms. Other theorists, such as Levinson or Pearlin, while agreeing that there are significant changes taking place over the adult years, do not see those changes as leading anywhere that is more mature, or more integrated, or more wise. Your great-aunt Elsie is different from you in specific, predictable ways; but she is not necessarily better (or worse), wiser or more mature.

Note that among the theorists I have listed in Figure 3–1 are several who fall at in-between points on the development/change dimension. It is not necessary to assert one position or the other; one might argue, for example, that both occur under some conditions.

The second dimension I have used to categorize theories of adulthood is that of the presence or absence of stages in each theory. This is a somewhat risky organizational rubric, since the term *stage* is used to describe several different concepts. Most generally, stages refer to fixed sequences of experiences or events over time, such as the family life cycle stages I mentioned briefly in chapter 1. More narrowly (and more commonly in psychological theories), stages imply systematic, sequential, *qualitative* changes in some skill or underlying psychological structure. When Jean Piaget talks about stages in children's cognitive development, for example, he does not mean merely that children learn to add and subtract before they learn to multiply and divide, but rather that the ability to multiply and divide requires fundamentally different understandings, logic, or mental structures. Each stage is thought of as being a structural whole, as having its own logic. Most stage theories of adult development make similar assumptions about the nature of changes in adulthood.

Stage theorists also differ on the extent to which they argue that the various stages are age-linked. Levinson's stages are strongly connected to specific ages, for example, while Loevinger's are not.

At the other end of the continuum are those theorists who do not see any stages in adult development at all, in any sense of the term stage. In this view, there is no such thing as a "midlife crisis," or "integrity" in old age, but only constant change or flux. In between these two extremes lie a number of theorists who argue that there are *sequences* but not stages. That is, there may be orderly, predictable sequences of experiences or changes in adulthood, but these changes may not be integrated into inclusive, shared internal or external structures.

When we put these two dimensions together, as in Figure 3–1, some combinations are obviously more common than others. (In fact, I cannot think of a theory that clearly belongs in the upper right-hand corner—a nonstage theory of development—although such a theory is logically possible. One could argue that individuals become more wise or more integrated, but that the paths they follow toward this end are highly individual, without shared stages or sequences.) At the moment, stage theories of development are probably the most common and the most influential. But many of the current attempts at theoretical integration, such as both Riegel's and Perun and Bielby's theories, lie in the middle.

Because of the current dominance of the stage/developmental theories, let me start the detailed discussion of these theories in the upper left and then work my way slowly toward the theories that lie in the middle. (The sequence I will use is indicated in Figure 3–1 by the numbers in parentheses after each theorist's name.)

# Developmental Stage Theories of Adulthood

## Erik Erikson's Theory of Identity Development

Erikson's theory (1950, 1959; 1980; Evans, 1969) has clearly been the most influential view of adult development proposed thus far. There are traces of this theory in every other stage theory of adulthood, and his terminology has been widely adopted.

He proposes that psychosocial development continues over the entire life span, resulting from the interaction between inner instincts and drives, and outer cultural and social demands. For Erikson, a key concept is the gradual, step-wise emergence of a sense of **identity**. Erikson explicitly stated that development follows a basic, built-in "ground plan" (1959, p. 53) which shapes a sequence of "potentialities for significant interaction" with those around the child or the adult. To develop a complete, stable identity, the individual must move through and successfully resolve eight "crises" or "dilemmas" over the course of the lifetime (see Table 3–1). Each dilemma emerges as the child or adult is challenged by new relationships, new tasks or demands. So the fourth stage of "industry versus inferiority" begins when the child starts school and is challenged by the demand to learn to read and write and to absorb great chunks of new information.

Each dilemma or stage is defined by a pair of opposing possibilities, one of which describes the optimum outcome of that dilemma, the other the potential

**TABLE 3–1 Erik Erikson's Stages of Psychosocial Development**

| Approximate Age | Stage | Description |
|---|---|---|
| 0–1 years | I. Basic trust versus mistrust | The infant must form a first, loving, trusting, relationship with the caregiver, or risk a persisting sense of mistrust. |
| 2–3 years | II. Autonomy versus shame and doubt | The child's energies are directed toward the development of key physical skills, including walking and grasping and sphincter control. The child learns control but may develop shame if not handled properly. |
| 4–5 years | III. Initiative versus guilt | The child continues to become more assertive, to take more initiative, but may be too forceful and injure others or objects, which leads to guilt. |
| 6–12 years | IV. Industry versus inferiority | The school-age child must deal with the demands to learn new, complex skills, or risk a sense of inferiority. |
| 13–18 years | V. Identity versus role confusion | The teenager (or young adult) must achieve a sense of identity—both who she is and what she will be—in several areas, including occupation, sex role, politics, and religion. |
| 19–25 years | VI. Intimacy versus isolation | The young adult must risk the immersion of self in a sense of "we," creating one or more truly intimate relationships, or suffer feelings of isolation. |
| 26–50 years | VII. Generativity versus stagnation | In early and middle adulthood, each adult must find some way to satisfy the need to be generative, to support the next generation, to turn outward from the self toward others. |
| 50+ years | VIII. Ego integrity versus despair | The culmination, if all previous stages have been reasonably well dealt with, is a sense of acceptance of oneself as one is. |

**Source:** Erikson, 1950, 1959, 1980.

negative or less healthy outcome, such as trust versus mistrust, or integrity versus despair. Erikson thinks that at each point in the life cycle each of us has to face the age-appropriate crisis and resolve it, one way or the other.

As you can see in Table 3–1, there are four dilemmas that describe adulthood, beginning with Stage 5, **identity versus role confusion**, which is the central task of adolescence and the early 20s. The young person must develop some specific ideology, some set of personal values and goals. In part this is a shift from the here-and-now orientation of the child to a future orientation; the teenager must not only consider what or who she *is* but who or what she *will be*. Erikson (and others who have explored this stage following Erikson's lead, such as James Marcia, 1980), suggests that the teenager or young adult must develop several linked identities: an occupational identity (What work will I do?), a sexual or sex role identity (How do I go about being a man or a woman?), a political identity, and a religious identity (What do I believe in?). If these identities are not worked out, then the young person suffers from a sense of diffusion, a sense of not knowing what or who he is.

Stage 6, **intimacy versus isolation**, builds upon the newly forged identity of adolescence. Erikson says:

> It is only after a reasonable sense of identity has been established that real *intimacy* with the other sex (or, for that matter, with any other person or even with oneself) is possible. Sexual intimacy is only part of what I have in mind. . . . The youth who is not sure of his identity shies away from interpersonal intimacy; but the surer he becomes of himself, the more he seeks it in the form of friendship, combat, leadership, love, and inspiration. (1959, p. 101)

Intimacy is "the ability to fuse your identity with somebody else's without fear that you're going to lose something yourself." (Erikson, in Evans, 1969, p. 48). Many young people, Erikson thought, make the mistake of thinking they will find their identity in a relationship, but in his view, it is only those who have already formed (or are well on the way to forming) a clear identity who can successfully enter this fusion of identities that he calls intimacy. For those whose identities are weak or unformed, relationships will remain shallow and the young person will experience a sense of isolation or loneliness.

In later writings (Erikson, 1968), Erikson suggests that this sequence of identity formation followed by intimacy may not be true for many women, for whom the identity may be created in a network of relationships. Other authors (e.g., Sangiuliano, 1978), argue that many women simply reverse the sequence of the tasks of identity and intimacy, while Carol Gilligan (1982), in her influential book *In a Different Voice*, argues that women's identity development is, from the beginning, *inter*dependent rather than *in*dependent. Women define themselves, and think about their choices and dilemmas, in terms of relationships, while men appear to define themselves more by what they do or what they are, separate from their relationships. For women, then, there may simply not be a separate stage of intimacy; rather, intimacy may form the backdrop for all women's stages.

Whatever the resolution of the controversy concerning the stage of intimacy, there is reasonably good agreement that for both men and women there is a subsequent stage, Stage seven in Erikson's model, **generativity versus stagnation**. This stage is difficult to describe. An adult in this stage takes her place in society and helps in the development of the next generation, or adds to the society in some fashion. The bearing and rearing of children is clearly the key element in generativity for Erikson, but he specifically expands the usage to include ''everything that is generated from generation to generation: children, products, ideas, and works of art'' (Erikson, in Evans, 1969, p. 51). I have come to think of this stage as the period in which each adult ''passes on the flame'' to a new generation—by rearing children, by training students, by serving as mentor to a younger worker, by creating ideas. Those adults who cannot achieve a satisfying sense of generativity may experience a sense of stagnation. Erikson also uses the term ''self-absorption'' to describe the flip side of generativity.

The final stage is **ego integrity versus despair**. I can best describe it using Erikson's own eloquent words:

> Only he who in some way has taken care of things and people and has adapted himself to the triumphs and disappointments of being, by necessity, the originator of others and the generator of things and ideas—only he may gradually grow the fruit of the seven stages. I know no better word for it than *integrity*. . . . It is the acceptance of one's own and only life cycle and of the people who have become significant to it as something that had to be and that, by necessity, permitted of no substitutions . . . and an acceptance of the fact that one's life is one's own responsibility. (1959, p. 104)

Erikson argues that this sense of integrity must be built upon the foundation of successful resolution of all the crises and dilemmas that came before. Those adults who cannot achieve a sense of integrity, perhaps because they carry forward a residue of distrust, guilt, diffusion, isolation or self-absorption from earlier stages, experience a sense of despair. They feel that time is too short, or that their life has been a failure, or that they wish they had it to do over again.

There are several key points about Erikson's theory that I want to make as clear as possible. First, the stages build on one another and affect onc another. The unsuccessful resolution of any one stage leaves the individual with ''unfinished business,'' unresolved conflicts, that are carried forward to the next stage, making it then more difficult to resolve the next stage successfully. But second, unlike some other stage theories (e.g., Loevinger), Erikson does not think that you simply stay at a given stage until you have completed it before going on to the next. He argues instead that each person is pushed through this sequence of dilemmas by biological maturation, by social pressures, by the demands of the roles she takes on. You can't stay a 20-year-old until you get it right! On that next birthday you are 21, and then 22, whether you are ready or not. And with increasing age there are new demands, new dilemmas. When you arrive at 60 or 70, the tasks you didn't fully deal with will remain as unresolved issues, interfering with your ability to find true integrity. The theory is thus sequential, but not fully hierarchical.

## Jane Loevinger's Theory of Ego Development

In contrast, Jane Loevinger's stage theory of ego development (1976) is hierarchical. She proposes 10 stages from birth through adulthood, each building on the one that precedes, and movement to the next stage occurring only when the individual has completed the development of the current stage. Although the first few stages typically occur in childhood, the stages have only very loose connections to particular ages. Among a group of adults of any given age, a wide range of stages of ego development would be visible. What Loevinger is describing, in essence, is a pathway (or, perhaps better, a flight of stairs) along which she thinks we all must move. But the rate of movement, and the final stage (step) achieved, differ widely from one person to the next.

The 10 stages or levels are listed in Table 3–2. Loevinger suggests that virtually all adults successfully move through the first three stages. Some then get stuck at the **self-protective stage**, while still others move to the **conformist stage** and no further. Most adults, however, reach at least the transition that she calls the **self-aware level**, and many go beyond this to the conscientious stage or further.

The final four stages are particularly interesting for a study of adulthood. The **conscientious stage** is really defined by the emergence of a set of self-chosen and self-evaluated rules. It is thus in some ways like Erikson's stage of "identity versus confusion," except that Loevinger argues that the transition to the conscientious stage often occurs well past adolescence, if it occurs at all. Another aspect of the conscientious stage is the ability to see other people in complex, three-dimensional terms, in contrast to the greater stereotyping and two-dimensionality of relationships of earlier stages. "With the deepened understanding of other people's viewpoints, mutuality in interpersonal relations becomes possible" (p. 22). An adult at this stage would no longer describe (or think of) some particular friend as "a stockbroker who grew up in New York," but perhaps as "a highly achievement-oriented, determined, but somewhat lonely man."

The key to the **individualistic level**, which represents a transition stage between the conscientious and the autonomous, is the development of greater tolerance for both self and others. Individuals are experienced as unique, their flaws and their virtues are seen clearly. There is also a renewed struggle with the problem of dependence on others. The individualistic adult realizes that independence is not achieved merely by earning your own money or having your own house. There is an inner level of independence as well. The individualistic person has not yet reached the point of full independence, but knows that it is possible.

The next full stage in Loevinger's model is the **autonomous stage**, when that inner independence has been reached. Autonomy does not at all imply indifference toward others. On the contrary, the autonomous adult cherishes

**TABLE 3–2 Jane Loevinger's Stages of Ego Development**

| Stage | Description |
|---|---|
| Presocial Stage | The baby must learn to differentiate himself from his surroundings, to develop object constancy. |
| Symbiotic Stage | Baby retains a symbiotic relationship with the mother (or other major caregiver). Major task is to emerge from that symbiosis, through language in part. |
| Impulsive Stage | The child asserts his separate identity, partly by giving free rein to impulses. Others are valued in terms of what they can give. Those remaining too long at this stage may be "uncontrollable" or "incorrigible." |
| Self-protective Stage | The child learns self-control of impulses by anticipating immediate, short-term rewards or punishments. The child understands existence of rules, but tries always to maximize his own gain. Some adults function at this stage. |
| Conformist Stage | Child or adult identifies his own welfare with that of the group and attempts to model his behavior along the lines of group expectations. Individuals in this stage tend to be insensitive to individual differences, to be highly stereotyped in response, particularly about sex roles. Inner life is seen in black and white: happy/sad, good/bad. |
| Self-aware Level | This is a transition level between conformist and conscientious stages. Self-awareness increases as does acceptance of individual differences and shadings of feelings and opinions. Stereotypic categories such as gender, marital status, education, however, are likely to be the basis of judgments, rather than other people's individual traits or needs. |
| Conscientious Stage | Individually created rules and ideals have now been formed, and the person attempts to live by them. Adults at this stage have a richer inner life, with many more shadings of feelings; similarly, the view of other people becomes more individualistic, the relationships more mutual. |
| Individualistic Level | This is a transition level between the conscientious and autonomous stages. Individuals at this level are focused heavily on the question of independence and dependence. They are also more aware of inner conflict. |
| Autonomous Stage | Adults at this stage (comparatively rare) are fully independent individuals, with a capacity to acknowledge and deal with inner conflict. Other people are accepted and cherished for what and who they are, with no attempt to make them over. |
| Integrated Stage | This final stage, which is extremely rare, transcends the conflict of the autonomous stage. |

**Source:** Loevinger, 1976.

the individuality of others and finds richness in personal relationships. But he is willing to let his friends and family be themselves. He has let his wife step off her pedestal, realized his father had been a partial failure in his business, but loves them both the more deeply for his acceptance of their flaws and failings.

Another key to this stage is the acceptance of the fact of conflict and paradox in human lives. The autonomous adult no longer sees the world in terms of opposites (good and bad, right and wrong) as the conscientious person tends to do; rather, he sees gradations, exceptions, complexities.

The highest stage in this model is the **integrated stage**. On the surface, it is somewhat like Erikson's stage of ego integrity, but Loevinger thinks that it is a more developed stage than "integrity." The person at this stage arrives at a personal reconciliation of the conflicts examined at the autonomous stage, and gives up the quest for the unattainable.

Loevinger's theory has become increasingly influential in the past 10 years, for several reasons. First of all, the fact that the stages are not linked to specific ages can be a real strength. As our empirical information about adult development has grown, it has become increasingly clear that strict age-linked stages, while appealing, are hard to find in real life. Adults of any one age are widely different from one another. Loevinger's theory can help to describe those differences. Second, Loevinger and her colleagues have developed an instrument, the Washington University Sentence Completion Test, to measure a subject's position in the stage continuum. It includes items like: "A woman feels good when ________" or "My main problem is ________." Subjects' answers are then evaluated according to well-defined criteria, to yield a stage score. The existence of such a measure has made it possible for Loevinger's model to be used in research on a range of aspects of adult development, as you will see as you move through this book.

## George Vaillant's View of Adaptation in Adult Life

A third theorist in the upper left quadrant of Figure 3–1 is George Vaillant, whose approach (1977a) has been strongly influenced by Erikson. Vaillant begins by accepting Erikson's stages as the basic framework of development, although he inserts an additional stage, which he calls **career consolidation,** between Erikson's stages of intimacy and generativity, some time at about age 30. Adults in this career consolidation stage, as Vaillant sees them, are intent on establishing their own competence, on mastering a craft, on acquiring higher status or a positive reputation.

Despite his acknowledgment of these stages, Vaillant's central interest has not been with stages, but in the ways in which adults adapt psychologically to the trials and tribulations they face. The major form of adaptation he discusses is the **defense mechanism**.

Freud used the phrase "defense mechanisms" to describe a set of unconscious strategies for dealing with anxiety. Everyone has some anxiety, so everyone uses some kinds of defense mechanisms. All involve self-deception or distortion of reality of some kind. We forget things that make us uncomfortable, or remember them in a way that is not so unpleasant; we give ourselves reasons for doing something we know we shouldn't do, and many more. The point is that the process of defending yourself against anxiety in this way is perfectly normal. What Vaillant has added to this concept is the notion that some defense mechanisms are more mature than others. Table 3–3 lists the four levels of

**TABLE 3–3 Levels of Defense Mechanisms Proposed by Vaillant**

| Level | Description |
|---|---|
| I. "Psychotic" Mechanisms | *Delusional Projection:* frank delusions, such as delusions of persecution.<br>*Denial:* denial of external reality.<br>*Distortion:* grossly reshaping external reality to suit inner needs, including hallucinations, wish-fulfilling delusions (Prince Charming will find me any day now). |
| II. Immature Mechanisms | *Projection:* attributing one's own unacknowledged feelings to others ("You're the one who's afraid, not me").<br>*Schizoid Fantasy:* the use of fantasy or inner retreat to resolve conflict.<br>*Hypochondriasis:* Reproach toward others turned into complaints of physical illness. Often used to avoid making dependency demands directly, or to avoid complaining directly about being ignored.<br>*Passive-Aggressive Behavior:* Aggression toward others expressed indirectly and effectively through passivity, or directed toward the self.<br>*Acting Out:* Direct expression of an unconscious wish, but without acknowledging the emotion that goes with it. It includes delinquent behavior, but also "tempers." |
| III. "Neurotic" Mechanisms | *Intellectualization:* Thinking about wishes or desires in formal, emotionally bland terms and not acting on them.<br>*Repression:* Memory lapses, or failure to acknowledge some information. Putting out of conscious memory.<br>*Displacement:* Directing your feelings toward something or someone other than the original object. (e.g., cuddling your cat, when you really want to hold a lover).<br>*Reaction Formation:* Behaving in a fashion directly opposite to what you would really (unconsciously) like to do (such as being exceptionally nice to a co-worker you detest, since you cannot acknowledge your hatred to yourself).<br>*Dissociation:* Temporary, drastic modification of one's sense of character, such as a sudden devil-may-care attitude, periods of irresponsibility. |
| IV. Mature Mechanisms | *Altruism:* Vicarious but constructive service to others.<br>*Humor:* Overt expression of ideas or feelings, but without discomfort, and without unpleasant effects on others (does not include sarcasm).<br>*Suppression:* Conscious or semiconscious decision to postpone dealing with some impulse or conflict.<br>*Anticipation:* Realistic expectation of future problem or discomfort, and planning for it.<br>*Sublimation:* Indirect expression of some desire or need, but without loss of pleasure or adverse consequences (such as expressing aggression through sports). Instincts are channeled, rather than dammed up. |

**Source:** Vaillant, 1977, p. 383–386.

defense mechanisms in Vaillant's classification. In general, mature defenses involve less distortion of reality. They reflect more graceful, less uncomfortable, ways of coping with difficulties. Vaillant's central thesis is that for an adult to be able to cope effectively with the slings and arrows of normal life, his defense mechanisms must mature.

Don't be confused by the levels listed in Table 3–3. Vaillant is not saying that an adult, at any one moment, uses only defenses that are at one and only one level. On the contrary, most of us use a wide range of defenses, covering several levels. And most of us show "regression" to less mature kinds of defenses when we are under stress. Facing a serious operation, most of us go through repression (of fear), or intellectualization (such as studying the details of the operation very abstractly), or projection ("My husband is the one who's afraid, I'm not"), or acting out (getting furious with the nurse for needing to jab you twice to get blood). Despite such regressions, according to Vaillant, in the normal course of adult life most adults add some of the more mature mechanisms or use them more frequently, and at the same time use the less mature mechanisms less often. Furthermore, Vaillant argues that individuals vary in the extent to which they show such maturing. It is those who move most toward mature defenses who will be most successful in their personal and professional lives.

Vaillant's theory is thus clearly developmental in emphasis, since he charts the progress each adult makes toward higher levels of maturity. But his theory is less easily categorized on the dimension of stage versus nonstage. He accepts Erikson's stages as the background against which adult development occurs. But the primary process of maturing he describes is not stage-like at all. The move from immature to mature defenses is a gradual one, not achieved by all adults at all, and not achieved all at once by any individual.

## Other Stage-Developmental Theories

There are many other theories of this same broad type which describe narrower dimensions of development, such as Lawrence Kohlberg's theory of moral development (Kohlberg, 1964, 1981, 1984), or James Fowler's theory of faith development (1981) both of which I will describe in chapter 10.

Still other theories in this group, while broad in scope, cover a narrower age range than do Erikson, Loevinger, or Vaillant, such as Roger Gould's extremely interesting theory of personal transformation (1978, 1980). Gould's theory effectively covers only the period from about 20 to about 45, and says nothing about the later years. He proposes, in essence, that the process of adult development is one of identifying, and then giving up, a series of "myths" about the world and your place in it. Some of these myths are individual, but Gould argues that there are also shared age-linked myths, such as the one common in one's early and middle 20s, that says something like "as long as I follow the rules, I will be rewarded and be happy." In midlife, there is the myth of immortality that must be faced and abandoned if full adult psychological potential is to be achieved.

Whether narrow or broad, covering all ages or only a portion of the age span, all of these theories share the basic assumption that adults actually develop—that we can become more mature, or can create more complex or higher orders of understanding—and that the development occurs in stages or steps.

# Stage Theories of Adult Change

When we move to the next group of theories, the concept of stages remains. What is eliminated is the assumption that movement through these stages involves ''development.'' Let me describe two such approaches, one drawn from sociology, the other representing a strongly psychological view.

## Family Life Stages: A Sociological Stage Theory

In order to understand the concept of family life stages it is necessary to understand the concept of a **role**. Sociologists describe social systems as being made up of linked or interlocking *positions* (also called *statuses*), such as teacher and student, parent and child, or employer and employee. The *content* of a particular position is called a role. A role is thus a kind of job description for a particular position, a set of skills or qualities expected in a person who occupies that position. The person who fills the role of Girl Scout leader is expected to know about camping, cooking, and crafts, and about organizing activities that will keep young children interested. Such a person is also expected to be friendly and cheerful.

The concept of role is an important one in any discussion of adulthood. We can, in fact, describe (or even define) any one adult's life in terms of the roles he or she performs. I am a mother, a daughter, a sister, a partner, a psychologist, an author, a friend, a school board member, and so on and on. Filling these roles takes up a good portion of my time and energy.

We can also examine the frictions that emerge when an individual attempts to fulfill the demands of two or more roles simultaneously (as virtually all of us do). **Role conflict** occurs when two or more roles are partially or wholely incompatible, logistically or psychologically. When you are trying to juggle the competing demands of your school, your job, and your family, you are experiencing role conflict. There are not enough hours in the day to fulfill the expectations of all three roles. **Role strain** occurs when a person's own qualities or skills are a poor match for the demands of any one role. If you have been out of school for a while, and your study skills are rusty, you may experience role strain when you go back to school. If you are promoted to a job for which you are only marginally prepared, you will feel role strain.

There are a number of roles that change somewhat systematically with age. As I pointed out in chapter 1, there are age strata in any society which have accompanying roles. In our culture, teenagers have one role, young adults another, retired persons still another. Work roles also change with age, as I'll detail in chapter 8. The one sequence of role changes that has been the focus of the greatest research and theoretical interest, however, is that of **family roles.**

A number of sociologists (e.g., Duvall, 1962) have proposed that adult life can be understood in terms of systematic changes in family roles. At least for those adults who marry and have children (the vast majority of adults), adult life marches to the rhythm of shifts in family roles. As you can see in Table 3–4, eight stages have been proposed, each reflecting either additions or deletions to the family (new child, or children leaving) or changes in the content of the parent role as the children shift from infancy to toddlerhood to school-age to adolescence.

You may note some interesting omissions in this list. The role of grandparent is not included. For most adults, this role coincides with the postparental and "aging family" stages. Nor is the role of caregiver to one's own aging parents included in this list, a role that many adults acquire in their 50s. These important family roles are omitted perhaps because they are less clearly sequential than are those associated with the bearing and rearing of one's own children. Grandparenthood might come at any of a wide variety of times, as could caring for an aging parent. But you should bear in mind that this conception of the family life cycle is an oversimplified description of the roles involved in family life.

Nonetheless, this conception has served as an organizing model for a great deal of sociological research on adulthood. Instead of comparing adults of different ages, adults in different life cycle stages are compared. You have already seen an example of this in chapter 1 (Figures 1–7 and 1–8), and there will be many more examples throughout the book. The basic idea, obviously, is that an individual's behavior and attitudes are shaped by the roles she occupies. And since these roles change with age in systematic and predictable ways, adults will also change systematically and predictably. There is no notion here

**TABLE 3–4 Stages in Family Life Cycle Proposed by Duvall and Others**

| Stage | Description |
|---|---|
| 1 | Newly married with no children. The role of spouse has been added. |
| 2 | New parents: first child is an infant, so the new role of parent has been added. |
| 3 | Families with preschool children: oldest child is between two and six; other younger children may also be in the family. |
| 4 | Families with school-age children: The oldest child is between 6 and 12; there may be younger children as well. |
| 5 | Families with adolescent children: Oldest child is now a teenager, which changes the parental role in specific ways. |
| 6 | Families with the oldest child gone from the home. There may well be still other children still at home, but the "launching center" role of the family has begun. |
| 7 | Families in which all children have left home. This is also often called the "post-parental" stage. |
| 8 | Aging families: One or both spouses has retired. |

**Source:** Duvall, 1962.

that some roles are better than others, or that the family life cycle (or any other age-related change in roles) leads to "growth" or "improvement" in some fashion. But there are definable stages, widely shared in this and other cultures. Knowing that a person has a new infant tells you something about his life. If you knew that another person's youngest child had just gone off to college, you would quite correctly infer very different things about her daily existence.

## Daniel Levinson's Theory of Seasons of Adulthood

Daniel Levinson (1978, 1980) has used the concept of roles in his theory of adult development, but has suggested a very useful, more inclusive concept, that of the **life structure**. According to this idea, each adult, at each of several ages, creates a life structure that is made up of some integrated combination of roles (work roles, family roles, relationships), adapted to, or filtered through, that person's specific personality and skills. In other words, each of us *adapts* to our environment, to the demands made upon us. We develop a pattern to our lives, a rhythm, a system. It is this adaptive pattern Levinson calls the life structure. As he puts it, "The life structure is the pattern or design of a person's life, a meshing of self-in-world" (1980, p. 278).

It is important to point out that this is an individual creation. Two individuals with the same roles and relationships to deal with will not create precisely the same life structure. But the demands of particular roles (such as family life cycle roles) do have a significant impact on the shape the life structure will have.

Because life structures are designed (by the individual) to adapt to a set of inner and outer conditions, they cannot remain stable throughout life. Life conditions change. Your satisfaction with constant life conditions might also change. So life structures must change, too. Levinson proposes, therefore, that adult life is made up of alternating periods of stable life structures and transitional periods during which the old life structure is reexamined, adjusted, or altered. Figure 3–2 shows his overall model.

Levinson suggests that each stable period, and each transition, has a particular content, some of which I have summarized in Table 3–5. The Early Adult Transition deals with the problem of independence, of establishing an identity and a life separate from one's family (thus it is similar in some respects to Erikson's stage of identity vs. diffusion). Young adults must explore the adult world, find work, create relationships. This inner and outer exploration leads to the creation of a first life structure in the 20s.

This first life structure is commonly distinguished by two elements that Levinson thinks play a critical part in an adult's life: The creation of a relationship with a mentor and the establishment of "the Dream."

The Dream is a sort of fantasy or a set of imagined possibilities showing what one wants to become—a picture of oneself winning the Nobel Prize, or playing professional basketball against Abdul-Jabbar, or bringing about racial equality in the country (Martin Luther King's "I have a dream" speech). Many young adults dream of becoming rich, or finding the perfect mate, or living

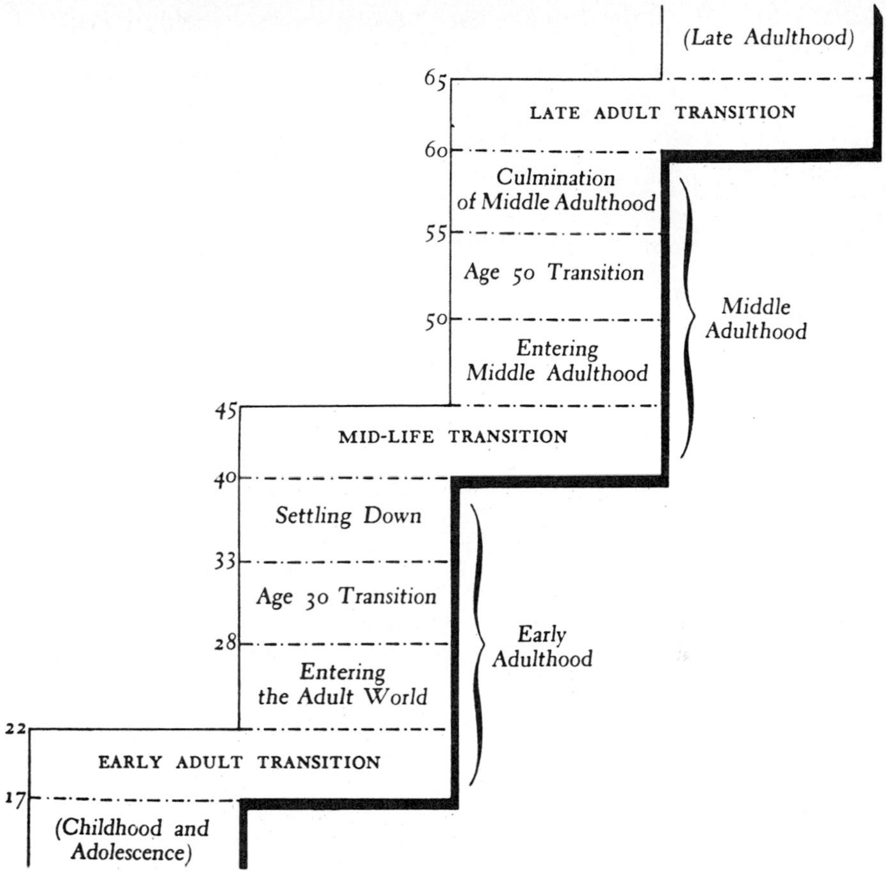


***Figure 3–2*** *Levinson's model of adult development. You can see the alternation of periods of stable life structures (such as "entering the adult world" and "settling down") and periods of transition. Certain transitions are likely to be particularly difficult or substantial, particularly those in early adulthood, at midlife, and at late adulthood. (Source: From* The Seasons of a Man's Life, *by Daniel J. Levinson. Copyright © 1978 by Daniel J. Levinson. Reprinted by permission of Alfred A. Knopf, Inc.)*

happily ever after in a lovely house in the suburbs with two well-behaved children. As the young person pursues this dream, he may establish a mentor relationship. The mentor is ordinarily 8 to 15 years older (someone, perhaps, in his own stage of generativity) who takes the young person under his wing, and teaches, advises, sponsors, supports, and serves as a model for the young person. A mentor is often found in a work setting, but it could also be an older relative or a friend. He is both a parent figure and a peer, and must be both if the relationship is going to work. The role of the mentor is to help the young person make the transition from reliance on the parents and their world to reliance on himself.

**TABLE 3–5 The Major Tasks of Each Developmental Period Proposed by Levinson**

| Development Period | Age | Tasks |
|---|---|---|
| Early Adult Transition | 17–22 | Terminate pre-adulthood, and move out of pre-adult world, taking preliminary steps into the adult world. Explore possibilities and make tentative commitments. |
| Entering the Adult World | 22–28 | Create a first major life structure, which may include marriage and a separate home, a mentoring relationship, and the Dream. Attempt to pursue the Dream. |
| Age 30 Transition | 28–33 | Become aware of the flaws of the first life structure and reassess it. Reconsider earlier choices and make new ones as needed. |
| Settling Down | 33–40 | Create a second adult life structure; invest yourself in work, family, friendships, community. Establish a niche in society and strive to "make it," to achieve the Dream. |
| Midlife Transition | 40–45 | A bridge from early to middle adulthood: Ask basic questions, such as "What have I done with my life?" or "What do I want for myself and others?" May or may not involve crisis. |
| Entering Middle Adulthood | 45–50 | Create a new life structure, often (but not always) with a new job, or a new marriage, or a change in nature of work life. |
| Age 50 Transition | 50–55 | Similar in function to the Age 30 Transition; a more minor adjustment to the middle adult life structure. However, if no crisis occurred at Midlife Transition, one is likely to occur now. |
| Culmination of Middle Adulthood | 55–60 | Build a second midlife structure, analogous to Settling Down in middle adulthood. May be a particularly satisfying time if the adult has successfully adapted the life structures to changes in roles and self. |
| Late Adult Transition | 60–65 | Termination of middle adulthood, and bridge to late adulthood. Conclude the efforts of middle adulthood, prepare for retirement and the physical declines of old age. A major turning point in the life cycle. |
| Late Adulthood | 65+ | Create a new life structure that will suit the new patterns in retirement, and the increasing physical declines. Cope with illness. Deal with the psychological issue of loss of youth. |

**Source:** Levinson, 1978.

The life structure of the 20s, including both the Dream and (for some) a mentor, does not last, in part because the goals may not be reached, but also because the roles and demands change. At the very least, the life structure of the 20s must be reexamined to see if it still fits, if the goals are still the same, if the strategies are working. The transition in the early 40s deals with another set of issues—with awareness of mortality, with the realization that the Dream may not have been fulfilled. A further major transition, at around age 60 or 65, is focused on the sense of loss of physical powers, with possible illness, with accepting that one has achieved as much as one can.

Levinson is quite specific in saying that these stages hold for all adults:

> The periods constitute a source of order in the life cycle. This order exists at an underlying level. At the day-to-day level of concrete events and experiences, our lives are sometimes rapidly changing and fragmented, sometimes utterly stationary. At the level of personality, we change in different ways, according to different timetables. Yet, I believe that everyone lives through the same developmental periods in adulthood . . . though people go through them in their own ways. . . . Our theory of life structure does not specify a single, "normal" course that everyone must follow. Its function, instead, is to indicate the developmental tasks that everyone must work on in successive periods, and the infinitely varied forms that such work can take in different individuals living under different conditions. (1980, p. 289)

But as I pointed out earlier, Levinson explicitly rejects the idea that these sequences of life structures, these "seasons of a man's life," involve any movement from worse to better or less mature to more mature. As he says, "The tasks of one period are not better or more advanced than those of another, except in the general sense that each period builds upon the work of the earlier ones and represents a later phase in the cycle. There are losses as well as gains in the shift from every period or era to the next" (Levinson, 1978, p. 320).] Thus, passage through these stages does not necessarily lead to any greater growth or wisdom. For some, it may. For others, it may not. But Levinson does clearly argue, rather like Erikson, that there are age-linked tasks that each adult must face and deal with in some fashion.

## Change Without Stages: Nonstage Theories of Adult Change

Stage or sequence theories are attractive in part because they describe the transit of adult life as an orderly process. But there is good reason to think that ordinary people's lives are not that orderly. Not all researchers who have looked for evidence of widely shared psychosocial or psychological stages have found them (e.g., Fiske, 1980; Pearlin, 1980). And certainly there are many men and women whose lives do not follow the clear pattern of the family life cycle. To use myself as an example again, I did not marry until I was 32, then I became the instant mother of two step children, who now no longer live with me. Where is the family life cycle here? It does appear to be true that some of the issues or tasks that Erikson, Levinson, and others describe are reflected in adult lives. But widely shared, clear stages are harder to find. In the view of some theorists, it is more fruitful to examine the ways adults adapt to the unique constellations of life experiences they may face.

Many of the theories in this group are really preliminary models rather than complete theories, proposed by researchers who have struggled to apply earlier, stage-like concepts to their observations of adult life, and who have found the stage theories wanting. "Eclectic" would be a reasonable general description of theories in this group. What they have in common, other than their strong data-based orientation, is skepticism about the usefulness of simple stage models of adult development, and similar doubt about conceptualizing changes in adulthood as "development." Leonard Pearlin's approach is a good example of a theory of this type.

## Leonard Pearlin's Model of Psychological Distress in Adults

Leonard Pearlin (1980, 1982a; Pearlin & Lieberman, 1979), working from a background of training in sociology, has offered a useful synthesis of concepts from both psychology and sociology. His major interest has been in sources of distress over the adult years, and in people's methods of coping with such distress. But his suggestions about the adult years are not limited to the domain of distress.

Pearlin grants that there may be life tasks or psychological issues that are characteristic of particular age periods. But in his view, such age-related issues form only a minor part of the experience of aging. Pearlin is much more struck by the diversity of pathways: "Because people are at the same age or life cycle phase, it cannot be assumed that they have either traveled the same route to reach their present locations or that they are headed in the same future directions" (1982, p. 64a).

The elements in individual lives that determine the route a person follows, in Pearlin's view, are several: (1) all the dimensions of individual difference I talked about in chapter 2, particularly the social or economic class in which the individual finds himself; (2) the range of skills the individual has for coping with stress or life change. The wider the range of such coping skills, the less distress the person will feel; (3) the availability and usefulness of social support networks. Adults with strongly supportive networks experience any form of potential distress less acutely; (4) the nature and timing of the sources of stress or distress the person must face.

Pearlin divides sources of distress into three types. First, there are the chronic or durable strains that are built into any life—the complaining mother-in-law, the boring job, the strain of trying to work and care for a family at the same time, the need to stretch the budget to meet inflation. Second, there are scheduled or predictable changes or events, such as the birth of a child, the departure of a young adult from home, retirement. These are all anticipated role changes. Finally, there are the unexpected, unscheduled changes, such as being laid off from work, or an automobile accident, or the unexpected death of a parent or close friend.

Pearlin's research findings persuade him that scheduled changes have rela-

***Figure 3–3*** *Stopping work when you are 65, at the normal or "scheduled" time to retire, seems to be much less stressful and destabilizing than losing your job in your early or middle adulthood, as these adults have experienced. (Source: Bruce Roberts, Photo Researchers Inc.)*

tively little effect on feelings of distress or wellbeing, while unscheduled changes frequently have major effects. But even unexpected or unscheduled events have most of their impact indirectly, by increasing the daily life strains. Being widowed, for example, has a relatively small impact on adults who have adequate financial and emotional resources. Those adults who are forced to change their daily lives sharply, however—go to work, or live at a lower economic level, or cope with rearing children alone—show far more distress, depression, and anxiety. Pearlin appears to be saying that the unplanned disruption of a life structure (to borrow Levinson's concept) is what causes maximum distress.

It should be clear from even this limited description of Pearlin's work that while this is a theory about changes in adult lives, it is definitely not a theory about development. Pearlin specifically rejects the idea that there is any inner unfolding, any "growth": "We hold, first, that adult emotional development does not represent the gradual surfacing of conditions that happen to reside within individuals. Instead, we see it as a continuing process of adjustment to external circumstances . . ." (1980, p. 180). Since adults of any given age are likely to share certain external circumstances, there may be common experiences at different points in the life course. But Pearlin is arguing that real understanding of adult lives will be found not in defining those shared experiences as universal stages, but in searching for those principles that govern the way individual adults cope with the changing demands of adult life.

## Additional Theoretical Complexities

The classification of theories I have offered in Figure 3–1 highlights two of the dimensions on which theories of adulthood differ from one another. But even the brief descriptions I have given of these theories point to other important dimensions of difference as well, two of which I think are critical.

First, there is the question of *universality versus diversity*. Are there ways in which all adults change or develop in the same way, in the same sequences, or at the same rates? Some theorists, such as Erikson or Loevinger, obviously think so. They are searching for underlying sameness in the face of apparent difference. Other researchers, including Pearlin and even Vaillant, have been much more struck by the diversity of adult pathways, sequences, and coping strategies. For theorists in this second group, understanding adulthood means to understand why people develop differently, or in different sequences, or more or less fully. What are the characteristics of the individual, the background characteristics, or the life experiences, that lead one adult to an integrated, satisfied old age, and another to a bitter, maladaptive, or lonely old age?

A second key issue that separates the theorists I have talked about is whether they see change (or development) as primarily an internal process, or as primarily an external one. As a general rule, theorists emerging from a psychological tradition have been most interested in internal change or growth—changes in personality, coping skills, ego states, mental skills, even physical capacities. In contrast, many theorists emerging from a sociological tradition have been more interested in external change, such as changes in roles, or age-related changes in the several forms of life strains described by Pearlin. To be sure, this line is often crossed, and some theorists talk about both (e.g., Levinson and Pearlin). Nonetheless, this disagreement about which aspects of adulthood should be studied runs through all of the literature on adulthood, and makes synthesis of theory and data extremely difficult.

Undaunted, a number of recent authors have attempted such syntheses, some of which I find intriguing. Let me describe two such attempts, and then add several suggestions of my own.

## Theoretical Syntheses

### Klaus Riegel's Dialectical Interpretation of Development

Klaus Riegel's synthesis (1975, 1977) is aimed precisely at the disgreement about whether change in adulthood is primarily internal or primarily external.

He argues that what we observe as development or change in adulthood results from both internal and external change. Specifically, Riegel sees two major sequences of change within each individual: inner-biological change and cultural-sociological change. The shifts in roles that accompany the family life cycle are an example of cultural-sociological change, as are broader historical changes in society as a whole (changes between cohorts). But there is also physical change/maturation/decline going on. As you will see in the next chapter, there are changes in hormones, in cell structure, in muscle strength, in tissue elasticity, in neural transmission. Individuals also experience disease or accidents, which significantly alter their bodies. For Riegel, the key to understanding development in any individual is the understanding of the dynamic interplay between these two threads of development. Psychological development—the sense of self, the development of defense mechanisms in Vaillant's sense, or the emergence of generativity or integrity in Erikson's sense—is a constructive dialectic of these several forces.

When your body changes, you are forced to develop new coping mechanisms, new strategies, which in turn affect your social conditions (what Levinson might call your life structure). When your cultural/sociological conditions change, as when your youngest child starts school, this, too, forces new adaptations, which will in turn affect biological functioning. Growth or development, in Riegel's view, occurs particularly when there is asynchrony between the patterns of change in the two domains. When such a "crisis" occurs, in order to maintain the sense of inner balance that Riegel assumes as a basic motive, you are forced to change your self-concept or your strategies for dealing with life.

The term *dialectic* used to describe this process is taken from philosophy or logic. The dialectical argument is one of thesis, antithesis, and synthesis. So in development, physical or social change unbalances the old synthesis, forcing a new antithesis and eventually a new synthesis. Whether Riegel intends to imply that the long chain of dialectical adaptations that makes up adulthood involves any development (in my sense of the word) or not is unclear. He does speak of "constructive" change resulting from the process of mutual adaptation of biological and social changes, but he appears not to have any general notion of growth or development.

On the issue of stages his position is clearer. He argues that there are biological stages of change in adulthood and social/cultural stages, such as the family life cycle and other role changes, but the dialectical process of integrating these two sets of stages does not, in his view, result in overarching psychological stages such as those proposed by Loevinger or Erikson.

As you can no doubt tell, I find Riegel's theory fuzzy in some respects, but he has been extremely influential for one key reason: He has gone beyond the psychologists' preoccupation with inner change, and beyond the sociologists' interest in changes in social roles or social structure, and focused our attention instead on the dynamic interaction between the two. Such an approach makes the theoretical and empirical task vastly more complex, but seems at the same time vastly more realistic.

A second type of synthesis, which in fact builds upon some concepts offered by Riegel, is what Janet Giele (1982a) calls a *timing model* of development. Pamela Perun and Denise Bielby's (1980) model is a particularly useful example.

## Perun and Bielby's Timing Model of Adult Development

Perun and Bielby conceive of adult life as made up of a large number of *temporal progressions*—sequences of experiences or internal changes each of which follows some timetable. The physical changes in the body over adulthood represent one such temporal progression, as do the changes in the family life cycle, or the ego developments described by Loevinger, or alterations in work roles or sex roles.

Figure 3–4 shows this model graphically, which may help to convey the complexity. Each of these disks, rather like machine gears moving at different rates, represents a single temporal progression, such as the life cycle within the nuclear family (marrying, having children, having those children grow up), or a separate life cycle within the extended family (such as the timing of one's parents' deaths). Each of these progressions moves at a different rate for each individual, thus creating a unique pattern for each adult. Laura Rogers, who married at 16, has speeded up the family life cycle progression; another adult who exercises three times a week for his whole adult life may slow down the rate of the physical change progression.

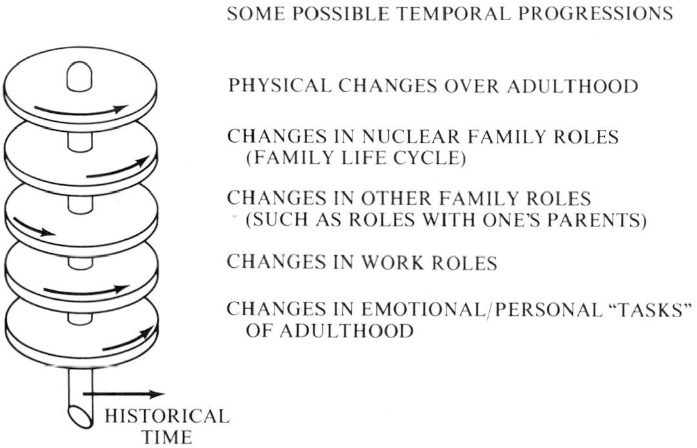


**Figure 3–4** *Perun and Bielby's timing model of the life course. Each of these disks represents one "temporal progression," a set of sequential changes in one aspect of adult functioning. (I have suggested some names for several progressions along the right-hand side.) Each of these progressions moves along its own timetable, at its own speed, creating a unique pattern of interlocking changes for each individual. (Source: From Perun & Bielby, 1980, Figure 1, page 102. Reprinted by permission of Westview Press, Boulder, CO.)*

Furthermore, this entire process is embedded within a particular period of historical time (a cohort), which will affect the process as well. For each of us, this collection of temporal progressions forms a whole. We do not experience this as a set of independent gears, crunching away inside. What we experience are the interrelationships among these progressions.

Following Riegel's lead, Perun and Bielby suggest that one of the key interrelationships is the *synchrony* or *asynchrony* of these temporal progressions. Do the several timetables dovetail, support one another, match? If so, then synchrony exists and the person will experience low levels of stress. In Levinson's terms, when there is synchrony, a stable life structure exists.

"Asynchrony occurs when one or more dimensions is off-time in relation to others" (Perun & Bielby, 1980, p. 105). This creates friction, as if the gears did not quite mesh. We experience such friction as stress, or as a crisis, and strive to change in one or more dimensions until synchrony is again achieved. To get the gears to mesh again, you may have to move one of the other gears to a new position. The man who, at 45, finds that he puffs when he walks up a flight of stairs, or can no longer beat his younger colleagues at tennis, may well experience this as asynchronous with his sense of increased effectiveness and responsibility at work. He could deal with this asynchrony in several ways, each of which involves "moving another gear." He might get into better physical shape (moving back or slowing down the rate of change of the progression of physical changes). Or he might go through some sort of internal reappraisal that would change the way he perceived the importance of physical competition. In coming to terms with his physical aging, he might shift to a higher level of ego development and again experience relative synchrony.

Thus, there are two sources of change within this model: First, the basic temporal progressions themselves describe changes, some of which are either inevitable or widely shared and some of which may be stage-like. Second, asynchrony triggers additional change.

Several intriguing and potentially useful implications or expansions of this model occur to me.

1. The rate of movement along any one temporal dimension may be influenced by those individual differences I talked about in chapter two—by gender, race, intelligence, temperament, education, or social class. For example, women from working-class families marry earlier and have their children earlier. This changes the timing of at least one of the "gears" in the model, which will in turn alter the points at which asynchrony will be experienced. If we could add to this model some equations describing factors that affect the rate of change in each progression, we could come closer to being able to predict individual life patterns.
2. Following Pearlin's lead, we might also hypothesize that anticipated or scheduled shifts on any one progression will create less disrupting asynchrony than will unanticipated or unscheduled changes. If I plan to retire at 65, I can think about the changes that will be involved and partially adjust to the change ahead of time.

3. Being significantly off-time in any one progression should produce relatively high rates of asynchrony throughout the life course. Women who have children in their teens, or those who do not have their first child until they are in their late 30s, would be two examples of such off-time patterns. Bernice Neugarten (1979), who was one of the first to talk about the impact of "on-time" and "off-time" events, has indeed found that there is a price to be paid for off-timeness. But Perun & Bielby's model also suggests that there is a potential reward to be reaped as well, in the form of higher levels of personal adaptation or growth.
4. Despite individual differences in the rate of movement along the several progressions, there are still widely shared points of asynchrony, such as at midlife. Those adults who follow a modal pattern are likely to have their children begin leaving home, their parents begin to fail in health, their own bodies begin to show signs of decline, and their jobs "peak out," all at approximately the same time. Such shared asynchronies may produce the somewhat illusory appearance of broad stages in adult lives. But those adults who, for any of a myriad of reasons, do not follow that modal path will not show the same stage-like patterns of adult change.
5. If asynchrony is one of the keys to personal change (and possibly to personal growth), then adults who find themselves in situations that force change are also likely to show the greatest growth. As an example, Melvin Kohn (1980) (whose work I'll describe more fully in chapter 8) has found that adults in complex jobs show greater growth in intellectual skill than do adults who have more routine jobs. Some of this is self-selection, of course: Adults with less intellectual skill to start with are more likely to end up with less complex jobs. But Kohn has shown that job complexity has an independent effect. High job complexity pushes everyone toward more complex and elaborate ways of thinking.
6. Given asynchrony, growth is not the only possible outcome. Synchrony can be recreated by regression or retreat in some progression. For example, if a new job requires you to learn a whole new set of complex skills, thus creating asynchrony, you could give up the job and go back to something more familiar. A midlife man may respond to the asynchronies of that age not by becoming physically fit, or accepting limitations, but by increased drinking or by depression. Each of these is a kind of adaptation. In Vaillant's terms, each of these is a defense against the anxiety produced by the asynchrony.

These implications and expansions illustrate, I hope, the potential richness of this model, or models like it. Nonetheless, there is a great deal that is not dealt with in such a model. As an example, when an individual is faced with asynchrony, what determines the coping method that he uses? Given what appears to be the same crisis, why do some people respond constructively, others destructively? And what determines the form that a new life structure will take? If we think of each of these asynchronies as a large freeway cloverleaf intersection, each represents a set of choices. You can choose to continue along the same road; you can turn off onto a new road, or you can turn around an go back on the road you came on. What determines such choices?

Erikson would undoubtedly suggest that each choice affects all that follow it. So unsuccessful resolutions of early dilemmas (perhaps particularly the very first dilemma of trust vs. mistrust) will increase the chances that later dilemmas will be unsuccessfully, or even destructively, resolved. To predict the future life course of any one individual, then, we would need to know his life history in detail. A very tall order indeed.

## Some Shared Flaws and Weaknesses in the Theories

Before leaving this excursion through the theoretical landscape and beginning a much longer journey through the empirical evidence on specific changes and continuities in adulthood, I would be remiss if I did not point out several major weaknesses shared by most or all of these theories.

First, the data base for these theories is typically extremely small. In Table 3–6 I have described briefly the major studies or clinical data from which these several theories have emerged. As you can see, most of the theories are based on only very limited observations of actual adults. Vaillant interviewed 100 middle aged men; Erikson's theory is based primarily on his own clinical observations. Of course, this need not mean that the theories are wrong. Many remarkable theoretical insights have been based on only a few clinical observations (Freud's work and that of Piaget come immediately to mind). But it does mean that the wide applicability of any one theory has not been well tested.

Second, there are several marked biases built into many (but not all) of the data sources and the the theories themselves. Most theorists have studied primarily middle-class, white adults. In addition, several of the major theories are based largely or entirely on interviews with or observations of men. Whether any theory emerging from such observations will be applicable to women, to working-class adults, or (more generally) to adults of other cultures, is open to doubt.

More particularly, any theory based on such limited observations that proposes that all adults develop in the same way or in precisely the same sequence seems to me to be particularly suspect. That does not mean that we cannot learn from such theories, but it does mean that we should be suitably skeptical about their wide applicability. Those theories that explicitly attempt to account for variations in individual responses to the tasks of adulthood seem to me the most flexible, and of these, I obviously find the timing model the most useful.

Incomplete as it is, and limited though the data base is, the timing model,

**TABLE 3–6 Major Sources of Data on Which the Several Theories of Adult Development Are Based**

| Theorist | Data Base |
|---|---|
| Erikson | Primarily Erikson's own clinical observations as a child analyst, and extensive reading of anthropological descriptions of other cultures. |
| Loevinger | Loevinger's own clinical judgment, supplemented and supported by fairly extensive research with the Sentence Completion Test of Ego Development, including studies of both black and white children, high school and college students studied longitudinally over four to six years, numerous college samples, and many studies relating this measure to other assessments. Less extensive evidence on the higher stages. |
| Vaillant | Vaillant's own clinical judgment as a psychiatrist, but primarily interviews with 100 of the all-male Grant study participants at about age 50, plus all other information on these Harvard men in the Grant Study files. |
| Family Life Cycle Theory | Proposed by several sociologists as a synthesizing concept, based on hundreds of studies of families in earlier decades, and since used as an organizational rubric and theoretical concept in hundreds more studies. Very extensive data base. |
| Levinson | Major source is an extensive set of interviews and assessments of 40 men between the ages of 35 and 45, equally divided into four occupations: hourly industrial workers, business executives, university biologists, and novelists. |
| Pearlin | Major source is a short-term longitudinal study of adults from wide range of socioeconomic levels, both male and female, ages 18 to 65; 2,300 adults were interviewed once, and a subset reinterviewed four years later, covering all aspects of labor and love—work and family roles and conflicts. |
| Riegel | A theoretical synthesis and reinterpretation of the theories and empirical work of others. |
| Perun & Bielby | A theoretical synthesis based on both theory and empirical evidence from others, but applied to a sample of forty-one married women with Ph.D's. |

in my view, comes closer to describing real-life adult patterns than any other single approach. What I need to do now is to look at each of the gears or cogs shown in Figure 3–4 one at a time, so that you can get some sense of the kinds of changes that occur in each dimension over the adult years. I will then come back to the task of putting the pieces back together in chapter 13, when I will attempt another synthesis.

## Summary

1. Theories of adulthood differ on a number of important dimensions, among them the distinction between development versus change theories, and between stage and nonstage theories. Development theorists assume that there is some direction in which adults move; change theorists do not assume direction.

2. Developmental stage theorists include Erik Erikson, Jane Loevinger, and Roger Gould.

3. Erikson's theory of identity development describes eight stages or dilemmas, spread over the entire life span, each of which is linked to a particular age. The individual moves into a new stage because of changes in cultural or role demands, or physical changes, and must then resolve the dilemma associated with that stage.

4. Incomplete or imperfect resolution of a dilemma leaves unfinished business to be carried forward to the next stage, increasing the likelihood that the next stage, too, will be imperfectly resolved.

5. The four stages Erikson describes that are part of adulthood are identity versus role confusion, intimacy versus isolation, generativity versus stagnation, and integrity versus despair.

6. The stages in Loevinger's theory are not tied to age. Children and adults move along a progression of 10 steps or levels, each built on the preceding ones, with movement occurring only when the preceding stage has been completed. A group of adults of a given age will thus contain individuals who may be functioning at any one of several different levels.

7. The stages particularly relevant to the study of adulthood are the conformist, the self-aware, the conscientious, the individualistic, the autonomous, and the integrated.

8. George Vaillant assumes the validity of Erikson's stages, but adds the concept of maturing defense mechanisms. He describes several levels of maturity of defenses, and suggests that adults may be characterized by the degree to which they use more mature forms.

9. Another group of theories retains the concept of stage, but eliminates the concept of directional development. Included in this group are models of family life cycles and Levinson's theory of seasons of life.

10. Life cycle theories emphasize the formative influence of the predictably changing set of roles associated with marriage, bearing and rearing children, and seeing the children leave home.

11. Levinson proposes a universally shared rhythm of stable life structures alternating with periods of transition. These alternations occur at particular ages, as adults come to terms with particular issues that are relevant for those ages.

12. More eclectic models, assuming neither development nor stages, also exist, such as Pearlin's model of methods of handling distress in adulthood.

13. These theories also differ on other dimensions, such as whether they assume universality or diversity of patterns, and whether they focus on internal or external change.

14. Several attempts at synthesis involve intermediate positions on the two key theoretical dimensions. Riegel's dialectical theory emphasizes that development emerges from the dynamic interaction between inner-biological change and external-cultural/sociological change.

15. Perun and Bielby's timing model is a second form of synthesis. They assume that within each adult there is a series of separate temporal progressions, each moving at its own speed. Asynchrony among these several progressions produces stress, which the individual resolves by some kind of change in one or more progression. This theory appears to provide a better (albeit much more complex) view of adult development than do many of the previous theories.

16. All of these theories, to a greater or lesser extent, share two weaknesses: They are based on a paucity of data, and they tend to be biased toward descriptions of the adult lives of white, middle-class, American males.

## Suggested Readings

GILLIGAN, C. (1982). *In a different voice.* Cambridge, MA: Harvard University Press.

Gilligan speaks here—eloquently and passionately—to the specific point of male bias in existing theories of adult development. She analyzes many existing theories, and presents evidence supporting the view that women's development is qualitatively different in key respects.

GOULD, R. (1978). *Transformations: Growth and change in adult life.* New York: Simon & Schuster.

I am particularly fond of this book, since it is written in a particularly engaging and clear style, with a great deal of clinical case material. It is perhaps the least technical and complex of the series of theoretical books (including also Vaillant's and Levinson's) that came out at about that same time.

SMELSER, N. J., & ERIKSON, E. H. (1980). *Themes of work and love in adulthood.* Cambridge, MA: Harvard University Press.

This is a wonderful collection of papers by many of the major theoretical figures I have talked about in this chapter, including Levinson, Gould, and Pearlin. The chapters are not overly technical, but each gives a good overview of that particular approach.

VAILLANT, G. E. (1977a). *Adaptation to life: How the best and the brightest came of age.* Boston, MA: Little, Brown.

Of all the individual books on adult life, I have found this one to be the most consistently fascinating. It is full of case studies of real men, moving through the years from 20 to 50. It is not particularly easy reading, but it is extremely informative and stimulating. Fair warning, though: If you are a man in your middle 40s or early 50s, you may find it somewhat depressing!

# 4

# Physical and Health Changes in Adulthood

My maternal grandparents both lived into their 90s, and were physically in quite good shape until their final few years. They remained active and vital people through the final decades, keeping house for themselves and each keeping up an extensive correspondence with friends and family. (My grandfather, in fact, always tried to answer letters the day he got them, so that no matter how hard I tried, I always seemed to owe him a letter!) My grandmother was working on her third book in her late 80s and early 90s. Despite their continuing vigor, though, they were both acutely aware of the physical changes that had significantly altered their lives. My grandmother complained particularly of the fact that she "couldn't taste anything anymore." Unless food was highly spiced, or had a strong natural taste (like strong coffee), it seemed totally bland to her. They also reported loss of energy and vitality; they simply couldn't carry on long at any one activity before they tired. And large groups of people were difficult for them to deal with; it got harder and harder to follow conversations in large groups, and there was too much noise and confusion. We also noticed that they both lost quite a lot of physical coordination in the last years, and both became extremely thin.

How typical are these changes? We all know that adults get grayer and more wrinkled and a bit slower as they age. But what other changes take place? We can catalogue quite a lot of changes—as I will do in a moment. But such a first level of description, however useful, does not tell the whole story. Equally important, we need to know whether the changes we observe are inevitable or resistant to intervention, and what impact they have on the daily functioning of adults. Isadore Rossman (1980) defines true aging processes (maturational changes in my terminology in this book) as "possessing the characteristics of universality, progressiveness, irreversibility, and being essentially detrimental'' (p. 125). Some (perhaps many) of the physical changes researchers have described in adulthood are aspects of aging in this sense. But some may not be. Some apparent ''aging'' changes could also be due to inactivity, or poor diet, or living among environmental hazards. And some universal and irreversible changes, while measurable, may have negligible or small impact on the ability of an older person to function on a day-to-day basis.

In exploring such questions, I want to begin at the simplest descriptive level: What changes do we observe in the physical body and its functioning, in health, and in resultant behavior? We can then turn to possible explanations of those changes, and to questions of individual differences and lifestyle differences in rate or pattern of aging.

# The Facts of Physical Aging

## Longevity

One of the most striking facts about physical aging at this point in history is that **longevity** has increased. That is, more of us (in the ''developed'' countries, at least) are living longer. Partly this is true because fewer people die in infancy, childhood, or early adulthood than was true several generations ago. Among children born in the United States in 1840, 25% were dead by the age of three. Among those born in 1910, in contrast, it wasn't till age 55 that a quarter of the cohort had died (Jacobson, 1964).

But **life expectancy** has also been extended at the upper end, primarily through the virtual elimination of infectious diseases. In 1940 in the United States, a woman of 65 could expect to live an average of another 13.6 years. In 1980, she could expect to live another 18.3 years. For men, the equivalent figures are 12.1 and 14.1 years (Verbrugge, 1984). What is more, this pattern of increased life expectancy is expected to continue. By the year 2050, according to at least some estimates, the average life expectancy at birth may be as high as 75 for men and 83 for women, and life expectancy for those who reach the age of 65 may then be another 17 years for men and 23 years for women (Crimmins, 1984).

Despite these advances, however, the upper limit of life expectancy has probably not changed at all. A few people have always lived to be 100 or a bit older; now more people live to be that old. But all the improvements in health care and disease prevention have not stretched that upper boundary, usually referred to as the **life span** (Hayflick, 1975; Yin & Shine, 1985).

One other fact about life expectancy—already apparent from Figure 2–4—is worth underlining: In our culture at least, women live longer than men do. In 1983, the average difference in life expectancy at birth was about seven years (78.3 for women, 71.0 for men, U.S. Bureau of the Census, 1984a). There are several possible reasons for this (Verbrugge, 1984): (1) women may have greater immunity to certain diseases, such as heart disease; (2) women's work may expose them less to environmental hazards; (3) women appear to seek medical attention earlier in any illness, improving the chances of cure or amelioration; and (4) women's personal health practices may be better (although with smoking rates increasing among women, one aspect of this difference is disappearing).

Taking all of these factors together, the vast majority of you now in your 20s or 30s can expect to live to be 65 or older, and many of you will live well into your 80s or even 90s. Just what will your bodies be like in those later years of adulthood?

## Changes in the Way You Look

For many adults, the most obvious changes with age are the ones they see in their mirror every day—those changes in physical shape and contour, in skin and hair, that visibly chart the passage of years. The catalogue of such changes includes the following:

**Loss of Height**. Longitudinal research shows that beginning at about age 40, adults lose one to two inches in height (Rossman, 1980). Most of this loss occurs in the spine, where the discs between vertebrae first shrink, and then the vertebrae themselves eventually lose height. The overall effect is that the trunk becomes shorter while the arms and legs remain about the same length.

**Body Shape Changes**. The contour of the body also changes. Up to about age 30 or 40, the head actually grows, following the pattern shown in Figure 4–1 (Guillen, 1984). And both the nose and ears grow fairly steadily until one's 70s (Smith, Bierman, & Robinson, 1978) (Pinocchio is not the only one whose nose grows!). More significantly, the fat deposits in the body shift locations. Past about age 50, fat is lost in the face and in the legs and lower arms, while it is added in the upper arm (particularly among women) and in the belly and buttocks. (One older male friend of mine says: "I'm not fat. My chest just slipped!"). These redistributions of fat deposits sometimes give the impression that the older person is heavier, but in fact the reverse is true. On the average, weight increases up to about age 40 or 50 (the famous middle-aged spread) and then declines slightly (about 10 lbs) past about age 50 (Bierman & Hazzard, 1978; Rossman, 1980).

**Changes in Skin and Hair**. Wrinkles, which become particularly evident beginning at 40 or 50, result in part from the loss of fat just under the skin. They also occur because of a loss of elasticity in the skin itself. This loss of elasticity is one of the pervasive changes of aging, and affects muscles, tendons, blood vessels, and internal organs as well as skin. It is especially noticeable in skin that has been continually exposed to the sun, such as the skin of the face and hands (Selmanowitz, Rizer, & Orentriech, 1977). Two other important changes in the skin are the reduction in the efficiency of functioning of

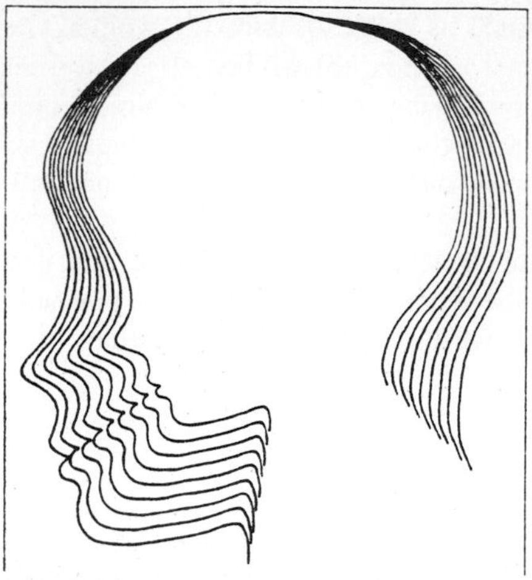

**Figure 4–1** *A computer simulation of the changes in head contours from infancy to adulthood. It turns out that these changes follow a specific mathematical formula (the "cardioidal-strain" formula), apparently as a result of the effect of gravitation on the structures of the head. There is a general "sinking" of both bone and tissue toward the lower part of the skull. Because these changes are so regular and predictable, most of us use them unconsciously as part of our basis for judging the age of a child or adult. (Source: Guillen, 1984, p. 77. Reprinted by permission of Dr. Leonard S. Mark, Psychology Department, Miami University, Oxford, OH.)*

both the sweat glands and the oil secreting glands. Older adults sweat less, which means that they cannot cool their bodies as effectively in high heat, and their skins become dryer, subject to cracking.

Hair loss is also a common characteristic of aging, in both men and women. Some men, of course, begin to lose hair very early in adulthood, but virtually all adults experience thinning of hair beginning in the 50s or 60s (postmenopausally for women). Graying of hair differs widely, but nearly all adults show some graying. (I was quite forceably struck by differences in hair graying patterns on a recent trip to China. Chinese gray very little, and only very late in life, while my hair has been almost white since my middle 30s. All foreigners in China are stared at a lot, but my hair was the occasion for considerable staring, pointing, and comment!)

## Changes in the Senses

A second series of body changes noted by many adults as they age affects vision, hearing, tasting, and feeling.

**Visual Changes.** Beginning in middle life (about 40 to 50 for most people) the lens in the eye begins to lose elasticity (like the skin). As a result, it becomes more difficult to focus both eyes on near objects. (As I write this, I am wearing my newly acquired reading glasses, without which the screen of my word processor is a total blur.) Total visual acuity also declines late in life. Fewer than 30% of 70 year olds still have 20/20 vision, and most older adults require more illumination to see well, and see less well in the dark. In addition, because of the generalized loss of elasticity of tissues, the reflexive adjustments of the eye lens to light or darkness is slowed, so that adults over the age of 60 or so find that it takes longer for their eyes to adjust to abrupt changes in light or darkness.

The combined effect of these changes is to make some tasks more difficult or somewhat risker. Driving a car, for example, may be trickier, especially at night when the eye must adjust quickly to changes in light and dark; finding your way to the bathroom in the middle of the night may be more difficult, as may reading or watching TV. However, many of these potentially increased difficulties can be compensated by wearing appropriate glasses, obtaining books with larger print, and the like. In general, these visual changes are noticeable but are not usually disabling.

**Changes in Hearing.** In contrast, a larger percentage of older adults experience a disabling loss of hearing. From about age 50 onward, virtually all adults lose some auditory acuity, especially for the high and very low frequency sounds (Corso, 1977). The basic cause of this loss appears to be gradual degeneration of the auditory nerves and structures of the inner ear.

For perhaps 15% to 30% of adults over 75, the degree of hearing loss is sufficient to impair their functioning. Firm figures are hard to come by, but perhaps 15% of adults over 75 can be classed as deaf (Corso, 1977) while another 15% to 20% report serious difficulty with hearing (Darbyshire, 1984; Verbrugge, 1984). There is some suggestion, by the way, that the percentage of older adults with significant hearing loss will go up in the decades to come, because current young adults have higher rates of ''acoustic trauma'' (a major cause of hearing loss) from listening to music at very high volume.

Some of both minor and significant hearing loss can be compensated by wearing hearing aids, but for those with major hearing loss, hearing aids do not compensate completely. These adults may experience markedly greater difficulty in social situations, particularly in settings in which there are several conversations going on at once. In general, even for those adults with only modest (normal) hearing loss, speech may have to be both louder and slower before it is understood (Eisdorfer & Wilkie, 1972).

**Smell and Taste.** My grandmother's complaint about losing her sense of taste is based on a real physical change: the number of taste buds on each bump on the tongue decreases from about 245 in early adulthood to perhaps 88 or 90 in an elderly adult. The salivary glands (like most glands) secrete less as we age so that many older people experience a dry or "woolly" mouth.

Since the senses of smell and taste are highly related (as you certainly know from your loss of taste sensitivity when your nose is clogged up with a cold), it is not surprising to find that there is also a loss of smell sensitivity over the adult years. Richard Doty and his colleagues (Doty, Shaman, & Dann, 1984) tested this in a cross-sectional study of nearly 2000 children and adults, using 40 different smells—ranging from pizza to mint to gasoline. He found that peak olfactory ability (best and most rapid discrimination) is found in early adulthood, between about the ages of 20 and 40. The sense of smell then declines slowly till about age 70, after which it declines rapidly. In this study, 60% of those adults between 65 and 80 have severe losses in the sense of smell, of whom a quarter had lost all sense of smell. (Incidentally, smokers lost their sense of smell more than nonsmokers did.)

The practical consequences of the loss of taste and smell can be substantial, since it is hard to work up enthusiasm for eating when you can't taste much. Poor eating habits may result—either eating too little, or skipping important nutrients, or adding too much salt.

**Pain and Touch.** There is less (and more conflicting) evidence about changes in both touch and pain sensitivity. Perhaps 25% of older adults experience a loss of touch sensitivity, and there is some indication that many adults become less sensitive to pain as they age (Kenshalo, 1977). But whether this reduced pain sensitivity is general, or applies only to particular tests of pain sensitivity, is not clear.

## Internal Physical Changes

Many of these changes in both appearance and sensory acuity are related to a much broader set of changes with age in internal organs or body systems.

**Changes in Muscles and Bones.** There is a significant loss of muscle tissue (actual muscle cells) over the adult years, with the most rapid decline occurring after age 50 (Rossman, 1980). There is some indication that the greatest loss is in so-called "fast twitch" muscle fibers, which are the ones primarily involved in rapid bursts of speed or strength (such as sprinting), with slower loss in "slow twitch" fibers, which are involved in prolonged activity (such as jogging) (Ostrow, 1984).

The major effect of this loss of fibers is a reduction in physical strength. Figure 4–2 gives one example of the pattern of strength decline, but it is important to emphasize that all muscles show these changes, including the muscles of the diaphragm and chest, used for breathing, and those of the bladder, used for elimination.

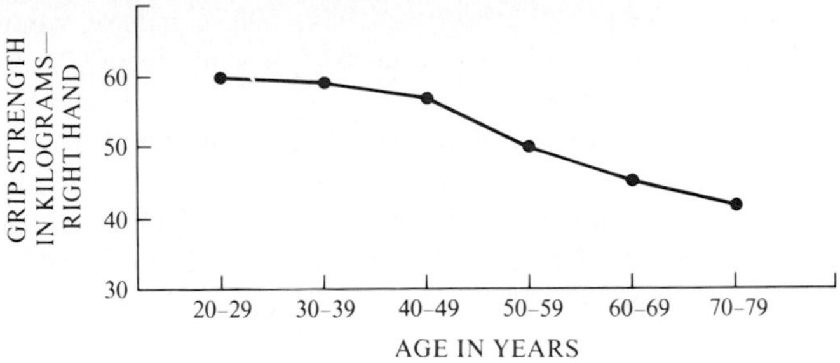


**Figure 4–2** *One of the consequences of loss of muscle tissue in adulthood is a loss of strength, such as these changes in grip strength in a group of men. Part of this loss of strength could also be the result of less use of the muscles, but that does not account for all of it. Muscle tissue is lost with age even among adults who do hard physical activity, or exercise regularly. (Source: Rossman, 1980, from Fig. 6.2, p. 128.)*

In the bones, there are several significant changes associated with age. First, bone marrow (in which blood cells are made) gradually disappears in arms and legs, and becomes concentrated in the bones of the trunk. Second, calcium is lost from the bones, making bones more brittle and porous, a process called **osteoporosis**. As a consequence, bone fractures increase markedly in frequency after about age 45 in women and 75 in men (Lindsay, 1985). Osteoporosis is far more likely to be severe in women, particularly postmenopausally. The loss of ovarian hormones that is part of the menopausal process (which I'll describe shortly) seems to be one of the causal factors, but diet and lifestyle factors also make a difference. The major known risk factors are listed in Table 4–1.

Third, changes in the bones of the joints, resulting primarily from the wear and tear of years of body movements, appear to be virtually universal. When such changes become marked, they are called **osteoarthritis** (Rossman, 1980).

**TABLE 4–1 Risk Factors for Osteoporosis**

| Factor | Direction of Effect |
|---|---|
| Race | Whites have higher risk than other races. |
| Gender | Females have considerably higher risk than males. |
| Weight | Those who are light for their height have higher risk. |
| Timing of Climacteric | Women with early menopause, or those who have had their ovaries removed, are at higher risk. |
| Family History | Those with family history of osteoporosis have higher risk. |
| Diet | Diet low in calcium and high in caffeine and or alcohol leads to higher risk. |
| Lifestyle | Sedentary lifestyle associated with higher risk. |
| Number of Children | Women who have borne any children are at higher risk. |

**Source:** Lindsay, 1985.

In one national health survey (Verbrugge, 1984, 1985), half of women and a third of men over 65 reported having "arthritis" of some form.

**Changes in the Cardiovascular and Respiratory Systems.** There is a host of changes in these body systems over the adult years: (1) The ability to take in and transport oxygen (**maximum oxygen uptake**, or VO2 max) to the various body organs decreases with age. Both longitudinal and cross-sectional studies show that VO2 max typically declines about 1% per year in adulthood (reviewed by Ostrow, 1984). (2) Cardiac output (blood flow from the heart) also declines, on the order of 30% to 40% from age 25 to age 65 (Rossman, 1980). (3) Blood pressure goes up, at least until about age 70 or 80, after which it may decline (Kohn, 1977). (4) Respiratory efficiency declines with age, because of decreased elasticity of the muscles in the chest and lung cavity, which in turn results in less efficient filling and emptying of the lungs. Collectively, these changes mean (among other things) that the cardiovascular system of the older adult is less able to support highly vigorous exercise or activity.

**Changes in the Nervous System.** Three broad changes in the nervous system that appear to be particularly important for the experience of aging have been documented. The broadest change is in loss of nerve cells. The brain loses cells and loses weight (Takeda & Matsuzawa, 1985); cells are also lost in the peripheral nerves. At the same time, connections between nerve cells become less numerous (Birren, Woods & Williams, 1980). Finally, and doubtless related to the other two, there is a slowing of speed of nerve response. If you measure the response of individual nerves to some stimulus (such as a sound), you find that in older adults the nerves "fire" somewhat more slowly than is true in young adults (Smith, Thompson, & Michalewski, 1980). The behavioral consequences of these changes will become especially clear when we look at changes in memory and other intellectual processes in the next chapter.

**Changes in the Reproductive System.** Major changes in the reproductive system do not typically begin until after age 40, often not until after age 50. The term **climacteric** is used to describe the gradual or rapid loss of reproductive capacity that occurs then in both men and women. It involves changes in hormones, resultant changes in the body and its functioning, and (for some) an overlay of psychological symptoms.

In men, there is a very gradual decline in testosterone (the major male hormone), which results in a number of changes: a diminished production of sperm, some shrinkage of the testes, and a reduction in volume of seminal fluid. It typically takes longer for an older man to achieve erection, and a longer latent period is required before the next erection can be achieved (Weg, 1983). Some men, particularly after age 60, experience temporary or long-term impotence. Estimates of the incidence of impotence vary considerably. For example, among men ages 60 to 65, the amount of impotence reported in various surveys ranges from 18% to 40% (Rossman, 1980).

There is also recent, and still very preliminary, evidence that at least some men experience a more significant emotional/physical upheaval during the climacteric, including insomnia or other sleep disturbances, other physical complaints, depression, and loss of interest in sex (Nolen, 1984; Weg, 1983). Just how large a segment of middle-aged men may experience such symptoms is not at all clear. Tamir's (1982) analysis of some of the cross-sectional results from the 1976 national sample of the Michigan Survey Research Center Study of Mental Illness and Health (recall Table 1–2) suggests that there are peaks between the ages of 40 and 50 in "psychological immobilization," in drinking problems and drug use, and in ill health *only* among college-educated men. But these same middle-aged, college educated men did not show any higher level of anxiety or depression symptoms—such as sleep disturbances, or nervousness, or loss of appetite. My best guess, based on very limited data, is that perhaps 5% to 10% of men may experience fairly extreme symptoms coinciding with the climacteric (Weg, 1983), but it is not at all clear whether these symptoms are physiological or psychological/cultural in origin.

Despite the physiological (and psychological) changes of the climacteric, however, the great majority of men can and do remain sexually vigorous well into old age (as I'll discuss in detail shortly). Men in their 70s and 80s may even produce enough sperm to father children.

For women, the climacteric is marked by the cessation of menses, called **menopause**, which occurs on average (in the U.S. today) at around age 50. The sequence of changes that leads eventually to menopause typically begins in the middle 40s with a decline in the production of estrogen, the major female hormone. The ovaries become less reponsive to the signals to release ova, which results in irregular menstrual cycles, and finally menopause.

As with men, this series of hormone changes is accompanied by changes in the genitals and other tissues. There is some loss of tissue in the genitals and the breasts, the ovaries and uterus become smaller, the walls of the vagina become thin and less elastic, and there is less lubrication produced during intercourse. The other major physical symptom experienced by the majority of women is the "hot flash," a brief, abrupt rise in body temperature which may be accompanied by sudden sweating and skin flushing. (This somewhat startling experience first happened to me when I was recently in China, recurring as often as 30 or 40 times per day. I was continually flushed and damp with sweat. I came to think of the entire trip as "Hot Flashing Through China.")

These various symptoms of the climacteric in women can be sharply reduced by the oral administration of estrogen. Such estrogen replacement therapy was extremely common in the United States in the 1950s and 1960s. In one survey in 1973–1974 (Stadel & Weiss, 1975), 51% of menopausal women had used estrogen, the majority for 10 years or more. Prescription of replacement estrogen has dropped markedly since that time, however, as evidence accumulated showing that the risk of endometrial cancer (cancer of the lining of the uterus) was multiplied three to 10 times when estrogen was used in this way (Nathanson & Lorenz, 1982). At the moment, short-term, low-dosage estrogen replacement is still often prescribed to help reduce hot flashes. The jury is still out on the long-term consequences of such a practice (see Nathanson & Lorenz, 1982, and Greenblatt, Natrajan, & Karpas, 1985, for alternative readings of the evidence).

One other aspect of the female climacteric deserves emphasis: Until quite recently, it was widely assumed that depression and other psychological symptoms were also a standard accompaniment of the climacteric in women. There is now a good deal of dispute about this (Eisdorfer & Raskind, 1975; Weg, 1983). Certainly some women do show depression or anxiety in their 40s and 50s, but there is no clear increase in such symptoms at midlife and no indication that such symptoms, when they do occur, are a result of the hormonal changes of the climacteric, rather than a response to significant life changes at the same ages. For example, Neugarten (1976) reports that in one extensive study of 100 normal women between 43 and 53, menopausal status (no irregularity of periods, some irregularity, or cessation) did not differentiate among the women on any of the psychological variables they had measured, including anxiety, life satisfaction, or self-concept.

It is clear that a small minority of women experience significantly unpleasant physical symptoms associated with menopause, such as more frequent hot flashes, often accompanied by headaches. But there is simply little support for the old stereotype of the inevitably disturbed, depressed, anxious, cranky, middle-aged, premenopausal woman. (The stereotype is not yet gone, though. I was recently told by a physician that the cause of dizziness I was experiencing was "premenopausal anxiety.")

## Body Changes in Adulthood: An Overview

There are several distinctly different ways to look at all the descriptive information I have given you about changes in the physical body over the adult years. The pessimistic approach (which some would say reflects "ageism") is to think of all of those parts of the body drooping, shifting, declining, shrinking, or becoming less efficient and to get depressed. A more optimistic reading of the evidence involves focusing on the role of judgment here: Gray hair and wrinkled skin are not inherently less attractive than dark hair and smooth skin. In addition, most of the changes I have described are both small and fairly gradual, so that effective loss of physical function may well occur only at age 70 or older, and even then there are relatively straightforward compensations that are possible.

My own position lies somewhere between these gloomy and sunny alternatives. It does seem clear that the body mechanism suffers from wear and tear, just as any machine does. We really do lose taste buds, nerve speed, aerobic efficiency. It is not ageism, but realism, to accept and recognize such changes. However it is also true that for most adults, the cumulative effect of these changes is not experienced as a real decline in functioning until the 50s or 60s, perhaps later. In general, as one ages, the body continues to function quite well for normal, day-to-day activities. What it does less and less well is to respond to sudden changes or stress. And with increasing age, there are increases in the compensatory actions or strategies required to maintain reasonable physical self-sufficiency—such as glasses, hearing aids, special books, louder sound on the TV, slower walking, and the like.

# Changes in Health in Adulthood

One way to see the effective result of the body changes I have described is to look at the healthiness of adults at different ages. (Once again, bear in mind that I am talking about health primarily in the United States; quite different patterns of health-over-age would be found in less developed countries.) What kinds of sicknesses do people of different ages have? How frequently? And what do they die of?

## Causes of Death over the Adult Years

Figure 4–3 condenses some of the key information about deaths, and their causes, at various ages. The upper part of the figure shows the probability of dying in any one year, for all adults in that age range. Thus, less than .1% of adults ages 15 to 24 die in any given year, while over 15% of adults over 85 die each year. The fact that older people are more likely to die is surely no great surprise (although you may be comforted to see how flat the curve is as late as 55 to 64). More interesting are the causes of death at each age.

If you examine the figure closely, you'll see that when young people die, they do not typically die of disease, but of accidents, suicide, or homicide. Nearly 58% of adults ages 24 to 34 who died in 1983 in the U.S., died from one of these three causes. In contrast, heart disease and cancer—the two leading causes of death at present—do not account for a significant percentage of deaths until the 35 to 44 age range, after which they account for the preponderance of deaths. What does seem to be true about the years from 20 to 40, however, is that adults are laying the groundwork for future disease—by the way they live, the health habits they practice, the risks in their workplaces. We can see this clearly when we look at incidence of disease, rather than death rates.

## Physical Illnesses

As you can see from Figure 4–4, the chance that you will have an "acute" illness (a short-term disease, like the flu) declines with age, while the chance that you will have a "chronic" illness (a continuing disorder, such as heart disease, or arthritis, or high blood pressure) goes up steadily with age. So in your 20s and 30s, you catch colds, the flu, maybe mononucleosis or even VD, but you have a less than 10% chance of having a diagnosed chronic disease. In contrast, postretirement age adults have about a 50% chance of having some chronic disorder. In the Duke Longitudinal Study sample (Siegler, Nowlin, & Blumenthal, 1980), among adults between the ages of 65 and 93, 57% had

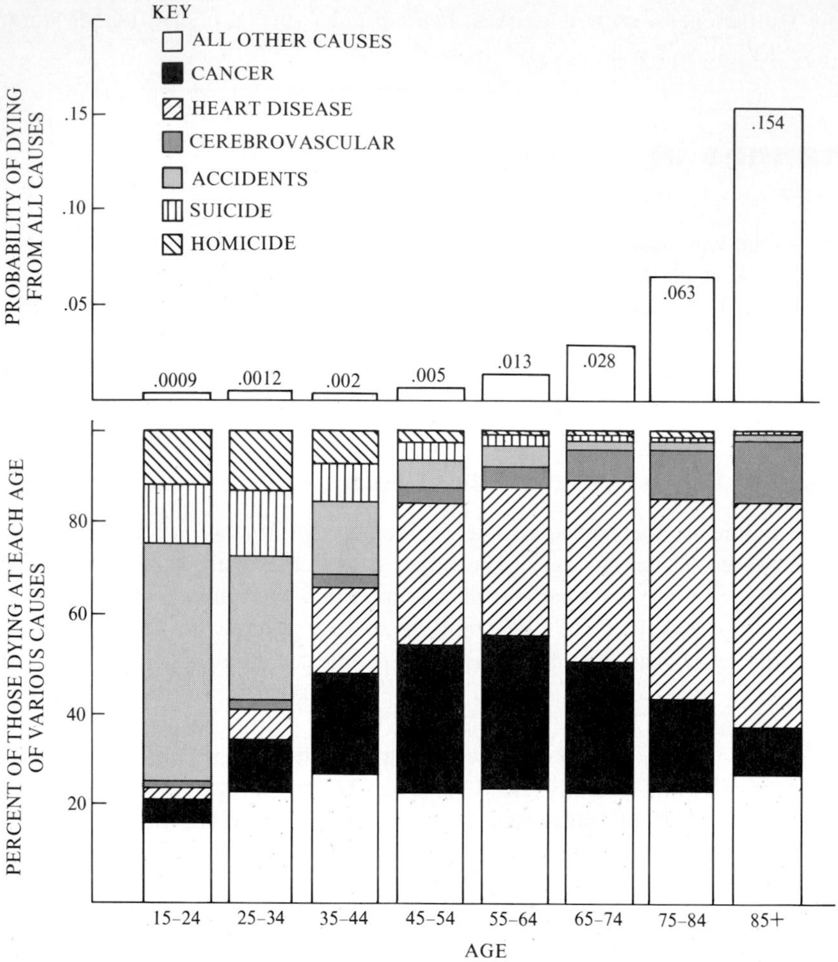


**Figure 4–3** *The upper part of this figure shows the probability of dying, for adults in each of a series of age groups, during 1983. The lower part of the figure shows what the people died of in 1983. Proportionately, many more young people die of accidents, suicide, and homicide, while beginning in the 45–54 age group, cancer and heart disease are the major causes of death. (Source: National Center for Health Statistics, Monthly Vital Statistics Report, 1984, 32(13).)*

arthritis, 25% had high blood pressure, another 23% had heart disease, with smaller percentages for other chronic disorders such as diabetes or emphysema. But even at these older ages the presence of chronic disease is not inevitable. Twenty-five percent of these older adults had no chronic disease at all (including 32% of those between the ages of 86 and 93).

There are some intriguing sex differences in these figures. Figure 4–4 shows that women appear to experience more acute illnesses, but fewer chronic ones.

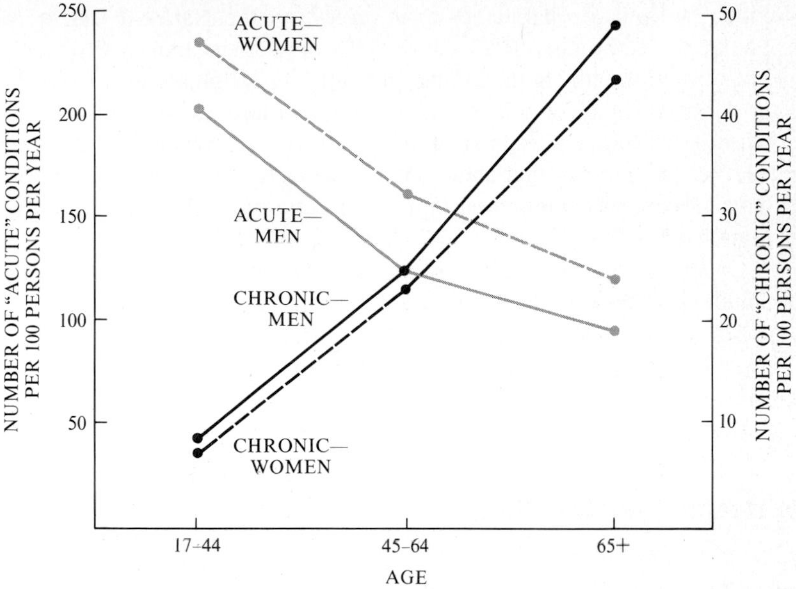


***Figure 4–4*** *The number of acute (short-term) illnesses tends to go down with age, while the number of chronic illnesses goes up. These particular figures, from 1978, are typical of health patterns in the United States in recent years. (Source: National Center for Health Statistics, Vital and Health Statistics, Series 10, No. 130.)*

The higher reported rate of acute illnesses for women is a very common finding, but no one is quite sure why (or even whether) women get sick more often. Pregnancy and all related disorders are not included in the numbers shown in this figure, so that's not the explanation. It is quite possible that in fact actual illness rates are the same for men and women, but that women are simply more likely than men to acknowledge sickness to someone who interviews them, or to take an illness seriously enough to seek medical attention for it.

## Physical Disability

Just as it is possible to experience measurable body changes without losing effective functioning, so it is possible to have a chronic disease without real functional disability. Just how many older adults are limited in their abilities to do everyday things like climbing stairs, or lifting a box, or stooping or kneeling? This is a difficult question to answer precisely, since we must rely on the self-reports of adults whose definitions of disability or difficulty may vary considerably. But there are some relevant findings.

For example, results from one longitudinal study (the National Longitudinal Surveys of Labor Market Experience, NLS, Chirikos & Nestel, 1985) involving several thousand black and white men indicate that 26% of the white men and 34% of the black men between 60 and 74 had difficulty going up stairs.

Findings from a separate national survey by the National Center for Health Statistics (Verbrugge, 1985) show 35% of women and 24% of men over 65 had difficulty with stairs. Lifting and carrying weights seems to be the activity in which most older adults are limited—perhaps as many as 50%—possibly because of loss of muscle strength, or arthritis, or other back disorders. Overall, Verbrugge finds that about 35% of women over 65 and about 43% of men have at least some limitation in a major activity, such as ability to work or do housework.

Overall, most of us experience fairly robust health in the first decades of adulthood, although the early, nonsymptomatic stages of disease may be present even then. Measurable symptoms of such diseases, and loss of function or disability associated with those diseases, are likely to appear for at least some adults in their 50s and 60s, which is reflected in the sharply increased rates of both illness and death in the decades past that.

## Mental Health over Adulthood

What I have said so far about health patterns relates to physical health, but what about mental health? Are there any age-related patterns in such symptoms of disturbance as alcoholism, or drug use, or suicide? Are there consistent age differences in depression, or anxiety, or other forms of identifiable mental illness?

Surprisingly, there seem to be very few, despite the prevailing view—among many health professionals as well as the lay public—that mental health problems increase with age. The President's Commission on Mental Health (1979), for example, asserted that "depression escalates decade by decade" (p. 3), and this is typical of statements in texts and government documents about the elderly. But this assertion is not at all well supported by the existing evidence.

Marjorie Feinson (1985) has reviewed 28 studies in which some aspect of emotional distress or mental health in random samples of adults of varying ages has been assessed. The most common finding is that there are no age differences, but when age differences are found, it is most often younger and not older adults who experience greater distress or more psychiatric symptoms. For example, in one very good study, Charles Holzer and his colleagues (Holzer, Leaf, & Weissman, 1985) interviewed a carefully selected sample of over 5,000 adults in New Haven, Connecticut. Each subject was asked in detail about the presence of a series of specific behaviors or symptoms. Their responses were then compared systematically to the standard diagnostic criteria for depression, including sadness or "the blues," changes in appetite and sleep patterns, loss of energy or fatigue, slowed thinking and indecisiveness, and the like. The findings, in Figure 4–5, reveal both the typically higher rate of depression for women, but also an age pattern of higher rates for younger adults in both sexes.

The one measure of disturbance or depression on which older adults do show higher rates is suicide. But as you can see in Figure 4–6, substantially heightened suicide rates after age 65 occur only in a subset of the population, namely

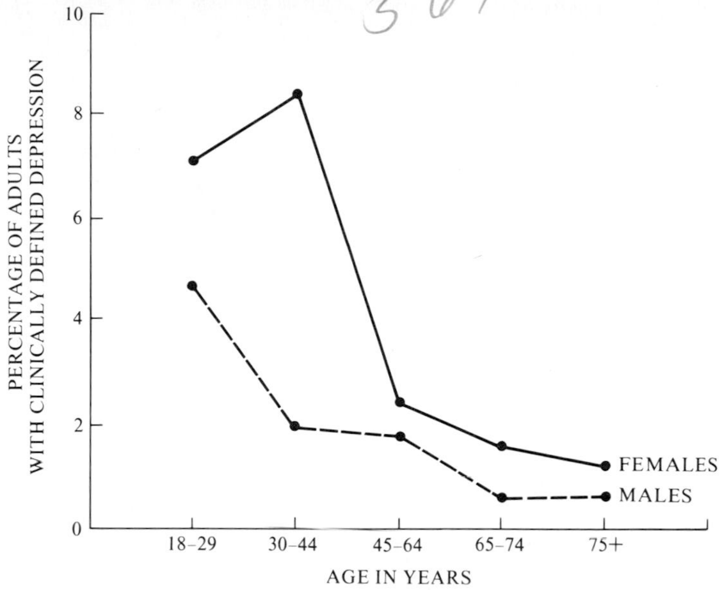


***Figure 4–5*** *Rates of depression in this large representative sample from a New England city are consistently higher for women and for young adults. This runs counter to the prevailing assumption that older adults are more prone to depression. (Source: Holzer, Leaf, & Weissman, 1985, from Table 7.4, p. 110.)*

white males (U.S. Bureau of the Census, 1984a). And the suicide rate for older males has halved since 1940 (McIntosh, 1985).

Before you draw the conclusion that old age is actually a time of generally lower risk of depression or other emotional distress, I need to point out a weakness in all the evidence I have cited: In all the major studies, only "community living" adults have been included; older adults in nursing homes or other institutions have been specifically excluded from the samples. Thus, the very older adults who may be most prone to depression or other distress, or who may be in an institution or nursing home precisely because they show some form of disturbance, are not counted in these statistics.

Given this limitation, and the inconsistency in the evidence, it is not reasonable at this point to draw any firm conclusion about the link (if any) between age and mental health. What would be more useful now would be some study of those factors that may interact with age to increase risk of emotional disturbance. Are some subgroups (such as college-educated, white males) more prone to depression or other disturbance at particular points in their life cycles? Is this different from the maximum risk times for women, or for blacks, or for widows? Patterns like these may be hidden in the apparent inconsistency of the present evidence. Beyond this, the one conclusion that does seem reasonable is that we can lay to rest the widely held belief that there is something inherent

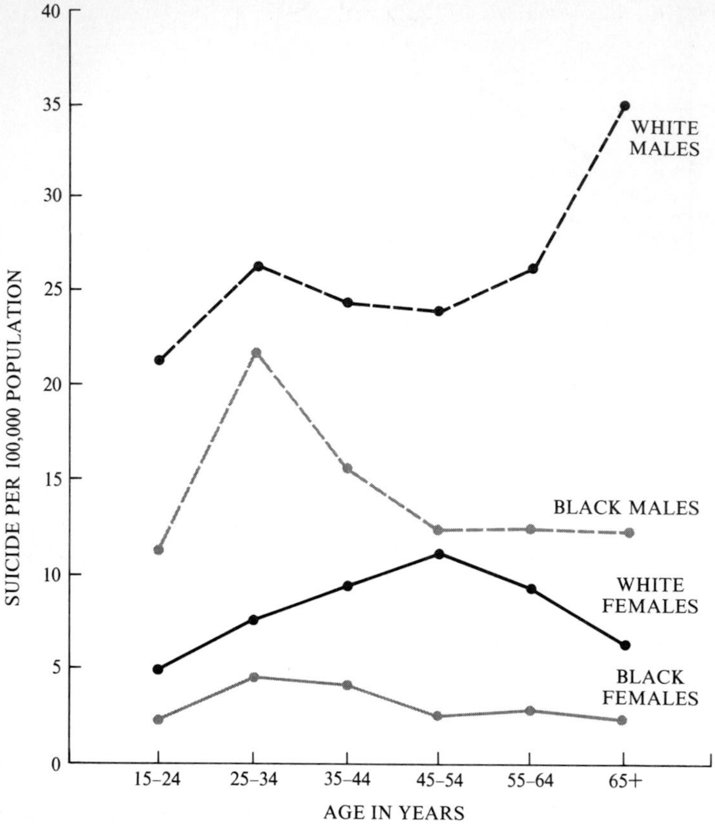


**Figure 4–6** *Suicide rates in the United States are markedly higher for white males than for any other group, and this group shows a sharp rise in rate of suicide past retirement age—a pattern unmatched by any other subgroup. Could this mean that retirement is a more difficult adjustment for white males? What other explanations occur to you? (Source: U.S. Bureau of the Census,* Statistical Abstract of the United States: 1985, *1984. Table 118, p. 79.)*

in the process of aging itself, or in the status of the elderly in our culture, which leads either commonly or inevitably to heightened depression or anxiety.

## The Effects of Physical Aging and Health on Behavior

While it is interesting to know what changes are going on in our bodies (or our emotions) as we age, or what risks of disease we may face, for most of us the crucial question is really this: How will this affect my daily life? I've alluded to bits of answers to this question already, but let me focus on it more directly.

## Slowing Down

The most significant general change in behavior resulting from all the body and health changes I have described is a quite distinct (and accurate) feeling of being slower as you get older. Reaction time is longer, so your reflexes as you drive are not quite as quick. You don't adapt as rapidly to heating or cooling, so you have more trouble dealing with sudden changes in temperature: Once you get cold, it is harder to warm up, and vice versa. In later years, it simply takes longer to do everyday tasks like tying your shoes or getting dressed. Not only is there a loss of some sensation in the fingers, there are also the arthritic changes in the joints to deal with. Stamina is also less for various reasons (e.g., the heart is less efficient, the lungs take in less air, the muscles are weaker), so older adults find that they can sustain mild or vigorous activity for shorter periods. (I have one extremely vital and vigorous friend of 67 who, after painting the inside of a house for 12 hours one day, complained that she was "a lot tireder than I used to be." It's all relative!)

## Sexual Activity

Another area in which many adults experience the consequences of all the changes of physical aging and health is in their sexual activity. As Kinsey reported years ago (Kinsey, Pomeroy, & Martin, 1948, 1953), sexual activity in married couples declines quite steadily over the adult years. Kinsey's own figures showed a drop in the average frequency of intercourse from about 10 times per month in the early 20s to perhaps two times a month past 65. Other authors have observed higher rates at every age (e.g., Hunt, 1974). Of course, the actual frequencies reported may be inflated, since these researchers are relying on self-reports from subjects (who tend to exaggerate sexual activity), but the overall decline with age is a consistent finding.

This is not just a "cohort problem," either, since longitudinal data show the same pattern, as you can see in Figure 4–7. These findings from the Duke Longitudinal Studies (Palmore, 1981) show that each group studied reported a decline in frequency of sexual intercourse over the years of the study.

The rates of sexual activity are generally lower for women than for men, in part because more women (especially in the older years) are unmarried and have difficulty finding a partner. But the age changes are common to both men and women.

What I find remarkable about the findings on sexual activity in adults is not that there is an average decline—a pattern we would expect, given the physical changes occurring—but how many adults remain sexually active well into old age. In one questionnaire study by Consumers Union (Brecher, 1984), including 4,246 respondents over 50, 81% of married women and 50% of unmarried women over 70 reported at least some sexual activity during the past month

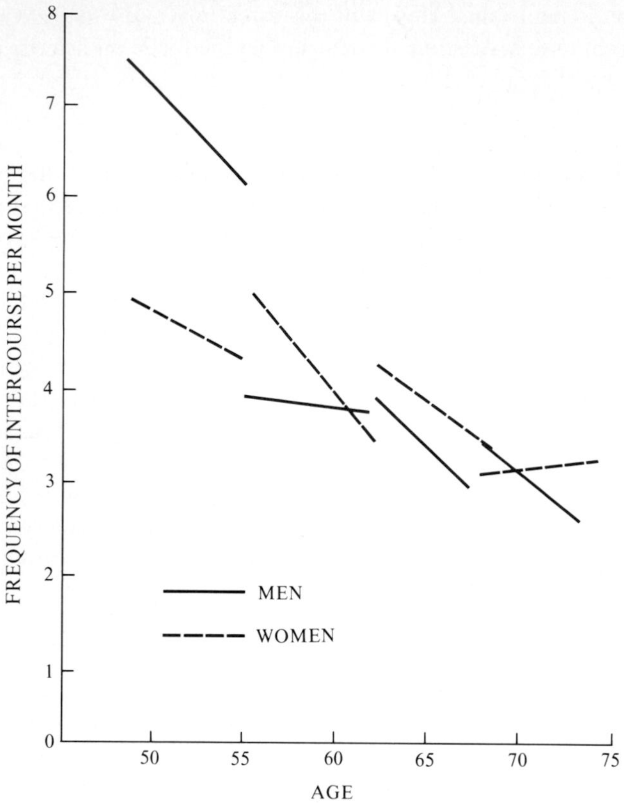


***Figure 4–7*** *These longitudinal data show clearly that the frequency of sexual intercourse declines with age even among married adults, but that regular sexual activity is typical even among adults in their 70s. Each line in this graph reflects the reported sexual activity of one group of men, or women, over a period of six years in a longitudinal study. So, for example, the line in the upper left shows that men who were 50 at the beginning of the study reported intercourse an average of 7.5 times per month. Six years later, when they were 56, they reported an average of slightly over 6 times per month. (Source: Palmore, Erdman,* Social Patterns in Normal Aging, *p. 88, Figure 6–4. Copyright © 1981 Duke University Press.)*

(including masturbation as well as sex with a partner). The equivalent figures for married and unmarried men over 50 were 81% and 75%. And of those sexually active in this study, the majority reported that they had sex at least once a week, that they enjoyed sex, and that they experienced orgasm every time or almost every time.

These numbers do not come from a random sample of adults, of course. The respondents in this study were all subscribers (or friends of subscribers) to *Consumers Report*, so they are, as a group, well educated and middle class. But similar findings have emerged from the Duke studies, which include a more representative sample of older adults. In this study, too, over half of adults over 70 were still sexually active. And as you can see in Figure 4–7, of those married and sexually active, frequency of sex was about once a week.

These findings underline yet again an important point about physical changes in adulthood that I have made before: Yes, there is a slowing down of many reactions, including sexual responses such as erection or lubrication. And yes, most adults experience an increase in physical ailments as they get older, some of which interfere with their daily functioning. But it is simultaneously true that most adults adapt to these changes with inventiveness and some grace, finding ways to continue activities that they enjoy.

The *frequency* or vigor of various activities may decline (as sex does), but *enjoyment* of them need not.

# Explanations of Physical Aging

At the descriptive level, most of the bodily changes I have been listing are well documented. But explanations of those changes are much harder to come by. As Joan Waring puts it:

> How the physical organism grows older is better understood than why. As yet there is no universally accepted theory as to what mechanism triggers the senescent changes that seem inevitably to increase the risk of death with increasing age. There is, however, an emerging consensus that more than one process is at work: Nature has an arsenal of fail-safe devices to ensure that people do not live forever. If disease or accident do not prove fatal, old age will. (Waring, 1981, p. 471)

Three main categories of explanations are presently competing for support. Each of the three may help to account for some of the changes that have been documented.

## Genetic Explanations

At the most basic level maturational changes associated with aging may be programmed directly in the genes, just as the maturational changes associated with growth in the early years of life appear to be. The bodily changes associated with puberty, for example, are triggered by a complex, specific series of hormonal changes, which are thought to be triggered, in turn, by some kind of unfolding code contained in the genes of each cell. Similarly, the hormonal changes of the climacteric, as well as such changes as the loss of elasticity of skin, muscles, and other structures, the loss of hair, or the loss of taste buds, may well be part of built-in sequences programmed by genetic codes.

A related genetic argument centers around the observation that each species has a characteristic maximum life span. As I pointed out earlier, 100 or 110 years appears to be the effective maximum life span for humans (Hayflick, 1977), despite improvements in health care and successful campaigns against infectious diseases. This persuades biologists that there is a genetic program setting the upper limit of functioning of each organism. Leonard Hayflick (1965, 1975) has provided further support for this idea from his research on the behavior of cells.

Hayflick observes that when human embryo cells (such as cells from the skin) are placed in nutrient solutions and observed over a period of time, the cells divide (doubling each time) only about 50 times, after which the cell colony degenerates. Even when the cells are frozen part way through this doubling process, when they are later thawed they "remember" where they were in the sequence, and still double only a total of about 50 times. When cells are taken from human adults, they double fewer times (perhaps 20 times) before the cell colony degenerates. Furthermore, cells from the embryos of longer-lived creatures (such as the Galapagos tortoise) double perhaps 100 times, while chicken cells double only about 25 times. Thus, there appears to be a rough correlation between the typical longevity of each species and the number of cell divisions each organism's cells are "programmed" to complete.

Another explanation of aging in this same general group is the argument that over time, the genetic material in clusters of cells is damaged in some fashion. Gerontologists who hold to this view (sometimes called the "hit" theory of aging) do not assume that the organism is actually programmed for specific maturational changes in senescence, but rather that the whole mechanism grinds slowly to a halt as the genetic information becomes more and more inaccurate through damage to the DNA within each cell. Such damage could occur from any of a series of random events, including exposure to low levels of radiation (which is present to some degree all the time).

## Nongenetic Cell Changes

Another group of gerontologists agree that cumulative cell changes are at the heart of bodily aging, but focus on modifications or deteriorations in other aspects of cell functioning (Shock, 1977a) rather than on changes in the genetic material itself. The proteins and enzymes in cells do not always operate optimally. Over time, "mistakes" occur in the various intra- and intercellular processes such as protein synthesis. These "mistakes," in turn, alter the way the cells or molecules function.

One particular change, called **cross-linking**, has been found to occur in cell proteins in older adults. In skin and in connective tissue, for example, two proteins called collagen and elastin form bonds, called cross-linkages, either between molecules, or within a given protein molecule. This decreases the efficiency of the protein. Since collagen and elastin are involved in the elasticity of the skin, the blood vessels and many other tissues, cross-linking helps to explain the increased wrinkling of the skin with age, and may also be one cause of some kinds of cardiovascular disease. It seems probable that similar accumulations of cellular malfunctions may lie at the heart of other observed patterns of bodily aging.

## Organ System Breakdown

The final group of explanations is focused not on the individual cell, but on whole organ systems (Shock, 1977a). The basic argument is that what we see as aging is the result of progressive failures of key organs in the body, particularly the cardiovascular system and the immune system.

We know, for example, that there are certain predictable changes that take place in blood vessels, such as increasing brittleness and loss of elasticity, as well as narrowing resulting from the accumulation of fatty acid deposits (such as cholesterol). Since circulation of the blood is one of the keys to the nourishment of the entire body, any decrease in the efficiency of circulation will affect all other organ systems.

A currently more popular whole-system theory of aging focuses on the immune system. The lymphatic system (including the thymus) protects the body in two ways: by producing antibodies which react to foreign organisms (such as viruses and other infectious agents), and by producing special cells (T cells) that are programmed to reject and consume harmful or mutant cells, such as cancers or transplanted organs. With age, both of these protective mechanisms work less efficiently. Adults produce fewer antibodies than do children or teenagers. In addition, T cells partially lose the ability to "recognize" a foreign cell, so that cancer cells, for example, may not be fought. More intriguing is the fact that the body, in adulthood, begins to form antibodies against its own cells. This *autoimmune* response seems to lie behind a number of diseases of adulthood, including rheumatoid arthritis, some kinds of diabetes, and perhaps multiple sclerosis (Shock, 1977b).

Of course, none of these system theories of aging tell us why the basic breakdown of the cardiovascular, or immune, or other system occurs in the first place. We can combine the several theories I have described, however, and come up with at least a general notion of why or how aging occurs. Over time, there appears to be an accumulation of changes at the cellular level, either because the system is reaching the end point of its genetically programmed reproductive capacity, or because small errors accumulate. Eventually these cellular changes are enough to alter the efficient functioning of many organ systems, which in turn makes us more susceptible to various diseases or major breakdowns. At the same time, hormonal changes, and perhaps others of the changes in body systems or cells, appear to be programmed in the genetic code itself.

Even this very preliminary notion of the process of aging implies that everyone ages at about the same rate. And in describing the body changes that take place, I have not placed much emphasis on individual differences in rate of change. But in fact there are wide differences among people in the rate with which their bodies age, and there are specific patterns of life that are associated with slower or faster aging.

# Individual Differences in Aging and Health

I have saved this topic for last because it is the aspect of physical aging that has the most obvious practical applications. If you wish to maintain fitness, to slow the rate of the physical changes of aging so as to maintain independence and effective functioning as long as possible, there are things you can do, starting now.

## Individual Heredity

One of the important factors in your physical health and longevity that you cannot control is the set of genes you inherited from your parents. Specific heredity affects a variety of aspects of the aging process.

Patterns of balding, for example, run in families (passed from mother to son, by the way, rather than father to son), as does the tendency to premature graying of hair (a gene I inherited).

If you have had a complete physical exam lately, in which a full medical history is taken, you'll also realize that susceptibility to some specific diseases runs in families as well. Most physicians will ask you about the disease history of your parents, your grandparents, even your aunts and uncles. In particular, they are likely to ask you about the family patterns of heart disease, diabetes, and cancer, each of which has been shown to be genetically influenced. Some other diseases that may have similar genetic components are ulcers, kidney disease, and perhaps Alzheimer's disease, a disease of middle and old age involving atrophy of the brain and considerable loss of brain cells which I will describe more fully in chapter 5 (Smith, Bierman, & Robinson, 1978; Upton, 1977). A propensity for alcoholism is also inherited (Schuckit, 1984). This is most clearly shown in studies of adopted children: Children of alcoholics who are adopted in early infancy and raised in nonalcoholic families are still about four times as likely to become alcoholics themselves in adulthood as are comparable adopted children born to nonalcoholic parents.

Longevity also seems to be partially inherited, which may mean that whatever body processes control the overall rate of aging are themselves controlled by specific genes or combinations of genes. If your grandparents and your parents have lived to ripe, old ages, the chances are very good that you will as well, barring accidents or infectious diseases (Kallman & Jarvik, 1959).

## General Life Circumstances

A second cluster of factors related to health and physical aging, over which an individual may have relatively little control, includes social class, income, and living arrangements. The relationships are easy to state: Better educated adults, and those with higher income, have better health, maintain their health better into old age, and live longer (e.g., Heinemann, 1985; Palmore, 1981). These patterns appear to hold both cross sectionally and longitudinally. Further, adults who live alone, particularly divorced adults and elderly men who live alone, have higher rates of both physical and mental illness, and higher mortality rates, than do adults living with someone else (e.g., Heinemann, 1985; Holzer et al., 1985; Palmore, 1981).

There are several fairly obvious possible causes for these patterns. First and most obviously, adults with lower incomes are less able to afford reasonable medical care or even decent food (Davis, Randall, Forthofer, Lee, & Margen, 1985). The cumulative effect of medical neglect, or undernutrition, over the years of adulthood will result in shorter life expectancy and higher rates of both acute and chronic diseases. Second, the less well educated adult may simply know less about good health practices, including good diet. And, of course, there are special strains associated with being poor which may take a physical toll over time.

Living alone, especially after a divorce or widowhood, seems to exact a psychological toll, which I'll discuss in more detail in later chapters. But one direct physical effect for at least some is a change in diet. This is particularly so for older widowers whose wives had always done the cooking. These men have few skills and little knowledge, and eat the least adequate diet (Davis et al., 1985).

## Personality, Aging, and Health

Yet a third element in the predictive equation is personality. There has not been a great deal of research on potential links between personality and physical aging, but there are some suggestive findings. For example, adults high in neuroticism (one of the dimensions of personality I talked about in chapter 2) complain more about their health than do those low in this dimension. They are also more likely to smoke (and have more trouble quitting) and to have drinking problems (Costa & McCrae, 1980b). Since smoking, in particular, has a demonstrable causal impact on both cancer and heart disease, the personality dimension of neuroticism may be an indirect contributor to ill health and reduced longevity in adulthood.

A second body of evidence linking personality and health comes from studies of the **Type A personality** and heart disease. This personality pattern, first described by two cardiologists, Meyer Friedman and Ray Rosenman (1974; Rosenman & Friedman, 1983), includes several key elements: (1) competitive achievement striving (always wanting to win, to do better than others, to turn simple situations into contests), (2) a sense of time urgency (including packing your day with tightly scheduled activities, timing things and trying to do them faster each time), and (3) hostility and aggressiveness, frequently expressed in chronic conflict with co-workers or family. Type A people hurry, press, strive, but they also approach new tasks with confidence. Type B people are more relaxed, put less pressure on themselves, and take time to "stop and smell the roses." Some people appear to show Type A behavior nearly all the time; some show it primarily under stress.

Friedman and Rosenman's research, and that of others (e.g., Glass, 1977), has shown a link between blood cholesterol and Type A behavior. Accountants, for example, show a rise in cholesterol before the April 15 tax deadline, as the time pressure of their work increases, and then a sharp drop in cholesterol after the deadline. Individuals who chronically show Type A behavior appear to have consistently higher cholesterol, as well as a higher risk of heart attack. Whether chronic Type A personality/behavior patterns can be significantly altered is not so clear. But if you are a Type A, or even an A−, it is probably worth the effort to try to slow down and ease up.

## Personal Health Habits, Aging, and Health

Personal health habits are much easier to control or change than is your heredity, your social class, or your personality. And health habits play a significant role in the rate with which you will experience the body changes of aging, the degree of good health you will have, and the length of your life.

The most striking demonstration of this comes from research by Nedra Belloc and her co-workers (Belloc, 1973; Belloc & Breslow, 1972). She identified seven good health practices, which I've listed in Table 4–2, each of which has been shown to increase life expectancy. Belloc's basic question was whether combining these good health practices would increase life expectancy still more.

The evidence she gathered was from a large sample of 6,928 adults in Alameda County, California, who had completed a health survey. Five and a half years after the first contact, Belloc checked the county records for all deaths, and was able to link the number of health practices initially reported to the probability of death over the five years. (Since she did not have information on the deaths of any of the sample who had moved from the county in the intervening years, the death rates are probably low, but the pattern of relationship between health practices and probabilty of death should not be affected by this limitation.)

**TABLE 4–2 Good Health Practices Identified by Belloc**

1. Usually sleep seven or eight hours per night.
2. Eat breakfast almost every day.
3. Eat between meals once in a while, rarely, or never.
4. Weight for a man between 5% under and 20% over desirable weight for height. Weight for a woman not more than 10% over desirable weight for height.
5. Often or sometimes engage in active sports, swimming, or take long walks, or often garden or do physical exercises.
6. Have not more than four drinks at a time.
7. Never smoke cigarettes.

**Source:** Belloc & Breslow, 1972, p. 415. Reprinted by permission of Academic Press, Orlando, FL and the author.

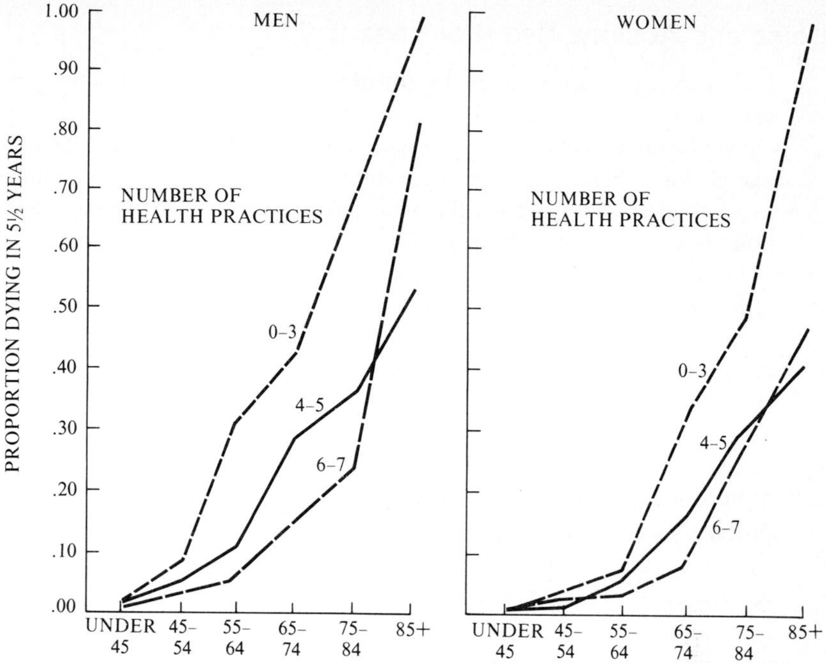


***Figure 4–8*** *These findings from Belloc's study show clearly that the risk of death over this five-year period increased the fewer the number of good health practices a person followed. The effect is clearest among older adults, but that does not necessarily mean that you can get away with poor health practices in early adulthood. Other evidence suggests that the impact of such poor health practices as smoking or inactivity is cumulative. (Source: Belloc, 1973, p. 75. Reprinted by permission of Academic Press, Orlando, FL and author.)*

You can see the results of Belloc's study in Figure 4–8. In early and midlife, it may appear that we can get away with poor health practices. But beginning at about 50 for men, and perhaps 60 for women, poor health practices catch up to us, and the risk of death is considerably higher for those with poor practices. The same conclusion comes from the Duke studies (Palmore, 1970). Adults who exercised less, smoked more, and were overweight died at an earlier age than one would predict from their age, sex, and race.

Data from the Duke studies also show that poor health practices are associated with more frequent illnesses. Those adults who were relatively sedentary at the beginning of the study, six years later had more illnesses that forced them to stay in bed, visited the doctor more, and rated their own health as worse than did originally active adults.

In sum, good health and long life are not entirely or largely the result of luck or good genes. They are at least partially under our own control.

## Exercise and Activity: Use it or Lose it

I want to say a further word specifically about exercise and activity as significant factors in aging and health in adulthood. My interest in this particular "good health practice" stems in part, I am sure, from my own decision (at the age of 38) to begin exercising and running regularly. Like most converts (such as ex-smokers,) I can be a bit of a bore on the subject. But in this case my point is well buttressed by research.

For example, I pointed out earlier that maximum oxygen uptake (VO2 max) typically declines about 40% in adulthood, which means that older adults are getting less oxygen to the brain, the muscles, and all other parts of the body. At any age, however, VO2 max can be significantly increased with exercise (Klocke, 1977; Ostrow, 1984; Shock, 1977b). And adults who have maintained fitness continuously beginning in their 20s have still higher levels of oxygen uptake.

In general, regular exercise or high levels of activity appear to slow the aging processes to some degree, and to reduce significantly the risk of some diseases, most particularly coronary heart disease (Paffenbarger & Hyde, 1984; Serfass & Gerberich, 1984). Current evidence suggests that the minimum amount of

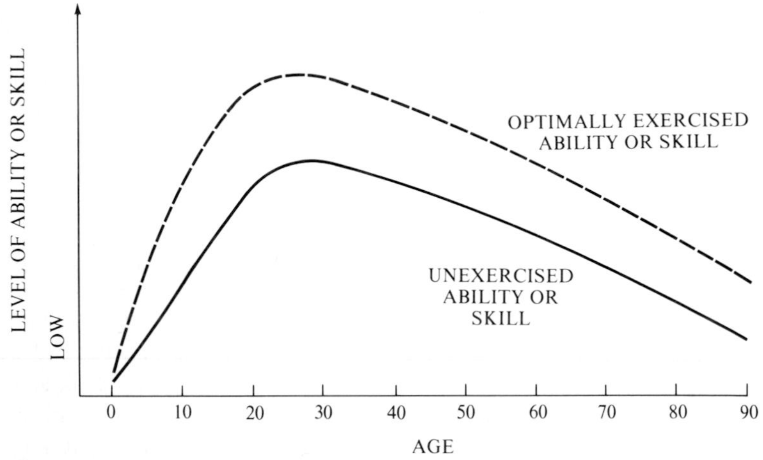


**Figure 4–9** *Nancy Denney has proposed this general model of age changes in "unexercised" and "exercised" activities. We might also use the term "base rate" instead of "unexercised." This lower curve is thus intended to represent the normal pattern of aging for any body function (or mental skill) without any special training or effort. The upper curve shows what the pattern of age changes may be like for the same function or skill if special training or effort are applied. (Source: N. W. Denney, "Aging and Cognitive Changes" in* Handbook of Developmental Psychology, *B. B. Wolman, Ed., © 1982, p. 819. Reprinted by permission of Prentice-Hall, Inc., Englewood Cliffs, NJ.)*

exercise required to maintain fitness is about 20 to 60 minutes, three times a week, at an intensity level that will bring the heart rate to about 75% of maximum (Serfass & Gerberich, 1984).

The growing body of evidence on the link between physical functioning and exercise points, in fact, to an intriguing possibility: At least some of the patterns of body change that we think of as inevitable facets of aging may instead (or in addition) be the result of disuse.

In specific support of this possibility, Walter Bortz (1982) points out that astronauts in weightlessness, and patients given prolonged bed rest, show many of the body changes we normally think of as aging, including increases in blood pressure, loss of a sense of balance, loss of red blood cells, loss of body weight, increase in body fat, loss of calcium in the bones, even decreased taste sensivitity. Since most adults (at least in Western societies) become less active as they grow older, at least some "aging" changes may be "disuse" changes. As the adage goes, "Use it or lose it."

Nancy Denney (1982) has proposed a very useful general model (Figure 4–9) to describe the relationship between activity/exercise and functioning. (The model works equally well for describing patterns of aging of intellectual abilities, by the way, so we will meet it again in chapter 5). She proposes that there is some pattern of rise and then fall, with age, in many skills, abilities, or body functions. The particular shape of the curve may differ for different abilities or functions, but the general pattern is certainly common. This basic curve holds whether the person "uses" or "exercises" that ability or body function or not. But the level of the curve is higher for those skills or functions that are well exercised.

Two implications of the model are worth emphasizing. First, at any given age, adults who have exercised some ability (who have increased their maximum oxygen uptake by aerobic exercise, or who have used their taste buds more by sampling a wide variety of flavors, or who have lifted weights or kept up typing skills, or whatever) will show a level of that skill or body function which is like that of a younger, unexercised person. So in this sense, the process of aging can be slowed.

A second implication of Denney's model is that it should be possible at any age to improve the level of any unexercised skill or body function by beginning to exercise it. The maximum level you will be able to reach will go down as you get older, but some improvement should be possible. Research on the effect of aerobic exercise on maximum oxygen uptake confirms this: Regardless of age, adults who begin physical exercise show some increase in aerobic capacity (Ostrow, 1984; Shock, 1977b).

Bortz sums up nicely:

> It is wrong to suggest that exercise might halt the fall of the grains of sand in the hourglass. It is proposed, however, that the dimension of the aperture may be responsive to the toning influence of physical activity, and consequently the sand may drain more slowly. A physically active life may allow us to approach our true biogenetic potential for longevity. (1982, p. 1206)

I would add that exercise and physical activity also increase the chances that we will spend our adult years in good health, and with higher life satisfaction (Palmore, 1981).

## A Review of Age Patterns

It may help in this chapter, and in each of the six largely descriptive chapters that follow, to take a moment to pull together information on physical and health changes with age, as I have done in Table 4–3. Physically, adults are clearly at their peak in the years from 20 to 35 or 40. They have the greatest strength, the most efficient functioning of body systems, the least likelihood of

**TABLE 4–3 Summary of Age Changes in the Physical Body and in Health**

| Age 20–40 | Age 40–65 | Age 65 and Older |
|---|---|---|
| The head grows and changes shape | Height is lost slowly<br>Skin and other tissues begin to lose elasticity | Height continues to be lost<br>Continuation of loss of elasticity in tissues |
| Peak of sensory acuity in all senses | Senses begin to be less acute starting at about age 50, but these changes are still small enough to make little difference in daily life | More rapid loss of sensory acuity, including vision, hearing, taste, smell. Loss of taste, smell, and hearing are particularly noticeable, and may have significant effects on daily living |
| Peak of physical strength, stamina, aerobic fitness | Beginning decline in strength, in heart capacity, and equivalent, but wide individual differences and little effect on daily life<br>Loss of brain cells and slowing of nerve conductance speed<br>Climacteric begins in this period for most men and women, with accompanying changes in hormones and genitalia | Continued loss of strength, stamina, and aerobic fitness, although this is less in physically active adults. Loss begins to have effect on daily life<br>Continued and more rapid loss of brain cells and speed<br>Climacteric usually completed, but sexual activity is typically maintained for those adults with partners |
| Deaths mostly from accidents or suicide | Deaths most commonly from heart disease or cancer | Cancer and heart disease continue to be the leading causes of death, with stroke, diabetes, and other diseases also occurring |
| Highest risk period for acute illness; lowest risk for chronic illness | Medium-level risk for both chronic and acute illness | Lowest risk for acute, and highest risk for chronic illness |
| Possibly highest risk for depression | No clear data on mental illness rates | |
| Peak of sexual activity | Sexual activity declines but is maintained by most | Sexual activity declines further, but is maintained by a majority |

chronic disease. Reaction times are fast, and everyday tasks are easily accomplished. In the years of midlife, from 40 to 60 or 65, the rate of physical change, or ill health, varies widely from one individual to the next, with some experiencing a loss of physical function quite early, others much later, in part as a response to health habits and exercise. Reaction time does begin to decline in this age span, however, as does strength, and there are measurable changes in cellular functioning beginning to accumulate. The risk of death rises, as does the risk of chronic disease.

In late adulthood, from 65 onward, the loss of speed of response continues, and is now matched by loss of sensory acuity, and by significant increases in chronic diseases. But here, too, there are wide individual differences in the rate of change, and effective compensations that can maintain perfectly adequate (or even excellent) physical functioning for many adults well into their 70s or 80s.

There is a fine line to be tread here between the overly optimistic and the overly pessimistic views of physical old age. The sands do run through the hourglass and cannot be permanently stayed. And certainly, many older adults, crippled by chronic disease, or restricted by loss of physical skill or function, find their older bodies painful, uncomfortable, or distressing. But it is also true that, within limits, there are choices we can each make that will ease these changes, and attitudes or strategies to adopt that make the adjustments easier.

## Summary

1. While the average life expectancy has been increasing steadily over the past decades, now reaching approximately 78 years for women and 71 years for men in the U.S., the maximum life span appears to have remained the same, at about 100 or 110.

2. Body changes in adulthood include changes in external appearance such as loss of height, redistribution of fat, loss of hair, and loss of elasticity in skin and other organs.

3. Loss of acuity in the senses also occurs, so that by age 65 or 70, 70% of adults have some visual loss, and 30% or more have significant hearing loss.

4. A loss of muscle tissue is another body change, as is a loss of bone marrow, and a loss of calcium in the bones (osteoporosis).

5. The cardiovascular system shows a steady decrease in maximum oxygen uptake and in cardiac output, and an increase in blood pressure with age.

6. The nervous system shows a steady loss of cells, in the brain and in the periphery, as well as a loss of connections between cells. Nerve conductive speed declines.

7. Both men and women experience a loss of reproductive capacity in middle and old age through a series of changes in hormones and reproductive organs collectively called the climacteric. In men, there is a reduced production of sperm, some loss of genital tissue, and greater difficulty in achieving and sustaining an erection. In women, menstruation ceases at about age 50 (on average), and this change is accompanied by other physical changes in the genitals. Many women also experience hot flashes during the years leading up to menopause.

8. The risk of death rises with increasing age, and the causes of death change markedly with age. Among young adults, accidents, suicide, and homicide account for more

than half of all deaths. By midlife, cancer and heart disease are the largest causes of death.

9. The probability of acute (short-term) illness declines over adulthood, while the probability of chronic illness increases, particularly after midlife. Women typically report more acute illnesses, but fewer chronic illnesses.

10. Evidence is mixed on age changes in probability of mental illness. Older white men are more likely to commit suicide, and there is some indication that young adults are more often depressed, but the findings are inconsistent.

11. The impact of these changes on behavior is seen in many areas, most broadly in a general slowing of responses and a loss of vitality and recuperative powers. Sexual activity also declines steadily with age, but the majority of adults remain sexually active well into old age.

12. Several explanations of physical aging have been offered, including genetic arguments emphasizing the role of unfolding genetic codes, genetic arguments emphasizing the limited capacity of the human cell to reproduce itself, and genetic arguments focused on cumulative damage to the genetic material in individual cells over time.

13. Other theories focus on progressive changes in nongenetic aspects of cell functioning, such as ''mistakes'' entering gradually into protein synthesis. Still other theories emphasize the importance of general breakdown of key body systems, such as the cardiovascular or the immune systems.

14. Both some specific diseases and longevity are at least partially influenced by heredity. Social class and living arrangements are also predictive of longevity and health risks.

15. Personality may also influence susceptibility to disease. In particular, a pattern of high achievement emphasis, time pressure, and aggressiveness has been associated with increased risk of heart disease.

16. Health habits that are associated with lower risk of disease and greater longevity include not smoking, getting regular exercise, not drinking to excess, eating three meals a day, getting sufficient sleep, and maintaining proper weight.

17. Exercise or physical activity, in particular, has been shown to be related to lowered risk of disease and greater capacity for physical exertion. At least some of the body changes normally thought of as ''aging'' may be the result of disuse.

## Suggested Readings

BRECHER, E. M. (1984). *Love, sex, and aging.* Boston, MA: Little, Brown.

This book reports on the results of a very interesting survey of over 6,000 adults over the age of 50, who described their sexual behavior over their life span. The sample is not altogether representative, but the report is still fascinating.

OSTROW, A. C. (1984). *Physical activity and the older adult. Psychological perspectives.* Princeton, NJ: Princeton Book Company.

Ostrow has not written this book for the layperson; it is written for psychologists, so is densely filled with research references and analyses. But it is a very readable, current, complete discussion not only of physical changes in aging, but the impact of exercise on those changes.

*The following two articles originally appeared in relatively unaccessible places, but have been reprinted in* Readings in Adult Development and Aging *(Little, Brown, 1982) edited by K. Warner Schaie & James Geiwitz. Both are excellent and not too complex.*

HAYFLICK, L. (1975). Why grow old? *The Stanford Magazine*, 3(1), 36–43.

ROSSMAN, I. (1980). Bodily changes with aging. In E. W. Busse & D. G. Blazer (Eds.), *Handbook of geriatric psychiatry*. New York: Van Nostrand Reinhold.

# 5

# Intellectual Changes in Adulthood

One of the most pervasive stereotypes about aging is that we all lose our intellectual powers as we age. The term *senile*, which the dictionary defines merely as "of or pertaining to old age," has acquired a colloquial meaning of "stupid" or "mentally dense" or merely "mentally slow." Most of us assume that as we age, we will lose our memory and our ability to reason or think clearly. When, perhaps in your 40s or 50s, you find you cannot remember the name of a familiar flower in your garden, or you go to the grocery store but forget to get the carton of milk that was on your mental list, you may say to yourself, "Good grief, I must be getting old. I can't remember anything anymore." Or, if your work requires some element of creativity, you may worry that you will never again have a good idea after the age of 40.

This assumption of inevitable loss of mental ability with age is so much a part of our cultural view of aging that it does not occur to most people to question it. But we should question it. There is now a large and sophisticated body of research on intellectual stability and change with age; many of the findings from that research show a much smaller, and much later, decline in mental abilities than the stereotype suggests.

Let me begin the exploration of intellectual changes with aging by looking at the broadest measures of intellectual functioning—scores on IQ tests of various kinds—and then break that down into subvarieties of intellectual skills, such as verbal versus nonverbal tasks, memory, and problem solving.

## Age Changes in IQ During Adulthood

Defining *intelligence* is one of the slipprier tasks in psychology, but one that many psychologists have nonetheless attempted. The typical definition goes something like this: Intelligence is "the aggregate or global capacity of the individual to act purposefully, to think rationally, and to deal effectively with his environment'' (Wechsler, 1939, p. 3).

Most psychologists assume that there is a central, general intellectual capacity (often called *g*) which influences the way we approach many different tasks. The total score on an intelligence test (usually labeled as IQ, or ''intelligence quotient'') is intended to describe this general capacity. The average IQ score is normally set at 100, with scores above 100 reflecting above-average performance, and scores below 100 reflecting below-average performance. The question to be addressed here is whether IQ changes systematically with age or remains constant.

Note that this is a different question from the one I addressed in chapter 2. There I was asking whether *individuals* remained in the same relative rank in IQ over time. The answer to that question, as you'll recall, was essentially ''yes.'' Here I am asking whether the *average score* goes up or down with age. That is, regardless of where an individual person may be in the distribution of IQ scores, are there common changes with age in the level of scores? Is the average IQ of 60-year-olds lower, higher, or the same as the average IQ of 30-year-olds?

## Cross-Sectional and Longitudinal Results

Most of the early information on age changes in IQ came from cross-sectional studies (e.g., Matarazzo, 1972), which seemed to show that declines in IQ began about age 30 and continued steadily thereafter. It was not until recently that data from several well-designed, long-term longitudinal studies cast significant doubts on that general conclusion.

The easiest way to show you the difference in results from these two strategies is to compare the cross-sectional and longitudinal findings from a single study. The best single example is K. Warner Schaie's cross-sequential study of intellectual patterns (the Seattle Longitudinal Study described in Table 1–2). Recall that Schaie (1983b; Schaie & Hertzog, 1983) began in 1956 with a set of cross-sectional samples, seven years apart in age, ranging from age 25 to age 67. A subset of subjects in each age group was then retested 7 years later, 14 years later, and then 21 years later. In 1963, another set of cross-sectional samples, covering the same age ranges, was also tested, and a subset of these was retested 7 and 14 years later. In 1970, and again in 1977, a third and fourth set of cross-sectional samples was studied, with a subset of the 1970 sample retested in 1977.

The contrast between the longitudinal and cross-sectional analyses of IQ scores emerges very clearly from the results of this study, as you can see in Figure 5–1. The numbers in this figure are not traditional IQ scores with a mean of 100. Instead, Schaie averaged the IQ scores on the first test given to each subject who participated at any time in the 21-year study. The average was set (arbitrarily) at 50 points on this scale, with a standard deviation of 10. Thus, two thirds of all adults should fall between scores of 40 and 60 (one standard

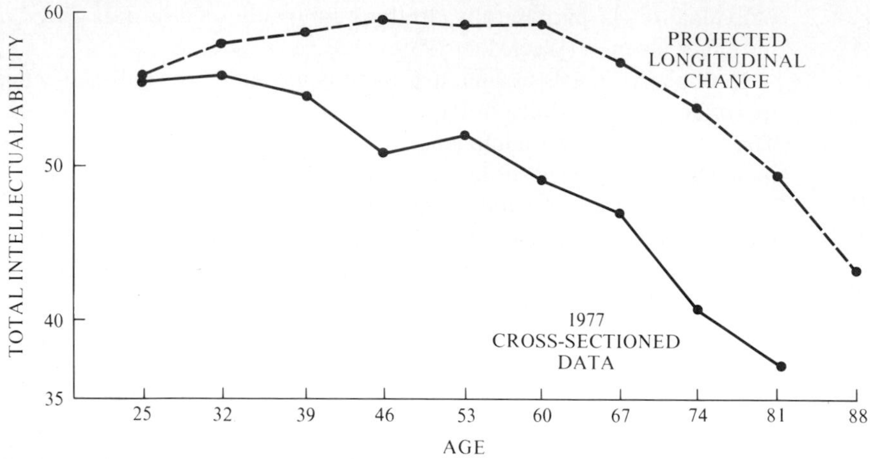


***Figure 5–1** Age changes in total IQ based on cross-sectional comparisons and on longitudinal data. As is clear from the figure, cross-sectional comparisons lead to the conclusion that mental performance begins to decline at about age 40, while longitudinal analyses lead to a much more optimistic conclusion about intellectual maintenance. (Source: Schaie, 1983b, data from Tables 4.5 and 4.9, pp. 89 and 100.)*

deviation on either side of the mean), and about 95% should fall between 30 and 70.

The lower line in the figure represents the average scores on this scale of adults of each age in the cross-sectional samples tested in 1977. The upper line is Schaie's estimate of the lifetime (longitudinal) pattern of change for someone born in 1952, who was thus 25 in 1977. Schaie arrived at this curve by calculating the average amount of change in the IQ score for each age interval that he had observed for the subjects studied longitudinally. For example, the average longitudinal change between age 25 and age 32 (based on three separate longitudinal samples) was +2.0 points. The upper curve is thus the smoothed sum of the observed seven-year longitudinal changes, projected for the group born in 1952 who began with an average score of 56 points at age 25.

When you compare the two lines in the figure, you can see that longitudinal and cross-sectional data yield very different answers to the question "Does IQ decline with age in adulthood?" The cross-sectional evidence, of which the lower curve is highly typical, seems to show a beginning decline in IQ starting somewhere between age 32 and 39. The longitudinal evidence does not show significant decline in total IQ until the period from age 60 to 67. But even that decline at age 60 to 67 does not bring the average score below the level observed at age 25. It isn't really until the period from 67 to 74 that total IQ scores (on average) dropped below that seen at age 25.

Since these findings are corroborated by the results from other longitudinal studies (Jarvik & Bank, 1983; Siegler, 1983), there is good support for a conclusion that general intellectual ability remains quite stable until perhaps 65 or 70, after which it declines.

This is a temptingly attractive and optimistic conclusion. But before we accept it fully, let me point out some wrinkles.

## Age Changes in Subvarieties of Intellectual Performance

The first and most substantial reason to be cautious about accepting a sweeping conclusion that there is "little change with age" is evident as soon as we look at subscores instead of total IQ scores. Although there is a general or *g* factor involved in virtually all measures of intellectual functioning, it is still useful to distinguish among more specific skills, such as verbal abilities, mathematical skill, spatial visualization, reasoning, or the like. In research on aging, such subskills have been grouped in at least three ways.

Some researchers (e.g., Cunningham & Birren, 1976; Cunningham & Owens, 1983; Jarvik & Bank, 1983; Owens, 1966) emphasize the difference between **speeded tasks** and **unspeeded tasks**. On any IQ test, some subtests require the subject to perform some actions within a stated period of time, or the subject's speed in completing some problem is measured. Other subtests, such as vocabulary tests, typically have no time limits. The general finding is that performance on speeded tests begins to decline earlier in the adult years than does performance on unspeeded tests.

An overlapping distinction is between **verbal** and **performance tests.** For example, one of the most often used adult intelligence tests, the Wechsler Adult Intelligence Scale (or WAIS) is divided into verbal tests (vocabulary, describing similarities, information, and comprehension) and performance tests (block design, coding, object assembly, and the like). Performance tests generally involve manipulation of objects in some fashion, while verbal tests involve manipulation of words or ideas. Since most verbal tests are untimed and many performance tests are timed, there is a strong parallel to the distinction between unspeeded and speeded tasks. So you will not be surprised to know that verbal abilities generally show increases or stability through the adult age span, up to as late as the 70s, while performance tests show much earlier decline (Denney, 1982; Matarazzo, 1972).

A third distinction, between **fluid** and **crystallized intelligence,** has been proposed by Raymond Cattell and John Horn (Cattell, 1963, 1971; Horn, 1982; Horn & Cattell, 1966; Horn & Donaldson, 1980). Crystallized intelligence is heavily dependent on education and experience. It consists of the set of skills and bits of knowledge that we learn as part of growing up in our culture, such as verbal comprehension, vocabulary, the ability to evaluate experience, the ability to reason with real-life problems, and technical skills you may learn for your job or your life (balancing a checkbook, making change, finding the salad dressing in the grocery store). In Nancy Denney's model, which I described in chapter 4, crystallized abilities are "optimally exercised" abilities. On standardized tests, crystallized abilities are usually measured by vocabulary and by verbal comprehension (e.g., reading a paragraph and then answering questions about it).

Fluid intelligence, in contrast, is thought to be a more basic set of abilities, not so dependent on specific education, and more dependent on the efficient functioning of the central nervous system. (In Denney's model, these are the "unexercised" abilities.) A common measure of this is a letter series test. You may be given a series of letters like *A C F J O*, and must figure out what letter should go next. This demands abstract reasoning, rather than reasoning about known or everyday events. Most tests of memory are also part of fluid intelligence, as are many tests measuring response speed and those measuring more difficult or abstract kinds of mathematics. Horn has concluded that crystallized abilities generally continue to rise or show stability over adulthood (until age 70 or so, at least), while fluid abilities begin to decline much earlier, beginning perhaps at 35 or 40 (Horn & Donaldson, 1980).

Whatever label we apply to these two broad categories of intellectual tasks (speeded versus unspeeded, verbal versus performance, crystallized versus fluid, or exercised versus unexercised), it seems clear that performance of one group (the unspeeded, verbal, crystallized task) is well maintained over the adult years, while performance on the other type of task (speeded, nonverbal, fluid) shows signs of earlier decline.

I can illustrate the difference again with results from Schaie's longitudinal study (1983b), as I have done in Figure 5–2. I have provided the findings for both the total "intellectual ability" score and for two subscores, vocabulary and number skills. The latter was a timed test involving simple addition problems which were either correctly added or incorrectly added. The subject had to decide if the sum was right or wrong. In Figure 5–2, I have shown the average change in scores on these three measures for each group of subjects who had been studied over 14-year intervals. The units are tenths of a standard deviation. Thus, a score of −2.0 means that the subjects studied during that particular 14-year age interval declined on that measure .2 of one standard deviation. Vocabulary, for example, shows increases during each age period until the 53 to 67 period. Subjects tested from age 53 to 67 showed a decline of 2.36 points (.236 of one standard deviation), those studied between 60 and 74 showed a decline of 5.0 points (.5 of one standard deviation), and so forth. I have marked with an asterisk each bar that represents a statistically significant change (increase or decline) from zero, so you can see that for the number score, significant decreases began in the 39 to 53 age range, while for the vocabulary score, a significant decrease was not seen until the 53 to 67 age interval.

Thus, the longitudinal line given in Figure 5–1 is somewhat misleading. On some kinds of tests, adults appear to show some decline beginning as early as their 30s or 40s. Typically the tests that show this early decline pattern are those that are timed, that involve abstract reasoning or memory, or that require speedy response. On tests that do not make such demands, particularly those that involve often-used skills such as language, decline occurs much later.

Furthermore, even the decline in speeded/performance/fluid test skill, while

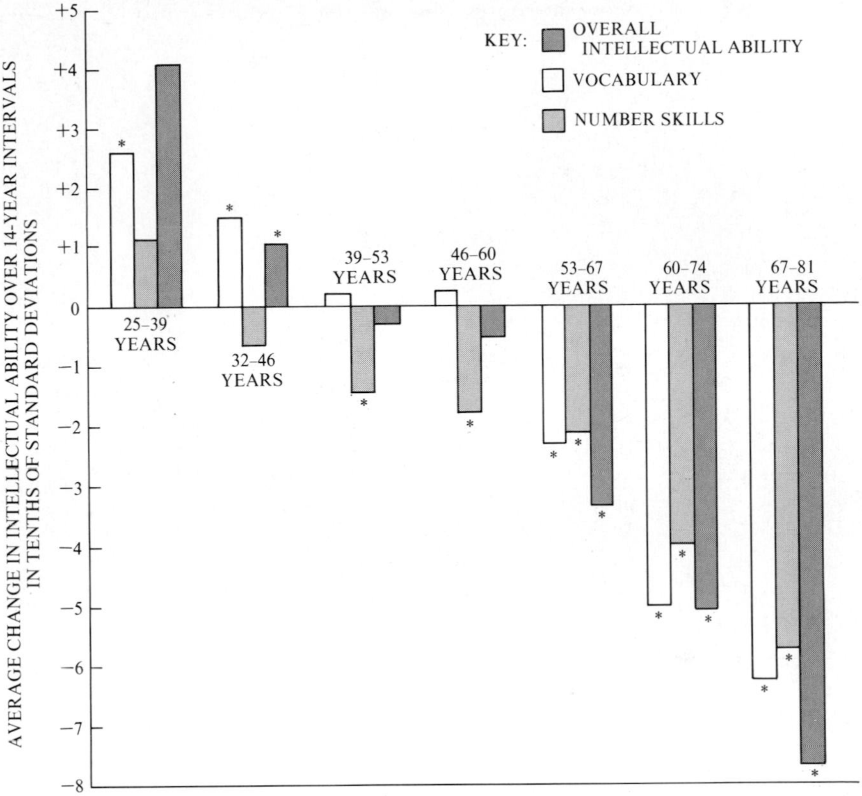


***Figure 5–2*** *Longitudinal changes in total intellectual ability, vocabulary, and number skills show somewhat different patterns, with number skills showing declines at earlier ages than vocabulary or total score. Each bar in this graph represents the average number of points of increase or decrease over that 14-year interval for all subjects who were tested longitudinally at those ages. An asterisk (*) at the end of a bar means that the average change for that group, for that test, was significantly different from zero. (Source: Schaie, 1983b, data from Table 4.10, p. 101.)*

statistically significant, may not represent psychologically significant loss until at least late middle age. Schaie concludes:

> At the risk of possible overgeneralization, it is my general conclusion that reliably replicable age changes in psychometric abilities of more than trivial magnitude cannot be demonstrated prior to age 60, but that reliable decrement can be shown to have occurred for all abilities by age 74. (Schaie, 1983b, p. 127)

I think that Schaie is generally correct for tasks or skills that lie within some average range of difficulty. As Paul Baltes and his colleagues point out, however (Baltes, Dittmann-Kohli, & Dixon, 1984), psychologically or functionally

**Figure 5–3** *The ability to read a road map is mostly dependent on what Horn calls crystallized intelligence. It requires specific map-reading experience, and is likely to be retained well into old age. (Source: Freda Leinwand, Monkmeyer Press.)*

relevant decrement may show up at earlier ages on highly complex or difficult tasks—tasks that stretch the individual's skills to the limit. Those adults whose occupations require them to function at these more taxing levels may thus (paradoxically) notice some loss of skill earlier than do those whose life circumstances make less stringent intellectual demands.

## One Last Caution

This, too, is a fairly rosy conclusion, but once again a caution is in order. Recall the point I made in chapter one about the attrition problem in longitudinal research. All longitudinal researchers have found that those adults who survive the longest had higher IQ scores to begin with (e.g., Jarvik & Bank, 1983; Siegler & Botwinick, 1979). This leads us to minimize the amount of decline that may be experienced by less capable, or less healthy, adults in their 60s or 70s or earlier. What does seem clear, however, is that broad decline in intellectual ability in middle age and early old age is not an inevitable accompaniment of aging. Just what factors predict decline for some and maintenance for others is an issue I'll talk about in more detail later in the chapter. First, though, let me turn away from measures of global IQ and standardized test scores and look at age changes in several other aspects of intellectual functioning.

# Changes in Memory over Adulthood

Complaints about memory loss are one of the common accompaniments of aging, at least in our culture. (As I write this, I can hear in my head the sound of one 70-year-old friend making small noises of frustration as he struggles to recall the name of a familiar person or a book he read the week before. ''Damn! What *was* the name of that book?'') There is thus a common sense of memory loss. But how accurate is this perception? Just how much memory do we actually lose, if any, as we get older?

There is a great deal of research touching on these questions, so you might suppose that the answers are definite. But as is often true, the more deeply researchers have explored the question, the more we have seen the complexity of the process. In addition, we are hampered by the fact that the majority of research has been cross-sectional rather than longitudinal, and in most cases involves only a comparison of ''young'' (usually 18-year-old) introductory psychology students and ''old'' adults, with little coverage of the ages of middle adulthood. Keep these limitations in mind as we go along.

## Some Terms

Before I describe the findings, I need to define some terms. Several sets of words have been used to describe memory processes. The earliest set of distinctions, still widely used, is between **encoding, storage,** and **retrieval.** Encoding refers to the processes by which information is committed to memory, which may include rehearsal, organizing the material into chunks, making mental pictures of it, or the like. Storage simply refers to what happens (if anything) to the memory over time, regardless of how it was encoded, while retrieval describes the processes by which you get information out of memory when you need it.

The distinctions are a bit like what you do when you put food in your refrigerator. Encoding is like what you do when you put it in the refrigerator in the first place. You organize all the vegetables together, all the cheese together, and put all the meat in a special drawer. Storage is what happens to the food over time if you don't eat it. Does it just sit there, staying essentially the same (like commercial mayonnaise, which will last virtually forever), or does it decay (like the cheese in the bottom drawer which grows green, furry stuff)? Retrieval is the process of finding the stuff you want when you need it and taking it out of the refrigerator.

Of the several kinds of retrieval, **recognition** is easier than **recall**. If I showed my 70-year-old friend a list of book titles, he could probably quite readily pick out the one he is trying to remember. That is, he recognizes it. What he has trouble with is recalling it spontaneously.

A second way of describing the processes of memory which has dominated more recent research is an information processing model. Again, three aspects are typically defined: **sensory memory, short-term memory** (also sometimes called **primary memory**), and **long-term memory**. In this way of looking at things, memory is seen in terms of a flow of information through the system. Think of what you do, for example, when you look up and then try to recall a phone number. When you first actually see the number, you have a very brief visual impression of the number. This is a sensory memory. If you do nothing more, you will not be able to recall the number even a second later. But if you pay attention to the number, you transfer it into short-term memory. So if you say it over to yourself once, you can usually remember it long enough to dial the number. If I then asked you a few minutes later to tell me the number, probably you couldn't do so. You had put the number into short-term memory, but it had not gotten into long-term memory. In order to put something into long-term memory further processing is required—more rehearsals or some further associations.

Obviously, these two ways of talking about memory are not mutually exclusive. Both sets of terms are useful in understanding what happens to memory with age.

## Evidence on Memory Changes

Whether we conclude there is a memory loss with age depends very much on which of these several facets of the memory process we study.

**Sensory Memory.** You might think that sensory memory, or the "sensory register" as it is sometimes called, would get less efficient as you get older. But there is no evidence for a systematic decline in the ability to hold information for a fraction of a second in this sort of sensory memory. Of course, older adults have poorer vision and poorer hearing, so there are some things they simply do not perceive as well. But assuming that something (like the numbers in the phone book) has been perceived, older adults seem to have as good a sensory memory as do younger adults (Baltes, Reese, & Lipsitt, 1980; Craik, 1977; Labouvie-Vief & Schell, 1982).

**Short-term Memory.** In contrast, there do appear to be slight declines in short-term memory with age. For example, if you read subjects a list of numbers or words and then ask them to repeat them back in the order given, younger subjects can repeat longer strings than can older adults. The difference is not large—on the order of one digit or one word fewer for someone in her 70s compared to someone in her 20s (Botwinick & Storandt, 1974)—but it is found quite consistently.

The effect of age on short-term memory is much larger, however, if the person is asked to do anything with the information—rearrange it, or recall it in some order other than the one in which it was given, or repeat back only the words of a particular type. So, for example, if you read off a list of words and then ask the subject to repeat them in backwards order, the discrepancy between the performance of older and younger subjects is larger than when the words are recalled in the order in which they were given. Thus, on simple short-term memory tasks, there is only a small age difference, but as soon as the task is made more complex in almost any way, older subjects are at a greater disadvantage.

**Long-term Memory.** It is in long-term memory that the largest age differences are found (Craik, 1977). Once you exceed the capacity of the short-term storage system, you must either transfer the information to long-term storage or you will forget it. Somewhere in this process the older adult seems not to do so well. The argument among researchers now is about just where in the system the difficulty may lie. In particular, does the problem lie at the point of getting things into long-term storage (an encoding process), or does it lie at the point of retrieval? Are the memories "in there," but you just can't get to them as easily as you get older? Or do you have trouble getting them "in there" in the first place? As is often the case in disputes of this kind, the answer seems to be "both."

Some of the problem does seem to be in the retrieval process. Perhaps most noticeably, retrieval become slower with age (e.g., Cerella, 1985; Madden, 1985) Some loss of retrieval speed or skill is also shown in the fact that older adults generally do about as well (although slower) as younger adults on tasks demanding recognition, but much less well on tasks demanding recall. If you give a subject a list of words to learn, for example, and ask them later to tell you merely whether particular words were in the list, older adults do quite well. But if you ask them to recall as many of the words as possible, they have more difficulty (Craik, 1977; Labouvie-Vief & Schell, 1982). Findings like these reinforce the impression of many older adults that they often "know" things that they cannot readily or quickly bring to mind. If they are given a hint, or reminded of the item at some later time, the memory comes back.

But it is in encoding, rather than retrieval, that the largest decrement with age seems to occur. Older adults appear to use less efficient or less effective strategies for organizing new material for learning. When older subjects are given clues ahead of time about what they will later have to remember, or are shown how to organize the material in an effective way, the age differences in recall decline (cf. Craik, 1977; Craik & Rabinowitz, 1985; Macht & Buschke, 1984; McFarland, Warren, & Crockard, 1985; Rankin & Collins, 1985).

**Familiar Versus Unfamiliar Material.** On reading this brief summary, many of you may well be asking yourself whether the tasks psychologists have invented to test memory ability have anything very much to do with real-life memory tasks. Isn't it possible that older adults do less well on these artificial tasks because they think the problems are boring or irrelevant? Would we see the same decrement with age if we studied memory for familiar things?

All of us, regardless of age, are better at remembering familiar things. In a classic study of this, M. T. Chi (1978), tested 10-year-olds and adults for two kinds of memory: the traditional digit-span test (repeating back a list of numbers that have been read aloud) and the placement of chess pieces on a chessboard. The catch was that the 10-year-olds were all expert chess players, while the adults were novices at the game. What Chi found was that the adults were better at remembering strings of digits, but less good at remembering chess placements. When adult expert chess players have been compared to adult novices in other studies (e.g., Chase & Simon, 1973), researchers noticed that the experts went about the task of remembering placements of pieces quite differently. The experts tended to look at, and then later reproduce, whole groups of pieces. That is, they used their knowledge of the game to help them encode the material more effectively. Thus, any adult, regardless of age, will find it easier to analyze, encode, and later recall material with which she is highly familiar. An experienced cook will recall a new recipe more readily than a novice; a carpenter will recall blueprints more completely than will a weekend handyman. This phenomenon is well documented by research. What is at issue here is whether, given familiar or known material, the age differences in memory disappear. Do older adults do less well on standard memory tasks simply because such tasks are less familiar to them? Or do we find the same differences when familiar material has to be recalled?

The findings are somewhat mixed. If you ask older adults to learn and remember material with which they are more familiar than are younger people, they show better recall. In one study, Hanley-Dunn and McIntosh (1984) had elderly adults (about 70 years old, on average) and young adults (undergraduate students) each memorize one of four lists of 14 names: (1) well-known politicians, (2) big band leaders from the 1930s and 1940s, (3) current popular singers, or (4) names of ordinary people, such as those you'd find in a phone book. Each subject studied his list for two-and-a-half minutes and then wrote down all the names he could recall. Hanley-Dunn and McIntosh found that the older adults were better than college students at remembering the politicians and band leaders, both groups with which they had greater familiarity. The college students did better on the list of current singers. The two groups did about equally well with the list of ordinary names.

The findings are not so clear, however, in studies in which the real-life material is equally familiar to both young and old. Fozard (1980), reviewing this evidence, concluded that older adults (again, if given enough time) remember as well as do younger adults under such conditions. But there are some inconsistent findings. Kausler, for example (Kausler, Lichty, & Freund, 1985), found that older adults were less good than younger ones at remembering whether they had performed some task—rather like the problem of remembering whether you turned the stove off before you left the house.

Another example comes from an intriguing study by Evans, Brennan, Skorpanich, and Held (1984), who studied the memory for the location of buildings in the downtown area of a small town. All the adults in this study, including a younger group averaging 32 years of age and an older group averaging 71 years, had lived in this town for at least a year, most of them much longer. (The older adults, in fact, had lived in the town longer, on average, than the younger ones.) Each subject was asked to list as many buildings in the downtown area as he or she could recall, and then to place a series of 13 familiar buildings on a street grid in their proper location. The results are shown in

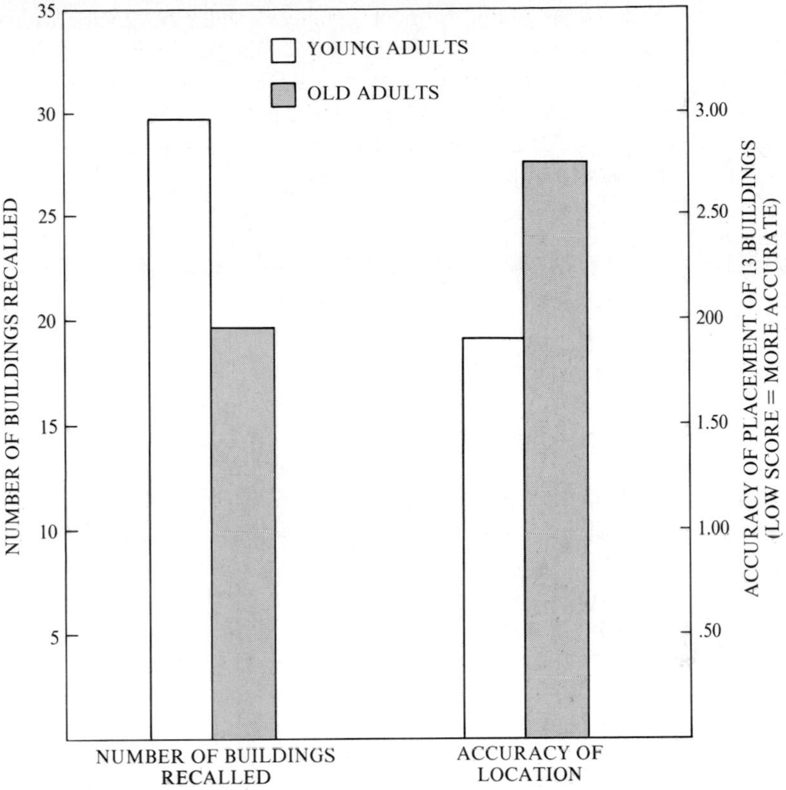


***Figure 5–4*** *In this study, elderly and young adults were asked to recall as many buildings as they could that were located in the downtown area of their town. The left-hand columns show the number of buildings recalled, and the right-hand columns show the accuracy with which the old and young subjects placed 13 well-known buildings on a street grid. In this instance, a low score means that the placement was more accurate. Older subjects remembered fewer buildings and placed them less accurately. (Source: Evans, Brennan, Skorpanich, & Held, 1984.)*

Figure 5–4. You can see that the older adults had poorer recall on both measures.

Overall, familiarity of material sometimes eliminates and sometimes lessens age differences in recall, but it does not make such differences disappear entirely. Older adults have trouble remembering recent news events, just as they have trouble remembering lists of numbers or words concocted by researchers (Craik, 1977).

**Summing Up.** There is some loss of memory ability as one ages, with the decrement appearing perhaps in the 60s or 70s. But except for those adults who are suffering from degenerative diseases (about whom I'll say more shortly), the loss is not terribly large in most instances. Older adults are a bit slower to bring things to memory, and their greatest difficulties lie not in very short-term recall but in longer-term memory. Part of the difficulty may be in some sort of central nervous system processing, which gets slower with age. But part of it appears to be a different (or less efficient) way of coding or analyzing information when it is first committed to memory.

## Changes in Problem-solving Ability over Adulthood

I could write a very similar summary paragraph about changes in problem-solving skill over the adult years. "Problem solving" refers to the complex set of processes that you use to figure out a solution to something. If your car doesn't start in the morning, the procedures you go through to figure out why, or to call for help, are all forms of problem solving. In traditional experiments, subjects are typically given bits of information from which they have to figure a "correct" solution. For example, a subject might be shown a large red square and asked whether this is an instance of some "right" category the experimenter is thinking of. Perhaps the subject guesses "yes," and is told that's correct. She is then shown a small red triangle, and guesses that this figure is not part of the "right" category, and so on until the subject figures out what combination of properties (color, size, and shape) is "right." On tasks like these, older adults do less well—it takes them more trials to arrive at the right answer, and they make more wrong guesses (Denney, 1982).

If you have played the game of 20 Questions you're familiar with another kind of problem-solving task. The experimenter thinks of some real-life object and the subject has to figure out what it is by asking questions that can be answered "yes" or "no." In this case the subject has two problems: to think up the questions and then to evaluate the answers to arrive at a solution. The kinds of questions a person asks can be divided into two main types, one of which is much more efficient and helpful than the other. Following the early labels proposed by Mosher and Hornsby (1966), the less effective question is called a *hypothesis* and consists of a specific guess ("Is it your red hat?" "Is it a gazelle?"). A *constraint question*, on the other hand, asks about a whole category of possibilities ("Is it living?" "Is it blue?" "Is it larger than a breadbox?").

Nancy Denney has used this game in a whole series of studies of problem solving in adults, and consistently finds that in cross-sectional comparisons older adults use fewer constraint questions than do younger adults, as you can see in Figure 5–5. Since asking constraint questions is more informative and is thus a better strategy, it also takes older adults more questions to arrive at the solution.

This rather striking change with age could have several explanations. It could, of course, be at least partially a cohort effect. As usual, the older groups in

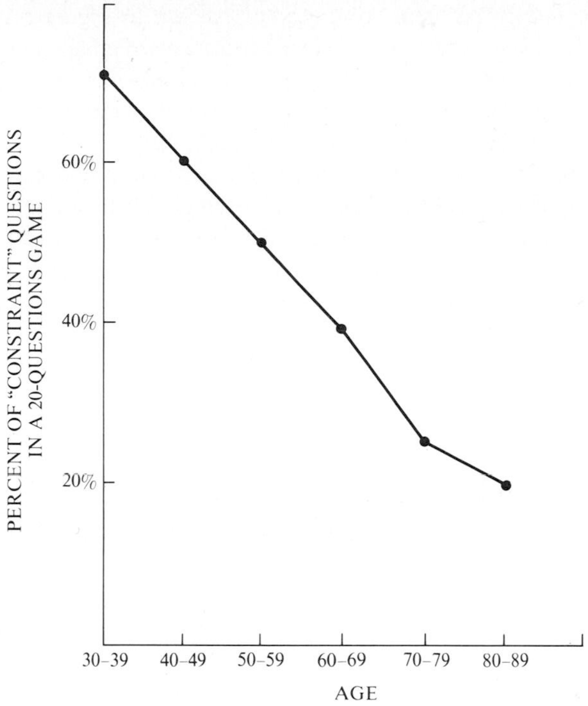


***Figure 5–5*** *When adults of various ages were asked to play 20 Questions, older adults used fewer "constraint" questions than did younger adults. (A constraint question is one that eliminates or confirms a whole group of possibilities, such as "is it larger than a breadbox?") These differences are quite striking, but they could reflect either cohort differences, or differences in familiarity with the task, rather than real "decline" in problem-solving skills. (Source: Denney & Denney, 1982, from Table 2, p. 192.)*

this study have had less education than the younger groups, and education may have an effect on the kinds of strategies people know how to use. The one longitudinal study of problem solving I know of, by Arenberg (1974; Arenberg & Robertson-Tchabo, 1977), lends some support to this possibility. Arenberg has studied problem solving ability in subjects aged 24 to 87 who have participated in the Baltimore Longitudinal Study (the same longitudinal study from which Costa & McCrae's analyis of personality consistency emerges). Each subject was tested twice, six years apart, and Arenberg found that declines in learning and problem solving occurred only in subjects 70 and older. Thus, the apparent earlier decline in problem-solving ability, like the apparent decline in cross-sectional comparisons of IQ scores, may reflect cohort differences and not real loss.

The apparent decline in problem solving skills shown in Figure 5–5 could also reflect the artificiality of the tasks used in experiments. Perhaps older adults are just as skilled as younger adults at solving real-life problems—the kind they encounter every day in their own lives—but are both less familiar with, and less interested in, the problems that researchers dream up.

Denney has attempted to discover whether familiarity and problem relevance play a part in the apparent decline of problem-solving skill by asking another group of subjects both to play 20 Questions and to give solutions to some more lifelike problems, such as "Let's say that one evening you go to the refrigerator and you notice that it's not cold inside, but rather, it's warm. What would you do?" (Denney & Palmer, 1981, p. 325). The answers that the adults gave to this kind of problem were scored for the number of solutions suggested and for the quality of the solutions. In this case, trying to fix it yourself (such as by checking to see if the refrigerator was plugged in, or checking the fuse box) was given three points; calling a repair person scored two points. Solving problems like this is a much more "exercised" (familiar) skill than is the game of 20 Questions, so we might expect to find that older adults did better on this task than on the 20 Questions game. That is, in fact, what Denney and Palmer found (1981). On the real-life task, the scores for the quality of solution peaked at about age 50, and 80-year-olds had about the same level of scores as 20-year-olds. Compared to adults in midlife, then, the 80-year-olds showed a lower level of problem-solving skill; but compared to young adults, they looked quite good.

There is not yet enough research of this kind to draw clear conclusions, but as with the research on memory, it appears that specific experience or knowledge ("exercise" in Denney's terms) improves the quality of intellectual performance in older adults. Nonetheless, there still appears to be some decline or "loss" of intellectual power in old age.

## Changes in Intellectual Structure over Adulthood

All of the measures of intellectual ability I have talked about so far emerge from the tradition within psychology that defines intelligence in terms of *power* or *skill.* IQ tests are designed to tell us how well someone can do something, or how quickly. But there is another way to think about intellectual changes with age, typified by Jean Piaget's theory of cognitive development (1952; 1964; Piaget & Inhelder, 1969). Piaget was interested in changes in cognitive *structure* with age, rather than in individual differences in intellectual power. What kind of logic does the child or adult use? How does the form of logic, the way of going about solving problems, change over the course of development? Piaget's work was almost entirely focused on cognitive development in children, but his theory has also influenced some of the work on cognition in adulthood and old age.

**TABLE 5–1 Piaget's Stages of Cognitive Development**

| Stage | Age | Description |
|---|---|---|
| Sensorimotor | birth–2 years | The baby interacts with the world, and understands the world around her, through senses and actions. Until at least age 1, according to Piaget, the infant does not represent objects internally. She "knows" objects only by what she can do with them or how she experiences them directly. |
| Preoperational | 2–6 years | Preoperational children are still tied to their own view ("egocentric" in Piaget's terms), but they can represent things internally, using words or images, they can engage in fantasy play, and they begin to be able to classify objects into groups. There is a primitive form of logic at this stage. |
| Concrete Operational | 6–12 years | The school-age child moves into a kind of intellectual third gear, discovering a whole series of powerful mental actions, which Piaget calls "operations," such as addition, subtraction, serial ordering, and the like. Children in this stage are capable of inductive logic (arriving at general principles by adding up specific experiences), and they are better able to understand others' points of view; but they are still tied to their own experience, and cannot yet imagine things they have not known directly. |
| Formal Operational | 12 years and into adulthood | Formal operations represents intellectual high gear. Those teenagers and adults who achieve this level of thinking (and not all do) are capable of deductive logic ("if . . . then" reasoning, for example); can approach problems systematically, examining all possible combinations or possibilities; and can think about ideas as well as about objects. This is vastly more abstract than concrete operations, although concrete operations are sufficient for most everyday experiences. |

Piaget proposed that there are four major stages of cognitive development, which I've sketched in Table 5–1. Shifts from one stage to the next occur gradually rather than suddenly, but each stage is thought to represent a general pattern of thinking. In Western cultures, virtually all adults think easily at the concrete operational level; perhaps half of adults think at the formal operational level at least some of the time.

When researchers studying adults have used some of the tasks Piaget devised to measure the structure of thought, the common result has been that older adults appear to "think like children." For example, Piaget was interested in the ways children grouped and classified objects. Young children in the preoperational stage often make stories or pictures out of objects and shapes (e.g., "The pipe and the matches go together because you use the matches to light the pipe"). Older children typically put objects together based on some more abstract similarity, such as shape or function. Nancy Denney (Pearce & Denney, 1984) gave a standardized version of this task to groups of children and adults, and found that the adults over 65, like the younger children, most often grouped things based on complementarity while the young and middle-aged adults based their groupings on more abstract similarities.

Other research using Piaget's tasks has yielded similar findings (reviewed by

Denney, 1982). But we have to be very careful about assuming that these findings reflect "regression" to earlier levels on the part of older adults. Denney has found, for example, that older adults are quite capable of making groupings based on similarity if they are told that is what is wanted. So the analytic skill is there, but the older adult normally chooses to approach the task in a different way, perhaps a more practical way. This interpretation raises the possibility that there may be types of thinking unique to adulthood that are developmentally beyond the stage of formal operations.

A number of theorists have made precisely this argument. Gisela Labouvie-Vief (1980), in particular, argues that we should not make the mistake of assuming that formal operations is the highest and best form of thought in all situations. Formal operations, with its emphasis on the exploration of all logical possibilities, is highly adaptive in early adulthood, when the young person is exploring options, establishing identity. But adult responsibilities require reasoning that is tied to specific concrete contexts. Adult thought thus becomes specialized and pragmatic. The adult learns how to solve the problems associated with the particular social roles she occupies, and discovers how to meet the specific difficulties or challenges. In the process, the deductive thoroughness of formal operations is traded off for contextual validity. In Labouvie-Vief's view, this trade-off does not reflect a regression or a loss, but a necessary structural change.

Another group of theorists has extended Piaget's stages using Riegel's concept of the dialectic. Riegel himself (1973) argued that, unlike formal operations in which a single "correct" solution is sought, mature thought is characterized by the acceptance of paradox. Things can be both true and not true at the same time. Following Riegel's lead, both Pascual-Leone (1983) and Basseches (1984) have argued that there is an additional stage of reasoning found in adulthood which might be called **dialectical thought.** As Basseches defines it:

> Dialectical thinking is an organized approach to analyzing and making sense of the world one experiences that differs fundamentally from formal analysis. Whereas the latter involves the effort to find fundamental fixed realities—basic elements and immutable laws—the former attempts to describe fundamental processes of change and the dynamic relationships through which this change occurs. (1984, p. 24)

Thus, dialectical thinking, made up of a continuous chain of thesis, antithesis, and synthesis, involves movement or change. A concrete example would probably help make this clearer.

An adult is facing the prospect of a divorce and is trying to understand what happened. In a formal operations analysis, he might ask, "Whose fault was it?" and search for all the options, examining each. But in a dialectical analysis, he might ask, "How have we each changed so that we no longer fit together well? How can the relationship change to adapt to the changes in each of us?"

You may note a certain resemblance between dialectical thinking and Loevinger's autonomous stage of ego development (recall Table 3–2). Both involve the acceptance of conflict and paradox as the very stuff from which understanding may develop.

There is little empirical evidence to support (or refute) these theories about special structures of adult thought. But the ideas are extremely interesting and may help to move us away from the dominant (but limited) view of adult thinking which focuses primarily on the gain or loss of specific skills. We also need to understand whether adult thought is organized differently, with different goals reached by different strategies.

## Age Changes in Creativity and Productivity

While all of the changes I have been describing are of considerable interest, you may find the questions rather abstract. For many of us, the more compelling set of questions is what effect, if any, the cumulative changes in intellectual speed, power, or structure have on our ability to do productive mental work as we get older. Do scientific breakthroughs—those rare, creative achievements—come mostly in early adulthood? Are older lawyers less effective advocates than younger ones? Do business executives have more difficulty solving problems later in life?

There is remarkably little research on questions of this kind, in part because in most areas of adult work there are no clear, agreed-on measures of skill or productivity. How do we judge the quality of a business person's solutions, or the quality of an architect's plans? What little we do know about productivity and quality of work over adulthood comes from studies of academic careers, where there are standard measures available, namely number and quality of publications.

Early research by Lehman (1953), widely quoted since then, indicated that major scientific discoveries over the past several hundred years were achieved primarily in early adulthood. That is, if you start by selecting scientific or theoretical breakthroughs and ask how old the researcher or theoretician was when he or she made that particular discovery, you find that most were quite young, especially in science and mathematics. But there is another way to ask the question that seems to me to be more relevant for those of us who are not in the same class as Einstein or Darwin: Over the adult life of the ordinary scientist or mathematician, does productivity peak in the early years and then decline? Does the quality of work suffer as you get older?

Apparently not, at least judging from Stephen Cole's (1979) thorough cross-sectional and longitudinal analyses of scientiic productivity. Cole studied samples of chemists, geologists, mathematicians, physicists, psychologists, and sociologists, and counted the number of research papers each person had published during a particular five-year span (a measure of productivity) and how often each paper had been cited (a measure of quality). When he divided the scientists into age groups and made cross-sectional comparisons, he found a slight curvilinear relationship between age and both productivity and quality.

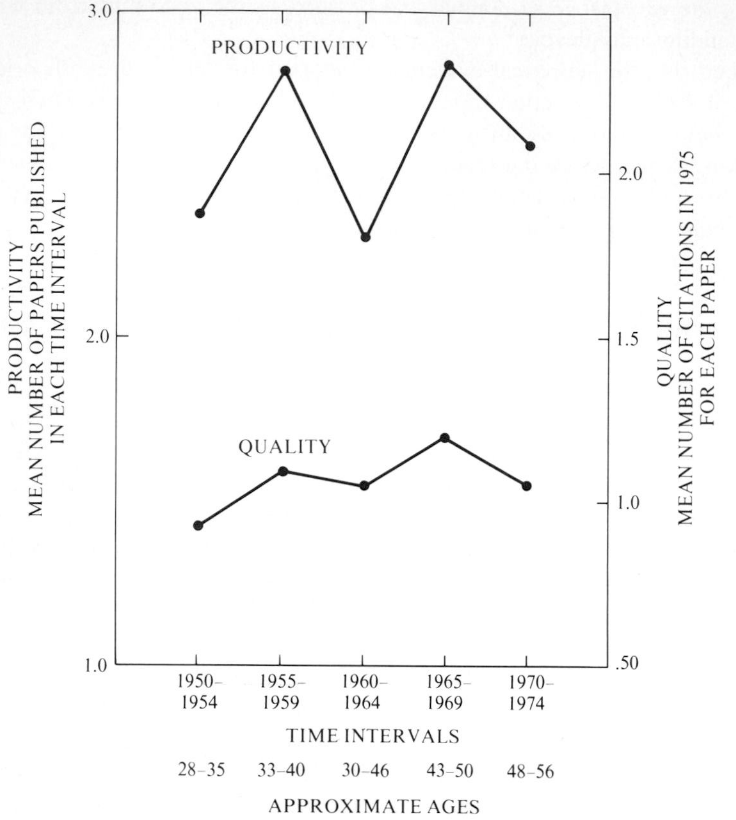


***Figure 5–6*** *When Cole studied the number of publications, and the number of citations of those publications, for a group of mathematicians who received their Ph.D.s between 1947 and 1950, he found essentially no changes with age in either productivity or quality of work. Whether this would be true for other professions (or other measures of productivity or quality) we do not know, but these findings at least do not show any signs of a significant decline in intellectual performance during the middle years. (Source: Cole, 1979, data from Table 4, p. 965.)*

The peak level of output and quality was at about age 40 to 44, with lower levels at both earlier and later ages. But when Cole examined a single cohort of scientists over time (mathematicians in this case), all of whom received their Ph.D. between 1947 and 1950, he found that both productivity and quality remained essentially unchanged through at least age 50 or 55 (the latest age studied), as you can see in Figure 5–6. Cole could also find no indication that the most often cited papers by each mathematician (which we might define as their "best work") were done when they were very young. It may still be true that major creative breakthroughs in science or mathematics are typically achieved by men and women in their 20s and 30s. But for the more ordinary scientist, productivity and quality of work appear to remain stable through adulthood.

Of course, this one study does not tell us that similar stability of performance is typical of all professions or occupations. But for those of you who had thought you were (or would be) intellectually over the hill at 40, these may be comforting findings.

## Terminal Drop

Perhaps equally optimistic is the concept of *terminal drop* or *critical loss* (although certainly these labels sound depressing enough!). The general idea, first proposed by Kleemeier (1962), is that intellectual power and skill is maintained virtually unchanged through adulthood until approximately five to seven years before death, at which point there is a fairly rapid decline. Since each older cohort in a cross-sectional study, and each subsequent testing in a longitudinal study, contains a larger and larger percentage of adults who are within five years of their eventual death, an average pattern of decline emerges. But perhaps we would not find the same declines if we measured "time till death" instead of age.

The only way to study this is in a longitudinal study in which it is possible to track backwards after the death of each subject and determine whether there was either steady decline or stability followed by rapid decline. Exactly this sort of analysis has been done in several studies (e.g., Jarvik & Bank, 1983; Siegler, McCarty, & Logue, 1982; Suedfeld & Piedrahita, 1984). In one fairly typical study, Palmore and Cleveland (1976) examined the pattern of earlier test scores in a group of 178 deceased men who had participated in the Duke studies. They found no indication of terminal drop on tests of physical functioning (which showed steady declines), but did find a pattern of terminal drop for the total IQ score. For these men, IQ remained relatively stable until a few years from death, at which point it dropped rather sharply.

On the whole, it appears that a sudden loss of performance on a nonspeeded or crystallized test (like vocabulary) is particularly predictive of impending death. Declines in performance on fluid/speeded tests are more gradual and seem not to show the pattern of terminal drop.

## Summary of Age Changes in Intellectual Performance

How can we add up all these pieces to the puzzle? The most optimistic statement would be something like this: "There is little significant loss in intellectual power, or memory, or problem solving ability until quite late in old age, perhaps as late as 70 or 80 on the average, and perhaps not until a few years before death.'' While there is support for this kind of statement in the findings I have been describing, as a general statement, I think this is overly optimistic. Some measurable loss in skill on fluid or speeded tasks appears earlier than this, and for many adults decline in total IQ, and in memory, is measurable in the 60s. As a general rule, it does appear to be true that well-practiced, familiar skills are retained well into old age, while less practiced skills, and those that demand speed, wane earlier.

What is perhaps most striking, however, in all of the research on intellectual functioning in adulthood, is the range of variation that we see. Some adults begin to show declines in mental abilities in their 40s or 50s; others show little loss of function well into their 80s. If we are to understand the processes of mental aging, we must not only explain the general or normative pattern, but also the sources of the individual differences.

# Individual Differences in Rate of Intellectual Changes in Adulthood

Of the myriad factors that no doubt contribute to individual differences in maintenance or loss of intellectual skill, two stand out as particiularly significant: (1) health and (2) ``exercise,'' including mental activity of various kinds as well as physical exercise.

## Health Effects on Intellectual Aging

Two specific diseases, senile dementia and cardiovascular disease, have been implicated in loss of cognitive functioning in adulthood.

**Senile Dementia.** The term *dementia* refers to a ``general deterioration in intellectual abilities due to some disorder of the nervous system . . . it involves a disintegration of personality and behavior as well as of intellect. The process of dementia eventually strips an individual of all those qualities that make him uniquely human'' (Seltzer & Frazier, 1978, p. 304). **Senile dementia** refers to any such organically based deterioration of intellectual functioning that is associated with aging. It has several possible causes, including multiple small strokes (which may be treatable), or specific genetic diseases such as Huntington's chorea. But by far the most common form of senile dementia is **Alzheimer's disease,** sometimes called ``pre-senile dementia,'' in fact, since it may strike adults as young as 45. The incidence of Alzheimer's disease is difficult to estimate, but it may affect as many as 10% of adults over 65 in the United States (Eisdorfer, 1985).

Bear in mind here that I am talking about *disease*, not normal aging. In Alzheimer's disease there is an overall loss of brain weight and size, but the most distinctive characteristic is a kind of tangling of brain fibers, particularly in the area of the hippocampus. Since the hippocampus is heavily involved in memory processes—both encoding and retrieval processes—it is not surprising that the major diagnostic symptom of Alzheimer's disease is a loss of memory.

The memory function does not disappear all at once, however. The first thing to go seems to be short-term memory (e.g., Vitaliano, Breen, Albert, Russo, & Prinz, 1984; Whelihan, Lesher, Kleban, & Granick, 1984). As the disease progresses, the patient eventually loses long-term memory as well, such as the recall of names, faces, dates, and addresses, and the ability to use a fork or tie shoelaces. Simple commands can still be followed fairly well in the early stages, but that ability, too, is lost as the disease continues.

Just what causes Alzheimer's disease is not clear. In some cases there appears to be a genetic pattern, since the disease has a slight tendency to run in families. But many Alzeimer's patients have no family history of the disease.

Since some individuals in the early stages of such senile dementia may be included in samples of older adults whose intellectual skill has been compared to younger adults', it is possible that some of the "normal aging" effects I have already described are in fact disease processes, and not normal aging at all. So far, we do not have the data to disentangle these processes.

**Cardiovascular Disease (CVD).** This general label is applied to a whole family of diseases involving the heart and blood vessels, including what laymen call a "heart attack" as well as high blood pressure (more properly called hypertension). In several of the major longitudinal studies I have been describing, the researchers had information about CVD as well as about intellectual performance. In the Duke studies, there is some indication that subjects with CVD showed greater declines in IQ and other test scores (Siegler, 1983).

Similar results come from Schaie's 21-year study of intelligence (described in Figures 5–1 and 5–2). Schaie (1983b), for example, found that those subjects with CVD showed greater declines with age than did non-CVD subjects in the total Intellectual Ability score and in the test of number ability. But Schaie makes two critical points about these findings: (1) The size of the effect is quite small, and (2) the effect may be indirect rather than direct. That is, adults who are diagnosed as having some form of cardiovascular disease may change their lifestyle, perhaps becoming less active. It could then be the lifestyle change, rather than the disease, that is the causal factor in the slightly greater intellectual decline. Furthermore, the analyses of the Duke studies indicate that the causality may run the other way entirely: Adults who show good maintenance of their intellectual abilities may be at lower risk for CVD (Woodbury & Manton, 1983).

At the other end of the health continuum, there is some evidence that adults in optimum health have better intellectual functioning than average. The most often quoted study of this kind is the Human Aging Study (Butler, 1968), an intensive longitudinal investigation of 47 healthy older men, who were 65 to 91 years old at the start of the study. Twenty-seven of the men had no indication of disease of any kind, while the remainder showed asymptomatic or subclinical levels of disease. As a group, these men scored higher on measures of intellectual ability than did a comparison group of young adults, and the healthier group had higher scores than the less healthy group.

When we combine this evidence with the information on the terminal drop hypothesis, we come once again to the possibility that intellectual decline in old age may be a reflection of disease processes and not a feature of normal, healthy aging.

## "Exercise" Effects on Intellectual Aging

I am using *exercise* rather broadly to describe a second major category of influences on intellectual abilities in adults. Obviously, physical exercise is one part of this category. But so is mental exercise of any form, including going to school, doing crossword puzzles, playing chess, reading the daily paper, and doing complex work. The basic hypothesis suggested by gerontologists and psychologists is that any intellectual ability that is used regularly will be maintained at a higher level, just as physically exercised bodies remain fitter. (''Use it or lose it'' strikes again!) If that is true, then individual adults who are more physically and intellectually active should show better maintenance of intellectual skill than less active adults.

There are several threads of information that support this hypothesis.

### Education Effects

The most indirect evidence comes from the repeated finding that better educated (or middle-class) adults not only perform intellectual tasks at a higher level but maintain their intellectual skill longer in old age (Jarvik & Bank, 1983; Palmore, 1981; Schaie, 1983b).

There are several possible explanations of this correlation between education and maintenance of intellectual skill. The most obvious possibility is that more intellectually able teenagers and young adults both complete more years of education and maintain their intellectual skill better into old age. Thus, it may not be education at all that is involved here, but underlying intellectual ability.

A second possible reason for the relationship between education and intellectual maintenance in old age is that better educated people remain more intellectually active throughout their adult years. It may thus be the intellectual activity (''exercise'' in the sense in which I have been using that term) which helps to maintain mental skills. From this viewpoint, education has only an indirect effect on maintenance of intellectual skills, by influencing the lifestyles and intellectual activities of adults.

### The Effects of Intellectual Activity

There is at least some evidence to support this possibility. In three separate longitudinal studies involving adults past the age of 60 (Gribben, Schaie, &

Parham, 1980; Jarvik & Bank, 1983; Schaie, 1983b; Siegler, 1983), a link between activity levels and intellectual maintenance was found. Adults who read books and take classes, or those who engage in more of both sedentary and physical activities, seem to do better intellectually over time. It is the more isolated and inactive adults (whatever their level of education) who show the most decline in IQ.

My hunch is that this is at least partially a real causal link, but at this point I can't argue for much more than a hunch. The evidence is neither extensive nor particularly strong. No researcher has really measured "activity" very precisely, and in every case level of activity is correlated with years of education. As I already pointed out in chapter 2, better educated adults are more likely to continue their education through adult education classes or seminars and to read more. What we have, then, is a complex interactive process. As Schaie puts it:

**Figure 5–7** *It makes sense that the older adult on the right, who is still mentally active, will stay alert and have better mental functioning longer than the less active adult on the left. Longitudinal research supports this hypothesis, but of course it is possible that the causality is complex: Those adults who are initially more intellectually able are likely to remain mentally active longer, and have generally had more education as well. Still, mental "exercise" seems like a useful (as well as interesting) activity throughout life. (Source: F. Grunzweig, Photo Researchers Inc. (right); Hugh Rogers, Monkmeyer Press (left).)*

> It appears that there are substantial relationships among social status, life-styles, and the maintenance of intellectual ability. But these relationships seem to be interactive rather than causal . . . early, favorable life experience may be implicated in attaining high levels of intellectual functioning in young adulthood; their maintenance into old age, however, may be related to an engaged life-style, but that life-style may also be a function of a high level of ability. (Schaie, 1983b, p. 119)

## Physical Exercise and Intellectual Abilities

The case for a causal link between physical exercise and intellectual skill is a bit better, since there is some experimental evidence here as well as the longitudinal findings I have just mentioned. For example, Elsayed, Ismail, and Young (1980) gave a battery of intellectual tests to a group of young and old men before and after a physical exercise program. Comparing the two scores, they found significant increases between the before-training and the after-training scores for both age groups in measures of fluid ability, but not in measures of crystallized ability.

Just what mechanism may be involved here is not yet clear. One likely possibility is that physical exercise increases the amount of oxygen to the brain, thus improving the overall functioning of the brain and the central nervous system (CNS). Men and women who maintain reasonable levels of physical exercise throughout their adult years may maintain better CNS function (and lower risk of CVD, too), which in turn may help to maintain optimum intellectual functioning.

## Work Patterns and Intellectual Maintenance

A fourth piece in this interactive puzzle is the impact of the level of complexity of an adult's job on intellectual functioning. Melvin Kohn (1980; Kohn & Schooler, 1978) has done some particularly fascinating and provocative work on this question.

Kohn has been interested in one particular facet of intellectual skill, intellectual flexibility, which has to do with the ability to meet complex intellectual demands. Kohn has measured this ability with an index based on a lengthy testing and interview session which includes a measure of IQ, measures of cognitive style, and an assessment of the range and flexibility of answers given to a simple question: ''What are all the arguments you can think of for and against allowing cigarette commercials on TV?''

Kohn has also measured a dimension of work which he calls ''substantive complexity.'' Each subject describes precisely what he does with written materials or data, what he does with his hands, and what he does with people. The complexity of each of these facets of each job can then be rated and given weights, depending on the amount of time the worker spends in each of the three kinds of activity. (Incidentally, this is very similar to the kinds of analyses that are now being used as a basis for ''comparable worth'' scores for different jobs.)

What Kohn wanted to know was the relationship, if any, between intellectual flexibility and job complexity over time. What he found in a sample of men interviewed twice, at 10-year intervals, was that both intellectual flexibility and job complexity were highly stable. A man who had been high in intellectual flexibility at the first interview was likely to be high at the second interview as well, and a man with a complex job at Time 1 was likely to have a complex job 10 years later. But there were also some fascinating connections between the two measures.

First, greater intellectual flexibility led to higher job complexity. That is, men who were high in flexibility in 1964, when the first interview was completed, had more complex jobs 10 years later than did those men whose initial intellectual flexibility was lower. Second, those men who were employed at complex jobs became more intellectually flexible. So job complexity helped to foster intellectual flexibility. And greater intellectual flexibility then led to more complex jobs.

If we add these findings to what I have already said about individual differences in intellectual performance in adulthood, a complex chain of influences is apparent. The starting points (as I discussed in chapter 2) are a key part of the equation. Adults who begin with high levels of intellectual flexibility (or who are better educated or who have higher intellectual ability) are likely to end up in more complex, intellectually demanding jobs. They may continue their education in order to advance in those jobs. The complexity of the job, in turn, stimulates or maintains intellectual flexibility, so the adult reads more, discusses issues more, thinks more about options and possibilities. These adults, barring significant disease, have a good chance of maintaining their intellectual power well into old age.

In contrast, those who begin their adult years with lower levels of education or intellectual flexibility are funneled into less complex and demanding jobs. Such jobs do not provide much mental challenge, so there is little growth of mental flexibility or skill, and in later years, perhaps less maintenance of intellectual abilities.

At any point along the way, however, it looks as if the trajectory can be altered by increasing physical or mental exercise, by moving into a more complex job, or by going back to school. I do not think that there is infinite flexibility here, nor that the ''fall of the sands through the hourglass'' can be totally halted or reversed simply by reading the newspaper every day, or teaching yourself a foreign language, or memorizing telephone numbers. But there is at least suggestive evidence that all of these activities help to maintain intellectual abilities in the later years of adulthood.

## A Theoretical Model

Much of what I have said in this chapter both about the modal pattern of intellectual decline through adulthood and about individual differences in maintenance of intellectual skill, can be combined by using Nancy Denney's model

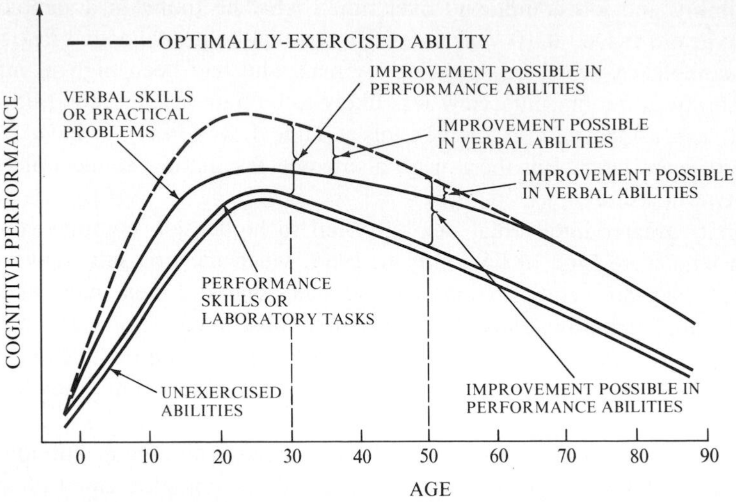


**Figure 5–8** *Figure 4–7 showed the simplest version of Nancy Denney's model of unexercised and optimally exercised abilities. Here, some of the further complexities of the model become clear. The center curve represents an approximation of the age changes for what we might think of as "semi-exercised" abilities, such as verbal skills or problem solving with practical problems. The hypothesized pattern of age change for performance skills or for laboratory tasks, however, follows the line of unexercised abilities. Also shown here are the estimated amounts of improvement possible, with training or exercise, for these two categories of skills. Since performance and laboratory task skills are typically less exercised (or less familiar), there is much more room for improvement than is the case for the "semi-exercised" abilities. Still, there is at least some room for improvement until quite late in life, according to this model. (Source: N. W. Denney, "Aging and Cognitive Changes" in* Handbook of Developmental Psychology, *B. B. Wolman, Ed., © 1982, p. 822. Reprinted by permission of Prentice-Hall, Inc., Englewood Cliffs, NJ.)*

of exercised and unexercised abilities. I described the general outlines of this model in the last chapter, referring there to the potential effects of physical exercise on physical aging. But the model was originally proposed to describe age changes in mental abilities. The general propositions are as follows:

1. The basic pattern of age change in mental abilities involves a rise until perhaps age 20 or 30, followed by a gradual decline (see Figure 5–8). The precise shape of this curve is yet to be determined by research. The research I have reviewed in this chapter suggests that there may be a longer, flatter, top to the curve than Denney proposes.
2. We can differentiate between "unexercised abilities" and "optimally exercised abilities." Unexercised abilities are those untrained or unpracticed

abilities that are thought to reflect the basic functioning of the nervous system and/or the effects of standard environmental experience. Many traditional laboratory tasks (such as those used to test memory ability) would fall in this category, as do most measures of "fluid" intelligence and many nonverbal tests of IQ. Optimally exercised abilities reflect the maximum ability that a normal healthy individual can attain with extensive practice and training. Of course, many abilities will fall between these two curves. As you can see in Figure 5–8, Denney suggests that the ability to solve practical problems falls between the curves, as does verbal ability for most adults.

3. The curve for the optimally exercised abilities represents an upper boundary of ability or performance at any one age. Training or exercise will thus help to raise the level of performance toward that maximum. Since exercised abilities, such as vocabulary or practical problem solving, are already closer to the maximum than are unexercised abilities, we should find that training has the largest effect on measures of fluid intelligence or on nonverbal tests, all of which are less fully exercised. Furthermore, with appropriate exercise or training, improvement in any unexercised ability should be possible at any age. But since there is also an underlying "decay" curve operating, training or exercise should not eliminate age differences entirely.
4. There are individual differences in the level of these curves (in the optimum that can be reached and in the lower boundary of unexercised abilities), reflecting differences in heredity, physical intactness, or early environmental stimulation. There are probably also individual differences in the trajectories, although that remains to be demonstrated. That is, some adults may be moving along a much slower "decay" curve than others.

If you think about the various facts I have provided in this chapter, you'll see that they fit this model reasonably well. Exercised abilities, such as verbal skills, show essentially the pattern that Denney has sketched in Figure 5–8: There is no practically significant decline until about age 60 or 70. Fluid abilities, such as many memory functions, show an earlier decline, following a pattern more like that of the unexercised abilities.

Furthermore, evidence from training studies does show that it is possible to raise the level of intellectual performance of middle-aged and elderly adults by providing training. But such training does not typically eliminate the age differences: Young adults with training still perform better than older adults with training, as we would expect from this model (Denney, 1982).

Finally, the model explicitly predicts that more mentally active adults will maintain higher levels of skill later into old age, which is confirmed by the findings on activity I just discussed. Denney suggests, however, that the effect of exercise is quite specific to a particular task. Reading the newspaper every day exercises certain kinds of verbal skills, but it doesn't provide much exercise for your memory. Memorizing phone numbers or Bible verses or poetry may help maintain memory skills but does little for your problem-solving ability. In other words, there does not appear to be any mental activity that in-

**TABLE 5–2 Summary of Age Changes in Intellectual Skills**

| Age 20–40 | Age 40–65 | Age 65 and Older |
|---|---|---|
| Peak intellectual ability between about 20 and 35 in both crystallized and fluid intelligence | Maintenance of skill on measures of verbal, unspeeded, or crystallized intelligence; some decline of skill on measures of performance, speeded, or fluid IQ; decline is usually not functionally significant till age 60 or later | Some loss of verbal or crystallized IQ, but this is most noticeable in adults with poorer health, lower levels of activity, and less education. Continued loss of skill on fluid IQ measures |
| Optimal performance on memory tasks | Little change in performance on memory tasks except perhaps some slowing later in this period | Slowing of retrieval processes and other memory processes; less skillful use of encoding strategies for new memories. |
| Peak performance on laboratory tests of problem solving | Peak performance on real-life problem-solving tasks | Decline in problem-solving performance on both laboratory and real-life tests |

creases basic mental ''fitness'' in the same way that aerobic exercise increases physical fitness. Rather, to maintain any given intellectual skill, one must practice or exercise that skill.

Obviously, Denney's model is only a preliminary statement. Over the next decades, as good research data become more plentiful, we will see whether this theoretical approach continues to offer both a good summary description and a heuristic basis for future work.

## A Review of Age Patterns

As in the last chapter, I have summarized the various age changes in intellectual functioning in a table (Table 5–2). Unlike the pattern of physical changes summarized in Table 4–3, in which some decline or change is measurable in many dimensions in the years of midlife, there is little indication of intellectual loss until later life. Just how these two sets of changes may be linked together remains the subject for further study.

## Summary

1. Cross-sectional comparisons of total IQ scores across the adult years show a decline beginning in the 30s or 40s; longitudinal studies show essential maintenance of IQ until approximately age 60 or 65, after which there is a decline.

2. Analyses of subscores of IQ tests suggest that performance on speeded, or nonverbal, or ''fluid'' tests declines earlier, perhaps as early as age 45 or 50, while performance on non-speeded verbal ''crystallized'' tests show little decline until perhaps age 65 or 70.

3. Age changes in memory appear to occur primarily in long-term memory, in both the encoding and retrieval processes. Adults in their 60s and 70s use less effective information-processing strategies for learning and remembering new material, and they have somewhat greater difficulty recalling already known material.

4. Age differences in memory are generally smaller when recall of familiar material is tested, but even with familiar material older adults typically remember somewhat less, or somewhat less rapidly.

5. Problem-solving performance also shows changes in the 60s or 70s, with older adults using less effective strategies. The difference is smaller when familiar, real-life problems are used instead of artificial laboratory tests.

6. Changes in intellectual structure with age are more difficult to determine. Older adults are often found to approach tasks using strategies that are similar to what we see in quite young children, but whether this represents a real "regression" or rather a more practical or even a dialectical approach is not clear.

7. The small amount of available research suggests that intellectual productivity remains essentially stable through at least the 50s, so whatever declines occur in performance on standardized tests are not necessarily reflected in poorer performance in job-related activities.

8. There is some evidence to suggest that intellectual skill is maintained, with little loss, until a period perhaps five years before death, at which point there is a fairly rapid drop.

9. In all the research, there are large individual differences in the timing and extent of intellectual maintenance or loss. Both physical health and mental "exercise" appear to shape those individual differences.

10. Two specific diseases are associated with earlier or more substantial decline in intellectual skill: senile dementia (e.g., Alzhiemer's disease) and cardiovascular disease (CVD). In Alzheimer's disease, the brain atrophies, and tangles appear in those nerves that are key to the processes of memory. Patients with this disease show very substantial loss of memory. CVD is associated with a slightly faster rate of decline in IQ and other measures of intellectual performance, perhaps because it is associated with a reduction in oxygen to the brain.

11. Those adults who maintain higher levels of physical and mental activity show slower rates of intellectual decline in old age. Since mentally active adults also tend to be better educated and higher in IQ in early adulthood, the causal links are not yet clear. Work complexity, however, appears to have a causal effect on intellectual flexibility.

12. Denney's theoretical model, contrasting the pattern of gain and loss in performance of "optimally exercised" and "unexercised" abilities, appears to be a useful description of our current knowledge about intellectual changes in adulthood.

## Suggested Readings

The agony of Alzheimer's disease. (1984, December 3). *Newsweek.*

This is an excellent article about Alzheimer's, with a very clear description of current research into the causes of the disease, as well as a good description of the lives of Alzheimer's patients and their families.

DENNEY, N. W. (1982). Aging and cognitive change. In B. B. Wolman (Ed.), *Handbook of developmental psychology*. Englewood Cliffs, NJ: Prentice-Hall.

This is not a simple article, but it is well worth the effort. Denney not only reviews much of the information I have described in this chapter, but she also presents her theoretical model of exercised and unexercised abilities.

# 6

# Sex Roles and Family Roles over the Adult Years

One of the things I remember most clearly about the transition from singlehood to marriage was that "wives" were treated very differently from "college professors." At academic gatherings, I had found that new acquaintances routinely asked each other "What do you do?" But at PTA meetings, or at gatherings where married couples met for the first time, no one ever asked me that. What I "did," clearly, was to "be a wife," and since everyone knew what that job involved, no one needed to ask. I was at first offended, and then amused, by the widely shared and totally unspoken assumption that wives didn't "do" other things, despite the vast evidence to the contrary.

Parenthood (a role I acquired simultaneously with marriage, which isn't the normal pattern, to be sure) had its own huge changes in roles. Aside from finding myself cooking and doing the laundry for four people instead of one—which takes a great deal more time, of course—I also found that the house got messy at the most astonishing rate, that the bathroom sink gathered toothpaste and other debris between one moment and the next, and that getting ready to go anywhere took at least five times as long as when I had been single. I was also suddenly in the business of listening to after-school tales from children, dealing with teachers and school problems, providing transportation to and from basketball games or friends' houses, and worrying about the prospective bad influence of some playmates.

All of these changes involve variations in roles, a concept I discussed in chapter 3. The patterns of change in physical and mental functioning I have been talking about in the past two chapters reflect the march of physical time in various ways, but role changes with age involve the march of "social time"—filling a series of socially defined positions, with their attendant roles, in a particular sequence. In this chapter I want to examine two particularly significant sets of such adult role sequences: sex roles and family roles. I'll explore the personal relationships within those family and sex roles in the next chapter, and then return to the description of adult role patterns in chapter 8, where the topic of work roles will be the central focus.

# Sex Roles in Adulthood

## Some Definitions

When we come to the study of sex roles, there is a whole collection of terms that get used rather imprecisely. If I do not define these terms at the outset, we will find ourselves in a tangle later on.

***Sex Roles.*** The definition of a sex role is much like the definition of any other role. Any role is a *job description*, a socially defined collection of behaviors and traits that a person occupying that role is expected to display. Thus, a sex role is the set of behaviors and traits that go with the social position of ''woman'' or ''man.'' The role describes what women and men are expected to do and how they should think or behave. In principle, either a male or a female could occupy the role of ''woman'' or the role of ''man.'' So when a woman becomes a top business executive, she is to some degree occupying a male role; when a man stays at home to care for an infant while his wife works, he is to some degree occupying a female role.

***Sex Role Stereotypes.*** When the job descriptions for men and women—including the prescriptions for personality traits as well as behavior—become highly fixed and widely shared, we can speak of sex role stereotypes. The presence of stereotypes is particularly evident when we make assumptions about the characteristics or behavior of an unknown individual based solely on his or her gender. When we do this, we move from descriptions of what men and women typically do, to assumptions about what men and women are or are supposed to be. In the process, we exaggerate both the similarities within each gender group and the differences between them.

***Sex Typing.*** The third concept, sex typing, refers to the extent to which any individual's behavior and attitudes match the sex role for his or her gender. A person who behaves in a way that is highly consistent with the sex role for his or her gender would be described as ''highly sex typed.''

***Masculinity, Femininity, and Androgyny.*** Finally, there are three terms now widely used to describe each person's perception or self-description of his or her own sex role-stereotyped qualities. Typically these personality traits or self-concepts are measured by giving individuals lists of adjectives and asking them the extent to which each adjective describes themselves. Some of the adjectives describe male-stereotyped qualities (such as assertiveness, independence, dominance, or self-confidence), and some describe female-stereotyped qualities (such as gentleness, emotionality, kindness, excitability, or passivity). (See Bem, 1974, 1977; Spence & Helmreich, 1978.)

Until the early 1970s, most psychologists thought of masculinity and femininity as opposite ends of a single dimension. One could be one or the other, but not both. But the current measures of these traits or self-concepts allow separate measurement of masculinity and femininity. You could, for example, describe yourself as both gentle and independent, both kind and assertive. Such a mixture of high levels of both masculine and feminine qualities is called **androgyny.** In contrast, adults who describe themselves as high in masculine traits, but low in feminine traits are labeled **masculine**, while those with the reverse pattern are labeled **feminine.** An individual who describes himself or herself as low in both masculine and feminine qualities is described as **undifferentiated.**

## The Content of Sex Role Stereotypes

We know a good deal more about the content of sex role stereotypes than we do about actual sex roles, in part because the roles themselves are changing rapidly while the stereotypes have remained remarkably stable over the past decades, even in the midst of the women's movement. Since the stereotypes form the basis of what most of us think men and women *ought* to be, let me start there.

**Sex Role Stereotypes in Adults.** The most extensive research on sex role stereotypes has been done by Inge and Donald Broverman and their colleagues (Broverman, Vogel, Broverman, Clarkson, & Rosenkrantz, 1972; Rosenkrantz, Vogel, Bee, Broverman, & Broverman, 1968). They asked subjects to go through long lists of traits (such as independent, talkative, optimistic, and grumpy), each of which was a label for a scale that ran from high to low. For each trait the subjects placed the ''typical male'' somewhere on the scale, and the ''typical female'' somewhere on the scale. For some traits, the researchers found that there was a consistent difference in the placement of men and women on these scales. They also found that if they asked other subjects to go through the same traits and pick out the ''good'' or ''desirable'' end of the scale, many more of the typical masculine qualities were also listed as ''good'' or ''desirable.'' Some of the highly valued masculine traits were aggressiveness, independence, objectivity, dominance, competition, ability to be leaders and to make decisions easily, ability to separate feelings and ideas, adventurousness, low levels of excitability in major crises, business skill, and logicalness. Some of the highly valued femimine traits were talkativeness, tactfulness, gentleness, neatness and quietness, awareness of others' feelings, and the ability to express tender feelings easily.

However, these stereotypes are not either/or statements. When Kay Deaux (1984) asked subjects to state a probability that men and women could have certain qualities, certain roles, and certain physical characteristics, she found a good deal of overlap, as you can see in Table 6–1. Obviously, although there are clear differences in subjects' expectations about men and women, the expected probability for ''cross-sex'' behavior or appearance is never zero. The

**TABLE 6–1 Sex Role Stereotypes: The Probability That the Average Man or Woman Will Show a Particular Trait, Behavior, or Physical Characteristic, According to Adult Raters**

| Characteristic | Judged Probability | |
|---|---|---|
| | *Men* | *Women* |
| Trait | | |
| Independent | .78 | .58 |
| Competitive | .82 | .64 |
| Warm | .66 | .77 |
| Emotional | .56 | .84 |
| Role Behaviors | | |
| Financial provider | .83 | .47 |
| Takes initiative with opposite sex | .82 | .54 |
| Takes care of children | .50 | .85 |
| Cooks meals | .42 | .83 |
| Physical Characteristics | | |
| Muscular | .64 | .36 |
| Deep voice | .73 | .30 |
| Graceful | .45 | .68 |
| Small-boned | .39 | .62 |

**Source:** Deaux, F. From individual differences to social categories: Analysis of a decade's research on gender. *American Psychologist,* 1984, *39,* 105–116. Copyright holder is American Psychological Association. Reprinted by permission of author.

pervasive male stereotype centers around qualities of competence and instrumentality, while the female stereotype centers around qualities of affiliation and expressiveness (Deaux, 1984), but we both observe and expect that there will be a good deal of overlap.

Such overlap does not mean, however, that the stereotypes are not powerful. They are. Among other things, Broverman and her colleagues (Broverman, Broverman, Clarkson, Rosenkrantz, & Vogel, 1970) have found that the male qualities are more highly valued and considered ''healthier'' by psychotherapists than are the female qualities. Further, jobs that women perform are also typically rated as less difficult than are those that men do (Deaux, 1984), and men and women who cross role lines and fill the opposite sex role experience a considerable amount of strain. Thus, although there is overlap in our conceptions of male and female roles, the stereotypes nonetheless shape our thinking about men and women in general, and about individual men and women.

**Sex Role Stereotypes in Children.** We can find virtually the same sex role stereotypes in children as young as five or six, and they are strongly established by fourth and fifth grade (Best et al., 1977; Ullian, 1981; Williams, Bennett, & Best, 1975). Children in these studies (in England and Ireland as well as in the U.S.) see men as strong, cruel, coarse, dominant, assertive, and ambitious. They see women as weak, soft-hearted, affectionate, and emotional.

**Age Changes in Sex Role Stereotypes.** The most rigid stereotypes are probably held by elementary school-age children. By adolescence, there is some softening, some recognition that while these are the qualities or activities of the average male or female, there are many exceptions. Among adults, older people are more likely to hold "traditional" views about sex roles (to be more stereotyped) than are younger people (Huston-Stein & Higgens-Trenk, 1978), but this seems to be a cohort difference rather than a developmental change. The current cohort of older adults grew up in an era when sex roles were much more clearly differentiated than they are today, and their own life patterns were likely to have followed the traditional pathways. Until cohort-sequential studies are completed, we won't know whether there are any genuine developmental changes in sex-role stereotypes over the adult years.

## The Content of Sex Roles

**Changes with Age in Sex Role Content.** Although the sex-role stereotypes are quite distinct and have remained remarkably stable over the past years, the actual job descriptions of the male and female role have been much more flexible. I should emphasize very strongly that what I can say about sex roles over the adult years is highly culture and cohort dependent. Sex roles have probably changed faster in the United States than in other countries—in no small part because of the massive, rapid change in labor force participation by women over the past decade—so what is true for the U.S. may well not be true elsewhere. And what is true for current cohorts in the U.S. may well not be valid for later groups.

Table 6–2 lists some of the present characteristics of the male and female roles for different age groups (based on Dobson, 1983; Hoffman & Manis, 1978, Katz, 1979; Rossi, 1980a, and others). There are clearly differences in roles at both a behavioral and an emotional level. Women not only bear and (primarily) rear children, they are also expected to provide the main source of nurturance and caring for both husband and children. It is also clear that the largest differences in sex roles appear in early adulthood, after the birth of children. Before marriage and childbearing, men and women have quite similar roles; after marriage and children there is a bifurcation of roles. This role separation continues until middle life (perhaps until age 45 to 50) when there are signs of a "crossing over," or of a reuniting of the two roles. Let me talk a bit more about each of these timepoints.

**The Intensification of Sex Role Differences in Early Adulthood.** There is now a good deal of evidence that the effect of marriage, and particularly the effect of having children, is to accentuate differences in sex roles (Abrahams, Feldman, & Nash, 1978; Feldman & Aschenbrenner, 1983; Gutmann, 1975; Hoffman & Manis, 1978). Even today, in this time of blending of sex roles and sex role stereotypes, after the birth of the first child women take on a larger share of the housework and primary responsibility for child care, and become

**TABLE 6–2 Present Content of Male and Female Roles at Different Ages**

| Age Group | Female Role | Male Role |
|---|---|---|
| 18–30 | Marry | Marry |
| | Bear children | Father children |
| | Be primarily responsible for childrearing | Have small role in caring for and rearing children |
| | Be primarily responsible for housework and cooking | Be secondarily responsible for cooking and housework |
| | Provide nurturance for all family members | Make major decisions for family |
| | Be secondary breadwinner (after children enter school particularly) | Be primary breadwinner |
| | Maintain contact with family and friends | Make progress in career or work |
| | Share in financial management | Manage finances |
| | Be sexual partner | Be sexual partner |
| | Be recreational partner | Be recreational partner |
| | Listen to others | Talk more |
| 30–45 | Continue rearing of children, including links with schools, other families with children, etc. | Minimal role in rearing of children |
| | Continue major responsibility for housework and cooking | Minimal responsibilities for house or cooking |
| | Continue provision of nurturance to children and spouse | Continue role as decision maker; provide strength and firmness |
| | Be secondary breadwinner | Be primary breadwinner |
| | Maintain contact with family and friends | Make major progress in work or career |
| | Share in financial management | Manage finances |
| | Sexual and recreational partner | Sexual and recreational partner |

less powerful in family decision making. The man becomes more preoccupied with the need to earn money to support the family, and his power within the family increases. In sum, egalitarianism declines. These changes are especially apparent if the woman also stops working when the first child is born, although some role separation appears to occur even when the woman continues to work (Hoffman & Manis, 1978).

Such changes occur in other cultures as well. David Gutmann (1975) refers to this process as the ''parental imperative.'' In the several cultures he has studied, including Navaho, the Mayan, and the Druze, he finds that men routinely describe themselves as having become more responsible, more selfless, and more moderate in habits after marriage and fatherhood. They become more focused on work, on supporting the family. Gutmann argues that these changes, and the matching increase in nurturance on the part of the woman, are a response to the obvious need of the child for both physical and emotional sustenance.

Another facet of this adaptation to parenthood may be a change in the way

| Age Group | Female Role | Male Role |
|---|---|---|
| 45–65 | Continue major role as rearer of children; help to launch children into independent life | Increase role with children, providing financial support for launching |
| | Continue major housekeeping role | Increase role in housekeeping |
| | Enter work force if have not already done so; increase levels of achievement and competence | Continue work or career; focus on training younger workers (mentor role) |
| | Assume primary role as caregiver or support for aging parent(s) and parents-in-law | Assume secondary role as caregiver or support for aging parents |
| | Continue major responsibility for maintaining contact with family and friends | Continue major responsibility for family decision making |
| | Become grandmother | Become grandfather |
| | Sexual and recreational partner | Sexual and recreational partner |
| | Assist in management of money | Primary financial manager |
| 65+ | Continue as primary link to children and grandchildren. Provide physical assistance to children if possible | Secondary role with children and grandchildren |
| | Retire from paid employment | Retire from paid employment |
| | Be in charge of, but share more in, household management | Share more in household management |
| | Share more in finances | Be in charge of finances |
| | Continue major role of support to aging parents if they are still alive | |
| | Sexual and recreational partner | Sexual and recreational partner |

young adults perceive their own masculinity and femininity. You can see the results of one study (Abrahams, Feldman, & Nash, 1978) in Figure 6–1. In this research, four separate groups of (white, middle-class, U.S.) adults were compared on their responses to a measure of masculinity-femininity-androgyny: cohabiting pairs, newly married pairs without children, couples expecting their first child, and couples with a first child between six and 12 months old. As you can see in the figure, masculinity scores were highest for males (and low for females) in the group of parents, while femininity scores were highest for women (and low for men) among parents. In a later replication of this analysis, Nash and Feldman (1981) again found that maximum sex differences in self descriptions on such dimensions as leadership, autonomy, compassion, and tenderness occurred among young parents and those expecting their first child, compared to single adults or more mature parents.

Other researchers have not invariably found this same pattern. For example, Feldman and Aschenbrenner, (1983) in a short-term longitudinal study of a group of highly educated, philosophically egalitarian couples, found that women

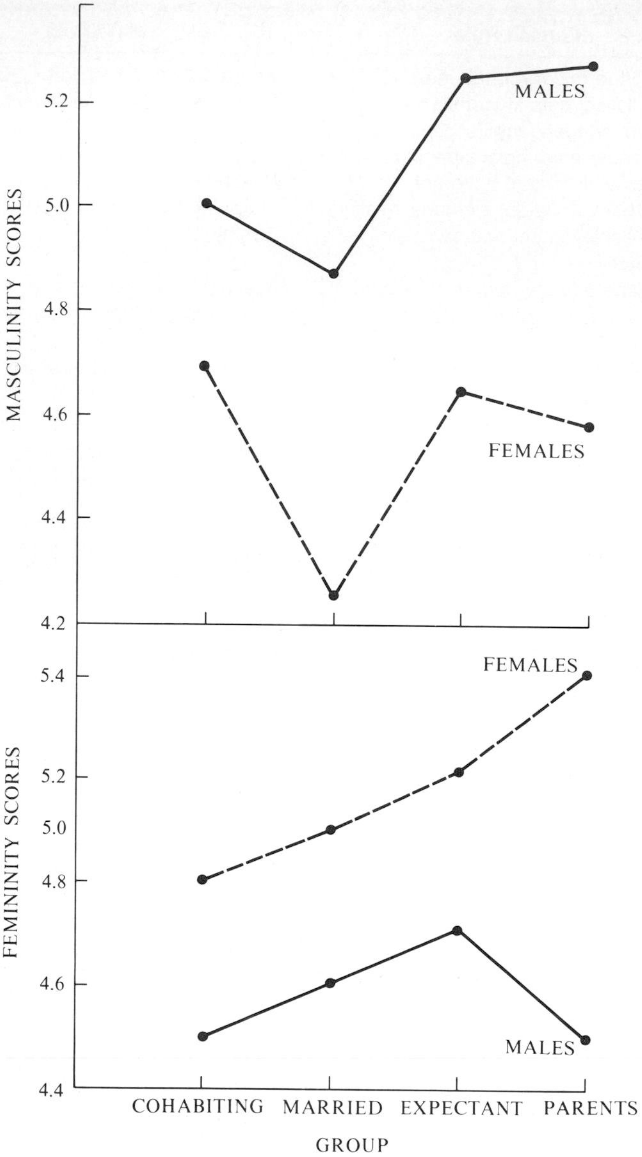


**Figure 6–1** *In this cross-sectional comparison, young adults in various "stages" of family formation were tested for their self-described masculinity and femininity. Masculinity was highest for males who were new parents, and femininity was highest for women who were new parents. This illustrates the intensification of traditional sex roles that appears to occur at the time of the birth of the first child. (Source: Abrahams, Feldman, & Nash, 1978, Figure 1, page 397. Copyright holder is American Psychological Association. Reprinted by permission of author.)*

became more feminine and men more androgynous (rather than more masculine) after the birth of a child. And in a study done in Australia, Cunningham and Antill (1984) found that working women had consistently lower femininity scores than did nonworking women, regardless of whether they were married or single, parents or nonparents. If we are to sort out the impact of the transition to parenthood on adults' self-perceptions of their own sex typing, more longitudinal research will be needed. For now, the pattern of results is suggestive, but not firm.

**The Crossover of Sex Roles at Midlife.** Equally suggestive is the evidence that sex roles may converge once again, perhaps even crossing over, at mid-life (Giele, 1982b; Rossi, 1980a). The data are fragmented, but intriguing. In one cross-sectional study, Feldman, Biringen, and Nash (1981) found that middle-aged women whose children were leaving home were more autonomous than were younger groups of women, while among men there was a higher level of compassion in the middle years than earlier. There is also some suggestion from recent research that, at least for current cohorts of middle-aged women, an increase in traditionally masculine role patterns in midlife is associated with lower rates of anxiety or depression and higher levels of life satisfaction. So, for example, middle-aged women who work outside the home are less likely to show psychiatric symptoms, while women who remain strongly family oriented show higher depression (Lowenthal, Thurnher, & Chiriboga, 1975; Powell, 1977).

Two theorists whose work I discussed in chapter 3 have also suggested a sex role crossover for men. George Vaillant, in his longitudinal study of Harvard men (1977a), found that the men became more "feminine" in middle age. In particular, they became more introspective, more concerned with feelings, more able to express emotions. Other researchers have found that men increase their involvement in housework after the children leave home (Model, 1981), although that is not a universal finding (e.g., Geerken & Gove, 1983). The role of "mentor," which Levinson (1978) describes as a common element in the midlife life structure, also involves many of the nurturing and supportive aspects of the traditional female role. At this point, many men (and some women, of course) take on the job of guiding younger workers, younger colleagues, through the thickets of the job world.

Finally, there is cross-cultural evidence from David Gutmann's studies (1975; 1977) that a typical pattern in many societies is for men's roles to become more nurturing, less achievement oriented in old age, while women's roles come to involve greater assertiveness, greater power.

I find the idea of sex role crossover at midlife appealing, possibly because it fits with my own biases. But I should emphasize again that the data base is thin, and nearly all the evidence—including the cross-cultural evidence—involves cross-sectional comparisons. We simply do not know whether, in individual adults, or in married couples, there is a change in sex roles at midlife, with an increasingly egalitarian division of labor and emotional responsibilities. Until we have decent longitudinal data, over several cohorts, we cannot be sure if this is a consistent developmental pattern.

## Sex Roles in Adulthood: A Brief Summary

Several points are worth emphasis about the impact of sex roles and sex role stereotypes on adult life patterns. First, as I pointed out earlier, adult life patterns are not firmly fixed by gender. The sex role definitions overlap: When we say that men are expected to be "instrumental" in their role, this means primarily that men are expected to be more instrumental than are women, not that women show none of this quality. In fact, most of us appear to learn both male and female roles, so that we are able, at least minimally, to fill the cross-sex role if the situation demands it. Women who find themselves unexpectedly needing to support their family are frequently able to take on the more assertive male role; men are quite capable of the nurturing and expressiveness involved in major caregiving to children. And when both men and women fill the same job role, they are very similar in their personal qualities (Deaux, 1984).

Sex roles appear to have their largest effect on the adult life course by influencing the choices that men and women make at crucial points in their lives. And those choices, in turn, typically set men and women on somewhat different pathways through adulthood.

The sequence of family roles operates in much the same way, influencing choices. Once the sequence of family roles has begun, it creates a predictable rhythm in the life pattern of the adult over a period of 20 or 30 years or more.

# Family Roles over the Adult Years

Just as individuals have roles, so the family, too, has a role or a set of tasks. Evelyn Duvall (1971) lists the following family tasks: allocation of resources, division of labor, reproduction, recruitment and release of family members, maintenance of order, placement of members in the larger society, and maintenance of motivation and morale. Both the extent to which any one task dominates, and the way the tasks are completed, will change from one phase to the next in the family life cycle, a concept I described briefly in both chapters 1 and 3. You'll recall that for families that remain together and have at least one child, eight steps in family composition are customarily distinguished: (1) newlyweds with no children, (2) families with one infant, (3) families with the oldest child of preschool age, (4) families with the oldest child of elementary school age, (5) families with the oldest child an adolescent, (6) families with the oldest child gone from home (to college, to marriage, or to single but independent living), (7) families with all children gone from the home ("empty nest"), and (8) aging families, in which one or both spouses has retired. Since the age at which adults begin this sequence varies considerably from one couple to the next, these stages do not describe chronological time. Rather, they describe social time, or the "family career" (Nock, 1982).

Each of the transitions involves one or more changes in roles. In some cases, roles are added (such as the role of parent between the second and third stages);

in some instances the content of the roles change, such as the shift in parental tasks that occurs when the oldest child starts school (all those PTA meetings and parent-teacher conferences, and the transporting of the child to special events), or the very large shift in the content of the parenting role when the last child leaves home. As Terkelsen (1980) points out, some of the role changes involve changes in things you *do,* and some require that the adult *be* something new (such as being a parent, or becoming more self-sufficient at midlife). The former involve changes in mastery or adaptation; the latter involve changes in status or meaning and are more profound and difficult.

## Secular Trends in the Family Life Cycle

Before I go on to describe some of the ways in which life experiences and attitudes are affected by the life cycle sequence, I want to explore some of the very large cohort differences in the timing of that cycle that have occurred in the United States during this century. In part this is designed to remind us all of the impact of cohort on the experiences of adulthood. But I also want to underline the cumulative effect of these changes for current cohorts and for our understanding of adult life.

Figure 6–2 shows the average age for three key events in the lives of women born in each of four decades, based on 1980 U.S. Census Bureau data on over 40 million women (Norton, 1983). All the women included in this graph had been married at least once. As you can see, the average age for a first marriage declined over these cohorts, as did the average age at the birth of the first and last children. Just what these numbers will look like for the cohort born between 1950 and 1959, or for later cohorts, we cannot yet tell, since these women have not yet completed their childbearing years. What is clear so far is that the cohort now in its 20s is marrying considerably later. (The median has risen to about 23 years for women and 25 years for men according to recent census numbers.) Young couples today also appear to be more likely to delay childbearing.

Whether these recent patterns reflect long-term trends or not, we can't say. We can draw some conclusions, though, about the family life cycles of those women born between 1910 and 1949, as depicted in Figure 6–2. The most striking change in that time is the declining age at the birth of the last child. Since, as you'll recall from chapter 4, the average life expectancy was going up dramatically during those same decades, the effect of these changes has been to expand markedly the number of years a man and woman can now expect to spend in the "postparental" and "aging parent" stages of the life cycle. Glick (1977, 1979) estimates that since 1900, 14 child-free years have been added to the life of the average adult, mostly in the postparental phase. Many other life pattern changes flow from the same shifts in the timing of marriage and childbearing. For example, in 1900, women were frequently widowed before their last child left home. Widowhood was thus a quite different state than it is likely to be today, when a woman is more likely to be widowed 10 or 15 years after her last child has grown and gone. Similarly, you can see

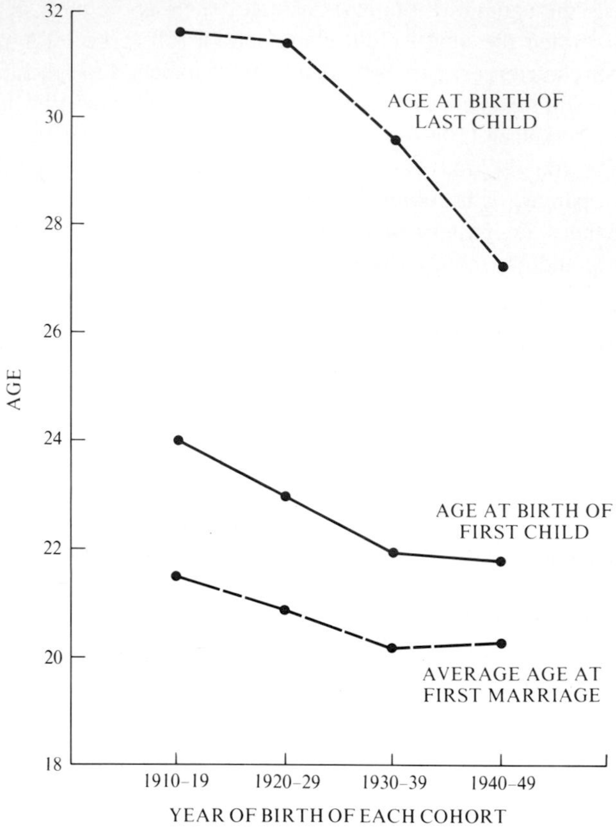


**Figure 6–2** *During this century in the United States, the trend has been for women to marry at younger and younger ages, and to have both their first and last children at younger ages as well. This change, along with the extension of life expectancy at older ages, has increased the total number of childless years in the average adult life by about 14. (Source: Norton, 1983, Table 1, p. 268.)*

from Figure 6–2 that those women born early in the present century were likely to complete menopause while there were still children at home. In contrast, the cohort born in 1940 was likely to experience the menopause, and the departure of the last child, at about the same time—a combination which may pose difficulties for some women.

Overall, it is clear that even rather small changes from one cohort to the next in the timing of marriage and childbearing, and in life expectancies, can have significant effects on the pattern of life experienced by generations of men and women.

## Life Experiences and the Family Life Cycle

Just how is an adult's life shaped by these steps or stages? To answer this question, let me first look at some trends across the full set of stages, and then focus on several specific stages more intensively.

**Marital Satisfaction, Life Satisfaction, and Mental Health over the Family Life Cycle.** Sociologists and psychologists who have studied the family life cycle have focused their attention primarily on the impact of the stages on three groups of dependent variables: marital satisfaction, overall life satisfaction or happiness, and aspects of mental health such as depression.

I have already described some of the major findings on family life cycle stages and marital satisfaction in chapter 1, as part of the illustration of cross-sectional research designs. You will want to go back and look at Figures 1–7 and 1–8 to refresh your memory. The general finding has been of a curvilinear relationship between marital satisfaction and family stage (Rollins & Galligan, 1978). The most well-documented, and reliably observed aspect of this curve is the decline in satisfaction that occurs with the birth of the first child, which has been demonstrated longitudinally (Ryder, 1973; Waldron & Routh, 1981) as well as cross-sectionally (Harriman, 1983; Polonko, Scanzoni, & Teachman, 1982). The rest of the curvilinear pattern has been shown only cross-sectionally, but it has reappeared in a number of studies, covering several different cohorts, so there is at least some reason to have confidence in the generality of the pattern.

However, as I pointed out in chapter 1, we also have evidence that this curve is more likely to appear in some subgroups than in others. Recall that Anderson and his colleagues (1983) did not find such a curve for spouses high in "marital conventionalization." In other research, Estes and Wilensky (1978) found that couples with low levels of financial worry showed roughly the same levels of marital satisfaction across the life cycle curve, while those who were experiencing financial strain showed the typical curve. And Abbott and Brody (1985) found that, in a group of wives, a decline in marital satisfaction after the birth of children occurred primarily for those with two or more children, or those with only sons. These findings lead to the hypothesis that marriages that enjoy highly positive (or less stressful) circumstances, such as low levels of discord, secure finances, and fewer children, are less likely to be disrupted by the presence of a child. When there are stresses present, however (as is nearly always the case), then children add to those stresses. One of the consequences is then a lower level of marital satisfaction.

A somewhat different curvilinear relationship appears if we look at overall happiness instead of marital satisfaction (Antonucci, Tamir, & Dubnoff, 1980; Campbell, 1981). Figure 6–3 shows some representative findings from the results of an analysis by Toni Antonucci and her colleagues (1980) of data from a time-sequential study, the Michigan Survey Research Center study of mental illness and health (described in Table 1–2). Recall that in this study the same

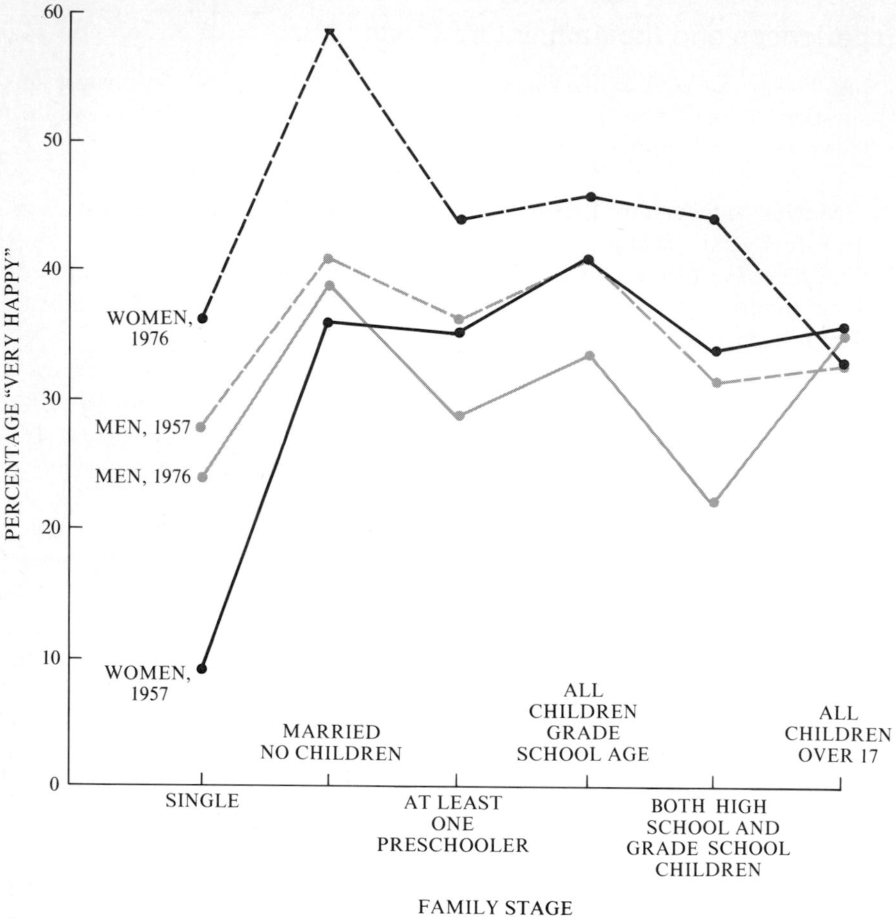


**Figure 6–3** *Two large national samples of adults, one in 1957 and one in 1976, were asked the following question: "Taking all things together, how would you say things are these days—would you say you're very happy, pretty happy, or not too happy?" This figure shows the percentage who said they were very happy, as a function of family life stage. You can see that single adults reported less happiness, as did adults with preschoolers. (Source: Antonucci, Tamir, & Dubnoff, 1980, data from Table 1, p. 40.)*

survey questions were used with two independent samples of over 2,000 adults each, interviewed nearly two decades apart (1957 and 1976). Comparison of the results in the two samples allows us to check whether the pattern is purely a cohort effect or not. In general, although more women described themselves as happy in 1957 than in 1976, the shape of the curves is quite similar. In each group there is a rise in happiness at marriage and a decline in reported happiness when there are preschool children in the family. The pattern at later stages is less clear, but there is only a very weak indication of an increase in happiness after the children leave home. In other research, however (e.g., Campbell,

1981), there are stronger signs of an upturn in overall life satisfaction. It seems that older people are less likely to describe themselves as either very happy or very distressed, but the balance between the two (sometimes called *affect balance*) is more strongly positive in the postparental stage than at earlier stages.

Finally, there is similar evidence of a family life cycle pattern in depression and other measures of mental health (consistent with the age-related pattern shown in Figure 4–5). Several studies have shown that women with preschool children are more prone to both depression and anxiety (Brown & Harris, 1978; Gove & Geerken, 1977), and this is true whether the woman also works or not. In Brown and Harris's study of a sample of British women (1978), however, the link between depression and age of children was apparent only for working-class women. Middle-class women, who have a greater range of options to deal with the role strains they experience, do not show elevated psychiatric symptoms when their children are small. In contrast, neither middle-class nor working-class men seem to show any change in depression or anxiety as a function of family life cycle stage.

Overall, then, we can see some effects of life cycle stages at several points: (1) at the transition from singlehood to marriage, (2) at the transition to parenthood, and (3) at the transition to the postparental (or "empty nest") stage. Let us explore each of these stages more fully.

**The Transition from Singlehood to Marriage.** From the point of view of roles, getting married marks one of the largest changes that occurs over the adult years. An entirely new role is added, that of husband or wife, each with its own prescriptions. Among other things (as is clear in Figure 6–3), being married is associated with higher levels of happiness, for both men and women. There is also abundant evidence that, compared to single adults, married adults are physically healthier and less prone to depression or other forms of psychiatric disturbances (Cargan & Melko, 1982; Doherty & Jacobson, 1982; Gove, 1972, 1979). Such a difference could be the result of self-selection processes. If mentally and physically healthier adults are more likely to get married, then the least healthy and poorest functioning adults would be left in the "single" group. There is some indication that self-selection processes work in this way for men, but probably not for women. In this culture at least, where men tend to marry "down" the social class ladder, and women tend to marry "up," unmarried women are likely to be relatively well educated, with above average IQs and white-collar jobs, while unmarried men are likely to have more average IQs and to be less educated. And, in fact, unmarried men have higher rates of physical and mental illness than do women (Spreitzer & Riley, 1974).

An alternative explanation of the relationship between marriage and health focuses on the role of **social support**, defined as the combination of affect, affirmation, and aid that a person receives from those around her (Kahn & Antonucci, 1980). We know that high levels of social support are associated with lower rates of physical disease and emotional disturbance (a relationship I'll discuss more fully in chapter 11). Since getting married increases the available social support for most individuals, we should expect that married adults would be healthier than unmarried adults, which they are. Furthermore, if this argument is valid, we should expect quite high rates of physical and mental illness among divorced adults, who experience a marked loss in social support, and this is precisely what researchers have found. In general, rates of physical and mental illness are even higher among the divorced than among the never married (Cargan & Melko, 1982; Doherty & Jacobson, 1982; Weingarten, 1985).

The emotional and physical benefits of the spouse role, however, do not seem to be evenly divided between men and women. In the majority of studies, married men are found to have better physical and mental health than married women. Walter Gove (1972, 1979) has suggested that this difference arises because the roles of husband and wife (in Western cultures, at least) are unequal in support, burdens, or gratification. For example, part of the wife's role is to provide nurturance and emotional support to all other family members, but the husband's role includes a much smaller expectation of support toward the wife. In addition, the wife role is lower in status and higher in the number of unpleasant or routine jobs than the husband role. Thus, men find marriage to be a better buffer against the slings and arrows of normal life than do women.

This difference in the two spousal roles is highlighted still further in the results of a study by Rosenfield (1980), who found that the typically higher levels of depression and physical illnesses for wives versus husbands occurred only for those wives who did not work outside the home. Working wives (who do less housework and have potential sources of emotional support and gratification in their work) had about the same levels of depression and sickness as did their husbands.

Overall, given the existing definitions of male and female roles and of spousal roles, the transition to marriage appears to be particularly beneficial for men: Married men show the lowest rates of illness or disturbances, while unmarried men (never married or divorced) show the highest. Married and unmarried women fall in between. But as role definitions change, these sex differences may change as well.

**The Arrival of the First Child.** Major role changes also occur at the birth of the first child. I have already talked about the changes in sex roles that seem to accompany this transition, but there are much broader role changes as well. Unlike the transition to marriage, which seems to be accompanied by an increase in happiness, initially the new role of parent brings a decrease in happiness and in marital satisfaction.

Longitudinal studies covering the period from pregnancy through the early months of the new baby's life seem to show that it is the increase in role conflict and role strain that is the source of the difficulty. Recall that role conflict occurs when two or more roles are physically or psychologically incompatible with one another; role strain occurs when an individual does not have the skills to fulfill some role. Sociologists have argued, with considerable empirical support, that any increase in the number of roles to be filled, or in role strain, will be accompanied by a decline in life satisfaction or marital satisfaction, and also a decline in the skill with which each of the person's roles is fulfilled. When you have too many jobs to do, you don't do *any* of them very well (e.g., Lerner & Galligan, 1978; Rollins & Galligan, 1978).

Since both role conflict and role strain commonly increase with the arrival of the first child, we should not be surprised at the accompanying decline in marital satisfaction. The role of major caregiver and the role of spouse are at least partially in conflict. The new baby demands time, attention, and nurturance, leaving less of all of these for the spouse. There are not enough hours in the day for the same kinds of recreational activities, for sex, or for quiet companionship between husband and wife as there were before. There is also less time for friends and less time alone. It is precisely this sense of not enough time, particularly affectionate or nurturant time with one's spouse, that marks this transition (Belsky, Spanier, & Rovine, 1983; Harriman, 1983; Myers-Walls, 1984). For some, there is also a sense of role strain, since caring for a child is a new and unfamiliar task. As you might expect, any factors that tend to increase the role conflict or strain is likely to make the marital satisfaction decline more. So, for example, couples that experience high levels of interference from their work—overtime demands or the need to bring work home, for example—show more strain after the birth of a child (Belsky, Perry-Jenkins, & Crouter, 1985) than do couples with less work interference. And when the infant has a particularly difficult temperament (making the parenting role more strained), parents show greater negative effects (Sirignano & Lachman, 1985).

Before I persuade you that having children is an unmitigated disaster, I should hasten to add two things. First, despite the drop in happiness and marital satisfaction at this point in the family life cycle, having a child also brings profound satisfactions, including a sense of purpose or worth, a sense of being "grown up," and a shared joy between husband and wife (Harriman, 1983; Hoffman & Manis, 1978). In Hoffman and Manis's large sample, 80% of subjects said that their lives had been changed in positive ways by the arrival of children.

Second, the role conflict and role strain of the transition to parenthood can be significantly mitigated in several ways, particularly by being very clear about the roles that husband and wife will fulfill with the child (Steffensmeier, 1982), by choosing priorities (which may mean giving up some other roles for a while), and even by changing your standards for other roles. That is, you can reduce the role conflict by redefining some roles (not vacuuming the living room every day, or eating convenience foods more often, for example), and by eliminating others. Those couples who apply these good coping strategies to the transition to parenthood experience less distress and more satisfaction (Myers-Walls, 1984).

**The Departure of the Children: The "Empty Nest."** We have much less information about the role changes and their effects that occur when all the children have left home. Extrapolating from data in Figure 6–2, and assuming that most young adults leave home by the age of 21 or 22 (an assumption which has become more dubious in recent years), we can estimate that women in the 1930–39 cohort will be on average about 50 to 52 years old when the last child leaves home, while men will be somewhat older.

This stage is sometimes called "postparental," as if the role of parent stopped when the last child walked out the door, suitcase in hand. Clearly it does not. Adults who have reared children go on being a parent until they (or their children) die. But the content of the role clearly changes, becoming less demanding, less time consuming. As a result, other roles within the family system change as well. Most importantly, the spousal roles change, as there is more time available for companionship. The spousal roles once again become more central, although the content of the husband and wife roles may have changed if some sex role crossover has occurred. Either husband or wife may also take on new roles (new work roles, for example, or community roles).

Folklore would have it that this "empty nest" stage is a particularly unpleasant and stressful period, especially for a woman, since she loses what may have been the most central role of her early and middle adulthood—that of mother. As a result she may lose a powerful sense of her own worth. The research findings, however, do not altogether support such a gloomy picture.

On the one hand, Marjorie Lowenthal and her colleagues (Lowenthal, Thurnher, & Chiriboga, 1975), in an often-cited comparison of newlyweds, middle-aged, and pre-retirement adults, found that the women in the middle-aged group, all of whom were on the verge of the postparental transition, were consistently the least happy, the most "desperate" with their lives. Another sign of an increased problem at this age come from the data on suicides, which you have already seen in Figure 4–6: There is a rise in the suicide rate for white women between ages 30 and 55, with the peak at around age 50. And there is evidence that alcohol use or abuse also increases among women in those same years from 30 to 50, as you can see in Figure 6–4.

The other side of the argument, however, seems to me to be more persuasive. First, note that both the rise in suicide and in heavy alcohol use occurs primarily in the years when children are still in the home, rather than postparentally. Second, there is other evidence that many women experience not distress, but relief, at the departure of children (Alpert & Richardson, 1980). Marital satisfaction typically goes up at this stage (recall Figure 1–7), and there is no evidence for a general rise in depression or physical symptoms accompanying the departure of the last child (recall Figure 4–5). On the contrary, adults in this life stage have fewer worries, fewer anxieties, than do those with young children (Antonucci, Tamir, & Dubnoff, 1981).

Those women who do experience heightened distress at this role transition—and there clearly are some—appear primarily to be those who attempt to maintain their old homemaking/parenting role, especially those who do not work outside the home.

I am not trying to suggest here that for most adults the postparental period is a continuous idyll, devoid of problems, any more than the advent of children ushers in continuous problems. Rather, I am trying to suggest that as a general rule, filling more roles is more stressful and difficult than filling fewer. So the addition of the full-time parenting role brings certain conflicts and strains, just as the partial shedding of that role at mid-life brings a reduction of certain conflicts and strains.

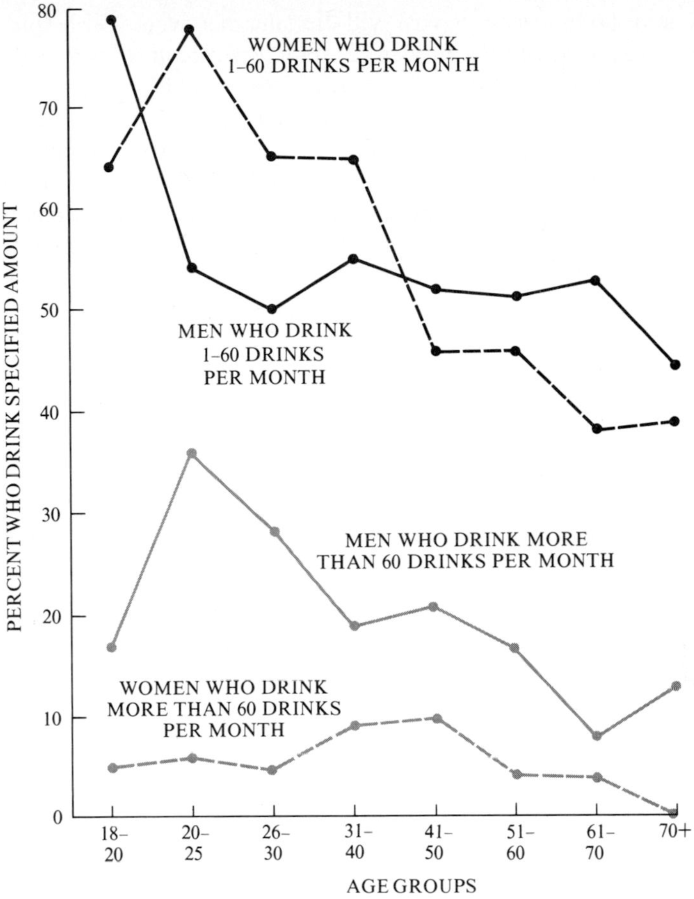


**Figure 6–4** *These figures, based on a national survey in 1979, don't tell us about rates of alcoholism, but they do say something about self-reported high levels of alcohol use. High use is most common in men in their 20s, and in women in their 30s and 40s. Self-reports of alcohol use are somewhat unreliable, so these figures may underestimate the amount of alcohol dependence or alcoholism. (Source: U.S. Bureau of the Census, 1984a, Table 192, p. 119.)*

At the same time, many adults at midlife take on a new role, namely, caring for (or arranging the care of, or worrying about) aging parents. The timing of the addition of this new role varies markedly from one adult to another, depending on their parents' age at their birth and on the health of the parents. Winsborough (1980) has estimated that the mothers of half the women born in 1930 were still alive when those women were 52. The parents of those of you born in 1970 will live still longer. Half of you, at age 58, will still have a living mother.

For most of you, however, sometime when you are between the ages of 40 and 65 one or both of your parents will die, and that event will be preceded by a period of years in which the older generation will require increased attention and assistance. Rueben Hill (1965) showed this ''middle generation squeeze'' very effectively in a study of three generations in 100 families. Each family included a set of grandparents over the age of 60, a set of parents aged 40 to 60, and a set of married children, aged 20 to 40. Each member of the family was asked how much help he or she gave to the other generations, and how much help was received. As you can see from Figure 6–5, the middle generation gave the most help and received the least. This midlife stage in the family life cycle thus involves not only a continued involvement in the life of children, but also an increase in role demands in the role of child-to-one's-parents.

The extent to which these overlapping roles will cause conflict or strain will depend very heavily on the luck of the draw or on timing. If you had your own children fairly late, then the likelihood that you will be facing economic strains at this midlife period are increased, with children in college requiring assistance just as your aging parents may require assistance. If you had your own children when you were quite young, and your parents are healthy and long-lived, then

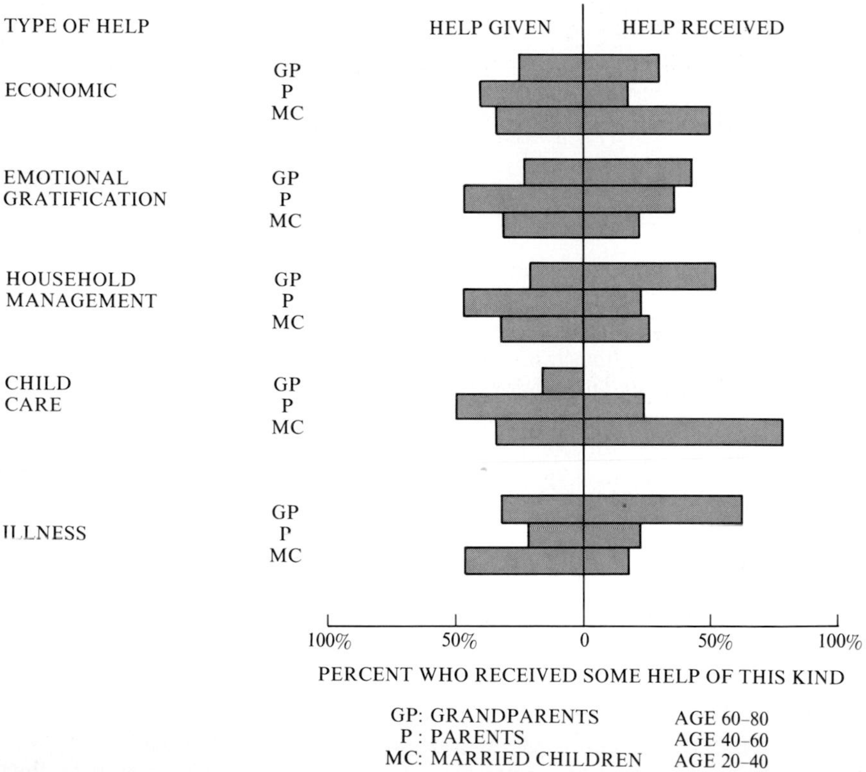


***Figure 6–5*** *The role of the middle-aged adult includes assistance given to both grown children and to aging parents, as you can see in these results from Hill's study of three generations in 100 families. (Source: Hill, 1965, data from Table 3, p. 125.)*

you are likely to have a period of a decade or more at midlife when the demands of both parent and child roles are at low ebb.

## Roles and Role Losses in Late Adulthood

One of the weaknesses of using family role stages as a basis for examining role changes in adult life is that old age tends to get short shrift. The final stage in Duvall's system is simply listed as "aged parent," and there is usually little said about the role changes involved at this point. But, in fact, there are myriad role changes in later life which have a profound effect on the life experiences of older adults.

There are two key points about the role changes in late life. First, most of these changes involve role loss rather than role gain. At earlier time points, adults add roles—spouse, parent, worker. In old age, adults shed roles. The role of worker is given up at retirement (which I'll discuss fully in chapter 8); the role of spouse is given up at widowhood for a great many adults. Friends die, children move away from the hometown, positions in organizations may be given up in favor of younger adults.

Second, as Irving Rosow so cogently pointed out (1976), the roles that do remain in later life have less content. That is, there is a social position or a label for the role, but there aren't as many duties or expectations as there were earlier in life. This was already apparent in Figure 6–5, where it was clear that the aging parent had fewer family responsibilities than had been true at earlier times. This is also true in whatever work or organizational roles may remain for the older adult. There are honorific titles and figurehead jobs in organizations. In this culture at least, the role of "being old" is a role with few prescriptions. "Enjoying yourself" or "taking it easy" may be the role dictates, and these are highly amorphous role prescriptions. Whether this loss of roles and role content means that older adults are less content with their lives is not so clear. I will be coming back to this issue in later chapters. But it is clear that simply labeling older adults as "aging family" is not adequate to describe the role experience of this age group.

**Grandparenthood.** One exception to the pattern of role loss in old age is the role of grandparent, which is typically added some time in the postparental period and retained throughout old age. About three fourths of adults over 65 in the United States have at least one living grandchild (Troll, 1980). Furthermore, most grandparents see or talk to their grandchildren regularly, often as frequently as every week or two. (My own grandfather would have written that often had I answered his letters more promptly!)

Despite the frequency of contact, however, the content of the grandparent role has the same fuzziness that characterizes many other roles in later life (Hagestad, 1985). To put it more formally, there are few normative expectations associated with the role of grandparent. The role is shaped quite differently in different families, in different ethnic groups, and in different contexts (Bengston, 1985).

For example, in a study of white, black, and Mexican-American grandparents and grandchildren, Vern Bengtson (1985) found that Mexican-American grandparents see their grandchildren more often, provide more help with their grandchildren, and report greater satisfaction with their relationships with their grandchildren. And Gunhild Hagestad (1985), in a study of three-generation families in Chicago, found that the role of grandmother seemed to be both broader and more intimate than the role of grandfather. The grandfathers gave advice, particularly about work or the world at large, and particularly to grandsons. The grandmothers gave advice about personal relationships as well.

But even within an ethnic group, or within groups of grandmothers and grandfathers, there are differences in the way the role is defined. Neugarten and Weinstein (1964), in one of the early studies of grandparenting style, identified five subsets: (1) formal, which involves clear separation between grandparent and grandchild, with occasional treats or a gift, or infrequent babysitting; (2) fun seeker, which involves informality and playfulness; (3) surrogate parent, a pattern in which the grandparent cares for the child part time; (4) reservoir of family wisdom, which is a largely authoritarian pattern in which the grandparent (nearly always the grandfather) is seen as the source of clear knowledge or authority; and (5) distant figure, a pattern in which the benevolent grandparent emerges "from the shadows" occasionally and fleetingly, such

***Figure 6–6*** *As life expectancy increases, more and more adults can expect to be grandparents, and a sizable number of us will be great-grandparents or even great-great-grandparents. Older adults seem to like this role best when they are in their 50s and 60s. Very young grandparents (who are "off time") like it less, as do older grandparents. (Source: Chester Higgins, Photo Researchers Inc.)*

as at birthdays and holidays. Neugarten's data and more recent studies (e.g., McCready, 1985) indicate that young grandparents are more likely to fall in the fun seeker or distant figure patterns. Older grandparents are more likely to follow a formal pattern, or perhaps (for a few grandfathers) a reservoir of family wisdom pattern.

Not only does the style of grandparenting differ from one adult to the next, but the psychological importance of the grandparenting role also undoubtedly varies. On the whole, however, the grandparenting role while extremely common appears not to be emotionally central to most older adults (Palmore, 1981). Life satisfaction in the elderly, for example, is not greatly influenced by the frequency of contact with grandchildren. Still, for many there may be considerable satisfaction from seeing one's family continue into the next generations.

# The Family Life Cycle in "Atypical" Families

Except for a few paragraphs on the unmarried, everything I have said so far in this chapter describes the life patterns of adults who follow a particular life course: They marry, have children, and remain married to the same spouse throughout adulthood. In fact, fewer than half of adults in the United States today follow such a life course. Approximately 5 to 10% remain unmarried. Of those that marry, approximately 10% have no children (Glick, 1977), and 40 to 50% of those who marry today will eventually divorce (Glick, 1984). Cumulatively, these figures mean that perhaps only 40% of all adults in the United States today actually follow the so-called "typical" pattern of the family life cycle. What can we say about the remaining 60%?

I want to focus my attention here on three kinds of "atypical" patterns: (1) married but childless adults; (2) adults who marry and have their children very early or very late, and who thus alter the timing of the family life cycle; and (3) divorced adults. Each of these groups is extremely interesting in its own right, and whole chapters could be written about them. (In fact, I will have more to say about divorce and its effects at several later points.) My interest at this point is quite selective: What is the impact of these deviations from the "normal" family life cycle on the roles and life experiences of an adult over the adult years?

## Childless Adults

One of the difficulties in analyzing the adult roles and life cycles of childless adults is that most researchers have not distinguished between the voluntarily and the involuntarily childless (just as those who study the impact of children on parents have not generally distinguished between intentional and accidental bearing of children). You should keep this point in mind, since I simply do not know to what extent the evidence fits both groups.

You should also bear in mind that most of the research on childless couples has focused on the early years of adulthood or (in a few studies) on the retired or elderly adult. We know very little about childlessness during middle age, and thus do not have a good view of the impact of childlessness over the full life cycle. The evidence we do have points to several conclusions.

First, childless women are more likely to work throughout their adult lives and to have somewhat higher-level jobs (Feldman, 1981; Hoffman & Manis, 1978). Hoffman and Manis, in their 1975 interviews with a sample of over 1,500 married women under age 40, found that over 80% of the childless women who had been married 6 to 10 years were working. This was considerably higher than the working rate of 43% for women with preschool children and 59% for women whose children were all over the age of five.

Whether women who have made a commitment to a career choose not to have children, or whether those who do not have children subsequently make a stronger career commitment is simply not clear from the available evidence. Probably both occur in different instances (Hennig & Jardim, 1976). Regardless of the reason, this difference in work pattern has an impact on career success, on income, and on the degree of investment the childless woman places in her work life, compared to the investment of a woman with children. In the Hoffman and Manis study, for example, 23% of the childless women who had been married 6 to 10 years chose "a sense of accomplishment" as their most important life value, compared to 7% of women with preschool children, and 13.5% of those with both teenagers and younger children. Childless men, in contrast, do not show any significantly different work pattern compared to men with children.

We know less about the impact of childlessness on other life roles. Childless men and women both report somewhat higher marital satisfaction than do couples with children (Anderson, Russell, & Schumm, 1983; Houseknecht, 1979). But we do not know whether childless adults show any consistent or age-related fluctuation in marital satisfaction over the duration of the marriages as we observe in those with children.

The final bit of information is perhaps the most surprising. You might expect to see some negative effect of childlessness in the later years, particularly when work roles diminish. But this seems not to be the case. There are several studies that show that among older adults (retirement age and later), happiness or life satisfaction is not related to the amount of contact the adult has with children or grandchildren (Lee & Ellithorpe, 1982; Lee & Ihinger-Tallman, 1980). Childless adults, at this life stage, also appear to be as happy as those with extended families (Glenn & McLanahan, 1981).

Collectively, these findings do not paint a picture of persisting sadness or distress among couples without children. On the contrary. But we are left with many questions: What are the differences, if any, between the voluntarily and the involuntarily childless? And what are the consequences for personality or personal growth of skipping the sequence of role changes associated with having children? We need to go beyond measures of "happiness" or "life satisfaction" as dependent variables in studies of childlessness and explore more subtle dimensions of adult functioning. Is it possible that, despite the increase in role conflict and role strain accompanying parenthood, parental roles may foster greater personal development, or higher levels of ego development in Loevinger's sense? Might substantive complexity of family roles have some effect on intellectual flexibility, just as substantive complexity of jobs does? These are questions that will need to be addressed by researchers in the future.

## Early and Late Marriage or Parenthood

Among those adults who do have children, a factor that may have a significant impact on the life course is the timing of marriage and children. Bernice Neugarten (1979) has long contended that each society lays out a typical timetable for major adult experiences. Any deviation from that timetable carries a price. Doing anything very early or very late ("unscheduled" in Pearlin's language) may have a significant impact on people's lives. Marrying and bearing children very early or very late seems to have a particularly marked effect.

In this case there is some decent longitudinal research to help sort out the effects of timing, although nearly all of it has focused on adults who marry and have their children very early. We know much less about those who delay childbearing until their 30s or 40s, although this is a growing (and extremely interesting) subgroup within the U.S. population, particularly among the better educated.

Marrying before the age of 18 has several distinct consequences, each of which helps to set the adult's life on a particular trajectory. Specifically, early marriage is associated with (1) having more children, more closely spaced together; (2) completing fewer years of education; (3) achieving lower levels of occupational success; (4) having lower income; and (5) having a higher probability of divorce (Doherty & Jacobson, 1982; Elder & Rockwell, 1976; Otto, 1979). These effects seem to hold even when social class is held constant, but the effects are generally larger for women than for men.

Let me give you some sample data from an eight-year longitudinal study of approximately 5,000 families who participated in the Panel Study of Income Dynamics (Moore, Hofferth, Wertheimer, Waite, & Caldwell, 1981). Figure 6–7 shows the percentage of women in this study who completed high school by the time they were 22 to 35, as a function of their age when the first child was born. You can see very clearly that in both black and white samples, having a first child while still in high school was associated with significantly lower rates of completion of high school. Given what we know about the effect of educational attainment on the life patterns of adults (recall chapter 2), you can see that early marriage and/or early childbearing has a long-term effect on the adult life course.

Being "off-time" or atypical in other ways also seems to exact a price. Hogan (1978), for example, has done an extremely interesting analysis of U.S. Census Bureau data for over 35,000 men ages 20 to 65. He argued that men who followed the expected or normal sequence of finishing school, getting a job, and then marrying should have lower divorce rates than men who deviated from this sequence, and this is precisely what he found. The highest divorce

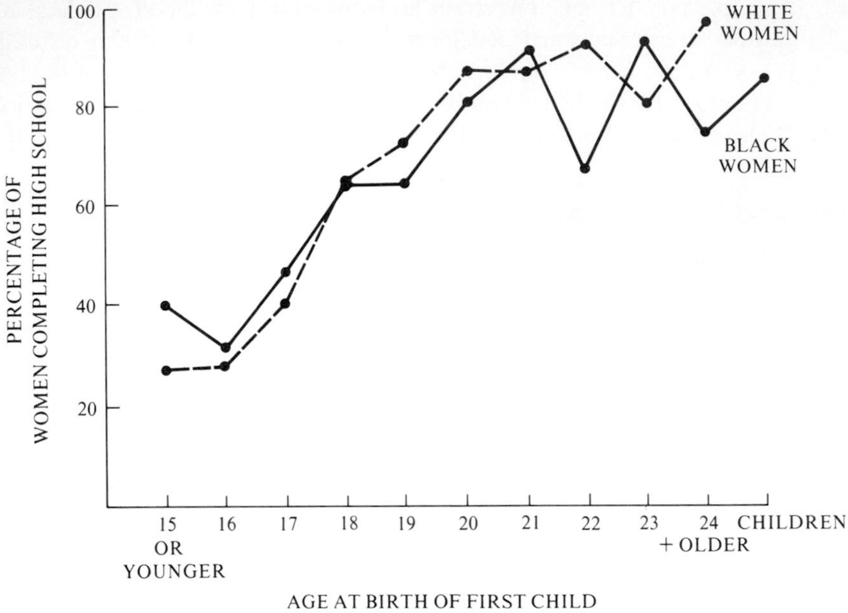


**Figure 6–7** *Women who bear their first child while they are still in high school (or under age 18) have a much smaller chance of completing high school. The particular group of women represented in this figure had been studied longitudinally over a period of eight years, so we also know that many of the early-birth groups did not go back to school at later points. (Source: Moore, Hofferth, Wertheimer, Waite, & Caldwell, 1981, data from Table 1, p. 39.)*

rates were for those who married before they finished school, regardless of their age or the level of school they completed; the lowest rates of divorce were for those who had followed the normative sequence.

In all of these studies, ''late'' marriage or childbearing is defined as anything past about age 24. But it is just as atypical to marry for the first time, or to have your first child, in your 30s or even 40s. If the ''off time is riskier'' theorum holds, we should find that such adults also pay a price. There are some supporting data. Divorce rates are higher, for example, among adults who marry after age 30 than they are for those who marry between 20 and 30, though not as high as among those who marry before age 20 (Kitson, Babri, & Roach, 1985). Beyond this, there are some obvious implications for family life among those who marry late. Delaying childbearing until one's 30s, for example, has the effect of pushing the entire family life cycle into the middle years, thus reducing the number of years spent in the postparental stage. Since this postparental period is one in which many adults experience heightened life satisfaction and higher marital satisfaction, delayed childbearing may reduce the pleasures of middle life. On the other side of the equation is the possibility that late childbearing may, in fact, be associated with greater pleasure in the parental role. Financial security may be higher, so that some of the role conflicts can be reduced by hiring assistance, and there may be greater willingness (on the part of fathers, particularly) to spend the time to create closer emotional bonds to their children.

At the moment, all of this is speculation. Until we have some data from studies of couples who significantly delay marriage and childbearing, we will not be able to determine the consequences of this form of ''off timeness.''

## Divorced and Remarried Adults

When we introduce divorce and remarriage into the family life cycle equation, the number of permutations and combinations becomes immense. I recall some years ago spending several hours with research colleagues trying to write a small set of questionnaire items that would clearly show the precise marital history and present family composition of each of our subjects. After we had found what we thought was a solution, I burst out laughing, realizing that the questions we were proposing would not have described my own family composition! Where in the normal descriptions of family constellations does an adoptive former-step-mother fit?

There are myriad ways in which we might explore the effect of divorce or remarriage on adult development. But since I will be talking about the personal and emotional impact of divorce on adults in chapter 11, when I discuss stresses of various kinds, let me focus here on the much narrower question of the impact of divorce or remarriage on family roles and the family life cycle.

Of the 40% to 50% of today's young adults who will eventually divorce, Paul Glick (1984) estimates that approximately 80% will eventually remarry. Most remarriages occur fairly shortly after a divorce. (The average interval between divorce and remarriage is about three years.) Men are more likely to remarry than are women, in part because they are likely to remarry a younger, never-married woman. Of those who remarry, about half will divorce a second time (Glick, 1984).

Although these patterns of marriage and remarriage produce a mind-boggling array of family types, divorce and remarriage patterns have a surprisingly small effect on some of the important points in the family life cycle, as you can see in Figure 6–8. What I have shown in this figure is Arthur Norton's (1983) analysis of 1980 census data, describing the cohort of women born between 1940 and 1949. (This is the same analysis, by the way, from which Figure 6–2 is drawn.) Norton divided this cohort into subgroups based on the women's marital history, and then compared these subgroups on the timing of significant family life cycle events. What I find surprising in these findings is that the total number of years in childbearing does not differ a great deal from one marital status group to the next, ranging from 4.6 years for the group married and divorced once, to 6.7 years for the group married three times. Obviously, most women who remarry do not start over with a new round of childbearing, which means that this aspect of family life cycle is not expanded a great deal because of divorce or remarriage.

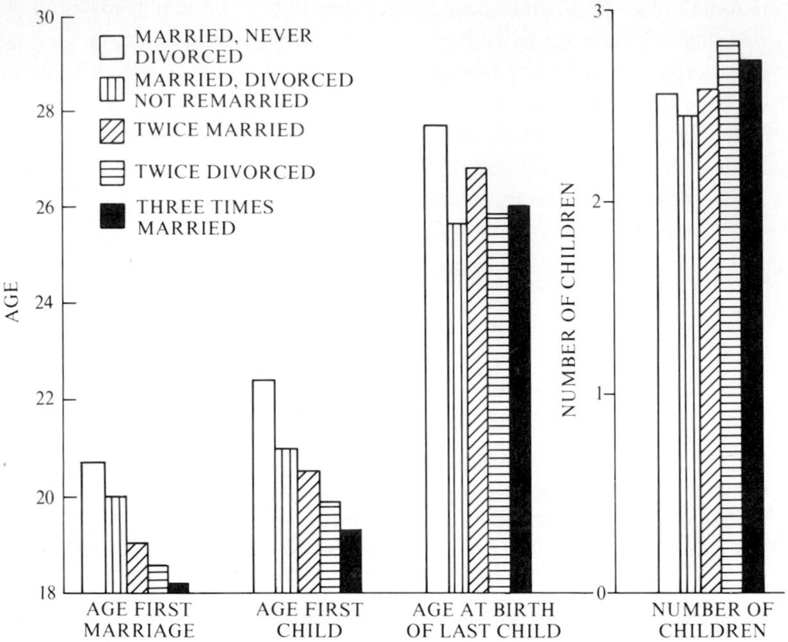


**Figure 6–8** *Surprisingly, there are only quite small differences in key family life cycle events for women who have remained married and those who have been divorced and remarried. These numbers are for the cohort of women born between 1940 and 1949, but similar patterns hold for women born in earlier cohorts as well. (Source: Norton, 1983, data from tables 2, 3, 4, 5, and 6, pp. 269–270.)*

At the same time, the years of childrearing may be increased for many divorced and remarried adults. This is especially true for men whose second marriage is to a woman much younger than themselves, who then have a second family or help to rear the new wife's young children. One effect of this is to shrink or even eliminate the postparental stage of the family life cycle for some.

While the effect of divorce on the timing of childbearing is relatively small, economic effects are large. There is ample evidence that divorce is accompanied by a precipitous drop in income, especially for women. In one recent study of a large sample of American families, Weiss (1984) found that among the middle class, income dropped by about a third, for the poor it dropped by about a fifth. For the adult with custody of children, there is also an enormous change in the family role structure. The single parent must fill essentially all of the adult roles (except spouse), including breadwinner, emotional supporter, housekeeper, caregiver, activities director, and chauffeur. For the adult without child custody, there are also new roles to be learned, including whatever roles the former spouse had been filling. Role conflict and role strain are thus virtually universal experiences accompanying divorce.

On remarriage, another set of roles is added. Spousal roles once again enter the repertoire, along with that of step-parent, or stepgrandparent, and those charmingly ambiguous role relationships with the former spouse of one's spouse, and with the spouse's former in-laws who remain the grandparents of your new stepchildren. If both spouses in a remarriage have children from former marriages, the family constellation now also includes stepsiblings.

Such expansion of the range of roles almost invariably increases both role conflict and role strain. In the short run, the effect of such role overload is to lower the quality of all role performances, and to lower marital satisfaction in remarried couples. Over the long term, however, it is at least possible that the increased adaptational demands, for at least some adults, could have positive effects on personal growth. As was true in the area of childlessness, this possibility remains to be explored.

## Match or Mismatch Between Personal Qualities and Role Demands

A particularly fruitful way to examine the impact of sex roles and family roles on personality and life experiences of individuals is to look at the extent to which an adult's personality or qualities matches the demands of the roles in which she finds herself. There is not a great deal of research of this type, but Florine Livson has provided some very provocative analyses of data from the Berkeley Intergenerational Studies that begin to move us in this direction (Livson, 1976; 1981).

Livson focused her attention on a group of men and women who, at age 50, were rated by the researchers as having particularly healthy and successful patterns of development. They were rated as having a high capacity for work and for satisfying interpersonal relationships, a realistic perception of themselves, and a sense of moral purpose. All of these adults had also been rated for overall health when they were about 40, so Livson was able to identify some who had been consistently healthy (the "stable" subjects), and some who had looked less integrated and healthy at 40, but looked good at 50 (the "improver" subjects).

When Livson then went back and looked at the information they had about each of these groups as adolescents and young adults, she found that for both men and women, those who had shown a pattern of stable, high emotional health were those whose personal qualities matched the sex and family roles prevailing for that cohort. In other words, both the men and women in this stable group were highly sex-typed. The men were focused on work achievement and supporting their families; the women were focused on providing nurturance to their families and on an array of friendships. By temperament, these women appeared to be highly extraverted and low in neuroticism. They liked staying at home and raising a family, and even at midlife, when the children were gone, they were quite content with their lives. The "improver" men and women, in contrast, had tried to fit themselves into the prevailing sex roles but the match had never been good. These groups included women who had been more strongly intellectually oriented as teenagers (not so acceptable in this cohort as it is now), but who had married at the expected time and followed the usual pattern of the family life cycle. By age 40, they were unhappy, thin-skinned, irritable. But by age 50, when they had reached the postparental stage, most had branched out into jobs or had returned to school.

Similarly, the "improver" men had been unconventional teenagers, but they tried to fit themselves into the gray-flannel-suit male role expectations of their generation. They too, at 40, were unhappy, with their emotions under tight, overly controlled rein. But by 50, they had allowed their artistic interests and humor to bloom.

Livson does not describe the life patterns of men and women who were less healthy at 50. But if the concept of "match" between personal qualities and role demands has any validity, we might expect to find that for this group an even greater mismatch occurred in the early life stages, or that they were unable to recover in midlife from the mismatches they had experienced at an earlier point.

Whether the concept of match or mismatch ultimately turns out to be fruitful or not I cannot say at this point; there is too little research. But I think that this concept points us in a very important direction in thinking about the impact of roles on adult lives. It is far too simple to think of a role as simply something that "shapes" the adult who occupies it. A role is, in some sense, like a piece of clothing that one puts on: It is bound to fit some people better than others. So it is the interaction between the demands and the flexibility of the role on the one hand, and the adult's qualities on the other that is crucial in determining the effect of the role. Thinking of roles in this way obviously makes the job of describing adult development far more complicated. But in my view it also brings us closer to the reality of adult developmental patterns.

# An Age Summary

As in earlier chapters, I have pulled together the various patterns of change with age in a summary table (Table 6–3) so that you can begin to build composite pictures of the qualities and experiences of adults in different age groups. The table points to at least one basic point about sex roles and family roles over the life cycle: The largest number of new roles are acquired in early adulthood. Family and sex roles change over the period of midlife, and there are a few new roles added (such as caregiver to an aging parent, and grandparent), but in later life it is the subtraction of roles and the loss of role content, that is striking. Thus, each of the three periods in the table is characterized by a different task or problem: In early adulthood, one must cope with learning new roles; in middle adulthood one must cope with changing definitions of existing roles; in late adulthood one must cope with the loss of roles.

**TABLE 6–3 Summary of Age Changes in Sex Roles and Family Roles**

| Age 20–40 | Age 40–65 | Age 65 and Older |
|---|---|---|
| Maximum sex role differentiation, particularly after birth of first child | Some sign of sex role crossover in this age range | Further indications of sex role crossover, with men becoming more emotional and expressive, and women more assertive |
| Role of spouse added | Spousal role changes after children leave home, when spousal roles become central | Spousal role changes further after retirement; role may be lost entirely at widowhood |
| Role of parent added | Role of parent changes after children leave home, becomes more distant, although assistance still provided | Role of parent changes significantly as the direction of assistance is reversed |
| Role of child to one's own parents continues, with young adults receiving more aid than they give | Role of child to one's own parents shifts toward more caregiving, less help received | Role of child to one's own parents lost when parents die |
| Grandchild role continues, but is usually not highly significant | Role of grandparent added | Role of grandparent continues, but becomes less central with increasing age |

# Summary

1. Sex roles, family life cycle roles, and work roles all show sequential changes over adulthood. Each sequence helps to shape the pattern and the rhythm of adult life for those who follow it.

2. Sex roles refer to the "job descriptions" for male and female behavior and qualities. Sex role stereotypes refer to the shared, excessively generalized beliefs about what men and women should be like. Sex typing refers to the extent to which any one adult's behavior or qualities matches the sex role for his or her gender. Masculinity, femininity, and androgyny describe aspects of the personality, or aspects of the self-concept, of individuals.

3. Sex role stereotypes are strong and have had a consistent content for at least several decades in the United States. The male stereotype centers around qualities of competence and instrumentality; the female stereotype centers around qualities of affiliation and expressiveness.

4. Stereotypes are not absolute; there is overlap between the expected behavior for men and women.

5. The content of sex roles changes over the adult years, with an intensification of traditional, differentiated sex roles apparent particularly in early adulthood, after the birth of the first child. In midlife, there may be a crossover of sex roles, with women expected to become more independent and assertive, and men becoming more affiliative and expressive.

6. Family roles also change in a sequence usually marked by the progression of the oldest child through a series of age stages. This sequence is typically referred to as the family life cycle. Each transition from one stage to the next involves addition, alteration, or deletion of roles.

7. Marital satisfaction, life satisfaction, and mental health all show some decline after the birth of the first child. Marital satisfaction rises again in midlife, after the departure of the last child.

8. The transition from singlehood to marriage for most adults involves an increase in happiness and a decline in the rate of physical and mental illness. In general, married men show the lowest rates of illness, with single men showing the highest. Married and single women fall in between.

9. The arrival of the first child ushers in a marked increase in the number of roles each adult must fill, with attendant increases in role conflict and role strain. The degree to which this disrupts the marital relationship depends on the extent to which the individuals can systematically reduce the role conflict or strain.

10. In midlife, the postparental period is marked by some increase in marital satisfaction for many adults, but it is also a time when adults may have increased role responsibilities with their own aging parents. Midlife adults give the most aid to both the older and younger generations.

11. The most marked change in roles in late adulthood is both a decline in the number of roles filled and a reduction in the content, or the clarity, of the roles still occupied. One new role of middle and late adulthood, grandparenthood, is a role filled by about three fourths of older adults. The content of this role varies widely from one adult to another.

12. The sequence of adult roles experienced by childless couples is quite different. Childless women are more likely to have jobs outside the home, and are more likely to devote themselves to a career. Childless couples report higher marital satisfaction, and in old age do not report lower life satisfaction than do adults who reared children.

13. Very early marriage and parenthood also alters the life pattern. For both men and women, but more strongly for women, marriage or parenthood under the age of 18 is associated with fewer total years of education, lower work success, lower income, larger families, and higher probability of divorce.

14. The divorced adult, too, shows somewhat different patterns of roles over adulthood. Divorced and remarried women do not spend appreciably more years in childbearing, but both men and women who have been divorced may spend more years in childrearing if they remarry someone with children of different ages from their own. The number and complexity of roles assumed by the divorced and remarried is also markedly higher than for the never-divorced.

15. Understanding the impact of role sequences and role demands on the development of individual adults requires us to go beyond the simple dependent variables so far studied. Particularly fruitful is the concept of the "match" between the personality or temperament of an individual and the demands of the roles he or she must fill. Where the match is good, we expect less stressful and perhaps more optimum adult development. Where the match is poor, the adult will experience higher levels of stress and lower levels of physical and mental health.

## Suggested Readings

Block, M. R., Davidson, J. L., & Grambs, J. D. (1981). *Women over forty: Visions and realities.* New York: Springer.

This is a very readable, brief, interesting book that addresses some of the questions I have been raising in this chapter.

DEAUX, K. (1984). From individual differences to social categories: Analysis of a decade's research on gender. *American Psychologist, 39*, 105–116.

This is a very good, current review of the topic. It deals less with sex roles than with other aspects of gender, but is an excellent source.

NEUGARTEN, B. L. (1979). Time, age, and the life cycle. *American Journal of Psychiatry, 136*, 887–894.

Neugarten has consistently talked about the impact of timing of events in adult lives. I find her style wonderful and her ideas provocative.

WINSLOW, T. S. (1980) Grandma. In R. Lyell (Ed.), *Middle age, old age: Short stories, poems, plays, and essays on aging*. New York: Harcourt Brace Jovanovich.

This is a short story about a grandmother who visits each of her three offspring and their families for four months. If you are tired of reading all the statistics and theories, you may find this a refreshing change.

# 7

# Development of Relationships in Adulthood

Take a moment and think about some of the most joyous and some of the most painful moments or times in your life. Perhaps graduating from high school or college, getting promoted, or becoming a parent are on your list of joys. Your list of painful moments may include getting fired from your job, or that day you got your first really bad grade in school. Certainly many of life's highs and lows have to do with family roles or work experiences. But I will wager that most of the joys and pains you thought of first were connected to a few key relationships—with your parents, with your partner, with your friends. In particular, the processes of attachment and detachment, of creating and breaking bonds with others, lie at the heart of many of the turning points in our lives.

In the last chapter I talked about some of the key roles that involve family and relationships, focusing primarily on the form and timing of those roles. Here I want to look inside the roles, at the quality of the relationships themselves. Are there age-linked changes in the quality or quantity of relationships over adulthood? Are there typical changes in the number or type of friends we have over adulthood? Does the relationship between partners (spouses or lovers) go through predictable changes over time or over age? Do relationships with our parents or our growing children change in specific ways over the adult years?

A second theme will be individual differences in relationships or relationship patterns. What differentiates satisfying or lasting marriages from dissatisfying marriages? What are the differences between adults who have many friends and those who have fewer?

# Attachment, Love, and Social Support: Some Definitions

If you begin to explore the literature on relationships in adults, you will find at least three descriptive words or phrases used: **attachment** (Bowlby, 1969, 1973, 1980; Kahn & Antonucci, 1980), **love,** (e.g., Rubin, 1973; Sternberg & Grajek, 1984), and **social support** (e.g., Kahn & Antonucci, 1980). There is a great deal of overlap in the use of these three terms, but it seems worthwhile to maintain at least some distinctions.

## Attachment and Attachment Behavior

The concept of attachment has been most fully used to describe the strong affectional tie formed by an infant to her major caregiver (e.g., Ainsworth, Blehar, & Waters, Wall, 1978; Bowlby, 1969). Typically, a distinction is made between the attachment itself, which is an invisible, underlying bond, and **attachment behaviors**, which are the ways that underlying attachment is expressed by the individual. Weiss (1982) suggests that in infants, three key features mark the presence of an attachment: (1) association of the attachment figure with feelings of security; (2) an increased liklihood of attachment behavior when the child is under stress or threat; and (3) attempts to avoid, or to end, any separation from the attachment figure. Infants smile more at the special person, explore new space more readily when the special person is nearby, turn to the special person in times of fright, and attempt to maintain contact with or nearness to that special person.

John Bowlby, one of the most influential attachment theorists, has maintained all along that the attachments of childhood persist into adulthood, and that new attachments are formed in adulthood to one's partner or friends (Bowlby, 1969, 1973, 1980). Following Bowlby's lead, in recent years the language of attachment theory has crept into a number of discussions of adult relationships (e.g., Kahn & Antonucci, 1980; Lerner & Ryff, 1978; Troll & Smith, 1976; Weiss, 1982). It is important, though, to be careful about such extensions of theoretical language. It is one thing to use ''attachment'' rather loosely to describe intimate adult relationships, but it is quite another to suggest that the bonds formed between adults are qualitatively the same as those formed by an infant for a parent.

At the very least, it is clear that the specific attachment behaviors change with age. Most adults do not burst into tears if their special person leaves the room; most adults maintain contact in a much wider variety of ways than what we see in children, including the use of letters, phone calls, fantasy, and imagery in addition to face-to-face interaction. But if we allow for these changes in the *form* in which the attachment is expressed, it does appear that strong attachments are formed in adulthood, particularly to one's spouse or partner, to some close friends, and possibly in a continuing way toward one's parents. As Weiss says:

> In all these instances individuals display need for ready access to the attachment figure, desire for proximity to the attachment figure in situations of stress, heightened comfort and diminished anxiety when in the company of the attachment figure, and a marked increase in discomfort and anxiety on discovering the attachment figure to be inexplicably inaccessible. (1982, p. 173)

A personal experience brought this final point home to me very clearly. I was recently separated from my partner under circumstances that made it impossible for me to contact him even by phone. Given the dictates of our separate careers, we have been apart many times. Separation itself is not anxiety provoking. But I found his inaccessibility quite surprisingly uncomfortable. I was plainly relieved when he was once again available, if only by phone.

Assuming that this use of the concept of attachment is valid for at least some adult relationships, it remains an open question whether all relationships between adults are forms of attachment. Are casual friendships merely "weak" attachments? Is your relationship to your grandparents, or your aunts or uncles, a kind of attachment? Many authors use the term in this way, but it seems useful to distinguish between attachments and what Weiss (1982) calls **affiliative relationships.** The latter category includes most friendships and a great many family relationships. For some adults even the relationship with their parents is an affiliative one rather than an attachment. If you are upset or lonely, does being with your parent still relieve that distress? Do you have friends whose presence eases any anxiety you may be feeling? If so, then it is an attachment; if not, then it is an affiliative relationship of some other kind. Thus, each person may have a small set of key relationships properly called attachments, which are different not just in intensity but also in quality from a broader range of friendships or personal connections.

## Love

A similar distinction between *loving* and *liking* is common in the theory and research on love in adulthood. As Zick Rubin (1973) defines it, liking includes the feelings of respect and affection, while loving includes caring and intimacy. (For example, Rubin includes the item "In my opinion, ______ is an exceptionally mature person" in his measure of liking, and the item "If I were lonely, my first thought would be to seek ______ out" as part of the love scale.) Both liking and loving are part of most relationships, but it is possible to like someone one does not love, and love someone one does not like. (Think about your own relationships for a moment, and see whether you can identify some examples of each kind.)

Research on love in adults suggests that the elements that make up a loving relationship are very similar across relationships. Your love for your parents,

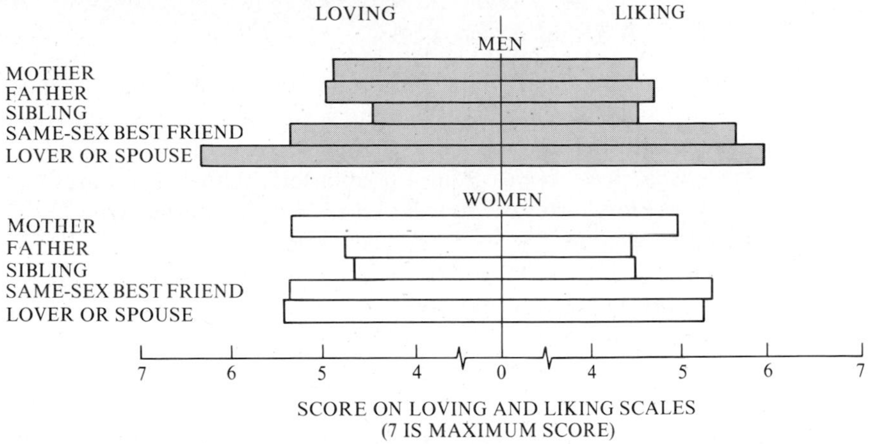


***Figure 7–1*** *Scores on Zick Rubin's Love scale and Liking scale for a group of adults describing their relationships with their mother, father, closest sibling, best same-sex friend, and spouse or intimate partner. In this study, the structure of the love and liking scales were essentially the same for all of these relationships, but as you can see, the level of love or liking felt by the respondents differed depending on the relationship. (Source: Sternberg & Grajek, 1984, data from Table 1, p. 318.)*

for your partner, for your friends is made up of very similar pieces, such as compatibility, a sense of personal benefit from the relationship, sharing, and a sense of mutual support (Sternberg & Grajek, 1984). But the level or amount of love differs from one relationship to the next, as you can see in Figure 7–1.

**Attachment and Love Compared.** There is clearly a great deal of overlap between the concept of attachment and that of love. In fact, Rubin includes attachment as one of the defining attributes of love. But there are nonetheless some differences in the ways these terms are used. Attachment seems to be more of an on/off phenomenon than is love. You are either attached or you are not. In contrast, you can love someone a lot or a little.

Furthermore, attachment can vary in quality. Ainsworth, for example, distinguishes between *secure* and *insecure* attachments (Ainsworth et al., 1978). In both cases there is a strong, compelling emotional bond, but in a secure attachment the child or adult is more readily comforted by the special person, and is less anxious or frightened when in the presence of that individual. Insecure attachments often involve more ambivalence, with the individual both approaching and avoiding the attachment figure at different times and receiving less comfort. In contrast, love appears to be a more unitary phenomenon, having much the same quality across relationships. I will use the term *attachment*, then, when talking about the presence (or absence) of some basic affectional bond between two individuals. I will use the term *love* to describe one dimension of an attachment or affiliative relationship.

## Social Support: A Third Approach

The third term currently used to describe relationships among adults is *social support*. Unlike attachment or love, however, both of which describe the quality or quantity of a person's link to some other individual, social support describes what one receives from a relationship. Although we also give support to those we love, like, or are attached to, most of the literature on support has focused on what we get back from such relationships.

Kahn & Antonucci (1980) suggest that social support has three elements—**affect, affirmation,** and **aid.** We receive social support to the extent that we receive affection, warmth, love (affect); expressions of agreement or acknowledgment (affirmation); and direct assistance, such as money, advice, information, and time (aid).

As you will see in chapter 11, the amount of social support available to an adult at times of stress has a powerful effect on nearly every facet of adult life and development. In this chapter, I want to focus less on these supportive effects of relationships, and more on the quality of the relationships themselves over the course of adulthood. Beginning with the relationship with a partner (spouse or lover), and then moving to consideration of other family ties and friendships, let me explore the developmental patterns and the individual differences in attachment and affiliation, loving and liking.

# Intimate Partnerships

I have quite purposely chosen to use the term *partnership*, rather than *marriage*, since I want to include here both long-term committed homosexual relationships and unmarried but committed heterosexual relationshps. The vast majority of the research, however, describes marital relationships, so those of you interested in other forms of partnership may find this discussion somewhat lopsided. Limited recent research on cohabiting heterosexual and homosexual couples, though, reveals that many of the same choice and interactional processes occur as are found in marriages.

## Finding a Partner

The process of mate selection preoccupies most of us in our teens and 20s (for many adults, it becomes a preoccupation again after a divorce). We are searching for a partner with whom we hope to spend the rest of our lives. Just what attracts one person to another? How does a couple move past acquaintance to commitment? Why do some early combinations break up, while others become stable? Social scientists have tried very hard to answer these questions, but despite the efforts, understanding still largely eludes us.

The most widely accepted theories describe mate selection as a series of "filters" or steps. Murstein, for example (1970, 1976, 1977), suggests that when you meet a prospective partner you first check for the degree of match on basic "external" characteristics, such as appearance, or manners, or apparent social class. If this first hurdle is passed, you then check for a match on attitudes and beliefs, such as politics, sex, or religion. Finally, if you are still interested in one another, the degree of "role fit" becomes an issue: Do your prospective partner's expectations fit with your needs or inclinations? Is there sexual compatibility or agreement on sex roles?

There is some support for filter theories of courtship, but the filtering process probably occurs very early in the courtship process rather than over a period of months or years, as Murstein originally suggested (Windle & Lerner, 1984), and may not follow a strict sequence. The one thing that is clear is that we chose our partners more on the basis of similarity than on any other single basis—similarity in background, religious involvement, interests, attitudes, and temperament (Huston, Surra, Fitzgerald, & Cate, 1981).

Several studies of couples who eventually marry also show that there are distinct changes in facets of the relationship as the couple moves from casual dating to greater commitment to marriage (Braiker & Kelley, 1979; Huston et al., 1981). Feelings of belongingness and attachment increase over time as do "maintenance behaviors" (disclosing feelings, trying to solve problems, being willing to change in order to please the partner). Both ambivalence and conflict also increase early in relationships, with the peak just before a commitment to marriage is made, after which they decline. Huston and his colleagues also found a sex difference in these patterns: Men, compared to women, reported higher levels of attachment early in the relationship during the phase of more casual dating, while women described higher levels than did men of "maintenance behavior" once a commitment had been made. Women appeared to be more cautious about forming an attachment or making a commitment; once it was made, they took on more of the task of relationship maintenance—a standard female sex role task in this culture.

**Marriage Versus Cohabitation.** Once a commitment has been made, today's couples face another choice: cohabitation or marriage. Graham Spanier (1983) estimates that in 1981 there were 1.8 million cohabiting heterosexual couples. This is about 5% of all couples, and is more than triple the number seen in 1970. Cohabiting couples come from all age groups and social backgrounds, but are on average somewhat less educated than are married couples. Cohabiting women are more likely to be working than are married women, though, and have somewhat higher-level jobs. Thus, cohabiting seems to be a choice made somewhat more by "two-career" couples.

Most couples who live together conceive of cohabitation as a final "filter," a sort of "test" before marriage. Can we really get along together? Are we sexually compatible? The assumptions are that relationships that pass this test will end in marriage, and that such marriages will be more satisfying and more durable. Interestingly, the current evidence, if anything, shows exactly the opposite. Recent studies show that cohabiting couples who eventually marry, in comparison to married couples who did not live together before marriage, are neither more nor less likely to divorce, but are less satisfied with their marriages and have poorer communication (DeMaris & Leslie, 1984; Watson, 1983).

The most likely explanation of this surprising set of research results is not that cohabiting somehow spoils people for marriage, but that adults who choose to live together before marriage are systematically different in key ways from those who reject such an option. DeMaris and Leslie (1984), for example, find that cohabiters are less traditional in sex roles, less likely to attend church, and less likely to agree that one should stick with a marriage no matter how bad it is. Whatever the explanation, these preliminary research findings do not support the idea that cohabitation is a good "training period" for marriage.

## Development of Partnerships over Adulthood

Of greater interest to me as a developmental psychologist is the nature of change in partnerships over time or over age. Are there predictable changes in the quality or content of the relationship as adults pass through various steps and stages?

I have already talked about one set of answers to such questions, namely, the curvilinear relationship between marital satisfaction and family life stage (recall Figures 1–7, 1–8, and the discussion in chapter 6). But such results only skim the surface.

Delving slightly deeper, we can look at the ingredients that make up marital satisfaction. At each age, elements such as emotional security, respect, communication, sexual intimacy, and loyalty enter into feelings of satisfaction. But some research shows that these are weighted somewhat differently by young and old couples, as you can see in the findings from one study (Reedy, Birren, & Schaie, 1981) in Figure 7–2. Older couples appear to place a somewhat higher value on loyalty and emotional security and a somewhat lower value on self-disclosure and sexual intimacy than do younger couples.

There is also some indication that satisfaction is composed of a different balance of positive and negative feelings at different points in the life cycle. This possibility emerges from one of my favorite studies, by Clifford Swensen and his colleagues (Swensen, Eskew, & Kohlhepp, 1981). Swensen's sample of 776 adults spanned the spectrum of family life cycle stages. Each subject was asked to describe aspects of both loving and problematic marital interactions. The resulting "love scale" describes the expressions of affection, self-disclosure, moral support and encouragement, material support, and toleration of the less pleasant aspects of the other person. The "marital problems" scale describes the degree of problems experienced in six areas: problem solving and decision making, childrearing and home labor, relationships with relatives and in-laws, personal care and appearance, money management, and expressions of affection. You can see the relationship between the scores on these two scales and family life cycle stages in Figure 7–3. The older age groups described their marriages as having fewer problems, but they also reported fewer expressions of love. Swensen calls these older marriages "devitalized," despite the fact that net marital satisfaction was quite high.

Support for both aspects of this pattern comes from the 1957 and 1976 na-

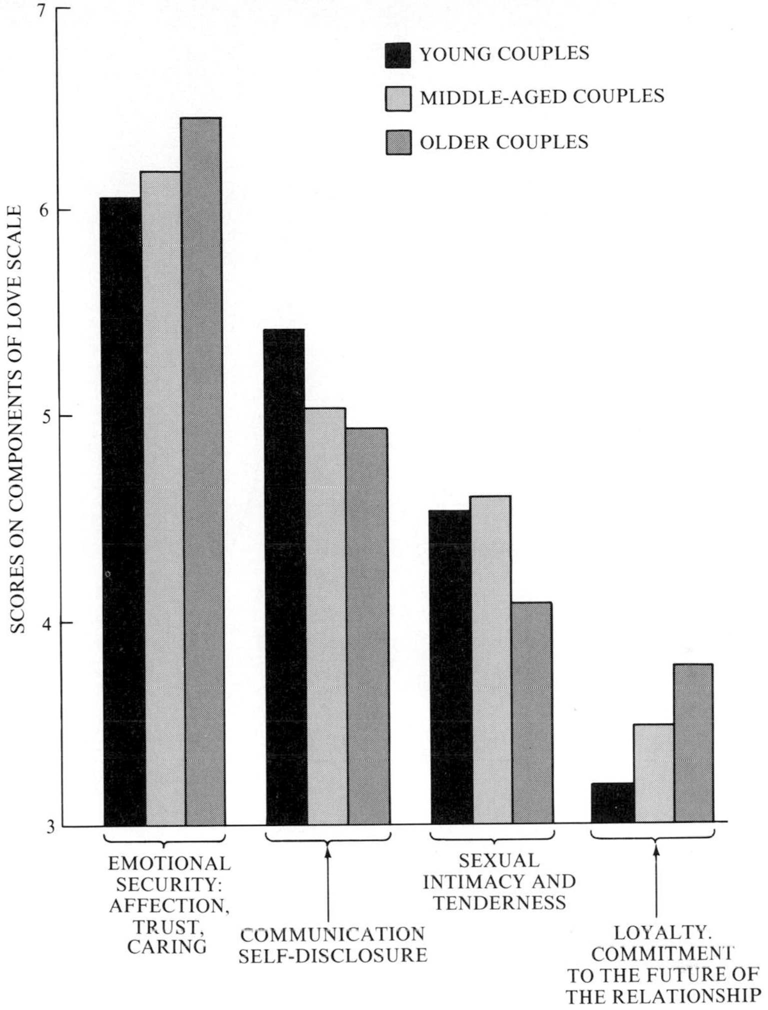


**Figure 7–2** *Love for one's spouse seems to be composed of the same basic ingredients at every age, but the relative importance of those ingredients is somewhat different for older and younger couples in this study. (Source: Reedy, Birren, & Schaie, 1981, data from Table II, p. 58.)*

tional survey samples studied by Veroff and his colleagues (see Table 1–2; Veroff, Douvan, & Kulka, 1981). At both time points there was a steady decline in marital problems reported by age groups from 21 to 65+. At the same time, the frequency of physical affection also declined with age. Interestingly, though, the researchers found that the frequency of reported "chatting" between spouses increased slightly with age, particularly for the least educated groups of men.

In attachment theory terms, then, it may be that one of the patterns of change

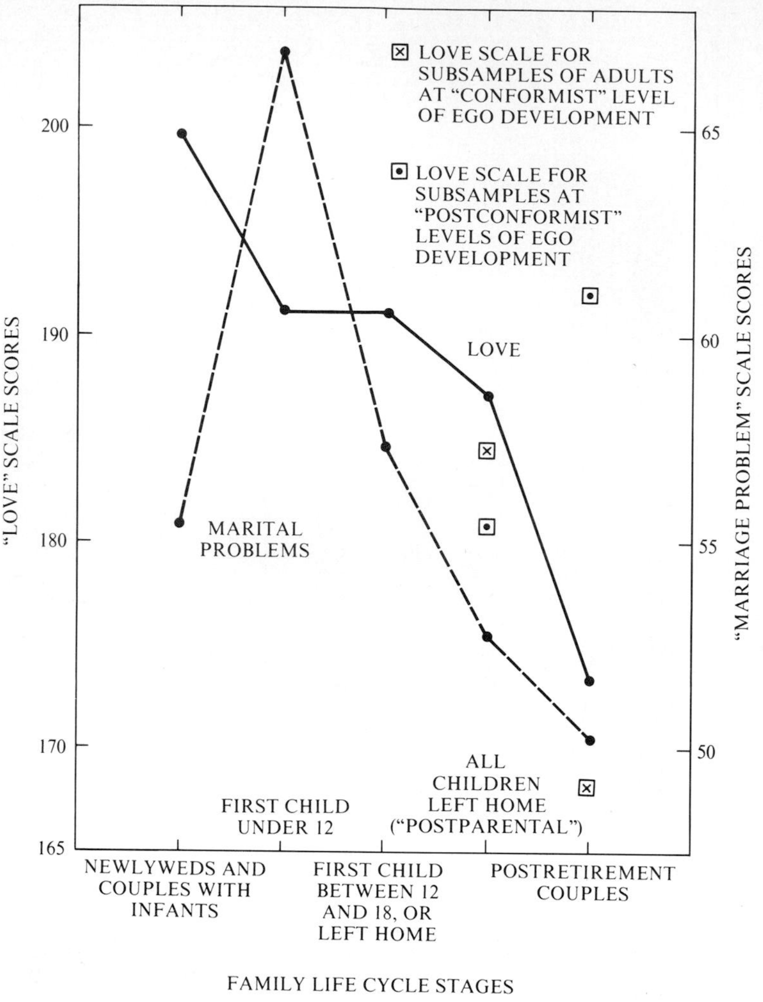


**Figure 7–3** *When these researchers measured expressions of love and marital problems in couples at various stages of the family life cycle, they found a pattern that helps to explain the curvilinear relationship between marital satisfaction and life stage. Satisfaction may be low when children are young because marital problems are high; satisfaction may rise later in life because problems decline, although expressions of love also decline. The latter pattern, however, was not typical of those retirement-age adults who scored at postconformist levels of ego functioning on Loevinger's scale. (Source: Swensen, Eskew & Kohlhepp, 1981, Figure 1, p. 848, and data from Table 3, p. 849. Copyrighted 1981 by the National Council on Family Relations, 1910 West County Road B, Suite 147, St. Paul, MN 55113. Reprinted by permission.)*

in marriages over the adult years is a decline in frequency of certain classes of attachment behaviors. Whether this signals a weakening of the attachment itself, I do not know. Certainly older adults continue to turn to one another in times of stress, and show marked distress at the death of the spouse—both signs of an enduring attachment. But attachment behaviors in the absence of stress may become less common, just as they do in children over the early years of life. And this reduction in overt expression of affection may affect the security of the attachment.

But not all late-life marriages show such emotional devitalization. Happily, Swensen pursued this possibility by assessing a subset of his two oldest groups of subjects on Jane Loevinger's measure of ego development (see Table 3–2 for a review). When the subjects were divided into those at the conformist level of ego development, and those at the post-conformist level, Swensen found (as you can see in Figure 7–3) that those older adults rated as functioning at the post-conformist level had very high scores on the love scale, compared to those rated at the conformist level. Swensen says:

> Post-conformists are able to transcend role expectations and form relationships based more upon the reality of needs, feelings, wishes, and aspirations of the individuals. They are more capable of coping with conflict through discussion rather than avoidance, and so form relationships in which vitality, as measured by the expression of love, may increase over time. (Swensen, Eskew, & Kohlhepp, 1981, p. 850)

A quite different way of looking at marriages over age has been offered by Jane Traupmann and Elaine Hatfield (1983). They have been interested in couples' perception of **equity** in relationships—the sense that oneself or one's partner is getting a "better deal," or that both are benefiting equally. When Traupmann and Hatfield asked married women aged 50 to 92 to rate the equity of their marriages in each decade of adult life, they found that, on average the women recalled their newlywed period as a time in which they had had a slightly better deal. The middle years of adulthood (30s, 40s, 50s, 60s) were a time the women remembered as inequitable in the other direction—they saw their husbands as having a somewhat better deal. But in their 70s and 80s, the women thought their relationships had become remarkably equitable. Whether men's reports of equity over adulthood would be a mirror image of this, I don't know, since equivalent data have not been collected for men. But these initial findings are suggestive and help to turn our attention away from a too thorough preoccupation with marital satisfaction as the major dependent variable.

Obviously, I would like to see a great deal more research focused on a wide range of potential changes (or stabilities) in aspects of partnership relationships over the adult years. Do communication skills within partnerships improve with age? Do partners share more and more interests with age, or do they branch out into independent activities? Does the role of confidant become more or less central a part of marriage over time? Further, I would like to see more research like Swensen and colleagues' study, in which change in partnership relationships is linked to changes in other dimensions of functioning—personality and physical and mental change. In particular, two hypotheses intrigue me: First, might the higher levels of marital satisfaction in late midlife observed by so many researchers occur in part because proportionately more adults at these ages have progressed to more mature levels of personal development? Second, among adults at any given age or family life cycle stage, might the quality of relationships be positively correlated with an individual's overall maturity or ego development? This is not to say that all of the changes with age that we see in the nature of relationships are due to individual growth. Relationships have histories and developmental dynamics. But relationships do not exist in a vacuum. They are influenced by, and influence in turn, each partner's personal developmental patterns or sequences.

It is wise to remember that virtually all of the information we have on age-related patterns of marital interaction comes from cross-sectional comparisons. In this case, in addition to the usual problems of interpretation of developmental trends from cross-sectional data, there is another serious problem: Length of marriage and age are totally confounded in virtually every study. This means, for example, that those couples who report quite high levels of satisfaction in their 50s and 60s are couples who have been married 25 or 30 years (or longer). Many of the couples who were dissatisfied have dissolved their marriges and are no longer in the population of middle-aged married couples. So far as I

**Figure 7–4** *If you go out to a restaurant and see a couple like this one, not talking to each other much, looking a bit bored, you are quite likely to conclude that they have been married a long time. One of our stereotypes is that old married couples don't have much to say to one another. Some of the research on devitalization of marriage, though, lends some support to this stereotype. (Source: Mimi Forsyth, Monkmeyer Press.)*

know, no one has yet looked at new marriages at each age to determine if the same curvilinear patterns would hold. Thus, we do not know whether the high level of satisfaction reported at 55 or 60 is characteristic of all marriages at that point in the life cycle, or only of long-term marriages.

## Good and Bad Marriages

A second way we can look at partnerships is through the study of good and bad or stable and unstable marriages. This very large body of research is non-developmental. No one, to my knowledge, has asked whether different elements contribute to marital breakdown or success at different points in the adult life cycle. But we may nonetheless glean some insights into the workings of this key relationship by a brief journey through the literature. I have summarized some of the key conclusions from this research in Table 7–1, giving recent references for each.

As you look at the items in this list you may be struck by some of the same points that stood out for me as I read this literature. When a marriage begins, some couples have a lot of good things going for them. Others start out with a few strikes against them. In general, as Lewis and Spanier (1979) point out, the more "resources" a couple has—such as more education, more commu-

**TABLE 7–1 Some Differences Between Satisfying or Lasting Marriages and Dissatisfying or Unstable Marriages**

| Personal Characteristics of Individuals in More Successful Marriages |
|---|
| They married between age 20 and 30 (Kitson, Babri, & Roach, 1985; Lee, 1977). |
| They come from high social-class families and have more education (Lewis & Spanier, 1979). |
| They have greater communication skill and greater cognitive complexity (Bruch, Levo, & Arisohn, 1984; Markman, 1981). |
| They are more likely to be highly involved in religion (Filsinger & Wilson, 1984; Heaton, 1984). |
| They have higher levels of self-esteem (Schafer & Keith, 1984; Skolnick, 1981). |
| **Qualities of the Interaction of Couples in More Successful Marriages** |
| They have high agreement on roles (including sex roles) and high satisfaction with the way the spouse is filling his/her role(s) (Bahr, Chappell, & Leigh, 1983; Bowen & Orthner, 1983). |
| They are roughly matched on levels of self-disclosure (high, medium, or low in both partners) (Davidson, Balswick, & Halverson, 1983; Hansen & Schuldt, 1984). |
| They have high levels of "nice" interactions and low levels of "nasty" ones (Gottman & Levenson, 1984). In particular, there is more reciprocation of negative behavior in poor marriages. |
| They have lower levels of stereotyped or highly predictable behavior patterns; in dissatisfied couples, behavior patterns are more strongly routinized (Gottman & Levenson, 1984). |
| They have better conflict resolution strategies, with low levels of both criticism and problem avoidance (Gottman & Levenson, 1984). |
| They are more symmetrical in their skill at reading each other's signals. In dissatisfied marriages, the husband appears to "read" the wife less well than she reads him (Gottman & Levenson, 1984; Gottman & Porterfield, 1981). |
| They like each other and consider their spouse to be their best friend (Lauer & Lauer, 1985). |

nication skill or problem-solving ability, better physical and emotional health, and greater individual self confidence—the better their chances of forming a satisfying intimate relationship (Ridley & Nelson, 1984). In the case of self-esteem, there are even some supportive longitudinal data. Using data from the Berkeley Intergenerational Studies, Skolnick (1981) compared the self-concepts at adolescence and early adulthood of three groups of middle-aged adults: happily married, unhappily married, and divorced. She found that those with satisfying marriages had the highest self-concept (the greatest self-esteem) at every earlier age at which they had been studied (adolescence and early adulthood). Those with unsatisfying but enduring marriages had the lowest self-esteem, with the divorced group falling in between.

If we use the language of Erikson's theory, then it looks like those young adults who have successfully completed the step of forming a clear (and positive) identity have a much better chance of creating a lasting and satisfying intimate partnership.

But the other point that struck home for me in this body of research was the fact that the personality or even the skills each partner brings to the relationship are by no means the most critical ingredients in a happy marriage. Far more important is the pattern of interaction the partners create together. Obviously, the skills each partner brings to the relationship affect the interaction pattern in some important ways. In particular, the ability to communicate clearly seems to be an especially important skill that some adults bring to their marriages, which enhances their interaction. But any partnership is a dynamic system, not merely the sum of the individual personal skills or qualities. Couples work out their own ways of dealing with conflict, of expressing affection, of handling day-to-day encounters.

The most consistent interactional difference between happy and unhappy couples is simply the "niceness" or "nastiness" of everyday encounters. In one typical finding, the ratio of pleasing encounters to displeasing ones was about 30 to one for happy couples, but about four to one for distressed couples (Birchler, Weiss, & Vincent, 1975).

Differences also appear when researchers have looked at more complex chains of interaction. John Gottman's research is particularly fascinating (e.g., Gottman & Levenson, 1984). He has studied conflict resolution in couples and finds distinct differences at every stage in the process, from the "agenda-building" stage, through the "arguing" phase, to the "negotiation" phase. For example, in the agenda-building phase, dissatisfied couples are more likely than satisfied couples to engage in what Gottman calls "cross complaining:"

WIFE: I'm tired of spending all my time on the housework. You're not doing your share.

HUSBAND: If you used your time efficiently, you wouldn't be tired.

Throughout a difficult discussion, satisfied couples are more likely to acknowledge a partner's comments—even with something so simple as "That's true, but . . ." or "Yeah"—before offering their own arguments or solutions. If one listens to prolonged sequences, the striking thing is the way in which satisfied couples continually de-escalate any build-up of negative feelings, while the dissatisfied couples allow (or encourage) such negative emotion to build.

Fortunately, the patterns are not immovable. Therapists who work with couples have found that marital satisfaction can be significantly increased by teaching couples how to solve conflicts, how to talk to one another, how to increase their positive interactions. So couples whose interactions have moved slowly toward stereotyped, negative, escalating discord can acquire new skills or relearn earlier patterns of interaction.

The direction of causality is difficult to determine in all this. Do couples develop negative, stereotyped, and insensitive ways of interacting because they are already dissatisfied, or do they become dissatisfied because their interactions are so negative? Probably it is both, but the fact that overall satisfaction can be increased by teaching couples how to interact more positively suggests that to at least some extent it is the interaction style that affects the satisfaction, and not merely the other way around. To a considerable degree, couples seem to be unhappy because they are negative, not negative because they are unhappy.

The final point that comes to my mind when I look at this research is the parallel between descriptions of interactions of satisfied couples and descriptions of interactions of "securely attached" infants with their caregivers. In both cases there is an atunement, a mutual rhythm, a smooth turn-taking. When this rhythm is disrupted in childhood—such as when an infant can't give good signals, or when the parent is not engaged or consistently available—then we see a pattern of insecure attachment, often characterized by alternating clinging and rejection or unconsolable distress. Similarly, the rhythm may be disrupted (or may never be established) in adult relationships if one or both partners comes to the relationship lacking the needed personal skills, or if one or both partners withdraws emotionally from the relationship, or if the particular combination of interaction patterns in the partnership meshes poorly. Then the interactions become less and less positive, with the partnership spiraling toward disruption.

Obviously, there are important differences between the relationship of an infant with her mother or father, and the relationship of two adults in a marriage or a long-term, committed relationship. But I find the parallel a helpful one in my own thinking about marital satisfaction. What I would like to see now is some exploration of the development of satisfying or dissatisfying relationships over time. How does a couple shift from smooth, positive interactions to more conflicting ones? More generally, do the same qualities characterize satisfying and dissatisfying relationships in couples of all ages, or at all stages of the family life cycle, or at all points in the length of a marriage? Only when we have research dealing with such questions will we be able to approach a truly developmental look at intimate partnerships in the adult years.

## Homosexual Relationships

Accurate numbers are virtually impossible to obtain, but perhaps 2% to 5% of adults in the United States are exclusively homosexual, with another 3% to 5%

typically, but not exclusively, homosexual (Paul & Weinrich, 1982). Virtually all surveys show higher rates of homosexuality for men than for women, but it is not clear whether this reflects greater willingness to report gay experiences among men, or a genuine difference in frequency.

All summary statements I can make about gay relationships must be taken with great caution. Since this group is a "hidden" minority, a large percentage is unwilling to participate in research or even to acknowledge their sexual orientation openly. Inevitably, what we know about adult homosexuals and their relationships comes from studies of a subset, primarily those who are fairly well educated and those who are "out" about their homosexuality. Whether this subgroup is at all typical of the larger group of gays, researchers do not know.

A number of recurrent findings have emerged from this research, however, which I can summarize briefly:

1. Long-term, committed relationships are very common among homosexuals, particularly among lesbians. Estimates vary, but perhaps 70% of lesbians are in committed relationships, in most cases living together (Peplau & Amaro, 1982). Among gay men, the percentage is lower, perhaps 45% to 50% (Bell & Weinberg, 1978; Larson, 1982). Among lesbians, monogamy within a

**Figure 7–5** *Long-term, committed relationships, largely monogamous, are the rule rather than the exception among lesbian couples. (Source: Hella Hammid, Photo Researchers Inc.)*

long-term relationship is about as common as in heterosexual relationships (marriage or cohabitation), but monogamy is much less commonly a feature of gay male relationships. In one large national study, for example, sociologists Philip Blumstein and Pepper Schwartz (1983) found that 72% of lesbians in long-term relationships had been monogamous, compared to 79% of married women. In contrast, only 18% of gay men had been completely monogamous within their current relationship, compared to 74% of married men.

2. Homosexual relationships are, on the whole, more egalitarian than heterosexual relationships, with less sharp role prescriptions. It is quite uncommon for homosexual couples to have one partner occupy a "male" role and the other a "female" role. Instead, power and tasks are more equally divided. Again, however, this is more true of lesbian couples—among whom equality of roles is frequently a strong philosophical ideal—than for gay males. Among male homosexual couples, the man who earns the most money is likely to have greater power within the relationship (Blumstein & Schwartz, 1983). For example, one gay male in the Blumstein and Schwartz study, who was the more economically successful of the pair, said:

> I'd like him to come up with some ideas for free time together. But then he can't come up with ideas for free time that require spending money, which he doesn't have. Like theater, plays, travel. If he made those decisions, he wouldn't have the money to do it . . . So we do those things when I suggest it and feel like doing it. (p. 60)

3. Satisfying and dissatisfying homosexual relationships differ in essentially the same ways as equivalent groups of heterosexual couples (Peplau & Amaro, 1982). Like marriages, gay relationships are more likely to persist and be satisfying if the two individuals are similar in background and interests and equally committed to the relationship. I know of no research that has explored the specific interactional patterns in satisfied and dissatisfied gay couples, but I would be surprised if the key dimensions of communication patterns were substantially different from what has been observed in heterosexual couples.
4. We know essentially nothing about age-related changes in relationship satisfaction or partner interaction patterns in homosexual couples. There are neither cross-sectional nor longitudinal studies available. There is some indication that long-term, committed relationships are more common among older than younger homosexuals, but no evidence one way or another about any curvilinear pattern of satisfaction within long-term relationships.

In sum, homosexual relationships are far more like heterosexual relationships than they are different. While long-term, committed, intimate pairings are less common among gay men than among other groups, when such commitments are made, they involve love and strong attachment. Many last a lifetime. Since homosexual relationships by definition involve two people who have both been socialized toward the same sex role, there are some differences in the dynamics of gay male and lesbian relationships. But the human urge to form one close, intimate, central attachment is as evident in gay relationships as it is in heterosexual relationships.

# Relationships with Other Family Members over the Life Span

With so many adults living longer, and with high divorce rates and remarriages, the term *family* these days may describe a far more complex set of relationships than was true even a few generations ago (Riley, 1983). At any one time, a family nearly always includes three generations, and many include four. As I write this, my own family includes four generations, and the oldest of the great grandchild generation is 24. So if my 92-year-old grandmother lives a few more years, there may be five living generations in the lineage. One of the key implications of this is a fact I pointed out earlier: Increasing numbers of middle-aged adults still have living parents.

With more generations, the sheer number of people with whom one is linked by family ties goes up, including not only one's own in-laws, but the in-laws of one's children or one's grandchildren. All of this is made still more complex when divorce and remarrige has occurred. To use my own family again as an (admittedly extreme) example, divorce and remarriage has occurred in three succeeding generations, which creates patterns so complex that I have to draw genealogical charts to explain the relationships to others. There are stepgrandmothers, step-stepuncles, and many stepcousins. As Matilda Riley points out (1983), when the family is so broad, personal relationships within the family group cease to be based on obligation or fixed kinship roles, and become more and more determined by choice. One can pick and choose among the array of relatives those with whom one wants a closer, more intimate relationship. I have, for example, very friendly relationships with two of my stepbrothers and their families, and, with the natural maternal grandmother of my two adopted children.

Research on family relationships in adulthood has not yet caught up to this complexity. Most research attention has been directed toward parent-child relationships, with a lesser emphasis on sibling relationships or grandparent-grandchild links. There is essentially no information available on relationships between stepsiblings, or even with in-laws (let alone former in-laws). Certainly parent-child relationships are among the most enduring and the most central for many adult lives. In the future, though, I hope we will see explorations of a broader array of family connections and their effects on adult pathways.

## General Patterns of Family Interaction in Adulthood

One of the consistent findings in research on family interactions in adulthood is the remarkable consistency with which we all maintain contact with our parents and siblings. Geoffrey Leigh's recent study shows this very clearly (1982).

Leigh interviewed a total of about 1,300 adults, spanning the full series of family lifecycle stages. Each adult reported how frequently he or she saw, spoke with, or wrote to parents, brothers and sisters, cousins, and grown children. Figure 7–6 shows the major findings for parents, siblings, and children. As you can see, there is no real sign of any age-related, or life cycle-stage variation in contacts with family members except for a slight decline in frequent contact during the "new parent" stage. In this study, virtually all adults, whatever their age, reported at least some kind of contact with their parents at least monthly, and the majority also had regular contact with siblings. Cicirelli (1983) estimates an even higher level of contact, suggesting that "between 78 and 90 percent of all older people with living children see their children once a week or more often and are in contact with them by telephone at about the same frequency" (p. 33).

As usual, these are cross-sectional results. We do not know that today's 20-year-olds will still have regular contact with their parents when they are 50 or 60, for example. But the consistency of such findings, in studies of several different cohorts, points to the stability of the pattern. Family relationships are a part of our lives throughout adulthood.

Just what is the content of those relationships? Do they involve strong attachments? Do we provide aid to our parents and our children? Do we continue to try to influence each other over time? The answer to these questions is, briefly, "sometimes," "yes," and "yes." Let me amplify.

## Parent-Child Relationships in Adulthood

**Attachments Between Adult Children and Parents.** Think about your relationship to your mother or your father, or your relationship with your own grown children (if you have any) and see whether you would agree with statements like these: "We're emotionally dependent on each other." "When we anticipate being apart, our relationship intensifies." "Our best times are with each other."

If you agreed with these statements about your relationship to your parents (or children), then it's fair to describe you as being attached. Clearly, some adults do retain strong attachments to their mothers or fathers and to their grown children. Still, despite the high rates of contact between family members, there are a number of reasons for supposing that a strong adult parent-child or child-parent attachment is the exception rather than the rule. Certainly for most adults the attachment to parents is weaker than the attachment to spouse.

One reason for thinking that parent-child attachments are not invariably strong is that when adults are asked to agree or disagree with the sort of statements I just gave, the average score (out of seven such statements) is only about four. Many adults simply do not describe their relationships with their parents in terms that fit the definition of attachment (Thompson & Walker, 1984). A more

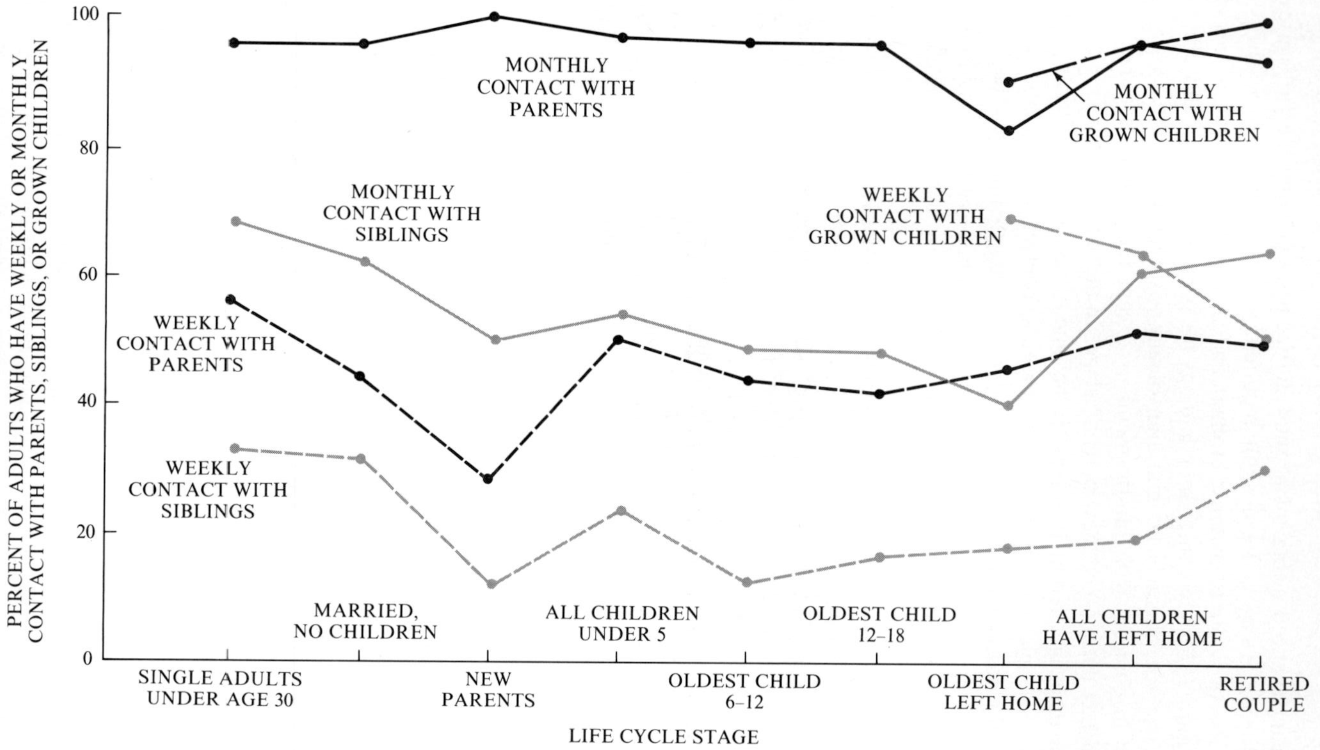


**Figure 7–6** *Contact between adults and their parents, siblings, and grown children seems to remain remarkably constant over adulthood, judging from these (and similar) results from a 1976 survey. Virtually all adults have at least monthly contact with their parents; about half talk to, write to, or see their parents at least weekly. Contact with siblings is less frequent, but still steady over the life span. (Source: Leigh, 1982, data from Table 2, p. 202.)*

significant piece of information comes from studies of life satisfaction among older adults. In several large, well-designed studies, Gary Lee (Lee & Ellithorpe, 1982; Lee & Ihinger-Tallman, 1980) found that for adults over 50, the amount of contact with children was not related to their overall pleasure or happiness. The adults in these studies did have regular contact with children and grandchildren, and said they enjoyed it. But family interaction was not necessary for their sense of wellbeing. That does not sound like a deep attachment.

Cicirelli's (1983) summary captures the quality of this relationship:

> While the [parent-child] relationship is not one of day-to-day contact or close personal intimacy, neither is it one of mere obligation, pseudo-intimacy, and estrangement. . . . Instead it is characterized by closeness of feeling between parent and child, an easy compatibility between them, a low degree of conflict, and a good deal of satisfaction. (p. 45)

Certainly some parent-child relationships can accurately be described as strong attachments, but many may be more accurately described as affiliative relationships or as weak attachments.

When a strong attachment does persist, it is more likely to involve a mother-daughter relationship than any other combination (Baruch & Barnett, 1983; Hagestad, 1984). But even mother-daughter relationships vary markedly. Two interesting studies by Linda Thompson and Alexis Walker (Thompson & Walker, 1984; Walker & Thompson, 1983) give us some insight into the elements in mother-daughter relationships that may affect attachment.

Thompson and Walker studied three-generational families of women, with a grandmother, a middle-aged mother, and a college student granddaughter. In general, whenever the pattern of assistance or support in these pairs is uneven—such as when a middle-aged mother is providing high levels of assistance to her aging mother, or to her college daughter but is not receiving assistance in return—intimacy and attachment are lower. The best predictor of high attachment in these women was a high level of reciprocal assistance or contact. Findings from studies of middle-aged adults (primarily women) who take on major caregiving responsibilities for an elderly parent underline the same point: The affection and attachment to the parent weakens as the interaction becomes less and less reciprocal, or more and more a burden (Cicirelli, 1983). For the parent generation, too, receiving aid from children but being unable to reciprocate is associataed with lower morale (Stoller, 1985).

These results are particularly interesting because they suggest that attachments in adults may be in this respect quite different from child-parent attachments in infancy or early childhood. The relationship between an infant and an adult involves some reciprocity, but there is certainly no reciprocity of assistance or even affection. Yet both the parent and the infant normally become strongly attached. In adults, if these studies can be generalized, unequal commitment or assistance patterns (a lack of "equity" in the terms of the Traupmann and Hatfield study I discussed earlier) seems to weaken attachments.

Another general point about parent-child attachments, at least in women, is that they appear to be somewhat stronger among unmarried than married women (Baruch & Barnett, 1983). Whether this is so because the unmarried woman has more time to create a pattern of reciprocal interaction with her parents, or whether the parent-child attachment in single adults in some sense takes the place of a central marital attachment, I do not know.

**Patterns of Aid Between Adult Children and Their Parents.** As is already clear from the discussion of attachment, a key dimension of the parent-child interaction in adulthood is the system of assistance, advice, and aid that they give to one another. I already discussed one of the significant elements of this aid system in chapter 6: The middle-aged generation gives the most assistance both upward and downward through the generations and receives the least (see Figure 6–5). They are, in a word, the "sandwich" generation.

But this heightened level of assistance does not fall equally on middle-aged men and women. In this culture at least, it is the woman who provides the most help—to her own parents and to her own children. Even when there is no daughter in the middle generation of a family, the son typically does not take over the major responsibility for assistance to the older generation. The responsibility is likely to fall instead on his wife, the daughter-in-law (Hagestad, 1984; Shanas, 1979).

Given the fact that so many more adults are living well into old age, and given the increasing number of middle-aged women now working full time, the heightened need to give aid and assistance both upward and downward in the family chain puts a significant strain on many middle-aged women. It creates a kind of "demographic double bind" (Treas, 1979). Gunhild Hagestad (1984) points out that this strain may be particularly acute if the youngest generation in the family chain has also gotten "off track," such as a mid-20s son or daughter who is still unemployed and living at home.

Just how much assistance these middle-aged women need to provide to their parents depends, of course, on the mental and physical health of the parents and on other sources of support the parents may have. It is comparatively uncommon for an older parent to share a house with a child. As you can see in Figure 7–7, in 1983, among those not in institutions, only 18% of women and 6% of men over 65 were living with relatives other than a spouse. Most of these "other relatives" are children.

Such figures may be misleading, however, since many older adults who live separately nonetheless require assistance—with shopping, or trips to the doctor, or dealing with Social Security or Medicare forms, or doing the housework, or preparing meals. In one study of a group of 161 middle-aged women and their mothers, Lang and Brody (1983) found that the daughters gave about eight to nine hours of all types of assistance per week to their mothers. About half of the daughters were involved in regular care, such as meals, housework, or helping with bathing and dressing. The older the mother, the more such care she was likely to need. And the more the daughters had other key roles to fill—such as their own marriages and jobs—the less assistance they provided.

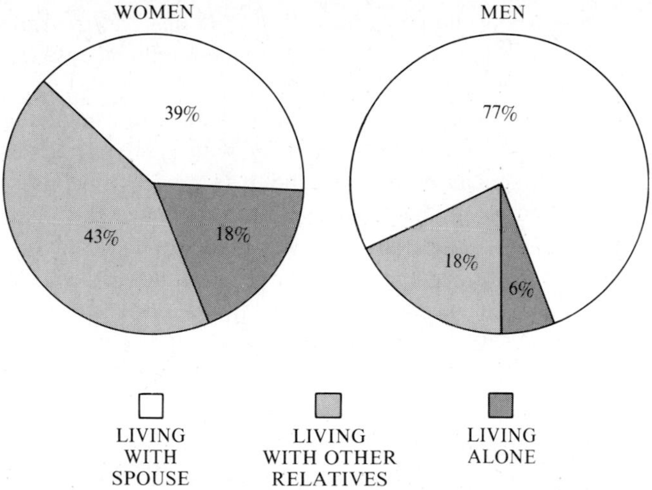


**Figure 7–7** *Living arrangements of men and women over age 65 in the United States in 1983. These figures include only those adults who were not institutionalized; an additional 5% of older Americans are in hospitals or nursing homes. Older women are more likely to live with other relatives (primarily their children), largely because they are so much more likely to be widowed. But for both sexes, living with one's children is the least common pattern. (Source: "A Profile of Older Americans, 1984," American Association of Retired Persons, based on data from the U.S. Census Bureau, Figure 3, p. 4.)*

I do not mean to imply here that relationships between middle-aged daughters and their parents are made up of nothing but long hours of somewhat grudging assistance. In most cases there is mutual respect and affection as well as the sense of obligation and responsibility. But it is clear that middle-aged daughters are likely to bear the brunt of the responsibility, and that their relationship with older parents is likely to become more strained when the parents' need for aid increases.

**Influence Attempts Between Parents and Children**. Parents and children not only provide affection and assistance to one another, they also give each other advice, try to change each other's opinions, and attempt to influence each other's behavior. You may try to get your parent or child to stop smoking or to eat better (however you define that). You may give advice about investments, or jobs, or how to handle money, or try to persuade your parents or children to vote in a particular way. Advice and influence attempts, in fact, make up a large percentage of the interactions within families. Gunhild Hagestad (1984), who has done some of the most interesting research on family interactions, interviewed three generations of adults in 150 families, asking each family member about the ways in which he or she had tried to influence the others, which other family members had tried to influence them, and how successful those influence attempts had been.

In these families, advice up the generational chain from middle-aged child to older parent dealt most often with health or with practical matters such as where to live, how to manage the household or money, and uses of time. Middle-aged adults also tried, but had less success, influencing their parents' attitudes on current social issues and on internal family dynamics. Older parents gave advice to their middle-aged children on subjects such as health, work, and finance. The youngest generation in these families tried to influence their own middle aged parents as well, particularly regarding health, social attitudes, and the uses of free time. These younger adults helped their parents "keep up with the times."

Two other suggestive patterns emerged from Hagestad's research, both of which gave me food for thought about my own family and other families I know. She observed that in these three-generation families, parents were more likely to try to influence their children than the reverse, and this was true in both generational pairs (grandparents/parents and parents/grown children). Interestingly, though, the influence attempts from children to parents were more likely to be successful. Only about a third of the advice or influence attempts from parents to children seemed to be effective, while about 70% of the influence attempts in the other direction found their mark. As parents, we don't seem to give up trying to influence our children, even when our children are in their 50s or 60s. But our children listen quite selectively! Perhaps in the process of emancipation from parents in the late teens, most young adults learn to tune out many kinds of parental advice, and this pattern persists. But as our children become adults, we begin to tune them in, listening more openly to their suggestions.

Another of Hagestad's observations was that each family seemed to have a certain set of themes or topics that acted like a kind of glue, holding the family together. Different members in the same family tended to talk about the same things, describing the same types of advice or influence. Some families talked about their relationships and spent a lot of time giving each other advice or trying to change each other's behavior in those relationships. ("Don't you think you should write to your brother?" "I wish you and Dad wouldn't argue so much about money.") Other families almost never talked about relationships, but talked instead about money or jobs. Generational chains of men (grandfather, father, grown son) were more likely to focus their advice and influence on such practical matters, while generational chains of women spent more time on relationships; but each family also had a characteristic "agenda," and this agenda seemed to be a powerful force for cohesion across the generations.

All in all, family interactions are clearly highly complex, with many layers of subtlety and depth that researchers have only begun to plumb. Some parent-child links seem not to be characterized by extremely strong emotional attachments, but they are nonetheless characterized by strong patterns of habit, family tradition, assistance, and influence. The most complex positions in the family chain appear to be the ones in the middle—the generations that have both parents and grown children. Over a lifetime, each of us moves through these generational positions, acquiring new roles and learning the changing "rules" of relationships at each step.

## Relationships with Brothers and Sisters

Emotional bonds with brothers and sisters appear to be generally weaker than those with parents, but they nonetheless persist over the entire lifetime for most adults. In fact for most of us, a relationship with a sibling will be the longest single family connection we will experience in our lives. The vast majority of adults (about 85%) have at least one living sibling, and for current cohorts at least, this continues to be true well into old age (Cicirelli, 1982). (Younger cohorts today, however, coming from smaller families, may be less likely to have living siblings in their later years.)

Descriptions of sibling relationships in everyday conversation range from exceptional closeness, to mutual apathy, to enduring rivalry. While rivalry and apathy certainly both exist, the research suggests that some kind of physical and emotional closeness is the most common pattern (Cicirelli, 1982; Scott, 1983). As you can see from Figure 7–6, the majority of adults have fairly frequent contact with siblings. It is really quite rare for a person to lose contact completely with brothers and sisters. Most write or call fairly regularly and see one another on family occasions or for brief visits.

When adults are asked to describe the closeness of their relationships with siblings, a very high percentage (about 80% in Cicirelli's studies) say they are "very close" or "close." And the closest relationships appear to occur between siblings who were close as children; it is rare for adults to become close for the first time in adulthood (Dunn, 1984; Ross & Milgram, 1982). Yet even those who describe their links to their siblings as close say that they do not often talk over important decisions or discuss intimate questions with their brothers or sisters. Mutual assistance is also fairly rare among siblings, especially in early and middle adulthood. Even in later years, when sibling relationships seem to be somewhat stronger, mutual assistance is the exception rather than the rule. Jean Scott (1983), for example, in a study of sibling relationships in a group of older adults (aged 65 to 90), found that 72% of her subjects received no help at all from siblings.

The impression I get from all these facts and figures is that many sibling relationships are pleasant and affectionate, but not terribly intense. There is an attachment of some kind, but it does not appear to be a central one for most adults. Nonetheless, that attachment is maintained across many decades, and may become stronger in old age. There is something about being the oldest living generation in a family that intensifies feelings of closeness. At that point, you and your brothers and sisters are the only ones alive who shared a particular set of experiences—a particular family in a particular era. Those shared memories form a solid basis for the continuing bond.

# Friendships in Adulthood

If you made a list of the significant people in your life, the list might well include your parents, your children, your brothers and sisters, or your boss or a significant co-worker. But a large portion of your list would be made up of friends. We do not get to choose our kin; often we have little control over work relationships. But we choose our friends.

## What Is a Friend?

How shall we define friendship? Psychologists and sociologists who have studied friendship in adulthood have used many different definitions, which makes it extremely difficult to add up the findings. If you think about your own friendships for even a moment it will be clear that they run the gamut from close confidants to rather casual pals with whom you share particular activities. John Reisman (1981) divides this continuum into two parts, which he calls **associative friendships** and **reciprocal friendships,** a distinction similar to the one I made earlier between affiliative relationships and attachments.

The stronger, more intimate, reciprocal friendships involve mutual feelings of affection, loyalty, and emotional disclosure. Such friends seek each other out, desiring and enjoying one another's company (Hartup, 1975; Reisman, 1981). In a talk on friendship I once gave to a group of middle-aged professionals, I suggested two somewhat homelier "tests" of a genuinely intimate friendship: A good friend is one who does not "keep score" of who owes whom a favor or time; a good friend is someone you are always glad to see, no matter what the circumstances—your hair in curlers, or while sick with the flu, or when the baby has just spit up all over your shirt.

In a great deal of the research on friendship in adulthood such a distinction between casual and reciprocal friendships has not been maintained. Most often, subjects have merely been asked to say how many friends they had, without being told just how "friend" should be defined.

Despite this serious limitation, and despite the (usual) lack of longitudinal information, there are still some consistent and interesting patterns.

## Choosing Your Friends

We do not choose our friends randomly. There are some well-established principles that seem to apply, many of them very similar to the principles of partner-selection I discussed earlier.

The most general statement is that we chose people as friends whom we see as similar to ourselves in age, in gender, in social class or education, in interests or attitudes, in family life cycle stage (Dickens & Perlman, 1981; Norris & Rubin, 1984). This does not mean that all of your friends are your own age or gender. Many adults (perhaps 30% to 40%) have cross-gender friendships, and older adults are more likely to have friends who are not their own age. Still, similarity is a powerful first filter. Propinquity is also part of the equation. Our friends come from among those who live near us, such as those who live on the same floor in a dorm, or those who live on the same block or in the same neighborhood as your family home. Work colleagues, who share both similarity and frequency of contact, are also a pool from which friends are drawn.

Past the point of first acquaintance, similarity and propinquity play a much smaller role. As is true of potential mates, a second filter seems to be the willingness of the other person to be open about feelings (Hays, 1984). Particularly in the early stages of friendship, and particularly for women, such intimacy is a key ingredient in those friendships that move beyond acquaintance to closeness. Other key qualities enhancing friendships are loyalty, warmth, affection, and supportiveness (Parlee, 1979).

## Friendships over the Adult Years

These "rules" for making new friends seem to apply at every age, but most of us make more new friends in adolescence and early adulthood than we ever will again. The general pattern is of a fairly steady decline in the numbers of friends adults have from early adulthood at least through late middle age. There may be an increase in number of friends later in life, but the evidence here is simply contradictory. Some researchers find that the decline continues through old age (e.g., Fischer & Phillips, 1982). Others find an increase in the 50s or 60s (e.g., Lowenthal et al., 1975). I suspect that the differences may lie in the way "friendship" is defined. My own hypothesis is that the sheer number of friends, counting both associative and reciprocal relationships, probably does decline steadily over all of adulthood. But the number of intimate friends, or the average level of intimacy of all friendships, may increase in the postparental or retirement periods.

You can see some of these trends in Figure 7–8, which shows the results of a study of 500 men aged 25 to 48 in the Boston area (Farrell & Rosenberg, 1981). These men were describing close friendships, and as you can see, they didn't have many. But the older men had fewer than the younger men. Frequency of contact and intimacy of the relationship also declined through about age 40 or 45, after which there is at least a hint of an increase.

It would be a mistake to read these (and comparable) data as saying that the older you get, the lonelier you will be. While personal networks do contract with increasing age, and 13% of adults over 65 report that loneliness is a serious problem for them (Harris, 1981), fewer older people describe themselves as lonely (Peplau, Bikson, Rook, & Goodchilds, 1982). As Peplau and Perlman define it, loneliness arises when there is a discrepancy between the amount of social contact you want and the amount you have. So although older adults have a smaller set of friends and kin with whom they interact, they apparently either want less or are more satisfied with the interations they do have.

The age differences in reported loneliness are very striking. In one survey,

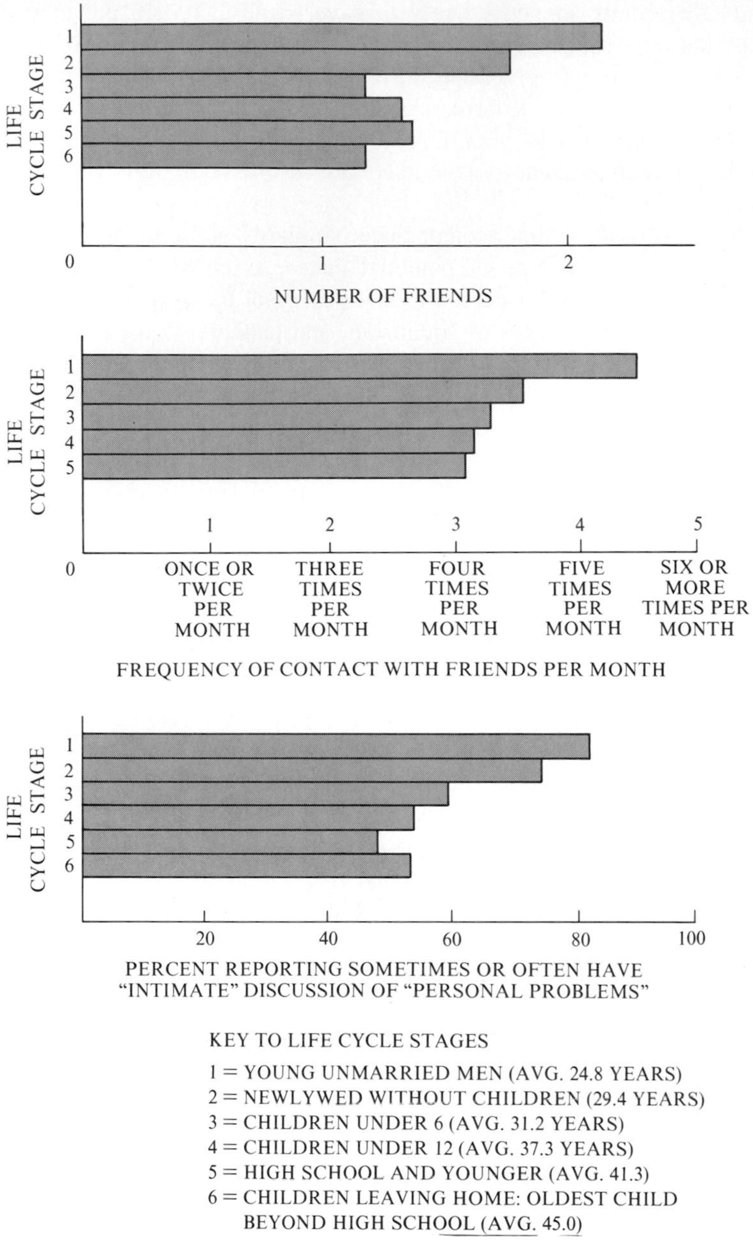


**Figure 7–8** *This group of working-class and middle-class men in the Boston area reported on the number of their friends, how often they had contact with them, and how often they discussed personal problems with their friends. All three measures decline with age, but there are hints of an increase in intimacy in the oldest group. (Source: Farrell & Rosenberg, 1981, data from Tables 9–3 and 9–4, pp. 195–196.)*

79% of young adults 18 to 24 years old said they felt lonely sometimes or often, compared to 60% of those 35 to 40 years old and 37% of adults over 55 (Parlee, 1979). These differences may mean that older people simply have more realistic expectations, or enjoy their own company more. But the decline in loneliness could also be the result of higher quality of friendships and family relationships over the adult years. In support of the latter interpretation is the fact that the older you get, the longer you are likely to have known your good friends (Dickens & Perlman, 1981).

If I can go beyond the data here, my sense of the developmental pattern is that in early adulthood, we make many friends and have a wide circle of acquaintances. Since it takes time to develop deeper, more intimate relationships, most of these early friendships are not very close. During the next decades, as family and work roles consume most of our time and energy, we make few new friends, but a few of the old friends remain, helping to create what Kahn and Antonucci call a relationship "convoy" that travels with us through the years. In late middle age, when work and family roles ease, there is time to extend the network of close friendships and to deepen existing friendships. This process continues into old age.

Of course, not everyone follows such a pathway. Some young adults do not form a large "convoy"; many of us find friendships weakened by distance, as we move away from our hometown, or when a good friend takes a job somewhere else. And in old age, good friends may die first, leaving the older person with a still smaller network. But there do appear to be broad developmental patterns in the number, intensity, and centrality of friendship in adult lives.

## Some Individual Differences

This general developmental picture differs in important ways, though, for several subgroups of adults. Most notably, there are consistent sex differences in friendship patterns in adulthood. Oversimplifying somewhat, I can state the difference baldly: Men have larger networks of friends (counting both "associative" and "reciprocal" friendships), but women's friendships are more intimate, involving more mutual self-disclosure (Dickens & Perlman, 1981; Reisman, 1981). Another way to describe the difference is to say that men do things together and women talk—usually about feelings (Bell, 1981).

One of my favorite quotes, from a 38-year-old male executive interviewed by Robert Bell (1981), makes the point clearly and poignantly:

> "I have three close friends I have known since we were boys and they live here in the city. There are some things I wouldn't tell them. For example, I wouldn't tell them much about my work because we have always been highly competitive. I certainly wouldn't tell them about my feelings of any uncertainties with life or various things I do. And I wouldn't talk about any problems I have with my wife or in fact anything about my marriage and sex life. But other than that I would tell them anything. [After a brief pause he laughed and said:] That doesn't leave a hell of a lot, does it? (p. 81–82)

I do not mean to imply that men have no close friends, nor even that men are necessarily less satisfied with their friendships. But these differences in the content or style of friendship may reflect a more fundamental sex difference. As Carol Gilligan has suggested (1982), women's identity may simply be more *interdependent* while men's identity is more *independent*.

There are some important implications of this difference in relationship pattern. There is a strong, accumulatiang body of evidence (which I will discuss in detail in chapter 11) pointing to the importance for emotional health and development of having at least one intimate relationship. If men's friendships are less intimate, it means that—in our society at least—men may be at greater risk for finding themselves in stressful situations without a confidant.

A second dimension of difference running through the research on friendships in adults is social class. In general, working-class adults (and most of this research is on men) appear to have fewer close friends than middle-class adults (e.g., Bell, 1981; Farrell & Rosenberg, 1981). In contrast, kin relationships (parents, children, siblings, etc.) seem to be closer in working-class families than in the middle class (Dickens & Perlman, 1981). In other words, the total size of the social network may be about the same for adults from different social strata, but the network is composed differently. Just what the causes, or consequences, of such differences in network compositions may be for adult development I do not know. But such a difference is definitely worth further study.

## Relationships in Adulthood: An Overview

Table 7–2 summarizes the myriad age-linked patterns in relationship I have talked about so far. Some of these are curvilinear patterns, some reflect increases, and some reflect declines in relationships. On the face of it, there seems to be little consistency. But there are some linkages that strike me.

In the very early years of adulthood, perhaps 18 to 25, it looks as if virtually all relationships are highly significant. This is the period that Erikson describes as the stage of intimacy versus isolation, and that label seems to capture the flavor well. Adults in early adulthood arc searching for and forming intimate partnerships, and typically are highly satisfied with their marriages. They also have large networks of friends, creating that "convoy" of relationships that will travel with them through the years. But a sense of isolation is also common. More young adults report feelings of loneliness than is true for any other age group. In other words, relationships matter very much at this age, and any lack in relationships is felt keenly.

In the years from 25 to 40, the period Erikson calls generativity versus stagnation, two things seem to happen. First of all, marital satisfaction is often at its lowest point. But at the same time, other relationships—with parents and friends—lessen somewhat in centrality. Energy is focused in the central partnership, in childrearing, and in work. Friends are fewer and are seen less often,

**TABLE 7–2 Summary of Age Changes in Relationships**

| Age 20–40 | Age 40–65 | Age 65 and Older |
|---|---|---|
| Marital satisfaction typically at peak in early part of this period, then declining; marital problems are high, but so are expressions of affection | Marital satisfaction often increases in the 50s and 60s; relationship includes fewer problems but also fewer expressions of affection: "devitalized" | Marital satisfaction appears to remain relatively high in this period, but there may be continued "devitalization" in many relationships |
| Women may perceive the relationship as benefiting themselves in early years, and then see themselves as receiving less than they give in remainder of this period | Women may perceive the partnership as inequitable, with themselves receiving less | Women aged 70 and 80 report their partnerships as highly equitable |
| Contact with parents remains steady and high, with satisfaction reported in this relationship | The "sandwich" generation; contact with own parents and with children remains high, but not necessarily strongly attached; direction of major aid shifts | Contact with parents ends when parents die; contact with children continues and is satisfying, but does not appear to be critical for overall life satisfaction |
| Contact with siblings remains relatively high and steady | Contact with siblings continues relatively high and steady | Some indication that relationships with siblings may be emotionally more important in old age than at earlier ages |
| Friendships are most numerous early on, then decline in 30s | Friendships lower in number and in intimacy | Friendships increase in number and may increase in intimacy |

and friendship relationships are less intimate. Contact with parents continues at a fairly high rate, but the young adult's relationships with his or her parents becomes temporarily less significant. The convoy is still there, but young adults spend little energy expanding or working on that convoy.

From 45 to 65, there is another pattern. As the adult moves into Erikson's period of integrity versus despair, the quality of relationships once again seems to become an issue. Marital relationships seem to improve, at least for many couples, perhaps as a result of new attention devoted to the interactions. Friendships, too, may become somewhat more intimate, although not more frequent. Finally, these are also the years in which most adults find themselves the "sandwich" generation in their own family lineage, and have heightened family responsibilities both upward and downward in the chain. As I pointed out in the summary of chapter 6, this is the time when roles, and the relationships within those roles, change significantly, demanding adaptation, but also bringing rewards.

Finally, in the years past retirement, the convoy continues to shrink in size, but is highly valued. Relationships with siblings may be renewed or revitalized; relationships with friends form an important part of older adults' social networks. There is some indication that these relationships with peers (siblings and friends) become more central even than family relationships for many older adults. Contact with families remains high, but life satisfaction in old age is more tied to friendships than to contact with family.

This ebb and flow is tied partly to family and work role cycles, but also may reflect underlying, internal, developmental processes, such as the stages Erikson proposes. Whatever the cause of the changes, it is clear that attachments to others are neither formed nor expressed equally throughout the life cycle.

## Summary

1. The term *attachment* is now quite commonly used to describe relationships between adults as well as between infants and caregivers. Not all adult relationships involve attachment; some are affiliative relationships. Relationships may also be described in terms of the amount of love or liking experienced or expressed, and the amount of social support received or given.

2. The relationship with an intimate partner is typically the most central relationship in adulthood. Selection of a partner is influenced initially by perceived similarity and by propinquity. As relationships develop, both love and conflict increase until the point of commitment is reached, when conflict declines.

3. Those couples who choose to live together before marriage (or instead of marriage) do not appear to have higher rates of later satisfaction or stability in their relationships than to couples who do not live together before marriage.

4. Satisfaction in marriage typically follows a U-shaped trend, with satisfaction highest before children, and after children leave home. Young couples' satisfaction is more influenced by self-disclosure and sexual intimacy, and less influenced by loyalty and emotional security.

5. Some couples, in middle and old age, can be described as "devitalized," with low levels of expression of affection, but also with low levels of reported problems. This pattern may be more common among those who do not progress past the conformist stage of ego development.

6. Satisfying and unsatisfying marriages differ on a number of key dimensions, such as niceness/nastiness, degree of role agreement, and adequacy of conflict resolution strategies.

7. Long-term partnerships are also common in homosexual couples, especially in lesbian pairs. Such partnerships appear to be more egalitarian in role allocation and power than are heterosexual partnerships.

8. Interactions with parents and siblings occur at high and apparently constant levels throughout adulthood. Nearly all adults have some contact with their parents at least once a month.

9. Child-parent relationships in adulthood may not always involve strong attachments, but they do include strong patterns of habit, obligation, and pleasure. Attachment seems to be strongest where the aid and assistance pattern is reciprocal.

10. The middle generation of adults provides the most assistance to both adult children and aging parents. For some, assistance to an aging parent becomes a dominant role in late midlife.

11. Parents and children continue to try to influence each other. More influence attempts are directed from parents to children than the reverse, but influence is more successful from child to parent.

12. Relationships with siblings, while constant over the life span, and perhaps inten-

sifying in old age, appear to be less central to most adults than are the relationships with partners.

13. Friendships, in contrast, appear to be quite central in early adulthood, and perhaps again in middle age and beyond. The number of friends declines with age, but the intimacy of friendships may rise in midlife.

14. Loneliness, however, does not rise as the number of friends goes down. Older adults are less lonely than younger adults.

15. Women's friendships are typically more intimate than men's. Working-class adults typically have fewer friends than middle-class adults.

16. These patterns of relationships can be partially understood by using the framework of Erikson's theory of developmental stages.

## Suggested Readings

BLUMSTEIN, P., & SCHWARTZ, P. (1983). *American couples.* New York: William Morrow.

This book was intended for a professional audience as well as the general public, so it is written in a less technical style. The authors report on the findings from their research, but also include a series of case studies of heterosexual and homosexual couples. I found it fascinating reading.

BRUBAKER, T. H. (1985). *Later life families.* Beverly Hills, CA: Sage.

This brief text covers many of the topics I have included in this chapter, though it emphasizes families at middle age and beyond, rather than covering the full adult life span. It is not too technical, and is more complete and detailed than I have been able to be.

LAUER, J., & LAUER, R. (1985). Marriages made to last. *Psychology Today, 19*(6), 22–26.

Like all articles that appear in *Psychology Today*, this is written for a nonprofessional audience, so it is perhaps more lively reading than many other sources I have suggested. In this case it reports on the responses of 351 couples who had been married 15 years or more.

PARLEE, M. B. (1979). The friendship bond: *PT*'s survey report on friendship in America. *Psychology Today, 14*(4), 43–54, 113.

This report on loneliness is based on several thousand responses to a survey published in *Psychology Today*. The sample is not at all random, but the results may strike a few responsive chords for you.

REISMAN, J. M. (1979). *Anatomy of friendship.* New York: Irvington Publishers.

This is a very clear, interesting, nontechnical book on friendship over the entire life span, from infancy through old age.

# 8

# Work and Work Roles in Adulthood

"I'm probably the youngest general foreman in the plant, yes, sir. I'm in the chassis line right now. There's 372 people working for us, hourly. And thirteen foremen. I'm the lead general foreman" (Terkel, 1972, p. 249). The speaker, Wheeler Stanley, was just 30 when Studs Terkel talked to him in 1972. Stanley had started at the Ford plant when he was 20, fresh out of the paratroopers. His goal in life was to be a "utility man," the man in the plant who can do all the assembly line tasks and spot-relieves other workers.

> I thought that was the greatest thing in the world. When the production manager asked me would I consider training for a foreman's job, boy! My sights left utility. I worked on all the assembly lines. I spent eighteen months on the line, made foreman, and eighteen months later I made general foreman. (p. 250)

Now Wheeler Stanley's goal is to be superintendent, and then maybe production manager. He likes his work, likes the company, but hopes his son will do something better.

Ray Wax (Terkel, 1972) has had a very different working life. He sold cakes in an outdoor market when he was 12 and caddied at a golf course at 14. As an adult he tried a whole range of jobs, all at least partially successful: He exported cars to South America, speculated in land, built houses, built and ran a hotel. Now in his 50s he is a stock broker. The restlessness that has been part of his work life all along is once again visible.

> I can't say what I'm doing has any value. This doesn't make me too happy. . . . When I built the houses, I hired a bricklayer, I hired the roofer, I determined who put the goddamned thing together. And when I handed somebody a key, the house was whole. I made it happen. I can't do that in the market. I'm just being manipulated . . . (Terkel, p. 446–447)

Not everyone gets promoted or shifts from job to job. Dolores Dante has been a waitress for 23 years, working in the same restaurant. She started working when her marriage broke up and she had three young children to support. Waitressing was a way to make good money from tips without a lot of training or schooling. She has stayed with it because she's very good at it and enjoys it.

> When somebody says to me, 'You're great, how come you're *just* a waitress?' *Just* a waitress. I'd say, 'Why, don't you think you deserve to be served by me?' It's implying that he's not worthy, not that I'm not worthy. It makes me irate. I don't feel lowly at all. I myself feel sure. I don't want to change the job. I love it. (Terkel, p. 391)

But it's tiring work. Delores Dante's feet hurt, she aches, she doesn't eat right, and at the end of a day's shift, at 2 A.M., she's drained and nerve-racked. But she wouldn't want to give up working. "I won't give up this job as long as I'm able to do it. I feel out of contact if I just sit at home" (p. 395).

Sigmund Freud was reportedly once asked to define maturity. His answer was that maturity was determined by one's capacity for work and love. I would probably add a few things to the list, but no one would argue about the centrality of both love and work in adult life. I talked about love in the last chapter; now I need to talk about work.

For Wheeler Stanley, Ray Wax, and Delores Dante, as for most of us, work is one of the most time-consuming, significant, identity-defining aspects of adult life. Your occupation, your "career," probably consumes a third to a half of your waking hours over a period of 40 or more years. As one example, the men in the Berkeley Intergenerational Studies—mostly white collar workers and professionals—reported that in their 40s they were working an average of 48 hours per week; the older professionals and top executives in this group were working an average of 51 hours per week (Clausen, 1981). And that doesn't count the time spent lying awake at night worrying about the report you're supposed to write, or the promotion you didn't get, or hours getting to and from work, or taking special classes.

I do not mean to imply by this that childrearing or homemaking (or unpaid volunteer work) are not "work." They are. I have talked about these roles in chapter 6, and I'll turn later in this chapter to the question of combining work and family roles. But here I want to focus on paid employment, on "jobs" or "careers."

It will not surprise you to hear that most of what we know about work and its effects over adulthood comes from studies of men. Only in quite recent years have large percentages of women been in the labor force, and even now—when over half of women over 16 are working—most women do not work continuously through adulthood. Sociologists, economists, and organizational psychologists who have studied work patterns have mostly been interested in continuous work patterns, so women have simply been left out. We know much less about the effect on women's lives of the various work/nonwork patterns that characterize women's employment histories. And even our knowledge of men's work patterns is limited largely to studies of middle-class occupations—business executives, lawyers, doctors, professors. We know a bit about men like Wheeler Stanley, who is in a job with a clear "career ladder," a sequence of steps or promotions from entry-level jobs on up. But we know almost nothing about the Dolores Dantes of the world—the waitresses, garbage collectors, meter readers, artists, flight attendants, and many others who work at jobs that don't have steps or clear promotion sequences, or who have little chance for advancement. What we know, then, is incomplete, but nonetheless fascinating.

## Choosing an Occupation

Most of us think of the process of choice of occupation as something one does only once, in early adulthood. The concept of a "career"—a lifelong sequence of jobs in a particular field or area—implies just such a permanent or long-term choice. In fact, most adults don't stay with the same job for their entire lives. Ray Wax (the stockbroker I described a few pages ago) is an extreme example of job shifting, but the average number of job shifts in a working life (as estimated by Alvin Toffler, in his book *Future Shock*, 1970) is somewhere between 5 and 10. Of course, most job changes are promotions or slight sideways shifts within a single job field, but a great many adults change careers entirely. Donald Super (1985), for example, in one study of a group of 100 men who had been followed longitudinally from high school to their mid-30s, found that 30% had shifted from one field of work to another. And Havighurst (1982) estimates that as many as 10% of men over 40 make radical shifts in careers. So while it is true that you are not permanently stuck with the first job you choose as a young adult, that first choice is a significant one.

Not surprisingly, that first choice is influenced by most of the factors I talked about in Chapter 2, including gender, race, intelligence, personality, family background, and education. These qualities of a young person affect the range of jobs that may be "open" to him or her, as well as the attitudes or goals the young adult may have.

For example, despite enormous changes in the work roles and opportunities available to women, it is still true in the United States (and in other developed countries) that many jobs are clearly labeled as "women's jobs" or "men's jobs." There are more traditionally male jobs, and those jobs are typically higher in both status and income (e.g., doctor, lawyer, business executive, carpenter, electrician) than are traditional women's jobs (Beyard-Tyler & Haring, 1984). "Women's jobs" are fewer in number and concentrated in the lower middle-class or working class levels (e.g., nurse, waitress, social worker, secretary).

The force of sex role socialization, beginning in early childhood and operating through the family, TV, books, and schools (Eccles & Hoffman, 1984) is such that young women are steered into traditional female jobs, and men into traditional male jobs (Schulenberg, Vondracek, & Crouter, 1984). The impact of these sex roles appears to be more powerful for young adults who grew up in working-class families. Young women who choose traditionally masculine jobs are more likely to perceive themselves as more masculine or androgynous, to come from families in which the mother works, and from middle-class families rather than blue-collar families (Huston-Stein & Higgens-Trenk, 1978; Waddell, 1983).

Intelligence serves as a second screening or filtering device for jobs. Since there are entrance tests for some jobs or educational requirements, more intellectually able adults have a wider range of job options open to them.

## Personality and Values in Job Selection

Even young people who, because of race or gender or low level of education, have somewhat restricted job choices, still have some range of options. And within that range, both personality characteristics and personal values affect the choice of job or career a young adult may make.

In one 25-year longitudinal study, for example, Huntley and Davis (1983) found that the values espoused by a group of men when they entered college and when they completed college were quite good predictors of their career choices over the next 21 years. Men who later became businessmen, for example, had placed greater emphasis on political and economic values as undergraduates than had those who later became physicians.

A more frequently used basis for the study of personality/occupational connections has been the work of J. L. Holland (1973) and his followers. Holland described six personality types and six parallel work environments, which I've listed in Table 8–1.

These six personality types can be measured using any one of several tests on which you are asked to say whether you like, dislike, or are indifferent to a whole range of jobs, school subjects, activities, amusements, situations, and people. From your answers, scores on each of the six dimensions are derived, as well as scores for a whole range of specific occupations.

Holland's fundamental hypothesis is that people tend to choose jobs or careers that match their personalities. Obviously, there are other forces at work in determining career choice, and most of us are not pure types. But research on Holland's category system lends a good deal of support to his basic thesis (e.g., Eberhardt & Muchinsky, 1984; Laing, Swaney, & Prediger, 1984). Among both men and women, for example, ministers score highest on the social scale, car salespersons on the enterprising scale, and engineers and doctors on the investigative scale (Benninger & Walsh, 1980; Walsh, Horton, & Gaffey, 1977).

The match is not always quite as predicted, however, and may differ by sex. For example, Benninger and Walsh (1980) found that women police officers scored highest on the social scale, while policemen were highest on the realistic scale. In general, however, among occupations that are "open" to a young person, given her or his gender, intellectual skill, education, and family background, personality characteristics appear to play a significant role in the choice.

## Family Influences on Occupational Choice

Families not only help to create the sex role socialization and the personality differences that Holland describes, they influence occupational choice in at least

**TABLE 8–1 John Holland's Six Personality Types and Six Work Environment Types**

| Type | Personality | Work Environment |
|---|---|---|
| Realistic | Aggressive, masculine, physically strong, low in verbal or interpersonal skills. Prefer mechanical activities and tool use, choosing jobs like mechanic or electrician or surveyor | Demand for explicit, ordered, or systematic manipulation of tools or machines or objects or animals |
| Investigative | Thinking, organizing, planning, particularly abstract thinking. These people like ambiguous, challenging tasks, but are generally low in social skills. They are often scientists or engineers | Demand for observation, creative symbol investigation of physical, biological, or cultural phenomena |
| Social | Similar to extraverts (see chapter 2). Humanistic, sociable, need attention. Avoid intellectual activity, dislike highly ordered activity. Prefer to work with people | Demand for training, caring for, enlightening of, informing, or serving others |
| Conventional | Prefer structured activities and subordinate role; like clear guidelines. See themselves as accurate and precise | Demand for systematic, ordered, precise, manipulation of data, such as keeping records, filing, bookkeeping, organizing written material, following a plan |
| Enterprising | Highly verbal and dominating, like organizing and directing others; persuasive, high in leadership | Demand for manipulating others, such as in sales of all types, or other manipulation to further organizational goals |
| Artistic | Asocial, preference for unstructured, highly individual activity | Demand for ambiguous, free, unsystematized activities to produce art or performance |

**Source:** Holland, 1973.

two other ways. First, as I pointed out in chapter 2, family background has a profound effect on educational attainment. Teenagers from middle-class families are more likely to attend college than are young people from working-class families, and this effect holds even when intellectual ability is held constant. A college degree, in turn, is a required credential for many entry-level jobs, particularly jobs in business.

Families also specifically and directly push their children toward specific careers and away from others. In particular, sons tend to follow in their fathers' career footsteps. Mortimer (1974, 1976), for example, has found that college men are likely to choose their fathers' occupations, or to choose occupations with similar values or rewards. Sons of professionals, for example, are likely to choose occupations that have similar levels of autonomy and work complexity; sons of businessmen are likely to choose occupations that are high in extrinsic rewards. These connections were stronger in families in which the relationship between father and son was particularly close.

Overall, families not only identify certain occupations as desirable or acceptable, they also inculcate values in their children that fit some occupations better than others. The young person follows these signposts in selecting an occupation.

Once the first occupational choice has been made, what happens next? Are there any consistent patterns in the next 20 or 40 years of work life? With due regard to the wide variability, the answer is a cautious "yes."

# General Age Trends in Work Experience

Research by sociologists and industrial psychologists shows several well-replicated patterns of work-related attitudes and behaviors over the adult years (reviewed ably by Susan Rhodes, 1983), most of which appear to hold for women as well as for men.

**Job Satisfaction.** The facet of work life that has been most frequently studied is overall job satisfaction, and here the findings are clear: Work satisfaction increases quite steadily throughout the work life, from age 20 to at least age 60, for both college-educated and noncollege-educated adults (Rhodes, 1983; Staines & Quinn, 1979; Tamir, 1982; Weaver, 1980). (Some typical data from Lois Tamir's cross-sectional study are shown in Figure 8–1.) Since this same pattern has been found over the past few decades, for women as well as for men, we can be reasonably sure that this is not a narrow single-cohort or male-only pattern.

Satisfaction seems to increase for several extrinsic reasons, such as better pay and more job security. But intrinsic satisfaction also goes up: Older people like the actual work they do better than younger workers do (Rhodes, 1983). In part this is an accurate reflection of differences between "young jobs" and "older jobs." Jobs held by younger workers tend to be physically harder and dirtier, and/or less complex and less interesting (Kunze, 1974). Jobs held by older workers are likely to have more authority (more "clout," to use Tamir's word), more prestige. It is not a great surprise, then, when we find that older workers like their jobs better.

There may also be self-selection operating here too: Workers who really dislike some line of work don't stay in it very long. Older workers in any given occupation are thus likely to be people who chose to stay in that line of work because they liked it.

**Job Involvement and Motivation.** Perhaps because older workers have more clout, or perhaps because of other internal changes in workers, researchers also observe an increase with age commitment to or involvement with work. Over time, workers become more and more committed to their specific job, or their specific employer, and more involved with the work itself (Rhodes, 1983). Men in their 40s and 50s are less likely to change jobs than are younger men; they see their current job as something they are likely to keep on doing until retirement; they show lower levels of avoidable absenteeism. All of these are

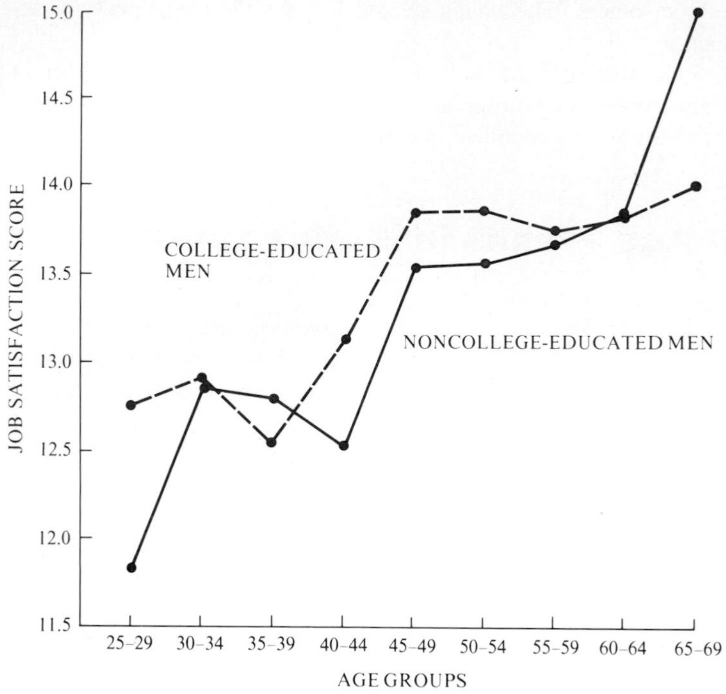


***Figure 8–1*** *These results are typical of findings on age changes in work satisfaction. The findings, from Lois Tamir's analysis, are cross-sectional, but are replicated in many studies with several different adjacent cohorts. (Source: Tamir, 1982, data from Table 4.1, p. 72.)*

indications of greater commitment to the job. Older men, in other words, take their work more seriously and find things about it that they like. Younger men are still experimenting, still searching for the right job or occupation, so they may be focused more on what is wrong with the current job, rather than what is right about it.

**Protestant Work Ethic.** Another reflection of this same age change is a general increase in what is often called the Protestant work ethic—the belief in the moral value of hard work. Older workers place greater emphasis on this value than do younger workers. (Of course, this could easily be a cohort effect rather than an age change.)

**Other Job Values.** At the same time, there is an interesting shift in job values that seems to occur among men in their mid-40s. (The research here is all on men, so we don't know if the same shift occurs for women.) For men younger than 40 or 45, job satisfaction seems to be strongly influenced by such intrinsic job characteristics as complexity or interest. Pay levels, fringe benefits, and job security are less influential in determining satisfaction. For men past 45 or 50, extrinsic job characteristics begin to play a bigger role. These older men begin to judge their job satisfaction not only in terms of interest and challenge, but also in terms of pay, convenience, and security (Gould, 1979; Rabinowitz & Hall, 1981).

One set of findings from the Oakland and Berkeley longitudinal studies, shown in Figure 8–2, (Clausen, 1981) illustrates this shift very nicely. The results

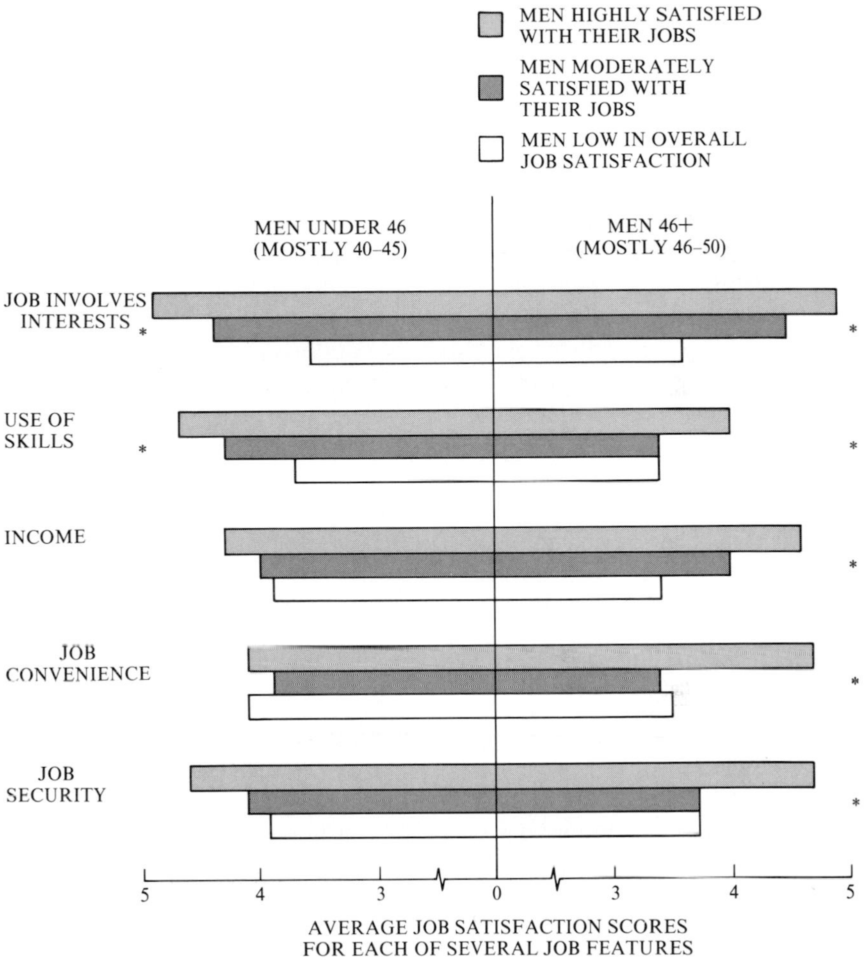


***Figure 8–2*** *Changes in work values at midlife are shown in these data from the Berkeley Intergenerational Studies. Men who rated their jobs as highly satisfying, moderately satisfying, and low in satisfaction also rated the individual qualities of their jobs. Among men under 46, only job interest and use of skills significantly (*) discriminate among the levels of satisfaction, but among older men, all the job qualities discriminate. (Each comparison that is statistically significant is marked with an asterisk *). (Source: Clausen, 1981, data from Table 13.4, p. 331.)*

here are from interviews with the subjects completed when they were between age 40 and 50. The men were divided into two age groups (45 and younger, and 46 and older), and then into three job-satisfaction groups, based on their overall evaluation of their job. As part of the interview, they also rated their degree of satisfaction with each of a series of features of their jobs. You can see that for both age groups, more satisfied men singled out the interest and skill demands of the job as positive features. For the younger group, however, income, job convenience, and job security were much less significant: Younger men highly satisfied with their jobs didn't rate their jobs as more convenient or having higher income than did men who were not satisfied with their jobs. But among the older group, these extrinsic job features contributed significantly to the overall rating of job satisfaction. Other research also shows this shift in emphasis from intrinsic to extrinsic job values in the mid or late 40s (Rhodes, 1983).

**Job Performance.** The one major feature of jobs that does not change systematically with age is job performance. Older workers are as good as younger workers by most measures (Rhodes, 1983). The major exceptions to this generalization are those occupations in which physical strength or speedy reaction time are critical elements, such as longshoremen, air traffic controllers, truck drivers, and professional athletes. In these jobs, there is a performance decline beginning in midlife or later. Many adults in such occupations change jobs at midlife in anticipation of, or because of, such declines.

In sum, while age does not influence work performance or productivity in systematic ways (at least in most occupations), age is related to most aspects of job satisfaction and job values. Older workers like their jobs better and are more committed to them.

## Career Ladders or Career Mobility

A quite different way of looking at overall work experience over time is to focus on the career pathways of individual adults in particular occupations. The metaphor of a *career ladder* is a pervasive one. Most of us think of our adult work life in terms of a series of definable steps, or rungs on a ladder. In the academic world this is very clear: You move from instructor to assistant professor to associate professor to full professor. In the Ford assembly plant where Wheeler Stanley worked, there is an equally clear ladder, from assembly line worker, to foreman, to general foreman, to superintendent, to pre-delivery manager, to production manager, and on up the line. Clearly, not all occupations have such sharply defined promotion steps. But most jobs have at least some features that distinguish beginners or low-level workers from advanced or high-level workers.

Just how does one move up this ladder, or through this sequence? Are the steps equidistant? Can you skip steps? Does everyone move along them at the same rate?

Answering such questions requires either retrospective reports from individuals about their work history or, preferably, longitudinal data. There is only a small amount of data that fits this bill. A particularly helpful study is James Rosenbaum's (1984) analysis of the work histories of a group of 671 workers who entered a large company (called ABCO by Rosenbaum) between 1960 and 1962, and were still employed by the company in 1975. Since company policy specified that all workers should enter the company at the submanagement level, Rosenbaum was able to trace career paths for a large group of individuals who had begun at roughly the same point. A second helpful study is the AT&T study of managers over a 20 year period (Bray & Howard, 1983; Thornton & Byham, 1982). In their analyses, the AT&T researchers focused less on sequences of individual career moves and more on factors that affected career success, but the results are illuminating nonetheless.

Several generalizations are possible from these and equivalent studies. First, as I pointed out in chapter 2, a college education makes a very large difference in the pathway an individual worker follows (Bray & Howard, 1983; Rosenbaum, 1984). Even with measures of intellectual ability held constant, a college degree is associated with earlier and more career advancements.

Second, those who are promoted early go further. Sample results from Rosenbaum's study in Table 8–2 illustrate this. Eighty three percent of those workers who received their first promotion (to foreman) within three years of joining the company had moved up to at least the first level of management within 13 years, but only 33% of those who took that first step to foreman at a later time made it to the management level. College-educated workers were more likely to be promoted early, so these are not independent bits of information. But even among the noncollege-educated, early promotion was associated with greater overall advancement.

Third, there is strong evidence that, at least in our culture at this point in history—most career advancement occurs early in adult life. By age 40 or 45, most adults have gone as far as they will go in their career ladder. Again, data from Rosenbaum's study of ABCO employees are illustrative (Figure 8–3). For this analysis Rosenbaum used data for all the workers in this company in the period from 1962 to 1965. Workers at the nonmanagement level had a very low probability of promotion past the age of 45; for foremen, the pattern is

**TABLE 8–2 The Relationship Between Earliness of First Promotion and Achievement of Middle-level Management in Managers in the ABCO Company Studied by Rosenbaum**

| | Achieved at Least Lower Management | | | |
|---|---|---|---|---|
| | *Yes* | *No* | *Total* | *Percentage* |
| *Period During Which Worker Was First Promoted:* | | | | |
| During first three years | 56 | 11 | 67 | 83% |
| Later than first three years | 42 | 86 | 128 | 33% |

**Source:** Rosenbaum, 1984, adapted from Table 2.4, page 56. Reprinted by permission of Academic Press, Orlando, FL and author.

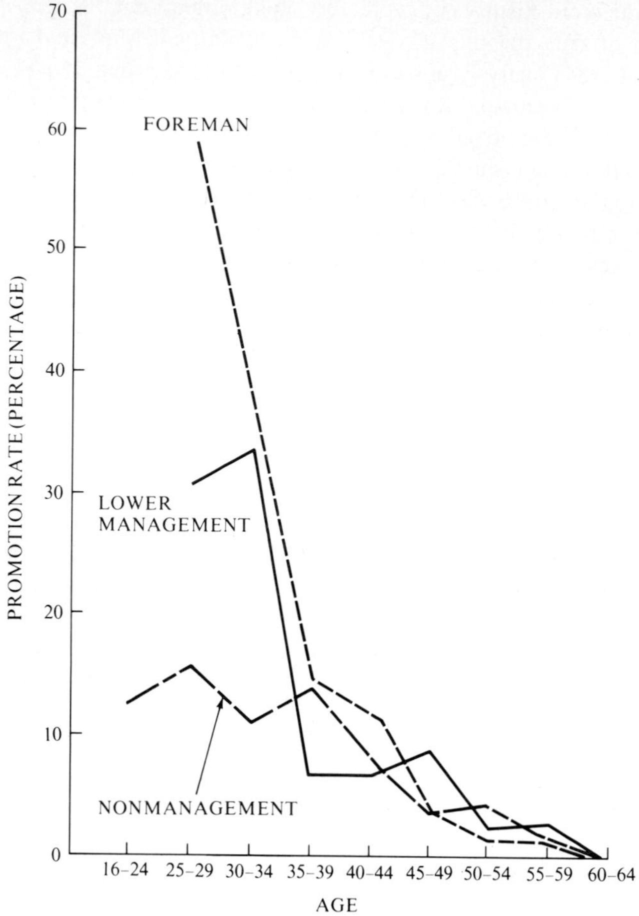


***Figure 8–3*** *Results from Rosenbaum's study of promotions in a large corporation show the promotions come early in workers' careers. Promotions are comparatively rare past about age 40, in part because the number of positions decreases at each successively higher level. (Source: Rosenbaum, 1984, Figure 3.1, p. 80. Reprinted by permission of Academic Press, Orlando, FL and author.)*

even more striking. There was a high probabilty of promotion until about age 30 or 35, and then a very sharp drop.

Rosenbaum describes the entire process using the metaphor of a tournament. Career paths are marked by decision points at which you either "win" (get promoted, get a raise, receive some bonus or new responsibility) or "lose" (are considered for but fail to receive a promotion, a raise, or increased responsibility). If you win, you are still in the tournament until the next decision point, and so on until you lose and thus remain at whatever level you had reached at that point.

This model fits the data quite well, but needs several supplements. First, it seems to make a difference just what sort of new responsibilities or skills the worker is given at the next-higher level of the system. In the AT&T studies, for example, the degree of challenge of the individual's job had a significant impact on later advancement: Workers at any given level who had more challenging jobs were more likely to be promoted (Bray & Howard, 1983). Given Kohn's work on the impact of work complexity on intellectual flexibility (which I discussed in chapter 5), this link makes very good sense. A complex job increases your intellectual flexibility, which in turn makes you a better prospect for further advancement. Since most promotions move a worker into more complex and challenging jobs, promotions themselves will tend to increase a worker's skills and capacities. The "fast track," then, is not just a reflection of entering skills; it creates skills.

The tournament model also needs to be modified to take account of the fact that, particularly at early steps in the career, "losing" does not put you totally out of the game. Many individuals do make slower or later progress in their careers; a few fail many times and then succeed spectacularly. Sports metaphors are risky; life is not really much like a tournament. But the metaphor does capture some of the features of career mobility patterns in at least some occupations. What it fails to show is that there are many games in this system. If a worker "loses" in one profession, with one company, he can try another. And that is precisely what most people do, especially during their 20s and early 30s, when the steps up the career ladder are taken.

All of what I have described so far appears to be roughly valid for both men and women. Women's job satisfaction increases with age, as does men's, and is influenced by roughly the same job characteristics (Weaver, 1978); job success in a company like AT&T can be predicted for women as well as for men, using essentially the same predictors (Ritchie & Moses, 1983); personality characteristics predict job choice about equally well for men and women. But there are clearly a great many ways in which the lifetime work patterns of men and women differ—differences I now need to explore.

## Men's Work Patterns

Donald Super (1957) describes four typical male work patterns: (1) The **conventional career pattern** is one in which the worker moves through a recognized series of steps, beginning perhaps with summer work or part-time work in high school or college, then an entry-level job in some field, and moving up slowly. (2) The **stable career pattern** is highly similar except that the man goes directly from school or college into his profession without as much preparatory work. This is common in professional and white-collar jobs. (3) The

**TABLE 8–3 Patterns of Continuous and Interrupted Work for Black and White Men and Women in a 1975 Study of 5,000 American Families**

| Work Pattern | Percentages | | | |
|---|---|---|---|---|
| | *White Men* | *Black Men* | *White Women* | *Black Women* |
| Continuous work | 55 | 61 | 36 | 42 |
| Nonwork followed by work | 11 | 15 | 29 | 42 |
| Work/nonwork/work | 29 | 22 | 15 | 5 |
| Nonwork/work/nonwork/work | 3 | 1 | 8 | 7 |
| At least five periods of alternating work and nonwork | 3 | 1 | 12 | 4 |

**Source:** Corcoran, 1978, Figure 2.3, p. 59–62. Reprinted by permission of John Wiley and Sons, Inc. and author.

**unstable career pattern** is one of a trial period, followed by a stable period, and then another trial period. The worker discards his first career choice and settles on another. (4) The **multiple trial career pattern** is the least constant, involving many shifts from trial to stable periods (and the least likely to be associated with high levels of job success, too, according to Super's data, 1985).

Some data from a study of 5,000 American families, in Table 8–3 (Corcoran, 1978), gives you some sense of the frequency of patterns like these. As you can see, 66% of white men and 76% of black men in this study had shown either conventional or stable patterns of work. Most men begin work in their early adult years and work more or less continuously—barring unemployment or a return to schooling—until retirement. Unstable patterns, and periods of nonwork, are more common among blue-collar and unskilled workers than among white-collar workers (Miller & Form, 1951), but continuous work is still the norm for men in this culture.

## Stages in Men's Work Patterns

These years of continuous work can be divided into several broad stages, each of which seems to have certain characteristics. You will recall from chapter 3 that several theorists, most notably Daniel Levinson, postulate such stages as an integral part of adult life. It seems doubtful that stages of work are as closely linked to age, or as highly specific in content, as Levinson suggests. Attempts to test Levinson's theory, for example, have shown only moderate links between age or career stage and career-related issues (Rush, Peacock, & Milkovich, 1980). But there is a good deal of evidence in the career development literature supporting the idea of a general sequence of career stages followed by many men.

**The Trial or Establishment Stage: Up to Age 30.** In the first stage, the young man must decide on a job or career, searching for a fit between his interests and personality and the jobs available. Young men particularly value jobs that are intrinsically interesting and challenging; neither salary nor job security is as critical in the job choice at this stage as is challenge. There is some trial and error involved in the whole process. Jobs may be tried and rejected and new jobs tried. Perhaps because many jobs available to young men are relatively low in challenge, and because many young men have not yet found the right fit, job changes are at their peak during this period.

Once he has chosen a job or career, though, the young man must learn the ropes. In many careers, this includes the task of finding a mentor—an older worker who will take you under his wing, show you the system, sponsor you for additional responsibilities, encourage your development (Levinson, 1978).

There is not a great deal of research on the significance or centrality of the role of mentor in men's work life. One study of scholars (Goldstein, 1979) indicated that having a mentor of the same gender was more predictive of later career success. Male graduate students whose major professor was a man, and female students whose major professor was a woman, went on to more productive academic careers than did those who had an opposite-gender mentor. But whether this is more broadly true in other professions (such as the business world) I do not know. Nor do we yet have the data to say whether having a mentor at all is a necessary, or even a common, ingredient in men's work experience. Still, it is an intriguing concept, one I hope researchers will explore in the future.

Another feature of this stage, at least as proposed by Levinson, is the creation of the Dream. Young scientists dream of winning the Nobel Prize; Wheeler Stanley dreamed initially of being a utility man and later modified his dream to being a production manager. Young businessmen may dream of being the company president. Each young man, according to Levinson, has such a secret ambition, a private fantasy of eventual success. The first career stage is one in which the young person takes the first steps toward realizing that dream.

**The Stabilization Stage: From 31 to 45.** In the next stage, the man strives hard to fulfill his Dream. In the early years of this period, the striving often pays off with promotion or improvement; toward the end of this period, there is a substantial slowing of progress. But satisfaction with the job is usually higher during this period than earlier, in part because the work itself is typically more complex and interesting than it was in the early stages.

**The Maintenance Stage: From 45 to 60.** Somewhere around age 45, opportunities and challenges in men's work stops increasing. Most men have by then gone as far as they will go in their work, and can look forward to 15 or 20 years at roughly the same level, at roughly the same job. A man can see if his dream has been achieved. Given the unrealistic quality of dreams, for most it has not.

Current folklore would have it that the mid life realization of having reached the ceiling in one's job, or of having failed to fulfill one's Dream, is commonly accompanied by depression or other symptoms of distress. The evidence on this point turns out to be mixed, just as was the evidence on the degree of upheaval associated with the male climacteric that I described in chapter 4. Many men do appear to go through a reassessment of their lives at this point

(Brim, 1976; Tamir, 1982). But the most typical reactions to the awareness of "falling short" seem to be redefinition of work values, or a deemphasis on the centrality of work for self-esteem or life satisfaction, rather than long-term depression or distress.

In the AT&T studies of the careers of managers, for example, Bray and Howard (1983) found that in their 40s and 50s, it was no longer the possibility of promotion that motivated men, but the challenge of the work itself. Or a man in a less challenging job may focus his attention on such extrinsic qualities of his job as better pay or greater security. Most interestingly, Tamir (1982) found that men at midlife seem to stop measuring their own value in terms of work success. In a cross-sectional study, there were no significant correlations between job clout or work satisfaction and self-esteem, zest, or life satisfaction among middle-aged men. Among younger men, these correlations were generally positive. That is, in the young man, being successful at one's job is one of the key elements in self-esteem or overall satisfaction. In middle-aged men it is not, despite the fact that this is the time in life when a man is likely to be maximally successful and to have the greatest clout in his work.

This is not to say that there is no pain involved in the transition. The fact that job values change, that deemphasis of job centrality occurs, indicates that there has been a significant readjustment occurring, and this readjustment may be painful for many men. But the data suggest that this is a transition that most men weather quite successfully.

**Adjustment to Retirement: 60+.** A final stage involves the transition to retirement, which occurs some time between 60 and 70 for most men. I will take up the subject of retirement more fully in a later section.

It is important to note that although approximate ages are given for each of the four stages, it is probably time-in-career rather than age that is the more critical variable. Despite Levinson's insistence that the steps are strongly age-linked, the research findings simply don't fit that model terribly well. New workers in any field, whatever their age, have certain characteristics in common. And a man coming to a new career at 40 will go through a period of trial and a period of stabilization before reaching a maintenance stage. For those of us interested in women's careers, this is a comforting statement, since the ages at which women enter (and leave) jobs and careers are frequently quite different from what we see in men's career patterns. If, as it seems, time-in-career is more helpful than age for predicting men's job-related attitudes and behavior, this suggests that women could successfully enter careers at later ages and still follow similar career paths. Research on women's career patterns lends at least some support to this possibility.

## Women's Work Patterns

It is not going to be news to you that women's work patterns have been changing radically over the past several decades. More and more, women's adult work histories have come to resemble men's, as a larger and larger percentage of women choose to follow a continuous work pattern. You can see the current state of affairs, as well as the change since 1970, in Figure 8–4.

Several points need to be made about this figure. Most obviously, there has been an increase in the percentage of women working in every category. The largest increases have occurred among married women living with their husbands, especially among those with young children. In 1960, only 18.6% of married women with preschool children were employed; this had risen to 30% by 1970, and to nearly 50% by 1982. That is an enormous change in a very short time. The changes are not nearly so vivid among separated and divorced women, however, who have been working in large numbers for some time.

Another curious point about this figure is the relatively low rate of work for women with no children under 18. The explanation lies in the fact that the numbers include a great many older women, from cohorts for whom work outside the home was simply less common. If only women between the ages of 16 and 44 are counted, 79.8% of married women with no children under 18 were in the work force in 1982.

Counting the number of women who are working at any given time, how-

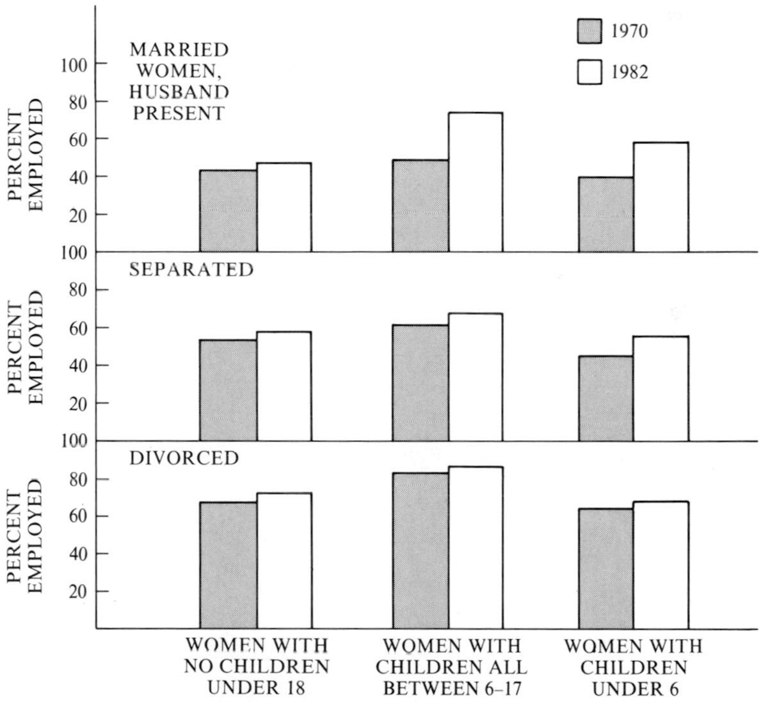


***Figure 8–4*** *The percentage of women in every category who are in the work force has increased from 1970 to 1982, but the change is especially large among married women with children under the age of 18. (Source: U.S. Bureau of the Census, Statistical Abstract of the United States: 1984, Table 686, p. 414.)*

ever, does not tell us much about the lifetime work patterns of women. How many of those working women have worked continuously? How many leave the work force when they marry, or have children? The patterns have been changing so fast that it is very hard to pin down, but there are several reasonably current sets of data that provide some answers.

One set of data you have already seen, in Table 8–3, was based on a study of 5,000 families from 1968 to 1975. A second source is a 1979 U.S.Census Bureau survey (U.S. Bureau of the Census, 1984b) of a representative sample of over 9,000 U.S. families. They found that among those who had ever worked, 28% had worked continuously (without a single work interruption of six months or more). Among those women aged 30 to 44, 22.5% had never had such a work interruption.

These findings are corroborated by Sorensen's (1983) longitudinal study of a random sample of 1958 graduates of Wisconsin high schools. Approximately 25% of these women had worked continuously. The remainder had either never worked or had left the work force, typically at marriage or at the birth of the first child. Of those women with children, about a quarter had not returned to work by their mid-30s. The remainder of those who had left the work force had returned at some point.

Continuous work patterns are more common in some subgroups of women than others: among black women (see Table 8–3), among those in non-traditional or "masculine" jobs (Betz, 1984), among those with strong commitments to work or career (Betz, 1984; Rexroat, 1985), and among the unmarried or those with no children. Highly educated women, whom one might expect to have a high likelihood of continuous employment, are in fact divided into two distinct groups. Some stop work when they marry and remain homemakers (presumably in part because they marry men who are able to provide good incomes); others pursue a continuous work pattern. Interrupted patterns are less common in this group (Sorensen, 1983).

In sum, something like one quarter of all women in recent cohorts have worked continuously through their adult lives. The modal pattern, however, describing the work histories of perhaps half of adult women, is to stop work for at least several years while children are young, with a later return to the work force. The remaining quarter of women either do not work at all, or stop work when they marry or have children and do not return to the work force.

## Impact of Differential Work Patterns on Women's Lives

Not surprisingly, given the enormous variability of work patterns for women, there has been no systematic attempt to describe common stages of work life for women. There has, however, been some attempt to examine the career consequences of choosing any one of the several work/nonwork patterns.

The question goes something like this: If you want to have a successful career *and* a family, is it better to establish the career before you marry or have children, or is it better to rear your children first and then pursue your career, or can you do both at the same time? Given the enormous practical importance of this question for today's young women, there is remarkably little information. The research is both relatively new and scarce. And with circumstances changing so rapidly, I am not confident of the generalizability of the results from one year to the next, let alone from one cohort to the next. So take what I am about to say with due caution.

If work achievement is one of your goals, continuous work patterns appear to be most successful. Van Velsor and O'Rand (1984), for example, have examined work success in a large seven-year longitudinal study of a national sample of women, all of whom were between 30 and 44 at the start of the study. In this group, the women who had worked continuously had the highest salaries. Another longitudinal study, by Ellen Betz (1984), covering the first 10 years since graduation of a group of 1968 college graduates, lends further support to this general conclusion. The women in Betz's sample who had the highest work commitments (most of whom had worked continuously) were much more likely to have moved upward in their jobs or careers than were less work-committed women. The latter group showed more horizontal job movement or change, shifting from one job to another at about the same level.

Studies of extremely successful women, such as the small group of chief executive officers interviewed by Hennig and Jardim (1976), also show that high success is achieved primarily by those women who worked continuously. In other words, the best way to succeed in the world of work is to follow an essentially "male pattern" of continuous work and high work commitment.

***Figure 8–5*** *Women executives and others with careers do not "dress for success" to quite this extent anymore, but high commitment and continuous work patterns among women are nonetheless associated with higher levels of professional success than are the more common intermittent work patterns. (Source: Michael Kagan, Monkmeyer Press.)*

For those women who do not work continuously, the one point that does seem clear is that working consistently in the same field, or along the same career path, is a better strategy for women than is switching from job to job. Further, those women who work before they have children and then return to the same type of job after the children are in school, earn higher salaries in the long run than do women who switch jobs, or than those who start work for the first time after they have had children (Van Velsor & O'Rand, 1984).

If I were to translate these bits of information into advice for today's young women interested in combining career achievement with family roles, I would offer two suggestions: (1) Work continuously if you can. (2) If you cannot, or if you would prefer to be at home with your children when they are young, then establish your career at least briefly before you stop work to have children, and return to the same type of work later. What I cannot tell from the available information is whether there is any optimal timing for these steps. Delaying childbearing into one's 30s (or even 40s) risks becoming significantly ''off time,'' which may carry an additional price. But such a delay may be optimal for job success in at least some fields. The trade-offs are extremely difficult to judge.

## The Effects of Work on Men and Women

I have been focusing so far on work itself and its role in adult lives. But an equally important issue for a developmental psychologist interested in adults is the effect of work on other facets of adult functioning or development. Very little of the research on this topic is really developmental in nature. Researchers have not asked, for example, whether certain kinds of work have more or less impact on personality change or growth at different points in the adult years. But there are several sets of studies that yield some interesting fragments.

### Effects for Men

To my surprise (my high work-commitment bias is showing, I guess), I can find little evidence that men who are more successful in their careers are a great deal happier or better adjusted than those who are less successful (e.g., Korman, Mahler, & Omran, 1983). In the most interesting study in this area, the 20-year longitudinal study of AT&T managers, Bray and Howard (1983) found that the men who had moved furthest up the corporate ladder at midlife were more satisfied with their jobs than were the less successful men, but they were not happier or better adjusted overall, nor did they have higher marital satisfaction.

It may be, as Tamir's analysis (mentioned a short time ago) suggests, that this lack of connection between job success (or job satisfaction) and overall adjustment is a peculiarly midlife phenomenon. More rapid career advancement in early adulthood may be more positively associated with life satisfaction in that age group. But my hunch is that, in general, work success is not the magic, automatic road to happiness that many young adults expect it to be. Support for this hunch comes not only from the AT&T studies, but also from the Berkeley Intergenerational Studies. In both cases, researchers found successful men and well-adjusted men to be distinctly different types. Contrasting these two groups of men—the successful, and the best adjusted—Bray and Howard said:

> The most successful and best adjusted were worlds apart. The most successful were cognitively astute; the best adjusted scored lower than others on cognitive tasks. The most successful were worldly Enlargers, had more general knowledge, and expanded themselves physically and intellectually; the best adjusted were less cynical, less oriented to heterosexual pleasures, and more religious than those who rated lower on life satisfaction. The most successful were less nurturant and deferential and more aggressive than their age peers; the best adjusted had steadier temperaments and were less selfish. (1983, p. 303)

The causality seems to run both ways. Some of these differences were already present at the beginning of the men's careers and influenced the men's work commitment and behavior. But to some extent, success and strong work commitment bring about changes in personality or values, just as intellectual flexibility increases with high levels of work complexity (Kohn, 1980). The moral seems to be that work success (or lack of it) does have an effect on men, but the effect is not primarily on overall happiness or life satisfaction.

## Effects for Women

The findings for women are more complicated. The major issue has not been the effect of job success, but more generally the positive or negative effects of work itself on women's lives, their satisfaction with their lives, or their psychological growth.

Research comparing the life satisfaction of working women and homemakers is highly inconsistent, in part because of the rapid changes in women's work roles in recent years. Recent research generally shows that working women are slightly more satisfied with their lives than are housewives, but this may be less true for working-class women than for the middle-class (Burke & Weir, 1976; Coleman & Antonucci, 1983). Several longitudinal studies of older cohorts of women, however, do not show this general positive effect of work. Willemsen (1980), for example, studied aspects of work commitment in a group of highly gifted women who have been part of a 50-year longitudinal study (Terman's study of the gifted). Examining the data up to the time the women were 60, Willemsen could find no indication that those women in this group who had had strong work commitments saw their lives any more positively than did women who had been primarily homemakers. The one difference between the two groups was that the strongly work-committed women were more likely than the less committed to see their lives as something they had shaped themselves, rather than having been shaped by external forces.

Stroud's analysis (1981) of work histories of the women in the Berkeley Intergenerational Studies also showed no overall benefit for the working woman in life satisfaction. Among college educated women, those who had been homemakers for all their adult lives had the highest morale and self-esteem at midlife, followed closely by those with a strong commitment to work. The lowest levels of esteem and morale occurred among women who had had uneven or interrupted work histories and who had only a moderate level of work commitment.

It appears that in the generation of women born from 1900 to about 1930, high life satisfaction could be found either through commitment to family or through commitment to work. Subsequent generations have, increasingly, tried to combine the two, assuming that women, like men, need to mature in both love and work. Studies of these more recent cohorts do show higher morale, life satisfacation, and self esteem for women who work than for those who do not. But the effect is not a large one, nor is it shared by all subgroups of women. Whether a woman finds that work helps to foster higher self-esteem or greater life satisfaction appears to depend at least in part on the way in which she combines work and family roles—a subject to which I now turn.

## Combining Work and Family Roles

In chapter 6, and so far in this chapter, I have largely talked about family roles and work roles as if they were quite separate. For most adults today, however, these two sets of roles are inextricably intertwined. I want to explore the connections by looking at the relationship from two directions: the effect of family roles on work experiences, and the effect of work on family.

### The Impact of Family Roles on Work Experiences

I have already touched on this linkage for women; one cannot talk about women's work patterns without examining the effect of family on work. But there is also a literature dealing with the effect of marriage and family on men's work experiences.

I mentioned in chapter 6 that married men are healthier and more satisfied with their lives than single men. It is also true that as a general rule married men are more successful in their jobs than are men who remain single (Aldous, Osmond, & Hicks, 1979). Some of this difference may be self-selection: Healthier and brighter men may simply be more likely to marry. But some of the difference undoubtedly reflects the impact of family life on the men. The responsibility of earning a living motivates the man to strive, and the assistance of a wife who provides emotional and logistical support frees the man to devote more attention to his work.

If the latter argument holds, then we ought to find that the most successful men are those with wives who do not work, and who thus can devote more time and attention to supporting their husbands in their careers. There is at least a bit of data to support this conclusion (e.g., Osherson & Dill, 1983). In role theory terms, a man can most readily fulfill the demands of his work role when he has low conflict or strain between work and family roles. Thus, the recent shift toward two-job or two-career family patterns may exact a career price for men, even while it adds career success for women.

## The Impact of Work on Family Roles

The preponderance of research exploring the effect of work on families has focused on the impact of *women's* work on family roles and functioning. When the husband works and the wife stays home, the husband's work does have some effect on the family. Marital satisfaction of women is higher, for example, if the husband is successful at his work, although wives of highly work committed men have somewhat lower marital satisfaction (Aldous et al., 1979). It is when both spouses work, however (increasingly the modal pattern), that role conflict and role strain rise. Who takes care of a sick child when both spouses have jobs? Who takes the cat to the vet or stays home when the repairman comes? (And repairmen will *never* tell you precisely when they are coming; you always have to wait around for at least half a day before they show up.) Who does the grocery shopping, reads the kids a story, or cleans the toilet when both adults are tired from long hours on the job? Dealing with these complexities and strains inevitably produces changes in family systems.

Because of our definitions of sex roles, the conflict and strain between work and family roles are felt more keenly by women than by men (a point nicely made in a panel of my favorite comic strip, in Figure 8–6). Strain and conflict are also higher when one or both spouses works odd hours, or weekends, or evening shifts (Staines & Pleck, 1984). Most of us find that there are simply

**Figure 8–6** *(Source: For Better or for Worse. Copyright © 1984 by Universal Press Syndicate. Reprinted with permission. All rights reserved.)*

not enough hours in the day to do a good job as worker, spouse, and parent. In addition, the actual demands of the different roles may be contradictory. The assertiveness and competitiveness that may be suitable or necessary in a work environment are out of place in the nurturing role of parent, for example.

Just how do couples cope with these complexities? In particular, how does the wife's employment affect the way decisions are made in the family, the way household labor is allocated, or the sense of overall marital satisfaction?

**Effect of Wife's Work on Decision Making and Power.** One of the important ways in which two-worker couples differ from those in which the husband is the only worker is that in the former, the wife has more power. Employed women, compared to housewives, have more say in important family decisions and more control of finances. In fact, the more money a woman earns, the more power she seems to have within the couple (Blumstein & Schwartz, 1983; Rallings & Nye, 1979). The general rule is that whoever earns the money has the largest say in how it is spent. When both partners earn money, there is greater equality in decision making.

**Effect of Women's Work on Division of Family Labor.** In this, as in so many areas, we are in a period of transition. Ten or 20 years from now I may write a very different summary statement. But today, despite the enormous increase in women's employment, despite the women's movement, despite an increase in egalitarian attitudes about childrearing and housework, it is still true that women have the major responsibility for both rearing children and keeping house, *whether they work or not.*

The research findings tell us several intriguing things about the ways that families take care of the endless chores of family life. Most importantly, when a woman works, she remains in charge of housework, cooking, cleaning, and childrearing. Working women nowadays do less of the actual physical work than do full time housewives. Husbands do some, children help with some of it, and some of it just doesn't get done as often. (I remember what a shock it was to me to realize that the living room rug really didn't *have* to be vacuumed every day.) But the wife remains the person who must organize, monitor, and supervise the work (Geerken & Gove, 1983; Johnson & Firebaugh, 1985; Maret & Finlay, 1984). Figure 8–7 shows some fairly typical data from a large sample of working wives (Maret & Finlay, 1984). It shows the percentage of women who describe themselves as "solely responsible" for each of several household jobs. If I added the percentages of women who are also "primarily" responsible (those who organize the work but have some help doing it), the figures would add to nearly 95% for every category, whether the woman works or not (Geerken & Gove, 1983).

An illustration of this comes from Anne Seiden (1980):

A distinguished woman professional, about to give a scientific paper, suddenly is distracted as she sits on the podium by the thought, "Oh, my God, I forgot to buy toilet

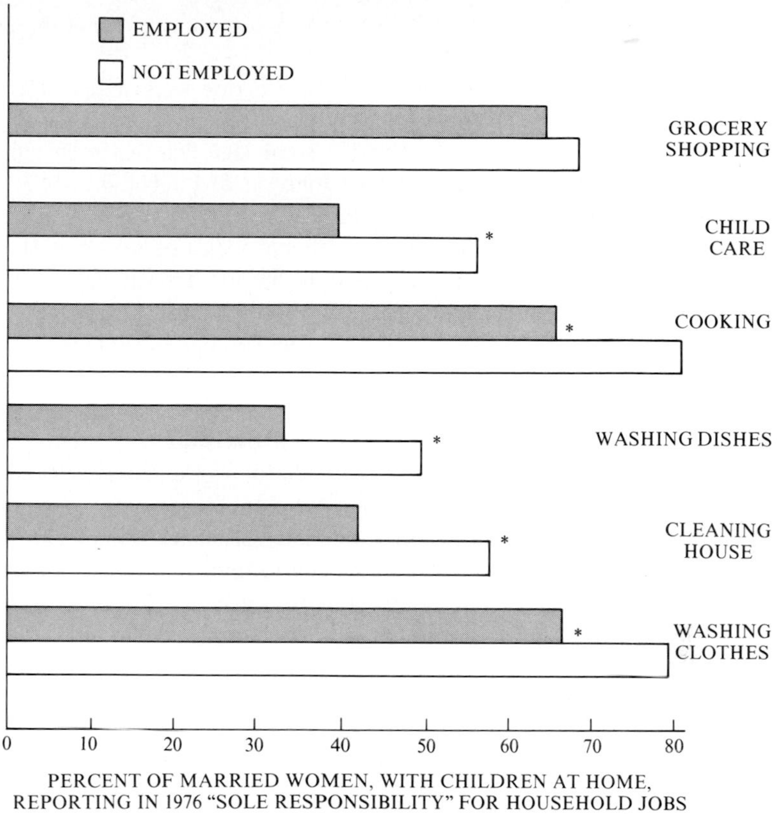


**Figure 8–7** *Working women share more of the household responsibilities with husbands or children than do full-time homemakers, but still bear the brunt of the responsibility, as you can see from these results from over 1,000 wives. The numbers represent the percentage of women, working or not working, who indicated they had sole and full responsibility for each task. (Source: Maret & Finlay, 1984, data from Table 1, p. 360.)*

paper.'' [These researchers] did not find male professionals of similar rank who as often felt a sense of personal responsibility for remembering, scheduling, and orchestrating the purchase and maintenance of routine or unusual domestic supplies. (p. 171)

Husbands of working women ''help'' with the housework when ''asked,'' but most of the research shows only a small or moderate increase in the number of hours per day or per week that husbands of working wives spend in household tasks (Geerken & Gove, 1983; Pleck & Rustad, 1980), compared to the household contribution of husbands with wives who are full-time homemakers. At least one study also shows a link between labor allocation and stage of the family life cycle. Suzanne Model (1981) found that husbands provided the least help during the time when children were in the household (a time when the husband's career demands may be greatest) and the most help at the newlywed and postretirement stages.

In sum, working women, compared to nonworking women, spend fewer hours doing housework or child care, but they still spend far more time at these activities than do their husbands. There is some sign that this is changing slowly toward more egalitarian arrangements (Johnson & Firebaugh, 1985; Maret & Finlay, 1984), and men with strongly egalitarian philosophies do appear to assist more than do men with more traditional views of sex roles (Bird, Bird, & Scruggs, 1984). At the moment, though, the job description for women still includes major responsibility for home, children, family. Clearly it is this expectation that is the major source of both role conflict and role strain for working women.

**The Effect of Wives' Work on Marital Satisfaction.** Given what I've said so far, you might expect that husbands of working wives would be less satisfied with their marriages. The men have lost some power in the relationship, and they are expected to provide more assistance around the house and with the children. It is somewhat surprising to find, then, that on average men whose wives work are neither more nor less satisfied with their lives, or their marriages, than are men whose wives are homemakers. This is the conclusion from a number of national surveys (reviewed and simultaneously analyzed by Fendrich, 1984). Some subgroups of men, however, show increased distress when their wives work: high-income men and men whose wives have salaries competitive with their own.

The general rule suggested by Blumstein and Schwartz in their book *American Couples* (1983), is that for a relationship to be satisfying and lasting, at least one member of the pair must be "relationship centered" rather than "work centered." In the vast preponderance of cases, it is the woman who is relationship centered. That is part of the job description for the role of "woman" in this culture. When the woman does not work, she can be strongly relationship centered. But even when she does work, the woman normally continues in the role of keeping the home fires burning. So long as she does so, or if the husband and wife are both relationship centered, satisfaction is reasonably high. It is when both husband and wife are strongly work centered that difficulties arise. Divorce seems to be higher in such couples (e.g., Philliber & Hiller, 1983), and marital satisfaction is lower.

If Blumstein and Schwartz are right, and I think they are, there are some troubling implications for women who are strongly motivated to achieve high-level success in a career, but who also want marriage and children. Such a "superwoman" combination has become the ideal for many young women in recent years. It is well to keep in mind that the research tells us this is an extremely difficult combination to carry off. A successful career virtually requires continuous employment and a strong work commitment. But a strong work commitment by a wife, especially if there are children, is likely to decrease marital satisfaction, increase the risk of divorce, and certainly increase overall role conflict and role strain. This does not imply that there is a conspiracy of some kind to prevent women from achieving both work success and family satisfaction. It does mean that our society has not yet evolved good methods to deal with such combinations of roles. Individual couples have worked out accommodations, but these are still exceptions. The difficulty at the moment is that large numbers of young women are aiming for something that is far harder to achieve than they may realize, especially in view of the sex role definitions still extant.

## Coping with the Conflict and Strain

There is no way to eliminate all of the overload and role conflict—for men or for women—that come from attempting to combine two paid jobs and family roles. But there are some strategies that help.

One strategy that does *not* help is simply trying harder to do it all. Women who attempt to do this report high levels of strain. But three other techniques seem to ease the strain somewhat:

1. Improving management skills, especially time management. Couples who successfully sail these reef-strewn waters need to be remarkably good at organizing their time. These are skills that can be learned (Seiden, 1980).
2. Redefining or restructuring the family roles. Douglas Hall in several studies (1972, 1975) has found that women who find ways to distribute tasks to other family members, or simply give up doing some tasks, experience less stress. The living room rug does not have to be vacuumed every day, men can clean toilets, teenage children can cook. And of course, given enough economic support, help can be hired.
3. Changing your ideas about what you *ought* to be. Sex role definitions are not written on stone tablets for all eternity. Each of us learned those sex role job descriptions as children and teenagers, and they are strongly ingrained. But it is possible to change the way one thinks about family roles and work roles. Women who undertake this kind of cognitive restructuring report lower levels of role conflict (Elman & Gilbert, 1984).

Dual-job or dual-career couples who are skillful in using these strategies are able to reduce their role conflict and achieve a reasonable balance of work and family life. But the balance is quite fragile, easily disrupted by unexpected demands such as a child's illness, or a car breakdown, or any of the myriad other small crises of everyday life. The simple fact is that there is no way to combine these roles that will completely eliminate the conflict or the strain. That may sound discouraging, but it is realistic.

# Retirement

I have talked so far about working and its effects. But what about the cessation of work at the time of retirement? What effect does it have on adult lives?

Two distinctly different images of retirement are part of our cultural lore.

On the one hand there is the vision of rest and relaxation, time at last to do as you please, release from the daily grind. Move to Florida and sit in the sun; get up at noon if you feel like it; stay up and watch the late movie on TV without worrying if that will make you too tired the next day.

The other vision of retirement is nicely captured by some comments I read recently in a one-page reprint making the rounds among faculty in a large university. "There is no way to describe adequately," it said, "the letdown many people feel when they retire from a responsible executive post." It went on to predict that retirees would undertake a desperate and doomed search for other sources of meaning and satisfaction, followed by depression and illness.

Which of these visions is valid? Does retirement bring large increases in satisfaction or happiness, or does it bring illness, depression, loss of a sense of self-worth, or something in between? In general, research on retirement supports the sunnier of these two visions.

## The Preparation for Retirement

Retirement is not something that just happens the day you turn 65. Barring an unexpected illness, disability, or job layoff as the cause of retirement, the vast majority of adults who retire do so after some period of planning and expectation. You may recall from earlier chapters Pearlin's (1980) concept of "scheduled" and "unscheduled" changes. For most, retirement is a scheduled change and as such is less distress-producing, less difficult.

Adults do, in fact, prepare for retirement in various ways, beginning perhaps as early as 15 or 20 years before the anticipated time of retirement (Evans, Ekerdt, & Bosse, 1985; Keating & Marshall, 1980). They talk with their spouse, relatives, and friends, read articles, do some financial planning, begin an IRA account. These activities seem to increase fairly steadily as the expected retirement date draws closer.

Such preparatory activities are not equally likely in all middle-aged workers, however. Evans and her colleagues, in one large-scale study (Evans, Ekerdt, & Bosse, 1985), found that men over 45 were more likely to report retirement-planning behavior if they were looking forward to retiring, if they enjoyed hobbies and pastimes, thought their pensions would be adequate, were dissatisfied with their jobs, or had a good friend who had retired. Those who dreaded retirement did the least preparation; but even in this group, those closest to retirement age showed more preparation than those more distant from it.

## The Timing of Retirement

Just as planning varies, so too does the actual timing of retirement. Figure 8–8 shows the percentage of men and women in each of several age groups who were still in the work force in the United States (full time or part time) in 1981 (U.S. Bureau of the Census, 1983b). You can see that retirement does not occur at the same time for all adults, but the current norm is between 62 and 65. For men, there has been a large change in retirement over the past decades.

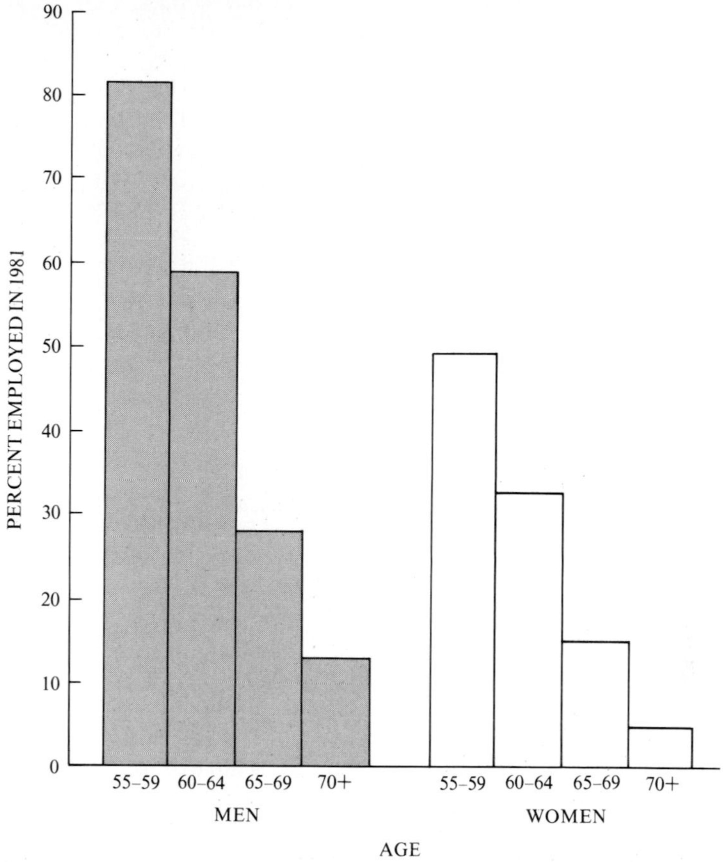


**Figure 8–8** *In the past decade, the average age at which men retire has been going down, while the average age at which women retire has been going up slightly. These figures show the percentages of men and women in each age group around age 65 who were employed in 1981. (Source: U.S. Bureau of the Census, Current Population Reports, Series p-23, No. 128, Table 12, p. 23.)*

In 1950, nearly half of men 65 and older were still working; in 1981 only about a fifth of that age group were in the work force. For women, however, there has been an increase in work rates for those 55 to 64 over the same decades, and a steady rate of employment of about 10% for those over 65. Thus, for men the average age of retirement has been coming down rapidly, while for women it has been rising somewhat.

Somewhere between 40% and 50% of retirement appears to be voluntary (Palmore et al., 1985). That is, the person stops work because he or she chose to, not because of ill health, or mandatory retirement age, or being laid off. Of those who retire involuntarily, perhaps two thirds do so because of ill health and the remainder for other reasons, such as mandatory retirement ages (Harris, 1981; Palmore et al., 1985).

## Who Retires, and Why?

Nearly everyone retires eventually, but there are clearly differences in the timing of the event. Evidence from both cross-sectional and longitudinal studies (e.g., Atchley, 1982; George, Fillenbaum, & Palmore, 1984; Palmore et al., 1985; Palmore, George, & Fillenbaum, 1982;) has converged on the following factors as influential in the timing of retirement:

**Health.** Those in poor health are likely to retire earlier than those in good health, but this is particularly so for those who retire before age 65.

**Social Class or Income.** In general, those in lower income and lower occupational status retire earlier than do those with higher income and status.

**Pension Programs.** Those who belong to a pension program (in addition to Social Security) are more likely to retire earlier than are those who lack this economic support during retirement.

**Attitudes Toward Work.** Those who have stronger committment to their work generally expect retirement to be a negative experience and retire later than do those with moderate or weaker commitment toward work.

**Marital Status.** Married men as a group retire later than single men, but married women retire earlier than single women, perhaps because their husbands have already retired.

In any individual case, these factors will interact in complex ways. For example, many workers with low incomes also have no pension program. Under these conditions workers retire somewhat later. Furthermore, all of the effects I have listed appear to be less significant predictors of retirement in women than in men (George et al., 1984). In women, the only really consistent predictor of retirement is age. Just why there should be this sex difference in the predictability of retirement is not at all obvious. It may reflect the effects of the changing status of women which has been accompanied by an increase in work participation by women in their 50s and 60s. This social change may work against the influence of other forces moving women toward retirement.

## What Are the Effects of Retirement?

The effects of retirement on the individual's income, health, activity, and attitudes are far fewer, and far smaller, than cultural stereotype would lead us to believe (George et al., 1984; Palmore et al., 1985; Palmore, Fillenbaum, & George, 1984; Szinovacz, 1982a). Furthermore, negative effects of retirement seem to be getting smaller over recent decades, as health care gets better and as cultural acceptance of retirement increases (Haring, Okun, & Stock, 1984).

**Effects on Income.** The largest single effect of retirement appears to be a reduction in income. Based on several large, national longitudinal studies, Erdman Palmore and his colleagues (Palmore et al., 1985) estimate that incomes drop an average of about 25% upon retirement. Because expenses, too, may be lower in retirement years (the mortgage may be paid off, the children are out of school and on their own, etc.) the adequacy of income does not drop by so much as 25% (Clark & Sumner, 1985). This is particularly true since the early 1970s as Social Security benefits and Supplemental Security Income (SSI) have increased sharply, raising the base income for most retired adults significantly. For example, in 1959 35% of adults over 65 lived below the poverty line; in 1981 it was only 15.3% (U.S. Bureau of the Census, 1983b). In fact, several analyses by Palmore show that the working poor may actually experience a net increase in income following retirement, since the combination of Social Security and SSI may be more than they were able to earn in their working lives.

This description of the economic condition of the retired, however, while accurate in the average, masks the existence of some significant subgroups who suffer extreme financial hardship in the retirement years. Women living alone represent the highest level of poverty among the elderly: 31.4% of such women were living below the poverty line in 1981 (U.S. Bureau of the Census, 1983b). And within this group, black women are markedly worse off, with as many as 70% living in poverty. (''Poverty,'' by the way, was defined as an annual income of $4,359 for one individual in 1981). Put another way, over 70% of elderly poor are women (Minkler & Stone, 1985). Many of these women did not, in fact, ''retire'' since they never worked. Their pension and Social Security benefits are tied to, but lower than, their spouse's, and many of them are widowed.

For the majority of adults, then, retirement does not bring as large a change in income as the common stereotype would suggest. But there is still a significant minority whose financial needs are not being met by any existing retirement programs.

**Effects on Health.** The effects of retirement on health, too, are smaller than you might expect. Summing across a number of studies, the best conclusion is that retirement itself has no direct effect on health. That is, people do not get sicker because they retire. Some retire because they are ill; Those in good health at retirement age show about the same levels of illness over the succeeding years whether they continue to work or not (Palmore et al., 1985; Palmore et al., 1984; Streib & Schneider, 1971).

**Effects on Activity Level.** The findings on changes in activities are more mixed, but as a rule retired adults increase the amount of time they spend in various nonwork activities compared to preretirement levels. They spend more time with friends, more time with hobbies or volunteer work.

**Effects on Attitudes.** Finally, contrary to the gloomier of the two visions of retirement, ''there is certainly no clear evidence . . . that retirement tends to make people depressed or dissatisfied with life'' (Palmore et al., 1985, p. 48). Cross-sectional studies, comparing life satisfaction of working adults (many younger than 65) and retired adults, show, on average, a small negative effect of retirement on life satisfaction or "subjective well being" (Haring, Okun, & Stock, 1984). But longitudinal studies, in which the same individuals have been questioned before and after retirement, generally do not show such an effect (Palmore et al., 1984; Streib & Schneider, 1971). In the Duke studies, men showed increases in self-worth, but also increases in perceptions of uselessness after retirement. Women increased in both sense of self-worth and in their belief in their ability to control their own lives. Other researchers have reported increases in a sense of autonomy after retirement among men (Palmore et al., 1984).

Given the fact that retirement does change people's everyday lives rather drastically, the paucity of physical and psychological effects seems a bit strange. The key to understanding this, I think, lies in the fact that this is a scheduled rather than an unscheduled change for most adults. Contrary to the general predictions of role theory then, major changes in roles do not always bring distress or upheaval. It is primarily the unexpected or unscheduled role changes that are linked to illness or distress.

## Who Adjusts Best to Retirement?

Despite the typically neutral effects of retirement, there are (as always) differences among adults in degree of adjustment. That is, both scenarios are true for some people. Those who adjust most easily (who are most satisfied with life and with retirement) are healthy, have an adequate income, are better educated, remain active or add new activities, have an extended social network of friends and family, think of themselves as "middle aged" rather than "old," and were generally satisfied with their lives before they retired (Block, 1982; Palmore et al., 1985; Szinovacz, 1982b). A small percentage of well-educated, highly work-committed adults find retirement particularly difficult, but this is not a general experience of well-educated, high-status workers. Such people retire later as a general rule, but normally make a good adjustment to retirement. Nor is it the case that single adults, who may have had greater work commitments, have more difficulty with retirement (Keith, 1985).

The least satisfied retirees are those with inadequate income and ill health, or those who must simultaneously cope with retirement and other major life changes, such as widowhood (Stull & Hatch, 1984). For these older adults, retirement brings serious hardship. For these adults, though, it is not the loss of the work role that is the problem, but the inadequacy of pension programs or the debilitating effects of ill health.

What predicts life satisfaction in later adulthood then, is not so much whether a person has retired or not, as much as the pattern of satisfaction or dissatisfaction in earlier adulthood. We take ourselves with us through the years; grumpy, negative young people tend to be grumpy, negative old people, and satisfied young adults find satisfactions in retirement as well. The consistency in this is quite striking, and provides very good support for consistency theories of adulthood (Palmore, 1981). Work does shape our daily lives for upwards of 50 years of our adulthood; but our happiness or unhappiness with life, our growth or stagnation, seems less a function of the specifics of the work experience than it is a function of the attitudes and qualities we bring to the process.

# A Review of Work Roles in Adulthood

As before, I have summarized the age-related changes described in this chapter in a table (Table 8–4). The pattern here is strongly reminiscent of the pattern of family and sex role changes I talked about in chapter 6. Early adulthood is marked by the acquisition and mastery of new work roles. A job must be found, and after each promotion or job change, the new job must be learned. In middle adulthood, in contrast, there are few totally new work roles, but the existing roles may be redefined. Emphases change, work values change, the relative importance of work may change. And as was true for family roles, late adulthood is a time in which work roles are lost, in this case through retirement.

Each of these tasks—acquisition of roles, redefinition of roles, and loss of roles—has its own set of issues, problems, and stresses. Different adults are

**TABLE 8–4 Summary of Age Changes in Work Roles**

| Ages 20–40 | Ages 40–65 | Age 65 and Older |
|---|---|---|
| Trial or establishment stage: first choice of occupation, influenced by personal qualities; formation of the dream; finding a mentor | Maintenance stage of career, during which there is not likely to be further career advancements; may take the role of mentor | Retirement for most workers accompanied by loss of income, but not marked reduction in health or satisfaction; some increase in social or volunteer activities |
| Stabilization stage (from 30 to about 45) after career is chosen, try to succeed at that path; most promotions and other advancements occur during this period | May be redefinition of importance of work in adult life | |
| Job satisfaction begins low and rises; job satisfaction tied in early years more to intrinsic work qualities than to extrinsic qualities | Job satisfaction at its highest, as is job involvement; job values shift somewhat, however, with greater emphasis on extrinsic values | |
| For women, this period has the greatest shifting in and out of the work force, with marriage and the birth of children | For those women who work, this is a more stable work period, with continuous work patterns more common than at earlier ages | |
| | Women who work at this age are generally more satisfied with their lives than are women who do not work | |

likely to find particular periods difficult or easy, depending on their temperament or circumstances. So for some, the heavy dosage of role acquisition in early adulthood may be particularly stressful, especially if many complex roles must be mastered simultaneously. For others, the redefinitions of midlife are more stressful, perhaps particularly so for adults who are low in openness to experience, or who lack the intellectual flexibility to reassess or redefine. For still others, the loss of roles in late life is most difficult. Thus, while we can identify a general pattern of role change over adulthood that seems to be common to the vast majority of adults, the experience of that pattern will vary markedly from one individual to another.

## Summary

1. We know more about men's work patterns than women's, and more about middle-class than working-class work histories.
2. While selecting an occupation occurs primarily in early adulthood, many adults change jobs and careers quite often over the 40 years of a working life.
3. Occupational choices are affected by gender, intelligence, personality, family background, and education.
4. Traditional ''men's jobs'' are more varied and higher in status than traditional ''women's jobs.''
5. Many jobs demand relatively high levels of intellectual skill, thus excluding young adults lacking such skills.
6. Adults tend to select occupations whose demands match their own personality charactistics or values. Six personality/job types have been suggested by Holland: realistic, investigative, social, conventional, enterprising, and artistic.
7. Families shape personality, but they also steer young people into some occupations and away from others. Young men are likely to select occupations like those of their fathers.
8. Over the adult years, job satisfaction is generally lowest among young workers and highest among workers in their 40s and 50s. Job involvement and motivation also increase over adulthood.
9. At all ages, workers attempt to find jobs that are interesting and challenging, but among workers over 45 or 50, jobs that are high in security and income are also preferred.
10. In progressing in an individual career, high levels of education are associated with more progress, as is early promotion. The most rapid career progress occurs early in adulthood.
11. Most men follow a pattern of continuous work through adulthood. The continuous flow can, however, be divided into broad stages.
12. In the establishment stage, the young man selects an occupation through trial and error and learns his work. In the stabilization stage, men pursue their career goals vigorously, striving to move as far as possible within the occupation. In the maintenance stage, men come to terms with their level of success.
13. Women's work patterns are far more variable, with up to half of married women today electing to remain at home while their children are young. Perhaps a quarter of women, however, choose a continuous work pattern.
14. Occupational success is greater for women who follow continuous patterns and for those who pursue the same field of work during interrupted work histories.

15. High levels of work success for men is not typically associated with greater life satisfaction or psychological adjustment. For women, having a job is generally associated with a slightly higher level of life satisfaction than is full-time homemaking.

16. Family life influences men's work: Married men are somewhat more successful than single men.

17. When both husband and wife work, role conflict and role strain increase, especially for women. In two-job families, compared to one-job families, women have more power, remain responsible for homemaking tasks and childrearing, but spend fewer hours actually doing housework.

18. Marital satisfaction is not generally higher or lower among two-job families, but is dependent on the presence of at least one relationship-centered partner.

19. The conflict and strain of a two-job family can be reduced by improving management skills, redefining the tasks, and rethinking and restructuring internal concepts of sex and work roles.

20. Retirement occurs between 60 and 65 for most working adults, although some remain in the work force well into their 70s. Most adults begin to prepare mentally and emotionally for their retirement some years before retirement age. Those who retire early, compared to those who retire late, are in poorer health, are lower in social class, are less committed to their work, and have decent pension programs.

21. The effects of retirement on the individual are generally smaller than popular lore would suggest. Income does go down and daily routines change, but health does not decline because of retirement, nor does life satisfaction go down.

22. Among the elderly, however, single women are far more likely than other groups to be poor.

## Suggested Readings

BLUMSTEIN, P., & SCHWARTZ, P. (1983). *American couples.* New York: William Morrow.

This book describes a series of extensive interviews with a broad range of couples about money, work, and sex. Included in the group are married couples, cohabiting couples, and both gay and lesbian couples, which gives the study a unique richness. The book is written for a lay audience, and includes a number of fascinating case studies.

GILBERT, L. A. (1985). *Men in dual-career families.* Hillsdale, NJ: Lawrence Erlbaum Associates.

For those who anticipate a marriage in which both husband and wife will have a career, this book may be especially interesting. The focus is on men's experience in dual-career families (based on extensive interviews with 51 such men), but Gilbert also reviews other theory and evidence. Food for thought.

TERKEL, S. (1972). *Working.* New York: Avon.

If you want to know what work feels like to Americans across an enormous range of occupations, read Studs Terkel's fascinating book.

# 9

# Changes in Personality, Motivation, and Values over the Adult Years

A 38-year-old friend, depressed over an accumulation of changes in his life, said to me recently, "This must be my midlife crisis, except that I'm not old enough yet!" Another expressed some surprise at her 75-year-old mother's vital and extensive social life. "I thought old people sat around and reminisced, or lived quiet, peaceful lives. She's still a whirlwind." Other friends, reaching their 40s and 50s, are telling me that the men their age are not quite so "macho" as they used to be. Men seem to cry more easily, or to be willing to talk about their feelings. But my men friends are saying that the women in their lives are restless and ready to try new things.

Lately, it seems, a great deal of the conversation that goes on among adults over coffee or dinner has to do with possible changes in personality at various points in the life cycle, a preoccupation fed by a string of best-selling books like *Passages, Making It from 40 to 50*, *Crisis Time!,* or *Love, Sex, and Aging*. The concept of a "midlife crisis," in fact, has reached such common acceptance that friends and acquaintances are routinely surprised when I express even the slightest doubt about the universality of this experience.

But is it all true? Are there predictable, widely shared changes in personality over the adult years? Do we all go through some kind of mid-life crisis? Do we become more androgynous in middle or later life, with men becoming more emotionally expressive and women more independent and assertive? Do older adults go through a process of "disengagement," as one widely quoted major theory would have us believe? Earlier chapters contain bits and pieces of information that give us part of the answers to these questions. But we need now to look systematically at the evidence on personality change or stability.

# Another Look at Change Versus Consistency

In chapter 2, I described some of the evidence for consistency in personality over the adult years. You will remember that on at least some dimensions, such as extraversion/introversion or neuroticism, adults appear to be notably consistent, at least over periods of 10 or 20 years. But as I pointed out then (and again in chapter 5, when talking about consistency and change in IQ) it is logically and theoretically possible to find both individual consistency and systematic developmental change at the same time. For example, even though adults tend to stay in the same relative position over time on measures of introversion, we could still find an average increase in introversion with age.

In this chapter I want to ask whether, in fact, there are any dimensions of personality, motivation, or values that show consistent average changes with age. That is, are there "developmental" patterns (in the sense in which I have used that word) in personality over individuals' lifetimes? Jane Loevinger (1984) uses the word "self" or the phrase "self system" to describe that "filter, template, or frame of reference for one's perception and conception of the interpersonal world" (p. 49). This template includes personality traits as well as values and motivations. Put in these terms, then, I am asking whether there are any predictable changes in our sense of self as we move through adulthood.

# Some Theories About Personality Change in Adulthood

I have already described several of the major theories of adult personality change in chapter 3, including Erikson's, Loevinger's, and Vaillant's. Let me review these briefly and explore in greater depth one other view, Abraham Maslow's theory of the hierarchy of motives.

## Erikson, Loevinger, and Vaillant: A Reprise

**Erikson's Stages of Identity Development.** Recall from chapter 3 that Erikson proposes a series of eight stages covering the ages from birth to death (Table 3–1). In each stage, a central task or dilemma is confronted and may be fully or only partially resolved. The sequence of dilemmas is heavily influenced by changes in social demands faced by the child and adult as she moves through the typical series of life roles. In adulthood, four stages are particularly relevant: identity versus role confusion (which Erikson placed in adolescence but which appears to continue into early adulthood for most of us), intimacy versus isolation (in early adulthood), generativity versus stagnation (in middle adulthood), and integrity versus despair (late adulthood and old age). If Erikson is correct, we should see shifts in the "self" or the "identity" over adulthood that reflect these different stages, moving from a focus on personal relationships and social roles in early and middle adulthood to greater "interiority" or reflectiveness in later life.

**Loevinger's Stages of Ego Development.** Loevinger, too, proposes stages (see Table 3–2 for a review) but in her theory they are caused less by changes in external roles or demands and more by internal, *structural* changes—fundamental changes in the way the individual experiences and understands his relationships and his world. Unlike Erikson, who thought that all adults eventually face all the dilemmas whether they have successfully worked out the earlier ones or not, Loevinger does not assume that all adults move through the sequence of stages she describes. But like Erikson, Loevinger's stages describe a general movement from dominance by social roles and conventionality to increasing individuality and autonomy, and increasing awareness of inner complexities.

If Loevinger's model is correct, then each succeedingly older age group should include more and more adults who have reached the "higher" stages, so the average scores on measures of autonomy or complexity should go up.

**Vaillant's Theory of Defense Mechanism Development.** Vaillant, like Loevinger, proposes a broad sequence of movement toward more maturity, while at the same time arguing that adults differ in the distance along this continuum that they move. Specifically, he proposes a hierarchy of defense mechanisms, from psychotic to immature to neurotic to mature forms (reviewed in Table 3–4). To the extent that adults successfully move toward a greater and greater use of mature mechanisms, we should find that older adults are more likely to display altruism, humor, and conscious awareness of their own inner processes.

## Maslow's Hierarchy of Needs or Motives

Like all three of the theorists I have just described, Abraham Maslow (1968, 1970a, 1970b, 1971) traces his theoretical tradition to Freud and other psychoanalytic thinkers, but he has offered some highly original insights.

Maslow's most central concern has been with the development of motives or needs, which he divides into two main groups: **deficiency motives** (also called D-motives) in contrast to **growth motives** or **being motives** (also called B-motives). Deficiency motives involve instincts or drives to correct imbalance or to maintain physical or emotional homeostasis, such as getting enough to eat, satisfying thirst, or obtaining enough love and respect from others. Deficiency motives are found in all animals. Being motives, in contrast, are distinctly human. Maslow argues that humans have unique desires to discover and understand, to give love to others, and to push for the optimum fulfillment of their inner potentials.

In general, the satisfaction of deficiency motives prevents illness, or cures illness, or recreates homeostasis (inner balance), while the satisfaction of being motives produces positive health. The distinction is like the "difference between fending off threat or attack, and positive triumph and achievement" (Maslow, 1968, 32).

But being motives are quite fragile and do not typically emerge until well into adulthood, and then only under supportive circumstances. Maslow's widely quoted needs hierarchy (Figure 9–1) reflects this aspect of his thinking. The lowest four levels on this hierarchy all describe different deficiency needs, while only the need for self-actualization is a being motive. Further, Maslow proposes that these five levels emerge sequentially in development, and tend to dominate the system from the bottom up. That is, if you are starving, the physiological needs dominate. If you are being physically battered, the safety needs dominate. In general, the need for self-actualization only emerges when all four types of deficiency needs are largely satisfied. Maslow's own estimates (1970b) were that among American adults about 50% of love needs, 40% of esteem needs, and only 10% of self-actualization needs are satisfied. The end point of the system may thus be the achievement of complete self knowledge, but few adults reach that point.

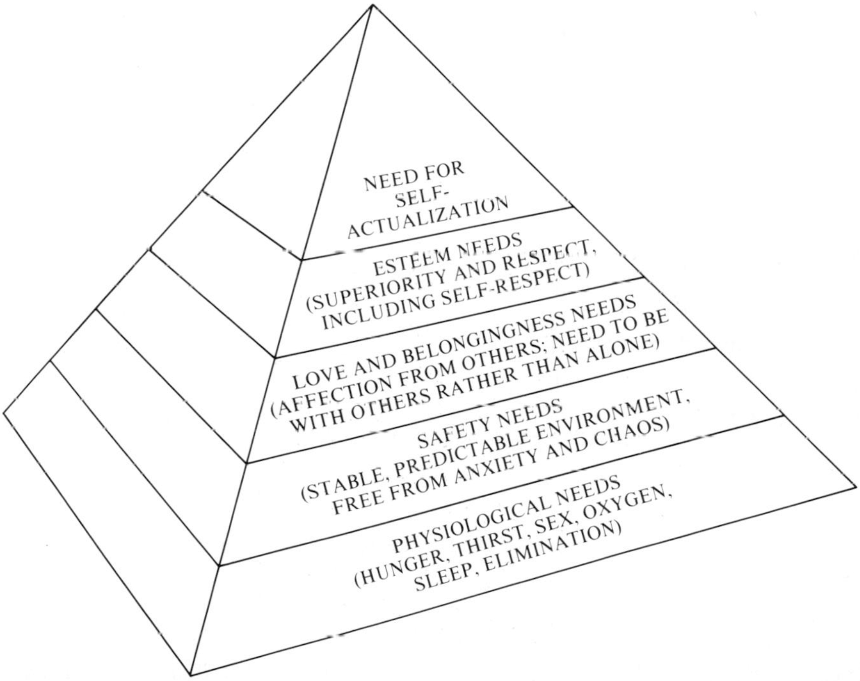


***Figure 9–1*** *Maslow's Need Hierarchy. Maslow proposed that these needs dominate the system from the bottom up, with higher level needs only coming to the fore later in life, and only when the lower needs were largely satisfied. (Source: Maslow, 1968, 1970b.)*

Despite the fact that Maslow's theory of motives has had little scientific testing, it has been widely accepted, perhaps because it has such a strong ring of truth for many of us. The theory also gains credence from the intriguing parallels between this hierarachy of needs and the stage theories offered by Erikson and Loevinger, and even Vaillant's theory. The need for belongingness and love, which dominates the motive system in the teens and 20s (and in later adulthood, too, for those who do not satisfy these needs earlier), is one aspect of what Erikson describes as the task of develping intimacy. Similarly, the need for the esteem of others and for high self esteem is one aspect of the process of generativity in Erikson's theory, and of the emergence of the conscientious adult in Loevinger's system. The pursuit of fulfillment of the need for self-actualization, in turn, sounds quite similar to the descriptions of the search for integrity offered by Erikson and Loevinger. In all these theories, a shift from essentially *external* to essentially *internal* definitions of the self is seen as a key part of a healthy adulthood.

**The Self-Actualizing Person.** No description of Maslow's theory would be complete without some further explication of his notion of self-actualization, and the self-actualizing person. Maslow's interest was in positive health, in genuine growth, not simply in the avoidance of illness or the creation of stability. So he sought to understand the personality and characteristics of those few adults who seemed to have risen to the top of the need hierarchy and to have achieved significant levels of self-understanding and expression—individuals like Eleanor Roosevelt, Albert Schweitzer, Albert Einstein, and Thomas Jefferson. Some of the key characteristics of such individuals, as Maslow saw them, are listed in Table 9–1.

As you read this list, you may wonder whether anyone—short of sainthood—is really like this! In fact Maslow thought that complete self-actualization was quite rare and likely to occur only quite late in life. But many adults, as they move into their middle years, may come to display at least a few of these characteristics, gradually adding more and more as lower level needs are satisfied, and as the need for self-actualization comes to dominate the motive system. Other adults, perhaps the majority, whose environments or relationships do not adequately satisfy their lower level needs, rarely experience the press of the need for self-actualization and may show few of these qualities.

# Personality Development: Some Hypotheses

Combining these theories, we can extract several broad hypotheses about the changes in personality or motives or sense of self that we might expect to see over the adult years:

1. There should be a shift from a preoccupation with relationships to a preoccupation with personal achievement or "generativity." This includes the

**TABLE 9–1 Some of the Characteristics of the Self-Actualizing Person, as Proposed by Maslow**

| | |
|---|---|
| More accurate perception of reality | The person is relatively free of defensive distortions or self-delusion and sees others and the environment clearly. |
| Greater acceptance of self and others | The person is more tolerant of both himself and others, accepting frailty as well as strength. They generally lack shame or anxiety about themselves, as a result. |
| Greater spontaneity and self-knowledge | These individuals are quite "natural," perhaps even eccentric in their behavior and life style, since they are not constrained by fear of what others think of them. They know themselves well, and follow that understanding. |
| Greater autonomy and resistance to acculturation | As a related quality, the self-actualizing person is more independent and not easily swayed by pressures of society, including role expectations. |
| Greater problem centering | Interestingly, despite their high level of self-knowledge, self-actualizing persons are typically not very introspective or "self-centered." Rather, they are typically involved in external problems, and may have a consuming mission in life, which often involves wider philosophical or ethical issues. |
| Greater freshness of appreciation and richness of emotional response | Self-actualizers live rich emotional lives and have the capacity to "see" things freshly, to experience again and again the wonder and joy of existence or the intensity of pain. |
| Greater frequency of "peak experiences" | A peak experience, in Maslow's language, is a brief (or sometimes prolonged) mystical moment, a sense of perfection or a sense of the loss of the sense of self altogether, and a submersion in a sense of unity. They may occur during sex, during creativity, or in profound insight or scientific discovery, or as the result of meditation or prayer. |
| Greater social interest | Self-actualizing individuals have deep sympathy and compassion for their fellow beings and a strong desire to help others. |
| Deeper, more loving interpersonal relationships | Not surprisingly, their personal relationships with spouse and close friends tend to be extremely deep, and not motivated by deficiency love needs. Sex is seen as meaningless without love; they are attracted to others who display goodness and considerateness. |
| Greater need for privacy | Paradoxically, self-actualizing adults also have stronger-than-normal needs for time alone, for solitude. There is a kind of emotional detachment that characterizes these individuals, even while their relationships are extremely loving. |
| Greater discrimination between good and evil, and between means and ends | These individuals have strong moral and ethical principles and live up to them quite fully. Their focus is nearly always on ends rather |

**TABLE 9—1 Some of the Characteristics of the Self-Actualizing Person, as Proposed by Maslow (*continued*)**

| | |
|---|---|
| | than means, although they would not argue that the "ends justify the means." |
| Greater creativity | Every self-actualizing person Maslow studied displayed some unusual form of creativity, whether artistic or otherwise. |
| More unusual sense of humor | These adults dislike humor that involves making fun of others, or insulting others. Their humor may take the form of anecdotes, but does not involve sarcasm. (Similar to "mature" humor as described by Vaillant.) |

**Source:** Maslow, 1968.

transition from the "conformist" to the "conscientious" or "autonomous" stages in Loevinger's model, from intimacy to generativity in Erikson's model, and from love needs to self-esteem needs in Maslow's hierarchy. We might expect to see this shift particularly clearly between early and middle adulthood.

2. There may be a second shift from the active, achieving, comparative emphasis of early midlife to a more reflective, inward-turned focus on self-understanding in late midlife and early retirement years. Bernice Neugarten (1976) has described this as an increase in **interiority**. To the extent that adults make this shift, we should see less and less concern with social roles, more concern with establishing personal values and personal life styles. This shift corresponds to the move toward the "integrated" stage in Loevinger, the period of "integrity" in Erikson, and the mature defense mechanisms described by Vaillant.
3. For a few, there may be still a third shift toward self-actualization, with its freedom from social conventions and its simultaneous focus on humanitarian values and actions. Thus, if these theorists are correct, after a period of new self-definition, of freeing oneself from some of the constraints of roles, the individual's values and behaviors may show another outward turn, toward compassion or altruism.
4. This sequence is not completed by all adults, perhaps not even by most adults. Thus, if we study adults longitudinally, the earlier steps or stages should be most apparent; the later changes may be much more difficult to detect in group comparisons.

## Some Difficulties in Testing These Hypotheses with Existing Evidence

Obviously, these hypotheses, like many theoretical statements, are broad and quite vague. They are inherently difficult to test precisely. The problem is made more difficult, however, by the fact that much of the information available on personality change in adulthood has not been structured around any explicit theory of adult development. Most frequently, researchers have simply used one or another of the many existing pencil and paper tests of personality, such as the California Personality Inventory, or Cattell's 16PF, or the Edwards Personal Preference Schedule, and have then compared the scores of younger and older adults. These inventories include items like "I easily become impatient with people," or "I am a happy person," or "I am superior to other people in some ways." The respondent is asked to indicate agreement or disagreement with a large number of such statements, from which a series of summary scores is then derived.

There is nothing inherently wrong with such personality inventories. Several are highly reliable and widely used. But none is linked to any developmental theory of adulthood, and since different researchers have used many different instruments, it is extremely difficult to add up the results. Furthermore, as usual, the cross-sectional studies have rarely included adults across the full age range, concentrating instead on comparisons of young and old, or middle-aged and old. We thus end up with a patchwork quilt of findings.

In recent years, however, a number of long-term longitudinal studies covering at least the early part of the adult years have come to fruition. Although widely different measures of personality have been used in these studies, collectively they begin to give us some picture of the changes (and the continuities) in personality, motives, values, and self-concepts of adults.

## Change and Continuity in Personality

### Results from Four Major Longitudinal Studies

Four of the most complete longitudinal studies, the Berkeley Intergenerational Studies, the AT&T studies, the Grant study, and the Seattle Longitudinal Study, have included at least some measure of personality in their testing batteries. You have met these studies before (see Table 1–2 for a quick review), but the specific measures of personality used in each case may require some further description.

**The Berkeley Intergenerational Studies.** The richest and most complex vein of information is found in the Berkeley studies. Recall that two separate studies were done—the Oakland Growth Study (OGS), involving a group of children born in 1920–21 who were first studied at about ages 12 to 14, and then again at 17, 37, and 47; and the Berkeley Guidance Study (GS), involving a group of subjects born in 1928 who were studied from infancy through adolescence, and then again at ages 30 and 40. Since each group included both males and females, four samples are included, with 26 to 41 subjects in each sample. To make comparisons simpler, the researchers have focused on the measurements in each sample at age 14, at 17, at "early adulthood" (age 37 for the OGS and 30 for the GS), and at "later adulthood" (age 47 for OGS and 40 for GS).

Norma Haan, who has been primarily responsible for the analysis of personality change in these samples (Haan, 1976, 1981; Haan & Day, 1974), has used several different methods of analysis. But in all analyses, the primary measure of personality has been the the **Q sort** (Block, 1971), a measurement technique that is unusual enough to require some elaboration.

The Q sort consists of a large number (90 for this investigation) of words or phrases that might describe an individual, such as "socially poised" or "feels guilty," or "satisfied with self." A rater (usually a highly trained psychologist, psychiatrist, social worker, or the like) reads through all the information available on a subject at any one age, from interviews, observations, or standardized test scores, and then sorts the many statements into a forced normal distribution of nine piles. The few statements that are seen by the rater as most characteristic of the individual are put in the #9 pile, and the few that are seen as the least characteristic are put in the #1 pile, with the remainder distributed in between. The number of items placed in each pile is specified ahead of time, and is the same for each subject. Each item is then given the score that represents the pile in which it is placed for that subject.

For the subjects in these two studies, separate Q sorts were completed (by different raters) at each of the four ages. It is important to understand that, given this type of measurement, change from one age to the next represents *intra*individual change—change in the relative position of particular descriptors within the structure for an individual. If we find that there are common changes, this means that there were shared reorderings. Thus, Q sort data do not tell us about any changes in the *absolute* level of any one characteristic, but only about changes in the *relative* levels within individuals.

Haan (1981) found that the 90 items could be grouped into six clusters, of which five showed some kind of pattern of change with age. Three of these patterns are shown in Figure 9–2. You can see that there was an increase with age in the relative prominence of items measuring "cognitive investment" (such as "values intellectual matters," "ambitious," "wide interests," "productive"), an increase in self-confidence (measured by items such as "assertive," "satisfied with self," "poised," and "values independence"), and an increase in "openness to self" (measured by high placement of items such as "insightful," "introspective," and "think unconventionally," and low placement of items such as "conventional," or "self-defensive").

On another cluster measuring nurturance/hostility, women showed relative increases in nurturance between age 17 and middle adulthood, while men did not. The OGS men showed a rise in nurturance between ages 37 and 47, but this pattern did not occur in the younger GS sample. On a fifth factor measuring basically interest in and expression of sexuality, all groups showed a decline from age 17 to early adulthood, and then an increase between the 30s and the 40s. Finally, there was no change with age on a factor measuring the degree of emotional control.

In sum, over the first half of adulthood, these adults became relatively more

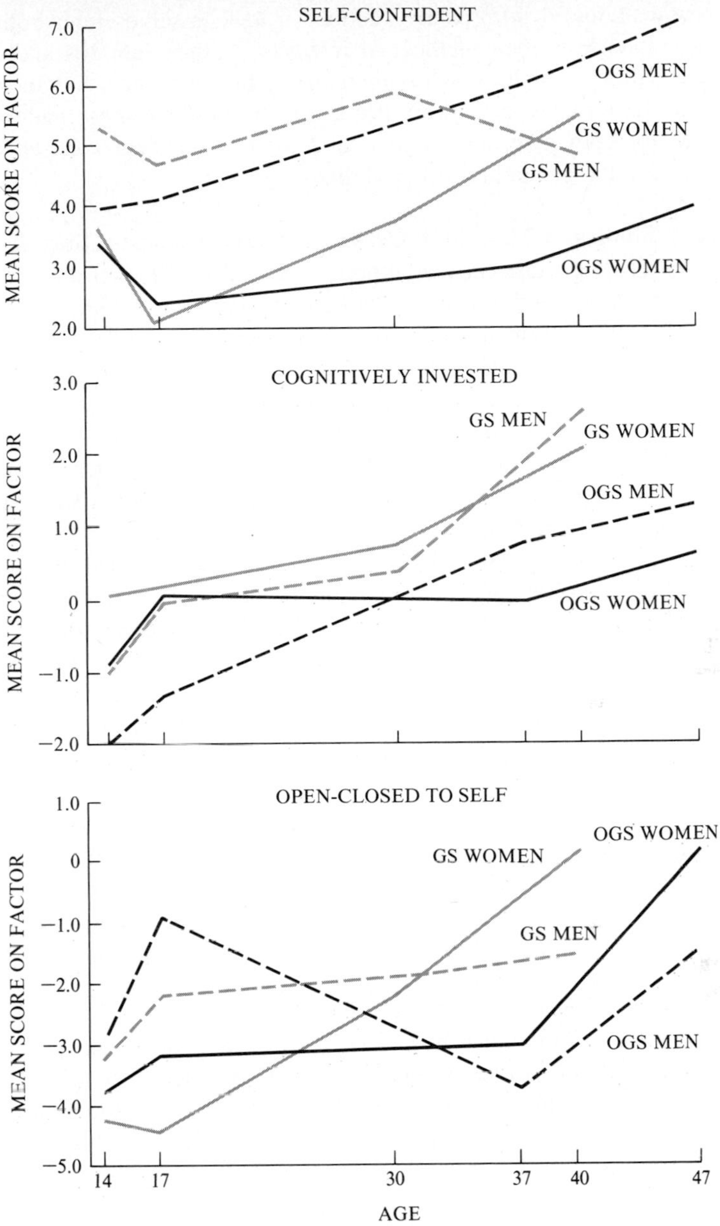


**Figure 9–2** *Haan's analysis of the Berkeley Q-Sorts revealed six clusters of items, three of which are shown here. The scores shown are the average scores on the clusters at each of four ages for each of the four samples. As you can see, there was a rise with age in the cluster called "cognitively invested," for self-confidence, and in openness to self. (Source: Haan, 1981, Figure 5.1, 5.3, and 5.6, pp. 132, 134. Reprinted by permission of Academic Press, Orlando, FL and author.)*

self confident, more introspective and open to themselves, and both broader and more intense in their intellectual interests. In their late 30s and 40s, they also showed some indication of an increase in nurturance and in sexuality. Although the samples studied are not large, the fact that these patterns generally held for both men and women, and for two adjacent cohorts, increases confidence in the generality of the findings.

**AT&T Studies of Male Managers.** The AT&T studies (Bray & Howard, 1983) covered the same early adulthood years. The 422 men included had all entered AT&T as low-level managers between 1956 and 1960, and were studied for 20 years. The men had been born between 1927 and 1936, so this is a slightly later cohort than the Berkeley Guidance Study sample. While the focus of the research was on work attitudes and prediction of work success, a number of personality measures were included in the various assessments. In particular, ratings were made on dimensions such as Need for Superior Approval and Need for Peer Approval, and the subjects completed several standardized pencil-and-paper personality tests.

Bray and Howard (1983) have not yet presented a detailed analysis of the personality continuities and changes, but do report several clear trends: (1) There was a decline over the 20 years in several measures of dependency, including both Need for Superior Approval and Need for Peer Approval. (2) There was an increase in independence, as measured particularly by a score on the Need Autonomy score from the Edwards Personal Preference Scales. I have shown this particular change in Figure 9–3, separately for college-educated and noncollege-educated men. To check to see if this pattern of rising autonomy was unique to this particular cohort, Bray and Howard also tested a new group of young managers in 1977. As you can see in the figure, this 1977 cohort of men (and women, too, in this sample) scored at the same approximate levels as had young managers in 1956, a finding which lends support to the assumption that this is an age-related or developmental change and not merely a pattern characteristic of a single cohort.

Changes in other scores provide additional evidence of the nature of this increased push toward independence and away from dependence. "The men showed a decline in motivation to make and enjoy friends, to understand others' motives or feelings, and to conform to authority and regulations" (1983, p. 293). Overall, Bray and Howard suggest that these men have become "harder" over the 20 year period.

**The Grant Study of Harvard Men.** A third study covering the years of early-to-middle adulthood is the Grant Study, which included 268 men originally studied when they were Harvard sophomores between 1936 and 1942 (and who were thus born between approximately 1917 and 1922). The men chosen were all thought to be relatively "healthy" and successful as undergraduates, so the sample includes few men who had any serious emotional problems. The men later completed questionnaires annually or biennially, and were interviewed at length in 1950–52. Finally, 100 men were interviewed by

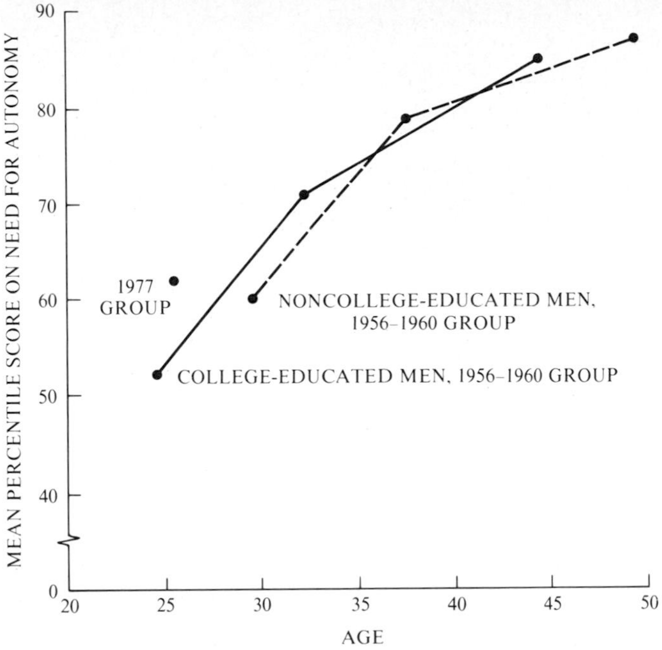


**Figure 9–3** *In the AT&T managers studied by Bray and Howard, the need for autonomy rose from early to middle adulthood, in both college-educated and non-college-educated groups. Twenty years later, another group of young managers reported a level of need for autonomy that was similar to that of the young managers in 1956–1960, which indicates that this is not merely a pattern typical of one cohort. (Source: Bray & Howard, 1983, Figure 8.5 adapted.)*

George Vaillant 30 years after they had entered the study, when the men were then in their late 40s or early 50s.

Vaillant's (1977a) report of the results of this study is cast primarily in the form of detailed case studies, with only a small amount of statistical analysis. He has, however, analyzed the defense mechanisms used by the men, as rated by judges reading transcripts of interviews and responses to open-ended questions on the questionnaires. As you can see in Figure 9–4, Vaillant found that with increasing age there was a shift toward more mature defenses and away from immature defenses.

Interestingly, such a change in defenses also appeared in some of the findings from the Berkeley studies. When Haan (1976) analyzed changes in individual Q sort items, rather than in clusters of items, she found decreases with age in self-defensiveness, fantasizing, and projection. Thus, we have two quite different studies reporting similar declines in immature defensive patterns between early adulthood and midlife.

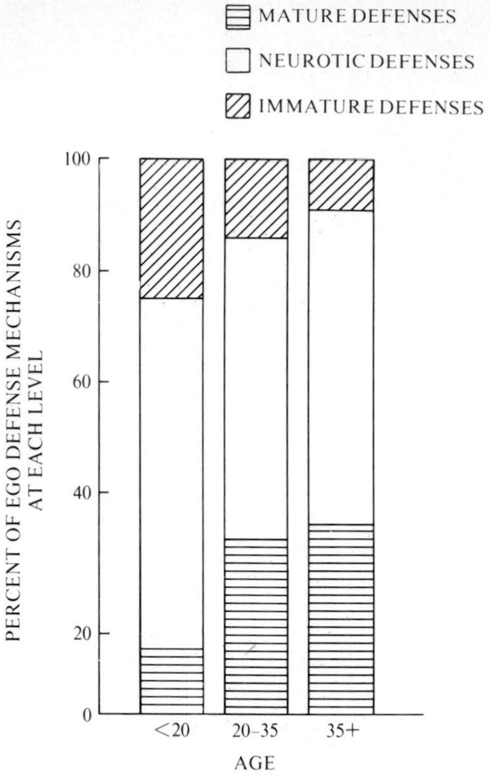


***Figure 9–4*** *These scores on the three categories of defense mechanisms come from analyses made by Vaillant of the interviews and questionnaires of 100 men in the Grant study who had been studied from college age to age 50. Immature defenses declined, and mature defenses increased over those years. (Source: From* Adaptation to Life *by George E. Vaillant. Copyright © 1977 by George E. Vaillant. By permission of Little, Brown and Company.)*

**Schaie's Cross-Sequential Study of Intelligence and Rigidity.** The fourth large study is one that should be particularly familiar by now, since I drew heavily upon it in chapter 5 (Schaie, 1983b). Recall that Schaie has completed both repeated cross-sectional comparisons covering the full adult age range, and has followed some of the subjects longitudinally for as long as 21 years. The majority of the testing of these subjects was of intellectual ability, but Schaie also included several measures of personality, such as a portion of the California Psychological Inventory, and a special set of items and tests designed to measure the dimension of rigidity-flexibility. Flexible individuals are those who can adapt quickly to changing circumstances, who are not made uncomfortable by new tasks or environments, who enjoy trying new things.

Figure 9–5 shows two cross-sectional comparisons (1970 and 1977) as well as an estimated longitudinal pattern for the measure of personality rigidity-flexibility. High scores here reflect flexibility, so you can see that adults appear to become more rigid as they age. (The longitudinal estimate here was calculated in the same way as the equivalent longitudinal estimate of total IQ, shown in Figure 5–1 and described in the text in chapter 5.) Since the pattern of declining flexibility was also found in the 1956 and 1963 cross-sectional comparisons for both men and women, the finding appears to be quite general.

Not all the measures of personality in this study showed patterns of change with age, however. Schaie and Parham (1976), using longitudinal and cross-sectional evidence from the 1963 and 1970 assessments, found that of 19 separate measures, only the dimension of "humanitarian concern" showed a consistent change with age in every cohort, with older adults displaying more concern

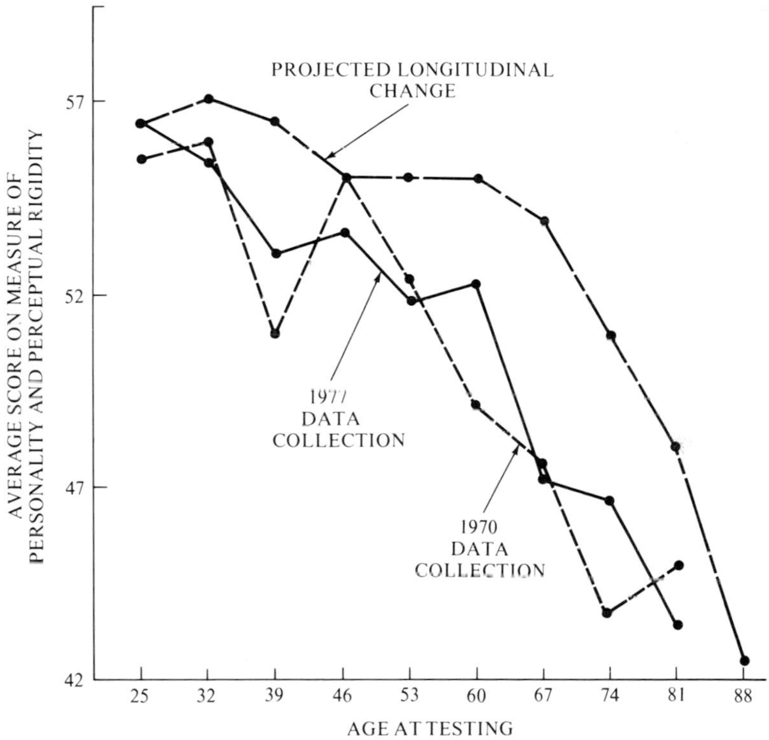


**Figure 9–5** *Schaie's study of a large number of adults, across the full span of adult years, included both repeated cross-sectional comparisons and longitudinal assessment of a subsample. This chart shows the cross-sectional data from two different assessments on a measure of personality rigidity, and an estimated longitudinal curve. Low scores on this measure indicate rigidity. (Source: Schaie, 1983b, adapted from Tables 4.21 and 4.23.)*

than younger adults. On other dimensions there were cohort differences, but no clear developmental change. For example, the more recent birth cohorts were more outgoing, less excitable, more internally restrained, more jealous and suspicious, less practical, more conservative, and higher in group dependency. But except for humanitarian concern, there were no clear age-related differences that appeared in all cohorts. Instead, considerable personal consistency was found over the seven-year interval studied longitudinally.

## Other Evidence on Personality Change

Other evidence, including several briefer or less extensive longitudinal studies and a host of cross-sectional comparisons, add to the complexity of the picture. For example, data from the Duke study of men and women ages 46 to 69 (Siegler, George, & Okun, 1979) show essentially no age changes on scores from the Cattell 16 Personality Factor test over an eight-year period. (These scores are similar to those on which Schaie found no age changes in his cross-sequential study.) Similarly, Woodruff and Birren (1972), who gave a general personality test to a group of adults who had been first tested as undergraduates 25 years earlier, found no change in the total score on the test over that long interval.

But two other longitudinal studies show changes with age. In one, personality change was studied longitudinally in a group of men between the ages of 37 and 77 who were part of a study of cardiovascular risk (Leon, Gillum, Gillum, & Gouze, 1979). The researchers found increases with age in depression, introversion, anxiety, and hypochondriasis, with particularly high scores on all these dimensions in old age. In the second, Whitbourne and Waterman (1979) followed a group of college students for 10 years after graduation, using a measure derived explicitly from Erikson's theory, with scores on scales of industry versus inferiority, identity versus role confusion, and intimacy versus isolation. They found increases in scores on all three scales over the 10 years. Since a new group of undergraduates tested at the same time as the 10-year follow-up showed low scores on the scales, the longitudinal results cannot be attributed to societal changes that have occurred during those years.

Cross-sectional studies, many of them involving comparisons of middle-aged and older adults, leave us with similarly conflicting results. Neugarten (1977) has concluded that the only consistent thread is an increase between middle age and old age in interiority. Older adults appear to be less likely to try to change the world, are less ''outer directed,'' and more focused on interior processes.

Such a shift from ''agency'' to ''interiority,'' or (as Carol Ryff, 1982, puts it) from ''implementation'' to ''culmination,'' is echoed in in David Gutmann's (1977) fascinating cross-cultural analysis (which I mentioned briefly in chapter 6). Gutmann has studied the personalities and the roles of middle-aged and aging men in a variety of Asian, Middle Eastern, and American Indian cultures, and has analyzed similar studies of women by other ethnographers. In general, he finds that for men there is a shift from active to passive mastery, and a reduction in dominance between midlife and old age. Older women, in contrast, appear in many cultures to increase in active mastery and power from midlife to old age, although this power is largely expressed through informal systems rather than in formal power structures, which continue to be dominated by men well into old age. Thus, in many cultures, men reach the peak of their "productive instrumentality" in middle age, after which they show a softening or mellowing. Women seem to reach a peak of nurturing or other-orientation at middle life, after which they show a rise in individual achievement and initiative.

Neugarten's analysis notwithstanding, the evidence for increased interiority in old age is not entirely consistent. Some particularly intriguing, disconfirming evidence comes from Carol Ryff's series of studies of adults' perceptions of their own change or stability in personality (Ryff, 1984; Ryff & Heincke, 1983). Not only did Ryff ask young, middle-aged, and old adults to describe their current selves, she also asked the older groups to describe themselves as they had been at earlier points, and the younger groups to describe how they thought they would be at later ages. In order to test both Erikson's theories about generativity and integrity and Neugarten's hypothesis about complexity in midlife and interiority in old age, Ryff devised scales to measure each dimension. She found that, as expected, generativity peaked at midlife, while integrity peaked in old age. Adults currently in those age groups described themselves more in those terms than did other groups. In addition, older adults recalled themselves as higher in generativity at midlife, and younger adults expected to become more integrated in old age. But Ryff could find no systematic age differences in interiority, and found the expected heightened levels of "complexity" at midlife only on concurrent (and not on retrospective or prospective) descriptions.

No doubt by now your head is swimming with data. The findings are complex and often contradictory. But before I attempt a synthesis, let me add several more bits to the mass of information by looking at patterns of change in motives and values in adulthood.

# Changes in Values and Motives

## Values

In chapter 8 I talked about some of the changes in work values found in studies of working men. Men younger than about 40 or 45 value work most highly if it is challenging and complex, while older men place value both on complexity and on such extrinsic job qualities as income and security. Studies of a wider range of life values generally corroborate this trend.

I can find no longitudinal studies that describe value changes, but there are several large cross-sectional studies available. The best of these is the Michigan Survey Research Center Study of Mental Illness and Health (see Table 1–2) by Joseph Veroff and his colleagues (Veroff, Douvan, & Kulka, 1981). Recall that this study involved interviews with large random samples of Americans in each of two years, 1957 and 1976.

To explore values, Veroff gave his subjects a list of the following items, and asked them to pick their first and second priorities: sense of belonging, excitement, warm relationships with others, self-fulfillment, being well respected, fun and enjoyment in life, security, self-respect, and a sense of accomplishment. These were then combined into five value orientations: (1) sociability (first choice of either belonging or warm relations), (2) hedonism (first choice of excitement or fun and enjoyment), (3) self-actualization (first choice of self-fulfillment or sense of accomplishment (note that this is not the same thing that Maslow means by self-actualization), (4) moral respect (first choice of being well respected or self-respect), and (5) security (first choice of security).

When Veroff compared the value orientations of younger adults (21 to 39) and older adults (40+), the pattern in Figure 9–6 emerged. Regrettably, Veroff did not subdivide the "older adult" group still further, so it is impossible to tell whether there would be further differences in values between those in their 40s and 50s, and those in their 60s and beyond. But the pattern shown in the figure is nonetheless interesting. Younger adults were more likely to place a high value on self actualization, on sociability, and on hedonism, while older adults were more likely to value self-respect and the respect of others.

It is worth noting that Veroff reports these value data only for men and women who are employed. No parallel information is given for women who are full-time homemakers.

A second set of information comes from Marjorie Lowenthal and her colleagues (Lowenthal, Thurnher, & Chiriboga, 1975), who have studied 216 men and women from four age groups, each in the midst of or preparing for a major role change: high school seniors (age 17), newlyweds (average age about 24), the parents of the high school seniors (average age about 50), and a group about to retire (average age about 60). Analysis of themes and values expressed during the extensive interviews showed that the two youngest groups placed the greatest value on instrumental-material goals (making money, being a success), the middle-aged group placed the strongest emphasis on interpersonal/expressive values, while the oldest group valued ease and contentment.

Finally, in two studies comparing middle-aged and older women, Carol Ryff (Ryff, 1982; Ryff & Baltes, 1976) found a significant shift from "instrumental" to "terminal" values. Instrumental values relate to desirable modes of conduct (being something), such as "ambitious," "capable," or "courageous." Terminal values describe desirable end states of existence (having something), such as a sense of accomplishment, freedom, or happiness. In both her studies, Ryff found that women in their 40s and 50s were more likely to select instrumental values, while women in their 60s and 70s were more likely to select terminal values. However, Ryff found no such difference in men. In fact, the men had significantly lower scores on instrumental values at middle age than did women (Ryff, 1982).

Collectively, these findings are intriguing but puzzling. There is some agreement that values in early adulthood center around making one's mark in the

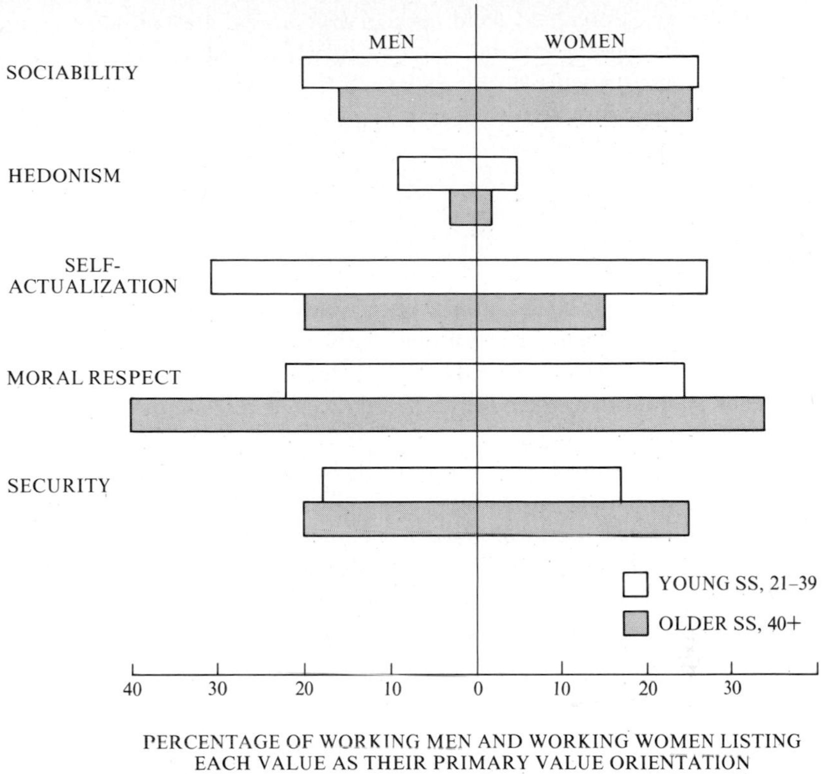


***Figure 9—6*** *Veroff asked men and women to pick the value that was most important to them, out of a list of nine, which were later grouped into these five categories. You can see that older men and women (over 40 in this case means "older") placed more value on moral respect and on security, while younger adults were more likely to select values reflecting sociability, hedonism, or self-actualization (self-fulfillment or a sense of accomplishment). (Source: Veroff, Douvan, & Kulka, 1981, adapted from Table 6.11, p. 263.)*

world. And there is some agreement that in old age, values center around end states such as security, happiness, or even inner satisfaction. But there is disagreement about the midlife values. Some investigators see midlife as the peak of social values (relating well to others), while other investigators see it as a time when self-respect values are at their peak.

In part, this confusion comes about because such widely different age groupings have been used. Veroff includes everyone over 40 in his "older" group, while for Lowenthal the middle-aged group is about 50. If there is a transition going on here, we need a more systematic look at the period from 35 to 55 to see if it can be identified.

Furthermore, there are probably differences between men and women in the pattern of value change over adulthood. Lowenthal and her colleagues, in fact, find that sex differences, and not age differences, are the most striking aspect of their findings. In general, and particularly at midlife, men appear to place a higher value on achievement, women a higher value on relationships. Another pattern of sex differences appears when we look at studies of motives over the adult years.

## Motives

If Maslow is correct about the sequence in which needs or motives will tend to dominate the system, then we ought to see a shift in emphasis from affiliative or love needs to esteem needs. In fact, there is some general support for such a shift in the results from several good recent studies of developmental changes in motives in adulthood.

Two studies in particular, one cross-sectional and one longitudinal, have yielded useful data. The cross-sectional evidence comes from Veroff's analysis of the same set of interviews of separate national samples of adults in 1957 and in 1976 that I described in the last section (Veroff, Reuman, & Feld, 1984). In this study, motives were measured with the Thematic Apperception Test (TAT), which is a widely used projective test requiring the subject to tell stories based on somewhat ambiguous pictures. The pictures are specifically selected so that they might trigger stories reflecting several major motives, including **affiliation** (the disposition to seek out or retain emotional relationships), **achievement** (the disposition to perform activities in competition with a standard of excellence), **fear of weakness** (the desire to avoid being controlled by others), and **hope for power** (the desire to have an impact on the world, often by focusing attention on the self). Veroff and his colleagues can compare the extent to which these motives appear as themes in the stories told by adults of different ages, and can check for the consistency of any age-related patterns by comparing the results in the 1957 and 1976 samples.

Good longitudinal data come from a recent study by David Stevens and Carroll Truss (1985). In 1978, they assessed three groups of adults using a pencil-and-paper measure of motives called the Edwards Personal Preference Schedule (EPPS): (1) group of 40-year-olds who had first taken the EPPS as college students in the late 1960s, (2) a group of 30-year-olds who had first taken the EPPS as college students in 1965, and (3) a group of current college students (about 20 years old). The inclusion of the third group allows researchers to identify cohort changes in levels of motives.

When the cohort differences have been sorted out in both of these studies, only a few consistent patterns of change remain that appear to be genuine developmental changes and not cohort-specific patterns:

1. The affiliation motive declines with age for women (but not clearly for men). The upper half of Figure 9–7 shows the findings from the cross-sectional comparisons. A similar decline in affiliation (at least up to age 40) was found in the longitudinal analysis.

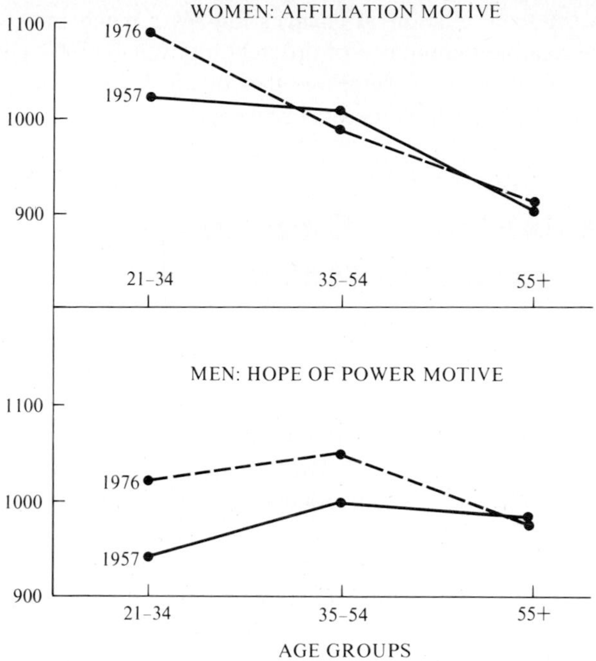


***Figure 9–7*** *Data from two large cross-sectional studies, two decades apart, show the same patterns of decline in affiliation motive with age in women, and a peaking in power motive in middle-age among men. (Source: Veroff, Rueman, & Feld, 1984, from Table 1, p. 1148.)*

2. Hope for power peaks at midlife for men in the cross-sectional study in evey cohort and every education subgroup, as you can see in the lower half of Figure 9–7. No such pattern emerged for women. (Since no comparable measure was included in the longitudinal study we cannot compare the results.) Veroff suggests that "increased power motivation seems to occur when men's expectations for having impact are in jeopardy" (Veroff et al., 1984, p. 1151), something which happens for many men in late midlife.
3. Longitudinal data show a rise in the motive for autonomy from age 30 to 40 in both men and women. Whether it goes down thereafter I cannot say, since no equivalent measure was included in the cross-sectional comparisons. However, Feldman, Biringen, and Nash (1981), in a separate cross-sectional study, found that autonomy rose for women in old age and remained relatively stable in men after midlife.
4. Achievement motivation shows a complex pattern that differs in the two studies. My best reading of the evidence is that achievement motivation increases between ages 20 and 30 for both men and women, and then levels off until midlife, after which it appears to decline.

On the whole, this constellation of changes implies a much more complex set of shifts in the relative importance of different motives over the adult years than Maslow's theory suggests. Nonetheless, the pattern is not inconsistent with the broad sweep of Maslow's hypothesized sequence.

## Adding Up the Evidence: Changes in Personality, Values, and Motives

Despite the contradictions and confusions in this array of evidence, there seem to me to be some common threads. In particular, I see signs of two changes occurring over the adult years, one between early and middle adulthood, and the other (more tentatively) occurring between middle and late adulthood.

The first change—which may occur gradually during the period from about age 30 to about age 50—seems to include several aspects: (1) an increase in "maturity" and in personality integration, as reflected in such findings as the reduction in immature defense mechanisms reported by both Vaillant and Haan, and in the increase in openness to self described by Haan; (2) an increase in "agenic" orientation—an emphasis on achieving, on doing, on succeeding, shown by the rise in power motive for men, the heightened achievement motivation for both men and women, and the rise in "cognitive investment" in both men and women. Ryff's finding of greater "instrumental" values for women at midlife is also consistent with such a midlife agenic orientation; (3) an increase in individuality and a decrease in dependence on others, perhaps particularly for men. The higher level of cognitive investment that Haan describes has some element of independence in it, and the marked shift toward heightened autonomy reported by Bray and Howard for the AT&T managers, and the rise in the autonomy motive shown in the Stevens and Truss longitudinal study, clearly show such a shift. Perhaps the decline in the affiliation motive for women is an aspect of this same change.

Information about a possible second shift between midlife and old age is scarcer, but there are at least some hints, including Schaie and Parham's finding of increasing philosophical concern with age, the greater introversion reported by Leon and colleagues in old age, and the greater perception of integrity among older subjects in Ryff's studies of self-perceived personality change.

Not all of the evidence fits neatly into these patterns, however. Schaie's finding of increased rigidity with age does not fit, nor does Leon's finding of greater anxiety and depression in later life. And there are some apparently direct contradictions, such as Haan's report of rising nurturance in midlife for women, while both Veroff and Stevens and Truss report a decline in affiliation motives among women at the same ages. Furthermore, there are a number of studies, including longitudinal studies, which show no age changes at all.

Several preliminary resolutions or partial explanations of these conflicts are possible. Let me suggest three.

## A Methodological Point

As I look over the array of evidence, I note that those studies showing no change with age (e.g., Siegler, George, & Okun, 1979; Woodruff & Birren, 1972), and those reporting the most discrepant findings (e.g., Leon et al., 1979; Schaie, 1983b), are those in which personality has been measured with standardized pencil-and-paper tests. In contrast, studies in which researchers have derived scores from open-ended written comments or from extensive interviews have generally shown systematic and reasonably consistent age effects. Since part of what I am searching for in these data is some indication of whether or not the basic structure of personality changes, rather than simply whether some traits have increased or decreased, I am inclined to place greater faith in those studies that have tested both broadly and deeply, including Haan's study of the Berkeley samples, the AT&T studies, Vaillant's analysis of the Grant Study sample, Ryff's research on self-perceived change, and probably Veroff's study of values and motives. This is obviously a matter of taste. Other psychologists may wish to place much greater weight on those studies in which reliable, standardized instruments were used, and may thus conclude that there is little evidence for age changes in personality.

## Cohort and Role Changes as Explanation

A second approach to the explanation of the disparate findings is one that I am sure has occurred to you. All of the changes I have described may be the result of either cohort differences or of specific role changes within cohorts that are correlated with age. If we take this approach, it should not surprise us that the findings are more consistent for men than for women, since women's roles have been undergoing much more radical changes in recent decades.

There is a good deal of research that can be mustered in support of a cohort-difference or role-change explanation. Carol Erdwins, for example, has found in two recent studies (Erdwins & Mellinger, 1984; Erdwins, Tyler, & Mellinger, 1983) that a woman's employment status is a better predictor of personality or motivation than is age. Full-time homemakers in these studies had higher affiliation motives than did married or single working women, regardless of age. The working women, of all ages, tended to be higher on self-acceptance, autonomy, and achievement via independence.

Further evidence that work status or work commitment is a critical variable comes from Veroff's study of motives (Veroff et al., 1984). He looked particularly at the pattern of age differences in affiliative motives for two subgroups: women in his samples who were highly work committed, and men who were weakly work committed. In contrast to the patterns for the samples as a whole, Veroff found that the work committed women showed no change in affiliative motivation over age, while the low work committed men showed the "feminine" pattern of declining affiliation with age.

**Figure 9–8** *If Veroff's findings are correct, this woman probably has a lower affiliation motive now than she did when her children were young. But is this caused by the change in her family role—by the fact that her children are older and need her less? Or is there a more basic, underlying change occurring that is largely independent of role changes? (Source: Sybil Shackman, Monkmeyer Press.)*

Veroff's explanation of these findings is that the traditional woman's role sequence (full-time homemaker, or working homemaker with low or moderate work commitment) is associated with maximum role uncertainty and anxiety in the 20s and early 30s, when women are struggling to juggle several conflicting roles—to learn to become a good mother, to be a wife at the same time, often to be a worker, too. When anxiety or uncertainty is high, people turn to their family or to friends, thus showing high affiliation. As women move through adulthood, however, the uncertainty and the anxiety decline as they learn the roles and as some of the roles are subtracted, such as the day-to-day care of infants or young children. Women's affiliation needs would thus go down with age. For men, in contrast, role uncertainty and anxiety remain at about the same level throughout the working life, so we should not see any age-related pattern in affiliation for most men. The fact that work-committed women show this "male" pattern thus makes sense.

In contrast, the need for power may peak at midlife precisely because this is the point in most men's careers when they experience a loss of authority or power in their jobs, the point when the career has reached a plateau and they doubt their effectiveness. But this is a work role-related change and only incidentally an age-related change. If careers peaked earlier or later, then the peak in the power motive ought to shift, too.

There seems no doubt that differences in role patterns, in the specific sequence and the timing of the sequence of role changes, have an impact on personality, motivation, values. Most adults enter several role "streams" in their early 20s and are carried along those streams for at least the next 30 or 40 years. The demands made on the adult at different points in such role sequences change in systematic ways, which will have an impact on values and motives.

But while an appeal to role sequences—and to cohort differences in the role patterns for women—does help to account for some of the disparities in the data, I am not convinced that all of the age differences in personality, motivation, or values that I've described in this chapter can be accounted for in this way.

Among other things, it is clear that roles alone do not impose personality patterns on adults. I have already pointed out in chapter 2 that there is considerable consistency in individual personality patterns over adulthood, despite role changes. Even more complicated is the fact that there is clearly self-selection into roles as a function of initial personality characteristics.

Helson and her colleagues (Helson, Mitchell, & Moane, 1984) have found some evidence for such self-selection in an intriguing longitudinal study of a group of college-educated women born between 1936 and 1938 and studied between the ages of 20 and 42. They divided the group into those who had followed a "feminine social clock" (marrying and having their first child before 28 and never being highly committed to a career) and those who had followed a "masculine social clock" (marrying late, or not marrying at all, with a strong committment to work). Those women who most consistently followed the masculine social clock had already been distinctly different from their peers in their early 20s. They were more dominant, more sociable, had the greatest self-acceptance, independence, empathy, and "social presence." In contrast, those women who most closely followed the feminine social clock were described, at 20, as seeking to follow the social norms. These young women had been quite well adjusted and content with themselves, but perceived that achievement could best be reached through conforming.

Thus, it may not be the roles of motherhood or work that shape the personality, but the personality that shapes the role sequence, or some complex combination of the two.

# A Theoretical Explanation

Still a third (and clearly my own favorite) way to organize the evidence on personality change (or consistency) in adulthood is within the framework of one or more of the major theories of personality development I have described in this chapter. Loevinger, Maslow, and Vaillant would agree that role changes are significant, but principally because they may be among those key life experiences that help to trigger or foster a change in personality structure or a change in dominant needs. These theorists also assert that the same underlying structure could be expressed in a number of different specific personality traits or emotions. If we are to make sense out of the data, we have to distinguish between those measures or variables that may tap basic personality structure, and those that reflect more short-term or role-related personality traits.

Let me use Loevinger's model as an example. She suggsts that in early adulthood, most adults are at the conformist stage, characterized by an external definition of what is good or right and a desire to live up to the expectations of the group to which one belongs. Note that Loevinger is not saying that all conformist behavior is the same. Rather, she is saying that each of us goes through a period in which we understand ourselves and experience ourselves in relation to the group norms. If all your peers are going to college and then combining work and motherhood, that may be the norm to which you conform. But if your peers (and parents) value the role of full-time homemaker, you will be likely to follow that path and derive your values and your motives from that role pattern.

Gradually, according to Loevinger, the adult moves away from this external definition of self and searches for an internal definition (Loevinger's conscientious and individualistic stages). In the process, adults often become focused on success or on striving, because these are ways of asserting and exploring their own individuality. At this stage, being uncomfortable with the dependence involved, many adults also show some turning away from relationships.

Finally, some adults reach a degree of security and comfort in their own independence/autonomy that allows them to turn outward, toward helping others, toward ''humanitarian concern.''

In Maslow's theory, these three broad steps are paralleled by the sequential dominance of love/belongingness needs, self-esteem needs, and self-actualization needs.

Many (but not all) of the research findings I have described fit such a sequence of changes fairly well. The transition from conformist to conscientious or individualistic stages may frequently occur in adults' 30s or 40s. And we've seen that both men and women move in those years toward greater openness to their own feelings, greater cognitive investment, greater self-confidence (Haan, 1981). At the same time, both men and women seem to become less gregarious (Haan, 1976) and autonomous (Stevens & Truss, 1985; Veroff et al., 1984) while studies of men show an increase in independence as well (Bray & Howard, 1983). Many adults moving through these years also become less defensive, more accepting of their own characteristics (Haan, 1976; Vaillant, 1977a), but it does not seem appropriate to describe this midlife change as ''mellowing.'' It may be ''maturing'' in Loevinger's sense, but for many adults the key midlife quality is one of intense individuality.

Depending on the role patterns they have chosen or have been thrust into, men and women may display this change quite differently. Individuality for the man, or for the woman who has initially conformed to a "male pathway," may be expressed in high achievement strivings or a motive for power; for women who began by conforming to a more traditional female role sequence, the midlife individuality may be expressed in changing patterns of interaction within the family, in reduced reliance on friendships (which decline in importance at midlife for both men and women, as I pointed out in chapter 7), in generativity expressed through a relationship with children. In other words, a woman need not abandon her family roles in order to become more individualistic. Some women may thus become more nurturant, some become less so, and both of these patterns may be expressions of this new personality organization.

In later life we see at least some hints of a move away from this heightened individuality and toward a broader set of concerns. Schaie and Parham (1976), for example, found an increase in "humanitarian concern" over the life span, and Ryff (1982) found a shift toward "terminal values" (at least for women). The apparent paradox is that there is also (albeit contradictory) evidence for a heightened interiority in old age, a focusing inward on questions about the meaning of one's life. These patterns make at least some sense if we think of the midlife period (the time when the conscientious stage and the individualistic level are likely to be achieved) as one in which the person attempts to do things (or to "generate" things, in Erikson's sense), to have an effect on the world, be it in work or in family life. The later life period (for those who make the transition to the autonomous stage) is more focused on being, on acceptance of the self.

Loevinger (and Maslow and Vaillant) has never said that all adults move through all these stages. On the contrary, most of us do not achieve the stage of an autonomous ego structure. Age, in fact, is only a very rough guideline for the kind of personality and motivational changes Loevinger is describing. Furthermore, the older the group studied, the more variability there should be in the stages or levels represented in the sample. Thus, while the transition from conformist to individualistic stages should be fairly widespread, the later shift toward autonomy should be much more difficult to detect. The contradictions contained within the research on personality development over adulthood are to be expected. Whether a particular pattern is found or not will depend very heavily on the particular subjects studied.

Helson (Helson et al., 1984) suggests something like this in her study of feminine and masculine "social clocks." She offers the hypothesis that those women who followed the masculine social clock were already, at 20, beyond the conformist stage. Those women who followed the most traditional feminine social clock, in contrast, appeared to be very much in the conformist stage.

Helson has gone still further and looked at the personality patterns of "feminine social clock" women who were later divorced or who stayed in unrewarding marriages. The former group appear to have been pushed into a new personality organization by the divorce. They increased in self-control and in "psychological mindedness" (a tendency to introspect and analyze their own and others' behavior). Those women who stuck with bad marriages—who may have remained at the conformist stage—showed a loss of poise, confidence, empathy, sociability, and sense of wellbeing. (When your understanding of yourself is determined by outside persons or groups, and you fail to live up to the expectations of those persons or groups, you are bound to lose confidence and poise.)

I do not want to suggest that every piece of evidence on personality change and continuity in adulthood can be fitted neatly together. There remain some glaring contradictions, most notably the increase in personal rigidity with age that Schaie found for both men and women (Schaie, 1983b). If Loevinger, Maslow, and Vaillant are correct, then decreasing rigidity ought to be characteristic of at least some older adults. But I am suggesting that it would be extremely fruitful to use theoretical models like these as a basis for future research designs. Simply using a standardized pencil-and-paper test of personality on adults of varying ages, without taking varying role patterns or personality structure into consideration is not going to lead to much insight.

With this as backdrop, let me return to the three popular hypotheses about personality change over adulthood that I raised at the beginning of the chapter: (1) Do all adults have midlife crises? (2) Do adults become more androgynous in late midlife? and (3) Do adults become disengaged emotionally and socially in late life?

# Evaluating Some Popular Hypotheses

## The Midlife Crisis

You'll remember from chapter 3 that Daniel Levinson (1978, 1980) argues that all adults go through some kind of significant reassessment and change of basic life structure in their early 40s, typically accompanied by depression, distress, and upheaval—the so-called "midlife crisis." I have talked about the possible physical aspect of such a midlife change in chapter 4 in discussing the climacteric. The subject came up again in chapter 8 in connection with adults' responses to the "topping out" of their occupational progress. Levinson's concept of a midlife transition or crisis includes both of these elements but is broader than either, and touches on some of the changes I have been describing in this chapter. He and others argue that there are several distinct developmental tasks associated with midlife: acceptance of death and mortality, recognition of biological limitations and health risks, restructuring of sexual identity and self-concept, reorientation to work, career, creativity, and achievement, and reassessment of primary relationships (Cytrynbaum, Blum, Patrick, Stein, Wadner, & Wilk, 1980; Levinson, 1978). The simultaneous resolution of these tasks, according to Levinson, can lead to a significant crisis for many adults.

The notion that a personal or emotional crisis at midlife is an integral part of adult experience, fed by characterizations in novels, plays, and films as well as by such popular books as *Passages* (Sheehy, 1974), has become so widely accepted that to raise doubts about it will align me against current popular culture. But doubts I do have.

To make any sense out of the evidence and theory in this area, I must first distinguish between a *transition* and a *crisis*. Levinson, as well as other theorists, proposes that adult life is made up of a series of transitions—times when existing life structures are reassessed and may be altered. Transitions may be experienced as stressful or crisis-like, but they can also be relatively smooth. A crisis occurs, as Cytrynbaum and his colleagues suggest, "when internal resources and external social support systems threaten to be overwhelmed by developmental tasks that require new adaptive resources" (Cytrynbaum et al., 1980, p. 464).

With this distinction in mind, at least three questions then need to be answered in order to decide whether a crisis is an inevitable or even a widely shared part of the physical and personality changes at midlife: (1) Do all adults experience a transition of some kind at midlife? (2) Is the content of this transition (the developmental tasks faced, the issues confronted) common to all adults and different from the content or tasks of other adult transitions? (3) Is this particular transition likely to be experienced as a crisis, especially in comparison to other transitions in adult life?

**Transition at Midlife?** No researcher has yet developed a real measure of the transition process, so it is difficult to answer this first question. But there is evidence that many adults, in this culture at this point in history, experience significant changes in roles or the content of continuing roles at midlife, brought about by such transitions as children beginning to leave home, jobs "topping out," or the death of a parent. Some of the evidence I have presented earlier in this chapter is also consistent with the notion that there is a psychological transition of some kind that occurs for many adults, including a shift toward greater self-confidence, greater openness, perhaps greater interiority. But whether all adults move through some sort of transition at this age is simply not clear from the existing evidence.

**Shared Content?** For those adults who do experience a transition at midlife, there is at least preliminary evidence pointing to common issues, including awareness of mortality, the loss of reliable physical skills, and the emergence of previously "submerged" aspects of the personality (Cytrynbaum et al., 1980; Levinson, 1978). But the data are extremely limited. Both white- and blue-collar men have been studied, but there is little information on the specific content of midlife transitions for women. Furthermore, no researcher (that I know of) has compared the reported issues or concerns of midlife adults with issues or concerns reported by younger or older adults. So while we know that awareness of mortality or awareness of unexpressed parts of the personality are frequently (but not invariably) described as issues for mid-life adults, we don't know whether those same issues are also part of other adult transitions.

**Is It a Crisis?** Once more I must say that we have relatively little evidence, but what little we have does not point to a widely experienced crisis at midlife. Some of the evidence against the midlife crisis hypothesis is compelling. Norma Haan (1981), in her analysis of the subjects in the Berkeley and

Oakland longitudinal studies, found no indication of a widespread upheaval. Similarly, no sign of an age-related crisis has emerged in the results of cross-sectional studies designed explicitly to search for evidence of midlife crisis. Costa and McCrae (1980a), for example, developed a midlife crisis scale which included items about a sense of inner turmoil, a sense of failing power, marital dissatisfaction, or job dissatisfaction. When they had over 500 men, ages 35 to 70, respond to these items they could find no age at which scores were particularly high. Some men at each age reported feelings of crisis. Farrell and Rosenberg (1981), whose study of friendship patterns in men I mentioned in the last chapter, similarly found no age difference on a scale measuring midlife crisis.

Finally, as Brim (1976) has noted, epidemiological evidence gives no sign of heightened rates of suicide, or divorce, or alcoholism at mid-life for mid-life adults as a whole.

The counterargument is that there is at least one subgroup—well educated white males—for whom there is some evidence of heightened problems at mid-life. Recall from chapter 4 that Tamir (1982) found higher rates of drinking problems and drug use and greater "psychological immobility" among college-educated men in their 40s in her cross-sectional study. Suicide rates are also high for this group (although lower than for still-older white men).

Just how these conflicting findings are to be integrated is not altogether clear. It may well be that for well-educated, successful men the period of midlife is particularly stressful in our society. But not all researchers have found this to be so. In the final analysis, my conclusion is in line with Costa and McCrae's summary: "These findings do not necessarily mean that there is no mid-life crisis. . . . They do, however, cast grave doubt on the claim that everyone goes through a crisis, or that there is any particular portion of the adult age span in which crises are concentrated" (Costa & McCrae, 1980a, p. 84).

In sum, it seems plausible that there is a psychological or role-related transition of some kind for many (perhaps even most) adults in this culture some time around midlife. The timing of this is quite variable, however, depending on the timing of various role changes, on the longevity of each adult's parents, on such unexpected events as unemployment, or divorce, or the like. There may be unique content to this midlife transition, consistent with the evidence presented in this chapter, but this transition is not routinely experienced as a crisis. Whether a crisis occurs probably depends on the specific personality or temperament of the individual and on whether there is a pile-up of role changes or other stressful life events within a short space of time. What we need now is much more research focused on the content of whatever transition occurs at this age, and much less emphasis on the "crisis" of midlife.

## Sex Role Crossover in Mid- and Late-Life: A Second Look

I raised the question of sex role crossover in chapter 6 and reached a tentative conclusion that such a shift toward androgyny may occur, but that the evidence was thin. That conclusion is not altered by the additional evidence I've described in this chapter. Certainly Gutmann, in his cross-cultural analysis (1977), asserts that there are many cultures in which men shift from active to more passive roles, and women from passive roles to more active ones in the second half of adulthood. And several of the longitudinal and cross-sectional studies I've described offer some support for this assertion within our own culture. Haan (1981) reports, for example, that at midlife, the women in the Berkeley Intergenerational Studies had become more masculine, and the men more feminine than they had been earlier in life. And Lowenthal and (1975) colleagues found that their midlife sample of women were less dependent and more assertive than were younger groups of women.

But there are also findings that do not fit. Lowenthal and associates (1975) did not find any parallel change in men, for example, and Carol Erdwins and her colleagues (Erdwins et al., 1983) found that the highest masculinity scores in their study were recorded by a group of college-age women and the lowest by a group of older homemakers (ages 40 to 75).

It may be, in other words, that the trend toward androgyny in the 40s and 50s noted by several authors is particularly evident in a particular set of cohorts—those born around the 1920s who reached midlife at the time the women's movement was beginning to be strongly felt. For these adults, a shift toward expressiveness in men and assertiveness in women may thus reflect social changes and not shared developmental processes. I lean toward the hypothesis that some sex role crossover is more than a pure cohort phenomenon, but we simply do not yet have adequate data to be sure.

## Disengagement in Later Life

Read almost any book on aging and you will come across the term disengagement, a term first proposed by Cumming and Henry (1961) to describe a psychological process in old age. The key elements of their disengagement theory, as restated by Cumming (1975) are that (1) adults' social "life space" shrinks with age. We interact with fewer and fewer others, and fill fewer and fewer roles as we move through old age; (2) the individual anticipates this change and actively participates in it; (3) the individual, in her roles and relationships, becomes more individualized, less governed by the "rules" and norms. Note that what is proposed here is a mutual withdrawal or disengagement: society withdraws from the older individual and the older individual withdraws from society.

Most researchers, and most popular discussions of this theory, have focused on the first of these points and on the implication that it is somehow healthier for adults to withdraw from many social roles as they grow older. On the first of these points, the evidence seems to offer some support. In old age, most adults show a decline in the number of social activities they engage in (Palmore, 1981). They participate in fewer clubs or organizations, go to church less often, see friends less often. This has been found in longitudinal studies (such as the Duke studies) as well as cross-sectional ones, so the pattern seems well established. But there is no indication that those who show the greatest decline in social activity (who disengage the most) are happier or healthier. On the contrary, the common finding in large studies is that the most socially active and involved (the least disengaged) adults also report the greatest satisfaction in their lives (Palmore, 1981).

I should point out that there is also good evidence that some older adults arrive at an independent, socially isolated (highly disengaged) life pattern that seems to satisfy them. Maas and Kuypers (1974), for example, in a study of some of the parents of the subjects in the Berkeley and Oakland longitudinal studies, describe a group of satisfied men they call "hobbyists," whose lives revolve around some solitary hobby such as woodworking or birdwatching. Similarly, in studies in England, Savage and his colleagues (Savage, Gaber, Britton, Bolton, & Cooper, 1977) found some introverted, socially-isolated aged adults who seemed largely content with their lives. But these groups are the exception. In most older adults, some continued social involvement is both a sign of, and probably a cause of, higher levels of satisfaction.

What all of this research does not address, though, is the part of the original disengagement hypothesis I find the most interesting: the proposed reduction in

**Figure 9–9** *While it is true that for older adults as a group, those who remain the most active are, on average, more satisfied with their lives and happier, there is a distinct subgroup, like this hobbyist, whose social withdrawal in old age is associated with high levels of satisfaction. (Source: Hedda Hammid, Photo Researchers Inc.)*

rule-following or conformity in relationships. Do older adults become disengaged from the role *definitions* even while they maintain the relationships? And more broadly still, as Labouvie-Vief suggested (1981), do adults in their later years become sufficiently freed of (disengaged from) the constraints of individual circumstances to allow them to become concerned with wider-reaching metaphysical issues—with the nature of personal integration or the meaning of life?

It is precisely to this question—the development of the search for meaning or ''wisdom'' over the adult years—that chapter 10 is addressed. So read on.

## Summary

1. Erikson's, Loevinger's, and Vaillant's theories of personality development in adulthood share the assumption that adults move sequentially through stages or dimensions of maturing. Loevinger and Vaillant, however, do not think that all adults necessarily pass through all stages.

2. Maslow's theory of the hierarchy of motives includes a distinction between deficiency motives and being motives. Deficiency motives include physiological, safety, love and belongingness, and self-esteem needs. The major being motive is the need for self-actualization.

3. Maslow suggested that these motives emerge in sequence over the life span, but that the being needs dominate only when the deficiency needs are largely met. Only a few adults reach the level of self-actualization.

4. Collectively, these theories suggest that adults may pass through several major transitions. One, often at midlife, includes the transition from love-belongingness to self-esteem, or from conforming to individualistic. The second, which may occur in late life, involves a shift to being needs, to integration.

5. Longitudinal evidence from several studies points to increases from early to middle adulthood in ''cognitive investment,'' openness to self, self-confidence, independence or autonomy, and nurturance (in women), and a decline in immature defense mechanisms. Over the full life span, researchers report increases in humanitarian concerns and in personal rigidity. Between midlife and late life there are some indications of a decline in active mastery for men and some increase in this for women.

6. Studies of age-related changes in values and motives show that older adults, compared to younger ones, are more focused on self-respect and less on a sense of accomplishment and self-satisfaction. Women show declines in affiliative motives, and men peak in the power motive in their 50s. Both men and women increase in autonomy and show somewhat heightened achievement motivation at midlife.

7. Collectively, the evidence fits the theoretical models reasonably well, but there are inconsistencies and gaps.

8. One methodological difference that separates those studies reporting systematic age differences in personality from those not finding such differences is that the latter studies typically use standardized pencil-and-paper instruments to measure personality, while the former use interviews or in depth, open-ended written answers.

9. The pattern of results may also reflect not age change per se but role-related changes. And some of what we take to be common developmental themes may be unique to the particular cohort most often studied—those who were born around 1920, who experienced (among many other changes) the women's movement in their 40s and 50s.

**TABLE 9–2 Summary of Age Changes in Personality, Motivation, and Values**

| Age 20–40 | Age 40–65 | Age 65+ |
|---|---|---|
| Lower levels of cognitive investment, self-confidence, and openness to self | Higher levels of cognitive investment, self-confidence, and openness to self | |
| Lower levels of independence, autonomy, and higher levels of dependency | Increased independence, autonomy, and decreased dependency | Probably increased autonomy and independence, but weak evidence |
| Highest levels of flexibility | Medium levels of flexibility; increased humanitarian concern | Lowest levels of flexibility; increased humanitarian concern |
| Lowest level of humanitarian concern | | |
| High values placed on material goals, getting things, achieving things | Highest values on self-respect and respect of others, and on expressive values | Highest value on ease, contentment, and reaching desired end states |
| Low scores on generativity and ego integrity | Peak scores on generativity | Peak scores on ego integrity |
| Lower scores on defensive maturity | Increased scores on defensive maturity | |
| For women: mixed signals on nurturance/affiliation; affiliation highest, nurturance lowest in early adulthood | Nurturance found to increase, affiliation to decrease in separate studies | |
| For men: Low scores on hope for power motive | Peak scores on hope for power | Lower scores on hope for power |

10. Loevinger's model can also be used to order the findings. Many of the personality traits found in young adults would be typical of adults at the conformist stage, while some of the changes reported at midlife would be characteristic of a shift to the conscientious or individualistic stages.

11. These several findings permit us to examine three common popular assumptions about personality change: that there is an invitable midlife crisis, that there is a crossover of sex roles in late midlife, and that in old age there is a disengagement, an increased introversion.

12. The midlife crisis appears to be more myth than substance. Some adults may experience transitions then, but there is no evidence that emotional upheaval, or internal transformation, is more common at that age than at any other—*except* among well-educated white males, among whom there are indications of greater stress at midlife.

13. Sex role crossover is more strongly supported, but there is a paucity of good longitudinal evidence to provide a firm basis for this assertion.

14. Disengagement in old age appears to be true in some respects and not others. Older adults do withdraw from many social activities, but those who withdraw the most are not the happiest or most satisfied. What remains open is the question of whether older adults become progressively disengaged from the confining and normative aspects of roles, or whether they engage in significant consideration of issues of meaning.

## Suggested Readings

*There are certainly a great many popular books that touch on this subject, but few seem to me to be worth recommending. An exception is*

SANGIULIANO, I. (1978). *In her time*. New York: William Morrow.

This is a book about women's development that I found stimulating when I read it some years ago. It includes some interesting case material as well as some more theoretical suggestions about the sequences of personality change in men and women.

*More technical but still highly readable is Vaillant's book (which I recommended in chapter 3). Other books are much more technical. Of these, the following are probably the most useful next steps.*

EICHORN, D. H., CLAUSEN, J. A., HAAN, N., HONZIK, M. P., & MUSSEN, P. H. (1981). *Present and past in middle life*. New York: Academic Press.

This book contains the bulk of the most current reports of the findings from the Berkeley and Oakland longitudinal studies. It assumes some knowledge of statistics, but most chapters are quite clearly written.

SCHAIE, K. W. (1983). *Longitudinal studies of adult psychological development*. New York: The Guilford Press.

Included in this book are reports of many of the most complete and interesting longitudinal studies covering intellectual and personality change in adulthood. Schaie's own study is described here, as is the AT&T study, the Duke study, and several others.

# 10

# Spiritual Development and the Search for Meaning

Ask yourself the following question:

> "What do you consider the one most fundamental or important issue for the human race; that is, what do you see as the basic and permanent question for mankind, the question of which all others are only parts?"

When Milton Yinger (1977) asked this question of 751 college students in Japan, Korea, Thailand, New Zealand, and Australia, 60% of them talked about some aspect of life's meaning as being the fundamental question for the human race.

This theme finds echoes in the writings of many clinicians and theorists (e.g., Frankl, 1984; Fromm, 1955). Erich Fromm listed the need for meaning as one of the five central existential needs of human beings. More recently, James Fowler, a theologian and developmental psychologist, has made a similar point: "One characteristic all human beings have in common is that we can't live without some sense that life is meaningful" (1983, p. 58).

In the last chapter, I talked about changes in personality and self-actualization, which is one aspect of inner development or growth in adulthood. But there is another aspect of inner development—perhaps more speculative, but certainly no less vital to most of us—that touches on questions of meaning, of purpose, of human potential. As we move through adulthood, does our sense of the meaning of life change? Does it become broader, more inclusive, or does it become narrower? Do we become more reflective, more tolerant of others, or do we become more fixed in our own views? Do we lose some of our preoccupation with our individual lives, our problems and triumphs, or do day-to-day concerns dominate more and more? Is there any sense in which, with age, we become wiser, more aware, even more spiritual?

You may well think that the answers to such questions lie in the province of religion, not psychology. Certainly one of the key functions of religion is to provide answers to fundamental questions about the meaning and purpose of life and about human beings' relationship to the universe. In fact one way to explore the search for meaning in adulthood is to look at the participation or involvement in organized religion over the adult years. Are there particular points in adulthood when people become more or less involved in religious practices such as church attendance? Does prayer (or meditation, or the equivalent) play a larger role in life at some ages than at others? One body of research has provided some answers to such questions.

Many theologians and developmental psychologists, however, have been dissatisfied with this approach. Involvement in organized religious activities may or may not change with age, but in any case such change or stability does not tell us about any changes in the purpose of religion in adults' lives, or about their more basic theories or concepts about the meaning of life. In an effort to probe more deeply, there has been a strong theoretical push in recent years toward a second kind of approach, focusing on questions of developmental changes in meaning systems. Can we detect any systematic changes, any "development" in the sense in which I am using that term in this book, in the structure or form of the meaning systems that adults create in order to make sense of their lives? More broadly still, we can ask—along with Maslow, Carl Jung, and many others—whether there is a systematic process of development of human potential over the adult years which is reflected in both the changes in personality I talked about in the last chapter and in the changes in meaning or understanding I want to address here.

I will pursue both of these approaches, although the second will occupy the greatest portion of space and time in the chapter. Before I move into this difficult and potentially touchy material, however, I need to make several key points.

## Some Caveats

**Theory versus Data.** I have said over and over throughout this book that we lack good data, or the right kind of data, to address some of what seem to me to be the most interesting questions about adult development. This is nowhere more true than here. Most of what I will be talking about in this chapter is theory only thinly tested or supported by empirical evidence. Lawrence Kohlberg's work on moral development is an exception—a large body of evidence consistent with his theory has accumulated over the past decades. But Fowler's theory of faith development, and the broader theories of the evolution of human consciousness such as the one proposed by Ken Wilber, go well beyond existing research evidence.

This relative lack of evidence reflects both the fact that psychologists have only recently begun systematic examination of such questions as faith development, but also the fact that some of the questions involved are not readily addressed by standard scientific methods.

What we do have in this area, however, in addition to a small collection of traditional scientific studies, is a very large body of autobiographical or introspective information, such as personal reports by religious adults, saints, philosophers, or mystics about the steps and processes of their own inner development. Collections of such independent reports have been analyzed, perhaps most impressively by William James, a distinguished early American psychologist, in his book *The Varieties of Religious Experience* (James, 1902), and by Evelyn Underhill (1911), in her book *Mysticism*.

Even detailed analyses of such personal reports do not fit with our usual concept of "scientific evidence." Only those few adults who who have chosen to describe their inner "journey" in writing can be included—hardly a random sample. Yet information from such sources has had a powerful effect on theories of the evolution of human potential. At the least, they tell us something about what *may* be possible, or about the qualities, meaning systems, or capacities, of a few extraordinary adults who appear to have plumbed the depths of the human spirit. William James made this point eloquently over 80 years ago:

> To describe the world with all the various feelings of the individual pinch of destiny, all the various spiritual attitudes, left out from the description—they being as describable as anything else—would be something like offering a printed bill of fare as the equivalent for a solid meal. Religion makes no such blunder. (James, 1902, p. 377)

But even if we accept such descriptions as valid reports of inner processes, it is a very large leap to apply the described steps or processes to the potential experiences of ordinary folks. I am going to take that leap in this chapter. You will have to judge for yourself whether it is justified.

**My Own Meaning System and Biases.** It is surely obvious (but nonetheless worth stating explicitly) that I bring my own meaning system to this discussion. Of course, that statement is true about this entire book (and about anyone else's book, too). I cannot report "objectively." Inevitably I select, place emphasis, integrate information in a way that is influenced by my basic biases, my assumptions about human nature. Such bias, although always present, is less troublesome in areas in which there is an extensive body of empirical evidence, such as in the study of physical or mental development. But it becomes far more troublesome when I talk about the development of ideas about life's meaning itself. So let me at least make my biases clear.

I approach this subject with a strong hypothesis that there are "higher" levels of human potential than most of us have yet reached, whether that is expressed in Maslow's terms as self-actualization, or in Loevinger's concept of the integrated personality, or in Fowler's concept of "universalizing faith," or in Ken Wilber's "transpersonal consciousness." When I describe the various models that have been proposed to describe the development of meaning and of human potential, I am inevitably filtering the theories and the evidence through this hypothesis, this meaning system. There is no way I can avoid this, any more than you can avoid filtering this chapter through your own assumptions, your own meaning system. Keep it in mind as you read further.

# Religious Participation over Adulthood

Part of the interest in participation in formal religious activities has been prompted by the concept of ''disengagement'' in old age, which I discussed in the last chapter. In order to determine whether adults become less socially active as they age, researchers have inquired about a whole range of activities, including church participation.

The findings (both longitudinal and cross-sectional) can be summarized quite briefly: (1) Church (or synagogue or temple) attendance appears to be relatively stable up through about age 50, when there is some increase in participation in formal church activities, followed by a decline in late adulthood, perhaps at age 70 and older (Blazer & Palmore, 1976; Moberg, 1965; Palmore, 1981). (2) In old age, however, the decline in participation in formal church activities is typically compensated by maintenance of or an increase in the number of informal or personal religious practices, such as private prayer or reading of religious books (Ainlay & Smith, 1984; Hunsberger, 1985; Mindel & Vaughan, 1978). (3) Some adults (at all ages) show very low levels of both formal and informal religious participation (e.g., Mindel & Vaughan, 1978).

This research indicates that religious disengagement is no more common than general social disengagement. It also reveals no particular age pattern in interest in or preoccupation with religious participation. There is evidence, however, that as adults age, they become more concerned with issues of personal morality or spirituality. The longitudinally observed increase with age in ''humanitarian concern'' that I reported in chapter 9 (Schaie & Parham, 1976) is one example of such a change.

Additional evidence consistent with this trend comes from two cross-sectional studies. Savage and his colleagues (Savage, Gaber, Britton, Bolton, & Cooper, 1977), in their study of a large group of elderly adults (70 and older) in Britain, found that the older the individual the more likely she was to select items that reflected moral qualities as key elements in her self concept (e.g., ''I am an honest person''). Similarly, Veroff and his colleagues (Veroff, Douvan, & Kulka, 1981), in both their 1957 and 1976 national samples, found that older adults were more likely than younger ones to use moral or virtuous qualities as self-descriptions (e.g., ''I lead a clean life,'' or ''I'm unselfish,'' or ''I don't go to church as often as I should''). Veroff and associates concluded:

> It is as though older people refocus identity from interpersonal relationships to broader social concerns. Older people indicate less need of social acceptance, and they less often feel inadequate in social roles. While we can interpret this as a diminishing energy for

***Figure 10–1*** *Adults of all ages attend church or temple, with possibly a peak in such attendance in late midlife, and a decline in attendance in old age, when it becomes physically more difficult for the elderly adult to manage movement and transportation. Private religious observances, however, do not decline. (Source: Katrina Thomas, Photo Researchers Inc.)*

role performance and interpersonal relationships, we can also think of these results as reflecting the fact that older people are more at peace with themselves and more invested in moral and spiritual values. (p. 378–79)

I read these findings as saying that if we are to understand changes in meaning or in the intensity or importance of broadly religious questions over the adult years, we must go beyond counting how often people go to church, or how often they pray or meditate, and begin to delve into their views of themselves, their "world views," their meaning systems.

# The Development of Meaning Systems over Adulthood

## Kohlberg's Theory of Moral Development

The theoretical underpinning of most of the current thinking about adults' evolving "world views" or "meaning systems" is Lawrence Kohlberg's theory of the development of moral reasoning (which is, in turn, an extension of Piaget's theory of cognitive development). Kohlberg first proposed this theory in 1958 in his Ph.D. dissertation, and has elaborated and modified it many times since (Colby, Kohlberg, Gibbs, & Lieberman, 1983; Kohlberg, 1958, 1964, 1973, 1976, 1981, 1984; Kohlberg & Kramer, 1969).

Although both this theory and the research it has prompted touch on only a corner of the subject I am examining here, I need to look at the theory in some detail in order to create a context for the later discusson of broader theories.

Kohlberg's concern has consistently been with children's and adults' *judgments* of morality, of what is right and wrong, of what is fair or just. Faced with conflict between different values, on what basis does a child or an adult decide what is morally right or wrong? Kohlberg makes an important distinction between the *form* of thinking and its *content*. The issue is not whether the child or adult thinks, for example, that lying is wrong, but *why* they think it is wrong. Kohlberg has been searching, then, for developmental patterns in the form of thinking about moral questions, just as Piaget was searching for developmental patterns in broader forms of logic (recall Table 5–1).

**The Stages.** After interviewing children and adults, asking their solutions to specially designed moral dilemmas, Kohlberg concluded that there were three basic levels of moral reasoning, each of which he divided further into two stages, resulting in six stages in all. Kohlberg's own descriptions of these stages are given in Table 10–1.

The **preconventional level** is typical of most children under age nine, but is also found in some adolescents and in some criminal offenders. At this level the child sees rules as something outside himself; what is right is what is rewarded or will get you pleasure; what is wrong is what is punished or what will bring displeasure. (Stage 2 is sometimes called "naive hedonism," which captures the flavor of this stage nicely.) At the **conventional level**, which is characteristic of most adolescents and most adults in our culture, the individual internalizes the rules and expectations of her family or peer group (at Stage 3), or of society (at Stage 4). In early presentations of the stages, Stage four was sometimes labeled as the "law and order" orientation, which again gives perhaps more flavor than does the phrase "social system and conscience."

The **principled level**, which is typical of only a minority of adults, involves a search for the underlying reasons behind society's rules. Since laws and con-

**TABLE 10–1** The Six Stages of Moral Development Proposed by Kohlberg

| Level and Stage | What Is Right | Reason for Doing Right | Social Perspective of Stage |
|---|---|---|---|
| **LEVEL 1: PRECONVENTIONAL**<br>Stage 1: Heteronomous morality | To avoid breaking rules backed by punishment, obedience for its own sake, and avoiding physical damage to persons and property. | Avoidance of punishment, and the superior power of authorities. | *Egocentric point of view:* Doesn't consider the interests of others or recognize that they differ from the actor's; doesn't relate two points of view. Actions are considered physically rather than in terms of psychological interests of others. Confusion of authority's perspective with one's own. |
| Stage 2: Individualism, instrumental purpose and exchange | Following rules only when it is to someone's immediate interest; acting to meet one's own interests and needs and letting others do the same. Right is also what's fair, what's an equal exchange, a deal, an agreement. | To serve one's own needs or interests in a world where you have to recognize that other people have their interests, too. | *Concrete individualistic perspective:* Aware that everybody has his own interest to pursue and these conflict, so that right is relative (in the concrete individualistic sense). |
| **LEVEL 2: CONVENTIONAL**<br>Stage 3: Mutual interpersonal expectations, relationships, and interpersonal conformity | Living up to what is expected by people close to you or what people generally expect of people in your role as son, brother, friend, etc. "Being good" is important and means having good motives, showing concern about others. It also means keeping mutual relationships, such as trust, loyalty, respect, and gratitude. | The need to be a good person in your own eyes and those of others. Your caring for others. Belief in the Golden Rule. Desire to maintain rules and authority which support stereotypical good behavior. | *Perspective of the individual in relationships to other individuals:* Aware of shared feelings, agreements, and expectations which take primacy over individual interests. Relates points of view through the concrete Gold Rule, putting yourself in the other person's shoes. Does not yet consider generalized system perspective. |
| Stage 4: Social system and conscience | Fulfilling the actual duties to which you have agreed. Laws are to be upheld except in extreme cases where they conflict with other fixed social duties. Right is also contributing to society, the group, or institution. | To keep the institution going as a whole, to avoid the breakdown of the system "if everyone did it," or the imperative of conscience to meet one's defined obligations. | *Differentiates societal point of view from interpersonal agreement or motives:* Takes the point of view of the system that defines roles and rules. Considers individual relations in terms of place in the system. |

| | | | |
|---|---|---|---|
| **LEVEL 3: POSTCONVENTIONAL OR PRINCIPLED**<br>Stage 5: Social contract or utility and individual rights | Being aware that people hold a variety of values and opinions, that most values and rules are relative to your group. These relative rules should usually be upheld, however, in the interest of impartiality and because they are the social contract. Some nonrelative values and rights like life or liberty, however, must be upheld in any society regardless of majority opinion. | A sense of obligation to law because of one's social contract to make and abide by laws for the welfare of all and for the protection of all people's rights. A feeling of contractual commitment, freely entered upon, to family, friendship, trust, and work obligations. Concern that laws and duties be based on rational calculation of overall utility, "the greatest good for the greatest number." | *Prior-to-society perspective:* Perspective of a rational individual aware of values and rights prior to social attachments and contracts. Integrates perspectives by formal mechanisms of agreement, contract, objective impartiality, and due process. Considers moral and legal points of view; recognizes that they sometimes conflict and finds it difficult to integrate them. |
| Stage 6: Universal ethical principles | Following self-chosen ethical principles. Particular laws or social agreements are usually valid because they rest on such principles. When laws violate these principles, one acts in accordance with the principle. Principles are universal principles of justice: the equality of all human rights and respect for the dignity of human beings as individual persons. | The belief as a rational person in the validity of universal moral principles, and a sense of personal commitment to them. | *Perspective of a moral point of view from which social arrangements derive:* Perspective is that of any rational individual recognizing the nature of morality or the fact that persons are ends in themselves and must be treated as such. |

**Source:** Kohlberg, 1976. Reprinted by permission of the author.

tracts are usually in accord with these underlying principles, most of the time obeying society's laws is quite in order. But when those underlying principles or reasons are at variance with some specific social custom or rule, the Stage 5 or Stage 6 adult argues on the basis of the fundamental principle, even if it means disobeying or disagreeing with a law. (Civil rights protesters in the early 1960s, for example, were typically supporting their civil disobedience with Stage 5 reasoning.)

Another way to look at the shifts from preconventional, to conventional, to principled levels of reasoning is as a process of *decentering* (a term Piaget used to describe cognitive development more generally). At Level 1, the child's reference point is herself—what the consequences of her actions will be, or what rewards she may gain. At Level 2, the reference point has broadened (moved away from the center of the self) to the family or society. Finally, at Level 3, the adult searches for a still broader reference point, namely, some set of underlying principles that lie behind or beyond social systems. This movement outward from the self is one of the constant themes in writings on the search for meaning or spirituality.

Kohlberg argues that these forms of moral reasoning emerge in a fixed sequence and that the stages are hierarchically organized. That is, each new stage grows from and replaces the one before it. Each successive stage is more differentiated and integrated than the last. This is the strictest form of a stage theory. Erikson's stages, for example, are described as sequential, but not hierarchically organized.

Only longitudinal data can tell us whether some set of stages fits this model. If Kohlberg is correct, then not only should children and adults move from one step to the next in the order he proposes, but they should also not show regression to earlier stages. The evidence Kohlberg and others have amassed supports this expectation.

**The Longitudinal Data.** Kohlberg and his colleagues have collected three sets of longitudinal data from (1) 84 boys from the Chicago area first interviewed when they were between 10 and 16 in 1956, some of whom were then reinterviewed up to five more times. The final interview was in 1976–77, when they were in their 30s (Colby et al., 1983); (2) a group of 23 boys and young men in Turkey (some from a rural village and some from large cities) followed over periods of up to 10 years, into early adulthood (Nisan & Kohlberg, 1982); (3) 64 male and female subjects from Kibbutzim in Israel (intentional collective communities), who were first tested as teenagers, and then retested once or twice over total periods of up to 10 years (Snarey, Reimer, & Kohlberg, 1985).

Figure 10–2 gives two kinds of information about the findings from these three studies. In the top half of the figure are total "moral maturity scores" derived from the interview. These scores are based on the stage scores, and can range from 100 to 500. As you can see, in all three studies the average score went up steadily with age, although there are some interesting cultural differences in speed of movement through the stages. In the bottom half of the figure are the percentages of answers reflecting each stage of moral reasoning

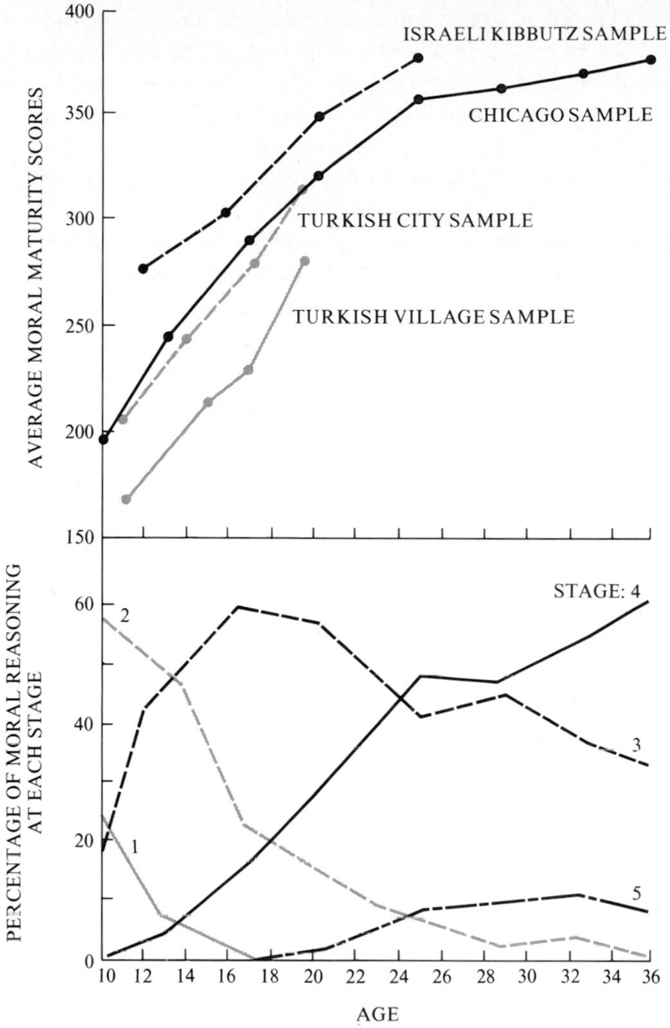


***Figure 10–2*** *The upper half of this figure shows Moral Maturity scores, which reflect level of reasoning on Kohlberg's moral dilemmas. Included are findings from teenagers and young adults in three countries. The lower half of the figure shows the percentages of answers to moral dilemmas among subjects in the Chicago study rated at each stage of reasoning at each age in the longitudinal study. As you can see, overall scores go up as age increases. It is also clear that principled reasoning is relatively rare, even in adulthood. (Sources: Colby et al., 1983; Nisan & Kohlberg, 1982; Snarey, Reimer, & Kohlberg, 1985. Colby et al. reprinted by permission of copyright holder, The Society for Research in Child Development, Inc. and author.)*

for subjects at each age. These data are for the Chicago sample only, since that sample has been studied over the longest period of time. As we would expect, the number of Stage 1 responses drops out quite early, while conventional morality (Stages 3 and 4) rises rapidly in the teenage years and remains high in adulthood. Only a very small percentage of answers, even of those in their 30s, show Stage 5 reasoning (principled reasoning), and none show Stage 6 reasoning.

Both analyses show the stages to be strongly sequential, a pattern even more strongly shown by the fact that in none of these three studies was there a single subject who skipped a stage, and only about 5% showed regressions—a percentage that would be consistent with scoring errors. Each subject also showed a good deal of internal consistency at any one testing, using similar logic in analyzing each of several quite different moral problems.

No equivalent longitudinal data exist for any adults past midlife. Results from several recent cross-sectional studies (Lonky, Kaus & Roodin, 1984; Pratt, Golding, & Hunter, 1983) show no age differences in overall level of moral judgment between young, middle aged, and older adults. Such findings might be taken to mean that the level of reasoning achieved in early adulthood remains relatively stable throughout adulthood. But the longitudinal data do not support such an assertion—at least not through the middle 30s. Among Kohlberg's sample were quite a few individuals who shifted from Stage 3 to Stage 4 while in their 20s, and a few who moved to Stage 5 while in their 30s. At least some adults may thus continue to develop through Kohlberg's stages throughout adulthood.

**Stage 6 and the Possibility of Stage 7.** In his early work, Kohlberg suggested that a fair number of college students reached Stage 6. As he has considered the theory further, however, he has concluded that this universalistic stage is extremely uncommon. The longitudinal data suggest that Stage 5 may be the typical end point of the developmental progression. Adults who reach Stage 5 (about 15% of those in their 30s in Kohlberg's samples) do indeed operate on some broad, general principles. What they lack, however, is "that which is critical for our theoretical notion of Stage 6; namely, the organization of moral judgment around a clearly formulated moral principle of justice and respect for persons that provides a rationale for the primacy of this principle" (Kohlberg, 1984, p. 271). In other words, at Stage 5 one develops some broad principles that go beyond (or "behind") the social system; at Stage 6, the rare individual develops a still broader and more general ethical system in which those principles are embedded. Among those individuals Kohlberg lists as Stage 6 thinkers are Martin Luther King and Gandhi.

Kohlberg has also proposed a still higher stage, Stage 7 (Kohlberg, 1973; Kohlberg, Levine, & Hewer, 1983). But here he makes an important distinction between what he calls *hard* and *soft* stages. By a "hard" stage he means a stage that conforms to the full Piagetian hierarchical model: The stages are sequential, show internal wholeness or consistency, and emerge from and restructure the earlier stages in a hierarchical manner. But not all stage sequences have those characteristics. ''Soft'' stages, in Kohlberg's terminology, may be sequential, but may not meet the other criteria of hard stages. In particular, soft stages may involve changes not only in structure, but also in content. Jane Loevinger's stages of ego development, for example, are soft stages in Kohlberg's terms, since they describe changes in motives, defenses, and functions of the self as well as changes in the overall structure of the ego.

With this distinction in mind, Kohlberg proposes a ''soft'' Stage 7 which may occur after the attainment of principled reasoning:

> We conceptualize Stage 7 as a high soft stage in the development of ethical and religious orientations, orientations which are larger in scope than the justice orientation which our hard stages address. Generally speaking, a Stage 7 response to ethical and religious problems is based on constructing a sense of identity or unity with being, with life, or with God. (Kohlberg et al., 1983, p. 249)

Such a sense, or experience, of unity is one of the defining characteristics of ''mystic'' or ''transcendent'' experience. The same sense of unity forms the end point of James Fowler's description of stages of faith, as you will see shortly.

**Evaluation and Comment.** The body of evidence that has accumulated concerning the development of moral reasoning provides strong support for several aspects of Kohlberg's theory:

1. There do appear to be stages that children and adults move through in developing concepts of fairness and morality.
2. Those stages, at least up to Stage 5, can legitimately be described as ''hard'' stages—they occur in fixed order, each emerging from and replacing the one that preceded it, and forming a structural whole.
3. The stage sequence appears to be universal. The specific content of moral decisions may differ from one culture to the next, but the overall form of logic seems to move through the same steps in every culture in which this has been studied, including Taiwan, Turkey, Mexico, Kenya, India, Israel, and the Bahamas.
4. The stages have some relevance for real life, as well. Edward Lonky and his colleagues (Lonky et al., 1984), for example, have found that adults who reason at the principled level are more able than are those at the conventional level to deal positively and constructively with significant losses in their lives, such as the death of a family member or the breakup of a relationship.

At the same time, a number of critics have pointed out that Kohlberg's theory is relatively narrow, focusing almost exclusively on the development of concepts of justice or fairness. Other aspects of moral/ethical reasoning are omitted, as are ''soft'' facets of adults' broader search for meaning.

The most eloquent of the critics has been Carol Gilligan (1977, 1982), whose approach I have mentioned before. She argues that Kohlberg's theory and research largely ignore an ethical/moral system based on caring for others, on responsibility, on altruism or compassion. Kohlberg has been interested in the concepts of justice, not concepts of care. In particular, Gilligan has found that women more often than men approach moral and ethical dilemmas from the point of view of responsibilities and caring, searching not for the "just" solution, but for the solution that best deals with the social relationships involved. Men, more often than women, use a morality of justice (Lyons, 1983).

In recent studies in which males and females have been compared on stage of moral reasoning using Kohlberg's revised scoring system, no sex differences are typically found (e.g., Pratt, Golding, & Hunter, 1984; Walker, 1984). That is, girls and women can and do use moral reasoning based on principles of justice when they are presented with dilemmas in which that is a central issue. So it is not so much that Kohlberg's system is somehow biased against women; rather, Kohlberg's concept of moral reasoning is more narrowly defined than Gilligan proposes. Gilligan, like Fowler, would include a much broader range of ethical stances.

Nonetheless, however narrow Kohlberg's theory may be, it has served as a highly heuristic jumping-off point for a whole group of thinkers concerned with issues of faith, meaning, or human potential, each of whom—like Gilligan—has attempted to extend or expand the theory. Of these, I find Fowler's theory the most fully stated and the most intriguing.

## Fowler's Theory of Faith Development

In talking about stages of faith development, James Fowler (1981, 1983) goes beyond questions of moral reasoning to search for the emergence of each individual's "world view," or "model" of her relationship to others and to the universe. He uses the word *faith* to describe such a personal model. Since faith is often used to refer to a specific set of religious beliefs, this usage may be somewhat confusing. But Fowler means the term much more broadly. In his view, each of us has a faith whether or not we belong to any particular church or organization. Moral reasoning is only a part (perhaps quite a small part) of faith. Faith is broader: It is both social and relational, dealing with our understanding of our connections with others, and with the common ground in which those relationships are embedded. Each of us, he argues, at any point in our lives, has a "master story" which is "the answer you give to the questions of what life is about, or who's really in charge here, or how do I live to make my life a worthy, good one. It's a stance you take toward life" (Fowler, 1983, p. 60).

Implicit in this definition of faith is a distinction between the form or structure of one's faith and the specific content, similar to Kohlberg's distinction between the structure and content of moral reasoning. Any given structure or "level" of faith may be expressed in a very wide variety of specific beliefs or religions. A Christian, a Hindu, a Jew, or an atheist could all have developed faiths that are structurally similar, even while they differ sharply in content.

Thus, when Fowler talks about the development of faith, he is not talking about specific religious beliefs or about conversions from one religion to another. He is searching for the underlying structure or logic that is common to many different specific beliefs or creeds.

**The Stages of Faith.** As you can see from the summary of the proposed stages in Table 10–2, Fowler is describing a general movement first toward individuation (which may consume most of the early adult years), and then a ''doubling backward'' toward participation and oneness. He says about the entire progression that ''each stage represents a widening of vision and valuing, correlated with a parallel increase in the certainty and depth of selfhood, making for qualitative increases in intimacy with self-others-world'' (1981, p. 274).

Some of the flavor of the differences that Fowler is attempting to codify will be clearer if I let a few adults speak for themselves. Here are three adults all operating with Stage 3 synthetic-conventional faith.

Mr. D. was a 63-year-old retired teamster who thought of himself mostly as ''one of the boys'':

> My views are quite the same as those of any teamster, or any working man. . . . I'm not now a religious man, never was, and never will be. Religion is just a lot of nonsense as I see it. As I see it, we are born, we live here, we die, and that's it. Religion gives people something to believe in, that there's something more, because they want there to be something more, but there isn't. So . . . you see, I'd rather put some money down on the bar and buy myself a drink, rather than put that same money into a collection plate! (Fowler, 1981, p. 165–166)

Anthony is a 40-year-old working man, married with two children, living in an Italian section of a large city. Speaking about what gives order or rightness to life, he says:

> When everything you're doing—let's face it—when you're abiding [by] the laws that were made—uh, not only the laws—it depends on your—uh, we won't get into the religious thing—say, laws. If you're going by—uh, what can I say? If you have, you know, a set of rules to live by—whether they write them down openly, you know—and let everybody know what they are actually—are—the rules and laws are or what they think their rights and wrongs are—if you're going by that, then what you're doing is right. (Fowler, 1981, p. 169)

Mrs. M. H. is a 61-year-old Southern woman who grew up on a tenant farm. After many years away from church activity, she has recently rededicated herself to the Baptist church. At one point she says:

> I feel very sad and ashamed for the way I have wasted my life. I do know that God has forgiven me for every wrong that I've done, and that He loves me. I feel very close to God most of the time, now that I am active in the work of the church again. Of course, there are times that I don't feel as close to Him as I'd like to, but I know that I

**TABLE 10–2 James Fowler's Proposed Stages of Faith**

| | |
|---|---|
| **Undifferentiated Faith** | This is very like what Erikson calls trust versus mistrust. In this early pre-stage, the child's identity is still largely merged with that of the mother (or other major caregiver). |
| 1: **Intuitive-Projective Faith** | From about two to seven, Fowler suggests that the child absorbs and combines in unique ways, bits and pieces of information about protective or threatening powers around him. The child at this age has differentiated self from other, but his ideas about the ways in which all of that is embedded in a larger context are heavily influenced by myth, by fantasy, by stories told to him by his parents or others. This is not yet integrated into a "system," but these early images (including perhaps images of terror or destructiveness, or taboos, as well as beneficent images) may have a powerful influence throughout his life. |
| 2: **Mythic-Literal Faith** | At school age, and continuing until at least adolescence, the child's thinking has become more abstract, and she searches for rules, for systems. Children this age absorb whole "stories" that are coherent and that guide, or are the basis for, faith at this stage. These stories—about death, life, God, why people are in the world—are taken quite literally. The child thus takes in as her own the specific beliefs and observances that are part of her "faith community," with literal meaning and without reflection. Some adults continue to show faith of this kind. |
| 3: **Synthetic-Conventional Faith** | At adolescence (for most of us) there is a wholesale reexamination of beliefs, of identity. Most adolescents, as part of this process, create a personal amalgam of beliefs and values. But while this is individual in some sense, it is still largely unreflected. The teenager or adult operating at this stage of faith does not perceive that there is a system or a kind of faith. The person, instead, chooses a set of beliefs from among those that are available. Another key feature of this type of faith is that authority is conceived of as outside the individual. Truth comes from external sources. |
| 4: **Individuative-Reflective Faith** | In young adulthood, for at least some, there is a further transition to a genuinely individually chosen set of principles or beliefs. "For a genuine move to Stage 4 to occur there must be an interruption of reliance on external sources of authority . . . there must be a relocation of authority within the self" (1981, p. 179). Frequently (but not invariably) this involves initially a rejection or moving away from the faith community to which one has belonged in the past, and the emergence of a genuinely self-chosen, self-created system of ideas or beliefs. For many adults this stage is heavily intellectual, oriented toward fact and science, and away from ritual or myth. |
| 5: **Conjunctive Faith** | Not typically found before midlife, conjunctive faith requires an integration of mind and emotion, of personal knowledge and objective fact. It also involves the realization that many different systems of belief can all be partially true, and that one's own specific religion or belief is "inevitably partial, limited to a particular people's experience of God and incomplete" (p. 186). Adults who display conjunctive faith are ready to hear about beliefs other than their own, and to |

**TABLE 10–2 James Fowler's Proposed Stages of Faith (*continued*)**

| | |
|---|---|
| | grant to those other beliefs some validity or partial truth. "What the previous stage struggled to clarify, in terms of the boundaries of self and outlook, this stage now makes porous and permeable. Alive to paradox and the truth in apparent contradictions, this stage strives to unify opposites in mind and experience" (p. 198). |
| 6: **Universalizing Faith** | The transition to Stage 6, relatively rare even in late adulthood, involves in some sense a step beyond individuality. At Stage 5, the individual may be "open" and "integrated," but is still very much centered in the self. The Stage 5 individual struggles with the paradox of searching for universality while still attempting to preserve individuality. "The transition to Stage 6 involves an overcoming of this paradox through a moral and ascetic actualization of the universalizing apprehensions. . . . Stage 6 becomes a disciplined, activist *incarnation*—a making real and tangible—of the imperatives of absolute love and justice of which Stage 5 has only partial apprehensions" (1981, p. 200). Such individuals are heedless of their own self-preservation and may be seen by others as subversive to the structures of society or traditional religion. Examples: Gandhi, Martin Luther King, Jr., Mother Theresa, and perhaps Dag Hammarskjold, Thomas Merton, Dietrich Bonhoeffer. |

am the one who moves away, not He. I've learned that we all have so much to be thankful for, if we only stop and count our blessings. (Fowler, 1981, p. 172)

The actual content of the beliefs of these three adults is quite different, but the sense of identity with a group, the definition of self and beliefs with reference to a specific community and a specific outside authority, are common to them all.

In contrast, let's listen to a woman with Stage 5 conjunctive faith: Miss T. was 78 when she was interviewed, and had at various times in her life been a Unitarian, a Quaker, and a follower of Krishnamurti and of other Eastern teachers. When asked if there were beliefs and values everyone should hold, she said:

If somebody asked me that and gave me just two minutes to answer it, I know what'd I'd say. It's a line from George Fox, the founder of Quakerism. It's old-fashioned English and it seems to me to have the entire program of anybody's life. Its a revolution, it's an enormous comfort, it's a peace maker. The line is: "There is that of God in every man." Now, you can start thinking about it. You can see that if you really did believe that, how it would change your relationships with people. It's far-reaching. It applies nationally and individually and class-wise; it reaches the whole. To anyone that I loved dearly I would say, "Put that in your little invisible locket and keep it forever." (Fowler, 1981, p. 194)

Other statements by Miss T. make it clear that her faith at this point involves a kind of return to some of the elements of her earlier religious teachings, but she has reframed it, casting it in language that has meaning to her now and that focuses on finding fulfillment in service to others—all of which are key elements of conjunctive faith.

Even these few examples suggest that many adults, like Anthony or Mr. D., come to a particular form of faith in their teens or 20s and remain essentially at that stage throughout their adulthood. Kohlberg's research similarly suggests that some adults remain at the level of moral reasoning they reached as young adults. There is a sequence, but it is only very roughly tied to age, and transitions from one stage to the next are not inevitable. (This is obviously similar, too, to Loevinger's or Maslow's accounts of the emergence of personality or motivation in adulthood which I talked about in the last chapter.)

Nonetheless, Fowler contends that each stage has its "proper" time of ascendancy in an individual's lifetime—a period at which that particular form of faith is most consistent with the demands of life. Most typically, Stage 3 (conventional faith) is in its ascendance in adolescence or early adulthood; Stage 4 (individuative-reflective faith) in the years of the late 20s and 30s; while a transition to Stage 5 (conjunctive faith), if it occurs at all, may occur at approximately midlife. (Those who experience such a transition may, in fact, think of it as part of their "midlife crisis.") Finally, Stage 6, if one can reach it, would be the optimal form of faith in old age, when issues of integrity and meaning become still more dominant. Each stage, at its optimum time, has the "potential for wholeness, grace and integrity and or strengths sufficient for either life's blows or blessings" (Fowler, 1981, p. 274). But remaining at a particular stage of faith past the "proper" time or age may bring problems. This is a potentially testable assertion, but one which has not yet been studied systematically.

No longitudinal data have yet been collected to test the sequential aspect of Fowler's theory. Fowler has, however, reported some cross-sectional data that show the incidence of the stages of faith at each of several ages (see Figure 10–3). The data included in this figure came from several different studies, from teenagers and adults living in several different parts of the United States (Boston, Chicago, Atlanta) and Canada (Toronto).

Since these are cross-sectional rather than longitudinal data, they do not tell us whether each individual has moved through the proposed stages in the sequence Fowler describes. But the findings fit the theory reasonably well. Stage 3 faith is most common in the teenage years, Stage 4 peaks among those in their 20s, while Stage 5 only really emerges in the 30s. Only one adult interviewed in any of these studies was scored at Stage 6, and he was a man in his 60s. Thus, the stages appear to emerge in the order, and at the approximate ages, that Fowler suggests. Further, these data are consistent with the idea that not all adults continue to shift from one stage to the next. Among adults of 30 or older, Stages 3 and 4 are as common as Stage 5 faith.

**A Preliminary Assessment.** What I find appealing about Fowler's theory is his attempt to add the element of faith or spiritual development to descrip-

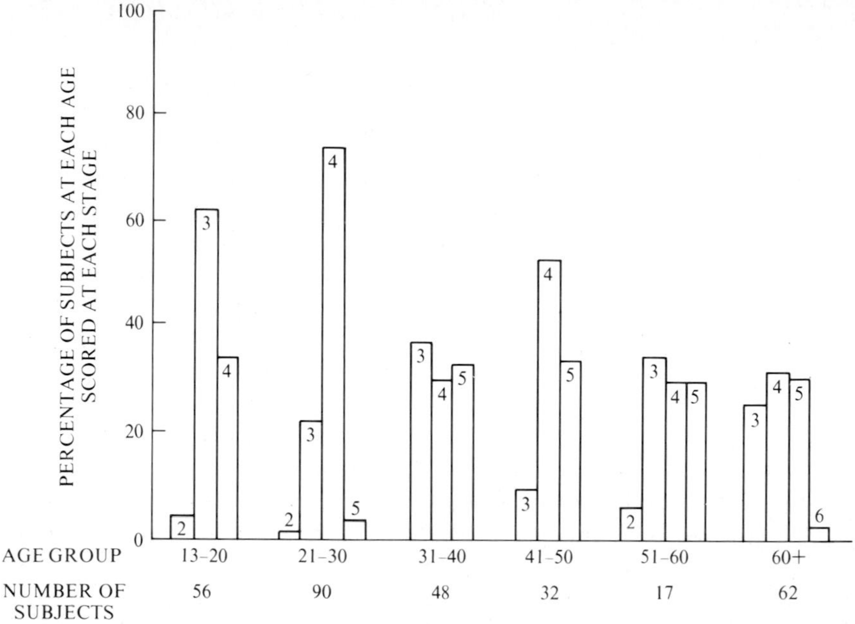


***Figure 10–3*** *Cross-sectional information about stages of faith from studies in several cities. Fowler actually scores interview responses in half steps. To simplify, I have combined each half step with the stage above it, so included in the bars reflecting Stage 4 are responses scored as both 3½ and 4. The findings suggest that Stage 3 is modal in the teenage years with Stage 4 emerging strongly in the 20s. Stage 5 does not appear frequently until the 30s, all of which is consistent with Fowler's theory. (Source: adapted from Fowler, 1981, Table B.3, p. 318.)*

tions of personality like Loevinger's, or of moral judgment like Kohlberg's. It is probably a mistake to assume that each adult functions as a single, cohesive whole, with moral reasoning, faith, and ego functioning all simultaneously at the same "level." Evidence accumulating about children's development points to the existence of sequences, but much less of broad, integrated stages (e.g., Flavell, 1982). But I think it is just as much a mistake to omit a consideration of faith—the fundamental, if often unreflected or unspoken, view that each of us has about the nature of ourselves and our world—from our examination of adult development.

Nonetheless, although theories like Fowler's supplement our thinking about adulthood in important ways, it is still very early in our empirical exploration of this and related theories. The greatest immediate need is for good longitudinal data, perhaps initially covering the years that are thought to be transitional for many adults, but ultimately for the entire adult age range. If the sequence that Fowler suggests stands up to such empirical tests, as have Kohlberg's stages of moral reasoning, then we will have taken a major step forward.

## Two Other Models

Fowler is not the only theorist groping for some overall model of adult development that will integrate our knowledge of personality development, the emergence of the sense of self, moral reasoning, motives, and emotions. Ken Wilber's approach, described in his book *The Atman Project* (1980), bears some striking similarities to Fowler's, but more explicitly attempts to integrate philosophical concepts from Eastern and Western traditions.

Like both Kohlberg and Fowler, Wilber proposes that there is a fundamental developmental process underlying the passage through childhood and adulthood. This process can be described in stages, with each stage emerging from and restructuring the previous stages. Of the several stages he suggests, two are particularly interesting for our purposes here: the **centaur stage** (also called the ''existential self'') and the **transpersonal stage.**

The stage of the centaur is roughly equivalent to Fowler's stage of conjunctive faith. It involves a shift from self-definitions in terms of roles or qualities, such as ''I am a psychologist,'' or ''I am a mother,'' or ''I am an introvert'' to a single sense I AM. The term *centaur* for this stage refers to the mythical beast that was half man and half horse. By using this term, Wilber is attempting to convey the flavor of this stage, that now the individual experiences mind and body as ''harmoniously one'' (p. 45).

The transpersonal stage, which (for a few adults at least) comes after the centaur stage, involves moving beyond the sense of individual self. There is a ''transcendance'' of self, such as what Maslow describes for his peak experiences or Fowler describes as part of universalizing faith.

A second recent theorist, Dwight Johnson (1983), similarly proposes a stage-like progression from childhood through adulthood, like Wilber attempting to draw on material from both Eastern and Western philosophy and psychology. I like Johnson's approach in part because the labels he has used for the several stages seem to me to be particularly simple and evocative of the key concepts. In his model, there are four adult stages (which he calls ''spirals''). The **social adult stage** is one in which the primary emphasis is on social roles. The social adult perspective is also dominated by black/white reasoning. Thoughts and emotions, in particular, are seen as opposites, and adults of this period tend to value one or the other.

This stage is followed by the stage of **the individual**, in which the person ''programs himself.'' The individual goes beyond the confines of social roles, often through developing highly individualized skill in some task or process. The suceeding stage Johnson calls **the free person,** which I think is a particularly apt description. In this stage the individual is free not only of the confines of role prescriptions, but also of the black/white thinking that characterized earlier stages. There is a turning away from the self-preoccupations of the previous stage, toward others.

Finally, Johnson proposes a stage he calls **the seer,** in which wisdom and compassion are both achieved, and their apparent inconsistencies resolved.

For neither of these theories is there any empirical evidence. But each contains some concepts that may be useful in arriving at some sort of theoretical synthesis.

## Integrating Meaning and Personality: A Preliminary Theoretical Synthesis

No doubt some of the parallels between these several theories, and those I discussed in chapters 3 and 9, have already struck you. But let me attempt an explicit integration by lining up the several sets of stages or hierarchies side by side, thus allowing direct comparison.

You will see that I have imposed my own order on the comparison. As I have read and thought about these several views of human development, a common pattern emerged, which I have used as the basis for the rows in this table. In the process of self-actualization, or in the development of self-understanding or of faith, there appears to me to be first, in childhood, a differentiation of self from other accompanied by an initial definition of self. This is followed by a period in which the self and the world view are experienced and defined in terms of the family, or society, or culture. Most theorists place the beginning of this phase in adolescence, but I would argue that to some degree at least it continues through the 20s and 30s, when socially defined roles dominate daily life. Life's meaning is given in terms of the fulfillment of roles or of the mores of a specific religion.

To some degree this "social adult" view (to use Johnson's helpful term) involves a submergence of the individuality. As a result, many adults in early adulthood begin to feel an urge to break free from the constrictions of social definitions. We are also pushed toward a deeper understanding of ourselves by specific experiences, failures, unhappinesses. For most of us, the implicit promise that "following the rules will lead to happiness" is broken. But if not rules, then what?

Most adults who confront this question seem then to move through an interesting period in which they may distance themselves from their own traditions, rethink old values and commitments, explore their emotions in a new way. Sam Keen (1983) calls this the period of the "outlaw," which I think is a bit strong, but conveys something of the quality of this period of individuality.

Some adults—not so very many, apparently—manage to emerge from this somewhat egocentric phase with a genuine integration of the various "parts" of the self—body, mind, emotion, intuition, faith. Maslow's description of the self-actualized person captures the potentialities of such an integration very nicely, as does Wilber's notion of the centaur. To achieve this integration, the individual must free herself from the self-preoccupation of the individualistic stage.

**The Transpersonal and Beyond.** As is clear from the Table 10–3, I do not think that development need cease at this point. Many theorists, and many

**TABLE 10–3** **Synthesis and Summary of Stages of Personality Development, Moral Development, Faith, and Spiritual Development**

| Suggested Synthesis of Stages | Loevinger's Ego Development Stages | Maslow's Needs Hierarchy | Kohlberg's Stages of Moral Development | Fowler's Stages of Faith | Wilber's Atman Project | Johnson's Spirals of Growth |
|---|---|---|---|---|---|---|
| Childhood: Undiff-erentaited body-self | Symbiotic, impulsive; self-protective | Physiological; safety | Level 1: Precon-ventional | Intuitive; mythic | Body-self | Childhood |
| Social or culture-bound self | Conformist; self-aware | Belongingness and love | Level 2: conven-tional morality | Synthetic-conventional | — | Social adult |
| Individuality | Conscientious; individualistic | Self-esteem | Stage 5: social contract and individual rights | Individuative | Verbal ego mind | The Individual |
| Integration: of body, mind, emo-tions, intuition | Autonomous; integrated | Self-actualized | Stage 6: Universal ethical principles | Conjunctive | Centaur; existential self | The Free Person |
| Transpersonal consciousness | — | Some peak experiences | Stage 7: Ethics based on unity | Universalizing | Transpersonal | Seer |
| Further reaches of transpersonal | — | Some peak experiences | — | — | "Subtle realms"; "causal realms"; Ultimate | |

**Sources:** Fowler, 1981; Johnson, 1983; Kohlberg, 1984; Loevinger, 1976; Maslow, 1954; Wilber, 1980.

individuals describing their own experience, propose still further steps. This is the period Wilber calls ''transpersonal,'' Fowler calls ''universalizing faith,'' and Kohlberg talks about as Stage 7 moral reasoning. It involves a ''standing outside of oneself'' and observing or experiencing the self and the world without the boundaries of individuality. There is a detachment from the individual, personal self, a new, profound ''decentering.'' Once again, Johnson's descriptive label for the stage (seer) seems particularly helpful. ''A seer, meaning one who 'sees,' is able to perceive the unity behind contradictions in specific structures of human expression or knowledge'' (Johnson, 1983, p. 115).

There is some interesting research evidence suggesting that many adults (even some children) experience at least moments in their lives that may be described as ''transpersonal.'' Such moments typically involve a loss of the sense of the separate self, a sense of insight or immediate ''knowing,'' and an emotional experience of joy (Hood, 1973; Stace, 1960). Researchers such as Ralph Hood (1970, 1973, 1975), who have developed interviews and standardized questionnaires to explore such experiences, report that they are widespread, even among young adults. Many of what Maslow calls ''peak experiences'' are included here, along with some moments of scientific insight, or of special creative power in an artist, as well as experiences described as mystical or religious revelation. I would argue (out of my own model of meaning) that the potential for such transcendance lies within each of us.

If that is so, then it is worth our while to examine, if only briefly here, the experiences of those who have described still further steps or stages along this same road. One of the richest veins of information about this further ''journey'' lies in the descriptions of inner steps or processes given by mystics of all religious traditions.

Evelyn Underhill (1911), in her remarkable book *Mysticism,* gave a splendid summary of the common developmental themes in the inner lives of mystics. Step 1, according to Underhill, is ''awakening,'' which may be brief (and corresponds to the glimpses or peak experiences I have just been describing). Step 2 Underhill calls ''purification.'' The individual, having ''seen'' herself from a broader perspective, also sees all her own imperfections, fruitless endeavors, her flaws. As St. Teresa of Avila (1562/1960, p. 181), one of the great mystics of the Christian tradition puts it, ''In a room bathed in sunlight not a cobweb can remain hidden'' (1562/1960, p. 181). There follows a period in which the person attempts to clean out the cobwebs by living a more saintly or more compassionate life. Many individuals at this stage also undertake special spiritual disciplines of one sort or another, including regular prayer or meditation, fasting, or the like.

Step 3 Underhill calls ''illumination,'' which is a much deeper, more prolonged awareness of a Light, or greater reality, or God. In Plato's metaphor of the cave, this is the step in which the individual, after realizing that the figures on the wall of the cave are only shadows, and after struggling to find the mouth of the cave, finally steps outside into the sun. This is accompanied by deep joy.

But even this illumination is not the end of the journey. Underhill finds two other ''steps'' described by many mystics that appear to lie beyond. The first of these, often called ''the dark night of the soul,'' involves a final purification of any sense of identification with the separate personality. At the stage of ''illumination,'' the individual still feels some personal satisfaction, some personal pleasure or joy, in having achieved illumination. Ultimately—at least according to mystics who have described these later stages—this personal pleasure, too, must be (or is) abandoned. And the process of abandonment requires a turning back into awareness of, and exploration of, all the remaining ways in which the separate self has survived. Only when this steep and slippery slope has been traversed does the individual achieve the end point, that of ''union''—with God, with Reality, with Beauty, with the Ultimate, however this may be described within a particular religious tradition.

**Development as a Spiral.** The series of stages reflected in Table 10–3, and the further steps or stages of the mystical experience described by Underhill, can be shown graphically in a number of ways, including the model I suggest in Figure 10–4. In this model, I am describing change, growth, or development along two dimensions: (1) the breadth of self-other orientation (that is, the size of the group with which one identifies oneself, moving from complete lack of differentiation of self from other, to a beginning sense of the separate self, to the dyad, to family, to society, to humanity, to all life), and (2) the degree of abstractness or ''decenteredness'' of the perspective. The process of decentering seems to me to be essentially continuous or sequential. The child originally views the world entirely from his own perspective, not even understanding that there are any other ways of experiencing or understanding. Gradually the child sees and is able to look at the world from the perspectives of friends and family, and then of society (Kohlberg's stage of conventional morality). In adulthood, the individual may transcend the societal perspective, too, and search for what lies behind it. Once an integrated individuality has been achieved, the individual then decenters (''steps beyond'') again, taking a perspective that lies outside of the separate self.

The interesting paradox is that it seems that in the process of achieving each new decentering, we repeatedly move backward on the dimension of self-other orientation. I am suggesting three such turns in the system: (1) At the stage of individuality we become more focused on ourselves, our own beliefs, our own personality or troubles or emotions, even as we are ''decentering'' from the social perspective. It is as if we must come to know ourselves fully in order to be ''free'' of ourselves in the transpersonal sense. (2) At the stage of purification, we must again look inward to become aware of the cobwebs, the flaws and residual selfishness. (3) Finally, at the point described as the dark night of the soul, there is another turning inward (often accompanied by a sense of complete loss of connection with the transcendant), as the person finds and abandons any remaining identification with the sense of separateness.

Also reflected in the figure is a concept advanced by Underhill that the stages of spiritual development involve fluctuations between periods of ''sunshine'' and ''shade,'' between pleasure and pain. Such fluctuation is a common theme

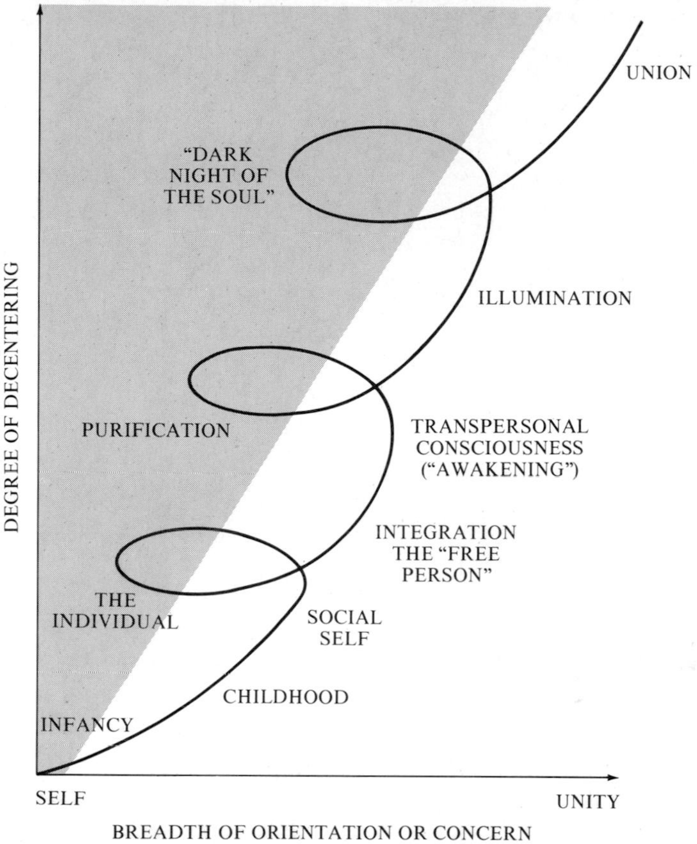


**Figure 10–4** *One possible way to represent the stages described in Table 10–3 is as a spiral. The interesting point is the apparent "regression" to a kind of preoccupation with the self at the fourth stage, and at later points, as if development were a constant movement back and forth from "inward" to "outward" orientations.*

in the descriptions given by mystics, with the period of purification, and the dark night of the soul both experienced as painful or ''dark'' in some sense. I have extended this idea into the earlier stages, proposing that the period of individuality may also have elements of ''shade'' or ''shadow,'' while the period of the social adult, and that of the integrated person, are both times of relatively greater light. In some sense I am suggesting something rather like Levinson's theory, that adult life is as an alternation between periods of upheaval and periods of stability. But I am going beyond Levinson to argue that some periods of upheaval may be not just transitions from one stability to the next, but are themselves critical elements in the developmental process.

Overall, I am proposing a model of development as a spiral. The process, in

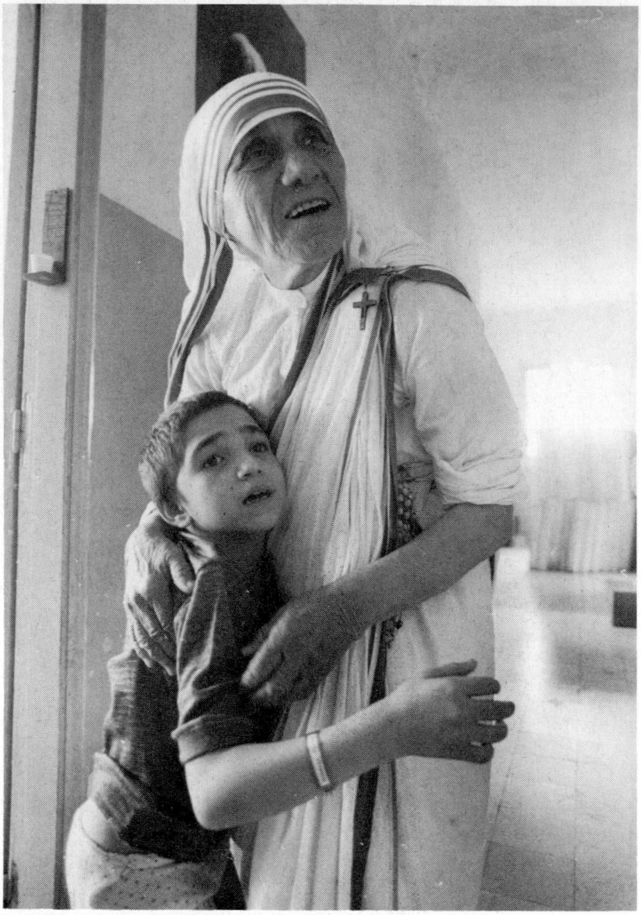

**Figure 10–5** *Mother Teresa appears to reflect at least the stage of Universalizing faith described by Fowler, with her profound commitment to compassionate action. Whether she has experienced stages beyond this, as described by Underhill, we do not know. (Source: Arnaud de Wildenberg, Sygma.)*

this view, is not linear. Rather, we continue to circle back to similar issues, but at higher and higher levels of decentering.

I cannot say, of course, whether this sequence, these spirals of inner human progress, reflects the inevitable or ultimate path for us all. I can say only that the developmental analyses of stages of morality, or stages of faith, or of personality that have been offered by many psychologists, for which we have at least some preliminary supporting evidence, appear to form a connected whole with the desciptions of stages of mystical illumination. At the very least, we know that a pathway similar to this has been trod by a long series of remarkable individuals, whose descriptions of their inner journeys bear striking similarities.

There may be many other paths or journeys. But the reflections of these remarkable few point the way toward the possibility of a far vaster potential of the human spirit than is apparent to most of us in our daily, humdrum lives.

## The Process of Transition

Coming down a bit from these lofty levels, but still assuming for the moment that there is some stage-like developmental process in meaning or spiritual development in adult lives, let me turn to the question that may be of special personal importance: What is the process by which transitions or transformations from one stage to the next take place? What triggers them? What are the common features of transitions? How are they traversed?

As a general rule, developmental psychologists who propose stages of adult development have focused more on the stages than on the transition process. But there are some common themes in the descriptions offered.

At a theoretical level, a number of authors have described transitions in parallel terms (James, 1902; Johnson, 1983; Kegan, 1980). Each time one shifts from one "level" or "stage" to the next there is a kind of death and rebirth—a death of the earlier sense of self, of the earlier faith, of the earlier equilibrium. Normally this seems to involve first some glimpses or precursors or premonitions of another stage or view, which are then followed by a period (which may be brief or prolonged) in which the individual struggles to deal with these two selves within. Sometimes the process is aborted, and the individual returns to the earlier equilibrium. Sometimes the individual then moves toward a new equilibrium, and identifies himself with that new equilibrium. There is, as William Bridges (1980) puts it simply and clearly, first an ending, then a middle, and then a beginning.

The middle part of this process, when the old self has been partially given up, but a new equilibrium has not yet been reached, is often experienced as profoundly dislocating. Sentences like "I am beside myself" or "I was out of my mind" may be used (Kegan, 1980). And like the transitions I described in the last chapter, the process of equilibration may be accompanied by an increase in symptoms of various kinds, including depression.

Kegan perhaps best summarizes the potential pain of the process:

> Development is costly—for everyone, the developing person and those around him or her. Growth involves a separation from an old system of meaning. In practical terms this can involve both the agony of felt meaninglessness and the repudiation of commitments and investment. . . . Developmental theory gives us a way of thinking about such pain that does not pathologize it. (1980, p. 439).

Such transitions may emerge slowly or may occur rapidly; they may be the result of self-chosen activities, such as therapy or exercise, or they may result from the happenstances of ordinary life or from unexpected experiences. In

Table 10–4 I have suggested some of the stimulants for such transitions, organized around three of the adult transitions I suggested in Table 10–3. I offer this list quite tentatively. We lack—again, as usual—the longitudinal evidence to allow us to say more fully what experiences may or may not stimulate a transition. We also need to understand much more completely why apparently equivalent experiences may lead to a transition for one person and not for another.

Note in Table 10–4 that I am suggesting that somewhat different experiences may be involved in each of these three transitions. Attending college, or moving away from home into a quite different community, seem to be particularly influential in promoting aspects of the transition to individuality. Both Kohlberg (1973) and Rest and Thoma (1985), for example, have found in longitudinal studies a correlation between the amount of college education completed and level of moral reasoning. Principled reasoning was found only in those who had attended at least some college. The transition seems to be precipitated, in this case, by exposure—often for the first time—to other assumptions, other faiths, other perspectives. Such a confrontation can produce disequilibrium, which may be dealt with by searching for a new, independent, self-chosen model.

I have also suggested that therapy may play some role by triggering or assisting with either of the first two transitions. Helping a client to achieve full integration is, in fact, the highest goal of many humanistically oriented therapies, such as those based on the work of Carl Rogers or Fritz Perls. But my hypothesis is that traditional forms of therapy do little to assist the transition

**TABLE 10–4 Transitions from One Stage to Another: Some Possible Triggering Situations or Experiences That May Assist in Passing Through a Transition**

| Transition | Intentionally Created Transition | Unintentional or Circumstantially Created Transition |
|---|---|---|
| From social or "culture bound" to individuality | Therapy<br>Reading about other religions or faiths | Attending college<br>Leaving home for other reasons such as a job or marriage<br>Usual failures or reverses while "following the rules" |
| From individuality to integration | Therapy<br>Introspection<br>Short-term programs designed to heighten self-awareness; e.g., some kinds of Gestalt workshops, est | Illness or prolonged pain<br>Death in the family or prolonged crisis<br>Peak experiences |
| From integration to transpersonal awareness | Meditation or prayer<br>Various forms of yoga<br>Self-disciplines and self-denials | Near-death experience<br>Transcendant experiences such as some peak experiences, or immediate mystical experience |

from integrated person to the transpersonal level of awareness. This transition, I think, requires (or is at least assisted by) a different form of active process, such as meditation or other forms of yoga or systematic prayer (LeShan, 1966).

Both painful experiences and transcendant ones can also be the occasion for a new transition. The death of a child or of a parent, for example, may reawaken our concern with ultimate questions of life and death. A failed marriage or discouragement at work may lead to questioning or to a loss of the sense of stability of one's present model. Peak experiences, too, by giving glimpses of something not readily comprehensible within a current view, may create a disequilibrium. Most adults who have had a near-death experience, for example, report that their lives are never again the same. Many change jobs or devote their lives to service in one way or another. Other forms of peak experiences, or religious "rebirth," may have the same effect.

I have been consistently using the word *may* in the last few paragraphs to convey the fact that such life changes do not invariably result in significant reflection or decentering. Patricia Gurin and Orville Brim (1984), in an argument reminiscent of the concept of "scheduled" and "unscheduled" changes, have recently offered an interesting hypothesis to explain such differences in the impact of major life changes. In essence, they argue that widely shared, age-linked changes are not likely to trigger significant reassessments of the sense of self. Most adults attribute such shared changes to causes outside of themselves. We do not, in other words, take so much personal responsibility for experiences that are common to others of our age or station in society. It is, instead, unique or off-time life changes that are most likely to lead to significant inner reappraisals, precisely because it is difficult to attribute such experiences to outward causes. If everyone at your job has been laid off because the company has gone out of business during a recession, you need not reassess your own sense of self-worth. But if you are the only one fired during a time of expanding economy, it is much more difficult to maintain your sense of worth.

Some shared experiences, such as college, may commonly trigger reappraisals or restructuring of personality, moral judgment, or faith (in Fowler's sense). But most age-graded experiences can be absorbed fairly readily into existing systems. It may then be the unique or misstimed experiences that are particularly significant for personal development. This hypothesis remains to be tested, but raises some intriguing issues.

## Commentary and Conclusions

For me, one of the striking things about the information I have presented in this chapter is that it is possible to find such similar descriptions emerging from such different traditions. But, of course, the fact that there is a great deal of apparent unanimity in the theoretical (and personal) descriptions of develop-

**Figure 10–6** *Attending college seems to have the effect of triggering a reassessment of moral reasoning (and perhaps faith more broadly) for many young people, as it brings the young adult into contact with others from different faith communities, with other forms of reasoning about rights and wrongs. (Source: Paulo Koch, Photo Researchers Inc.)*

ment of moral judgment, meaning systems, motive hierarchies, and spiritual evolution does not make this shared view true.

It does seem to be fair to say that most adults are engaged in some process of creating or searching for meaning in their lives. But this is not necessarily a conscious, deliberate process. Thus the word *search* in the title of this chapter may be misleading. Some adults appear to engage in a conscious search, and their descriptions of the process are remarkably similar. But as I pointed out earlier, this may or may not mean that such a search, or even a nonconscious, or nonintentional, sequence of faiths, is a ''natural'' or essential part of adult development.

Furthermore, it is important to realize that all of what I have said—and all of what these various theorists have said—is based upon a single metaphor of development, the metaphor of ''life as a journey'' (a kind of pilgrim's progress). We imagine the adult trudging up some hill or along some road, passing through steps or stages as she moves along. Implicit in this metaphor is the concept of a goal, an end point, a *telos* (a Greek word from which our word *teleological* comes, meaning having purpose or moving toward a goal). This is a journey going somewhere. As Sam Keen says (1983), ''If we use the idea of stages and journey we are obliged to follow the logic of our metaphors and ask where we are going and why. If life is a journey, the end of life may be death but it cannot be its telos'' (p. 30). If, for example, the purpose of the journey

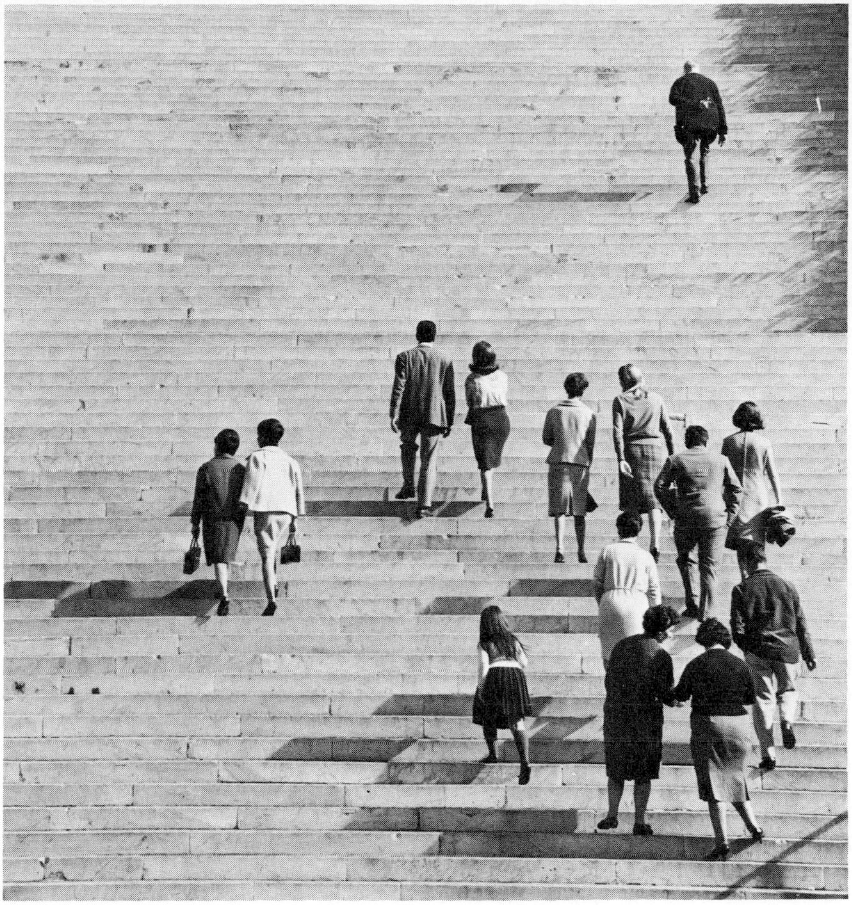

***Figure 10–7*** *The metaphor of the journey, like some endless flight of stairs, is at the root of many theories of adult personality development or search for meaning. But it is not the only metaphor we might adopt, and may be a misleading one by placing too great an emphasis on linearity, on telos. (Source: Louis Goldman, Photo Researchers Inc.)*

is thought of as "growth" or "evolution," then we must have some concept of "highest growth."

Such a journey metaphor is implicit or explicit in virtually all existing theories, but the linearity of the metaphor may well be a serious limiting feature. Keen suggests several other ways in which we might think of the process, of which I find two particularly appealing: (1) "When we think of this eternal dimension of our being, the circle is more appropriate than the line. If life is a journey, then, it is not a pilgrimage but an odyssey in which one leaves and returns home again" (p. 31). Each step may be a circling back, a remembering of the "still point" within (to use T. S. Eliot's phrase). Progressively, we understand or "know" ourselves and our world differently at each stage, but there is no necessary end point. (2) We could think of the entire process as "musical themes that weave together to form a symphony; the themes that are central to each stage are anticipated in the previous stage and remain as resonant subthemes in subsequent stages" (p. 32). Still another metaphor is that of a tapestry, in which one weaves many colors. An individual who creates many different life views or faiths may thus be weaving a tapestry with more colors, but it may be no more beautiful or pleasing than a tapestry woven intricately of fewer colors.

The basic point I want to make is a simple one, although often hard to absorb thoroughly: Our theories are based in part on metaphors. We begin our search for understanding of adult development with such a metaphor, and it colors all of what we choose to examine and all of what we see. The journey metaphor has dominated most of the current thinking, but it is not the only way to think about the process.

If we are to understand this process further, if we are to choose among these several metaphors, what we need is a great deal more empirical information to answer questions such as the following:

1. Is there a longitudinal progression through Fowler's stages of faith or equivalent sequences proposed by others, including Loevinger's stages of ego development? I pointed out in chapter 9 that Loevinger's theory is at least roughly consistent with some of the evidence from existing longitudinal studies. But more direct tests are needed.
2. What are the connections, if any, between movement through the several parallel sequences described in Table 10–3? That is, if we look at the rows in the table, would we find most people describing their faith, their moral development, their sense of self in similar ways? Alternatively, it is possible that such integration occurs only at the final steps—at the level of the "centaur" or the "free person." Or we may be dealing here with timing models like those I described in chapter 3, with each sequence developing somewhat independently, but disequilibrium created when two or more sequences are significantly out of synchrony.

We do not yet have the evidence that would allow us to choose among these alternatives, but several existing studies point to at least some consistency across the sequences. For example, measures of Loevinger's ego development and moral reasoning are typically found to be correlated moderately, in the range of $r = .50$ (Loevinger, 1984; Sullivan, McCullough, & Stager, 1970). Similarly, Leean (1985) reports a moderate relationship between scores on a measure of stage of faith development and on a measure of extent of completion of Erikson's stages. Data from still another recent study suggest a link between principled moral reasoning (Stage 5 in Kohlberg's system) and "openness to experience," which we might take as an aspect of the shift to individualistic/integrated stages (Lonky, Kaus, & Roodin, 1984). But these are merely the first whiffs of evidence. Much more is needed.

3. Assuming that longitudinal data confirm that there are stages of meaning-development, we need to know what prompts a shift from one to the next. What supports a transition? What retards it?
4. Is there any relationship between stages of faith (or models of meaning, or constructions of the self) and a sense of wellbeing, or greater physical health, or greater peace of mind? If I am correct in the proposal implicit in Figure 10–3, then we might find higher levels of wellbeing or life satisfaction during the conscientious and integrated stages, and lower levels during the individualistic stage (or its equivalent).

To check this hypothesis, it is not enough to look at changes with age in life satisfaction. Rather, one must measure stages of faith or stages of ego development (preferably longitudinally) and examine life satisfaction at the same time. No longitudinal study fits this bill, but one cross-sectional study goes part way. Costa and McCrae (1983) measured the ego development stage for each subject, using Loevinger's sentence completion test, personality (extraversion and neuroticism), and feeling of wellbeing. They found that the ego development stage was not correlated with sense of wellbeing, but they did not check for the possibility of alternating higher and lower levels of wellbeing. Being cross-sectional, their data also cannot tell us whether individuals experience predictable fluctuations in positive or negative effects as they move through the stages of faith.

Answers to some of these questions may be forthcoming in the next decades, as researchers devise better ways to measure and explore these elusive dimensions of adult lives. For now, much of what I have said in this chapter remains tantalizing and intriguing speculation—but speculation that points toward the potential for wisdom, compassion, even illumination within each adult.

## Summary

1. In addition to studying inner development by examining personality change over adulthood, we can also ask about any changes in meaning systems or faith or spirituality.

2. In this area there is more theory than data, but some evidence does exist.

3. Participation in the formal aspects of religion (e.g., church attendance) appears to peak some time around age 50 and then decline. This decline is compensated by an increase in private religious practices.

4. Theories of the development of systems of meaning have been strongly influenced by Kohlberg's theory of the development of moral reasoning.

5. Kohlberg describes three sequentially achieved levels of moral reasoning, with two stages at each level. Level 1 is preconventional reasoning, in which right is understood as that which brings pleasure or approval. Level 2 is conventional reasoning, in which right or justice is defined by the rules or mores of the family and later of society. Level 3 is principled reasoning, in which right or justice is defined by appeal to a set of principles that lie behind social customs or laws.

6. Longitudinal data show that teenagers and young adults do move through these stages, without skipping, and with little indication of regression. In adults, conventional reasoning is most common.

7. Fowler's theory of faith development is broader in concept than Kohlberg's model, and extends to "higher" levels. He seeks to describe the ways in which adults explain to themselves the purpose of life.

8. Fowler proposes six stages, of which the final four are characteristic of adulthood: synthetic-conventional (dominated by external sources of authority), individuative-reflective (dominated by an individual, internally located meaning system), conjunctive (reflecting an integration of mind and emotion), and universalizing (going beyond individuality to a sense of universal connectedness).

9. Cross-sectional data are consistent with Fowler's theory, with Stages 3, 4, and 5 first found at approximately the points in adult life that he proposes. Among adults, however, Stages 3, 4, and 5 are all about equally common.

10. Integration of Kohlberg's and Fowler's theories with those of Loevinger and Maslow, and two other still broader theories of the evolution of human consciousness proposed by Wilber and Johnson, suggests a common set of stages, moving first toward individuation, and then back toward universalizing or "transpersonal" experience.

11. This common set of stages can be linked coherently to descriptions of steps in mystical or transcendant experience, in which the individual moves from glimpses of transpersonal awareness to the experience of complete unity with Reality, or Beauty, or God.

12. Transitions from one stage to the next in this progression are frequently experienced in terms of loss or "death" of the old self or the old view. Transitions may thus be profoundly dislocating.

13. Transitions may be triggered by unique life changes, by suffering, by peak experiences, by intentionally pursued self-knowledge, or by self-disciplines.

14. To move beyond the speculative aspect of these theories, additional longitudinal and cross-sectional data will be required.

## Suggested Readings

*Given my obvious interest in this area, you will not be surprised that I have a long list of books to recommend to you. Any of these would be provocative; none is too technical since they were all written for a lay audience as well as for professionals.*

Fowler, J. (1981). *Stages of faith.* New York: Harper & Row.

You may find the case material he gives as fascinating as the theory.

Fowler, J. (1983). Stages of faith. *PT* conversation with James Fowler. *Psychology Today, 17,* 56–62.

If you want a briefer look at Fowler's theory, try this short article.

Frankl, V. E. (1984). *Man's search for meaning* (3rd ed.). New York: Simon & Schuster.

Frankl is a psychiatrist who came to the conclusion that an understanding of a patient's model of meaning was the key to any successful therapy. But the roots of this conclusion came from his own experience in a concentration camp. He describes both in this book.

JAMES, W. (1958). *The varieties of religious experience.* New York: Mentor. (Original work published in 1902)

I find this a delightful book, remarkably free of the convoluted style that otherwise seems to be common in this area.

KEEN, S. (1983). *The passionate life: Stages of loving.* New York: Harper & Row.

Keen's views, like most in this area, have been influenced by Kohlberg, so this is not totally new stuff. But his focus on the emotional/loving side of the developmental process makes this book particularly relevant for our lives.

KEGAN, R. (1982). *The evolving self.* Cambridge, MA: Harvard University Press.

Kegan is another of the group of theorists at Harvard, influenced by Kohlberg among others. I find his style clearer and more elegant than many of the others.

PECK, M. S. (1978). *The road less travelled.* New York: Simon & Schuster.

In this book, Peck offers a highly original, very readable, provocative theory of love and spiritual growth in adulthood, and of the potential role of therapy in promoting that growth.

ST. THERESA OF AVILA. (1961). *Interior castle* (E. Allison Peers, Trans.). Garden City, NY: Image Books. (Original work published 1577)

Many experts consider St. Theresa's several descriptions of her inner spiritual journey to be the most complete and the most comprehensible available. I found it astonishing: delightfully written, provocative, and stimulating.

UNDERHILL, E. (1961). *Mysticism.* New York: E. P. Dutton. (Original work published 1911)

This book is a scholarly tour de force. Underhill combined and distilled the essence of the reports of hundreds of mystics and other religious teachers, from all religious traditions, into a single, coherent account. Her style is clear and straightforward.

# 11

# Dealing with the Stresses of Adult Life

There may be a few exceptionally lucky people in this world who rarely face crises, upheavals, or loss. But most of us encounter these quite regularly. I consider my own adult years (so far, at least) to be relatively crisis-free, but in the 26 years since I turned 20, I have gone through the usual failed love affairs, a divorce, 16 moves, seven or eight job changes, assorted minor car accidents, assorted small surgeries and the usual collection of illnesses, the death of a close friend and of two grandparents, and have twice been the victim of a crime. Most people, no doubt, have had to cope with far more.

As I have pointed out all along, some crises and upheavals are predictable and are quite widely shared by adults as they move through the various normative roles and stages. But many of these experiences, and the timing of them, are unique to each individual. If we are to understand the various pathways through adulthood that may be taken by an individual, we need to take a look at the effect of such stresses on adults. We also need to look at those qualities of adults, or their environments, that may soften or shorten the effect of stress.

Fortunately, the study of ''stress'' has been a hot research topic in recent years, so there is an extensive literature. Less fortunately, almost none of the research is developmental in conception or design. Nonetheless, some extremely interesting concepts and provocative findings have emerged that expand our understanding of adulthood.

## Definitions of Stress

Before I can go further, I need to talk about the definition of stress. Writing a definition would be a much simpler task if there were agreement among stress researchers. But at this stage in the evolution of theory and research in this area, there are still at least three types of definitions, each associated with a different body of theory and research: response-oriented theories, stimulus-oriented theories, and interactionist theories.

**Response-Oriented Theories.** The one name most prominently associated with this theoretical tradition is Hans Selye, who is really the "father" of modern stress research (1936; 1976; 1982). Selye defines stress as "the non-specific (that is, common) result of any demand upon the body, be the effect mental or somatic" (1982, p. 7). That is, stress is the body's response to demand. So the more demands there are on a person—demands from roles, from environmental hazards such as heat or noise, from time pressures, and so on—the more stress the person experiences.

According to Selye, the body's stress reaction occurs in three stages, which he calls collectively the **general adaptation syndrome** (GAS). First comes the **alarm reaction**, which has two phases. In the "shock" phase there is an initial, immediate effect of some noxious stimulus on the body's tissues. Typically there is a loss of body temperature and a lowering of blood pressure. Then there is a "countershock" phase in which some kind of physiological defenses are mounted. The adrenal cortex enlarges and secretes higher levels of hormones, and the body temperature and blood pressure rise again. If the stressor continues, these alarm reactions fade and are replaced by a stage Selye calls **resistance,** in which the body strives to achieve homeostasis. Three physiological changes are particularly notable in this stage: enlargement of the adrenal gland, shrinkage of the thymus gland (especially critical since the thymus is involved in immune responses), and gastrointestinal ulceration. Thus, in this phase the individual is able to control the shock or alarm reaction to the stressor, but does so in a way that lowers resistance to other stressors or stimuli. Eventually, however, if the stressor continues long enough (and many chronic stressors do continue over very long periods of time), the somewhat fragile adaptation of the resistance phase breaks down and the person reaches the stage of **exhaustion**, when some of the alarm-responses reappear. If the stressor is severe enough, exhaustion is accompanied by physical illness or even death.

These three stages are rather like what happens when you exercise. When you first begin a several-mile run, or at the start of an aerobics class (or the equivalent), your body may initially feel tired and it may be difficult to keep moving. But then you get into a rhythm (a kind of homeostasis) and for a while you feel as if you could go on forever. Eventually, though, if you continue long enough, you will reach the stage of exhaustion.

Physical illness, or even death, can be associated with any of these stages. Some of the body's adaptations in the middle stage may, in fact, promote illness in the long run. For example, the Type A pattern of behavior I talked about in chapter 4, which is associated with a heightened risk of heart disease, is a kind of resistance pattern. Thus, although the intermediate stage is more stable than the initial alarm reaction or the ultimate exhaustion stage, the body's response to heightened physical or emotional demand is not perfect. And in general, the greater the demand, the greater the risk of disease or injury. Fur-

**TABLE 11–1 Life Change Events Included in the Holmes and Rahe Social Readjustment Rating Scale**

| Life Event | Points Assigned |
|---|---|
| 1. Death of spouse | 100 |
| 2. Divorce | 73 |
| 3. Marital separation from mate | 65 |
| 4. Detention in jail or other institution | 63 |
| 5. Death of a close family member | 63 |
| 6. Major personal injury or illness | 53 |
| 7. Marriage | 50 |
| 8. Being fired at work | 47 |
| 9. Marital reconciliation with mate | 45 |
| 10. Retirement from work | 45 |
| 11. Major change in the health or behavior of a family member | 44 |
| 12. Pregnancy | 40 |
| 13. Sexual difficulties | 39 |
| 14. Gaining a new family member (e.g., through birth, adoption, oldster moving in, etc.) | 39 |
| 15. Major business readjustment (e.g., merger, reorganization, bankruptcy, etc.) | 39 |
| 16. Major change in financial state (e.g., a lot worse off or a lot better off than usual) | 38 |
| 17. Death of a close friend | 37 |
| 18. Changing to a different line of work | 36 |
| 19. Major change in the number of arguments with spouse (e.g., either a lot more or a lot less than usual regarding child-rearing, personal habits, etc.) | 35 |
| 20. Taking out a mortgage or loan for a major purchase (e.g., for a home, business, etc.) | 31 |
| 21. Foreclosure on a mortgage or loan | 30 |
| 22. Major change in responsibilities at work (e.g., promotion, demotion, lateral transfer) | 29 |
| 23. Son or daughter leaving home (e.g., marriage, attending college, etc.) | 29 |
| 24. Trouble with in-laws | 29 |

thermore, Selye specifically postulates that the return to "rest" after the stressor has stopped and the GAS is terminated is never complete. One gets back almost to the old level but not quite. The process of what we call aging may thus be simply the accumulation of the effects of many GASs, each leaving a residue of effects on the hormone system, the cardiovascular system, the immune system.

Much of the work that has followed this line of reasoning has been done by physicians and physiologists attempting to identify the specific physiological patterns that are part of the "stress response" or GAS. Psychologists, in contrast, have generally approached the problem from the other end, starting with the stressor.

**Stimulus-Oriented Theories.** Taking this approach, we might define *stress* as an environmental circumstance that demands change and adaptation. (This comes closer to the everyday use of the word, I think. When you say, "I'm

**TABLE 11–1 Life Change Events Included in the Holmes and Rahe Social Readjustment Rating Scale (*continued*)**

| | |
|---|---|
| 25. Outstanding personal achievement | 28 |
| 26. Wife beginning or ceasing work outside the home | 26 |
| 27. Beginning or ceasing formal schooling | 26 |
| 28. Major change in living conditions (e.g., building a new home, remodeling, deterioration of home or neighborhood) | 25 |
| 29. Revision of personal habits (dress, manners, associations, etc.) | 24 |
| 30. Trouble with the boss | 23 |
| 31. Major change in working hours or conditions | 20 |
| 32. Change in residence | 20 |
| 33. Changing to a new school | 20 |
| 34. Major change in usual type and/or amount of recreation | 19 |
| 35. Major change in church activities (e.g., a lot more or a lot less than usual) | 19 |
| 36. Major change in social activities (e.g., clubs, dancing, movies, visiting, etc.) | 18 |
| 37. Taking out a mortgage or loan for a lesser purchase (e.g., for a car, TV, freezer, etc.) | 17 |
| 38. Major change in sleeping habits (a lot more or a lot less sleep, or change in part of day when asleep) | 16 |
| 39. Major change in number of family get-togethers (e.g., a lot more or a lot less than usual) | 15 |
| 40. Major change in eating habits (a lot more or a lot less food intake, or very different meal hours or surroundings) | 15 |
| 41. Vacation | 13 |
| 42. Christmas | 12 |
| 43. Minor violations of the law (e.g., traffic tickets, jaywalking, disturbing the peace, etc.) | 11 |

**Source:** Reprinted with permission from *Journal of Psychosomatic Research, 14,* Holmes, T. S. and Holmes T. H. Short term intrusions into Life-Style routine (pp. 121–132). Copyright 1970, Pergamon Press, Ltd. (Original publication of the Social Readjustment Rating Scale appeared in the *Journal of Psychomatic Research, 11,* 1967, pp. 213–218. Copyright 1967, Pergamon Press, Ltd.

under stress,'' you are describing the environment's demands on you, rather than your body's reaction.) For a researcher using such a definition of stress, the task is to specify just what classes of circumstances are stressful, and what the effects of that stress may be on the individual.

A number of different lists of stresses have been developed (e.g., Chiriboga & Dean, 1978; Paykel, 1974; Sarason, Johnson, & Siegal, 1979) of which by far the most famous and widely used is the Social Readjustment Rating Scale (SRRS) developed by Thomas Holmes and Richard Rahe (1967). This scale consists of the 43 ''life change events'' listed in Table 11–1. The subject is asked to check off those that have occurred in the past 6 or 12 months. The basic idea is that any change, be it positive or negative, requires adaptation. The more changes, the more the adaptation. Of course, some life changes are more profound or severe than others, so different numbers of points are assigned to reflect the degree of adaptation each life change requires. A subject's score on this instrument is thus the sum of the points for all the changes he or she has recently experienced. Holmes and Rahe hypothesized that the higher the score, the greater the likelihood that the person would become physically ill or emotionally disturbed within the next year. In particular, a score of over 300 was thought to reflect a major life change crisis or stress.

There is a great deal of research evidence (which I'll describe shortly) supporting Holmes and Rahe's original hypothesis. At the same time, there have been serious questions raised about this definition of stress and this method of measurement (e.g., see Derogatis, 1982; Dohrenwend & Dohrenwend, 1978; Perkins, 1982). First of all, it is not so obvious that all kinds of life change are equivalent in their stress-producing effects. Are positive life changes and negative life changes really equally stressful? And even among life changes that may be classed as negative, are there some subvarieties that are more stress-producing or more likely to lead to illness than others?

Several researchers have lately suggested some interesting subcategories of life changes or stress experiences that may prove to be more helpful descriptors or predictors than the original Holmes and Rahe list. For example, Pearlin (1980, 1982b), whose approach I have described several times, makes a distinction between chronic life strains and life changes. And among life changes, as you know, he distinguishes between those that are scheduled and those that are unscheduled. Richard Lazarus and his colleagues (DeLongis, Coyne, Dakof, Folkman, & Lazarus, 1982; Lazarus & DeLongis, 1983; Lazarus & Folkman, 1984) similarly suggest that we will better understand the links between stress and illness if we count not just major life changes, but also "daily hassles" and "daily uplifts." Hassles, which may be transient or chronic, include such familiar experiences as misplacing your keys, having to fill out forms, finding you've gained a pound when you step on the scale in the morning, or getting caught in a traffic jam on your way to an important meeting. Uplifts may include laughter, pleasant times with your family, or other joyous or satisfying moments. These newer expansions of the concept of life stresses, while not as thoroughly studied as life changes, have proven to be useful predictors.

A second major question raised about defining stress only in terms of major life changes is whether the same life change is equally stressful for all people. Perhaps, instead, it is the person's *subjective interpretation* (the **appraisal,** to use Lazarus's word) of an event that is critical, and not the objective event itself. Questions of this kind have led to a third, interactionist, view of stress.

**Interactionist Approaches.** Interactionist definitions of stress focus on the individual's perception of an event or on the extent to which some experience exceeds the individual's adaptational capacity. For example: stress may be defined as "a (perceived) imbalance between demand and response capability, under conditions where failure to meet demand has important (perceived) consequences" (McGrath, 1970, p. 20), or as "a particular relationship between the person and the environment that is appraised by the person as taxing or exceeding his or her resources and endangering his or her well-being" (Lazarus & Folkman, 1984, p. 19).

Looked at this way, stress occurs when the individual perceives an experience as demanding or threatening and cannot readily cope with the demand. Only then would we expect some potential stressor to be related to disease or emotional disturbance.

**A Combined View.** Taking the best of the elements of each definition, we can define a set of experiences as potentially stressful if they demand change or adaptation. Whether those experiences will trigger the physiological stress response (GAS), and thus increase the risk of illness, however, will depend on an individual's interpretation of the event, temporary or long-term vulnerability (such as lack of social supports), and internal coping skills. Figure 11–1 shows this system schematically.

Note that age does not appear in this figure. But age or developmental stage may affect the stress response system at any one of several points. Adults of different ages may be exposed to differing numbers or types of potentially stressful experiences. Or as they move through the life span, adults may perceive such life changes differently, or become more skilled at coping with the stressful experiences they encounter. Most of the research I'll be talking about is not cast in such a developmental framework, but there are at least some bits and pieces that I will weave into the discussion as we move along.

Let me begin the exploration of the elements in this system by looking at the most studied portion of the figure, the link between potentially stressful experiences and illness.

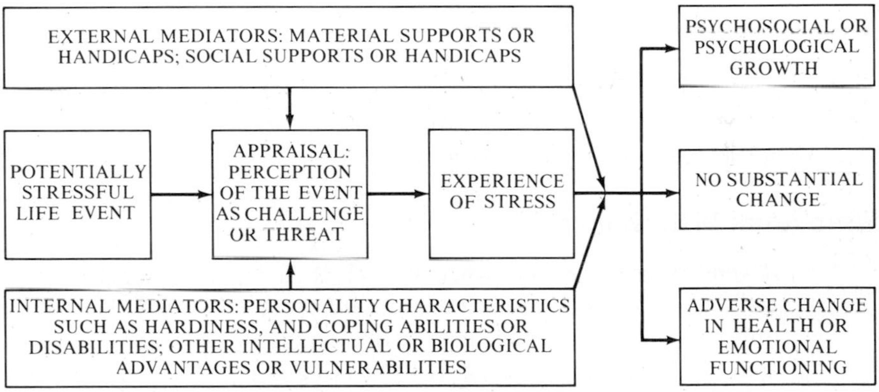


**Figure 11–1** *A first approximation of a model of the link between stress and adverse or positive changes during adulthood. Whether a particular potentially stressful life event (such as a major life change or an accumulation of daily hassles) will lead to illness or not depends on how you perceive the event, whether you have adequate support to help you meet the stress, and what specific coping strategies you use. (Source: adapted and modified from a similar model by Dohrenwend & Dohrenwend, 1980, Figure 1.1, p. 2.)*

# Effects of Stress on Adult Functioning

## Physical Disease

Most of the research examining the links between stress and disease is based on the Holmes and Rahe scale (Table 11–1). Even with the limitations of this scale, a consistent finding has emerged: The larger the number of life changes a person has experienced within the past 6 to 12 months, the greater the likelihood of physical illness, such as tuberculosis, diabetes, arthritis, cancer, heart disease, complications of pregnancy, accidents, and athletic injuries (Perkins, 1982). This does not mean that if your score on the scale is over 300 you will contract all these diseases, nor even that you will automatically get sick. It does mean that the risk goes up. Similarly, high levels of life change are also associated with lowered resistance to pain or discomfort (Harney & Brigham, 1985).

High rates of daily hassles, too, are associated with increased risk of illness. Of course, major life changes usually bring with them an increase in daily hassles, but the more ordinary strains add up as well (DeLongis et al., 1982; Holahan, Holahan, & Belk, 1984; Lazarus & DeLongis, 1983).

Despite this consistency in the findings, however, the size of the effect is quite small. The correlation between subjects' scores on the SRRS and illness is typically around .30. Such a correlation converts to the statement that stress (measured in this way, at least) accounts for only about 10% of the variation in the presence or absence of disease (Dohrenwend & Dohrenwend, 1981). It is possible, of course, that the effect of stress is really much larger than this, and that we will detect it better as our measures of stress become more refined, and as we begin to take into account the other elements in the model in Figure 11–1. But it is important to emphasize that stress theorists are *not* saying that stress is the only cause of disease. People obviously get sick, or have accidents, for a whole lot of reasons other than stress.

## Emotional Disturbance

A similar picture emerges when we look at the relationship between life change and emotional disturbance (Rabkin, 1982). There is a link, but the size of the effect is fairly small. Let me describe one study in some detail to give you some sense of the kind of effect I'm talking about.

E. S. Paykel (1974) has explored the link between life change and depression. He compared a group of 185 patients being treated in psychiatric hospitals for depression with a nonhospitalized sample from the general population, matched with the patients on age, sex, marital status, race, and social class. He then determined the number of life changes (out of a list of 61) each of these subjects had experienced during the six months prior to the depressive episode (or the equivalent period for the nondepressed subject). Paykel found that the depressives had experienced more life changes than had the nondepressives in several categories: employment (beginning or ending a job, being demoted or fired, being promoted or retiring), health, and marital relationships (marriage, separation, divorce, or increase in arguments with spouse). There were no differences between the depressed and nondepressed subjects in the number of in-family changes (child marrying, family member leaving home, etc.) or in legal difficulties.

Paykel also found, however, that only *undesirable* life changes were really at work here, and among the undesirable changes, the key ones appeared to be what he called ''exits''—loss of some relationship, such as the death of a close family member, divorce, or a child leaving home. You can see these results in Table 11–2.

These findings are confirmed by a large study of depression in women in England by Brown and Harris (1978). They found that severe, negative events were common within a few weeks before the onset of a depression, both in women who were actually being treated for depression and among those who had not sought professional help but who nonetheless reported depressive symptoms. Approximately 60% of depressed women had experienced at least one severe event within the three weeks just prior to their depression. Only about 20% of the nondepressed patients had experienced an equivalently severe event during an equivalent three-week period. And like Paykel, Harris and Brown found that the key event seemed to be some loss or ''exit.''

But as with physical disease, a high level of life change or loss does not guarantee depression (or other emotional disturbance). It merely increases the likelihood. Paykel estimates that only about 10% of the people who experience a significant ''exit'' in their lives become clinically depressed.

**TABLE 11–2 Frequency of Undesirable, Desirable, "Exit," and "Entrance" Life Changes in the Recent Experiences of Depressed and Nondepressed Adults**

| Category of Life Change | Percentage of Subjects Who Had Reported at Least One Such Change in the Past Six Months | |
|---|---|---|
| | *Depressed Patients* | *Controls* |
| Desirable life changes (e.g., engagement, marriage, promotion) | 3.2% | 5.4% |
| Undesirable life changes (e.g., death of family member, separation, demotion, serious illness of family member, jail, major financial problems, unemployment, divorce, business failure, stillbirth) | 44.3% | 16.8% |
| Entrances (engagement, marriage, birth of child, new person in home) | 11.4% | 9.7% |
| Exits (death of a close family member, separation, divorce, family member leaves home, child married, son drafted) | 24.9% | 4.9% |

**Source:** Paykel, 1974, adapted from Tables 2 and 3, p. 139–140. Reprinted by permission of John Wiley & Sons, Inc.

## Positive Effects of Stress

To make the picture still more complex (and far more interesting from my perspective), there are a few studies suggesting that stressful life changes may be beneficial to some individuals—increasing life satisfaction, improving overall mental health, perhaps prompting the kind of inner changes I discussed in chapters 9 and 10.

The best evidence for such growth-producing effects of stress comes from several longitudinal studies by Chiriboga (Chiriboga, 1984; Chiriboga & Cutler, 1980; Chiriboga & Dean, 1976). This research is based on a sample I have described earlier (Lowenthal, Thurnher, & Chiriboga, 1975), which originally included a group of high school seniors, a group of newlyweds, a group of adults around age 50 whose children were leaving home, and a group of older adults (about age 60) who were getting ready to retire. These adults were re-interviewed and tested 3, 5, 7, and 11 years later and completed lengthy assessments of life changes at the later contacts. Chiriboga has been interested in the relationship between subgroups of life changes and various outcomes for the individuals, including life satisfaction, depression, other psychological symptoms, and health.

Chiriboga's results parallel those of other researchers studying stress and life change: Negative life events were more likely to be related to later negative outcomes than were positive life changes; and life changes that involved changes in close personal relationships, particularly marital relationships (marriage, separation, divorce, death of a spouse, etc.) were more consistently related to negative outcomes than were other kinds of life changes.

But Chiriboga also found a few indications that some kinds of stresses may have led to improved functioning. For example, among the younger men (those in their 20s at the time of the retesting) "negative preoccupation" with (dwelling on and worrying about) work and personal changes was associated with a decline in depression over several years. And among older men, a group of changes that Chiriboga calls "disharmony," which includes changes in political or religious beliefs, in hobbies, and in anticipation of impending stress, were associated with lower levels of reported emotional problems.

Some evidence from the Berkeley Intergenerational Studies confirms the possible positive effect of life changes. Haan reports that those subjects who had been hospitalized or ill more often were later rated as more empathic and more tolerant of ambiguity than were those who had been physically healthier (Haan, 1982).

The amount of research suggesting such potentially positive effects of stress or life change is small, so I need to be careful about placing too much emphasis on these specific results. But the possibility obviously fits with the general view of personality and spiritual development I have proposed in the last two chapters. Major stresses or life changes may, under some circumstances or for some people, be the stimulus or the occasion for reassessment and transformation, and thus for growth.

## Developmental Differences in Stress Experiences and in Responses to Stress

In those few studies in which age differences in stress experiences have been examined, the consistent finding is that older adults experience fewer major life changes than do younger adults (DeLongis et al., 1982; Goldberg & Comstock, 1980; Lazarus & DeLongis, 1983). Figure 11–2 shows some typical findings from Chiriboga's studies. (The figure shows the average number of changes reported by each age group out of a maximum total of 138 events.) In Chiriboga's studies, younger adults were also more likely to describe themselves as preoccupied with the stresses they were encountering (e.g., "I can't forget it," or "I think about it all the time").

This pattern certainly fits with what I have said in several earlier chapters about the high number of role changes that occur in early adulthood, compared to the number that occur later. Since major role changes (e.g., getting married, having a child, changing jobs) are typically accompanied by a whole set of other life changes, it is logical that younger adults would characteristically report higher numbers of life changes than would middle-aged adults. It is some-

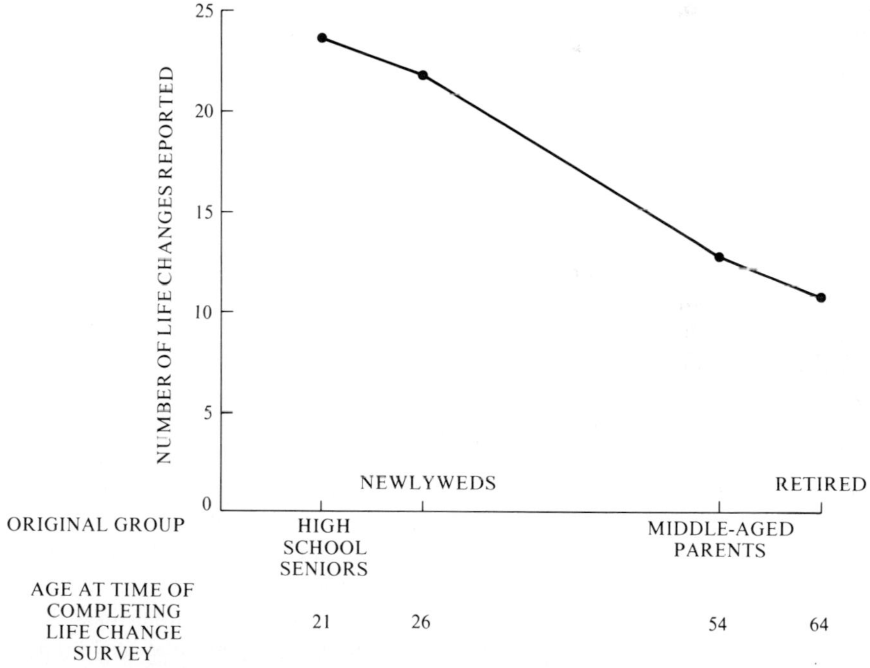


***Figure 11–2*** *These findings are typical of the few studies that have looked at the relationship between age and the number of life changes adults encounter: The older you get the fewer life changes you are likely to have to deal with. (Source: Chiriboga & Dean, 1976, from data in Table 1, p. 50.)*

what more surprising that older adults also report low levels of life change, given the number of role losses (often "exits" in Paykel's language) that occur in old age. But bear in mind that the data shown in Figure 11–2 extend only to about age 65. No comparable study I can find reports equivalent findings for old age. Thus, it is possible that elderly adults, experiencing extensive role losses, possibly relocation or institutionalization, would describe higher levels of life change than is common in midlife.

### A Quick Summary

To summarize all of this, we have evidence that increased rates of life change, particularly life changes that involve emotional losses or losses of relationships ("exits") are modestly predictive of physical illness and emotional disturbances such as depression. Daily hassles, too, accumulate and increase the risk of both physical and emotional illness. The absolute incidence of life changes appears to be higher in early adulthood than in later adulthood, but adults of different ages may also interpret life changes differently. Finally, for some adults, life changes and hassles may lead to emotional or personal growth, rather than disease or depression.

## Resistance Resources

This summary leaves a great many questions unanswered. In particular, if we wish to understand the reactions of individual adults to stress, and if we want to know why it is that some adults do not become ill or depressed in the face of major life changes, we must turn our attention to those personal and social resources that may buffer the individual from the potential impact of stress. Such resources may be collectively called **resistance resources.** Central among these are social support and coping responses.

### Social Support and Response to Stress

In Chapter 7, I gave an initial definition of social support, namely, the receipt of affect, affirmation, and aid from others. For further clarity, I also need to distinguish between a **social network** and social support.

A social network is a "specific social envelope" (Lieberman, 1982), a collection of relationships with family and friends that each of us maintains. Social networks can be described along any of a variety of dimensions, including (1) size (How many people are there with whom you have any kind of regular contact?), (2) composition (Is your network composed mostly of family or of friends? Does it include people you have known a short time and those you have known a long time?), (3) rate or frequency of contact (Do you see network members often or rarely?), (4) interconnectedness (Do the people in your network know and interact with each other, or do you have separate groups of family and friends who do not have contact with one another?), (5) intimacy (Are at least some of the relationships within your network close and intimate?), and (6) duration (How long have you known the people in your network?). Any or all of these features may be important in understanding the effect of social networks on a person's life.

What a social network provides is social support, which is a general term describing the content of the exchange between members of a social network. Support, in turn, is usually subdivided still further, such as the categories of affect, affirmation, and aid I already mentioned (Kahn & Antonucci, 1980) or emotional, tangible, and informational support (Schaefer, Coyne, & Lazarus, 1982).

Many interactions with family or friends obviously include all these elements. If a friend of yours who is facing a personal crisis calls you up one evening, you may commiserate with her pain, suggest the name of a good therapist, and offer to babysit with her kids while she goes to see that therapist. Equally often, you may receive (or give) only one of these several kinds of support in any one exchange.

**Evidence on the Buffering Effect of Social Support.** Research on the impact of social support on responses to stress has been confused by a lack of agreement on just how social support should be measured. Despite this difficulty, however, consistent information has accumulated.

For example, Nuckolls, Cassel, and Kaplan (1972) studied a group of pregnant women and found the highest level of physical complications of pregnancy in the group that had high levels of life change *and* low levels of "psychosocial assets" (an aspect of social support). Similarly, in the British study of depression in women I mentioned earlier (Brown & Harris, 1978), the link between severe life changes and depression was significantly weaker when the woman had a close, intimate relationship with her husband or boyfriend, as you can see in Table 11–3.

**TABLE 11–3 Percentage of Women in a Large British Study Who Experienced Significant Depression Following a Major Life Change as a Function of the Presence of an Intimate Confidant in Their Lives**

| | Husband or Boyfriend Was Intimate Confidant (*N*=281) | Family Member or Friend Other Than Boyfriend or Lover Was Confidant; Seen at Least Once a Week (*N*=86) | Either No Confidant, or Confidant Seen Less Than Weekly (*N*=52) |
|---|---|---|---|
| At least one severe life event within the past year | 10% | 26% | 41% |
| No severe event in past year | 1% | 3% | 4% |

**Source:** Brown, G. W. & Harris, T. Social origins of depression: A study of psychiatric disorder in women. Publishers Tavistock Publications, Ltd., London and the Free Press (division of Macmillan, Inc.), New York.

Similarly, in a short-term longitudinal study of men who had been laid off from work because their companies had gone out of business, Kasl and Cobb (1982) found that those men who felt that they had adequate social support from their wives and friends showed fewer physical and emotional symptoms than did those men with lower levels of perceived support.

These studies, and others like them, certainly confirm the common sense assumption that having friends helps you ride out the various storms of life. But the connection between social support and response to stress is not nearly so straightforward or so general as these findings may lead you to think. Researchers who have simply counted the number of different people an adult in crisis turns to, or the frequency of contact, have often found either very weak or no relationship between these network properties and the degree of disturbance or illness the individual shows in response to the stress (e.g., Lieberman, 1982; Spanier & Thompson, 1984). Only certain specific relationships seem to have a buffering effect, and the particular "optimal" relationship may vary depending on the stress being experienced. As Lieberman puts it, "It is not the total amount of help that is salient, but rather the fit between a particular kind of problem and the help provider" (1982, p. 771).

The source of support that is most often critical is that of a spouse or lover. For example, women who are expecting or have just given birth to their first child suffer fewer physical and emotional effects if they have their husband's support. If such spousal support is missing, it apparently cannot be compensated for by the support of lots of friends (Lieberman, 1982). You can see some of this effect in Table 11–3. In the table, an intimate relationship with a family member was better than no intimate relationship at all, but it was not as good a buffer against severe stress as was the support of a husband or lover.

For a life change like widowhood (which I'll talk about in detail shortly), where it is precisely the loss of that central intimate source of social support that must be dealt with, the optimal (most buffering) source of support appeared in one study to be the widowed person's parents or other widowed friends (Bankoff, 1983), especially during the early phases of mourning.

Lieberman offers an interesting additional hypothesis: "It may very well be that when the salient support person is available but does not provide needed [support], substitution becomes almost impossible; this may not be the case when the critical relationship no longer exists" (1982, p. 773). In Bankoff's study of widows, for example, those widows who had the most difficult time were those whose parents were still alive but not providing help and emotional support. For these women, substitute support from friends did not appear to have a buffering effect. But those widows whose parents were deceased appeared to be able to use the support of widowed friends as a replacement. Similarly, we would expect that for unmarried adults (including the divorced), other intimate relationships would become more salient in the face of stress.

Summing up this complex set of findings, I conclude several things. First, to create a buffering effect, the most critical property of a social network is its intimacy. Even very small networks can be helpful if the relationships are intimate. The smallest number of intimate relationships that seems to be abso-

***Figure 11–3*** *If you are facing a life crisis of some kind, having at least one good friend you can talk to like this seems to be critical in helping you weather the storm without too much ill effect. (Source: Warren D. Jorgensen, Photo Researchers Inc.)*

lutely necessary is one. Five out of six adults (according to Campbell, in his national survey, 1981) have at least one such intimate relationship, most often with a spouse, so the majority of adults are at least minimally buffered against the most serious effects of stress. But there is a significant minority who do not have a confidant, and who may thus be particularly vulnerable to the negative effects of stressful life experiences.

Second, however, different types of life crises may require different forms or sources of support. The individual who has only one key relationship is therefore at higher risk in any life change in which that single relationship will not suffice, or in which that relationship itself is in jeopardy. Divorcing or widowed adults, for example, whose only intimate relationship has been with the spouse (as is true for many men), should experience more difficulty than would those adults whose network contains alternative sources of intimacy and assistance (Kahn & Antonucci, 1980).

Third, it begins to look as if the key variable in the buffering effect is the individual's perception that his support network is sufficient to aid him in critical ways (Cohen & Wills, 1985). Feeling let down by a key person alters that perception of support adequacy and limits or eliminates the buffering effect, even for an individual with an extensive network.

If I convert these general statements into advice, I would urge you not to put all your social support eggs into one basket. An array of intimate relationships—with spouse or lover, with friends, with family members—is most likely to meet your needs across a wide variety of stressful situations.

**Some Negative Effects of Social Networks.** Lest I give the impression that there is nothing but sweetness and light in the world of social relationships, let me hasten to add that there are costs associated with social networks. Network systems are generally reciprocal. Not only do you receive support, you give it as well. And as I pointed out in chapter 6 and 7, there are particular points in the life cycle when the giving side of the equation seems to be more heavily weighted than the receiving side, which may increase stress and daily hassles.

Everyday social interactions can also be a significant source of hassles. Most of us have at least some regular interactions with individuals we do not like or who irritate us to distraction: your co-worker who picks her nose, your neighbor who stops by for a chat every time you have settled down for an hour of pleasant solitude, your mother who invariably tells you how to rearrange your living room furniture each time she comes to visit. Karen Rook (1984) argues that an adult's overall sense of wellbeing and happiness may be more affected by the presence of such irritating or problematic social ties than by the presence of positive and supportive relationships. Results from her study of older widows (all over 60) support this argument. The women with the lowest level of life satisfaction were those with the largest number of problematic social ties.

Rook's study is quite limited, since it includes only elderly women, all widowed. And she did not ask about the impact of these negative relationships on the women's response to life change or stress. But it important to keep in mind that maintaining social networks involves costs as well as potential benefits.

**Age Differences in Social Support.** So far as I know, no researcher has searched for a possible relationship between age and the buffering effect of social support. We do not know, for example, whether older adults are more skillful in using their social networks than are younger ones, or vice versa. Our developmental information is limited to comparisons of the properties of networks of adults of different ages, much of which I have already described in chapter 7. Recall that contact with family members remains largely constant across adulthood. Young adults, however, appear to have the largest networks and to place the greatest emphasis on the importance of friends (e.g., Veroff et al., 1981). The number of friends adults report is usually lower among adults in their 30s and 40s than among those in their 20s and 50s, but there seem to be no major changes in the total size of adults' networks between middle age and old age (Antonucci, 1985).

The one change in the functioning of social networks that does appear to occur in the later years of adulthood is a reduction in the amount of support given. Once an adult leaves the years of the "sandwich generation," when maximum help is given in both directions in the generational chain, there is a gradual drop in the amount of help or other social support given to the members of one's network. This may imply a decline in the amount of reciprocal interactions that occur between family members or with friends. Since most adults report preferring reciprocal relationships, there may develop some reluctance to call on the assistance of the network in times of stress, or some loss of the buffering effect of the support system, but that possibility has not been tested empirically.

## Personality and Coping Strategies

The second major category of resistance resources for dealing with stress are those personal qualities or skills that may help reduce the impact of the stress. Most researchers (e.g., Pearlin & Schooler, 1978) distinguish between two aspects of such personal responses: (1) psychological resources, which are enduring qualities a person has, including such things as intellectual skill, temperament, or personality; and (2) coping behaviors, which are the things a person does in the face of stress or potential harm. The two are clearly interconnected. Adults with particular personality patterns are more likely to use some coping behaviors than others, and certain kinds of coping behaviors require at least a minimal level of intellectual skill. But for initial clarity, let me continue the distinction here.

**Personality as a Mediator of Stress.** The one dimension of personality that has been most thoroughly studied as a mitigator of stress is what Suzanne Kobasa (1979, 1982; Kobasa, Maddi, & Kahn, 1982) calls **hardiness.** Hardiness includes three facets:

1. Commitment: "The ability to believe in the truth, importance, and interest value of what one is doing, and the willingness to exercise influence or control in the personal and social situations in which one is involved" (Kobasa, 1981, p. 708). Adults high on commitment are likely to disagree with statements like "The attempt to know yourself is a waste of effort," or "Life is empty and has no meaning in it for me."
2. Control: A disposition to see oneself as in control of or influential over (rather than helpless) in the face of problems or tasks. This is very similar to the dimension of inner versus outer **locus of control** proposed by Rotter (1966, 1975). Rotter argues that a person's locus of control affects responses particularly when a situation is ambiguous. Since many life changes involve just such ambiguity (in roles, for example), this aspect of personality may be particularly salient.
3. Challenge: "The belief that change rather than stability is normal in life and that the anticipation of changes are interesting incentives to growth rather than threats to security" (Kobasa, Maddi, & Kahn, 1982, p. 170). People low in challenge are those for whom safety, stability, and predictability are higher values.

To my ear, there is a certain strong similarity between these descriptions of "hardiness" and some of the descriptions of the "individualized" or even the "integrated" stages of personality or spiritual growth. Perhaps what Kobasa is describing here is not just an enduring personality dimension, but the achievement of a particular level of ego development. Be that as it may, the key point for the present discussion is that Kobasa has consistently found that adults who are high in hardiness are less likely to become ill in the face of high levels of stress than are adults low in hardiness (Kobasa, 1979, 1982; Kobasa et al., 1982). The relationship also holds longitudinally. Hardiness measured at the beginning of a two-year study predicted the response of a group of business executives to subsequent stress or life changes. The hardiest subjects were least likely to respond to such stress with illness (Kobasa et al., 1982). Hardiness also seems to help stave off depression in the face of stress (Ganellen & Blaney, 1984).

James Crandall (1984) offers a somewhat different personality dimension as a potential buffer against stress: *social interest*. Crandall (following the lead of Alfred Adler) defines social interest in terms of "valuing (being interested in and caring about) things that go beyond the self. It is the opposite of complete self-centeredness or self-preoccupation" (p. 164). It not only includes interest in and concern for others, it also covers an interest in nature, art, the cosmos. The non-self-centered, altruistic element in this description once again sounds rather similar to the descriptions of particular developmental stages in chapters 9 and 10, in this case to the description of the integrated personality or even the stage of "universalizing" faith described by Fowler, both of which also contain a strong element of altruism.

Social interest is not unrelated to hardiness. In particular, individuals high in social interest are also typically high in the control dimension of hardiness. And like hardiness, the quality of social interest appears to serve as a buffer. In one group of undergraduates, those who were higher in social interest were less likely to become depressed, anxious, or hostile in the face of high levels of life change (Crandall, 1984).

In all of this research the consistent finding is that the buffering effect of specific personality characteristics is only apparent when the individual is under high stress. Under low stress, there is no difference between hardy and nonhardy, or socially interested or disinterested adults in the rate of depression or illness.

These studies point us toward an answer to one of the key questions about stress: Given the same level of life change or external threat, why do people react so differently? Part of the answer seems to lie in the way each individual defines or perceives the problem, and the extent to which the individual feels in personal control of the solution. Another part of the answer lies in the particular coping behaviors the person uses to deal with stress.

**Coping Behaviors in the Face of Stress.** Suppose you have been trying for a particular promotion and find out that you didn't get it. Or suppose that your father has just died. How do you cope with these stresses? "Coping" is a very broad and fuzzy word to describe all the things you might think, feel, and do in response to such events in an effort to handle the stress. Lazarus and Folkman (1984) define it as "constantly changing cognitive and behavioral efforts to manage specific external and/or internal demands that are appraised as taxing or exceeding the resources of the person'' (p. 141). The number of different specific actions that might fall under this rubric is almost unlimited, so various theorists have attempted to categorize the possibilities. Kobasa, following the lead of Maddi (Kobasa, 1982) suggested two categories, *transformational* and *regressive* coping actions. Moos and Billings (1982; Billings & Moos, 1981) suggest a division into *problem-focused* (what you do), *emotionally-focused* (how you feel), and *appraisal-focused* (what you think) strategies. In Table 11–4 I have combined the two into a six-type matrix. Again there are some interesting parallels between this classification system and a similar classification given in an earlier chapter, namely, Vaillant's categories of defense mechanisms (Vaillant, 1977a). Some of what are listed here as transformational coping strategies would be included in Vaillant's list of mature defenses, while regressive coping strategies overlap with the categories of immature or neurotic defenses.

In general, we ought to find that adults who use more transformational coping strategies deal with stress more effectively. They should be less likely to get sick, depressed, or anxious in the face of major life changes or chronic life strains. On the whole, that is what the research shows (Billings & Moos, 1981; Pearlin & Schooler, 1978), but there are some interesting exceptions.

Pearlin and Schooler (1978), in the most extensive study, found that advice seeking in the face of stress was associated with higher rather than lower rates

**TABLE 11–4 Types of Coping Strategies in the Face of Stress**

| | Transformational | Regressive |
|---|---|---|
| Problem-focused Coping: DOING something | Seek information or advice<br>Take specific action, such as negotiation or compromise<br>Develop alternative rewards<br>Learn new skills<br>Make alternative plans | Withdraw physically, such as taking time off, sleeping a lot, or moving to another place to avoid a problem |
| Emotion-focused Coping: FEELING things | Postpone paying attention to impulses and feelings (suppression)<br>Try not to be bothered or to worry too much | Discharge emotion, such as by crying, increased drinking, smoking or eating<br>Show resigned acceptance<br>Show apathy<br>Keep things to yourself |
| Appraisal-focused Coping: THINKING about the problem | Analyze the problem logically<br>Reassess priorities<br>Redefine the problem, such as with positive comparisons ("It could be worse"; "Other people are worse off") | Deny fear or distress<br>Try to forget it<br>Avoid thinking about the problem |

**Source:** Kobasa, 1982; Moos & Billings, 1982.

of distress. Self-reliance, rather than help seeking, seemed to be a more effective coping strategy. The researchers also found that selective ignoring (a regressive coping device) was actually an effective coping device if the stress was experienced in the area of finances, but counterproductive if the stress was in marriage or family relationships. Among transformational strategies, too, particular coping devices worked better for some stresses than others. So negotiation was a particularly good strategy for a marital stress, while a reassessment of values or priorities worked when the problem was economic.

Thus, while it is roughly true that coping strategies from the transformational list are more likely to eliminate or alleviate the worst effects of stress, the best coping strategies will vary from one kind of stress situation to the next. Having a wide variety of coping strategies in your repertoire, and using them appropriately, is thus probably most helpful.

**Age or Developmental Differences in Personality or Coping Strategies.** As usual, most of the research I have just described has not been cast in a developmental framework. Obviously, such a framework is possible, especially given the potential links between hardiness, or social interest, or transformational coping styles and personality development. In future research, it will be extremely interesting to see whether such a connection is found. For the moment, the little information we have suggests that age is not consistently related to particular coping strategies (Lazarus & DeLongis, 1983). It is clear that adults have different stress experiences and may define those experiences differently at different ages, as I have already pointed out. Values change, commitments change, systems of meaning change. So the same life change may not be experienced as equally stressful at different points in the adult life cycle. But there is no clear indication that older adults use consistently different coping strategies than do younger adults except for the fact that older adults are less likely to use denial, fantasy, or hostility—all ''regressive'' strategies (Lazarus & DeLongis, 1983; McCrae, 1982; Vaillant, 1977a).

## Other Resistance Resources

Social support and good coping strategies are not the only resistance resources that make a difference in adults' responses to stress. A decent income helps, as does good health and vitality. Specific beliefs may also help an individual cope with major life changes. Any source of hope, for example, be it a belief in God or in justice, or simply in the efficacy of a particular doctor, or diet, may be helpful. Personal skills may also have an effect. An adult with a wide range of occupational skills may face divorce or relocation more easily; an adult with good social skills—including those skills that allow one to relate easily and well to others and to form close relationships—may be able to form new networks if old ones are disrupted. All of these additional resources may affect the range of coping strategies or options that are available to the individual in the face of some stress, as well as affecting the individual's choice among the options that are available.

## Responding to Stress: An Overview

All of these pieces can be put together, at least in a preliminary way, using a model like the one in Figure 11–1. Stressful stimuli are most likely to result in illness or depression (or other adverse change) if a person appraises the potential stressor as a threat; has a low level of social support, particularly if he lacks a close confidant appropriate for that stress; lacks suitable transformational coping strategies. The opposite set of conditions seems to lead to at least some chance of growth or maturing in the face of stress.

To make all this more real to you, let me explore at least briefly the impact of a few particularly critical or interesting life changes or stress experiences, in this case widowhood, divorce, and relocation (such as moving to a nursing home) in old age.

## Application of the Basic Principles to Specific Life Changes

### Widowhood

Approximately 12 million adults in the United States have lost a spouse by death. Of these, 11 million are women. (This does not mean, by the way, that 11 husbands die for every wife. In fact, approximately one out of every five spouses who dies is a woman [Carter & Glick, 1976]. But since women live a lot longer than men, more of the widows survive for many years. Thus, in the population at large, 11 of 12 living adults who have lost a spouse are women.) About half of these deaths occur when the surviving spouse is 56 or younger, so widowhood is most commonly an experience of women in middle and early old age. Not surprisingly, most of the research on widowhood (a term I shall use interchangeably to describe both men and women) describes the adaptation of women. When researchers have studied both men and women, however, the pattern of response to bereavement seems to be very similar. So for the following discussion, unless I say otherwise, assume that the findings hold for both sexes.

The death of a spouse is itself a huge life change, and it triggers a whole string of other changes. It involves not only the loss of a relationship, but also the loss of the support and assistance of the spouse and the role of spouse itself. Justine Ball (1976–77) describes one widow as saying she ''felt she had no name or label now. She was not a 'wife' or 'housewife' and with no job, it gave her no concept of who she was'' (p. 329). For a man, the loss of identity may be less severe, but the loss of the support from his wife may be far greater, particularly since men (in this culture, at least) are less likely to have other close, supportive relationships outside of their marriage (recall chapter 7).

Given the information I have already reported on the link between life changes and physical illness or emotional disturbance, you will not be surprised that the year following bereavement is one of heightened disease, depression, and risk of death. Mortality rates go up, with deaths from both disease and suicide heightened. Depression is also much more common among the widowed than among nonwidowed persons of the same age (Balkwell, 1981; Stroebe & Stroebe, 1983).

To give just one specific example, Ball (1976–77) found that among the 80 widows she studied (all women), 44% reported pronounced sleep disturbances, 38% described themselves as frequently irritable, 34% had appetite problems, and 20% reported thoughts of suicide during the six to nine months following their husband's death. Half had taken some kind of tranquilizing drug.

**Age Differences.** These effects appear to be much greater for younger men and women than for widowed adults in their 60s, 70s, and 80s. Ball's results, shown in Figure 11–4, are fairly typical. She divided her sample into three age groups (18 to 46, 47 to 59, and 60 to 75), and then further subdivided it by the suddenness or unexpectedness of the death. As you can see, younger widows were much more disturbed by the death than were older widows, and this was particularly true if the death was unexpected.

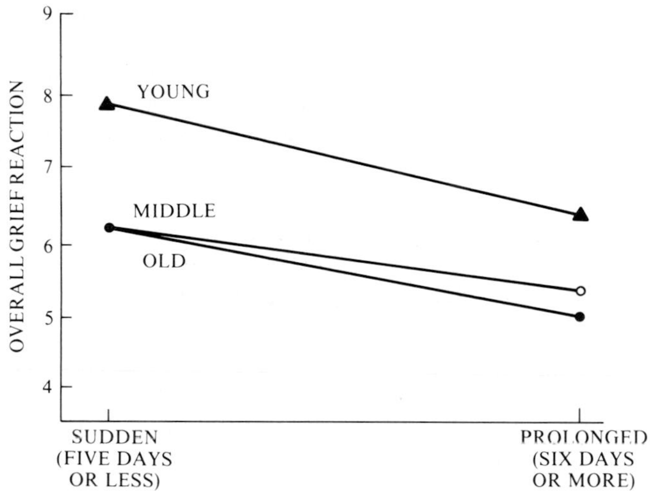


**Figure 11–4** *These results from a study of young and older widows are an illustration of the general principle that unexpected or unscheduled life events are generally harder to deal with—are more likely to result in illness—than are scheduled or expected life events. (Source: Ball, Justine F., 1976–77, Widow's Grief: The Impact of Age and Mode of Death.* Omega—Journal of Death and Dying, *7(4), Fig. 1, p. 319. Reprinted by permission of Baywood Publishing Co., Inc.)*

This pattern of findings fits nicely into Pearlin's model of the effect of scheduled and unscheduled changes (1980, 1982b). If you are over 65 or so, then the death of your spouse is, if not exactly "scheduled," at least not altogether unanticipated. But having your spouse die when you are in your 30s or 40s is clearly "unscheduled," or "off time" in Neugarten's language (1979), and should (if Pearlin is right) be associated with greater experience of stress and heightened physical and emotional effects. Since a very sudden death is still less "scheduled" or anticipated than is a more prolonged illness, we should find greater negative impact from a sudden than from a prolonged death. This is precisely what the findings in Figure 11–4 show. Certainly the death of a spouse at any age is associated with at least some consequences. But the effects seem to be markedly less severe—both physically and emotionally—when the death is anticipated.

**Sex Differences.** The pattern of findings I have reported is essentially the same for both men and women, but the effects of widowhood seem to be somewhat more severe for men (Stroebe & Stroebe, 1983). When widows and widowers are compared with married adults of the same ages and social backgrounds, researchers quite consistently find that widowers show more greatly increased mortality rates, suicide rates, and illness than do widows. For men, the most critical point seems to be the first six months after the spouse's death. If they survive that period in reasonable health, then they generally adapt quite well, most of them remarrying.

The most plausible explanation of this is that men are more likely to be socially isolated at the death of their wife than are women at the death of their husband. As I mentioned in chapter 7, men's social support networks are typically less extensive and less intimate than women's. In particular, men are more likely to have only a single confidant, their wife. And when she dies, they are left without that key element of the social network.

**Social Networks, Personality, and Coping Skills.** In general, it is true that those widows who show the fewest physical and emotional symptoms following bereavement are those with the most supportive social networks. But as I pointed out earlier, not all elements in a social support network are interchangeable. Recall Bankoff's study (1983), which showed that the most buffering relationships were with the widow's parents or with widowed friends. Contact with children, interestingly enough (and perhaps surprisingly), does not appear to increase very much following widowhood, and seems to provide only limited buffering against the negative effect of bereavement (e.g., Ferraro, 1984). Helena Lopata, in several classic studies of widows (Lopata, 1969, 1973, 1979; Lopata, Heinemann, & Baum, 1982), does find that widowed women with children report less loneliness than do widows without children, but there is no indication that widows with children show lower rates of disease or depression than do widows without children. Friendships, in contrast, do appear to increase in number following bereavement, and to serve some buffering function.

Researchers studying widowhood have not explored personal dimensions such as hardiness or social interest, nor the several types of coping strategies listed in Table 11–4. But extrapolating from Lopata's findings, there is some indication that those widows who tend to reach out to others, maintaining or even increasing social contacts (a transformational, problem-focused form of coping) show least loneliness and best adjustment. In addition, Lopata (Lopata et al., 1982) has found that those widows with a positive attitude toward themselves and others report lower levels of loneliness and distress than do those whose self-concept and social interactions are more negative. Similar patterns emerge from studies of divorced adults.

## Divorce

In chapter 6 I talked about what may happen to family roles after a divorce, but I sidestepped the question that I want to address now, namely, the impact of divorce on the individual's functioning. As I pointed out then, between 40% and 50% of adults marrying today will eventually divorce (Glick, 1984). Half of all divorces occur within the first seven years of marriage; most therefore occur when adults are fairly young. Only about 10% of divorces are granted to adults over 50. So to the extent that this is a "scheduled" life event, it is normative in early adulthood and not in late adulthood—at least in present cohorts.

Among life changes, divorce is one of the most stressful and difficult. But unlike widowhood, which is almost uniformly experienced as painful, reactions to divorce are more varied. In Albrecht's (1980) large study of 500 divorced adults (who were looking back on the period of their divorce from the vantage point of 10 to 15 years beyond it), 27% of the women and 16% of the men reported that their divorce had been "traumatic, a nightmare." Another 40% of men and women described it as "stressful but bearable." But 13% of the women and 20% of the men said it had been "relatively painless." And Spanier and Thompson (1984), who interviewed 50 divorcing adults, found that both relief and distress were fairly common feelings.

Divorce is like widowhood, however, in that both require a process of detachment, a breaking or a giving up of that powerful affectional bond that formed the core of the initial partner relationship. But in the case of divorce, the emotional components of this detachment process are, if anything, more complex than for the widowed. A number of researchers have found that most divorcing adults continue to maintain an emotional attachment to the now departed spouse for some period of time after the separation (Hetherington & Camara, 1984; Kitson, 1982; Weiss, 1979), while at the same time experiencing anger and distress over the spouse's contribution to the dissolution.

The period of maximum upheaval appears to be the period from just before the divorce through the first year afterward (Albrecht, 1980; Kolevzon & Gottlieb, 1983). Mavis Hetherington has provided us with the most detailed look at this period in a longtitudinal study of a group of divorcing adults (Hetherington & Camara, 1984; Hetherington, Cox, & Cox, 1978) over the two years following the decree. In those months, daily routines became chaotic with meals taken at irregular hours. Discipline of the children became erratic. The men in the study, most of whom had moved out of the family house, often felt rootless and lacking an identity. The divorced women felt unattractive and helpless. Both often felt isolated from their still-married friends.

Divorce also causes financial upheaval. However, as I pointed out in chapter 6, this effect is far more marked for women than for men. For men, in fact, while divorce may involve some loss of assets (such as interest in the family home), actual income typically does not decline much, if at all (Hetherington & Camara, 1984). Women, in contrast, typically experience a dramatic loss of income and standard of living (Colletta, 1983; Spanier & Thompson, 1984; Weiss, 1984).

**Effects of Divorce on Physical and Emotional Illness.** I already pointed out in chapter 6 that married adults as a group are happier and healthier than single adults (recall Figure 6–3), but it is primarily the divorced, rather than the never-married, among the single who show the highest levels of problems. As is true for widowhood, divorce is followed by a temporary rise in physical illness and emotional disturbance. Figure 11–5 shows two typical findings, one for the incidence of admissions to outpatient psychiatric clinics, and the other for the number of days that adults report they are restricted in activity because of illness. In each case I have given the rates for separated and divorced adults, and, for comparison purposes, the rates for never-married, married, and widowed adults. You can see that divorced and separated adults are more likely to seek psychiatric help and are sick more than are married or never-married adults. (Interestingly, widowed adults had low levels of psychiatric care, but levels of physical sickness comparable to those for the divorced.)

Other research shows that divorced and separated adults, compared to married (or never-married) adults, have more car accidents, commit suicide more often, and are also more likely to be the victim of homicide (Bloom, White, & Asher, 1979). In the group of 50 recently divorced adults interviewed by Spanier and Thompson, for example, 24% of the women and 9% of the men said they had either attempted suicide or made specific suicide plans, while another 20% of the women and 9% of the men had seriously considered suicide.

In most of the large surveys on which these conclusions are based, subjects were merely asked to indicate their current marital status. We do not ordinarily know how long it has been since the separation or divorce for each subject. But if we assume that the split was more recent for the separated group than for the divorced group, then there is evidence here that the time of maximum risk is in the first few months after a couple separates. Car accidents, for example, seem to peak in this time, and psychiatric admissions (as you can see in Figure 11 5) are markedly higher for the separated, compared to the divorced.

Obviously there are several possible explanations for these heightened levels of sickness, death, and disaster among the divorced. One possibility, usually called the *selectivity theory*, is that people who eventually get divorced were less stable to begin with. No doubt that is at least partially true. In one five-

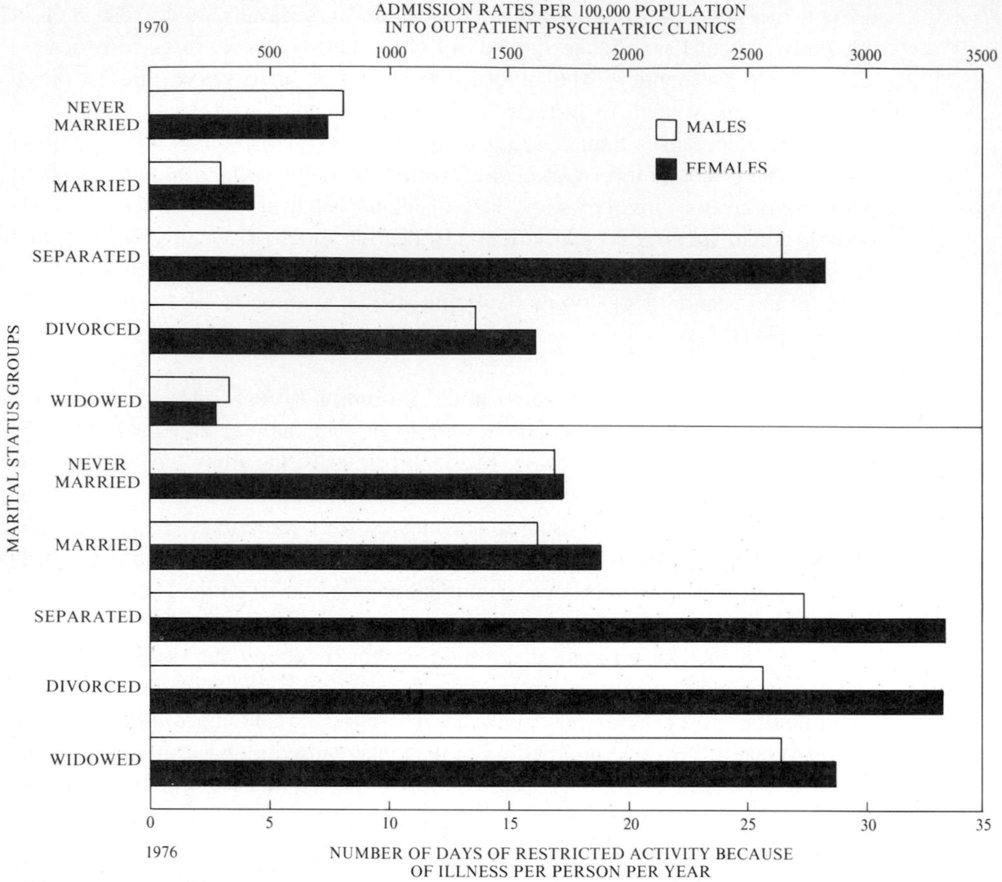


***Figure 11–5*** *Divorced and separated adults, compared to married, never-married, and widowed adults, are more likely to be seen in psychiatric outpatient clinics, and are sick more days of the year. Since this is especially so for separated adults, who have presumably gone through the stress more recently, it suggests that the risk of illness is particularly high immediately following this particular life change. (Source: adapted from Bloom, White, & Asher, 1979, data from Tables 11–1 and 11–2, p. 186.)*

year longitudinal study, for example, Erbes and Hedderson (1984) found that on a measure of psychological wellbeing, those men who eventually divorced had lower scores as many as five years before the divorce than had continuously married men.

But selectivity does not seem to account for all of the results (Bloom et al., 1979). Among other things, selectivity cannot readily account for heightened rates of illness, death, and emotional disturbance in widowed persons. Doubtlessly a bidirectional effect is at work. Initial instability or unhappiness may increase the likelihood of divorce (or other life changes). But the life change itself also increases the risk of later disease or disturbance.

**Age Differences in Effects of Divorce.** In the few cases in which age has been studied as a variable in epidemiological studies, researchers have consistently found that older divorcing persons have a more difficult time adjusting to this life change than do younger adults (Bloom, White, & Asher, 1979). This is the precise opposite of what was true for widowhood. But both patterns make sense within Pearlin's theory of scheduled and unscheduled changes. If we expand his concept somewhat and talk of *normative* and *non-normative* life changes, perhaps we can do an even better job of explaining the age differences.

My hypothesis, like Neugarten's concept of on-time and off-time events, is that any life change that is atypical or non-normative for one's age group (or one's cohort) will produce greater stress and poorer adaptation than a life change that is typical or normative for one's age or cohort. Since (at present, at least) divorce is more common in the early decades of adulthood, it should be (relatively) easier for the younger person to handle. A younger divorcing adult, for example, is much more likely than an older adult to know someone else who has recently been through the same experience. In addition, of course, the cohorts of adults now in their 60s and 70s had much lower divorce rates at all ages. So at present, divorce in one's 60s or 70s is non-normative both by age and for that cohort, which should make it still more stressful.

**Sex Differences in the Stressfulness of Divorce.** The differences in men's and women's responses to divorce are much less clear than in the case of widowhood. Women certainly suffer far greater economic upheaval, and most must deal with the complexities and stresses of single-parenting. But when we look at the effects of these stresses, as indicated by rates of disease or disturbance, there are hints, as there are with widowed adults, that men may have a slightly more difficult time than women. More divorced men end up as inpatients in psychiatric hospitals than do divorced women, for example (Bloom et al., 1979).

**Social Support and Coping Strategies in Divorce.** It is plausible that the sex differences in the effect of divorce may again be related to the availability of adequate emotional support from friends and family members. The one clear finding is that for both men and women, adequate emotional and social support from friends and kin helps to speed the process of recovery (Hetherington & Camara, 1984). Development of new intimate relationships also plays a significant role in the recovery process for both men and women. To the extent, then, that men's friendships and kin relationships are less intimate and thus possibly less supportive, men may have fewer social resources on which to draw.

Those personal qualities other than social support that appear to assist an adult in dealing effectively with the crisis of divorce are readily predictable from what I said earlier about hardiness and transformational coping. Better adjusted divorced adults have higher self-esteem. stronger feelings of internal control, are open-minded and tolerant of change (see Hetherington & Camara, 1984, for a review). Those divorcing adults who have these qualities and who also have a supportive social network, are likely not only to weather the immediate crisis of the divorce without major symptoms, but may also show real personal growth in the process.

## Relocation in Old Age

The third life change I want to talk about is quite different from either widowhood or divorce primarily because it is normally far less stressful. If you take another look at Table 11–1, for example, you will see that death of a spouse and divorce head the list of stressful life changes, while a "change in residence" is 32nd on the list. My particular interest here, however, is not in changes of residence early in adulthood, but in those changes that may occur after retirement such as a voluntary move to a sunnier climate, a forced relocation because the older person can no longer afford the housing she previously occupied, or a move to a nursing home or other special residence for the elderly. Current popular articles have painted highly romanticized pictures of the first of these, and highly gloomy pictures of the latter two. But what does the evidence tell us?

First, there is really far less moving after age 65 than I had thought. In 1976, for example, 59% of older adults in the United States who owned their own homes had lived there for 16 years or more; 55% of older renters had been in the same apartment for 6 years or more. Only about 1% of older adults move from one state to another in any given year (Lawton, 1977, 1985).

Second, those older adults who choose to move, or have some clear control over their move or their destination, typically show increases in morale or life satisfaction and little sign of increased physical disease or other symptoms. The move itself is likely to be stressful (as any of you who have moved can surely understand!), but these effects are quite short-term.

It is the involuntary moves, including those to nursing homes, that are likely to cause the greatest stress—at least as indicated by rises in mortality and morbidity (death and disease). As a group, involuntarily relocated elderly adults show sharp increases in death rates compared to roughly equivalent groups who have remained at home. However, the quality of the new care facility makes an enormous difference, as you would suppose. Those elderly adults who move to institutions or other settings that are characterized by warmth, individuation, autonomy, and self-control actually show improvement in morale and health (Lawton, 1977, 1985).

Two points emerge from these findings that are particularly relevant for the issues I have been discussing in this chapter. First, it is the perception or appraisal of the residential move that seems to be critical in determining any stressful effect. When the move is voluntary, the effects are positive rather than negative.

Second, the ability of the individual to control his life circumstances appears

***Figure 11–6*** *For those who move to Florida, or Arizona, or even to special retirement communities voluntarily, the relocation seems to be associated with low levels of stress and improvement in morale. But the same is not true of many involuntary relocations in old age. (Source: Eric Kroll, Taurus Photos.)*

to be a particularly significant element in determining the appraisal of some potential stressor. I have already pointed out that adults who typically see themselves in control of their environments (part of hardiness) generally show smaller effects from potentially stressful events than do those who feel helpless in the face of circumstances. But even highly internally controlled adults will experience stress in circumstances in which actual control is reduced. The corollary of this statement is obviously that even in involuntary or low-control circumstances, the more perception of individual choice and control that can be built into the situation, the less stress that will be perceived.

Presumably this same principle applies to life changes other than relocation. Looked at in this way, "on-time" life changes are low in stress because the individual can plan ahead and thus control the timing or the circumstances to some extent. "Off-time" events, such as being fired, however, are far less controllable.

This principle may be worth bearing in mind the next time you face a major life change or even an accumulation of daily hassles. To the extent that you can control your choices (a kind of transformational, appraisal-focused coping), your experience of stress can be reduced.

## Summary

1. Stress is defined in at least three ways: as a physical response to demand, as a life change or hassle that demands adaptation, or as the result of some interaction between a demanding environmental event and the individual's coping capacity.

2. Research based on the second of these definitions (a stimulus-oriented definition) has most commonly involved instruments that measure the number of major or minor life changes experienced by an individual in a given space of time.

3. Standard measures of life changes have been criticized because they treat positive and negative changes as equal, do not take into account the individual's interpretation or perception of the event, and do not include daily hassles.

4. A small but consistently observed increase in the risk of disease or emotional disturbance has been found associated with heightened levels of life changes or hassles. Undesirable life changes, particularly those involved in a loss of a relationship, appear to be especially stressful.

5. Life changes may also be associated with some positive outcomes, such as personal growth, although this is much less established.

6. Older adults experience fewer major life changes than do younger adults.

7. The effects of stress may be mitigated ("buffered") in individuals by any of several resistance resources, including social support, certain personality patterns, and certain coping strategies.

8. Studies of social support in stressful conditions suggest that the intimacy of the relationships within a social network is the key variable. Adults with emotionally supportive, intimate relationships are less likely to respond to stress with illness than are adults without such support.

9. There are indications that the optimal supportive relationship may vary from one type of life change to another.

10. Social networks also have some negative effects, since their maintenance may increase daily hassles, and they may include genuinely negative interactions.

11. Two personality characteristics thus far shown to be related to reduced impact of stress are hardiness and social interest. Hardiness includes a belief in yourself and in your ability to control and influence the world around you as well as a perception of stress experiences in terms of challenge rather than threat. Social interest describes a quality of selfless interest in and caring about others.

12. Of the many varieties of coping strategies in the face of life changes or hassles, those described as "transformational" are generally more effective than those described as "regressive." Taking positive actions, rethinking priorities, evaluating alternatives are all transformational strategies, while ignoring and emotional outbursts (including increased drinking, smoking, and eating) are all regressive strategies.

13. Other resistance resources include adequate income, health or vitality, and a generally positive outlook on life.

14. These same general patterns of results hold for specific major life changes such as widowhood, divorce, and relocation in old age.

15. Widowhood is associated with heightened rates of illness, depression, suicide,

and auto accidents. The effects are generally larger for men and for any adult widowed early in life or unexpectedly.

16. Divorce similarly is associated with heightened rates of depression and illness, with effects slightly larger for men. Divorce has a greater impact on older adults, however, suggesting that any life event that is non-normative for an age group or a cohort is particularly likely to lead to illness.

17. Relocation in old age has relatively little negative effect if the move is voluntary, or if involuntary, is to a setting or institution in which the individual has some personal autonomy or control. Involuntary moves to non-optimal institutions are the only ones consistently associated with increased levels of mortality or illness.

18. Overall, in the face of some kind of potentially stressful experience, illness or emotional disturbance is most likely if the individual appraises the experience as a threat, has a low level of social support, lacks options or control, and lacks suitable transformational coping strategies.

## Suggested Readings

*Bookstores are full of titles on "stress management." If you find yourself facing major life changes or accumulated hassles, any of these books may be helpful to you. If you are interested in the more academic side of the question, I can recommend one excellent collection of papers on which I have drawn:*

GOLDBERGER, L., & BREZNITZ, S. (Eds.). (1982). *Handbook of stress. Theoretical and clinical aspects.* New York: The Free Press.

Included in this collection are papers by nearly all of the big names in stress research, such as Hans Selye, Richard Lazarus, Rudolph Moos, Leonard Pearlin, Norma Haan, and Barbara Dohrenwend. The papers are somewhat technical, but most are quite clear.

# 12

# The End of the Journey: Death and Dying

In chapter 2 I talked about some of the beginnings, the starting points of adult life. Now I need to close the parentheses by talking about endings, about death and about the process of dying. It is a mistake, though, to think that a discussion of death and dying should cover only the very last years or months of each adult's life. Each adult has attitudes about death, fears of death, and makes preparations for death long before the final confrontation with dying. So let me begin the story by looking at these attitudes, fears, and preparations over the adult years.

## The Meaning of Death

> The one invariant of the meaning of death for both the individual and society is that death matters. And so does the process of dying. The event of death and the process of dying have immense impact on individuals and on the community, whether judged by emotional feelings, social relationships, spiritual well-being, financial stresses, or changes in daily living. (Kalish, 1985, p. 149)

Understandings of death change over the life span. Preschool children, for example, normally do not understand the irreversibility of death (perhaps aided and abetted by the tendency of adults, when explaining death to young children, to say things like ''Grandma has gone to heaven.'' In the child's experience, ''going'' implies ''coming back''). Elementary school-age children (between about ages five and nine), personify death—they may imagine a ''death-man'' of some kind who comes to take people away. Finally, at perhaps age 10, children not only understand fully that death is final but also that it is inevitable, that it will happen to them, too (Kastenbaum & Aisenberg, 1976; Nagy, 1948).

In adulthood, there are still some remnants of these earlier views, particularly various personifications of death (''the pale horse,'' ''the Grim Reaper,'' and the like). But most adults have a far more complex conception of death. Kalish (1977, 1985) suggests four different meanings for death among adults, which are typically mixed in any individual's meaning system:

**Death as an Organizer of Time.** Death defines the end point of one's life, so the concept of ''time till death'' may be an important one for an individual trying to organize his life. Bernice Neugarten (1968, 1977), in fact, suggests that one of the key changes in thinking in middle age is a switch in the way one marks one's own lifetime, from ''time since birth'' to ''time till death.'' Her interviews with middle-aged adults frequently yielded statements like the following:

> Time is now a two-edged sword. To some of my friends, it acts as a prod; to others, a brake. It adds a certain anxiety, but I must also say it adds a certain zest in seeing how much pleasure can still be obtained, how many good years one can still arrange, how many new activities can be undertaken. (Neugarten, 1968, p. 97)

Such a change in time perspective, accompanied by a greater awareness of (and worry about) death, does not occur at midlife for every adult. Nor do all older adults think of their lives in terms of time till death. In one study of elderly adults, for example, Keith (1981–82) found that only about half of her sample of 72- to 99-year-olds seemed to think about or precisely define ''time remaining.'' But such a recognition of ''time remaining'' may be a useful (perhaps even a necessary) aspect of coming to terms with one's own death. In Keith's study, those adults who did talk about time remaining also had more favorable attitudes (less fear) of death. Other research confirms this pattern: Older adults who continue to be preoccupied with the past, who avoid thinking about the future, are more likely to be fearful or anxious about death than are those who face the future (and their own deaths) more fully (Pollak, 1979–80).

**Death as Punishment.** Many religious traditions emphasize that death is a punishment for sins, and many adults believe that a ''good'' person will be rewarded with longer life.

**Death as Transition.** Death involves some kind of transition, from life to some sort of life after death, or from life to nothingness. Kalish and Reynolds (1976) have found that in the United States, about three fourths of adults would like to believe in some kind of life after death; only 10% said they would prefer no such life after death.

**Death as Loss.** Perhaps most pervasively, death is seen by most of us as a loss of some kind—loss of the ability to complete projects or carry out plans, loss of one's body, loss of experiencing, loss of taste, smell, touch, loss of relationships with people. No more hot fudge sundaes, no more delight in the reds and golds of autumn leaves making a pattern on the ground, no more

**TABLE 12–1 What Would You Do If You Knew You Were to Die in Six Months? Subjects in a Los Angeles Study Gave These Types of Answers**

| | Age Groups | | |
|---|---|---|---|
| | *20–39* | *40–59* | *60+* |
| Make a marked change in lifestyle, (e.g., travel, sex, experiences, etc.) | 24% | 15% | 9% |
| Center on inner life (read, contemplate, pray) | 14% | 14% | 37% |
| Focus concern on others, be with loved ones | 29% | 25% | 12% |
| Attempt to complete projects, tie up loose ends | 11% | 10% | 3% |
| No change in lifestyle | 17% | 29% | 31% |
| Other | 5% | 6% | 8% |

**Source:** Kalish & Reynolds, 1976, p. 205. Reprinted by permission of University of Southern California Press.

caresses or kisses, no more Bach chorales, no more trips to exotic new places. Of course, some of these losses may occur during a person's lifetime. A loss of hearing will already cut out the Bach chorales; widowhood may deprive an adult of caresses. But death guarantees all of these losses.

It will not surprise you that there are age differences in the particular losses that seem to be most critical in adults' thinking about death. Young adults are more concerned about loss of opportunity to experience things and about the loss of family relationships; older adults may be more concerned with the loss of time to complete some inner work. These differences are reflected in Table 12–1 in the results Kalish and Reynolds (1976) obtained when they asked a group of adults what they would do with their time if they were told they had a terminal disease and six months to live. (You may want to think about your own answer to this question before you look at the table.) As you can see, the younger adults were more likely to plan to spend time either experiencing things or on relationships, while older adults much more often said they would read, contemplate, or pray—more evidence, perhaps, for the greater "spiritual" preoccupation in later life that I proposed in chapter 10.

## Fears of Death

This final aspect of meaning of death, that of loss, is strongly linked to the most studied aspect of death attitudes, namely, the fear of death. If we fear death, it is in part the losses of experience, sensation, relationships that we fear. Fear of death may also include fear of the pain or suffering or indignity that may be involved in the process of death itself, fear of whatever punishment may come after death, and a fundamental fear of loss of the self.

Pervasive as it is, fear of death is extremely difficult to study, in part because we defend ourselves against this fear in various ways, most typically with repression or denial. So if you ask adults directly whether they are afraid of death, the majority will say no. A greater reported degree of fear emerges if you ask a whole series of more specific questions, such as some dealing with feelings about the deaths of others, expectation of or fear of pain, and the like. A still different picture of fear of death appears when researchers attempt to tap unconscious fear. For example, Feifel and Branscomb (1973) gave subjects lists of words, printed in various colors. The subject's task was to read off the color of the word, not the word itself. Half the word series were made up of death-related words, half of neutral words. If it takes subjects longer to read the colors of death words than neutral words, this implies some resistance to these words, and may reflect unconscious anxiety or fear about death. On this measure, even subjects who had reported no conscious fear of death typically showed a difference in response time to the two kinds of words.

## Age Differences in Fear of Death

Using all these various types of measures, researchers have attempted to plot age changes in the strength of fear of death. Several possible age-related patterns seem plausible. On the one hand, I can argue that young adults might be highly fearful, since they have in some sense the most to lose—all those experiences not yet enjoyed, those relationships uncompleted. On the other hand, I could argue that since older adults are (on average) much closer to death, they may be much more fearful of the impending pain or suffering, and so fear death more.

To some degree, the pattern of age differences in fear of death that one finds depends on the particular measure one uses. But in general, neither of my two conjectures receives much support. Instead, the peak of fear of and worry over death seems to be at midlife rather than in early adulthood or later life.

Such a pattern emerges, for example, from a set of interviews with a large national sample by Riley (unpublished, cited in Riley & Foner, 1968). Riley asked subjects to say if they agreed or disagreed with certain statements about death, such as "Death always comes too soon," or "To die is to suffer." Table 12–2 gives the percentages who agreed with the first of these statements, by age, for each of three levels of education. You can see that in all three groups, the middle-aged adults were most likely to agree that death always comes too soon. There were no parallel age differences in agreement with the statement that "To die is to suffer," so these age differences do not appear to reflect a pervasive negative attitude or expectation about death or dying. They do suggest that at middle age, many adults shift from an assumption of unlimited time to a recognition that life is finite.

A higher level of explicit, conscious fear among middle-aged adults also appeared in a well-designed study by Bengtson and his colleagues (Bengtson, Cuellar, & Ragan, 1977). Bengtson's sample, all between 45 and 74 years of age, was selected to be representative of adults in the Los Angeles area, and

**TABLE 12–2 Percent of Adults of Various Age Groups and Education Groups Who Agreed with the Statement, "Death Always Comes Too Soon"**

| Age | Education | | |
|---|---|---|---|
| | *Junior High School or Less* | *High School* | *College* |
| 30 and under | 65 | 53 | 40 |
| 31–40 | 58 | 50 | 24 |
| 41–50 | 75 | 64 | 49 |
| 51–60 | 70 | 50 | 53 |
| 61+ | 58 | 59 | 29 |

**Source:** From *Aging and society. Volume One. An Inventory of Research Findings* by Matilda White Riley and Anne Foner. Copyright © 1968 by Russell Sage Foundation. Reprinted by permission of Basic Books, Inc., Publishers.

included approximately equal numbers of whites, blacks, and Mexican Americans. The measure of fear of death was quite simple (perhaps too much so, in fact). He asked each subject, ''How afraid are you of death? Would you say you are: not at all afraid?/somewhat afraid?/or very afraid?'' Only 37% said they were either somewhat or very afraid, but these were mostly the younger subjects, as you can see in Figure 12–1. Of course, since adults younger than 45 were not included in this study, we don't know whether fear of death would be lower at earlier ages. But these results do point to a decline in overt fear from middle age to old age.

My sense of these findings is that in midlife, many adults are forced in some way to recognize and come to terms with their own mortality. The stimulus for such renewed awareness of death may be the loss of or decline in some taken-for-granted physical or intellectual skill—finding yourself unable to read the phone book without glasses, or losing some hearing, or having more trouble remembering names or learning new skills. It could be the premature death of a friend. Most commonly, however, it is the death of one's parents that serves as the trigger. Many adults find the death of their parents unexpectedly shocking and disturbing. Not only is there the specific loss to be mourned; there is also the realization that you are now the oldest generation in the family lineage, and thus ''next in line'' for death. Any one (or several) of these experiences may heighten a middle-aged adult's awareness of death, which is reflected in the rise in reports of overt fear. But then each adult comes to terms with this inevitability in some way, defending against the anxiety, redefining the problem, accepting that life has been full and fairly complete and that death is an inevitable and natural ending.

This does not mean that older adults are unconcerned with death. On the contrary, they are more likely to talk about it and think about it than are younger adults (Kalish, 1985). But while death is highly salient to the elderly, it is not as frightening as it was in mid-life.

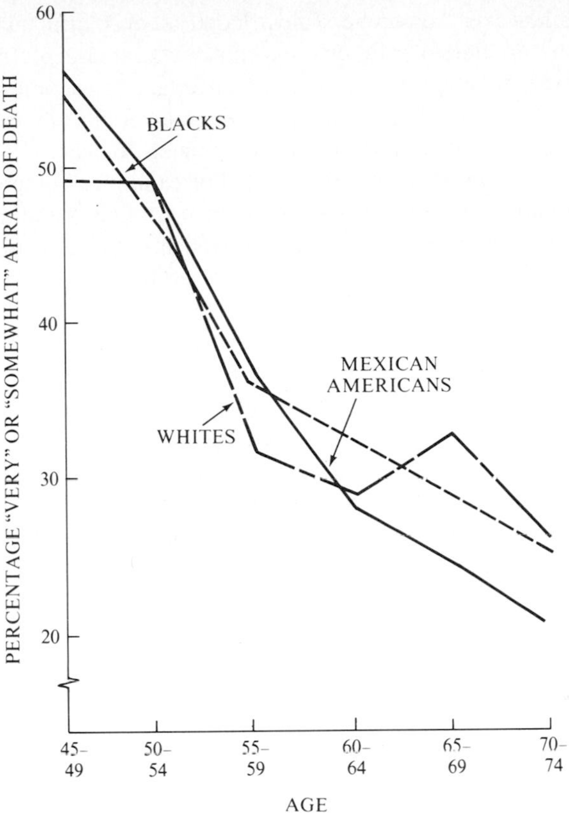


**Figure 12–1** *The remarkable similarity of the patterns of age-change in overt fear of death in these three different groups lends credence to the view that older adults are less consciously fearful. There may be a peak of such fear in middle age, but since no young adults were included in this study, we cannot be sure. (Source: Bengston, Cuellar, & Ragan, 1977, Figure 1, p. 80. Reprinted by permission of* The Journal of Gerontology, *32(1), 1977.)*

## Other Correlates of Fear of Death

Age is not the only element in fear of death. Several other personal qualities—many of which will be familiar from the last two chapters—appear to be related to conscious fearfulness.

First of all, the degree of religious feeling seems to make some difference. Kalish (1985), after reviewing the few studies addressed to this link, concludes that, in general, adults who describe themselves as deeply religious or who go to church regularly are less afraid of death than are those who describe themselves as less religious or who participate less regularly in religious activities.

In some instances, however, researchers have found a curvilinear relationship, with both those who are deeply religious and those who are deeply irreligious less fearful than those in between, who may be uncertain or uncommitted.

Individual temperament or personality is a second variable in the fear of death equation. Extraversion is not consistently related to fear of death, but measures of neuroticism are (Pollak, 1979–80). For example, Templer (1972) reported a correlation of .36 between a measure of neuroticism and a measure of conscious fear of death in a group of college students. Since neuroticism is generally characterized by greater fear or negative attitudes toward many aspects of life, this pattern is quite predictable.

More interesting, I think, is the link between fear of death and a sense of personal worth or competence. Several facets of this domain have been studied. Adults who feel they have achieved the goals they set out to achieve, or who think of themselves as not too discrepant from the person they wanted to be, are less fearful of death than are those who are disappointed in themselves (Neimeyer & Chapman, 1980–81). Adults who feel that their life has some purpose or meaning also appear to be less fearful of death (Durlak, 1972), as do those who feel some sense of personal competence (Pollak, 1979–80).

Such findings suggest at least the possibility that those adults who have successfully completed the major tasks of adult life, who have adequately filled the roles they occupied, who developed inwardly, are able to face death with greater equanimity. Those adults who have not been able to resolve the various tasks and dilemmas of adulthood face their late adult years more fearfully, more anxiously, with despair (to use Erikson's term). Fear of death is merely one facet of such despair.

In some sense, then, all of adult life is a process of moving toward death. An adult's attitude toward death and his approach to it are influenced by many of the same qualities that affect the way he approaches other life changes or dilemmas.

# Preparation for Death

Despite the fear, and despite the frequent avoidance of the very subject, adults do make preparations for death, particularly as they get older. In his national survey, Riley (Riley & Foner, 1968) found that 80% of adults of all ages thought that one should make plans for one's death, and most did have life insurance. But those over 60 years of age were more than twice as likely as those under 40 to have made out a will or to have made funeral or cemetery arrangements.

## Life Review

A quite different form of preparation for death, proposed by Robert Butler (1963, 1968) is the process of the **life review,** which is the "naturally occurring, universal mental process . . . prompted by the realization of approaching dissolution and death, and the inability to maintain one's sense of personal invulnerability'' (1968, p. 487).

Life review is partly a process of reminiscence, of running the mind over past experiences. But according to Butler, there is more going on here than mere recall. The individual, through the process of reminiscence, is reorganizing her image of herself, integrating the various experiences, the various roles and ''selves'' that have populated her life. One behavioral manifestation of this process is mirror gazing—staring at oneself in the mirror, perhaps with a sense of shock. One adult quoted by Butler said, ''I was passing by my mirror. I noticed how old I was. My appearance, well, it prompted me to think of death—and of my past—what I hadn't done, what I had done wrong'' (Butler, 1968, p. 489).

The resemblance between this concept and Erikson's concept of ego integrity versus despair is strong. In a sense, the life review as Butler describes it is the process by which an adult deals with the task of attempting to achieve ego integrity.

## Intellectual and Psychological Changes Before Death

At a much less conscious level, adults seem to prepare physically and psychologically for death. In chapter 5 I introduced the concept of ''terminal drop'' as a description of the rather rapid decline in intellectual performance that seems to occur in the years immediately prior to death. Related kinds of terminal changes seem to occur in personality and in emotional patterns.

Morton Lieberman provided the best description of such changes based on a series of short-term longitudinal studies of elderly adults, matched in age, sex, marital status, and education. Half of the subjects died within one year of the assessments, while the other half survived at least three years past the final assessment. Lieberman was thus able to compare those who were near death with those who were further from death (Lieberman, 1965; Lieberman & Coplan, 1970).

Lieberman found that those nearer to death not only showed the expected lower performance on tests of memory and learning, but also differed on measures of emotion and self-image. Near death subjects displayed fewer different emotions and were less introspective than were adults of the same age who were further from death. Those near death also perceived or described themselves as less aggressive or assertive, more conventional and conforming, more docile and dependent, more warm, more responsible. Since Lieberman gave the same tests to these subjects repeatedly over a period of several years, he was able to show that these characteristics emerge more strongly as the individual moves closer to death. So it is not that conventional, docile, unaggressive adults die sooner, but that these characteristics are accentuated as death nears.

Some of these changes are the result of (or are influenced by) physiological processes occurring immediately prior to death. But some may be a reflection of a psychological preparation for death. Adults very near death are less active both physically and psychologically. They give up tilting at windmills, cease fighting the daily battles. In that sense they become more passive, more accepting, perhaps more inwardly turned.

# The Process of Dying

A similar movement toward acceptance of death has been described by Elizabeth Kübler-Ross, based on her interviews with hundreds of terminally ill adults and children (1969, 1975). Kübler-Ross was (and is) a remarkable clinician, with enormous empathy and compassion for dying patients. Her observations, and her proposed stages of dying have been widely accepted and have helped greatly to humanize the process of dying for millions.

## Stages of Dying

After watching and listening to many patients, Kübler-Ross suggested that the process of dying involves five steps or stages, occurring in a particular order: denial, anger, bargaining, depression, and acceptance.

**Denial.** When confronted with a terminal diagnosis, the first reaction most patients report is some form of ''No, not me!'' ''It must be a mistake.'' ''The lab reports must have been mixed up.'' ''I don't feel that sick, so it can't be true.'' ''I'll get another doctor's opinion.'' All these are forms of denial, which Kübler-Ross argues is a valuable, constructive first defense. It gives the patient a period of time in which to marshall other strategies of coping with the shock. Some patients, of course, continue to use denial right up to the end. But for most, according to Kübler-Ross, the extreme versions of denial fade within a short time and are replaced by anger.

**Anger.** The classic second reaction is ''Why me?'' The patient resents those who are healthy, and becomes angry at whatever fate put her in this position. This may be reflected in angry outbursts at nurses, family members, doctors—anyone within reach. In part, this anger may be a response not just to the verdict of death, but also to the typically dependent and helpless position of a patient. There is a ''Hey, pay attention to me! I'm still here!'' aspect to this anger.

**Bargaining.** At some point, Kübler-Ross saw anger being replaced by a new kind of defense. The patient now tries to ''make a deal'' with doctors, nurses, with God. ''If I do what I'm told, and don't yell at everyone, then I'll be able to live till Christmas.'' Kübler-Ross (1969) describes one woman with terminal cancer who wanted to live long enough to attend the wedding of her oldest, favorite son. With help from the hospital staff she learned how to use self-hypnosis to control her pain for short periods, and was able to attend the

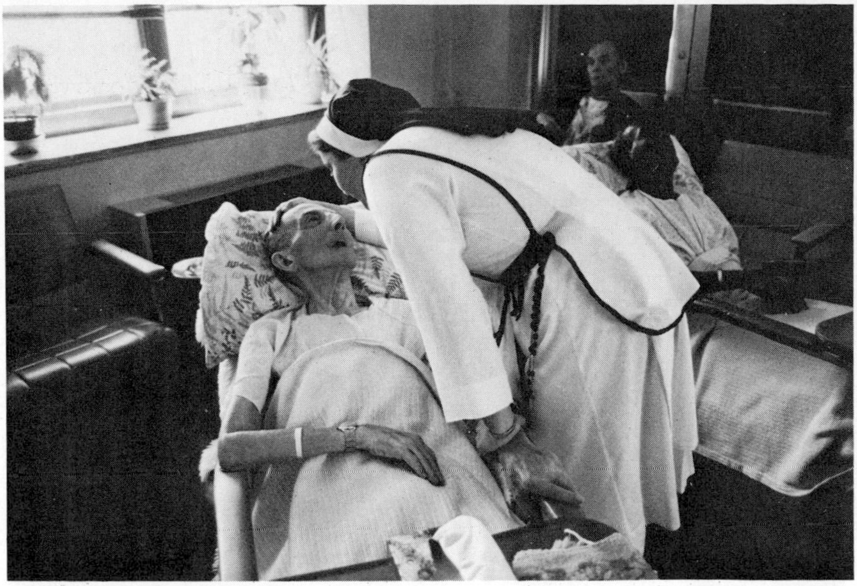

***Figure 12–2*** *Kübler-Ross's theories about stages of dying, and the sensitivity with which she listened to dying patients, have strongly influenced the care of dying patients in many hospitals. Nurses and doctors now try to take the patient's feelings and emotional patterns into account and to comfort and listen to the patient more as well. (Source: Abraham Menashe, Photo Researchers Inc.)*

wedding. As Kübler-Ross reports, "I will never forget the moment when she returned to the hospital. She looked tired and somewhat exhausted and—before I could say hello—said, 'Now don't forget I have another son!' " (1969, p. 83).

**Depression.** Bargaining only works for so long, however, and as disease processes continue and the signs of the body's decline become more obvious, patients typically become depressed. This is, in a sense, a kind of mourning—for the loss of relationships as well as of one's own life. Often the dying person sinks into a sort of despair, which may last for a prolonged period. But Kübler-Ross argues that this depression is part of the preparation for the final step, acceptance. The dying person must grieve for, and then give up, all the things of the world. Only then can acceptance of death occur.

**Acceptance.** The final step is a quiet understanding, a readiness for death. The patient is no longer depressed, but may be quiet, even serene. In a widely quoted passage, Stewart Alsop (1973), who was dying of leukemia, described his own acceptance: "A dying man needs to die as a sleepy man needs to sleep, and there comes a time when it is wrong, as well as useless, to resist" (Alsop, 1973, p. 299).

Through all of these stages, Kübler-Ross thought, runs a current of hope. Patients hope for a new form of therapy, a new drug, a miraculous cure. And patients hope that they can die "well," without too much pain and with some acceptance.

## An Assessment of Dying Stages

Kübler-Ross's description has been enormously influential. She has provided a common language for those who work with dying patients, and her highly compassionate descriptions have, without doubt, sensitized health care workers and families to the complexities of the process of dying. There are moments when what the patient needs is cheering up, and moments when he needs simply to be listened to; there are times to hold his hand quietly, and times to provide encouragement or hope. Many new care programs that arrange for terminally ill patients to be cared for and to die at home (about which I'll have more to say shortly) are without doubt outgrowths of this greater sensitivity to the dying process.

These are all worthwhile changes. But there has been perhaps too-ready an acceptance of the description of stages of dying. Kübler-Ross's hypothesized sequence was initially based on clinical observation of perhaps 200 patients, and she does not provide information about how frequently she talked with them or spent time with them, or over how long a period they continued to be observed. Other clinicians and researchers who have attempted to study the process more precisely have not found that all dying patients exhibit these five emotions at all, let alone in a specific order (Schulz & Aderman, 1974). Of the five, only some type of depression seems to be consistently present in dying patients. Edwin Shneidman (1980, 1983), a major theorist and clinician in the field of thanatology (the study of dying) puts it this way:

> I reject the notion that human beings, as they die, are somehow marched in lock step through a series of stages of the dying process. On the contrary, in working with dying persons, I see a wide panoply of human feelings and emotions, of various human needs, and a broad selection of psychological defenses and maneuvers—a few of these in some people, dozens in others—experienced in an impressive variety of ways. (1980, p. 110)

Schneidman goes on to describe some of the many themes that can appear, disappear, and reappear in the process of dealing with death in any one patient: terror ("I was really frightened"), pervasive uncertainty ("If there is a God . . ."), fantasies of being rescued ("Somebody . . . that maybe could perform this miracle"), incredulity ("It's so far fetched, so unreal . . . it is a senseless death"), feelings of unfairness, a concern with reputation after death, the fight against pain, and so forth.

Thus, instead of each person following a series of five fixed stages, each person moves back and forth, in and out of a complex set of emotions and defenses. Kübler-Ross herself would not now disagree with this view. In later writings she says, "Most of my patients have exhibited two or three stages simultaneously and these do not always occur in the same order" (1974, p. 25–26). Given this variability, the term *stage* does not seem to be an appropriate label for these several emotions or themes. But we can nonetheless ask what aspects of an individual's history or character may affect the dominant themes or emotions surrounding his death.

## Individual Adaptations to Dying

How shall we measure a patient's adaptation to terminal illness? One approach, used by Weisman and Worden (1975), is to compare patients who survived longer than expected (considering the diagnosis and the stage of the patient's disease) with those who died sooner than expected. Weisman and Worden studied 46 cancer patients, varying in age and specific diagnosis, and found that those who survived longer than expected were those who had a history of good relationships with others and maintained those relationships quite well during their illness. The patients asked for and received emotional and medical support. They accepted the reality of their illness, but actually showed a fair amount of denial of the inevitability of their death. They were seldom deeply depressed, but did show anger or resentment at times.

Those who died sooner than expected were typically patients with a history of poor social relationships, often with early separations from parents or other family members. They did not have close friends and did not maintain good relationships with family during the illness. These patients became much more depressed, and the depression often deepened to the point at which they wished to die.

Another approach has been to measure the degree of depression, anger, or anxiety the patient experiences. Thus, Carey (1974) had hospital chaplains rate each of a series of terminal patients on "emotional adjustment," which included ratings of the amount of anger, guilt, anxiety, depression, and the ability to verbalize feelings with family and friends shown by each patient. What Carey hoped this measure reflected was a sense of inner peace or self-possession, not resignation or despair or even acceptance of death.

Similarly, in one of the most widely cited studies, Hinton (1975) interviewed patients, their spouses, and nurses and rated each patient's depression, anxiety, anger, and withdrawal separately based on the information from each source. He also rated the patients' attitudes toward dying and their awareness of the fact that they were dying.

Results from these two studies suggest that there are several qualities that differentiate better adjusted patients from less well-adjusted patients. Those who show the least persistent depression or anger are those who:

- are in the least pain. Carey found that the patient's report of pain or discomfort was negatively related to adjustment (the more pain, the least "adjustment")

- have had previous close contact with a person who was dying (Carey, 1974)
- have good marriages, or supportive relationships with friends and family members during the illness (Carey, 1974; Hinton, 1975)
- have a previous history of coping well with life's problems and crises (Hinton, 1975)
- have a previous history of being satisfied with their lives. In Hinton's study, this is particularly predictive of the amount of depression and anger shown by the patient, and may reflect a characteristically positive versus negative mood
- describe their religious orientation as "intrinsic" rather than "extrinsic" (Carey, 1974)

An individual with an intrinsic religious orientation is one who attempts to integrate beliefs into actual living, taking the specific tenets and ethical concerns seriously and personally. An extrinsically oriented person is more likely to focus on the forms of religious observance—church attendance, specific times of prayer or the like—and on personal gains from religious observance, such as gains in social standing.

Clearly we should be cautious about overgeneralizing from the findings of these two studies, or from the other limited work on differing adaptations to dying. Not only is this work limited to our own culture, it is also almost completely limited to patients dying of a particular type of disease—cancer. It is not obvious that we should assume the same processes in those dying of cardiovascular disease, or pneumonia, or any other type of nonmalignant disease. Still, these findings are intriguing. Among other things, they suggest the (not surprising) conclusion that adults die very much as they live. Each of us brings to the process of dying the same personality, the same level of coping skills, the same degree of capacity for secure, satisfying relationships that we evinced throughout our lives.

It is also interesting that this list of characteristics of "well adjusted" dying adults sounds so similar to the list of factors I mentioned as resistance resources to stress or life change in the last chapter. And if we can take "intrinsic" religious orientation as a reflection of, perhaps, an individualistic or a conjunctive faith (in Fowler's sense), while an "extrinsic" orientation may reflect conventional faith, then Carey's results suggest once again that the process of personal growth, of inner development, affects the way we approach death as much as the way we approach life.

## Where Death Occurs

The vast majority of people in our culture die in hospitals. But in part because of Kübler-Ross's work and the subsequent awakening of interest in the process of dying, a number of health professionals and other caring adults began to ask whether a traditional hospital setting was, in fact, the most supportive and compassionate place for a dying person to be cared for. If an "appropriate death" (to use Weisman's phrase, [1972])—a death according to the wishes of

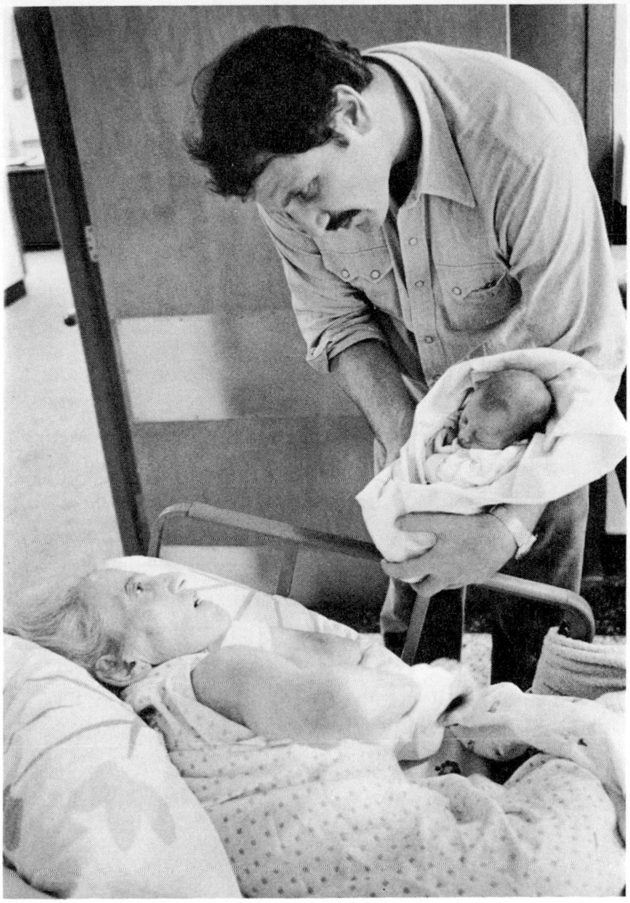

***Figure 12–3*** *Hospice care offers some terminally ill patients and their families an alternative to traditional hospital care, and can be a strongly enriching and deepening experience. (Source: Ray Ellis, Photo Researchers Inc.)*

the dying person, with dignity—can most readily be accomplished when the individual has frequent contact with loving friends and family, with familiar surroundings, then hospital wards designed to maximize efficiency rather than contact will not be as supportive as would a home setting, or a home-like setting.

Considerations like these have led to a movement generally known as **hospice care**. The original concept came from England (Saunders, 1977) and emerged as an alternative form of care for the terminally ill patient. The idea spread rapidly to the United States, where it is to be found not only in special wards within hospitals, but (most commonly) in supervised home-care programs.

The philosophy that underlies this alternative setting or situation for the dying patient has several aspects (Bass, 1985): (1) that death should be viewed as a normal, inevitable part of life, not to be avoided but to be faced and accepted; (2) that the patient and the family should prepare for the death, by examining their feelings, by planning for their later life; (3) that the family should be involved in the care to as full an extent possible. This permits each family member to come to some resolution of his or her relationship with the dying person; (4) that the control over the care and the care-receiving setting should belong to the patient and family.

In home-based hospice programs, there is typically one family caregiver (most often the spouse) who may spend as long as 19 hours a day caring for the patient. Other family members may help, but the central person has the organizational responsibility. This key person is then assisted and supported by one or more nurses or other hospice personnel, who visit regularly (often daily when death is near), train family members in care procedures, help the family to prepare for the death, and provide emotional support throughout the process.

So far as I know, there is no decent research comparing the effect or effectiveness of hospice care with that of traditional hospital care. There are, instead, many case studies of families who have undertaken hospice care who describe the richness and profound impact of the experience. Many dying adults in such programs describe their experiences as enormously supportive and enriching (Bass, 1985; Kalish, 1985).

Still, this is not an option to be undertaken lightly. The burden of care is enormous and may require skills that the caregivers do not have; care is much less medically aggressive than may be true of hospital care, so it may not be appropriate for any except the clearly terminally ill for whom no further aggressive care seems reasonable. Bass (1985) finds that some families that initially chose hospice care later placed their dying relative in a hospital setting because they could no longer cope. But as with new (or renewed) health care options at the beginning of life (such as the return of midwifery and home delivery), it seems to me to be a very good thing that in many communities today, dying adults and their families have some choices about where and how the process of dying will occur. Since that sort of choice and control is one of the coping strategies that seems most effective in helping adults deal with other life crises, it is likely to have the same beneficial effect in the case of the ultimate life change—death.

## After Death: Rituals and Grieving

Whether a death is sudden or prolonged, anticipated or unexpected, it leaves survivors who must somehow come to terms with the death and eventually pick up the pieces of their lives. I talked a bit about widowhood in the last chapter, in discussing the impact of several major life changes. But my emphasis there was primarily on the epidemiological effects—the rate of illness, or emotional disturbance, or premature death among the survivors. Let me turn here to a more general discussion of the process of grieving itself.

## Ritual Mourning: Funerals and Ceremonies

Every culture has some set of rituals associated with death. Far from being empty gestures, these rituals have at least three clear and important functions. First, in these rituals the bereaved person is given a specific role to play. Like all roles, this one includes a clear set of expected behaviors and an equally clear set of prohibited or discouraged behaviors. The content of these roles differs markedly from one culture to the next, but the clarity of the role in most cases provides a clear shape to the days or weeks immediately following the death of a loved person. (I have an unreasoning bias, by the way, against the phrase "loved one," which sounds to me like unctuous funeral director language.) In our culture, the rituals prescribe what one should wear, who should be called, who should be fed, what demeanor one should show, and far more. Depending on one's religious background, one may need to arrange to sit shiva, or gather friends and family for a wake, or arrange a memorial service. There are a large number of details to be taken care of, all of which keep the grieving person busy during the first numbing hours and days.

***Figure 12–4*** *Funeral rituals may sometimes seem overly elaborate or draining of the energy of the recently bereaved. But they serve important functions for the bereaved individuals and for their friends. (Source: Katrina Thomas, Photo Researchers Inc.)*

At the same time, the rituals provide less central but significant roles for friends, most particularly that of support-giver. Friends and family bring food to the home of the bereaved person, for example, or drop in to offer help, or send letters of condolence. (I shall never forget my gratitude to one friend who appeared, uninvited, on my mother's doorstep the day my stepfather died. I had to pick up other family members at the airport, but I did not want to leave my mother alone. The friend appeared at precisely the right moment.)

Finally, the rituals, particularly the religious rituals, may give a sense of transcendant meaning to the death itself, at a time when the bereaved person very much needs an answer to the question "why?"

## Stages of Grief

When the funeral or memorial service is over, what do you do then? How does a person handle the grief of this kind of loss, whether it be a spouse, parent, child, a friend, or lover?

The short answer to that is "slowly and with difficulty." Grief over the death of someone to whom you have been strongly attached is not a quick process. And as has been proposed in the case of dying, grieving may occur in stages.

Both Parkes (1970) and Bowlby (1980) have suggested four such phases, strongly reminiscent of Kübler-Ross's stages of dying:

1. Numbness. This stage may be very brief, or may last weeks or months. Typically it is operative during the ritual period after the death. The loss is partially disregarded; it has not yet "sunk in."
2. Yearning. This period is one in which the bereaved person desires to recover the lost object. She or he may actively search for the dead individual, or may wander around as if searching. Not infrequently, adults report that they actually do see the dead person in some familiar setting (Kalish, 1985; Kastenbaum & Aisenberg, 1976). Interestingly, anger may also occur during this phase, although neither Parkes nor Bowlby lists anger as a separate stage. The anger may sometimes be directed at the deceased, but is more often directed at those thought to have contributed to his death ("The doctors didn't try hard enough"; "His boss should have known better than to ask him to work so hard"). Bowlby suggests that this searching or yearning has some of the elements of what we see when a young child is temporarily separated from his mother. In the young child, such searching is a sign of a powerful attachment, so it is not surprising that we should see it in adults permanently separated from their own objects of strong attachments.
3. Disorganization and despair. The third phase, very similar to the period of depression in dying described by Kübler-Ross, is one in which searching ceases and the loss is accepted. But with that acceptance comes despair. Immense loneliness may be experienced, immune to the ministrations of kind friends or family members (Lopata et al., 1982).
4. Reorganization. Finally, the grieving person realizes that he must get on

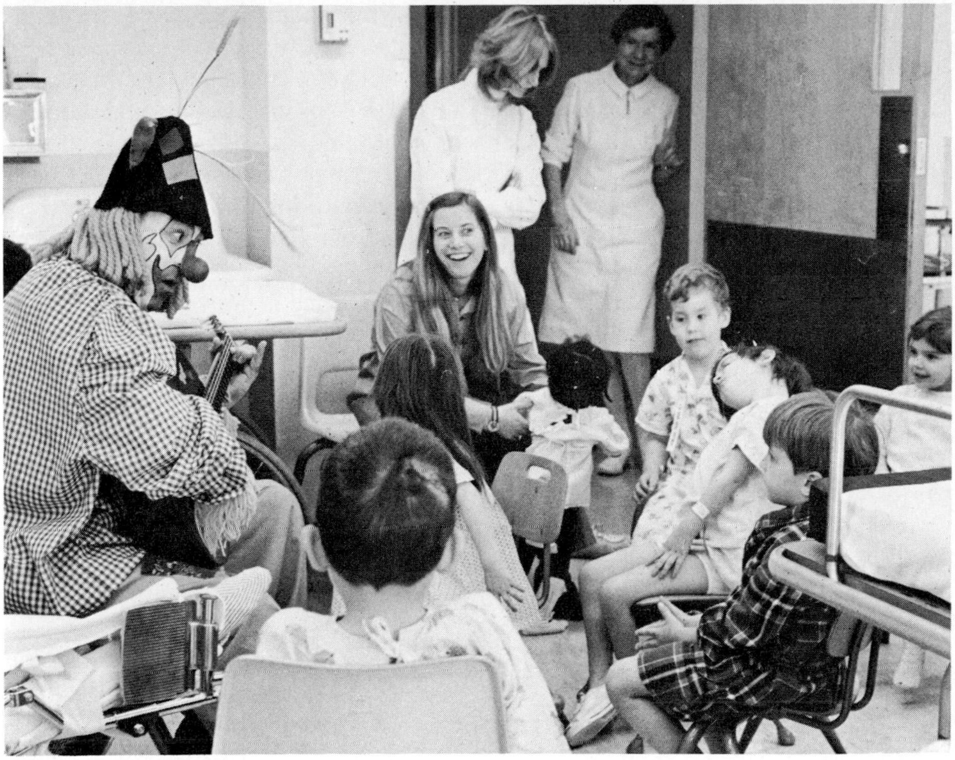

***Figure 12–5*** *One of the hardest things for an adult to deal with is the death of a child. The parents of these terminally ill children are struggling with all the aspects of grief, even before the child dies. But painful as it is, this anticipatory grief can sometimes ease the pain after the child's death. (Source: John Robaton, Leo de Wys Inc.)*

with his life, must take up his usual activities or find new relationships. This is equivalent to the stage of acceptance in Kübler-Ross's system, although in the case of grief there is less an element here of resignation as there is constructive and active restructuring of one's life.

These stages are not confined to the grief an adult shows on the death of another adult. Bowlby has observed very similar processes among parents coping with the dying and death of young children (Bowlby, 1980). But in this case, at least some of the grief work appears to be done during the terminal illness rather than after the child's death. Some parents, at least, particularly those who have already accepted the inevitability of the child's death, seem to be able to move very quickly through the period of despair to a time of reorganization after the child's actual death. Some such anticipatory grief may occur in the case of adults grieving for dying adults, but for reasons that are not clear, it seems to be less effective in such cases than it is with dying children (Kalish, 1985).

Whether the deceased is a child or adult, the process of grieving takes time. The sequence may be completed in a few months, or a few years, or in some cases may never be completed. Judging from the epidemiological data I reported in the last chapter, the time of highest risk for disease or disturbance (including depression and suicide) among the widowed is the first year after the bereavement. This points to a period of a year or two as perhaps the modal duration for the grieving process. (Urging your widowed mother to "get back into the swing of things" only a few months after your father's death may thus be both insensitive and counterproductive.)

As in the case of stages of dying, there is some controversy over whether these proposed stages of grieving are really sequential, widely shared steps in a linear process (e.g., Barrett & Schneweis, 1980–81; Kalish, 1985). As with the stages of dying, we would be better advised to think of themes or aspects rather than stages. The themes of grief clearly include anger, guilt, depression, anxiety and restlessness, and preoccupation with the image of the deceased. And as with other life changes and life crises, how quickly and how fully an adult absorbs the loss and restructures her life seems to depend on the same personal qualities and resources I talked about in the last chapter, and that I will return to in the next chapter.

## Living and Dying: A Final Word

If it is true that we die as we have lived, then it is also true that to some extent we live as we die. Our understanding of death and its meaning, our attitude toward the inevitability of death, the way in which we come to terms with that inevitability, affects not only the way we die, but the way we choose to live our lives throughout adulthood. David Steindl-Rast (1977), a Benedictine monk, makes this point:

> Death . . . is an event that puts the whole meaning of life into question. We may be occupied with purposeful activities, with getting tasks accomplished, works completed, and then along comes the phenomenon of death—whether it is our final death or one of those many deaths through which we go day by day. And death confronts us with the fact that purpose is not enough. We live by meaning. (Steindl-Rast, 1977, p. 22)

An awareness of death is thus not something we can put off till, one day, we hear a diagnosis of our own impending death. It can, instead, help to define and give meaning to daily life.

### Summary

1. Four different aspects to the meaning of death have been identified: death as an organizer of time, death as punishment, death as transition, and death as loss.

2. Anxiety or fear of death seems to peak in midlife. Younger adults are still partially convinced of their own immortality, and older adults have to some degree accepted the inevitability.

3. Adults who are more afraid of death are also likely to be higher in neuroticism and to have lower opinions of their own competence or worth. Higher fear is also associated with uncertain positions on religious questions.

4. Preparations for death include wills and insurance (more common among older adults), and may include a process of reminiscence called the life review. Immmediately prior to death, there are also signs of "terminal" changes in intellectual performance and emotional response. Adults within a year of death show declining intellectual performance, declining memory, reduced emotional complexity and introspectiveness, and a more passive, accepting self-concept.

5. Kübler-Ross proposes five stages in the actual dying process: denial, anger, bargaining, depression, and acceptance. Research, however, does not support the contention that all dying individuals show all these emotions, in this order or any other order. The process of dying is more individual, more varied, less sequential than Kübler-Ross proposed.

6. Individual variations in adaptation to dying are parallel, to at least some degree, to individual variations in handling other life dilemmas or changes. Adults who are least depressed or anxious and appear to cope best with their own deaths are likely to have strong and supportive relationships, to have had contact with someone else who was dying, to have a history of coping well with earlier crises, and to report an intrinsic religious orientation.

7. Where a death occurs may also have an impact on the degree of acceptance and comfort the individual experiences. Hospice care is a relatively new form of care in which the dying individual is largely cared for by family members (often at home) and controls major decisions about care.

8. Those left to mourn after a death are helped by clear rituals which provide roles for the bereaved and for friends, and may give a sense of transcendant meaning to the death.

9. Once past the rituals, the grieving person must move through a complex grief process which may be accomplished in four stages: numbness, searching and yearning (with accompanying anger), despair and disorganization, and reorganization.

## Suggested Readings

KASTENBAUM, R., & AISENBERG, R. (1976). *The psychology of death.* New York: Springer.

In many ways this is quite an amazing book, since it explores all possible aspects of death: definition, meaning, causes, cultural milieu, the costs of health care, and many more.

KÜBLER-ROSS, E. (1969). *On death and dying.* New York: Macmillan.

This was the original major book by Kübler-Ross that significantly changed the way many physicians and other health professionals viewed the dying process. It is full of case material, and reflects very well Kübler-Ross's great skill as a listener and clinician.

SHNEIDMAN, E. S. (1983). *Deaths of man.* New York: Jason Aronson.

This is a less clinical book than Kübler-Ross's, but much broader and equally sensitive. Shneidman deals with some of the medical and legal aspects of death as well as the personal process.

# 13

# Pathways Through Adulthood

Eleanor Roosevelt had a largely loveless childhood. She was orphaned at 10, reared by a domineering grandmother, and was painfully shy and lacking in self-confidence. She spent the first 20 years of her adult life in the role of wife and mother, bearing and rearing five children (under the highly critical eye of her mother-in-law) and serving as helpmate to her husband in his rising political career. She was in her late 30s when she learned that Franklin had a mistress, and nearing 40 when he became ill with polio. These enormous stresses did not break her. On the contrary, they forced her to transcend the limitations of her upbringing and of the socially prescribed roles in which she had spent her early adulthood. She went on to lecture widely, to protest injustice, to work for the poor during the Depression, to serve as ambassador to the United Nations. In Loevinger's terms, she appeared (to an outside observer, at least) to have become an integrated human being, a self-actualized, compassionate woman.

Others of us, often with much easier and more loving early years, facing equivalent stresses and demands, do not respond in the same way, perhaps do not "develop" to the same degree. We may lead reasonably happy lives, with more joys than sorrows, with contentment rather than frustration. But few of us transcend our early patterns, our roles, our early sense of self as fully as Eleanor Roosevelt seemed to do. Some adults, in fact, respond to the inevitable stresses and strains by regression to immature defenses, by prolonged emotional disturbance, or by forms of self-destruction such as alcoholism or drug abuse. How can we understand these differences in the pathways people follow through the adult years?

I have suggested a few answers to this question as I have gone along. But it is now time to attempt at least a preliminary integration of the many facts and age-related patterns I have described in the preceding chapters. I need to pull together the threads of both common patterns of experience and change over the adult years, and the individual differences in life experiences and growth.

The simplest place to begin is with an essentially normative approach: What is the "normal" life pattern for adults in this culture? What sorts of changes with age do we see, and which of those appear to be genuinely age-linked? Which are maturational changes, and which are related to changing life experiences?

## A Normative Approach

In each of the earlier descriptive chapters (chapters 4 through 9) the major trends and age changes were summarized in a table. So we already have the ingredients on hand for a normative analysis. What we need to do now is to look at all of these age-change patterns simultaneously, as in Table 13–1. Note that I have subdivided the ages somewhat more than in the earlier summary tables, with both the early adulthood and the late adulthood periods divided into smaller age ranges. Such a further subdivision helps to highlight several key points about age patterns.

Also note that the table describes the "average" or typical sequence of events for an adult who follows the culturally defined sequence of roles at the modal ages. The normative pattern is clearly to marry in one's early 20s and begin having children before 25. The children then typically leave home by the time one is about 50. Each row of the table represents a highly condensed version of one facet of change we might see over the lifetime of an individual who follows such a modal pattern.

Of the eight rows in the table, four seem to me to describe genuinely maturational or developmental sequences. Both the physical and mental changes summarized in the first two rows are strongly related to highly predictable and widely shared physical processes. While the rate of change is affected by lifestyle and habits, the sequences appear to be maturational. More tentatively, I have argued that the sequences of change in personality and in systems of meaning may also be "developmental" in the sense in which I have used that term throughout the book. These are not strongly age-linked changes, but there is at least some evidence that they are sequential and not merely a function of particular or culture-specific changes in roles or life experiences. The remaining four rows, describing roles, tasks, and relationships, seem to describe sequences that may be shared by many adults, but that are a product of specific role patterns, specific experiences. If the timing or the sequence of those roles or tasks is changed, then the pattern described in the table changes as well.

A second way to look at the table is to read down the columns rather than across the rows. This gives some sense of the various patterns that may occur simultaneously—the several "gears" in Perun and Bielby's timing model which I described in chapter 3 (recall Figure 3–4).

When you look at the information in this way, some interesting relationships may jump out at you. For example, the table makes clear a point I made in chapters 6 and 8, that the period during which adults face the largest number of changes, the most new tasks, is not midlife but the period of young adulthood, from 18 to 25. But this is also the time at which adults are at their physical and mental peak, and when most young adults have excellent opportunities for coming into contact with prospective friends and partners. Thus, at a time when life change is high, some key personal resources are also high.

The period from 25 to 40 is similarly blessed with maximum or near-maximum levels of health and intellectual skills, enabling the individual to meet the challenges of childrearing and establishment of an occupation. Most adults work extremely hard during these years, with their energies focused on their immediate families, on their work, or (increasingly) on both.

These two periods together, from about age 18 to about age 40 or 45, seem to represent the period in which socially prescribed work and family roles most fully dominate the personal agenda. To the extent that any given adult's life has been guided by the ticking of the widely prescribed and shared social clock, we can make quite good predictions about the timing of particular experiences or particular concerns during these years. We know that adults who marry early and have their children fairly soon are likely to hit a low point in marital satisfaction in their late 20s or early 30s. We know that those adults who enter a career in their 20s are likely to have a number of promotions or raises in their early 30s, and then reach a plateau. We know that during these years, personal friendships take a back seat, as energy and attention are devoted to family and work.

During middle adulthood, the pattern changes. For one thing, the years from 40 to 65 are marked by the beginning signs of some physical and mental deficits. Fortunately, for most adults these early signs, while distressing, are not yet functionally very significant. A more significant change, from my view, is the easing of the strictures of this social clock. Social roles certainly do not disappear when an adult hits 45 or 50. We go on being parents, even after our children have left home; the role of child to our aging parents may loom larger than before; we continue to go to work every day. But as the children leave home (and as the job is fully learned and offering, perhaps, fewer challenges), this collection of roles may fit less tightly, may be less constraining. In some sense, in midlife an adult is allowed to redefine her roles, to say "I don't want to do that anymore," or "I want to go back to school," or "Enough of this dishwashing; the rest of you can help out now."

For many adults such a lessening of the dominance of role-defined life patterns forms the occasion for a new look at themselves. The transition from a conformist to a conscientious or even an autonomous sense of self begins. For some, the sequence may operate the other way around: An emerging conscientious or autonomous sense of self leads an adult to a reexamination of his roles. Whatever the sequence, for many adults these middle years are a time of high work satisfaction and high marital satisfaction. My own reading of the evidence is that such heightened satisfactions are in part the result of whatever reassessment or redefinition has occurred. But the simple reduction in role demands, with or without reassessment, undoubtedly contributes as well.

In late adulthood (from 65 on), roles are lost, and those that are retained may become even less dominating. At the same time, however, there is a new

**TABLE 13–1 A Summary of Changes in Eight Different Domains of Adult Functioning Over the Years from 18 to Late Old Age**

| | Young Adulthood 18–25 | Early Adulthood 25–40 | Middle Adulthood 40–65 | Late Adulthood 65–75 | Late, Late Adulthood 75+ |
|---|---|---|---|---|---|
| Physical Change (chap. 4) | Peak functioning in most physical skills; optimum time for child-bearing | Still good physical functioning in most areas; health habits during this time establish later risks | Beginning signs of physical decline in some areas, e.g., strength, elasticity of tissues, height, cardiovascular function | Significant physical decline on most measures | Marked physical decline on virtually any measure, including speed, strength, work capacity, elasticity, system functioning |
| Cognitive Change (chap. 5) | Cognitive skill high on most measures | Peak period of cognitive skill on most measures | Some signs of loss of cognitive skill on "fluid," timed, unexercised skills; high cognitive investment | Small declines for virtually all adults on "crystallized" and "exercised" skills and larger losses on "fluid" skills | Functionally significant loss in virtually all areas, including memory, and both fluid and crystallized abilities |
| Family & Sex Roles (chap. 6) | Major role acquisition: marriage & family formation; clear separation of male and female roles | Family roles strongly dominant, with continued differentiation of sex roles; women do most family and home work | Launch children; postparental phase; begin care for elderly parents; possibly some sex role cross-over | Grandparent role; significantly less dominance of family roles and sex roles | Family roles now relatively unimportant |
| Relationships (chap. 7) | Maximum emphasis on forming friendships and partnership; usually high marital satisfaction till birth of first child | Lower marital satisfaction; fewer new friends made and lower contact with friends | Increased marital satisfaction; possibly some increase in importance of friends | High marital satisfaction and possibly some increase in importance of friends and siblings | Continued importance of friendship and sibling relationships |

| | | | | | |
|---|---|---|---|---|---|
| Work Roles (chap. 8) | Choose career, which may involve several job changes; low work satisfaction is common | Rising work satisfaction; major emphasis on career or work success; most career progress steps made | Plateau on career steps but higher work satisfaction | Retirement | Work roles now unimportant |
| Personality Development (chap. 9) | Conformist; task of intimacy | Perhaps self-aware or conscientious level; task of generativity | Perhaps individualistic or autonomous level; increase in self-confidence, openness; lower use of "immature" defenses | Perhaps integrated level; perhaps more interiority; perhaps self-actualized; task of ego integrity | Perhaps integrated or self-actualized |
| Systems of Meaning (chap. 10) | Social self; conventional faith | Social self continues, with a move toward individual; individuative-relective faith | Individual moving toward integrated sense of self; conjunctive faith | Integrated level to potentially transpersonal (rare); for some, universalizing faith | Continuation of previous pattern |
| Major Tasks | Separate from family; form partnership; begin family; find job; create individual life pattern | Rear family; establish personal work pattern and strive for success | Launch family; redefine life goals; redefine self outside of family and work roles; care for aging parents | Cope with retirement; cope with declining body and mind; redefine life goals and sense of self | Come to terms with death |

form of shared "clock" now ticking more audibly, namely the physiological clock of aging. We see the effects of this clock in the measurable decline in intellectual power in the late 60s and early 70s, and in the fairly steady physical changes in strength, speed, and elasticity of the body. These widely shared changes form a common backdrop against which other late-adult patterns are played out.

In contrast, rates of personality and spiritual development are much less consistent or shared in late adulthood than was true in earlier years. In Loevinger's system of stages and levels, most young adults are at the conformist or self-aware level. But among adults in their 60s and 70s there may be some at the conformist level, but significant numbers also at each level beyond that. (Recall Figure 10–3, too, which shows similarly large variability in stages of faith among older adults.)

In sum, for those who follow a typical social clock, the first half of adulthood is marked by many shared, age-related patterns of family and work roles. And in late adulthood, there are shared, age-related patterns of change in physical and mental functioning. In this normative pattern, it is in the years of middle adulthood when there is the greatest freedom and the greatest variability, when social roles are less confining and physical and mental decline has not yet begun to be significant. Middle adulthood may thus provide the opportunity for the redefinition of values and goals that will make the years of late adulthood more satisfying and fulfilling.

There is at least some suggestive evidence supporting this view of the heightened variability of middle life. Haan (1981), for example, has found that the range of scores on the dimension of "openness to self" in the Berkeley Intergenerational Studies subjects was significantly larger at midlife than it had been when the subjects were in their teens or 30s. Other such analyses would be useful.

This normative approach to the adult years tells us something about the "average" or "expectable" pattern of adulthood, which is surely useful. Among other things, the mere existence of an average or modal pattern affects all adult expectations, goals, and aspirations. We compare ourselves to the expectable pattern and judge our progress (or lack of it) accordingly.

But the normative approach, however accurate, cannot give us a full description or explanation of adult life. For one thing, most of us are not "average." And even for those adults who do roughly follow the timing and sequence reflected in Table 12–1, there are wide variations in attitude, satisfaction, and inner growth. The normative approach simply does not inform us about such differences, or about the rules that govern individual choices and individual responses to the tasks of adulthood. So to come to a synthesis of our knowledge of adulthood, we must go beyond averages and look at individuals.

There are several ways I might tackle the problem of summarizing information on individual differences in adult trajectories or experiences. Ultimately, I will try my hand at a model that combines the normative information in Table 13–1 with an analysis of individual differences. But let me begin at a simpler level, by asking what aspects of adults, or their experiences, are predictive of "successful" or "unsuccessful" lives.

Success might be defined in any of a variety of ways. We might call someone successful who makes a lot of money or becomes famous. We might say someone is a successful adult if he or she has fully traversed the sequence of stages or levels I described in chapters 9 and 10. Or, most commonly, we might say that someone is successful if she is satisfied with her life.

## A First Look at Individual Differences: Life Satisfaction as a Measure of Success

One of the questions about adulthood that has most fascinated psychologists and sociologists is why some people are happier than others. Why do some adults have high subjective wellbeing or life satisfaction, while others are much less satisfied with their lives?

In the pursuit of answers to such questions, social scientists have devised dozens of measures of happiness, wellbeing, or life satisfaction (Diener, 1984). Some have used only a single question, such as "Taking all things together, how would you say things are these days—would you say you are very happy, pretty happy, or not too happy?" (Campbell, 1981). Others, such as Cantril (1965), give subjects a nine-rung ladder marked at the top with "best life for you" and at the bottom with "worst life for you." Each subject is asked to mark the rung that best represents her current life. Among researchers who use more than one question to tap life satisfaction, Bradburn's (1969) affect balance approach is one of the most widely used. Bradburn argues that overall life satisfaction reflects the combination of positive and negative feelings. His scale includes a set of items about negative emotions (loneliness, depression, boredom, restlessness, or being upset with criticism) and positive emotions (feeling on top of the world, excited or interested in something, pleased with an accomplishment, pride). The resultant sum of the positive and negative feelings Bradburn calls "affect balance."

Each of these measures captures a somewhat different facet of life satisfaction or happiness, but all of these measures normally correlate quite highly with one another, suggesting that there is a single dimension being tapped by all. Studies of happiness using these many measures also have yielded quite consistent findings.

### Age and Life Satisfaction

Interestingly, age seems to have very little systematic relationship to happiness or wellbeing (Stock, Okun, Haring, & Witter, 1983). Longitudinal data from the Duke studies (Palmore, 1981), covering the years from 45 to 75, illustrate this point (Figure 13–1). There is some suggestive evidence from other studies

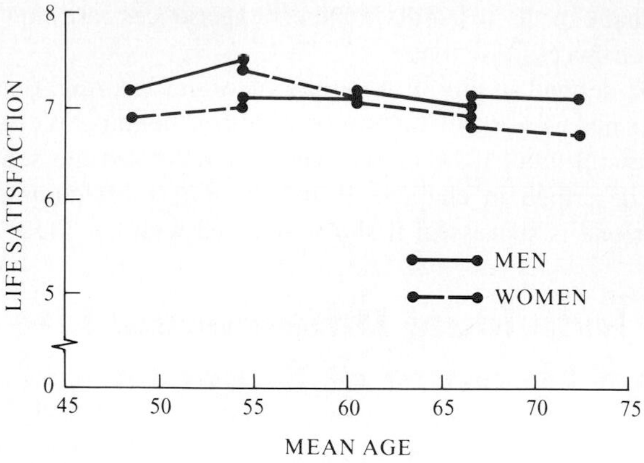


***Figure 13–1*** *In these cross-sequential data from the Duke Longitudinal Studies, you can see that there were no age changes in life satisfaction (on Cantril's "ladder") over the period from 47 to 73. Each line on this graph represents the score on life satisfaction for each age group at the beginning of the study, and again 6 years later. (Source: Palmore, Erdman,* Social Patterns in Normal Aging, *p. 98, Figure 7–2. Copyright © 1981 Duke University Press.)*

that younger adults may experience both positive and negative feelings more strongly (higher highs and lower lows) than do older adults. Older adults, on the other hand, may have higher affect balance than younger adults (Diener, 1984). But these age differences are neither large nor found consistently.

In contrast, many other demographic and personal variations among adults are related to their reported happiness or wellbeing. I've summarized the findings in Table 13–2, but let me comment further on a few of the especially interesting or significant patterns.

## Demographic Differences in Life Satisfaction

One of the items in the table that may surprise you is the statement that the effect of income on happiness appears to be relative rather than absolute. (Money really can't buy happiness after all!) If you have more money than others with whom you compare yourself, you are likely to be slightly happier than those who are lower on the comparative totem pole. But if everyone in your comparison group experiences a rise in income, such an increase in your ability to purchase goods and services will not make you happier (Campbell, 1981; Diener, 1984). The general lack of age differences in happiness is further evidence for the same point. Middle-aged adults, as a group, have much higher incomes than they did when they were younger, as well as being higher in income than the current younger cohort. But middle-aged adults are not on

**TABLE 13–2 Factors Associated with Life Satisfaction Among Adults**

| | |
|---|---|
| | **Demographic Variables** |
| Income | Higher income is associated with higher life satisfaction but the effect appears to be relative rather than absolute. |
| Education | A very weak relationship: higher education adults are only slightly more satisfied. |
| Gender | Essentially no difference, although women may have higher highs and lower lows than men. |
| Employment | Employed adults (including those employed as homemakers) are more satisfied than unemployed adults, even when income is matched. |
| Marital status | Married adults are more satisfied than unmarried. This difference is generally larger for men. |
| Parenthood | Either a zero or a slight negative effect: Adults with children are sometimes found to be slightly less happy. |
| | **Personal Qualities** |
| Personality or Temperament: | |
| Extraversion | Extraverted adults are higher in life satisfaction than introverts. |
| Neuroticism | Adults high in neuroticism are less satisfied than those low on this dimension. |
| Sense of personal control | Those adults who feel they can and do control their own choices and opportunities are more satisfied than those who think they are mostly controlled by outside forces. |
| Amount of social interaction | Adults with more social interactions or social contacts generally have higher life satisfaction than those with low levels of contact or interaction. |
| Quality of social interaction | Adults whose social interactions are more intimate and more supportive have higher satisfaction. This is especially true for marital interaction. If marital relationship is poor, life satisfaction is adversely affected. |
| Health | Those adults with better self-perceived health are more satisfied than those who perceive themselves as ill or disabled. This is especially important in later years of adulthood. |
| Religion | Adults who describe themselves as religious, or who say that religion is important in their lives, are more satisfied. |
| Life events | The more "negative" life changes an adult has recently experienced, the lower the life satisfaction. |
| Goals | Adults who are committed to very long-term goals, with little short-term reward, are less satisfied than are adults whose goals are shorter-term or less difficult to achieve. |

**Sources:** Many, but particularly Diener, 1984, and Campbell, 1981.

average more satisfied with their lives than are young adults. This makes sense if we assume that an adult's primary comparison group is his own cohort. Since the whole cohort has risen in income between the age of 20 and 45, there will be no overall increase in happiness. Only those adults who gained comparatively more than their cohort are likely to be more satisfied with their lives.

Combining income and education into a single analysis, Campbell (1981) reports the interesting finding from several large national surveys that income or standard of living is least predictive of wellbeing among the college-educated. Such a finding fits roughly with what Maslow might predict on the basis of his hierarchy of needs. College-educated adults are likely to earn enough money to take care of their basic physiological and safety needs. Once these more fundamental needs are met, higher-order needs emerge, such as the need for love, for self-esteem, and for self-actualization. And these higher needs are not readily met by more money.

## Personal Qualities as Predictors of Happiness

Among the most interesting effects listed in Table 13–2 are those connecting personality or temperament with life satisfaction. I have mentioned this connection in earlier chapters, but let me provide some specific numbers.

Costa and McCrae have found such relationships both concurrently and predictively in longitudinal studies of men (Costa & McCrae, 1980b; Costa, McCrae, & Norris, 1981). Those men who score higher on measures of extraversion and lower on measures of neuroticism described themselves as happier at first testing, and still described themselves as happier 10 to 17 years later when happiness was again measured. Some sample findings from these studies are given in Table 13–3. In related research, Carp (1985) found that among elderly adults, happiness among those who recently moved to living in public housing or in a

**TABLE 13–3 The Relationship Between Extraversion, Neuroticism, and Life Satisfaction**

| | *Correlation with Neuroticism* | *Correlation with Extraversion* |
|---|---|---|
| **Concurrent Relationships** | | |
| Scores on the Bradburn Affect Balance Scale: | | |
| Positive Affect | −.10* | .25* |
| Negative Affect | .34* | −.12* |
| Affect Balance | −.27* | .25* |
| **Predictive (Longitudinal) Relationships** | | |
| Scores on the Affect Balance Scale 10 years after Neuroticism and Extraversion were measured: | | |
| Positive Affect | −.08 | .23* |
| Negative Affect | .39* | .03 |
| Affect Balance | −.30* | .14* |
| Scores on a single measure of life satisfaction 10–17 years after Neuroticism and Extraversion were measured: | | |
| Life Satisfaction Score | −.08 | .35* |

**Note:** Those correlations marked with an asterisk are statistically significant at the .05 level or better.

**Sources:** Costa & McCrae, 1980b, data from Table 4, p. 674 and from text; Costa, McCrae, & Norris, 1981, data from Table 3, p. 81.

senior citizens' center could be predicted from measures of neuroticism and extraversion.

Paul Mussen and his colleagues (Mussen, Honzik, & Eichorn, 1982) have found some corroboration of these general findings in their analysis of life satisfaction among the mothers of the children who participated in the Berkeley Intergenerational Studies. The mothers were first interviewed and tested when they were around age 30, and then again 40 years later. A personality assessment of the mothers was derived from the age–30 contact, while life satisfaction was measured at the age–70 contact. Amazingly enough, the researchers found they could predict life satisfaction at age 70 from several qualities at age 30, including mental alertness, cheerfulness, self-assurance, poise, freshness (lack of fatigue), and "satisfaction with lot." Each of these correlations was around .30, even with social class differences removed from the correlation, reflecting a consistent, if small, relationship.

The third personality dimension listed in Table 13–2, a sense of personal control, has a similarly small but consistent relationship with life satisfaction. Those adults who feel they are in charge of their own lives and responsible for their own decisions are generally happier than those who feel that their lives are controlled by others, or by fate or chance. Furthermore, adults who feel that they have some choices and options are generally happier than those who perceive themselves as being trapped in circumstances they cannot control (Diener, 1984). You may recall that the sense of personal control is also part of the dimension of "hardiness" I talked about in chapter 11. Thus, adults high in "internal" rather than "external" control may be more satisfied with their lives in part because they are better able to deal with the major problems and life strains that come along.

Taken together, these studies tell us that it is possible to make some prediction of happiness in middle or old age from knowing something of the personality or temperament of young adults. In particular, some adults appear to meet the vicissitudes of life with a cheerful, outgoing attitude. I find these correlations extremely interesting, but before I make too much of them, two caveats are in order.

First, although these relationships have been found repeatedly on different samples, both longitudinally and concurrently, the correlations are not terribly large. At most, about 5% to 10% of the variation in reported happiness can be predicted by knowing an individual's characteristic extraversion, neuroticism, or sense of inner control. Being extraverted clearly does not guarantee happiness, just as a high level of neuroticism does not guarantee grumpiness or unhappiness.

Second, as I pointed out in Chapter 1, correlations do not describe causal relationships. For example, it is difficult to know whether extraverts are happier because they simply interpret more life experiences in a positive way, or whether happy people are more outgoing. Or, alternatively, extraversion may operate indirectly, by affecting the quality and quantity of relationships with others that an individual creates. The key to life satisfaction may be in the relationships rather than in the extraversion itself. The fact that extraversion can predict later happiness helps to rule out one of these causal chains: Extraversion seems to lead to happiness, rather than the other way around. But choosing between the direct and indirect effects is not so simple.

Certainly both the quantity and quality of relationships is related to life satisfaction (Campbell, 1981; Deimling & Harel, 1984; Diener, 1984; Veroff et al., 1981). And when socially isolated adults are helped to increase their total social contact, their life satisfaction increases (Fordyce, 1977), which suggests that social contact itself has a significant effect. But extraversion may have a separate, independent effect as well.

Similar intricacies are involved in interpreting the relationship between perceived health and life satisfaction. A direct effect is highly plausible, since adults whose health deteriorates report lowered happiness. But it is interesting that an adult's perception of health is a better predictor of happiness or life satisfaction than are more objective measures such as physicians' assessments or checklists of symptoms (Diener, 1984; Palmore, 1981). Since adults high in neuroticism are (among other things) more likely to be preoccupied with and negative about their own health, it is clear that perception of health may be influenced by personality as well as by actual health.

## Relative Importance of Predictors of Happiness

The list in Table 13–2, while informative, doesn't tell you how these different variables are weighted. Which factors are the most important? How do they add or interact?

The one thing that is clear is that there is no magic happiness pill. There is no one element in adult life that guarantees high life satisfaction, nor any one experience or quality that leads automatically to unhappiness. Happiness seems to be made up of a great many small things which are probably weighted differently by each person. All the demographic variables (income, gender, education, marital status) combined account for no more than about 10% of the variation in happiness (Diener, 1984), and even health and personality each account for no more than a similar 10%.

But of the variables listed in the table, the one that appears to be the single most potent variable in predicting overall happiness has been the person's reported happiness in marriage or family relationships (Campbell, 1981; Campbell, Converse, & Rodgers, 1976; Glenn & Weaver, 1981). Satisfaction with work has been consistently found to be a less powerful predictor of happiness, even among those for whom work commitment is typically high, such as highly educated men.

In his autobiography, Chrysler chairman Lee Iacocca makes this point clearly: "Yes, I've had a wonderful and successful career. But next to my family, it really hasn't mattered at all" (1984, p. 289). Robert Sears (1977) often heard similar comments from 60- to 70-year-old men he interviewed as part of Terman's 50-year longitudinal study of a group of gifted subjects. Sears reports that of six areas studied (family, occupation, friends, culture, service, and joy), "family experience was reported retrospectively to have been the one most

***Figure 13–2*** *These pleasant moments with family members, or with one's spouse, are the ones adults remember as being the biggest single ingredient in their overall life satisfaction. (Source: David M. Grossman.)*

important for securing satisfaction'' (p. 125–126). In several national surveys, the correlations between satisfaction with marriage or family life and overall life satisfaction are in the range of .40—.50, which means that about 20% of variation in happiness is attributable to this feature of adult life (Campbell, 1981; Glenn & Weaver, 1981).

Since the amount of social contact is also related to happiness, it appears that the size and variety of your social network, as well as the quality of social support available in your key intimate relationships, not only affects your ability to handle stress or life change, but also strongly affects your ongoing level of life satisfaction or happiness.

# Other Measures of Success

The degree of happiness an adult experiences may be one measure of success in the adult years. But there are other ways of defining successful adulthood that rely more on professional assessments of an individual's psychological health than on self-reports of happiness. Two approaches, both involving analyses of rich longitudinal data, are particularly interesting.

Researchers working with the Berkeley longitudinal data have developed a measure of ideal adult adjustment or ''psychological health'' based on the Q sort of personality I described in chapter 9. In this research, psychotherapists and theorists agreed on the pattern of qualities of an optimally healthy person, which included the "capacity for work and for satisfying interpersonal relationships, a sense of moral purpose, and a realistic perception of self and society" (Peskin & Livson, 1981, p. 156). According to this view, ideally healthy adults are high in warmth, compassion, dependability, and responsibility, insight, productivity, candor, and calmness. They value their own independence and autonomy as well as intellectual skill, and behave in a sympathetic and considerate manner, consistent with their own personal standards and ethics.

The Q sort for each subject in the study could then be compared to this "ideal" profile, and each adult could be given a score on psychological health. When this measure was correlated with the subjects' reported satisfaction with work, with family life, and with the closeness or affection in marriage, researchers found that adults who are rated by observers as having "healthy" qualities also describe themselves as more satisfied with their lives.

The Berkeley researchers (Livson & Peskin, 1981; Peskin & Livson, 1981) were also able to trace some of the precursors of psychological health in childhood and adolescence. In general, adults who were higher in psychological health at age 30 or 40 grew up with parents who were rated as more open minded, more intellectually competent, with good marital relationships. Their mothers were typically warmer, more giving and nondefensive, more pleasant and poised. Those adults who were low in psychological health at 40 came from families that were more negative and conflictful, less cheerful (Siegelman, Block, Block, & von der Lippe, 1970).

As teenagers, adults who went on to be high in psychological health at 40 were rated as intellectually competent. Healthy men were also rated as high in responsibility as teenagers, as low in defensiveness, and as somewhat amoralistic. For women, the key predictors of later psychological health were a tendency not to complain about their health and higher scores on the masculine end of a masculinity-femininity scale (Livson & Peskin, 1981).

It is interesting that intellectual competence or interest appears so consistently as a predictor of later psychological health. Intelligence is only very weakly related to self-reports of life satisfaction, but it is consistently related to ratings of psychological health. A willingness to break the rules a bit (especially for girls) is also part of the equation, suggesting the interesting hypothesis that moving beyond the "conformist" stage of ego development may be a key to long range psychological health. Some capacity for intellectual analysis or introspection may be a prerequisite for such a transition, a hypothesis I will return to shortly.

A somewhat different look at psychological adjustment as a measure of success in adulthood comes from Vaillant's (1977a) assessment of the group of Harvard students studied from college age through about age 50 as part of the Grant Study. Using all the information available on these 100 men over the 25 years of the study, Vaillant rated each subject on a 32-item Adult Adjustment Scale, which describes specific features of an *unsuccessful* or maladjusted adult life. Scale elements included

Failure to receive steady promotion or increasing responsibility, if possible, every five years since graduation.

Has not actively participated over the years in extracurricular public service activities.

Occupational success clearly does not equal father's.

Failed to achieve 10 years or more of marriage (without separation) or failed to express overt satisfaction with that marriage on two or more occasions after the first year.

One-third or more of children are markedly underperforming scholastically, delinquent, or getting psychiatric care.

Maintained no contact with surviving family of origin, except by duty or necessity.

For more than half of years described, did not use full allotted vacation time or spent it at home doing chores or on dutiful visits to relatives.

Evidence of detrimental . . . use of alcohol, or use of sedative or stimulant drugs weekly for more than three years, or more than six ounces of hard liquor a day for three years, or use of tranquilizers for more than a year.

On the average misses five or more workdays a year due to illness. (Vaillant, 1977a, pp. 389–390)

When the 30 men with the best scores on these items (those who showed the fewest such maladaptive characteristics) were then compared to the 30 men with the worst (highest) scores, the findings in Table 13–4 emerged. The list in the upper part of this table may be somewhat confusing. Listed here are those of the 32 items in the Adjustment Scale on which high scorers and low scorers showed the widest divergence. Out of all the 32 items, then, these are the ones that most fully carry the difference between a well adjusted and a less well-adjusted man. The lower part of the table shows the results on a set of independent measures that also discriminated between these "successful" and "unsuccessful" men.

As you can see, worst-outcome men are likely to be dissatisfied with their lives, so these measures of success are at least partially linked to the research on life satisfaction. Many of the other variables that are related to life satisfaction also appear in this list, including poor physical health, low marital satisfaction, and some indication of neuroticism (use of immature defenses, pessimism, self-doubt). These men came from relatively unloving families, and were likely to be less mature or psychologically healthy at college age as well as later.

What emerges from these two studies is a strong sense that Freud was right when he said that the key to a successful adulthood lay in the capacity for working and loving. Those young adults who, by dint of inborn temperament or early family history, are able to create and sustain loving, intimate relationships with a spouse, with friends, with their children, and who have both the intellectual enthusiasm and the capacity for commitment required for satisfying work, are much more likely to show increasing maturity and better health over the adult years.

**TABLE 13–4 Differences Between Men with the "Best" and "Worst" Outcomes on the Adult Adjustment Scale in Vaillant's Study of Harvard Men in the Grant Study**

| | Best Outcomes | Worst Outcomes |
|---|---|---|
| *Items from the Adjustment Scale itself:* | | |
| No steady career progress | 10% | 57% |
| Real income less than father's at same age | 13% | 53% |
| Less than 20 years of enjoyable marriage | 23% | 77% |
| No real evidence of friends | 0% | 30% |
| Heavy use of alcohol and/or tranquilizers | 17% | 52% |
| *Other pieces of information about the subjects not included in the Adjustment Scale:* | | |
| Ever unemployed for 3 months | 3% | 47% |
| 10 or more vignettes (in interviews and questionnaires) of passivity, dependence, pessimism, self-doubt, or fear of sex | 3% | 50% |
| Dissatisfied with life | 0% | 40% |
| Often used immature defenses | 0 | 60% |
| Clinical evidence of psychopathology | 3% | 67% |
| Children have social and emotional problems | 23% | 67% |
| Poor physical health or dead (by age 50) | 3% | 50% |
| Dominated by mother in adult life | 0% | 40% |
| Failure to marry by 30 | 3% | 37% |
| Average yearly charitable contribution | $3,000 | $500 |

**Source:** Adapted from Vaillant, 1977a, Table 4, p. 275, with added items from Vaillant 1977b. From *Adaptation to Life* by George E. Vaillant. Copyright © 1977 by George E. Vaillant. By permission of Little, Brown and Company. (Adaptation approved by author.)

These longitudinal studies take us beyond the somewhat superficial (and non-developmental) study of life satisfaction and begin to point to some of the elements that may affect the way in which different adults will move through the sequence of tasks outlined in Table 13–1. But there is still a great deal of distance to be traveled between these studies of mental health in adulthood and a full model describing and explaining the many possible pathways through adulthood. As a final step in this synthesis, let me try my hand at such a model.

## A Model of Adult Growth and Development: Trajectories and Pathways

On the several occasions when I have tried to create a visual picture of the pathways of adult development, it has been clear that no two-dimensional drawing, however skillful, can successfully depict the process. Three dimensions, at least, are required, and even that does not quite capture the many possibilities and pathways. Since three- and four-dimensional models are impossible to depict on these two-dimensional pages, I shall have to content myself with a set of four propositions, several of which can be converted into schematic drawings.

---

Proposition 1: There are shared, basic, sequential physical and psychological developments occurring during adulthood, roughly (but not precisely) age-linked.

---

The sequences of physical and mental changes summarized in the top two rows of Table 13–1 surely belong in this category. Whatever other processes may influence adult life, it is clear that the entire journey is occurring along a road that has certain common features. The body and the mind change in predictable ways with age. These changes, in turn, affect the way adults define themselves and the way they experience the world around them. As I said earlier, I also place the sequence of changes in self-definitions or meaning systems outlined by Loevinger, Fowler, and others in this same category. The difference is that unlike physical and mental changes, the process of ego development or spiritual change is not an inevitable accompaniment of aging, but a *possibility* or potentiality.

Within the general confines of these basic processes and sequences of development, however, there are many individual pathways—many possible sequences of roles and relationships, many different levels of growth or life satisfaction or "success." Which brings me to the second major proposition:

---

Proposition 2: Each adult's development occurs primarily within a specific pathway or trajectory, strongly influenced by the starting conditions of education, family background, ethnicity, intelligence, and personality.

---

I can best depict this individuality by borrowing from Waddington (1957) the image of the **epigenetic landscape**, shown in Figure 13–3. (Waddington introduced this idea in a discussion of the strongly "canalized" development of the infant years, but the same general concept can serve for a discussion of adulthood.)

The original Waddington image, like Figure 13–3, was of a mountain down which ran a series of gullies. In this metaphor, old age represents the bottom of the mountain, and early adulthood represents the top. Each of us, in our adult years, must somehow make our way down this mountain. Since we are all going down the same mountain (following the same basic "rules" of physical, mental, and spiritual development), all journeys down the mountain will have some features in common. But this metaphor also allows for wide variations in the specific events and outcomes of the journey.

Imagine a marble placed at the top of the mountain. The particular pathway it follows to the bottom of the mountain will be heavily determined by the

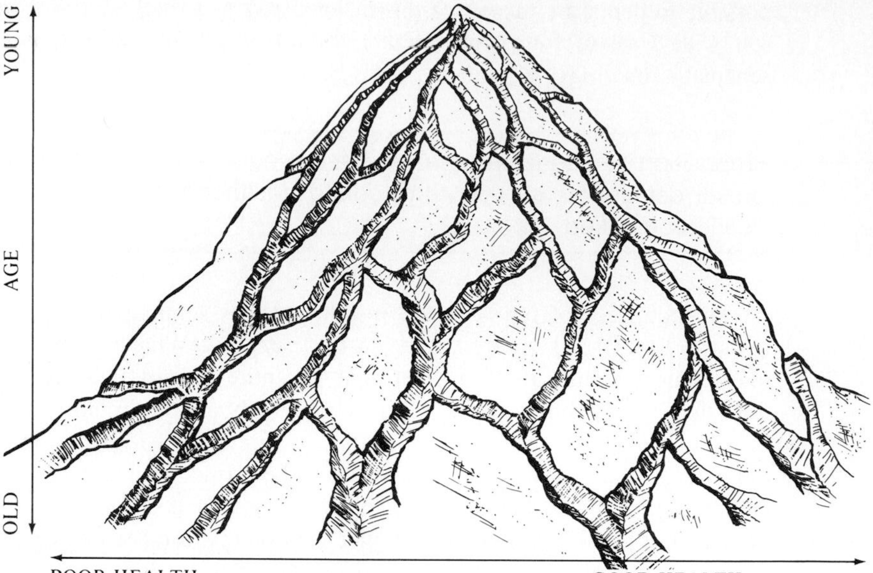


**Figure 13–3** *The image of a mountain with gullies running down it is one way to depict the alternative pathways through adulthood. The journey down the mountain (from youth to old age) can begin in any one of many tracks. As the adult moves down that track, there are periods of stability and choice points at which the individual may shift from one track to another.*

gully in which it starts. If I also assume that the main pathways are deeper than the side tracks, then shifting from the track in which one starts is less probable than continuing along the same track. Nonetheless, the presence of choice points or junctions does make it possible for a particular marble to start in any gully and still end up at the bottom of the mountain at almost any point. Given a particular starting point, some pathways and some outcomes are much more likely than others. But many possible pathways diverge from any onc gully.

This model obviously takes us back to the ideas and the evidence I presented in chapter 2. The research evidence points quite clearly to the general statement that good health and greater psychological maturity in late adulthood are much more likely for those adults who begin this journey with reasonable intelligence, a good education, an extraverted, nonneurotic temperament, and an openness to change. Thus, young adults who start the journey with few of these resources will begin in the gullies at the left-hand side of the mountain, while those who start out with more of these resources will begin in the right-hand gullies. Since we know that intelligence, education, and personality are all somewhat stable characteristics, it is reasonable to depict the main pathways as deep or relatively resistant to change. But we also know that consistency is not perfect. Adults do change, do grow and mature or regress and deteriorate. While such change is possible at any point in adulthood, it seems to be particularly likely at certain times, when the system becomes unbalanced in some fashion.

---

Proposition 3: Each pathway is made up of a series of alternating episodes of stable life structure and disequilibrium.

---

In the mountain-and-gully metaphor, the stable life structures are reflected in the long straight stretches between junction points, while the junctions represent the disequilibria. This aspect of the model is obviously borrowed from Levinson's theory of adult personality development (1978, 1980). Like Levinson, I conceive of each stable life structure as a balance achieved by an individual among the collection of role demands she is then facing, given the skills and temperamental qualities at her command. This balance is normally reflected in a stable externally observable life pattern—getting up at a particular time every day to get the kids off to school, going off to your job, doing the grocery shopping on Saturday, having dinner with your mother every Sunday, going out to dinner with your spouse every Valentine's Day, or whatever. These patterns are not totally fixed, of course. We all make small adjustments regularly, as demands or opportunities change. But there do appear to be times in each adult's life when a temporary balance is achieved.

**The Relationship of Stable Periods and Age.** These periods of stability (and the alternating periods of disequilibrium or transition) appear to be related to age. I've suggested such a rough age-linkage in Figure 13–3 by showing the choice points more frequently at certain levels on the mountain than at others. But I think this age-linkage is much more approximate than Levinson originally proposed. The evidence I have described throughout the book simply does not conform well to the strict age-grading of stability and transition that Levinson suggests.

Nonetheless, the content of the stable structures at each approximate age, and the issues dealt with during each transition, seem to be somewhat predictable (after all, we are going down the same mountain). There is a set of tasks or issues that confront most adults in a particular sequence as they age, as I outlined in Table 13–1. In early adulthood this includes separating from one's family of origin, forming one's own family and creating a stable central partnership, and establishing satisfying work.

In middle adulthood the tasks include launching one's children into independence, caring for aging parents, redefining parental and spousal roles, exploring one's own inner nature, coming to terms with the body's aging and with the death of one's parents. An adult who follows the modal "social clock" will thus be likely to encounter transitions at particular ages, and to deal with shared issues at each transition. But I am not persuaded that there is only one order, or only one set of ages, at which those tasks are or can be confronted. Among other things, it appears that (in our culture at least, for cohorts born in the early part of this century) women may deal with the tasks of identity and intimacy in a different order than do men. In this respect the mountain-and-gully model is misleading since it does not convey variability in timing of major choice points that clearly does exist, such as when an adult does not marry, or does not have children until his or her 30s or 40s, or becomes physically disabled, or widowed, or ill in his early adult years, or the like.

But whatever the variations in timing, it still appears to me to be valid to describe adult life as alternating between periods of stability and transition.

**Disequilibrium.** The periods of disequilibrium may be triggered by any one (or more than one) of the following (sketched on the left-hand side of Figure 13–4).

*Role changes*, such as marriage, or the birth of a child, or the departure of the last child from home, or retirement, changes in jobs, and so on.

*Asynchrony of timing* in the several different dimensions of adult change or growth. This is part of Perun and Bielby's timing model of development, which I talked about in chapter 3. When physical development, or mental development, or role patterns are not synchronous, there is tension or disequilibrium in the system. Being significantly ''off time'' in any one dimension of adulthood (physical, mental, role sequence, relationship change, or the like) creates such asynchrony automatically, and is thus associated with higher rates of stress. Having a first child in your late 30s is not only a role change, it is also an asynchronous role change, which should increase the likelihood of a major disequilibrium. In a recent paper, Gurin and Brim (1984) offer the interesting hypothesis that on-time role changes, in fact, seldom trigger major crises or self-reexamination precisely because, since such changes are shared with one's peers, the individual can easily explain both the change and the strain it may cause as originating ''outside'' of himself. Non-normative changes, in contrast, are hard to explain away in any way except with reference to one's self—your own choices, failures, or successes. These more individual experiences, then, are far more likely than the normative ones to bring about reassessment or redefinition of the self, of values, of systems of meaning.

*Lack of match* between the demands of a particular set of roles and an adult's own temperament or personality. This is, in some sense, another kind of asynchrony. The study by Florine Livson of the several ''pathways'' to high-level health in middle age that I described in chapter 6 is one example of matching or nonmatching patterns. As you'll recall, Livson found that those adults who looked psychologically health at 50, but had shown signs of distress or disturbance at 40, were likely to be those whose qualities as teenagers didn't match the then-prevalent sex roles. The less social and more intellectual young women in this group tried to fit into a mold of full-time homemaking and found it distressing; the more creative and emotional men tried to fit into the mold of the gray-flannel-suit society and were disturbed at 40. Both groups went through

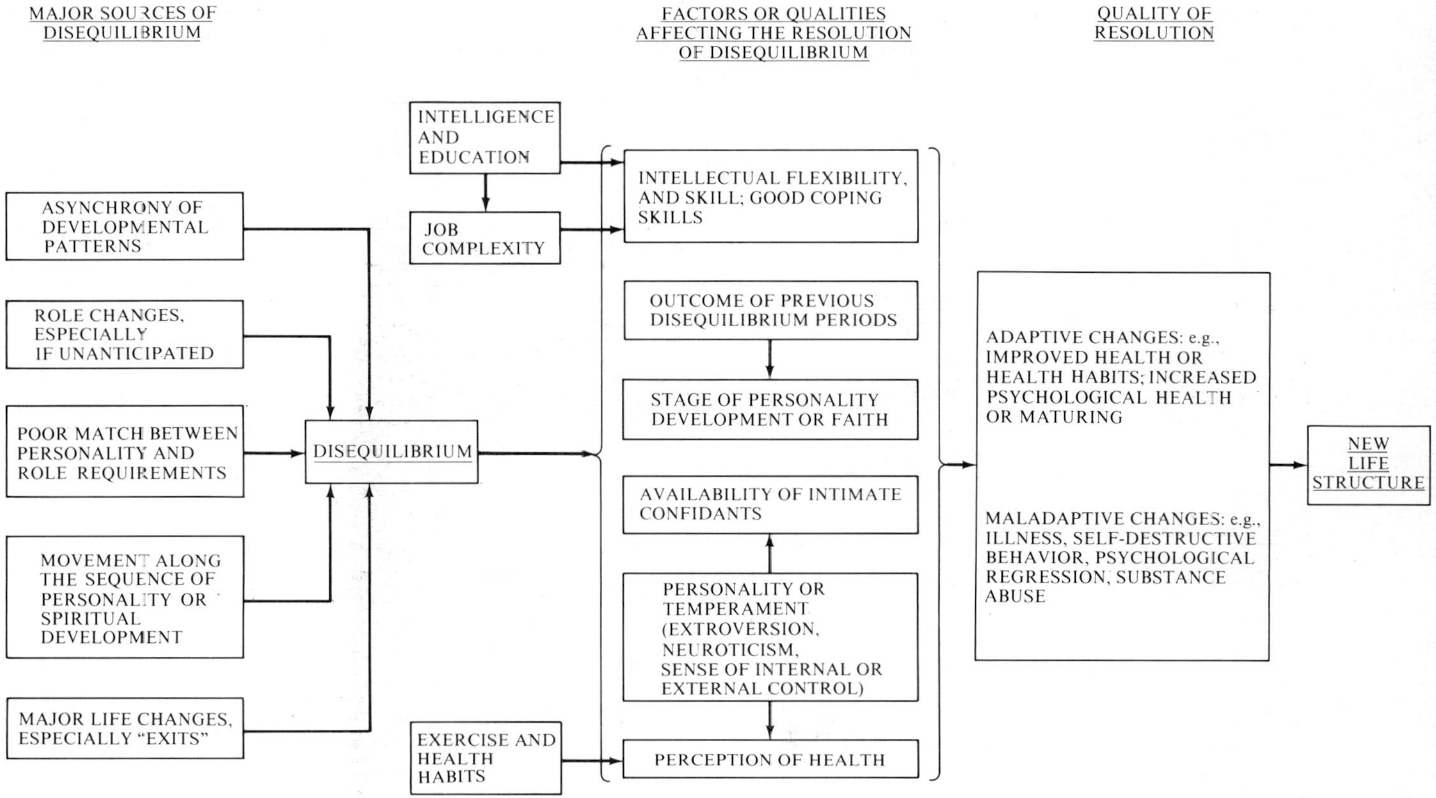


**Figure 13–4** *A model of disequilibrium and its resolution. I am suggesting that such a process occurs repeatedly during adulthood, with each such transition affecting the pathway (the gully) along which the adult then moves.*

a process in their 40s of freeing themselves of the constraints of those early, ill-fitting roles, and emerged at 50 looking very much put together.

Some findings I reported a few pages ago, also from the Berkeley studies, provide further evidence: Those young women who did not fit well into the then-prevailing pattern of traditional femininity when in their late teens actually looked healthier at 40 than did those who had experienced a better match early on. If one of the necessary ingredients in the emergence of health or maturity is the successful traversing of several periods of disequilibrium/reassessment, then a mismatch may be initially uncomfortable but ultimately fruitful. At the very least, the lack of a good match clearly produces strain in the system. One can only sustain a nonmatching life structure for so long before the system breaks down.

*Major life changes or major chronic stresses,* particularly "exits" such as the death of a close family member or friend, or the loss of a friendship or love relationship. While unanticipated or off-time changes may be the most difficult in most instances, even some anticipated changes, such as the death of your parents when you are in your 40s or 50s, still call for significant reassessment and reorganization.

Finally, disequilibrium can be triggered by a *change in inner psychological tasks*, such as any movement along the dimension described by Erikson or Levinson, or by Fowler's stages of faith. Such inner changes typically occur in response to the disequilibrium-causing agents I have just described. But once begun, a transition such as from conformist to conscientious ego structure, or from individuative to conjunctive faith, carries its own disequilibrium. Any new stable life structure that emerges at the end of the disequilibrium period must be built on the new sense of self, or faith, that has evolved.

The severity of the disequilibrium—whether the individual experiences it as a crisis or merely as a rather transitory phase—seems to depend on at least two things: the number of different sources of disequilibrium and the individual's own personality and coping skills (as I outlined in chapter 11). When there is a pile-up of disequilibrium-producing events, such as changes in roles, major relationship losses, and asynchronous physical changes, any individual is likely to experience a major transition. But the tendency to respond to this as a crisis may also reflect relatively high levels of neuroticism, low levels of extraversion, or the lack of effective coping skills.

---

Proposition 4: The outcome of a period of disequilibrium may be either positive (psychological growth, maturity, improved health, etc.), neutral, or negative (regression or immaturity, ill health, or the like).

---

Each choice point on this mountain has several avenues opening from it. Which of these several kinds of outcome may occur at any choice point—which channel one follows—appears to be influenced by a wide range of variables, which I have sketched in the middle of Figure 13–4.

***Figure 13–5*** *Not all "resolutions" of disequilibrium are adaptive or positive. Some, like increasing alcohol or drug usage, may temporarily deaden the pain or help to repress the problem, but leave the adult less able to cope with both current or future tasks. (Source: Mimi Forsyth, Monkmeyer Press.)*

Intellectual flexibility or skill seems to be a particularly critical ingredient in leading to the later stages of maturity and growth that Vaillant or Loevinger describe. Janet Giele puts it well:

> It is the degree of social complexity on the job or in other aspects of everyday life that appears critical. Those who must learn a great deal and adapt to many different roles seem to be the most concerned with trying to evolve an abstract self, conscience, or life structure that can integrate all these discrete events. By contrast, those with a simple job, limited by meager education and narrow contacts, are less apt to experience aging as a process that enhances autonomy or elaborates one's mental powers. (1982a, p. 8)

As I have suggested in Figure 13–4, an individual's level of flexibility is affected by the complexity of her job, either a job outside the home or even the complexity of housework (Schooler, 1984), while the job complexity is in turn partially determined by the level of original education she has attained.

Underlying temperamental tendencies also seem to be a key ingredient. Adults who are high in what Costa and McCrae call neuroticism appear to be more likely to respond to disequilibrium by increases in substance abuse, illness, depression, or regressive patterns of defense. Adults with less neurotic or more extraverted temperament, in contrast, respond to disequilibrium by reaching out to others, by searching for constructive solutions.

The availability of close supportive confidants is another key variable, clearly not independent of temperament. Adults who lack close friends or the supportive intimacy of a good marriage are more likely to have serious physical ailments in midlife or to have significant emotional disturbances, to drink or use drugs and to use more immature forms of defense (Vaillant, 1977a). Such friendless or lonely adults more often come from unloving and unsupportive families, but even such a poor early environment can be more readily overcome if the adult manages to form at least one close, intimate relationship. Vaillant, in his longitudinal study of Harvard men, describes several men who had grown up in unloving or highly stressful families, who were withdrawn or even fairly neurotic as college students, who nonetheless went on to become "successful" and emotionally mature adults. One of the common ingredients in the lives of these men, especially compared to those with similar backgrounds who had poorer outcomes, was the presence of a "healing" relationship with a spouse.

Health may also make some difference in the way an adult responds to a period of disequilibrium. Poor health reduces options; it also reduces your level of energy, which affects the range of coping strategies open to you or the eventual life structures you can create.

Finally, I am suggesting in this figure that the effects of these several disequilibrium periods are cumulative. Such a cumulative effect of earlier stages or transitions is a key element in Erikson's theory of development, as you'll recall from chapter 3. Unresolved conflicts and dilemmas remain as unfinished business, as excess emotional baggage that make each succeeding stage more difficult to resolve successfully. Vaillant and others who have studied adults from childhood through midlife have found some support for this notion. Men in the Grant Study who could reasonably be described as having failed to develop "trust" in their early childhood did have many more difficulties in adulthood. They were more pessimistic, self-doubting, passive, and dependent as adults, and showed many more maladaptive or unsuccessful outcomes compared to those with more "trusting" childhoods.

I think Erikson is right, but I have in mind other varieties of cumulative effect, too. For example, one possible result of a disequilibrium (perhaps particularly transitions at midlife) might be the adoption of a regular exercise plan. This would not only change the subsequent life structure, it would also be likely to increase the individual's actual health or perception of health. The next transition point would then be faced with a different set of resources. For

***Figure 13–6*** *Choosing to get more education, as these adults are doing, may be an adaptive response to a current problem or task. It is also likely to increase the range of resources an adult has available when facing subsequent tasks. Thus, the choices we make at each point along the way accumulate and interact with one another. (Source: Hugh Rogers, Monkmeyer Press.)*

another adult, one of the resolutions of a prior disequilibrium point might be a change to a more complex job or a return to school. Such a change not only alters the life structure, it also increases the adult's intellectual flexibility, which in turn affects the range of cognitive coping skills in his repertoire. The next transition might thus be faced more adaptively.

It is important for me to emphasize that the range of possible outcomes I have labeled "adaptive" or "maladaptive" changes are not isomorphic with happiness or unhappiness. Maladaptive changes, such as illness, substance abuse, suicide attempts, or depression, obviously are correlated with unhappiness. But such adaptive changes as improved health habits, increased social activity, or movement along the sequence of changes in ego or spiritual development, are not uniformly associated with increases in happiness. McCrae and Costa, for example (1983), did not find that adults who were at the conscientious or higher levels of ego development reported any higher affect balance than did adults at the conformist stage. Thus, profound changes can result from a disequilibrium period without such changes being reflected in alterations of overall happiness or life satisfaction. Instead, a change in ego development stage may alter the criteria of happiness the person applies to his life. As McCrae and Costa said:

> We suggest that the quality and quantity of happiness do not vary with levels of maturity, but that the circumstances that occasion happiness or unhappiness, the criteria

of satisfaction or dissatisfaction with life, may vary with ego level. The needs and concerns, aspirations and irritations of more mature individuals will doubtless be different—more subtle, more individualistic, less egocentric. The less psychologically mature person may evaluate his or her life in terms of money, status, and sex; the more mature, in terms of achievement, altruism, and love. (1983, p. 247)

Maturing clearly does not make an adult happy, as demonstrated by the lack of correlation between age and happiness. Maturing and other adaptive changes alter the agenda, and thus alter the life structures we create and the way we evaluate those life structures.

## Five Young People: Some Forward Predictions

With this model in mind, is it possible to make any predictions about the course of adulthood for the five young people I introduced at the beginning of chapter 2? Certainly unexpected future events will have an impact on their passage through the years, but some reasonable guesses are certainly possible.

Tom Kleck, the extraverted, bright, working class young man, has already, by age 22, gotten more education than his father had and has a more complex job. He is also open to new experiences, willing to experiment, low in neuroticism. Certainly he begins his trip down the mountain in a gully fairly far to the right. The fact that he has already established an apparently satisfying relationship with his girlfriend also bodes well. The most straightforward prediction would be that he would make fairly rapid progress in his career for the next 10 or 15 years, reaching his career peak by about age 40. He is likely to be accompanied on this journey by a reasonably large convoy of friends and family, which will make passage through the several transitions somewhat smoother. In general, I would expect Tom to be fairly happy as an adult. I also expect that he will mature. His openness to new experience, his willingness to buck tradition, are two qualities that especially point in this direction. Such maturing may be particularly likely if Tom has to face some major life changes or disequilibria.

Cathy Stevens (the All-American Girl), in contrast, is likely to be happy, but is probably less likely to mature. She is following a traditional social clock, marrying fairly early, having her children at normative times, beginning work only in her 30s or later. For her, some of the issues of identity and independence will be postponed until her 40s or even her 50s. The fact that she is likely to be economically quite well off will buffer her against some of the strains of the roles of wife/mother/worker, thus maintaining the life structure of her 20s or 30s for a longer period. Stability is also indicated by the fact that Cathy's temperament (extraverted, low neuroticism) matches quite well the roles she anticipates filling. For her, the most significant disequilibrium may occur at 40 or 50 (as was true for Eleanor Roosevelt), when the role demands of motherhood will wane. If her parents should die when she is in that age range, or some other disequilibrium-producing event coincides with the role changes, she is likely to experience a period of depression or distress. Whether she emerges from that time with adaptive growth or not will depend on all the factors I've just listed. She enters the process, like Tom Kleck, with a range of excellent resources, so the likelihood of truly maladaptive responses is not large. But her generally conventional approach may reflect greater resistance to change than is true of Tom.

A quite different prediction can be made for Laura Rogers, who was a mother at 16 and divorced by 22. She has few resources and begins the journey down the mountain in a left-hand track. The sorts of stresses and traumas Laura has already faced can have the effect of producing greater maturity. But in Laura's case, given her temperament (high in neuroticism), her lack of education, and the "off timeness" of her family life cycle, the greater likelihood is for maladaptive changes. Several events could change that prognosis, however, chief among them the advent a satisfying and supportive second marriage. She has several close friendships, so she is obviously capable of establishing an intimate relationship. Another "lucky" event would be a job that challenged her or the opportunity to go back to school. It is not so clear, though, that Laura would seize such opportunities if they were offered. She is low in "hardiness." She sees the world as largely outside of her own control, and this attitude will make adaptive growth and maturing much less likely.

Making predictions about Walter Washington, the black, inner-city, former basketball player, is harder, in part because he has such a mixture of qualities. He shows the kind of intellectual interest and determination that is often associated with psychological growth and health. In addition, his pursuit of further schooling, and the more complex job he is likely to end up in because of that schooling, predict a high level of cognitive complexity. On the positive side of the ledger there is also his relatively low level of neuroticism. At the same time, Walter is quite introverted, and has some trouble establishing really intimate relationships with other people. And, of course, he is black, with all the continuing experience of discrimination that still may imply. My prediction is that Walter will be quite successful in his work, achieving satisfaction from that success. But should Walter encounter some really unexpected life change, or when his mother dies, he is likely to have more difficulty dealing with the stress than would someone with stronger social support systems. Walter has the intellectual coping skills that would assist him, but not the skill to form the relationships that would be beneficial. This is a man who may very well have a classic midlife crisis, but his inner resources are good enough that he may emerge from such an experience strengthened by it.

Chris Linton, the highly intellectual, introverted law student, also has an interesting mixture of qualities. In some respects he begins adulthood with a high chance of external success. He is extremely bright, has an excellent education, and possesses the drive to succeed. He will probably become quite wealthy. But he is also likely to be fairly dissatisfied and unhappy most of the time. Like Walter, faced with the inevitable disequilibria in his future, Chris will have the intellectual skill to analyze the alternatives, but he is likely to lack the friendships and intimate relationships to buffer him from the effects of the stress. Unlike Walter, who is low in neuroticism, Chris's characteristic approach to problems is pessimistic or negative. I will not be surprised if he has a heart attack at 45 or develops some other chronic illness, such as an ulcer. Nor would I be surprised if he became an alcoholic. Barring that, he may have serious difficulties at retirement, when his self-definition through work is lost. What could save him from these maladaptive outcomes, among other things, would be a strong, secure, supportive marriage, or even a close relationship with a mentor or friend. Given his personality, the chances of his finding a partner who could provide such unconditional support is not great. But it is possible.

You may have gathered in what I have said about these five young people that I think that some stress or disequilibrium is necessary for growth or maturity to occur. Stable life structures (including stability in stage of ego development or faith) remain in place so long as they work, so long as they provide balance in the system. Fortunately, the normal course of adult life contains a number of inescapable, built-in stresses or changes. So every adult must cope with some transitions or potential disequilibrating experiences. The ideal arrangement for maximum growth seems to be for those stresses or disequilibria to be substantial enough to stretch the capacity of the individual to cope, but not to overwhelm the adult's resources. An adult who begins life with more personal resources—intellectual, temperamental, physical—can respond with maturing to more complex or pervasive transitions. Other adults, like Laura Rogers, have few resources and are likely to be overwhelmed by the ordinary sequence of life changes, let alone the off-time sequence of experiences she is already coping with.

## A Last Look at the Model

I am sure it is clear to you already that the model I have sketched in this chapter, complex as it is, is nonetheless too simplistic. It is doubtless also too culture-specific, although I have tried to state the elements of the model broadly enough to encompass patterns in other cultures. It may also be quite wrong in a number of respects. Among other things, I have assumed throughout this discussion that something like Loevinger's sequence of ego development stages actually exists, and that all adults mature in this pattern if they mature at all. But as you know from chapters 9 and 10, that assumption is based on quite limited evidence.

Despite these obvious limitations, however, the model may give you some sense of the ''rules'' or ''laws'' that seem to govern the richness and variety of adult lives. In the midst of a bewildering array of adult patterns there does appear to be order, but the order is not so much in fixed, age-related sequences of events as in *process*. To understand adult development it is useful to uncover the ways in which all pathways, all gullies, are alike. But it is equally important to understand those factors and processes that affect the choices an adult will have, and the way she will respond to those choices. Perhaps the most remarkable thing about this journey is that with all its potential pitfalls and dilemmas, most adults pass through it with reasonable happiness and satisfaction, acquiring a modicum of wisdom along the way. May you enjoy your own journey.

## Summary

1. Taking a normative approach to the synthesis of information about adulthood, we can identify several age-related patterns or sequences that appear to be maturationally based or developmental in character.

2. Sequences of physical and mental changes appear to be maturationally based, while the sequence of personality change and spiritual development may reflect basic underlying processes that emerge over time.

3. Role sequences, in contrast, may be age-linked and widely shared but they are a product of the specific culture.

4. Early adulthood, from 20 to at least 40, is marked by dominance of family, work, and sex roles. Late adulthood (from 65 on) is marked by shared physical and mental changes. The period in between may be the most "free," providing the opportunity for greatest personal growth.

5. Life satisfaction is not strongly related to age, however, although the ingredients in satisfaction undoubtedly change with age.

6. More highly satisfied adults are likely to have relatively higher income than their peers, to be slightly better educated, to be employed, and to married. They are more likely to be extroverted, to be low in neuroticism, and to have a sense of personal control. They are also higher in quantity and quality of social interactions, are healthier, are more likely to be religious and to have achievable, short-term goals.

7. The causal links among these various factors, and between these predictors and life satisfaction, are complex and bidirectional. For example, greater life satisfaction or happiness may lead to increased contact with others, as much as the other way around.

8. No one predictor of happiness accounts for a very large percentage of the variation in satisfaction among adults. Individual happiness is composed of many ingredients, many of them highly individual.

9. Adults rated as psychologically healthy or adjusted are likely to have come from warm, affectionate families and to have had histories of intellectual competence or interest.

10. A preliminary model of adult development includes the metaphor of a mountain with gullies running down it. Each adult, with his own combination of beginning characteristics, moves down the mountain (through adulthood) in a particular gully, somewhat resistant to change.

11. Each pathway (gully) can also be thought of as being made up of alternating periods of stable life structures and disequilibrium periods. During the disequilibria, the adult may shift to another track or gully, or continue along the same pathway.

12. In any one culture, the stable periods are age-linked because they are largely defined by the set of family and work roles assumed by adults of particular ages.

13. Disequilibrium may be triggered by role changes, by asynchrony in timing of the several aspects of development, by a lack of match between an individual's characteristics and particular role demands, by unanticipated life changes or stress, and by psychological growth such as movement to a new level in Loevinger's stages of ego development.

14. Whether the outcome of a period of disequilibrium will be positive/adaptive, or

negative/maladaptive, or neutral, will depend on the intellectual flexibility and coping resources of the individual, underlying temperamental qualities, availability of close, supportive confidants, physical health, and the outcomes of previous disequilibrium periods.

## Suggested Readings

BLOCK, J. (1971). *Lives through time.* Berkeley, CA: Bancroft.

Like Vaillant's description of the Grant Study men, Block's discussion of the early results of the Berkeley/Oakland longitudinal study gives some sense of the elements that affect the pathways of adulthood. At the time this book was written, the subjects were only in their 30s, so this does not describe as long a span of adult years as does Vaillant's discussion, but it is still of great interest.

VAILLANT, G. E. (1977). *Adaptation to life.* Boston: Little, Brown.

I have recommended this book before, so you may already have dipped into it. I recommend it again here because it is one of the really good descriptions of actual lives over time.

# Glossary

**Achievement Motive** The disposition to perform activities in competition with a standard of excellence.

**Adulthood** Arbitrarily defined here as the period from age 18 to death.

**Affect** General term used by psychologists to mean roughly "emotion," but used more specifically here as a defining attribute of social support.

**Affiliation Motive** The disposition to seek out or retain emotional relationships.

**Affiliative Relationships** Term used by Weiss to describe relationships between adults that do not involve clear attachment. May vary in liking or degree of contact.

**Affirmation** A second defining attribute of social support suggested by Kahn and Antonucci, including expressions of agreement or acknowledgment.

**Age** Number of years since birth.

**Age Strata** Layers or groupings by age within any given society. Individuals in each age stratum are expected to occupy certain roles and have certain privileges.

**Aging** The passage of years in an individual's life—without any connotation of loss or deterioration.

**Aid** Third defining attribute of social support suggested by Kahn and Antonucci, including direct physical, financial, or informational assistance.

**Alarm** The first phase of the General Adaptation Syndrome suggested by Selye, in which the body reacts immediately with "shock" to a noxious stimulus.

**Alzheimer's Disease** One of several causes of *Senile Dementia,* involving loss of brain weight and tangling of neurofibers of the brain resulting in gradual and permanent loss of memory and other cognitive functions.

**Appraisal** Term used by Lazarus to refer to the perception or analysis of an event (such as a potentially stressful event).

**Associative Friendship** Term used by Reisman to describe more casual, less-close relationships between friends.

**Attachment** A positive affective bond between any two individuals presumed to underlie attachment behaviors.

**Attachment Behaviors** Outward expressions of underlying attachment, such as smiling, trying to be near, writing letters to, hugging, etc. Specific attachment behaviors change over the life cycle.

**Autonomous Stage** The next-to-highest stage proposed by Jane Loevinger, characterized by the capacity to acknowledge and deal with inner conflict.

**Being Motives** Term used by Maslow for a cluster of motives found in humans, to discover and understand, to give love, to find optimum fulfillment of inner potential. Also called "growth motives."

**Career Consolidation** A stage suggested by George Vaillant as an addition to Erikson's stages of adulthood, said to occur in one's early 30s, when attention is focused on work success and achievement.

**Centaur Stage** Stage proposed by Wilber, also called the stage of the existential self, in which the adult integrates the sense of body and mind, and all the separate definitions of self into a single encompassing sense of being.

**Change** Term used in this book to describe observed patterns of variation over age on any given dimension of human functioning.

**Climacteric** The general term used to describe the period (in both men and women) in which reproductive capacity is gradually lost during adulthood. *Menopause* is used to describe the climacteric in women.

**Cohort** A group of individuals born at approximately the same time who share the same pattern of historical experiences in childhood and adulthood.

**Cohort Difference** An observed difference between the performance of older and younger subjects on any given measure that can be most readily explained as the result of the different historical experiences of the two cohorts.

**Cohort-sequential Design** A subvariety of sequential research design in which successive cohorts are each studied longitudinally over the same age ranges (e.g., a group born in 1940 is studied from age 20 to age 35, and then another cohort born in 1950 is studied from age 20 to age 35).

**Conformist Stage** A stage proposed by Loevinger in her theory of adult development, characterized by the identification of one's self with group norms and values.

**Confounding** The covarying of two measures or properties of individuals or groups such that it is impossible to determine the independent effect of each. In cross-sectional research, age and cohort are confounded.

**Conjunctive Faith** Fifth stage of faith development proposed by Fowler, involving openness to other views, other faiths, and to paradox, myth, and metaphor.

**Conscientious Stage** A stage proposed by Loevinger to follow the conformist and the self-aware level, characterized by the creation of individual rules and ideals.

**Conventional Career Pattern** Phrase used by Super to describe a career moving steadily through a recognized series of steps or up a "ladder."

**Conventional Level of Moral Reasoning** The middle of the three levels of moral reasoning suggested by Kohlberg, involving reasoning based on the rules or expectations of the family or society.

**Correlation** A statistic used to describe the degree to which the scores on two variables covary. A correlation can range from +1.00 to −1.00, with numbers nearer 1.00 reflecting stronger relationships.

**Cross-linking** A process of bond formation between proteins either within or between molecules, occurring in adulthood, and thought to be one of the causes of the loss of elasticity in body tissues with age.

**Cross-sectional Design** Type of research in which different age groups are compared on the same measures at one time point.

**Cross-sequential Design** A type of sequential research design in which several adjacent cohorts are simultaneously studied longitudinally (e.g., a group of 25-year-olds, a group of 30-year-olds, and a group of 35-year olds might each be simultaneously studied for 20 years).

**Crystallized Intelligence** An aspect of intelligence that is primarily dependent on education and experience: knowledge and judgment acquired through experience.

**Decline** Term used in this book only as a description of some observed lowering or drop in performance over age on some measure.

**Defense Mechanism** In psychoanalytic theories, a strategy of the ego for coping with anxiety, including such patterns as denial, repression, projection, and intellectualization. May be organized by levels of maturity.

**Deficiency Motives** Term used by Maslow to describe basic instincts or drives to correct imbalance or to maintain physical or emotional homeostasis.

**Development** Term used in this book to refer to any changes with age that appear to involve some systematic improvement, integration, or "growth."

**Dialectical Thought** Proposed form of adult thought that involves recognition and acceptance of contradiction and paradox, and the seeking of synthesis.

**Ego Integrity versus Despair** The final stage of development proposed by Erikson, confronted in late life, when the adult must come to terms with who she is and has been, or face despair.

**Encoding** The processes by which information is committed to memory.

**Epigenetic Landscape** Phrase used by Waddington to describe a metaphor for genetic canalization in development.

**Equity** A major theory in social psychology dealing with the degree of equality of exchange (thus the fairness) of any given relationship.

**Exhaustion** The third phase of the General Adaptation Syndrome proposed by Selye in which the body's temporary adaptation to a stressor breaks down.

**Experiment** A research design in which the experimenter systematically manipulates one or more variables, assigning subjects randomly to one or more experimental and control groups.

**Fear of Weakness Motive** The desire to avoid being controlled by others.

**Fluid Intelligence** That aspect of intelligence reflecting fundamental, biological processes and less dependency on specific experience.

**The Free Person** Stage of development proposed by Johnson, roughly analogous to Fowler's stage of *Conjunctive Faith,* in which the individual is freed from preoccupation with self, turning outward to caring and compassion.

**Gain** Term used in this book to describe patterns of change with age that involve increases or rises on some measure.

**General Adaptation Syndrome** A complex sequence of physiological reactions to stressors proposed by Selye, including initial alarm, intermediate resistance, and finally exhaustion.

**Generativity versus Stagnation** The seventh stage proposed by Erikson, occurring from perhaps age 25 to 50, when the adult must find some way to rear or support the next generation.

**Growth Motives** See *Being Motives.*

**Hardiness** A dimension of personality proposed by Kobasa, including the tendency to respond to situations with commitment, a sense of personal control, and a sense of challenge.

**Hope for Power Motive** The desire to have an impact on the world, often by focusing attention on the self.

**Hospice Care** Relatively new pattern of care for terminally ill patients in which the majority of care is provided by family members, with control of care and care-setting in the hands of the patient and family. May be at home or in special wards or separate institutions.

**Identity** The term used in Erikson's theory of development to describe the gradually emerging, and continually changing, sense of self.

**Identity versus Role Confusion** The fifth stage in Erikson's theory of development, typifying the teenager and young adult, when the individual must form specific occupational, sexual, and religious identities.

**The Individual** Stage proposed by Johnson, roughly equivalent to Fowler's *Individuative* stage of faith, in which the young or middle-aged adult moves beyond (or outside of) the perspective of social roles, searching for individual rules and understanding.

**Individualistic Level** In Loevinger's theory of development, the transitional point between the conscientious and the autonomous stages; central issue is that of dependence and independence.

**Individuative-Reflective Faith** Fourth stage proposed by Fowler, in which the source of authority for the adult's model of the world shifts from external to internal.

**Integrated Stage** The final stage of adult development proposed by Loevinger, rarely reached, in which the conflicts of the autonomous stage are transcended.

**Interiority** Term used by Neugarten to describe the personality pattern of elderly adults, including a lowered investment in social relationships, reflectiveness, and a freedom from norms or role restrictions.

**Intimacy versus Isolation** The sixth stage proposed by Erikson, typically occurring in the early 20s, when the young adult forms several key, intimate relationships.

**Intuitive-Projective Faith** First stage of faith proposed by Fowler, found in children up to about age seven, in which bits of myth and information are combined into a set of "stories" about the world.

**Life Expectancy** The average number of years a person of some designated age (e.g., birth, or age 65) can still expect to live.

**Life Review** A mental process proposed by Butler and thought to be characteristic of the elderly in which reminiscence of past experience serves as the vehicle for integration and restructuring.

**Life Span** The theoretical maximum number of years of life for a given species, which is thought will not be exceeded even with improvements in health care.

**Life Structure** Concept suggested by Levinson to describe the pattern of existence, combining roles, relationships, and particular personality adaptations, created by each individual at several points in the adult life.

**Locus of Control** Dimension of personality proposed by Rotter, ranging from internal control (the sense of being in charge of one's life, of having choices and personal responsibility) to external control (the sense of being managed by outside events, of having no say or choice, of not being responsible for one's own circumstances).

**Longevity** A word literally meaning "long life," but used generally in gerontological literature to mean roughly the same as life expectancy.

**Longitudinal Design** Research design in which the same individuals are studied repeatedly over a period of time.

**Long-term Memory** Memory retained over more than a few minutes by means of some encoding process.

**Love** In this context, refers to Rubin's more attached and intimate form of relationship, in contrast to "liking."

**Marital Homogamy** The selection of a spouse from among those similar to the self in social class, background, and race.

**Maturation** Any sequential unfolding of physical changes that is governed by the genetic code, or by other biological processes, and that is shared by all members of the species.

**Maximum Oxygen Uptake (VO2 max)** The amount of oxygen that can be taken into the bloodstream and hence carried to all parts of the body. A major measure of aerobic fitness, VO2 max decreases with age, but can be increased again with exercise.

**Menopause** Term used to refer to the female climacteric, that set of physical and hormonal changes associated with the loss of reproductive capacity in women in their 40s and 50s.

**Multiple Trial Career Pattern** A career pattern described by Super in which the individual shifts careers or jobs many times, alternating stable and trial periods.

**Mythic-Literal Faith** Second stage of faith development proposed by Fowler, typical of children from about age seven to adolescence. Child absorbs from family and religious teachings a coherent, literally-understood, "story" about life, death, God, and the universe.

**Osteoarthritis** Term used generally to describe any significant changes in the bones of the joints of the body associated with the wear and tear of aging.

**Osteoporosis** The changes in bones, including increased brittleness and porousness, resulting from loss of calcium in the bone.

**Performance Tests** Those tests on many IQ tests that rely less on verbal skills and more on basic analytic or memory processes.

**Personality** An individual's unique, relatively consistent and enduring, patterned methods of behaving in relation to others and the total environment.

**Preconventional Level of Moral Reasoning** First level of reasoning suggested by Kohlberg, in which the child sees as fair or just that which is rewarded. Self-serving, egocentric view.

**Primary Memory** See *Short-term Memory.*

**Principled Level of Moral Reasoning** Third major level of moral reasoning proposed by Kohlberg, in which the adult looks behind the rules of society or family for a set of underlying principles on which to base moral judgments.

**Q Sort** A method of assessing or describing an individual's characteristics involving the sorting of a set of descriptors into a forced normal distribution of "typical" and "atypical" traits.

**Recall** A type of memory in which an item is brought from long-term memory without prompting or other clues.

**Reciprocal Friendship** The more intimate, close, attached friendships as defined by Reisman, in contrast to *Associative Friendship.*

**Recognition** A type of memory in which the item to be remembered is selected from among several alternatives, or merely recognized as known.

**Resistance** The second phase of the General Adaptation Syndrome proposed by Selye, during which the body attempts to achieve homeostasis in the face of a stressor.

**Resistance Resources** Phrase used to refer to the collection of resources that may help an individual respond effectively to environmental or internal stressors, such as *Social Support* and a repertoire of coping responses.

**Retrieval** The process of bringing a particular memory out of short-term or long-term memory.

**Role** A concept from sociology describing the expected behavioral and attitudinal content of any one social position, such as teacher, mother, or employer.

**Role Conflict** The experience associated with occupying two or more roles that are wholly or partially logistically or psychologically incompatible.

**Role Strain** The experience associated with occupying a role, the demands of which do not match one's own qualities or skills.

**The Seer** Highest stage of development proposed by Johnson, in which the individual "sees" clearly the syntheses behind paradox; reflected in both compassion and wisdom.

**Self-aware Level** A transitional level proposed by Loevinger, occurring between the conformist and the conscientious stages and characterized by increased flexibility of judgment.

**Self-protective Stage** The fourth stage proposed by Loevinger, typically occurring in middle childhood or adolescence, but found occasionally in adults as well. Characterized by attempts to maximize one's own gain in any situation.

**Senile Dementia** Any deterioration of intellectual abilities in old age that is due to some disorder of the nervous system rather than to any normal aging process. See also *Alzheimer's Disease.*

**Sensory Memory** The initial, very brief, sensory impression of some experience that is retained in memory, without encoding, for a very short time.

**Sequential Designs** A family of research designs which combine some of the features of cross-sectional and longitudinal research. Most typically, several adjacent age groups are each studied longitudinally.

**Sex Roles** Socially defined collections of traits and behaviors expected to be displayed by male and female persons in any given culture.

**Sex Role Stereotypes** Relatively inflexible, widely shared concepts about the personality and behavior expected from men and women in any given culture.

**Sex Typing** The degree of match between an individual's behavior and the prescriptions of the sex role assigned to his or her gender.

**Short-term Memory** That portion of the memory process in which information in the sensory store is attended to and retained for a slightly longer time. Such memory decays rapidly if there is no further encoding of the item. Also called primary memory.

**Social Adult Stage** Stage proposed by Johnson, roughly equivalent to Fowler's stage of synthetic-conventional faith, in which the individual's view of the world and of herself is dominated by social roles.

**Social Class** Strata within any society defined by the power, prestige, and control of resources characteristic of members of that strata. An individual's social class is typically measured in terms of years of education, income, and prestige of occupation.

**Social Mobility** The movement of individuals from one social stratum to another within any given society.

**Social Network** The collection of relationships with family, friends, and acquaintances from whom social support may be received.

**Social Status** A term very similar in usage to *Social Class*. The level of prestige and power describing any one individual or group of individuals in a social system.

**Social Support** The combination of *Affect, Affirmation,* and *Aid* that an individual receives from those with whom she has relationships.

**Speeded Tasks** Term used for those measures of intellectual ability which have time limits.

**Stabilization Stage of Career Development** Typically a time in an adult's 30s and early 40s, when the career direction has been set, and the individual strives to achieve the maximum career advancement.

**Stable Career Pattern** Pattern described by Super in which there is a single trial period followed by a stable continuation in the same job or career.

**Storage** The third basic memory process (in addition to encoding and retrieval), involving placing some memory in short-term or long-term memory.

**Synthetic-Conventional Faith** Third stage of faith proposed by Fowler, in which the individual selects a model (a faith) from among those available in the social system. Authority is external to the individual.

**Temperament** A subclass of characteristics included under the general term of *Personality*. Normally refers to those aspects of personal style and emotional responsiveness that are detectable early in infancy and appear to have a constitutional basis.

**Time-sequential Design** A variety of sequential design in which parallel cross-sectional studies are completed several years apart (e.g., 20-, 40-, and 60-year-olds might be studied in 1960, and then separate groups of 20-, 40-, and 60-year-olds studied in 1980).

**Transpersonal Stage** Stage proposed by Wilber as the highest level of development typically available to the individual, characterized by a loss of the sense of the individual self, an awareness of connection with some unity or whole.

**Type A Personality** A combination of competitiveness, a sense of time urgency, and hostility or aggressiveness, which has been found to be associated with higher risk of coronary heart disease.

**Undifferentiated** Term used by psychologists to describe an individual whose self-description includes low levels of both feminine and masculine qualities; the opposite of *Androgynous*.

**Undifferentiated Faith** A kind of "pre-faith" proposed by Fowler, characteristic of infants, and preceding the first full faith stage, *Intuitive-Projective Faith*.

**Universalizing Faith** The highest (sixth) stage of faith proposed by Fowler, like Wilber's *Transpersonal Stage,* involving some loss of the sense of individuality.

**Unspeeded Tasks** Those measures of intellectual skill that do not have time limits, such as a test of vocabulary or reasoning.

**Unstable Career Pattern** As described by Super, this is a pattern of a trial period followed by a stable work period, followed by another trial period. Less varied than the *Multiple Trial Career Pattern.*

**Verbal Tests** In contrast to *Performance Tests,* those measures of intellectual ability that rely heavily on the ability to manipulate verbal symbols.

# References


ABBOTT, D. A., & BRODY, G. H. (1985). The relation of child age, gender, and number of children to the marital adjustment of wives. *Journal of Marriage and the Family, 47,* 77–84.

ABRAHAMS, B., FELDMAN, S. S., & NASH, S. C. (1978). Sex role self-concept and sex role attitudes: Enduring personality chracteristics or adaptations to changing life situations? *Developmental Psychology, 14,* 393–400.

ACHENBACH, T. M. (1978). *Research in developmental psychology: Concepts, strategies, methods.* New York: The Free Press.

AINLAY, S. C., & SMITH, D. R. (1984). Aging and religious participation. *Journal of Gerontology, 39,* 357–363.

AINSWORTH, M. D. S., BLEHAR, M. C., WATERS, E., & WALL, S. (1978). *Patterns of attachment.* Hillsdale, NJ: Lawrence Erlbaum & Associates.

ALBRECHT, S. L. (1980). Reactions and adjustments to divorce: Differences in the experiences of males and females. *Family Relations, 29,* 49–68.

ALDOUS, J., OSMOND, M. W., & HICKS, M. W. (1979). Men's work and men's families. In W. R. Burr, R. Hill, F. I. Nye & I. L. Reiss, (Eds.), *Contemporary theories about the family.* New York: The Free Press.

ALPERT, J. L., & RICHARDSON, M. S. (1980). Parenting. In L. W. Poon (Ed.), *Aging in the 1980s. Psychological Issues.* Washington, DC: American Psychological Association.

ALSOP, S. (1973). *Stay of execution.* New York: Lippincott.

AMERICAN ASSOCIATION OF RETIRED PERSONS. (1984). *A Profile of older americans, 1984,* (PF 3049) (585). Washington, DC: American Association of Retired Persons.

ANDERSON, S. A., RUSSELL, C. S., & SCHUMM, W. R. (1983). Perceived marital quality and family life-cycle categories: A further analysis. *Journal of Marriage and the Family, 45,* 127–139.

ANTONUCCI, T. C. (1985). Personal characteristics, social support, and social behavior. In R. H. Binstock & E. Shanas, (Eds.), *Handbook of aging and the social sciences* (2nd ed.). New York: Van Nostrand Reinhold.

ANTONUCCI, T., TAMIR, L. M., & DUBNOFF, S. (1980). Mental health across the family life cycle. In K. W. Back (Ed.), *Life course: Integrative theories and exemplary populations.* American Association for the Advancement of Science Selected Symposium No. 41. Boulder, CO: Westview Press.

ARENBERG, D. (1974). A longitudinal study of problem solving in adults. *Journal of Gerontology, 29,* 650–658.

ARENBERG, D., & ROBERTSON-TCHABO, E. A. (1977). Learning and aging. In J. E. Birren & K. W. Schaie (Eds.), *Handbook of the psychology of aging.* New York: Van Nostrand Reinhold.

ASHER, S., RENSHAW, P. D., & HYMEL, S. (1982). Peer relationships and the development of social skills. In S. G. Moore & C. R. Cooper (Eds.), *The young child: Reviews of research* (Vol. 3). Washington, DC: National Association for the Education of Young Children.

ATCHLEY, R. C. (1982). The process of retirement: Comparing women and men. In M. Szinovacz (Ed.), *Women's retirement.* Beverly Hills, CA: Sage.

BAHR, S. J., CHAPPELL, C. B., & LEIGH, G. K. (1983). Age at marriage, role enactment, role consensus, and marital satisfaction. *Journal of Marriage and the Family, 45,* 795–803.

BALKWELL, C. (1981). Transition to widowhood: A review of the literature. *Family Relations, 30,* 117–128.

BALL, J. F. (1976–77). Widow's grief: The impact of age and mode of death. *Omega, 7,* 307–333.

BALTES, P. B., DITTMANN-KOHLI, F., & DIXON, R. A. (1984). New perspectives on the development of intelligence in adulthood: Toward a dual-process conception and a model of selective optimization with compensation. In P. B. Baltes & O. G. Brim, Jr. (Eds.), *Life-span development and behavior* (Vol. 6). Orlando, FL: Academic Press.

BALTES, P. B., REESE, H. W., & LIPSITT, L. P. (1980). In M. R. Rosenzweig & L. W. Porter (Eds.), *Annual review of psychology.* Palo Alto, CA: Annual Reviews.

BANKHOFF, E. A. (1983). Social support and adaptation to widowhood. *Journal of Marriage and the Family, 45,* 827–839.

BARRETT, C. J., & SCHNEWEIS, K M. (1980–81). An empirical search for stages of widowhood. *Omega, 11,* 97–104.

BARUCH, G., & BARNETT, R. C. (1983). Adult daughters' relationships with their mothers. *Journal of Marriage and the Family, 45,* 601–606.

BASS, D. M. (1985). The hospice ideology and success of hospice care. *Research on Aging, 7,* 307–328.

BASSECHES, M. (1984). *Dialectical thinking and adult development.* Norwood, NJ: Ablex.

BELL, A. P., & WEINBERG, M. S. (1978). *Homosexualities: A study of diversity among men and women.* New York: Simon & Schuster.

BELL, R. R. (1981). *Worlds of friendship.* Beverly Hills, CA: Sage.

BELLOC, N. B. (1973). Relationship of health practices and mortality. *Preventive Medicine, 2,* 67–81.

BELLOC, N. B., & BRESLOW, L. (1972). Relationship of physical health status and health practices. *Preventive Medicine, 1,* 409–421.

BELSKY, J., PERRY-JENKINS, M., & CROUTER, A. C. (1985). The work-family interface and marital change across the transition to parenthood. *Journal of Family Issues, 6,* 205–220.

BELSKY, J., SPANIER, G. B., & ROVINE, M. (1983). Stability and change in marriage across the transition to parenthood. *Journal of Marriage and the Family, 45,* 567–577.

BEM, S. L. (1974). The measurement of psychological androgyny. *Journal of Consulting and Clinical Psychology, 42,* 155–162.

BEM, S. L. (1977). On the utility of alternative procedures for assessing psychological androgyny. *Journal of Consulting and Clinical Psychology, 45,* 196–205.

BENGTSON. V. L. (1985). Diversity and symbolism in grandparent roles. In V. L. Bengtson & J. F. Robertson (Eds.), *Grandparenthood.* Beverly Hills, CA: Sage.

BENGTSON, V. L., CUELLAR, J. B., & RAGAN, P. K. (1977). Stratum contrasts and similarities in attitudes toward death. *Journal of Gerontology, 32,* 76–88.

BENNINGER, W. B., & WALSH, W. B. (1980). Holland's theory and non-college-degreed working men and women. *Journal of Vocational Behavior, 17,* 81–88.

BENTLER, P. M., & NEWCOMB, M. D. (1978). Longitudinal study of marital success and failure. *Journal of Consulting and Clinical Psychology, 46,* 1053–1070.

BEST, D. L., WILLIAMS, J. E., CLOUD, J. M. DAVIS, S. W., ROBERTSON, L. S., EDWARDS, J. R., GILES, H., & FOWLES, J. (1977). Development of sex-trait stereotypes among young children in the United States, England, and Ireland. *Child Development, 48,* 1375–1384.

BETZ, E. L. (1984). A study of career patterns of women college graduates. *Journal of Vocational Behavior, 24,* 249–263.

BEYARD-TYLER, K., & HARING, M. J. (1984). Gender-related aspects of occupational prestige. *Journal of Vocational Behavior, 24,* 194–203.

BIANCHI, S. M., & FARLEY, R. (1979). Racial differences in family living arrangements and economic well-being: An analysis of recent trends. *Journal of Marriage and the Family, 41,* 537–551.

BIERMAN, E. L., & HAZZARD, W. R. (1978). Adulthood—the middle years. In D. W. Smith, E. L. Bierman, & N. M. Robinson (Eds.), *The biologic ages of man.* Philadelphia: W. B. Saunders.

BILLINGS, A. G., & MOOS, R. H. (1981). The role of coping responses and social resources in attentuating the stress of life events. *Journal of Behavioral Medicine, 4,* 139–157.

BIRCHLER, G. R., WEISS, R. L., & VINCENT, J. P. (1975). Multidimensional analyses of social reinforcement exchange between maritally distressed and non-distressed spouse and stranger dyads. *Journal of Personality and Social Psychology, 31,* 348–360.

BIRD, G. W., BIRD, G. A., & SCRUGGS, M. (1984). Determinants of family task sharing: A study of husbands and wives. *Journal of Marriage and the Family, 46,* 345–355.

BIRREN, J. E., WOODS, A. M., & WILLIAMS, M. V. (1980) Behavioral slowing with age: Causes, organization, and consequences. In L. W. Poon (Ed.), *Aging in the 1980s.* Washington, DC: American Psychological Association.

BLAZER, D., & PALMORE, E. (1976). Religion and aging in a longitudinal panel. *The Gerontologist, 16,* 82–84.

BLOCK, J. (1971). *Lives through time.* Berkeley, CA: Bancroft Books.

BLOCK, J. (1981). Some enduring and consequential structures of personality. In A. I. Rabin, J. Aronoff, A. M. Barclay, & R. A. Zucker (Eds.), *Further explorations in personality.* New York: John Wiley & Sons.

BLOCK, M. R. (1982). Professional women: Work pattern as a correlate of retirement satisfaction. In M. Szinovacz (Ed.), *Women's retirement* (pp. 183–194). Beverly Hills, CA: Sage.

BLOCK, M. R., DAVIDSON, J. L., & GRAMBS, J. D. (1981). *Women over forty: Visions and realities.* New York: Springer.

BLOOM, B. L., WHITE, S. W., & ASHER, S. J. (1979). Marital disruption as a stressful life event. In C. Levinger & O. C. Moles (Eds.), *Divorce and separation: Context, causes, and consequences.* New York: Basic Books.

BLOOM, B. S. (1964). *Stability and change in human characteristics.* New York: John Wiley & Sons.

BLUMSTEIN, P., & SCHWARTZ, P. (1983). *American couples.* New York: William Morrow.

BOOTH, A., & EDWARDS, J. N. (1985). Age at marriage and marital instability. *Journal of Marriage and the Family, 47,* 67–75.

BORTZ, W. M., II. (1982). Disuse and aging. *Journal of the American Medical Association, 248* (September), 1203–1208.

BOTWINICK, J., & STORANDT, M. (1974). *Memory, related functions and age.* Springfield, IL: Charles C. Thomas.

BOWEN, G. L., & ORTHNER, D. K. (1983). Sex-role congruency and marital quality. *Journal of Marriage and the Family, 45,* 223–230.

BOWLBY, J. (1969). *Attachment and loss: Vol. 1. Attachment.* New York: Basic Books.

BOWLBY, J. (1973). *Attachment and loss: Vol. 2. Separation, anxiety, and anger.* New York: Basic Books.

BOWLBY, J. (1980). *Attachment and loss: Vol. 3. Loss, sadness, and depression.* New York: Basic Books.

BRADBURN, N. M. (1969). *The structure of psychological well being.* Chicago: Aldine.

BRAIKER, H. B., & KELLEY, H. H. (1979). Conflict in the development of close relationships. In R. L. Burgess & T. L. Huston (Eds.), *Social exchange in developing relationships.* New York: Academic Press.

BRAY, D. W., & HOWARD, A. (1983). The AT&T longitudinal studies of managers. In K. W. Schaie (Ed.), *Longitudinal studies of adult psychological development.* New York: Guilford Press.

BRECHER, E. M. (1984). *Love, sex, and aging.* Boston, MA: Little, Brown.

BRIDGES, W. (1980). *Transitions.* Reading, MA: Addison-Wesley.

BRIM, O. G. JR. (1976). Theories of the male mid-life crisis. *The Counseling Psychologist, 6,* 2–9.

BRODY, E. B., & BRODY, N. (1976). *Intelligence: Nature, determinants and consequences.* New York: Academic Press.

BROVERMAN, I. K., BROVERMAN, D. M., CLARKSON, F. E., ROSENKRANTZ, P. S., & VOGEL, S. R. (1970). Sex-role stereotypes and clinical judgments of mental health. *Journal of Consulting and Clinical Psychology, 34,* 1–7.

BROVERMAN, I. K., VOGEL, S. R., BROVERMAN, D. M., CLARKSON, F. E., & ROSENKRANTZ, P. S. (1972). Sex-role stereotypes: A current appraisal. *Journal of Social Issues, 28,* 59–78.

BROWN, G. W., & HARRIS, T. (1978). *Social origins of depression.* New York: The Free Press.

BRUBAKER, T. H. (1985). *Later life families.* Beverly Hills, CA: Sage.

BRUCH, M. A., LEVO, L. C., & ARISOHN, B. A. (1984). Conceptual complexity and skill in marital communications. *Journal of Marriage and the Family, 46,* 927–932.

BURKE, R. J., & WEIR, T. (1976). Relationship of wives' employment status to husband, wife and pair satisfaction. *Journal of Marriage and the Family, 32,* 29–37.

BUSS, A. H., & PLOMIN, R. (1984). *Temperament: Early developing personality traits.* Hillsdale, NJ: Lawrence Erlbaum & Associates.

BUTLER, R. N. (1963). The life review: An interpretation of reminiscence in the aged. In B. L. Neugarten (Ed.), *Middle age and aging.* Chicago: University of Chicago Press, 1968.

BUTLER, R. N. (1968). The facade of chronological age: An interpretataive summary. In B. L. Neugarten (Ed.), *Middle age and aging.* Chicago: University of Chicago Press.

CAMPBELL, A. (1981). *The sense of well-being in America.* New York: McGraw-Hill.

CAMPBELL, A., CONVERSE, P. E., & ROGERS, W. L. (1977). *The quality of American life.* New York: Russell Sage Foundation.

CANTRIL, H. (1965). *The pattern of human concerns.* New Brunswick, NJ: Rutgers University Press.

CAREY, R. G. (1974). Living until death: A program of service and research for the terminally ill. *Hospital Progress,* Reprinted in E. Kübler-Ross (Ed.), *Death: The final stage of growth.* Englewood Cliffs, NJ: Prentice Hall, 1975.

CARGAN, L., & MELKO, M. (1982). *Singles. Myths and realities.* Beverly Hills, CA: Sage.

CARP, F. M. (1985). Relevance of personality traits to adjustment in group living situations. *Journal of Gerontology, 40,* 544–551.

CARTER, H., & GLICK, P. C. (1976). *Marriage and divorce: A social and economic study* (rev. ed.). Cambridge, MA: Harvard University Press.

CATTELL, R. B. (1963). Theory of fluid and crystallized intelligence: A critical experiment. *Journal of Educational Psychology, 54,* 1–22.

CATTELL, R. B. (1971). *Abilities: Their structure, growth, and action.* Boston: Houghton Mifflin.

CERELLA, J. (1985). Information processing rates in the elderly. *Psychological Bulletin, 98,* 67–83.

CHASE, W. G., & SIMON, H. A. (1973). The mind's eye in chess. In W. G. Chase (Ed.), *Visual information processing*. New York: Academic Press.

CHI, M. T. (1978). Knowledge structure and memory develoment. In R. S. Siegler (Ed.), *Children's thinking: What develops?* Hillsdale, NJ: Lawrence Erlbaum & Associates.

CHIRIBOGA, D. A. (1984). Social stressors as antecedents of change. *Journal of Gerontology, 39,* 468–477.

CHIRIBOGA, D. A., & CUTLER, L. (1980). Stress and adaptation: Life span perspectives. In L. W. Poon (Ed.), *Aging in the 1980s. Psychological issues.* Washington, DC: American Psychological Association.

CHIRIBOGA, D. A., & DEAN, H. (1978). Dimensions of stress: Perspectives from a longitudinal study. *Journal of Psychosomatic Research, 22,* 47–55.

CHIRIKOS, T. N., & NESTEL, G. (1985). Longitudinal analysis of functional disabilities in older men. *Journal of Gerontology, 40,* 426–433.

CICIRELLI, V. G. (1982). Sibling influence throughout the life span. In M. E. Lamb & B. Sutton-Smith (Eds.), *Sibling relationships.* Hillsdale, NJ: Lawrence Erlbaum & Associates.

CICIRELLI, V. G. (1983). Adult children and their elderly parents. In T. H. Brubaker (Ed.), *Family relationships in later life.* Beverly Hills, CA: Sage.

CLARK, R. L., & SUMNER, D. A. (1985). Inflation and the real income of the elderly: Recent evidence and expectations for the future. *The Gerontologist, 25,* 147–152.

CLAUSEN, J. A. (1981). Men's occupational careers in the middle years. In D. H. Eichorn, J. A. Clausen, N. Haan, M. P. Honzik, & P. H. Mussen (Eds.), *Present and past in middle life.* New York: Academic Press.

COHEN, S., & WILLS, T. A. (1985). Stress, social support, and the buffering hypothesis. *Psychological Bulletin, 98,* 310–357.

COLBY, A., KOHLBERG, L., GIBBS, J., & LIEBERMAN, M. (1983). A longitudinal study of moral judgment. *Monographs of the Society for Research in Child Development, 48* (Whole No. 200).

COLE, S. (1979). Age and scientific performance. *American Journal of Sociology, 84,* 958–977.

COLEMAN, L. M., & ANTONUCCI, T. C. (1983). Impact of work on women at midlife. *Developmental Psychology, 19,* 290–294.

COLLETTA, N. D. (1983). Stressful lives: The situation of divorced mothers and their children. *Journal of Divorce, 6,* 19–32.

CORCORAN, M. (1978). Work experience, work interruption, and wages. In G. J. Duncan & J. N. Morgan (Eds.), *Five thousand American families—patterns of economic progress.* Ann Arbor, MI: University of Michigan, Institute for Social Research.

CORSO, J. F. (1977). Auditory perception and communication. In J. E. Birren & K. W. Schaie (Eds.), *Handbook of the psychology of aging.* New York: Van Nostrand Reinhold.

COSTA, P. T., JR., FOZARD, J. L., & MCCRAE, R. R. (1977). Personological interpretation of factors from the Strong Vocational Interest Blank scales. *Journal of Vocational Behavior, 10,* 231–242.

COSTA, P. T., JR., & MCCRAE, R. R. (1980a). Still stable after all these years: Personality as a key to some issues in adulthood and old age. In P. B. Baltes & O. G. Brim, Jr. (Eds.), *Life-span development and behavior.* New York: Academic Press.

COSTA, P. T., JR., & MCCRAE, R. R. (1980b). Influence of extraversion and neuroticism on subjective well-being: Happy and unhappy people. *Journal of Personality and Social Psychology, 38,* 668–678.

COSTA, P. T., JR., & MCCRAE, R. R. (1983). Psychological maturity and subjective well-being: Toward a new synthesis. *Developmental Psychology, 19,* 243–248.

COSTA, P. T., JR., & MCCRAE, R. R. (1984). Personality as a lifelong determinant of wellbeing.

In C. Z. Malatesta & C. E. Izard (Eds.), *Emotion in adult development*. Beverly Hills, CA: Sage.

COSTA, P. T., JR., MCCRAE, R. R., & ARENBERG, D. (1983). Recent longitudinal research on personality and aging. In K. W. Schaie (Ed.), *Longitudinal studies of adult psychological development*. New York: Guilford Press.

COSTA, P. T., JR., MCCREA, R. R., & NORRIS, A. H. (1981). Personal adjustment to aging: Longitudinal prediction from neuroticism and extraversion. *Journal of Gerontology, 36,* 78–85

CRAIK, F. I. M. (1977). Age differences in human memory. In J. E. Birren & K. W. Schaie (Eds.), *Handbook of the psychology of aging*. New York: Van Nostrand Reinhold.

CRAIK, F. I. M., & RABINOWITZ, J. C. (1985). The effects of presentation rate and encoding task on age-related memory deficits. *Journal of Gerontology, 40,* 309–315.

CRANDALL, J. E. (1984). Social interest as a moderator of life stress. *Journal of Personality and Social Psychology, 47,* 164–174.

CRIMMINS, E. M. (1984). Life expectancy and the older population: Demographic implications of recent and prospective trends in old age mortality. *Research on Aging, 6,* 490–514.

CUMMING, E. (1975). Engagement with an old theory. *International Journal of Aging and Human Development, 6,* 187–191.

CUMMING, E., & HENRY, W. E. (1961). *Growing old*. New York: Basic Books.

CUNNINGHAM, J. D., & ANTILL, J. K. (1984). Changes in masculinity and femininity across the family life cycle: A reexamination. *Developmental Psychology, 20,* 1135–1141.

CUNNINGHAM, W. R., & BIRREN, J. E. (1976). Age changes in human abilities: A 28-year longitudinal study. *Developmental Psychology, 12,* 81–82.

CUNNINGHAM, W. R., & OWENS, W. A., JR. (1983). The Iowa State study of the adult development of intellectual abilities. In K. W. Schaie (Ed.), *Longitudinal studies of adult psychological development*. New York: Guilford Press.

CYTRYNBAUM, S., BLUM, L., PATRICK, R., STEIN, J., WADNER, D., & WILK, C. (1980). Midlife development: A personality and social systems perspective. In L. W. Poon (Ed.), *Aging in the 1980s. Psychological Issues*. Washington, DC: American Psychological Association.

DARBYSHIRE, J. O. (1984). The hearing loss epidemic: A challenge to gerontology. *Research on Aging, 6,* 384–394.

DAVIDSON, B., BALSWICK, J., & HALVERSON, C. (1983). Affective self-disclosure and marital adjustment: A test of equity theory. *Journal of Marriage and the Family, 45,* 93–103.

DAVIS, M. A., RANDALL, E. FORTHOFER, R. N., LEE, E. S., & MARGEN, S. (1985). Living arrangements and dietary patterns of older adults in the United States. *Journal of Gerontology, 40,* 434–442.

DEAUX, K. (1984). From individual differences to social categories: Analysis of a decade's research on gender. *American Psychologist, 39,* 105–116.

DEIMLING, G. T., & HAREL, Z. (1984). Social integration and mental health of the aged. *Research on Aging, 6,* 515–527.

DELONGIS, A., COYNE, J. C., DAKOF, G., FOLKMAN, S., & LAZARUS, R. S. (1982). Relationship of daily hassles, uplifts, and major life events to health status. *Health Psychology, 1,* 119–136.

DEMARIS, A., & LESLIE, G. R. (1984). Cohabitation with the future spouse: Its influence upon marital satisfaction and communication. *Journal of Marriage and the Family, 46,* 77–84.

DENNEY, N. W. (1982). Aging and cognitive changes. In B. B. Wolman (Ed.), *Handbook of developmental psychology*. Englewood Cliffs, NJ: Prentice-Hall.

DENNEY, N. W., & DENNEY, D. R. (1982). The relationship between classification and questioning strategies among adults. *Journal of Gerontology, 37,* 190–196.

DENNEY, N. W., & PALMER, A. M. (1981). Adult age differences on traditional and practical problem-solving measures. *Journal of Gerontology, 36,* 323–328.

DEROGATIS, L. R. (1982). Self-report measures of stress. In L. Goldberger & S. Breznitz (Eds.), *Handbook of stress. Theoretical and clinical aspects.* New York: The Free Press.

DICKENS, W. J., & PERLMAN, D. (1981). Friendship over the life-cycle. In S. Duck & R. Gilmour (Eds.), *Personal relationships 2. Developing personal relationships.* New York: Academic Press.

DIENER, E. (1984). Subjective well-being. *Psychological Bulletin, 95,* 542–575.

DOBSON, C. (1983). Sex-role and marital-role expectations. In T. H. Brubaker (Ed.), *Family relationships in later life.* Beverly Hills, CA: Sage.

DOHERTY, W. J., & JACOBSON, N. S. (1982). Marriage and the family. In B. B. Wolman (Ed.), *Handbook of developmental psychology.* Englewood Cliffs, NJ: Prentice-Hall.

DOHRENWEND, B. S., & DOHRENWEND, B. P. (1978). Some issues in research on stressful life events. *The Journal of Nervous and Mental Disease, 166,* 7–15.

DOHRENWEND, B. S., & DOHRENWEND, B. P. (1980). What is a stressful life event? In H. Selye (Ed.), *Selye's guide to stress research* (Vol. 1). New York: Van Nostrand Reinhold.

DOHRENWEND, B. S., & DOHRENWEND, B. P. (1981). Life stress and illness: Formulation of the issues. In B. S. Dohrenwend & B. P. Dohrenwend (Eds.), *Stressful life events and their contexts.* New York: Watson.

DOHRENWEND, B. S., KRASNOFF, L., ASKENASY, A. R., & DOHRENWEND, B. P. (1982). The Psychiatric Epidemiology Research Interview Life Events Scale. In L. Goldberger & S. Breznitz (Eds.), *Handbook of stress. Theoretical and clinical aspects.* New York: The Free Press.

DOTY, R. L., SHAMAN, P., & DANN, M. (1984). Development of the University of Pennsylvania Smell Identification Test: A standardized microencapsulated test of olfactory function. *Physiology and Behavior, 32,* 489–502.

DUNN, J. (1984). Sibling studies and the developmental impact of critical incidents. In P. B. Baltes & O. G. Brim, Jr. (Eds.), *Life-span development and behavior* (Vol. 6). Orlando, FL: Academic Press.

DURLAK, J. A. (1972). Relationship between attitudes toward life and death among elderly women. *Developmental Psychology, 8,* 146.

DUVALL, E. M. (1962). *Family development* (2nd ed.). New York: Lippincott.

DUVALL, E. M. (1971). *Family develoment* (5th ed.) Philadelphia: Lippincott.

EBERHARDT, B. J., & MUCHINSKY, P. M. (1984). Stuctural validation of Holland's hexagonal model: Vocational classification through the use of biodata. *Journal of Applied Psychology, 69,* 174–181.

ECCLES, J. S., & HOFFMAN, L. W. (1984). Sex roles, socialization, and occupational behavior. In H. W. Stevenson & A. E. Siegel (Eds.), *Child development research and social policy* (Vol. 1). Chicago: University of Chicago Press.

EICHORN, D. H., CLAUSEN, J. A., HAAN, N., HONZIK, M. P., & MUSSEN, P. H. (Eds.) (1981). *Present and past in middle life.* New York: Academic Press.

EICHORN, D. H., HUNT, J. V., & HONZIK, M. P. (1981). In D. H. Eichorn, J. A. Clausen, N. Haan, M. P. Honzik, & P. H. Mussen (Eds.), *Present and past in middle life.* New York: Academic Press.

EISDORFER, C. (1985). Overview of dementia: The scope and impact of the problem. *Recent advances in geriatric medicine: Dementia in the elderly.* San Diego, CA: San Diego School of Medicine, Office of Continuing Medical Education and Institute for Research on Aging.

EISDORFER, C., & RASKIND, M. (1975). Aging, hormones and human behavior. In B. Eleftheriou & R. Sprott (Eds.), *Hormonal correlates of behavior: Vol. 1, A lifespan view*. New York: Plenum Press.

EISDORFER, C., & WILKIE, F. (1972). Auditory changes. *Journal of the American Geriatrics Society, 20,* 377–382.

ELDER, G. H., JR. (1974). *Children of the great depression.* Chicago: University of Chicago Press.

ELDER, G. H., JR. (1979). Historical change in life patterns and personality. In P. B. Baltes & O. G. Brim, Jr., (Eds.). *Life-span development and behavior* (Vol. 2). New York: Academic Press.

ELDER, G. H., LIKER, J. K., & CROSS, C. E. (1984). Parent-child behavior in the Great Depression: Life course and intergenerational influences. In P. B. Baltes & O. G. Brim, Jr. (Eds.), *Life-span development and behavior* (Vol. 6). New York: Academic Press.

ELDER, G. H., & ROCKWELL, R. C. (1976). Marital timing in women's life patterns. *Journal of Family History, 1,* 34–53.

ELMAN, M. R., & GILBERT, L. A. (1984). Coping strategies for role conflict in married professional women with children. *Family Relations, 33,* 317–327.

ELSAYED, M., ISMAIL, A. H., & YOUNG, R. S. (1980). Intellectual differences of adult men related to age and physical fitness before and after an exercise program. *Journal of Gerontology, 35,* 383–387.

ERBES, J. T., & HEDDERSON, J. J. C. (1984). A longitudinal examination of the separation/divorce process. *Journal of Marriage and the Family, 46,* 937–941.

ERDWINS, C. J., & MELLINGER, J. C. (1984). Mid-life women: Relation of age and role to personality. *Journal of Personality and Social Psychology, 47,* 390–395.

ERDWINS, C. J., TYLER, Z. E., & MELLINGER, J. C. (1983). A comparison of sex role and related personality traits in young, middle-aged, and older women. *International Journal of Aging and Human Development, 17,* 141–152.

ERIKSON, E. H. (1950). *Childhood and society.* New York: Norton. (Reissued 1963).

ERIKSON, E. H. (1959). *Identity and the life cycle.* New York: International Universities Press. (Reissued by Norton, 1980).

ERIKSON, E. H. (1968). *Identity: Youth and crisis.* New York: W. W. Norton.

ERIKSON, E. H. (1980). Themes of adulthood in the Freud-Jung correspondence. In N. J. Smelser & E. H. Erikson (Eds.), *Themes of work and love in adulthood.* Cambridge, MA: Harvard University Press.

ESTES, R. J., & WILENSKY, H. L. (1978). Life cycle squeeze and the morale curve. *Social Problems, 25*(3), 277–292.

EVANS, G. W., BRENNAN, P. L., SKORPANICH, M. A., & HELD, D. (1984). Cognitive mapping and elderly adults: Verbal and location memory for urban landmarks. *Journal of Gerontology, 39,* 452–457.

EVANS, L., EKERDT, D. J., & BOSSE, R. (1985). Proximity to retirement and anticipatory involvement: Findings from the Normative Aging Study. *Journal of Gerontology, 40,* 368–374.

EVANS, R. I. (1969). *Dialogue with Erik Erikson.* New York: E. P. Dutton.

FARRELL, M. P., & ROSENBERG, S. D. (1981). *Men at midlife.* Boston: Auburn House.

FEATHERMAN, D. L. (1980). Schooling and occupational careers: Constancy and change in worldly success. In O. G. Brim, Jr. & J. Kagan (Eds.), *Constancy and change in human development.* Cambridge, MA: Harvard University Press.

FEATHERMAN, D. L., & HAUSER, R. M. (1975). Design for a replicate study of social mobility in the United States. In K. Land & S. Spilerman (Eds.), *Social indicator models.* New York: Russell Sage Foundation.

FEIFEL, H., & BRANSCOMB, A. B. (1973). Who's afraid of death? *Journal of Abnormal Psychology, 81,* 282–288.

FEINSON, M. C. (1985). Aging and mental health. *Research on Aging, 7,* 155–174.

FELDMAN, H. (1981). A comparison of intentional parents and intentionally childless couples. *Journal of Marriage and the Family, 43,* 593–600.

FELDMAN, S. S., & ASCHENBRENNER, B. (1983). Impact of parenthood on various aspects of masculinity and femininity: A short-term longitudinal study. *Developmental Psychology, 19,* 278–289.

FELDMAN, S. S., BIRINGEN, Z. C., & NASH, S. C. (1981). Fluctuations in self-related self-attributions as a function of stage of family life-cycle. *Developmental Psychology, 17,* 24–35.

FENDRICH, M. (1984). Wives' employment and husbands' distress: A meta-analysis and a replication. *Journal of Marriage and the Family, 46,* 871–879.

FERRARO, K. R. (1984). Widowhood and social participation in later life: Isolation or compensation? *Research on Aging, 6,* 451–468.

FILSINGER, E. E., & WILSON, M. R. (1984). Religiosity, socioeconomic rewards, and family development: Predictors of marital adjustment. *Journal of Marriage and the Family, 46,* 663–670.

FISCHER, C. S., & PHILLIPS, S. L. (1982). Who is alone? Social characteristics of people with small networks. In L. A. Peplau & D. Perlman (Eds.), *Loneliness.* New York: John Wiley & Sons.

FISKE, M. (1980). Changing hierarchies of commitment in adulthood. In N. J. Smelser & E. H. Erikson (Eds.), *Themes of work and love in adulthood.* Cambridge, MA: Harvard University Press.

FLAVELL, J. H. (1982). Structures, stages, and sequences in cognitive development. In W. A. Collins (Ed.), *The concept of development: The Minnesota symposia on child psychology* (Vol. 15). Hillsdale, NJ: Lawrence Erlbaum & Associates.

FORDYCE, M. W. (1977). Development of a program to increase personal happiness. *Journal of Counseling Psychology, 24,* 511–521.

FOWLER, J. W. (1981). *Stages of faith.* New York: Harper & Row.

FOWLER, J. W. (1983). Stages of faith. *PT* conversation with James Fowler. *Psychology Today, 17* (November), 56–62.

FOZARD, J. L. (1980). The time for remembering. In L. W. Poon (Ed.), *Aging in the 1980s. Psychological issues.* Washington DC: American Psychological Association.

FRANKL, V. E. (1984). *Man's search for meaning* (3rd ed.). New York: Simon & Schuster.

FRIEDMAN, M., & ROSENMAN, R. H. (1974). *Type A behavior and your heart.* New York: Knopf.

FROMM, E. (1955). *Escape from freedom.* New York: Holt, Rinehart & Winston.

GANELLEN, R. J., & BLANEY, P. H. (1984). Hardiness and social support as moderators of the effects of life stress. *Journal of Personality and Social Psychology, 47,* 156–163.

GEERKEN, M., & GOVE, W. R. (1983). *At home and at work: The family's allocation of labor.* Beverly Hills, CA: Sage.

GEORGE, L. K., FILLENBAUM, G. G., & PALMORE, E. (1984). Sex differences in the antecedents and consequences of retirement. *Journal of Gerontology, 39,* 364–371.

GIELE, J. Z. (1982a). Women in adulthood: Unanswered questions. In J. Z. Giele (Ed.), *Women in the middle years.* New York: John Wiley & Sons.

GIELE, J. Z. (1982b). Women's work and family roles. In J. Z. Giele (Ed.), *Women in the middle years.* New York: John Wiley & Sons.

GILBERG, L. A. (1985). *Men in dual-career families.* Hillsdale, NJ: Lawrence Erlbaum & Associates.

GILLIGAN, C. (1977). In a different voice: Women's conceptions of the self and of morality. *Harvard Educational Review, 47,* 481–517.

Gilligan, C. (1982). *In a different voice: Psychological theory and women's development.* Cambridge, MA: Harvard University Press.

Glass, D. C. (1977). *Behavior patterns, stress, and coronary disease.* Hillsdale, NJ: Lawrence Erlbaum & Associates.

Glenn, N. D., & McLanahan, S. (1981). The effects of offspring on the psychological well-being of older adults. *Journal of Marriage and the Family, 43,* 409–421.

Glenn, N. D., & Weaver, C. N. (1981). The contribution of marital happiness to global happiness. *Journal of Marriage and the Family, 43,* 161–168.

Glick, P. C. (1977). Updating the life cycle of the family. *Journal of Marriage and the Family, 39,* 5–13.

Glick, P. C. (1979). The future of the American family. *Current Population Reports* (Special Studies Series P-23, No. 78). Washington, DC: U.S. Government Printing Office.

Glick, P. C. (1984). Marriage, divorce, and living arrangements: Prospective changes. *Journal of Family Issues, 5,* 7–26.

Goldberg, E. L., & Comstock, G. W. (1980). Epidemiology of life events: Frequency in general populations. *American Journal of Epidemiology, 111,* 736–752.

Goldstein, E. (1979). Effect of same-sex and cross-sex role models on the subsequent academic productivity of scholars. *American Psychologist, 34,* 407–410.

Gottman, J. M., & Levenson, R. W. (1984). Why marriages fail: Affective and physiological patterns in marital interaction. In J. C. Masters & K. Yarkin-Levin (Eds.), *Boundary areas in social and developmental psychology.* New York: Academic Press.

Gottman, J. M., & Porterfield, A. L. (1981). Communicative competence in the nonverbal behavior of married couples. *Journal of Marriage and the Family, 43,* 817–824.

Gould, R. (1978). *Transformations: Growth and change in adult life.* New York: Simon & Schuster.

Gould, R. (1980). Transformations during early and middle adult years. In N. J. Smelser & E. H. Erikson (Eds.), *Themes of work and love in adulthood.* Cambridge, MA: Harvard University Press.

Gould, S. (1979). Age, job complexity, satisfaction, and performance. *Journal of Vocational Behavior, 14,* 209–223.

Gove, W. R. (1972). Sex roles, marital roles, and mental illness. *Social Forces, 51,* 34–44.

Gove, W. R. (1979). Sex, marital status, and psychiatric treatment: A research note. *Social Forces, 58,* 89–93.

Gove, W. R., & Geerken, M. R. (1977). The effect of children and employment on the mental health of married men and women. *Social Forces, 56,* 66–76.

Greenblatt, R. B., Natrajan, P. K., & Karpas, A. (1985). The endocrine and reproductive system of aged women. In M. R. Haug, A. B. Ford, & Scheafor, M. (Eds.), *The physical health of aged women.* New York: Springer.

Gribben, K., Schaie, K. W., & Parham, I. A. (1980). Complexity of life style and maintenance of intellectual abilities. *Journal of Social Issues, 36*(2), 47–61.

Guillen, M. A. (1984). The face of change. *Psychology Today, 18*(10), 76–77.

Gurin, P., & Brim, O. G., Jr. (1984). Change in self in adulthood: The example of a sense of control. In P. B. Baltes & O. G. Brim, Jr. (Eds.), *Life-span development and behavior* (Vol. 6). Orlando, FL: Academic Press.

Gutmann, D. (1975). Parenthood: A key to the comparative study of the life cycle. In N. Datan & L. H. Ginsberg (Eds.), *Life-span developmental psychology: Normative life crises.* New York: Academic Press.

Gutmann, D. (1977). The cross-cultural perspective: Notes toward a comparative psychology of aging. In J. E. Birren & K. W. Schaie (Eds.), *Handbook of the psychology of aging.* New York: Van Nostrand Reinhold.

HAAN, N. (1976). ". . . change and sameness . . ." reconsidered. *International Journal of Aging and Human Development, 7,* 59–65.

HAAN, N. (1981). Common dimensions of personality development: Early adolescence to middle life. In D. H. Eichorn, J. A. Clausen, N. Haan, M. P. Honzik, & P. H. Mussen (Eds.), *Present and past in middle life.* New York: Academic Press.

HAAN, N. (1982). The assessment of coping, defense, and stress. In L. Goldberger & S. Breznitz (Eds.), *Handbook of stress: Theoretical and clinical aspects.* New York: The Free Press.

HAAN, N., & DAY, D. (1974). A longitudinal study of change and sameness in personality development: Adolescence to later adulthood. *International Journal of Aging and Human Development, 5,* 11–39.

HAGESTAD, G. O. (1984). The continuous bond: A dynamic, multigenerational perspective on parent-child relations between adults. In M. Perlmutter (Ed.), *Minnesota symposia on child psychology* (Vol. 17). Hillsdale, NJ: Lawrence Erlbaum & Associates.

HAGESTAD, G. O. (1985). Continuity and connectedness. In V. L. Bengtson (Ed.), *Grandparenthood.* Beverly Hills, CA: Sage.

HALL, D. T. (1972). A model of coping with role conflict: The role behavior of college educated women. *Administrative Science Quarterly, 17,* 471–486.

HALL, D. T. (1975). Pressures from work, self, and home in the life stages of married women. *Journal of Vocational Behavior, 6,* 121–132.

HANLEY-DUNN, P., & MCINTOSH, J. L. (1984). Meaningfulness and recall of names by young and old adults. *Journal of Gerontology, 39,* 583–585.

HANSEN, J. E., & SCHULDT, W. J. (1984). Marital self-disclosure and marital satisfaction. *Journal of Marriage and the Family, 46,* 923–926.

HARING, M. J., OKUN, M. A., & STOCK, W. A. (1984). A quantitative synthesis of literature on work status and subjective well being. *Journal of Vocational Behavior, 25,* 316–324.

HARNEY, M. K., & BRIGHAM, T. A. (1985). Tolerance of aversive stimuli in relation to life change. *Journal of Behavioral Medicine, 8,* 21–35.

HARRIMAN, L. C. (1983). Personal and marital changes accompanying parenthood. *Family Relations, 32,* 387–394.

HARRIS, L. (1981). *Aging in the eighties: America in transition.* Washington, DC: National Council on the Aging.

HARTUP, W. W. (1975). The origins of friendships. In M. Lewis & L. A. Rosenblum (Eds.), *Friendship and peer relations.* New York: John Wiley & Sons.

HAUSER, R. M., & DICKINSON, P. J. (1974). Inequality of occupational status and income. *American Educational Research Journal, 11,* 161–168.

HAUSER, R. M., & FEATHERMAN, D. L. (1976). Equality of schooling: Trends and prospects. *Sociology of Education, 49,* 99–120.

HAVIGHURST, R. J. (1982). The world of work. In B. B. Wolman (Ed.), *Handbook of developmental psychology.* Englewood Cliffs, NJ: Prentice-Hall.

HAYFLICK, L. (1965). The limited *in vitro* lifetime of human diploid cell strains. *Experimental Cell Research, 37,* 614–636.

HAYFLICK, L. (1975). Why grow old? *The Stanford Magazine, 3*(1), 36–43.

HAYFLICK, L. (1977). The cellular basis for biological aging. In C. E. Finch & L. Hayflick (Eds.), *Handbook of the biology of aging.* New York: Van Nostrand Reinhold.

HAYS, R. B. (1984). The development and maintenance of friendship. *Journal of Social and Personal Relationships, 1,* 75–98.

HEATON, T. B. (1984). Religious homogamy and marital satisfaction reconsidered. *Journal of Marriage and the Family, 46,* 729–733.

HEINEMANN, G. D. (1985). Negative health outcomes among the elderly: Predictors and profiles. *Research on Aging, 7,* 363–382.

Helson, R., Mitchell, V., & Moane, G. (1984). Personality and patterns of adherence and nonadherence to the social clock. *Journal of Personality and Social Psychology, 46,* 1079–1096.

Hennig, M., & Jardim, A. (1976). *The Managerial Woman.* Garden City, NY: Doubleday (Anchor Books).

Hetherington, E. M., & Camara, K. A. (1984). Families in transition: The processes of dissolution and reconstitution. In R. D. Parke, R. N. Emde, H. P. McAdoo, & G. P. Sackett (Eds.), *Review of child development research: Vol. 7. The family.* Chicago: University of Chicago Press.

Hetherington, E. M., Cox, M., & Cox, R. (1978). The aftermath of divorce. In J. H. Stevens, Jr., & M. Matthews (Eds.), *Mother-child, father-child relations.* Washington, DC: National Association for the Education of Young Children.

Hill, R. (1965). Decision making and the family life cycle. In E. Shanas & G. F. Streib (Eds.), *Social structure and the family: Generational relations.* Englewood Cliffs, NJ: Prentice-Hall.

Hinton, J. (1975). The influence of previous personality on reactions to having terminal cancer. *Omega, 6,* 95–111.

Hoffman, L. W., & Manis, J. D. (1978). Influences of children on marital interaction and parental satisfactions and dissatisfactions. In R. M. Lerner & G. B. Spanier (Eds.), *Child influences on marital and family interaction.* New York: Academic Press.

Hogan, D. P. (1978). The variable order of events in the life course. *American Sociological Review, 43,* 573–586.

Holahan, C. K., Holahan, C. J., & Belk, S. S. (1984). Adjustment in aging: The roles of life stress, hassles, and self-efficacy. *Health Psychology, 3,* 315–328.

Holland, J. L. (1973). *Making vocational choices: A theory of careers.* Englewood Cliffs, NJ: Prentice-Hall.

Holmes, T. H., & Rahe, R. H. (1967). The Social Readjustment Rating Scale. *Journal of Psychosomatic Research, 11,* 213–218.

Holmes, T. S., & Holmes, T. H. Short-term intrusions into life-style routine. *Journal of Psychosomatic Research, 14,* 121–132.

Holzer, C. E. III, Leaf, P. J., & Weissman, M. M. (1985). Living with depression. In M. R. Haug, A. B. Ford, & M. Sheafor (Eds.), *The physical and mental health of aged women.* New York: Springer.

Hood, R. W., Jr. (1970). Religious orientation and the report of religious experience. *Journal for the Scientific Study of Religion, 9,* 285–291.

Hood, R. W., Jr. (1973). Religious orientation and the experience of transcendence. *Journal for the Scientific Study of Religion, 12,* 441–448.

Hood, R. W., Jr. (1975). The construction and preliminary validation of a measure of reported mystical experience. *Journal for the Scientific Study of Religion, 14,* 29–41.

Horn, J. L. (1982). The aging of human abilities. In B. B. Wolman (Ed.), *Handbook of developmental psychology.* Englewood Cliffs, NJ: Prentice-Hall.

Horn, J. L., & Cattell, R. B. (1966). Refinement and test of theory of fluid and crystallized ability intelligences. *Journal of Educational Psychology, 57,* 253–270.

Horn, J. L., & Donaldson, G. (1980). Cognitive development in adulthood. In O. G. Brim, Jr. & J. Kagan (Eds.), *Constancy and change in human development.* Cambridge, MA: Harvard University Press.

Houseknecht, S. K. (1979). Childlessness and marital adjustment. *Journal of Marriage and the Family, 41,* 259–265.

Houston, J. P., Bee, H. L., & Rimm, D. C. (1983). *Invitation to psychology* (2nd ed.). New York: Academic Press.

HUNSBERGER, B. (1985). Religion, age, life satisfaction, and perceived sources of religiousness: A study of older persons. *Journal of Gerontology, 40,* 615–620.

HUNT, M. (1974). *Sexual behavior in the 1970s.* New York: Playboy Press.

HUNTLEY, C. W., & DAVIS, F. (1985). Undergraduate study of value scores as predictors of occupation 25 years later. *Journal of Personality and Social Psychology, 43,* 1148–1155.

HUSTON, T. L., SURRA, C. A., FITZGERALD, N. M., & CATE, R. M. (1981). From courtship to marriage: Mate selection as an interpersonal process. In S. Duck & R. Gilmour (Eds.), *Personal relationships: Vol. 2. Developing personal relationships.* New York: Academic Press.

HUSTON-STEIN, A., & HIGGENS-TRENK, A. (1978). Development of females from childhood through adulthood: Career and feminine role orientations. In P. B. Baltes (Ed.), *Life-span development and behavior* (Vol. 1). New York: Academic Press.

IACOCCA, L. (1984). *Iacocca: An autobiography.* Toronto: Bantam Books.

JACOBSON, P. H. (1964). Cohort survival for generations since 1940. *Milbank Memorial Fund Quarterly, 42*(3), 36–53.

JAMES, W. (1902). *The varieties of religious experience.* New York: Mentor edition, 1958.

JARVIK, L. F., & BANK, L. (1983). Aging twins: Longitudinal psychometric data. In W. K. Schaie (Ed.), *Longitudinal studies of adult psychological development.* New York: Guilford Press.

JOHNSON, D. (1983). *Spirals of growth.* Wheaton, IL: Theosophical Publishing House.

JOHNSON, P. J., & FIREBAUGH, F. M. (1985). A typology of household work performance by employment demands. *Journal of Family Issues, 6,* 83–106.

KAGAN, J. (1980). Perspectives on continuity. In O. G. Brim, Jr. & J. Kagan (Eds.), *Constancy and change in human development.* Cambridge, MA: Harvard University Press.

KAGAN, J., & MOSS, H. A. (1962). *Birth to maturity.* New York: John Wiley & Sons.

KAHN, R. L., & ANTONUCCI, T. C. (1980). Convoys over the life course: Attachment, roles, and social support. In P. B. Baltes & O. G. Brim, Jr. (Eds.), *Life-span development and behavior* (Vol. 3). New York: Academic Press.

KALISH, R. A. (1977). Death and dying in a social context. In R. H. Binstock & E. Shanas (Eds.), *Handbook of aging and the social sciences.* New York: Van Nostrand Reinhold.

KALISH, R. A. (1985). The social context of death and dying. In R. H. Binstock & E. Shanas (Eds.), *Handbook of aging and the social sciences* (2nd ed.) New York: Van Nostrand Reinhold.

KALISH, R. A., & REYNOLDS, D. K. (1976). *Death and ethnicity: A psychocultural study.* Los Angeles: University of Southern California Press. Reprinted 1981, Farmingdale, NJ: Baywood Publishing Co.

KALLMAN, E. J., & JARVIK, L. F. (1959). Individual differences in constitution and genetic background. In J. E. Birren (Ed.), *Handbook of aging and the individual.* Chicago: University of Chicago Press.

KAPLAN, B. (1983) A trio of trials. In R. M. Lerner (Ed.), *Developmental psychology: Historical and philosophical perspectives.* Hillsdale, NJ: Lawrence Erlbaum & Associates.

KASL, S. V., & COBB, S. (1982). Variability of stress effects among men experiencing job loss. In L. Goldberger & S. Breznitz (Eds.), *Handbook of stress. Theoretical and clinical aspects.* New York: The Free Press.

KASTENBAUM, R., & AISENBERG, R. (1976). *The psychology of death.* New York: Springer.

KATZ, P. A. (1979). The development of female identity. *Sex Roles, 5,* 155–178.

KAUSLER, D. H., LICHTY, W., & FREUND, J. S. (1985). Adult age differences in recognition memory and frequency judgments for planned versus performed activities. *Developmental Psychology, 21,* 647–654.

Keating, N., & Marshall, J. (1980). The process of retirement: The rural self-employed. *The Gerontologist, 20,* 437–443.

Keen, S. (1983). *The passionate life: Stages of loving.* New York: Harper & Row.

Kegan, R. (1980). There the dance is: Religious dimensions of develpmental theory. In J. W. Fowler & A. Vergote (Eds.), *Toward moral and religious maturity.* Morristown, NJ: Silver Burdett.

Kegan, R. (1982). *The evolving self.* Cambridge, MA: Harvard University Press.

Keith, P. M. (1981–82). Perceptions of time remaining and distance from death. *Omega, 12,* 307–318.

Keith, P. M. (1985). Work, retirement and well-being among unmarried men and women. *The Gerontologist, 25,* 410–416.

Kenshalo, D. R. (1977). Age changes in touch, vibration, temperature, kinesthesis, and pain sensitivity. In J. E. Birren & K. W. Schaie, (Eds.), *Handbook of the psychology of aging.* New York: Van Nostrand Reinhold.

Kinsey, A. C., Pomeroy, W. B., & Martin, C. E. (1948). *Sexual behavior in the human male.* Philadelphia: W. B. Saunders.

Kinsey, A. C., Pomeroy, W. B., & Martin, C. E. (1953). *Sexual behavior of the human female.* Philadelphia: W. B. Saunders.

Kitson, G. C. (1982). Attachment to the spouse in divorce: A scale and its application. *Journal of Marriage and the Family, 44,* 379–393.

Kitson, G. C., Babri, K. B., & Roach, M. J. (1985). Who divorces and why: A review. *Journal of Family Issues, 6,* 255–293.

Kleemeier, R. W. (1962). Intellectual changes in the senium. *Proceedings of the Social Statistics Section of the American Statistics Association, 1,* 290–295.

Klocke, R. A. (1977). Influence of aging on the lung. In C. E. Finch & L. Hayflick (Eds.), *Handbook of the biology of aging.* New York: Van Nostrand Reinhold.

Kobasa, S. C. (1979). Stressful life events, personality, and health: An inquiry into hardiness. *Journal of Personality and Social Psychology, 37,* 1–11.

Kobasa, S. C. (1982). Commitment and coping in stress resistance among lawyers. *Journal of Personality and Social Psychology, 42,* 707–717.

Kobasa, S. C., Maddi, S. R., & Kahn, S. (1982). Hardiness and health: A prospective study. *Journal of Personality and Social Psychology, 42* 168–177.

Kohlberg, L. (1958). *The development of modes of thinking and choices in the years 10 to 16.* Unpublished doctoral dissertation, University of Chicago.

Kohlberg, L. (1964). The develoment of moral character and ideology. In M. L. Hoffman and L. W. Hoffman (Eds.), *Review of child development research* (Vol. 1). New York: Russell Sage Foundation.

Kohlberg, L. (1973). Continuities in childhood and adult moral development revisited. In P. B. Baltes & K. W. Schaie, (Eds.), *Life-span developmental psychology: Personality and socialization.* New York: Academic Press.

Kohlberg, L. (1976). Moral stages and moralization: The cognitive-developmental approach. In T. Lickona (Ed.), *Moral development and behavior: Theory, research and social issues.* New York: Holt, Rinehart and Winston.

Kohlberg, L. (1981). *Essays on moral development: Vol. 1. The philosophy of moral development.* San Francisco: Harper & Row.

Kohlberg, L. (1984) *Essays on moral development: Vol. 2. The psychology of moral development.* San Francisco: Harper & Row.

Kohlberg, L., & Kramer, R. (1969). Continuities and discontinuities in children and adult moral development. *Human Development, 12,* 225–252.

Kohlberg, L., Levine, C., & Hewer, A. (1983). Moral stages: A current formulation and a response to critics. *Contributions to human development 10*. Basel, Switzerland: S. Karger. (In L. Kohlberg, *Essays on Moral Development,* Vol. 2, The psychology of moral development, p. 249. New York: Harper & Row, 1984).

KOHN, M. L. (1980). Job complexity and adult personality. In N. J. Smelser & E. H. Erikson (Eds.), *Themes of work and love in adulthood.* Cambridge, MA: Harvard University Press.

KOHN, M. L., & SCHOOLER, C. (1978). The reciprocal effects of the substantive complexity of work and intellectual flexibility: A longitudinal assessment. *American Journal of Sociology, 84,* 24–52.

KOHN, R. R. (1977). Heart and cardiovascular system. In C. E. Finch & L. Hayflick (Eds.), *Handbook of the biology of aging*. New York: Van Nostrand Reinhold.

KOLEVZON, M. S., & GOTTLIEB, S. J. (1983). The impact of divorce: A multivariate study. *Journal of Divorce, 7,* 89–98.

KORMAN, A. K., MAHLER, S. R., & OMRAN, K. A. (1983). Work ethics and satisfaction, alienation, and other reactions. In W. B. Walsh & S. H. Osipow (Eds.), *Handbook of vocational psychology: Vol. 2. Applications*. Hillsdale, NJ: Lawrence Erlbaum & Associates.

KÜBLER-ROSS, E. (1969). *On death and dying*. New York: Macmillan.

KÜBLER-ROSS, E. (1974). *Questions and answers on death and dying*. New York: Macmillan.

KÜBLER-ROSS, E. (1975). *Death. The final stage of growth*. Englewood Cliffs, NJ: Prentice Hall.

Kunze, K. R. (1974). Age and occupations at Lockheed-California: Versatility of older workers. *Industrial Gerontology, 1,* 57–64.

LABOUVIE-VIEF, G. (1980). Beyond formal operations: Uses and limits of pure logic in life-span development. *Human Development, 23,* 141–161.

LABOUVIE-VIEF, G. (1981). Proactive and reactive aspects of constructivism: Growth and aging in life-span perspective. In R. M. Lerner & N. A. Busch-Rossnagel (Eds.), *Individuals as producers of their own development: A life-span perspective*. New York: Academic Press.

LABOUVIE-VIEF, G., & SCHELL, D. A. (1982). Learning and memory in later life. In B. B. Wolman (Ed.), *Handbook of developmental psychology*. Englewood Cliffs, NJ: Prentice Hall.

LAING, J., SWANEY, K., & PREDIGER, D. J. (1984). Integrating vocational interest inventory results and expressed choices. *Journal of Vocational Behavior, 25,* 304–315.

LANG, A. M., & BRODY, E. M. (1983). Characteristics of middle-aged daughters and help to their elderly mothers. *Journal of Marriage and the Family, 45,* 193–202.

LARSON, P. C. (1982). Gay male relationships. In W. Paul, J. D. Weinrich, J. C. Gonsiorek, & M. E. Hotvedt (Eds.), *Homosexuality: Social, psychological, and biological issues.* Beverly Hills, CA: Sage.

LAUER, J., & LAUER, R. (1985). Marriages made to last. *Psychology Today, 19*(6), 22–26.

LAWTON, M. P. (1977). The impact of the environment on aging and behavior. In J. E. Birren & K. W.Schaie (Eds.), *Handbook of the psychology of aging*. New York: Van Nostrand Reinhold.

LAWTON, M. P. (1985). Housing and living environments of older people. In R. H. Binstock & E. Shanas (Eds.), *Aging and the social sciences* (2nd ed.). New York: Van Nostrand Reinhold.

LAZARUS, R. S., & DELONGIS, A. (1983). Psychological stress and coping in aging. *American Psychologist, 38,* 245–254.

LAZARUS, R. S., & FOLKMAN, S. (1984). *Stress, appraisal, and coping.* New York: Springer.

LEE, G. R. (1977). Age at marriage and marital satisfaction: A multivariate analysis with implications for marital stability. *Journal of Marriage and the Family, 39,* 493–504.

LEE, G. R., & ELLITHORPE, E. (1982). Intergenerational exchange and subjective well-being among the elderly. *Journal of Marriage and the Family, 44,* 217–224.

LEE, G. R., & IHINGER-TALLMAN, M. (1980). Sibling interaction and morale: The effects of family relations on older people. *Research on Aging, 2,* 367–391.

LEEAN, C. (1985). *Faith development in the adult life cycle, Module 2.* Working paper of the Faith Development in the Adult Life Cycle Project, The Religious Education Association of the United States and Canada, 1985.

LEHMAN, H. C. (1953). *Age and achievement.* Princeton, NJ: Princeton University Press.

LEIGH, G. K. (1982). Kinship interaction over the family life span. *Journal of Marriage and the Family, 44,* 197–208.

LEON, G. R., GILLUM, B., GILLUM, R., & GOUZE, M. (1979). Personality stability and change over a 30-year period—middle age to old age. *Journal of Consulting and Clinical Psychology, 47,* 517–524.

LERNER, R. M., & RYFF, C. D. (1978). Implementation of the life-span view of human development: The sample case of attachment. In P. B. Baltes (Ed.), *Life-span development and behavior* (Vol. 1). New York: Academic Press.

LESHAN, L. (1966). *The medium, the mystic, and the physicist.* New York: Ballantine.

LEVINSON, D. J. (1978). *The seasons of a man's life.* New York: Knopf.

LEVINSON, D. J. (1980). Toward a conception of the adult life course. In N. J. Smelser & E. H. Erikson (Eds.), *Themes of work and love in adulthood.* Cambridge, MA: Harvard University Press.

LEWIS, R. A., & SPANIER, G. B. (1979). Theorizing about the quality and stability of marriage. In W. R. Burr, R. Hill, F. I. Nye, & I. L. Reiss (Eds.), *Contemporary theories about the family* (Vol. 1). New York: The Free Press.

LIEBERMAN, M. A. (1965). Psychological correlates of impending death: Some preliminary observations. *Journal of Gerontology, 20,* 182–190.

LIEBERMAN, M. A. (1982). The effects of social supports on responses to stress: In L. Goldberger & S. Breznitz (Eds.), *Handbook of stress. Theoretical and clinical aspects.* New York: The Free Press.

LIEBERMAN, M. A., & COPLAN, A. S. (1970). Distance from death as a variable in the study of aging. *Developmental Psychology, 2,* 71–84.

LINDSAY, R. (1985). The aging skeleton. In M. R. Haug, A. B. Ford, & M. Sheafor (Eds.), *The physical and mental health of aged women.* New York: Springer.

LIVSON, F. B. (1976). Patterns of personality development in middle-aged women: A longitudinal study. *International Journal of Aging and Human Development, 7,* 107–115.

LIVSON, F. B. (1981). Paths to psychological health in the middle years: Sex differences. In D. H. Eichorn, J. A. Clausen, N. Haan, M. P. Honzik, & P. H. Mussen (Eds.), *Present and past in middle life.* New York: Academic Press.

LIVSON, N., & PESKIN, H. (1981). Psychological health at 40: Prediction from adolesacent personality. In D. H. Eichorn, J. A. Clausen, N. Haan, M. P. Honzik, & P. H. Mussen (Eds.), *Present and past in middle life.* New York: Academic Press.

LOCKSLEY, A. (1982). Social class and marital attitudes and behavior. *Journal of Marriage and the Family, 44,* 427–440.

LOEVINGER, J. (1976). *Ego development.* San Francisco: Jossey-Bass.

LOEVINGER, J. (1984). On the self and predicting behavior. In R. A. Zucker, J. Aronoff, & A. I. Rabin (Eds.), *Personality and the prediction of behavior.* New York: Academic Press.

LONKY, E., KAUS, C. R., & ROODIN, P. A. (1984). Life experience and mode of coping: Relation to moral judgment in adulthood. *Developmental Psychology, 20,* 1159–1167.

LOPATA, H. Z. (1969). Loneliness: Forms and components. *Social Problems, 17,* 248–262.

LOPATA, H. Z. (1973). *Widowhood in an American city.* Cambridge, MA: Schenkman Publishing Co.

Lopata, H. Z. (1979). *Women as widows: Support systems*. New York: Elsevier.

Lopata, H. Z., Heinemann, G. D., & Baum, J. (1982). Loneliness: Antecedents and coping strategies in the lives of widows. In L. A. Peplau & D. Perlman (Eds.), *Loneliness*. New York: John Wiley & Sons.

Lowe, G. D., & Witt, D. D. (1984). Early marriage as a career contingency: The prediction of educational attainment. *Journal of Marriage and the Family, 46,* 689–698.

Lowenthal, M. F., Thurnher, M., & Chiriboga, D. (1975). *Four stages of life*. San Francisco, CA: Jossey-Bass.

Lyons, N. P. (1983). Two perspectives: On self, relationships, and morality. *Harvard Educational Review, 53,* 125–143.

Maas, H. S., & Kuypers, J. A. (1974). *From thirty to seventy*. San Francisco: Jossey-Bass.

Macht, M. L., & Buschke, H. (1984). Speed of recall in aging. *Journal of Gerontology,* 39, 439–443.

Madden, D. J. (1985). Age-related slowing in the retrieval of information from long-term memory. *Journal of Gerontology, 40,* 208–210.

Magnusson, D. (1982). Situational determinants of stress: An interactional perspective. In L. Goldberger & S. Breznitz (Eds.), *Handbook of stress: Theoretical and clinical aspects*. New York: The Free Press.

Marcia, J. E. (1980). Identity in adolescence. In J. Adelson (Ed.), *Handbook of adolescent psychology*. New York: John Wiley & Sons.

Maret, E., & Finlay, B. (1984). The distribution of household labor among women in dual-earner families. *Journal of Marriage and the Family, 46,* 357–364.

Markman, H. J. (1981). Prediction of marital distress: A 5-year follow-up. *Journal of Consulting and Clinical Psychology, 49,* 760–762.

Maslow, A. H. (1968). *Toward a psychology of being* (2nd ed.). New York: Van Nostrand Reinhold.

Maslow, A. H. (1970a). *Religions, values, and peak experiences*. New York: Viking. (Original work published 1964.)

Maslow, A. H. (1970b). *Motivation and personality* (2nd ed.). New York: Harper & Row.

Maslow, A. H. (1971). *The farther reaches of human nature*. New York: Viking.

Matarazzo, J. D. (1972). *Wechsler's measurement and appraisal of adult intelligence* (5th ed.). Baltimore: Williams & Wilkins.

McCall, R. B. (1977). Childhood IQ's as predictors of adult educational and occupational status. *Science,* 197, 482–483.

McCrae, R. R. (1982). Age differences in the use of coping mechanisms. *Journal of Gerontology, 37,* 454–460.

McCrae, R. R., & Costa, P. T., Jr. (1983). Psychological maturity and subjective well-being: Toward a new synthesis. *Developmental Psychology, 19,* 243–248.

McCready, W. C. (1985). Styles of grandparenting among white ethnics. In V. L. Bengtson & J. F. Robertson (Eds.), *Grandparenthood*. Beverly Hills, CA: Sage.

McFarland, C. E., Warren, L. R., & Crockard, J. (1985). Memory for self-generated stimuli in young and old adults. *Journal of Gerontology, 40,* 205–207.

McGrath, J. E. (1970). A conceptual formulation for research on stress. In J. E. McGrath (Ed.), *Social and psychological factors in stress*. New York: Holt, Rinehart & Winston.

McIntosh, J. L. (1985). Suicide among the elderly: Levels and trends. *American Journal of Orthopsychiatry, 52,* 288–293.

McLaughlin, S. D., & Micklin, M. (1983). The timing of the first birth and changes in personal efficacy. *Journal of Marriage and the Family, 45,* 47–55.

Menaghan, E. (1983). Marital stress and family transitions: A panel analysis. *Journal of Marriage and the Family, 45,* 371–386.

Miller, D. C., & Form, W. H. (1951). *Industrial sociology*. New York: Harper & Row.

MINDEL, C. H., & VAUGHAN, C. E. (1978). A multidimensional approach to religiosity and disengagement. *Journal of Gerontology, 33,* 103–108.

MINKLER, M., & STONE, R. (1985). The feminization of poverty and older women. *The Gerontologist, 25,* 351–357.

Mischel, W. (1966). *Personality and assessment.* New York: John Wiley & Sons.

MISCHEL, W. (1984). Convergences and challenges in the search for consistency. *American Psychologist, 39,* 351–364.

MOBERG, D. O. (1965). Religiosity in old age. *The Gerontologist, 5,* 78–87.

MODEL, S. (1981). Housework by husbands. Determinants and implications. *Journal of Family Issues, 2,* 225–237.

MOORE, K. A., HOFFERTH, S. L., WERTHEIMER, R. F., WAITE, L. J., & CALDWELL, S. B. (1981). Teenage childbearing: Consequences for women, families, and government welfare expenditures. In K. G. Scott, T. Field, & E. G. Robertson (Eds.), *Teenage parents and their offspring.* New York: Grune & Stratton.

MOOS, R. H., & BILLINGS, A. G. (1982). Conceptualizing and measuring coping resources and processes. In L. Goldberger & S. Breznitz (Eds.), *Handbook of stress: Theoretical and clinical aspects.* New York: The Free Press.

MORTIMER, J. T. (1974). Patterns of intergenerational occupational movements: A smallest-space analysis. *American Journal of Sociology, 5,* 1278–1295.

MORTIMER, J. T. (1976). Social class, work and family: Some implications of the father's occupation for family relationships and son's career decisions. *Journal of Marriage and the Family, 38,* 241–156.

MOSHER, F. A., & HORNSBY, J. R. (1966). On asking questions. In J. S. Bruner, R. R. Olver, & P. M. Greenfield (Eds.), *Studies in cognitive growth.* New York: John Wiley & Sons.

MURRAY, J. (1979). Subjective retirement. *Social Security Bulletin, 42,* 1–7.

MURSTEIN, B. I. (1970). Stimulus-value-role: A theory of marital choice. *Journal of Marriage and the Family, 32,* 465–481.

MURSTEIN, B. I. (1976). *Who will marry whom? Theories and research in marital choice.* New York: Springer.

MURSTEIN, B. I. (1977). The stimulus-value-role (SVR) theory of dyadic relationships. In S. W. Duck (Ed.), *Theory and practice in interpersonal attraction.* New York: Academic Press.

MUSSEN, P., HONZIK, M. P., & EICHORN, D. H. (1982). Early adult antecedents of life satisfaction at age 70. *Journal of Gerontology, 37,* 316–322.

MYERS-WALLS, J. A. (1984). Balancing multiple role responsibilities during the transition to parenthood. *Family Relations, 33,* 267–271.

NAGY, M. (1948). The child's view of death. *Journal of Genetic Psychology, 73,* 3–27.

NASH, S. C., & FELDMAN, S. S. (1981). Sex role and sex-related attributions: Constancy and change across the family life cycle. In M. E. Lamb & A. L. Brown (Eds.), *Advances in developmental psychology* (Vol. 1). Hillsdale, NJ: Lawrence Erlbaum & Associates.

NATHANSON, C. A., & LORENZ, G. (1982). Women and health: The social dimensions of biomedical data. In J. Z. Giele (Ed.), *Women in the middle years.* New York: John Wiley & Sons.

NATIONAL CENTER FOR EDUCATIONAL STATISTICS (1981). *Participation in adult education.* Washington, DC: U.S. Department of Education.

NATIONAL CENTER FOR HEALTH STATISTICS (1979). Current Estimates from the Health Interview Survey, United States, 1978. *Vital and Health Statistics,* Series 10, No. 130.

NATIONAL CENTER FOR HEALTH STATISTICS, (1984). Annual summary of births, deaths, marriages, and divorces: United States, 1983. *Monthly Vital Statistics Report, 1984* (32, No. 13).

NEIMEYER, R. A., & CHAPMAN, K. M. (1980–81). Self/ideal discrepancy and fear of death: The test of an existential hypothesis. *Omega, 11,* 233–239.

NEUGARTEN, B. L. (1968). The awareness of middle age. In B. L. Neugarten (Ed.), *Middle age and aging*. Chicago, IL: University of Chicago Press.

NEUGARTEN, B. L. (1976). Adaptation and the life cycle. *The Counseling Psychologist, 6,* 16–20.

NEUGARTEN, B. L. (1977). Personality and aging. In J. E. Birren & K. W. Schaie (Eds.), *Handbook of the psychology of aging*. New York: Van Nostrand Reinhold.

NEUGARTEN, B. L. (1979). Time, age, and the life cycle. *American Journal of Psychiatry, 136,* 887–894.

NEUGARTEN, B. L., & WEINSTEIN, K. (1964). The changing American grandparent. *Journal of Marriage and the Family, 26,* 199–204.

NISAN, M., & KOHLBERG, L. (1982). Universality and variation in moral judgment: A longitudinal and cross-sectional study in Turkey. *Child Development, 53,* 865–876.

NOCK, S. L. (1982). The life-cycle approach to family analysis. In B. B. Wolman (Ed.), *Handbook of developmental psychology*. Englewood Cliffs, NJ: Prentice-Hall.

NOLEN, W. A. (1984). *Crisis time! Love, marriage, and the male at midlife*. New York: Dodd, Mead.

NORRIS, J. E., & RUBIN, K. H. (1984). Peer interaction and communication: A life-span perspective. In P. B. Baltes & O. G. Brim, Jr. (Eds.), *Life-span development and behavior* (Vol. 6). Orlando, FL: Academic Press.

NORTON, A. J. (1983). Family life cycle: 1980. *Journal of Marriage and the Family, 45,* 267–275.

NUCKOLLS, K. B., CASSEL, J., & KAPLAN, B. H. (1972). Psychosocial assets, life crises, and the prognosis of pregnancy. *American Journal of Epidemiology, 95,* 431–441.

O'RAND, A., & HENRETTA, J. C. (1982). Midlife work history and retirement income. In M. Szinovacz (Ed.), *Women's retirement*. Beverly Hills, CA: Sage.

OSHERSON, S., & DILL, D. (1983). Varying work and family choices: Their impact on men's work satisfaction. *Journal of Marriage and the Family, 45,* 339–346.

OSTROW, A. C. (1984). *Physical activity and the older adult. Psychological perspectives*. Princeton, NJ: Princeton Book Co.

OTTO, L. B. (1979). Antecedents and consequences of marital timing. In W. R. Burr, R. Hill, F. I. Nye, & I. L. Reiss (Eds.), *Contemporary theories about the family* (Vol. 1). New York: Free Press.

OWENS, W. A. (1966). Age and mental ability: A second adult follow-up. *Journal of Educational Psychology, 57,* 311–325.

PAFFENBARGER, R. S., JR., & HYDE, R. T. (1984). Exercise in the prevention of coronary heart disease. *Preventive Medicine, 13,* 3–22.

PALMORE, E. (1970). Health practices and illness. *The Gerontologist, 10,* 313–316.

PALMORE, E. (1981). *Social patterns in normal aging: Findings from the Duke Longitudinal Study*. Durham, NC: Duke University Press.

PALMORE, E. B., BURCHETT, B. M., FILLENBAUM, G. G., GEORGE, L. K., & WALLMAN, L. M. (1985). *Retirement: Causes and consequences*. New York: Springer.

PALMORE, E., CLEVELAND, W. (1976). Aging, terminal decline, and terminal drop. *Journal of Gerontology, 31,* 76–81.

PALMORE, E. B., FILLENBAUM, G. G., & GEORGE, L. K. (1984). Consequences of retirement. *Journal of Gerontology, 39,* 109–116.

PALMORE, E. B., GEORGE, L. K., & FILLENBAUM, G. G. (1982). Predictors of retirement. *Journal of Gerontology, 37,* 733–742.

PALMORE, E. B., & KIVETT, V. (1977). Change in life satisfaction: A longitudinal study of persons aged 46–70. *Journal of Gerontology, 32,* 311–316.

PALMORE, E., & STONE, V. (1973). Predictors of longevity. *Gerontologist, 13,* 88–90.

Parkes, C. M. (1970). "Seeking" and "finding" a lost object. *Social Science and Medicine, 4,* 187–201.

Parlee, M. B. (1979, October). The friendship bond. *Psychology Today, 14,* 43–54, 113.

Parnes, H. (1981). *Work and retirement.* Cambridge, MA: Massachusetts Institute of Technology Press.

Pascual-Leone, J. (1983). Growing into human maturity: Toward a metasubjective theory of adult stages. In P. B. Baltes & O. G. Brim, Jr. (Eds.), *Life-span development and behavior* (Vol. 5). New York: Academic Press.

Paul, W., & Weinrich, J. D. (1982). Whom and what do we study: Definition and scope of sexual orientation. In W. Paul, J. D. Weinrich, J. C. Gonsiorek, & M. E. Hotvedt (Eds.), *Homosexuality: Social, psychological, and biological issues.* Beverly Hills, CA: Sage.

Paykel, E. S. (1974). Life stress and psychiatric disorder: Applications of the clinical approach. In B. S. Dohrenwend & B. P. Dohrenwend (Eds.), *Stressful life events: Their nature and effects.* New York: John Wiley & Sons.

Pearce, K. A., & Denney, N. W. (1984). A lifespan study of classification preference. *Journal of Gerontology, 39,* 458–464.

Pearlin, L. I. (1980). Life strains and psychological distress among adults. In N. J. Smelser & E. H. Erikson (Eds), *Themes of work and love in adulthood.* Cambridge, MA: Harvard University Press.

Pearlin, L. I. (1982a). Discontinuities in the study of aging. In T. K. Hareven & K. J. Adams (Eds.), *Aging and life course transitions: An interdisciplinary perspective.* New York: Guilford Press.

Pearlin, L. I. (1982b). The social contexts of stress. In L. Goldberger & S. Breznitz (Eds.), *Handbook of stress: Theoretical and clinical aspects.* New York: The Free Press.

Pearlin, L. I., & Lieberman, M. A. (1979). Social sources of emotional distress. In R. Simmons (Ed.), *Research in community and mental health.* Greenwich, CT: JAI Press.

Pearlin, L. I., & Schooler, C. (1978). The structure of coping. *Journal of Health and Social Behavior, 19,* 2–21.

Peck, M. S. (1978). *The road less traveled.* New York: Simon & Schuster.

Peplau, L. A., & Amaro, H. (1982). Understanding lesbian relationships. In W. Paul, J. D. Weinrich, J. C. Gonsiorek, & M. E. Hotvedt (Eds.), *Homosexuality: Social, psychological, and biological issues.* Beverly Hills, CA: Sage.

Peplau, L. A., Bikson, T. K., Rook, K. S., & Goodchilds, J. D. (1982). Being old and living alone. In L. A. Peplau & D. Perlman (Eds.), *Loneliness.* New York: John Wiley & Sons.

Peplau, L. A., & Perlman, D. (1982). Perspectives on loneliness. In L. A. Peplau & D. Perlman (Eds.), *Loneliness.* New York: John Wiley & Sons.

Perkins, D. V. (1982). The assessment of stress using life events scales. In L. Goldberger & S. Breznitz (Eds.), *Handbook of stress: Theoretical and clinical aspects.* New York: The Free Press.

Perun, P. J., & Bielby, D. D. (1980). Structure and dynamics of the individual life course. In K. W. Back (Ed.), *Life course: Integrative theories and exemplary populations.* AAAS Selected Symposium 41. Boulder, CO: Westview Press.

Peskin, H., & Livson, N. (1981). Uses of the past in adult psychological health. In D. H. Eichorn, J. A. Clausen, N. Haan, M. P. Honzik, & P. H. Mussen (Eds.), *Present and past in middle life.* New York: Academic Press.

Philliber, W. W., & Hiller, D. V. (1983). Relative occupational attainments of spouses and later changes in marriage and wife's work experience. *Journal of Marriage and the Family, 46,* 161–170.

PIAGET, J. (1952). *The origins of intelligence in children.* New York: International Universities Press.

PIAGET, J. (1964). Development and learning. In R. Ripple & V. Rockcastle (Eds.), *Piaget rediscovered.* Ithaca, NY: Cornell University Press.

PIAGET, J., & INHELDER, B. (1969). *The psychology of the child.* New York: Basic Books.

PLECK, J., & RUSTAD, M. (1980). *Husbands' and wives' time in family work and paid work in the 1975–76 study of time use.* Wellesley, MA: Wellesley College Research Center on Women.

POGUE-GEILE, M. F., & ROSE, R. J. (1985). Developmental genetic studies of adult personality. *Developmental Psychology, 21,* 547–557.

POLLACK, J. M. (1979–80). Correlates of death anxiety: A review of empirical studies. *Omega, 10,* 97–121.

POLONKO, K. A., SCANZONI, J., & TEACHMAN, J. D. (1982). Childlessness and marital satisfaction: A further assessment. *Journal of Family Issues, 3,* 545–574.

POWELL, B. (1977). The empty nest, employment, and psychiatric symptoms in college-educated women. *Psychology of Women Quarterly, 2,* 35–43.

PRATT, M. W., GOLDING, G., & HUNTER, W. J. (1983). Aging as ripening: Character and consistency of moral judgment in young, mature, and older adults. *Human Development, 26,* 277–288.

PRATT, M. W., GOLDING, G., & HUNTER, W. J. (1984). Does morality have a gender? Sex, sex role, and moral judgment relationships across the adult lifespan. *Merrill-Palmer Quarterly, 30,* 321–340.

PRESIDENT'S COMMISSION ON MENTAL HEALTH (1979). *Mental health and the elderly: Recommendations for action.* Reports of the task panel on the elderly and the secretary's committee on mental health and illness of the elderly (OHDS 80–20960). Washington, DC: Government Printing Office.

RABINOWITZ, S., & HALL, D. T. (1981). Changing correlates of job involvement in three career stages. *Journal of Vocational Behavior, 18,* 138–144.

RABKIN, J. G. (1982). Stress and psychiatric disorders. In L. Goldberger & S. Breznitz (Eds.), *Handbook of stress: Theoretical and clinical aspects.* New York: The Free Press.

RALLINGS, E. M., & NYE, F. I. (1979). Wife-mother employment, family, and society. In W. R. Burr, R. Hill, F. I. Nye, & I. L. Reiss (Eds.), *Contemporary theories about the family* (Vol. 1). New York: The Free Press.

RANKIN, J. L., & COLLINS, M. (1985). Adult age differences in memory elaboration. *Journal of Gerontology, 40,* 451–458.

REEDY, M. N., BIRREN, J. E., & SCHAIE, K. W. (1981). Age and sex differences in satisfying love relationships across the adult life span. *Human Development,* 24, 52–66.

REISMAN, J. M. (1981). Adult friendships. In S. Duck & R. Gilmour (Eds.), *Personal relationships 2. Developing personal relationships.* New York: Academic Press.

REISMAN, J. M. (1979). *Anatomy of friendship.* New York: Irvington Publishers.

REST, J. R., & THOMA, S. J. (1985). Relation of moral judgment to formal education. *Developmental Psychology, 21,* 709–714.

REXROAT, C. (1985). Women's work expectations and labor-market experience in early and middle family life-cycle stages. *Journal of Marriage and the Family, 47,* 131–142.

RHODES, S. R. (1983). Age-related differences in work attitudes and behavior: A review and conceptual analysis. *Psychological Bulletin, 93,* 329–367.

RIDLEY, C. A., & NELSON, R. R. (1984). The behavioral effect of training premarital couples in mutual problem-solving skills. *Journal of Social and Personal Relationships, 1,* 197–210.

RIEGEL, K. F. (1973). Dialectic operations: The final period of cognitive development. *Human Development, 16,* 346–370.

RIEGEL, K. F. (1975). Adult life crises. A dialectic interpretation of development. In N. Datan & L. H. Ginsberg (Eds.), *Lifespan developmental psychology: Normative life crises.* New York: Academic Press.

RIEGEL, K. F. (1977). History of psychological gerontology. In J. E. Birren & K. W. Schaie (Eds.), *Handbook of the psychology of aging.* New York: Van Nostrand Reinhold.

RILEY, M. W. (1976). Age strata in social systems. In R. H. Binstock & E. Shanas (Eds.), *Handbook of aging and the social sciences.* New York: Van Nostrand Reinhold.

RILEY, M. W. (1983). The family in an aging society. A matrix of latent relationships. *Journal of Family Issues, 4,* 439–454.

RILEY, M. W., & FONER, A. (1968). *Aging and society: Vol. 1. An inventory of research findings.* New York: Russell Sage Foundation.

RILEY, M. W., JOHNSON, M., & FONER, A. (1972). *Aging and society: Vol. 3. A sociology of age stratification.* New York: Russell Sage Foundation.

RITCHIE, R. J., & MOSES, J. L. (1983). Assessment center correlates of women's advancement into middle management: A 7-year longitudinal analysis. *Journal of Applied Psychology, 68,* 227–231.

ROLLINS, B. C., & FELDMAN, H. (1970). Marital satisfaction over the family life cycle. *Journal of Marriage and the Family, 32,* 20–28.

ROLLINS, B. C., & GALLIGAN, R. (1978). The developing child and marital satisfaction of parents. In R. M. Lerner & G. B. Spanier (Eds.), *Child influences on marital and family interaction. A life-span perspective.* New York: Academic Press.

ROOK, K. S. (1984). The negative side of social interaction: Impact on psychological well-being. *Journal of Personality and Social Psychology, 46,* 1097–1108.

ROSENBAUM, J. E. (1984). *Career mobility in a corporate hierarchy.* New York: Academic Press.

ROSENFIELD, S. (1980). Sex differences in depression: Do women always have higher rates? *Journal of Health and Social Behavior, 21,* 33–42.

ROSENKRANTZ, P., VOGEL, S., BEE, H., BROVERMAN, I., & BROVERMAN, D. M. (1968). Sex-role stereotypes and self-conceptions of college students. *Journal of Consulting and Clinical Psychology, 32,* 287–295.

ROSENMAN, R. H., & FRIEDMAN, M. (1983). Relationship of Type A behavior pattern to coronary heart disease. In H. Selye (Ed.), *Selye's guide to stress research* (Vol 2). New York: Scientific and Academic Editions.

ROSOW, I. (1976). Status and role change through the life span. In R. H. Binstock & E. Shanas (Eds.), *Handbook of aging and the social sciences.* New York: Van Nostrand Reinhold.

ROSS, H. G., & MILGRAM, J. I. (1982). Important variables in adult sibling relationships: A qualitative study. In M. E. Lamb & B. Sutton-Smith (Eds.), *Sibling relationships.* Hillsdale, NJ: Lawrence Erlbaum & Associates.

ROSSI, A. S. (1980a). Life-span theories and women's lives. *Signs: Journal of Women in Culture and Society, 6,* 4–32.

ROSSI, A. S. (1980b). Aging and parenthood in the middle years. In P. B. Baltes & O. G. Brim Jr., (Eds.), *Life-span development and behavior* (Vol. 3). New York: Academic Press.

ROSSMAN, I. (1980). Bodily changes with aging. In E. W. Busse & D. G. Blazer (Eds.), *Handbook of geriatric psychiatry.* New York: Van Nostrand Reinhold.

ROTHBART, M. K., & DERRYBERRY, D. (1981). Development of individual differences in temperament. In M. E. Lamb & A. L. Brown (Eds.), *Advances in developmental psychology* (Vol. 1). Hillsdale, NJ: Lawrence Erlbaum & Associates.

ROTTER, J. B. (1966). Generalized expectancies for internal versus external control of reinforcement. *Psychological Monographs: General and Applied, 80,* (Whole No. 609).

ROTTER, J. B. (1975). Some problems and misconceptions related to the construct of internal versus external control of reinforcement. *Journal of Consulting and Clinical Psychology, 43,* 56–67.

ROWE, I., & MARCIA, J. E. (1980). Ego identity status, formal operations, and moral development. *Journal of Youth and Adolescence, 9,* 87–99.

RUBIN, Z. (1973). *Liking and loving: An invitation to social psychology.* New York: Holt, Rinehart & Winston.

RUSH, J. C., PEACOCK, A. C., & MILKOVICH, G. T. (1980). Career stages: A partial test of Levinson's model of life/career stages. *Journal of Vocational Behavior, 16,* 347–359.

RYCHLAK, J. F. (1982). *Personality and life-style of young male managers.* New York: Academic Press.

RYDER, R. G. (1973). Longitudinal data relating marriage satisfaction and having a child. *Journal of Marriage and the Family, 35,* 604–606.

RYFF, C. (1982). Self-perceived personality change in adulthood and aging. *Journal of Personality and Social Psychology, 42,* 108–115.

RYFF, C. (1984). Personality development from the inside: The subjective experience of change in adulthood and aging. In P. B. Baltes & O. G. Brim, Jr., (Eds), *Life-span development and behavior* (Vol. 6). Orlando, FL: Academic Press.

RYFF, C., & BALTES, P. B. (1976). Value transition and adult development in women: The instrumentality-terminality sequence hypothesis. *Developmental Psychology, 12,* 567–568.

RYFF, C., & HEINCKE, S. G. (1983). The subjective organization of personality in adulthood and aging. *Journal of Personality and Social Psychology, 44,* 807–816.

SANGIULIANO, I. (1978). *In her time.* New York: William Morrow.

SARASON, I. G., JOHNSON, J. H., & SIEGAL, J. M. (1979). Assessing the impact of life changes. In I. G. Sarason & C. D. Spielberger (Eds.), *Stress and anxiety* (Vol. 6). New York: John Wiley & Sons.

SATTLER, J. M. (1974). *Assessment of children's intelligence.* Philadephia: W. B. Saunders.

SAUNDERS, C. (1977). Dying they live: St. Christopher's Hospice. In H. Feifel (Ed.), *New meanings of death.* New York: McGraw-Hill.

SAVAGE, R. D., GABER, L. B., BRITTON, P. G., BOLTON, N., & COOPER, A. (1977). *Personality and adjustment in the aged.* London: Academic Press.

SCARR, S. (1981). *Race, social class, and individual differences in IQ.* Hillsdale, NJ: Lawrence Erlbaum & Associates.

SCHAEFER, C., COYNE, J. C., & LAZARUS, R. S. (1982). The health-related functions of social support. *Journal of Behavioral Medicine, 4,* 381–406.

SCHAFER, R. B., & KEITH, P. M. (1984). A causal analysis of the relationship between the self-concept and marital quality. *Journal of Marriage and the Family, 46,* 909–914.

SCHAIE, K. W. (1983a). What can we learn from the longitudinal study of adult psychological development? In K. W. Schaie (Ed.), *Longitudinal studies of adult psychological development.* New York: Guilford Press.

SCHAIE, K. W. (1983b). The Seattle longitudinal study: A 21-year exploration of psychometric intelligence in adulthood. In K. W. Schaie (Ed.), *Longitudinal studies of adult psychological development.* New York: Guilford Press.

SCHAIE, K. W. (Ed.) (1983c). *Longitudinal studies of adult psychological development.* New York: Guilford Press.

SCHAIE, K. W., & HERTZOG, C. (1983). Fourteen-year cohort-sequential analyses of adult intellectual development. *Developmental Psychology, 19,* 531–543.

SCHAIE, K. W., & PARHAM, A. IL. (1976). Stability of adult personality traits: Fact or fable? *Journal of Personality and Social Psychology, 34,* 146–158.

SCHOOLER, C. (1984). Psychological effects of complex environments during the life span: A review and theory. *Intelligence, 8,* 259–281.

SCHUCKIT, M. A. (1984). Prospective markers for alcoholism. In D. W. Goodwin, K. T. Van Dusen, & S. A. Mednick (Eds.), *Longitudinal research in alcoholism.* Boston: Kluwer-Nijhoff.

SCHULENBERG, J. E., VONDRACEK, F. W., & CROUTER, A. C. (1984). The influence of the family on vocational development. *Journal of Marriage and the Family, 46,* 129–143.

SCHULZ, R., & ADERMAN, D. (1974). Clinical research and the stages of dying. *Omega, 5,* 137–143.

SCOTT, J. P. (1983). Siblings and other kin. In T. Brubaker (Ed.), *Family relationships in later life.* Beverly Hills, CA: Sage.

SEARS, R. R. (1977). Sources of life satisfactions of the Terman gifted men. *American Psychologist, 32* 119–128.

SEIDEN, A. M. (1980). Time management and the dual-career couple. In F. Pepitone-Rockwell (Ed.), *Dual-career couples.* Beverly Hills, CA: Sage.

SELMANOWITZ, V. J., RIZER, R. L., & ORENTREICH, N. (1977). Aging of the skin and its appendages. In C. E. Finch & L. Hayflick (Eds.), *Handbook of the biology of aging.* New York: Van Nostrand Reinhold.

SELTZER, B., & FRAZIER, S. H. (1978). Organic mental disorders. In A. M. Nicholi, Jr. (Ed.), *The Harvard guide to modern psychiatry.* Cambridge, MA: Belknap Press of Harvard University Press.

SELYE, H. (1936). A syndrome produced by diverse nocuous agents. *Nature, 138,* 32.

Selye, H. (1976). *The stress of life* (rev. ed.). New York: McGraw-Hill.

SELYE, H. (1982). History and present status of the stress concept. In L. Goldberger & S. Breznitz (Eds.), *Handbook of stress. Theoretical and clinical aspects.* New York: The Free Press.

SERFASS, R. C., & GERBERICH, S. G. (1984). Exercise for optimal health: Strategies and motivational considerations. *Preventive Medicine, 13,* 79–99.

SHANAS, E. (1979). The family as a social support system in old age. *The Gerontologist, 19,* 169–174.

SHEEHY, G. (1974). *Passages.* New York: E. P. Dutton.

SHNEIDMAN, E. S. (1980). *Voices of death.* New York: Harper & Row.

SHNEIDMAN, E. S. (1983). *Deaths of man.* New York: Jason Aronson.

SHOCK, N. W. (1977a). Biological theories of aging. In J. E. Birren & K. W. Schaie (Eds.), *Handbook of the psychology of aging.* New York: Van Nostrand Reinhold.

SHOCK, N. W. (1977b). System integration. In C. E. Finch & L. Hayflick (Eds.), *Handbook of the biology of aging.* New York: Van Nostrand Reinhold.

SIEGELMAN, E., BLOCK, J., BLOCK, J., & VON DER LIPPE, A. (1970). Antecedents of optimal psychological adjustment. *Journal of Consulting and Clinical Psychology, 35,* 283–289.

SIEGLER, I. C. (1983). Psychological aspects of the Duke Longitudinal Studies. In K. W. Schaie (Ed.), *Longitudinal studies of adult psychological development.* New York: Guilford Press.

SIEGLER, I. C., & BOTWINICK, J. (1979). A long-term longitudinal study of intellectual ability of older adults: The matter of selective attrition. *Journal of Gerontology, 34,* 242–245.

SIEGLER, I. C., GEORGE, L. K., & OKUN, M. A. (1979). Cross-sequential analysis of adult personality. *Developmental Psychology, 15,* 350–351.

SIEGLER, I. C., MCCARTY, S. M., & LOGUE, P. E. (1982). Wechsler memory scale scores, selective attrition, and distance from death. *Journal of Gerontology, 37,* 176–181.

SIEGLER, I. C., NOWLIN, J. B., & BLUMENTHAL, J. A. (1980). Health and behavior: Methodological considerations for adult development and aging. In L. W. Poon (Ed.), *Aging in the 1980s.* Washington, DC: American Psychological Association.

SIRIGNANO, S. W., & LACHMAN, M. E. (1985). Personality change during the transition to parenthood: The role of perceived infant temperament. *Developmental Psychology, 21,* 558–567.

SKOLNICK, A. (1981). Married lives: Longitudinal perspectives on marriage. In D. H. Eichorn, J. A. Clausen, N. Haan, M. P. Honzik, & P. H. Mussen (Eds.), *Present and past in middle life*. New York: Academic Press.

SMITH, B. D., THOMPSON, L. W., & MICHALEWSKI, H. J. (1980). Averaged evoked potential research in adult aging: Status and prospects. In L. W. Poon (Ed.), *Aging in the 1980s.* Washington, DC: American Psychological Association.

SMITH, D. W., BIERMAN, E. L., & ROBINSON, N. M. (1978). *The biologic ages of man.* Philadelphia: W. B. Saunders.

SNAREY, J. R., REIMER, J., & KOHLBERG, L. (1985). Development of social-moral reasoning among kibbutz adolescents: A longitudinal cross-cultural study. *Developmental Psychology, 21,* 3–17.

SORENSEN, A. (1983). Women's employment patterns after marriage. *Journal of Marriage and the Family, 45,* 311–321.

SPANIER, G. B. (1983). Married and unmarried cohabitation in the United States: 1980. *Journal of Marriage and the Family, 45,* 277–288.

SPANIER, G. B., & THOMPSON, L. (1984). *Parting: The aftermath of separation and divorce.* Beverly Hills, CA: Sage.

SPENCE, J. T., & HELMREICH, R. L. (1978). *Masculinity and femininity.* Austin, Texas: University of Texas Press.

SPREITZER, E., & RILEY, L. E. (1974). Factors associated with singlehood. *Journal of Marriage and the Family, 36,* 533–542.

STACE, W. T. (1960). *Mysticism and philosophy.* Philadelphia: Lippincott.

STADEL, B. V., & WEISS, N. S. (1975, September). Characteristics of menopausal women: A survey of King and Pierce Counties in Washington, 1973–74. *American Journal of Epidemiology, 102,* 209–216.

STAINES, G. L., & PLECK, J. H. (1984). Nonstandard work schedules and family life. *Journal of Applied Psychology, 69,* 515–523.

STAINES, G. L., & QUINN, R. P. (1979, January). American workers evaluate the quality of their jobs. *Monthly Labor Review,* 3–12.

STAPLES, R., & MIRANDE, A. (1980). Racial and cultural variations among American families: A decennial review of the literature on minority families. *Journal of Marriage and the Family, 42,* 887–904.

STEFFENSMEIER, R. H. (1982). A role model of the transition to parenthood. *Journal of Marriage and the Family, 44,* 319–334.

STEINDL-RAST, BROTHER DAVID. (1977). Learning to die. *Parabola, 2,* 22–31.

STERNBERG, R. J., & GRAJEK, S. (1984). The nature of love. *Journal of Personality and Social Psychology, 47,* 312–329.

STEVENS, D. P., & TRUSS, C. V. (1985). Stability and change in adult personality over 12 and 20 years. *Developmental Psychology, 21,* 568–584.

STOCK, W. A., OKUN, M. A., HARING, M. J., & WITTER, R. A. (1983). Age and subjective well-being: A meta-analysis. In R. J. Light (Ed.), *Evaluation studies: Review annual* (Vol. 8). Beverly Hills, CA: Sage.

STOLLER, E. P. (1985). Exchange patterns in the informal support networks of the elderly: The impact of reciprocity on morale. *Journal of Marriage and the Family, 47,* 335–342.

STREIB, G. F., & SCHNEIDER, C. J. (1971). *Retirement in American society.* Ithaca, NY: Cornell University Press.

STROEBE, M. S., & STROEBE, W. (1983). Who sufers more? Sex differences in health risks of the widowed. *Psychological Bulletin, 93,* 279–301.

STROUD, J. G. (1981). Women's careers: Work, family, and personality. In D. H. Eichorn, J. A. Clausen, N. Haan, M. P. Honzik, & P. H. Mussen (Eds.), *Present and past in middle life*. New York: Academic Press.

ST. TERESA OF AVILA. (1960). *The life of Teresa of Jesus* (E. Allison Peers, Trans.). Garden City, NY: Image Books. (Original work published in 1562)

ST. TERESA OF AVILA. (1960). *Interior castle* (E. Allison Peers, Trans.). New York: Image Books. (Original work published in 1577)

STULL, D. E., & HATCH, L. R. (1984). Unravelling the effects of multiple life changes. *Research on Aging, 6,* 560–571.

SUEDFELD, P., & PIEDRAHITA, L. E. (1984). Intimations of mortality: Integrative simplification as a precursor of death. *Journal of Personality and Social Psychology, 47,* 848–852.

SULLIVAN, E. V., MCCULLOUGH, G., & STAGER, M. (1970). A developmental study of the relationship between conceptual, ego, and moral development. *Child Development, 41,* 39–411.

SUPER, D. E. (1957). *The psychology of careers*. New York: Harper & Row.

SUPER, D. E. (1985). Coming of age in Middletown: Careers in the making. *American Psychologist, 40,* 405–414.

SWENSEN, C. H., ESKEW, R. W., & KOHLHEPP, K. A. (1981). Stage of family life cycle, ego development, and the marriage relationship. *Journal of Marriage and the Family, 43,* 841–853.

SZINOVACZ, M. (Ed.). (1982a). *Women's retirement*. Beverly Hills, CA: Sage.

SZINOVACZ, M. (1982b). Personal problems and adjustment to retirement. In M. Szinovacz (Ed.), *Women's retirement*. Beverly Hills, CA: Sage.

TAKEDA, S., & MATSUZAWA, T. (1985). Age-related brain atrophy: A study with computer tomography. *Journal of Gerontology, 40,* 159–163.

TAMIR, L. M. (1982). *Men in their forties: The transition to middle age*. New York: Springer.

TEMPLER, D. (1972). Death anxiety: Extraversion, neuroticism, and cigarette smoking. *Omega, 3,* 53–56.

TEMPLER, D., RUFF, C., & FRANKS, C. (1971). Death anxiety: Age, sex and parental resemblance in diverse populations. *Developmental Psychology, 4,* 108.

TERKEL, S. (1972). *Working*. New York: Avon.

TERKELSEN, K. G. (1980). Toward a theory of the family life cycle. In E. A. Carger & M. McGoldrick (Eds.), *The family life cycle*. New York: Gardner Press.

THOMAS, A., & CHESS, S. (1977). *Temperament and development*. New York: Brunner/Mazel.

THOMPSON, L., & WALKER, A. J. (1984). Mothers and daughters: Aid patterns and attachment. *Journal of Marriage and the Family, 46,* 313–322.

THORNTON, G. C., III, & BYHAM, W. C. (1982). *Assessment centers and managerial performance*. New York: Academic Press.

TOFFLER, A. (1970). *Future shock*. New York: Random House.

TRAUPMANN, J., & HATFIELD, E. (1983). How important is marital fairness over the lifespan? *International Journal of Aging and Human Development, 17,* 89–101.

TREAS, J. (1979). Intergenerational families and social changes. In P. Ragen (Ed.), *Aging parents*. Los Angeles: Andrus Gerontology Center, University of Southern California.

TROLL, L. (1980). Grandparenting. In L. W. Poon (Ed.), *Aging in the 1980s. Psychological issues*. Washington, DC: American Psychological Association.

TROLL, L., & SMITH, J. (1976). Attachment through the life span: Some questions about dyadic bonds among adults. *Human Development, 19,* 156–170.

ULLIAN, D. Z. (1981). The child's construction of gender: Anatomy as destiny. In E. K. Shapiro & E. Weber (Eds.), *Cognitive and affective growth*. Hillsdale, NJ: Lawrence Erlbaum & Associates.

UNDERHILL, E. (1961). *Mysticism.* New York: E. P. Dutton. (original work published 1911).

U.S. BUREAU OF THE CENSUS. (1983a). *Statistical Abstract of the United States: 1984.* (104th ed.) Washington, DC: U.S. Government Printing Office.

U.S. BUREAU OF THE CENSUS. (1983b). *America in Transition: An Aging Society.* Current Population Reports, Series P–23, No. 128). Washington, DC: U.S. Government Printing Office.

U.S. BUREAU OF THE CENSUS (1984a). *Statistical Abstract of the United States: 1985.* (105th ed.) Washington, D.C.: U.S. Government Printing Office.

U.S. BUREAU OF THE CENSUS, (1984b). *Lifetime work experience and its effect on earnings: Retrospective data from the 1979 Income Survey Development Program* (Current Population Reports, Series P-23, No. 136). Washington, DC: U.S. Government Printing Office.

UPTON, A. C. (1977). Pathobiology. In C. E. Finch & L. Hayflick (Eds.), *Handbook of the biology of aging.* New York: Van Nostrand Reinhold.

VAILLANT, G. E. (1977a). *Adaptation to life: How the best and brightest came of age.* Boston: Little, Brown.

VAILLANT, G. E. (1977b). The climb to maturity: How the best and the brightest came of age. *Psychology Today, 11*(4), 34–42, 48–49.

VAN VELSOR, E., & O'RAND, A. M. (1984). Family life cycle, work career patterns, and women's wages at midlife. *Journal of Marriage and the Family, 46,* 365–373.

VERBRUGGE, L. M. (1984). A health profile of older women with comparisons to older men. *Research on Aging, 6,* 291–322.

VERBRUGGE, L. M. (1985). An epidemiological profile of older women. In M. R. Haug, A. B. Ford, & M. Sheafor, (Eds.), *The physical and mental health of aged women.* New York: Springer.

VEROFF, J., DOUVAN, E., & KULKA, R. A. (1981). *The inner American. A self-portrait from 1957 to 1976.* New York: Basic Books.

VEROFF, J., REUMAN, D., & FELD, S. (1984). Motives in American men and women across the adult life span. *Developmental Psychology, 20,* 1142–1158.

VITALIANO, P. P., BREEN, A. R., ALBERT, M. S., RUSSO, J., & PRINZ, P. N. (1984). Memory, attention, and functional status in community-residing Alzheimer type dementia patients and optimally healthy aged individuals. *Journal of Gerontology, 39,* 58–64.

WADDELL, F. T. (1983). Factors affecting choice, satisfaction, and success in the female self-employed. *Journal of Vocational Behavior, 23,* 294–304.

WADDINGTON, C. H. (1957). *The strategy of the genes.* London: Allen & Unwin.

WALDRON, H., & ROUTH, D. K. (1981). The effect of the first child on the marital relationship. *Journal of Marriage and the Family, 43,* 785–788.

WALKER, A. J., & THOMPSON, L. (1983). Intimacy and intergenerational aid and contact among mothers and daughters. *Journal of Marriage and the Family, 45,* 841–849.

WALKER, L. (1984). Sex differences in the development of moral reasoning: A critical review. *Child Development, 55,* 677–691.

WALSH, W. B., HORTON, J. A., & GAFFEY, R. L. (1977). Holland's theory and college-degreed working men and women. *Journal of Vocational Behavior, 10,* 180–186.

WARING, J. (1981). The middle years: A multidisciplinary view. In A. C. Eurich (Ed.), *Major transitions in the human life cycle.* Lexington, MA: D. C. Heath.

WATSON, D., & CLARK, L. A. (1984). Negative affectivity: The disposition to experience aversive emotional states. *Psychological Bulletin, 96,* 465–490.

WATSON, R. E. L. (1983). Premarital cohabitation versus traditional courtship: Their effects on subsequent marital adjustment. *Family Relations, 32,* 139–147.

WEAVER, C. N. (1978). Sex differences in the determinants of job satisfaction. *Academy of Management Journal, 21,* 265–274.

WEAVER, C. N. (1980). Job satisfaction in the United States in the 1970s. *Journal of Applied Psychology, 65*, 364–367.

WECHSLER, D. (1939). *The measurement of adult intelligence.* Baltimore: Williams & Wilkins.

WECHSLER, D. (1955). *Manual for the Wechsler Adult Intelligence Scale.* New York: Psychological Corporation.

WEG, R. B. (1983). The physiological perspective. In R. B. Weg (Ed.), *Sexuality in the later years: Roles and behavior.* New York: Academic Press.

WEINGARTEN, H. R. (1985). Marital status and well-being: A national study comparing first-married, currently divorced, and remarried adults. *Journal of Marriage and the Family, 47,* 653–662.

WEISMAN, A. D. (1972). *On dying and denying.* New York: Behavioral Publications.

WEISMAN, A. D., & WORDEN, J. W. (1975). Psychosocial analysis of cancer deaths. *Omega, 6,* 61–75.

WEISS, R. S. (1979). The emotional impact of marital separation. In C. Levinger & O. C. Coles (Eds.), *Divorce and separation: Context, causes, and consequences.* New York: Basic Books.

WEISS, R. S. (1982). Attachment in adult life. In C. M. Parkes & J. Stevenson-Hinde (Eds.), *The place of attachment in human behavior.* New York: Basic Books.

WEISS, R. S. (1984). The impact of marital dissolution on income and consumption in single-parent households. *Journal of Marriage and the Family, 46,* 115–127.

WERNER, H., & KAPLAN, B. (1956). The developmental approach to cognition: Its relevance to the psychological interpretation of anthropological and ethnolinguistic data. *American Anthropologist, 58,* 866–880.

WHELIHAN, W. M., LESHER, E. L., KLEBAN, M. H., & GRANICK, S. (1984). Mental status and memory assessment as predictors of dementia. *Journal of Gerontology, 39,* 572–576.

WHITBOURNE, S. K., & WATERMAN, A. S. (1979). Psychosocial development during the adult years: Age and cohort comparisons. *Developmental Psychology, 15,* 373–378.

WILBER, K. (1980). *The atman project: A transpersonal view of human development.* Wheaton, IL: The Theosophical Publishing House.

WILLEMSEN, E. W. (1980). Terman's gifted women: Work and the way they see their lives. In K. W. Back (Ed.), *Life Course: Integrative theories and exemplary populations.* AAAS Selected Symposium, #41. Boulder, CO: Westview Press.

WILLIAMS, J. E., BENNETT, S. M., & BEST, D. L. (1975). Awareness and expression of sex stereotypes in young children. *Developmental Psychology, 11,* 635–642.

WINDLE, M., & LERNER, R. M. (1984). The role of temperament in dating relationships among young adults. *Merrill Palmer Quarterly, 30,* 163–175.

WINSBOROUGH, H. H. (1980). A demographic approach to the life cycle. In K. W. Back (Ed.), *Life course: Integrative theories and exemplary populations.* AAAS Selected Symposium, #41. Boulder, CO: Westview Press.

WINSLOW, T. S. (1980). Grandma. In R. Lyell (Ed.), *Middle age, old age: Short stories, poems, plays, and essays on aging.* New York: Harcourt Brace Jovanovich.

WOODBURY, M. A., & MANTON, K. G. (1983). A theoretical model of the physiological dynamics of circulatory disease in human populations. *Human Biology, 55,* 417–441.

WOODRUFF, D. S., & BIRREN, J. E. (1972). Age changes and cohort differences in personality. *Developmental Psychology, 6,* 252–259.

YIN, P., & SHINE, M. (1985). Misinterpretations of increases in life expectancy in gerontology textbooks. *The Gerontologist, 25,* 78–82.

YINGER, J. M. (1977). A comparative study of the substructures of religion. *Journal for the Scientific Study of Religion, 16,* 67–86.

# Index

## Author Index

# Subject Index